THE AFRICAN WORLD

A Survey of Social Research

THE AFRICAN WORLD

A SURVEY OF SOCIAL RESEARCH

Edited for the African Studies Association
by Robert A. Lystad

FREDERICK A. PRAEGER, Publishers
New York · Washington · London

FREDERICK A. PRAEGER, *Publishers*
111 Fourth Avenue, New York 3, N.Y., U.S.A.
77–79 Charlotte Street, London W.1, England

Published in the United States of America in 1965
by Frederick A. Praeger, Inc., Publishers

Library of Congress Catalog Card Number: 65-10753

Printed in the United States of America

Editor's Preface

AFRICA'S POST-WAR ENTRY onto the stage of world politics in a greatly changed and grander role has coincided with its equally momentous entry onto the stage of research in the social sciences, humanities, and related fields and disciplines. Nearly every contributor to this volume recognises the second world war as marking an intellectual turning point, for subsequent years have witnessed the emergence of what previously had been only partially anticipated bodies of theory, methodological approaches and techniques of social research. In these decades, too, Africa has come increasingly to be recognised as an area of the world that offers unusual, though not unique, opportunities for the extension of knowledge, for the application of knowledge to the solution of difficult problems of thought and action, and for the training of scholars and technicians in both the 'pure' and the 'applied' aspects of the sciences and humanities.

Aware of these phenomena and opportunities, the African Studies Association — itself in part a product of this social and intellectual ferment — proposed, late in 1960, to undertake a review of the current and recent, as well as the most relevant earlier, social research in the African field. This volume brings that project to fruition.

The Ford Foundation generously assumed the cost of the project as part of its grant to the Association in that year. The organisation and administration of the plan was initiated by the appointment of a Committee of the Board, composed of Drs Robert D. Baum, William O. Brown, L. Gray Cowan and Joseph H. Greenberg. This Committee discharged its essential duties by affirming the broad outlines of the project, selecting the Editor, aiding in the selection of contributors, and maintaining a steady and encouraging, if not actively committed, interest in the progress of the work.

It should perhaps be pointed out that the contents of this publication do not bear any official endorsement by the African Studies Association or by the Ford Foundation. Neither has read the manuscript nor prescribed any portion of the text apart from the guidelines originally established and approved. The Editor's accountability to the Board of Directors and the membership of the Association has been administrative, interpreted in the strictest sense; the contributors' responsibilities to the Editor have been primarily administrative. Once informed of the broad objectives of the project and of their specific roles in it, the contributors

have proceeded as scholars subject only to their own understanding of the highest standards of their disciplines and to their estimates of the most useful contribution they could make to the achievement of the project's goals.

The lapse of time between the writing and publication of several of the essays is more than two years. In a certain, substantive sense, therefore, some of these studies are already outdated, for the pace of research and publication during the intervening months has not only continued unabated but, indeed, has increased. As a result, the bibliographies lack the latest items; but the essays remain timely to a degree which largely obviates the necessity for contributors who early submitted studies to revise their materials — however desirable this might be in ideal circumstances. Their value is not dependent upon their recency, for they deal with fundamental issues.

The purpose of the book is to summarise and show relationships among current, recent, and pertinent earlier research 'within' a particular discipline or area of knowledge, in such a manner as effectively to inform scholars in other disciplines. However useful to specialists in a field these essays may prove to be, they are principally directed towards scholars and students with other primary but related interests.

The studies indicate the systematic theories or the theorising that have informed research, the methodologies that have helped to organise it, the types of research problems scholars have defined, and the nature of what are judged to be the more significant findings. Trends in research, gaps in knowledge, and the probable directions of future research are discussed. These various aspects are assessed from the standpoint of one who is encouraging cross-disciplinary understanding and recommending closer and more productive relationships among disciplines.

The book is not a handbook, manual, compendium or encyclopedia of past and current research. Specific studies are reported in a context of related studies within and between disciplines. Reference is made in it to materials derived from research throughout Africa, including North Africa, to the work of scholars of any nationality, and to publications in several languages. The greatest attention, however, is given to sub-Saharan materials published in the English language.

The emphases on theory and method, on an explanation of the fundamental problems of the disciplines, and on the possibilities of interdisciplinary stimulus and integration, more than compensate for the inability to report the findings of the most recent studies. Radically new departures and astounding breakthroughs are rare. These studies, therefore, should continue to be of value for some time to come.

The continued relevance of these essays is also enhanced by the emphasis of each author on the probable directions of future research. Disciplinary patterns once established are only seldom subject to rapid revision; and, although the predictions of trends are primarily those of one individual, they are not likely to be grossly misleading. Some contributors, too, have felt more constrained than others to outline the fundamental nature of their disciplines. In the interest of enlightening only vaguely informed specialists in other crafts, they have departed further from the permissively prescribed format; in so doing, they have strengthened the continuing, broad utility of the volume.

Area studies possess far less unity than do disciplines: a phenomenon reflected in the format of the book, which devotes each of its successive chapters to a discipline or area of knowledge. No comprehensive systematic theory, which can subsume all social or socially oriented research, is as yet available. Indeed, it may never be available. No embracing methodology serves to integrate or co-ordinate the foci and styles of research. At no stage in the book's preparation was this condition more apparent than when decisions were made about ordering the chapters in the Table of Contents. In many ways, the only satisfactory rubric under which each of the essays could be subsumed was the general one adopted as the book's subtitle: 'A Survey of Social Research'. So deeply do the disciplines interpenetrate without actually converging, so acutely conscious are the authors of the interdependence of their disciplines, so overlapping are some of their problem areas, that it was difficult to order the chapters in a manner which would ensure smooth transitions and a logical flow of ideas. Yet it was also clear that random placement was impossible: the disciplines do retain their distinctive qualities, and these link some more closely than others. Many, moreover, participate simultaneously in more than one sub-family of disciplines, and their proper placement occasioned some difficulty.

The ordering principles eventually adopted relate to those disciplines that seem more largely to share similar foci of interest: I. *Historical and socio-structural aspects* (pre-history, history, anthropology, sociology, political science, law, education, economics, and economic development); II. *Physico-biological aspects* (geography, demography, biological studies, agricultural studies, medical research); and III. *Psycho-cultural aspects* (psychology, linguistics, visual arts, music and dance, folklore and literature). The principle of 'similar foci', however, is not wholly satisfactory, as the reading of any chapter will indicate. In any event, it must be emphasised that location in the book is by no means a ranking of significance or an ordering of priorities.

At various stages in the preparation of most of the manuscripts, expert readers have contributed their knowledge to the criticism, proposed modification or confirmation of the authors' appraisals. Appreciation is therefore due to Philip D. Curtin (History), Lloyd A. Fallers (Anthropology), Immanuel Wallerstein (Sociology), David E. Apter (Political Science), James C. N. Paul (Law), Betty George (Education), Walter A. Chudson (Economics), Walter W. Deshler (Geography), Dudley Kirk (Demography), Sherwood L. Washburn (Biological Studies), Richard Bradfield (Agricultural Research), Marshall H. Segall (Psychology), Desmond T. Cole (Linguistics), Jan Vansina (Visual Arts), and David McAllester (Music and Dance).

R. A. L.

Contents

EDITOR'S PREFACE   v

CONTRIBUTORS   xi

INTRODUCTION: THE INTEGRATION OF SOCIAL
RESEARCH   Robert A. Lystad   1

I   Historical and Socio-Cultural Studies

1. PREHISTORY   J. Desmond Clark   11
2. HISTORY   J. D. Fage   40
3. ANTHROPOLOGY   P. H. Gulliver   57
4. SOCIOLOGY: SOME ASPECTS OF URBAN PLURAL
    SOCIETIES   Leo Kuper   107
5. POLITICAL SCIENCE   Harvey Glickman   131
6. LAW   A. Arthur Schiller   166
7. EDUCATION   David Scanlon   199
8. ECONOMICS AND ECONOMIC DEVELOPMENT   Andrew M. Kamarck   221

II   Physico-Biological Studies

9.   GEOGRAPHY   Benjamin E. Thomas   245
10. DEMOGRAPHY   Frank Lorimer,
                                      William Brass and
                                      Etienne van de Walle   271
11. BIOLOGICAL STUDIES   Neil C. Tappen   304
12. AGRICULTURAL RESEARCH   John J. McKelvey, Jr.   317
13. MEDICAL RESEARCH: SOME ANTHROPOLOGICAL
     ASPECTS   Robert F. Gray   352

III Psycho-Cultural Studies

14.	PSYCHOLOGY	Leonard W. Doob	373
15.	LINGUISTICS	Joseph H. Greenberg	416
16.	THE VISUAL ARTS	Roy Sieber	442
17.	MUSIC AND THE DANCE	Alan P. Merriam	452
18.	FOLKLORE AND LITERATURE	William Bascom	469

Chapter Notes and Bibliographies   493

Tables and Map:

Table I: *Chronology of African Pleistocene Cultures*   19, 20–21

Table II: *Terminal and Post-Pleistocene Cultures*   22–23

Map: *Prehistoric sites referred to in Chapter 1*   24–25

Index of Contents   561

General Index   567

Contributors

Introduction

ROBERT A. LYSTAD is Professor of African Studies at the School of Advanced International Studies of The Johns Hopkins University, Washington, DC. After receiving the PhD in Anthropology at Northwestern University, where he studied with Professor Melville J. Herskovits, he became a member of the faculty of Tulane University. He taught there for ten years prior to assuming his present position. In 1949-50 he conducted field research on comparative cultural change in two rural communities in the Gold Coast and the Ivory Coast; in 1957-58 he returned to Ghana for field work as a participant in an interdisciplinary, comparative study of socio-political change. His publications include *The Ashanti: A Proud People*.

1 Prehistory

J. DESMOND CLARK, CBE, FBA, FSA, PhD, is Professor of Anthropology at the University of California, Berkeley. Until 1961, he was Director of the Rhodes-Livingstone Museum in Northern Rhodesia. For twenty-five years he has worked on the prehistory of central and southern Africa, and published his results in books on the archaeology of Northern Rhodesia, the Horn of Africa, and north-eastern Angola; he is also the author of *The Prehistory of Southern Africa* (1959). He is currently engaged on the preparation of publications based on materials from the rich Stone Age site at Kalambo Falls in Northern Rhodesia, and in compiling, with the assistance of colleagues, an *Atlas of African Prehistory*.

2 History

JOHN D. FAGE graduated from Magdalene College, Cambridge, and was awarded the PhD of that university. In 1949 he took the post of lecturer at the new University College of the Gold Coast (now University of Ghana), becoming Professor of History there in 1955. He returned to England in 1959 as Lecturer in the History of Africa at the School of Oriental and African Studies in the University of London. In 1963 he was appointed first Director of the Centre of West African Studies in the University of Birmingham, where he is also Professor of African

History.   His publications include: *An Introduction to the History of West Africa* (1955); *An Atlas of African History* (1958); *Ghana: A Historical Interpretation* (1959); and (with Roland Oliver) *A Short History of Africa* (1962).   He is co-editor of the *Journal of African History*.

3 Anthropology

PHILIP H. GULLIVER is Reader in African Anthropology at the School of Oriental and African Studies in the University of London.   Formerly Research Sociologist to the Tanganyikan Government (1952–58), he was, in turn, Visiting Lecturer in Social Anthropology at Harvard University (1958–59), and Research Associate and Associate Professor of Anthropology in the African Studies Program of Boston University (1959–62).   He carried out extensive anthropological research in East Africa (1948–58), and was awarded the Wellcome Medal for Anthropological Research by the Royal Anthropological Institute (1957).   Among his publications are: *A preliminary survey of the Turkana* (1951); *The Family herds* (1955); *Labour migration in a rural economy* (1955); *Land tenure and social change among the Nyakyusa* (1958); and *Social control in an African society* (1963).

4 Sociology

LEO KUPER is Professor of Sociology at the University of California, Los Angeles.   He was for many years on the faculty of the University of Natal, South Africa.   His main interests have been in the areas of sociological theory and social structures, with particular reference to African societies.   He is the author of 'Blueprint, for Living Together' in *Living in Towns* (1953), *Passive Resistance in South Africa* (1956), and co-author (with H. Watts and R. Davies) of *Durban: A Study in Racial Ecology* (1958). *A study of An African Bourgeoisie* is now in process of publication.

5 Political Science

HARVEY GLICKMAN is Assistant Professor of Political Science at Haverford College, Pennsylvania.   He received his PhD in Political Science at Harvard University.   He has taught there, and also at Princeton University.   His initial work was on British politics, and he has published *The Problem of Internal Security in Great Britain* (1954; with H. H. Wilson), and several articles on British parties and political thought.   African political systems have engaged his attention since 1959. He was Book Editor of *Africa Report* for two years, and in 1962–63 he did field work in Tanganyika on a Ford Foundation Foreign Area Training Fellowship.   He has contributed a chapter on the crisis in the Congo in *New Forces in Africa* (1962: edited by W. H. Lewis), and is currently preparing a study of nationalism and party ideology in Tanganyika.

6 Law

A. ARTHUR SCHILLER is Professor at the Law School of Columbia University, New York, where he has been a member of the faculty for over thirty years.   He took his degree in law at the University of California, where he was also awarded a Master's degree in Egyptology.   At Columbia he combined the two fields of interest in his doctoral thesis, 'Ten Coptic Legal Texts', edited and translated with commentary.   His major field of work has been in Roman Law, but he has long been interested in the problems of the interaction of indigenous and Western legal systems. Before the war he reached into Dutch and *adat* law in the Netherlands East Indies, transferring his attention during the last ten years to indigenous and Western-based legal systems in Africa. As legal counsel for the Commissioner of the United Nations in Eritrea he helped in drafting the Eritrean Constitution. He has made several visits to Africa in recent years, the latest being in 1963 when he attended the African Conference on Local Courts and Customary Law at Dar es Salaam. He is the author of several articles on African Law and of a booklet, *Syllabus in African Law* (1961) which is to be published in a revised and extended version in 1964. Professor Schiller is a vice-president of the International African Law Association and a director of the African Studies Association.

7 Education

DAVID SCANLON is Professor of Education at Columbia Teachers' College, New York, and Director of Studies in the Institute for Education in Africa at Columbia University. He is the author of *International Education: A Documentary History* (1960), and of *Traditions of African Education* (1964).

8 Economics and Economic Development

ANDREW MARTIN KAMARCK is Senior Economic Adviser on Africa for the World Bank Group, Washington. During the first academic semester, 1964-5, he was on leave from the World Bank as Regents Professor, University of California, Los Angeles. Before joining the Bank in 1950, he worked for the US Treasury on international economic and financial problems, engaging in various assignments including the chairmanship of the interdepartmental Financial Policy Committee in the preparation of the Marshall Plan, and acting as the US Treasury representative in Italy. During the war he served as a major in the field artillery and then as Central Banking Adviser for the Allied Control Commission in Italy, and as deputy-director of the Finance Division of the US Group Control Council in Germany. He has headed World Bank economic missions to many African countries, in particular the Kariba and the Volta missions. The opinions he expresses are his own and do not necessarily reflect the views of the institutions with which he is associated.

9 Geography

BENJAMIN E. THOMAS worked under Professor Derwent Whittlesey at Harvard University, where he was awarded the PhD in geography in 1947. Since 1949 he has given courses on African geography at the University of California, Los Angeles, and has travelled widely during six study-visits to Africa. His work on northern and western Africa from 1949 to 1956 resulted in monographs on *Trade Routes of Algeria and the Sahara* (1957), and *Transportation and Physical Geography in West Africa* (1960). In 1957–58 he was Ford Foundation Fellow in East Africa, and in 1959–60 he lectured at Makerere College at Kampala in Uganda.

10 Demography

FRANK LORIMER is Professor Emeritus of Sociology at American University, Washington, and Visiting Professor, University of the Philippines, Manila. His early interests were in the areas of religion, social work and philosophy, but his subsequent contributions have been in the field of demography. He joined Frederick Osborn in a study of the social and genetic aspects of population trends: *Dynamics of Population* (1934). His other publications include: *The Problems of a Changing Population* (1938) —as study director, the US National Resources Committee; *The Population of the Soviet Union* (League of Nations 1946); and *Culture and Human Fertility* (UNESCO 1954). His survey, *Demographic Information on Tropical Africa* (1961), was prepared during his association with Boston University, and he has more recently participated with other demographers at Princeton University in a program of critical investigations and analysis of such data. From 1956 to 1958 he was President of the International Union for the Scientific Study of Population: an organisation for which he had been Administrative Director from 1948 to 1956.

WILLIAM BRASS is Reader in Medical Demography at the London School of Hygiene and Tropical Medicine. From 1955 to 1964 he lectured on Statistics at Aberdeen University, Scotland. Graduating MA with honours in Mathematical and Natural Philosophy at Edinburgh University in 1947, he served as a statistician in the East Africa Statistical Department from 1948 to 1955. In 1961–62 he was Visiting Research Associate and Co-director of the African Demography Program of the Office of Population Research at Princeton University. His main research interests and publications are in the development of statistical techniques for medical studies and the application of mathematical and biometric methods in demography, particularly to data from underdeveloped areas.

ETIENNE VAN DE WALLE is Research Associate of the Office of Population Research at Princeton University. A Doctor in Law and MA in Economics of the University of Louvain, he has served as researcher at the Institut pour la Recherche Scientifique en Afrique Centrale, and has done field work in demography in Rwanda and Burundi.

11 Biological Studies

NEIL C. TAPPEN is Associate Professor of Physical Anthropology at Tulane University, New Orleans. A graduate of the University of Florida, he studied anthropology at the University of Chicago, gaining his PhD in 1952. His main interests include primate biology, primate and human evolution, and the structure and functions of bones and muscles. He has studied primates in the field in East Africa (1956–57) and in West Africa (1963).

12 Agricultural Research

JOHN J. MCKELVEY, JR. was educated at Oberlin College, Virginia Polytechnic Institute and Cornell University, specialising in the study of plant disease and insect control. He joined the Rockefeller Foundation as an Entomologist in its Mexican Agricultural Program in 1945, and later travelled throughout Latin America in connection with the awarding of grants and fellowships. Since 1959 Dr McKelvey has had initial responsibility for the Foundation's agricultural activities in Africa. He is now an Associate Director for Agricultural Sciences. In 1960 he served on an ICA-FAO team surveying the natural resources of Northern Nigeria. He is a member of the National Academy of Science's Advisory Committee for Africa.

13 Medical Research: Some Anthropological Aspects

ROBERT F. GRAY is Associate Professor of Anthropology at Tulane University, New Orleans. He holds the MD degree of Northwestern University Medical School, Illinois, and the PhD degree in Anthropology of the University of Chicago. During the war he was a medical officer in the British and American armies in Africa, returning to the continent for field work in anthropology in 1950–51 and 1954–56. He is the author of The Sonjo of Tanganyika (1963). Before going to Tulane University in 1961 he held a research position with the Human Relations Area Files, and taught at the University of Illinois.

14 Psychology

LEONARD W. DOOB received his BA from Dartmouth College, New Hampshire, and did graduate work at Duke University, North Carolina, and the University of Frankfurt. He was awarded the PhD of Harvard University. Except for the war years, he has taught at Yale University since 1934. During the war he held various positions connected with psychological warfare and became Policy Co-ordinator of the Overseas Branch of the US Office of War Information. His research has been conducted largely in the field of public opinion, propaganda and communications. His research in Africa began in 1952 and provided material for his Becoming More Civilised (1960) and Communication in Africa (1961). He does not regard himself as an Africanist, because his interest there is not in the continent or in the Africans as such, but in using the countries and their peoples as a way of testing hypotheses cross-culturally.

15 Linguistics

JOSEPH H. GREENBERG is a professor of Anthropology at Stanford University. His main fields are African ethnology, African linguistics and general linguistics. In the course of his research, he visited West Africa for extended field trips in 1938–39 (ethnological field work among the Hausa) and in 1954–55 (linguistic survey of the Plateau Provinces, Nigeria). His publications include: The Influence of Islam on a Sudanese Religion (1946); Languages of Africa (1963); Universals of Language (1963, editor); and Essays in Linguistics (1957).

16 The Visual Arts

ROY SIEBER was appointed Associate Professor of Art at Indiana University in 1962. He graduated with a degree from the New School for Social Research, New York, and was later awarded the PhD of the State University of Iowa. He is chairman of the Committee of Fine Arts and the Humanities of the African Studies Association in the United States, and has served as consultant and member of several foundation committees concerned with research in Africa. In 1958–59 he conducted research at the British Museum and in Nigeria on a grant from the Ford Foundation. His publications include Sculpture of Northern Nigeria (1961).

17 Music and the Dance

ALAN P. MERRIAM, an anthropologist and ethnomusicologist, is Professor of Anthropology at Indiana University. He has taught at the universities of Wisconsin and Minnesota, and at Northwestern University. In 1951–52 he carried out field research in the former Belgian Congo and in Ruanda-Urundi, and again in the Congo in 1959–60. He also studied the Flathead Indians of western Montana in 1950 and 1958. His publications include: *Congo; Background of Conflict* (1961); *A Prologue to the Study of the African Arts* (1962); *The Ethnography of Flathead Indian Music* (1955); and *The Anthropology of Music* (1964).

18 Folklore and Literature

WILLIAM BASCOM is Professor of Anthropology and Director of the Robert H. Lowie Museum of Anthropology at the University of California, Berkeley. He carried out field research among the Yoruba of Nigeria in 1937–38, in 1950–51 and in 1960; and was in government service in the Gold Coast (now Ghana) from 1942 to 1945. He taught at Northwestern University, where he received his PhD, from 1939 to 1957, and later was associated with the Program of African Studies. He was President of the American Folklore Society from 1952 to 1954.

Introduction:
The Integration of Social Research   Robert A. Lystad

A T THE MOST general level of integration, the methods of science inform research
in all, or nearly all, the disciplines, but they do so in greater and lesser degrees.
So difficult does the rigorous application of its methods appear to be for many
disciplines, so loosely and haphazardly have they been applied, and, probably, so
various are their interpretations that only in the general sense of wishing and striving
can scientific methods yet be regarded as creative of unity in African areal studies.
That this is the case need be neither surprising nor dismaying, for there is something less than total agreement on general theory, 'middle-range theory', methodologies, and the interpretations of findings within most of the disciplines themselves.

The suffusion of at least a strongly scientific orientation into all the disciplines,
nonetheless, is apparent. This has occurred in research conducted with predominantly historical or predominantly directly observable materials and with
predominantly qualitative or predominantly quantifiable materials. The spirit of
the 'hard', 'exact' sciences, if not precisely their experimental methods, increasingly infuses the 'softer' sciences, the social sciences, history, education and the
humanities, as they intensify their studies of man in the African area. Although
this is most clearly seen in those disciplines that already are part of the hard tradition
and in those that attempt to employ the exact sciences in the solution of social
problems, it is evident elsewhere as well. Had other areas of knowledge, regrettably omitted as entities, been more specifically reported—areas such as religion,
values or international relations, to identify a few—the influence, sometimes
surprisingly, would have been further underscored. This community of scientific
outlook is expressed in several themes that appear in nearly all the essays in this
volume.

There is a vast concern with the extension or amplification of theory, and so
frequent are the acknowledgments of, or calls for help from, other disciplines that
it is almost possible to say that the universal objective is the construction of a
general, systemic, predominantly behavioural theory or theories. At the same
time, there is universal recognition that Africa offers no unique theoretical problems: a viewpoint thoroughly consistent with scientific endeavour. With reference to the analysis of his behaviour at higher levels of theoretical abstraction and

generalisation, man in Africa is man anywhere. There is no essential need, inherent in any discipline, to conduct research in Africa *per se*. What does confront the researcher in Africa is a rare—not unique—opportunity to test hypotheses and generalisations derived from theories that have been devised principally on the basis of non-African materials. The African setting, African histories and African solutions to fundamental human problems differ from others only in their particulars; they do not differ in kind.

At lower levels of generalisation, however, warnings are voiced against the uncritical adoption of 'Western' categories of analysis for the ordering of African materials. The feeling is strong that the distortion of concrete African social realities is too great, the omission of relevant, even crucial, data too likely when the data are injected into categories predefined on the basis of non-African materials and from 'Western' models. Writers in nearly all disciplines have encountered these conceptual difficulties on the level at which raw data are minimally organised and at the next higher levels on which relationships among minimum categories are being determined. At the same time, the need to define new (or to modify 'Western') categories has the salutary effect of forcing a discipline's non-Africanists to review and revise those categories that fail adequately to comprehend African data. This, more than perhaps any other, is the principal service African areal studies can provide to theoreticians in any discipline working toward general models and theories.

What also impresses researchers in these respects is the abundant opportunity to study the phenomena of social change in settings marked by an astonishing diversity and variety. Varying degrees of instability and discontinuity—rather than stability and continuity—are the primary characteristics of African societies in the process of dissolution or of becoming. Certainly these are the aspects of change that have most captured the attention of the researcher. The modern and the pre-modern, the old and the new, the past and the present, the fast-moving and the slow, the radical and the conservative exist side by side, between and within each other. If this factor of juxtaposition, partial assimilation in various directions, and confusion—and it occurs all along the continuum between any polar points—perturbs the scientist in Africa, it does not defeat him. It rather stimulates him to a heightened concern with the construction of new classifications and typologies and a search for new hypotheses that are, after all, among the essential building blocks of theory and are a primary concern of science.

Perhaps the very observation of so much social change contributes to a certain reticence to make theory explicit or to relate specific research to a general body of theory. Perhaps the not infrequent occurrence of events that are apparently unpredictable in their timing, exact content, intensity and duration contribute to a certain reticence to predict outcomes in advance or at least to record advance predictions. The concern with the construction of theories that will enable researchers to make predictive hypotheses, nevertheless, is widespread.

These concerns, activated as they are in a setting characterised by a great diversity of social situations, are sustained by still another element essential to scientific research. In some ways and in many places, Africa presents the researcher with conditions resembling, though by no means duplicating, an experimental laboratory. The spatial juxtaposition of historically identical or highly similar social groups, which have been subjected to slightly different stimuli for change, makes possible modes of analysis not unlike those ideally conducted in laboratories. The possibility of discovering and analysing the emergence of similar—or different—social characteristics in previously different groups after subjection to identical stimuli provides a delightful prospect for the scientist. The persistence of identifiable groups, which have previously and fairly recently been studied and for which documents record at least some of the events of the intervening period, also sets the stage for simulated experimentation. Any scientifically oriented scholar tries to define a research problem in which at least some of the variables and social units are controlled or controllable.

The African area certainly does not provide a laboratory in the hard sense of the term. Situations in which a small number of independent, known variables have operated must be discovered, and such situations are difficult to come by. When they have been found, the ensuing experiment is still one of the *ex post facto* variety, in which the experimenter is forced to identify and attempt to manipulate variables he himself did not contrive. However carefully the research methods and techniques are employed, the results of such experimentation are always less than completely persuasive and satisfying. They nevertheless can heighten the degree of certainty with which conclusions can be stated, increase the probability of subsequent verification, and strengthen the plausibility, if not the 'proof', of the argument for the reader. In the absence of an exact laboratory and in the welter of multiple, complex variables that almost always and everywhere plague the social scientist, the African approximations of a laboratory hold out attractive possibilities.

The increase in numbers of researchers and greater co-ordination among them may increase the frequency with which the tools of science are put to use. Most disciplines are only now beginning to take hold in any strength on the continent, and many cannot even claim that. Without exception they call for greatly increased research activity, and, almost without exception (at least with respect to some aspects of the discipline), all have truly elemental needs. Considerably below the levels of sophisticated theory and method there persists the need for facts at the empirical level; there is a paucity of data that is descriptive in sufficient detail.

Facts and theories, of course, are not disparate entities. There are numerous facts lying around, so to speak, but many of them have been collected by researchers with purposes other than those derived from theories, which, in all disciplines, have had greater significance imputed to them since the second world war. Many of these facts are of little contemporary use even when they have been well-reported. They may have been selected on the basis of outmoded concepts, or they may have become less relevant because of the rapid flow of events since they were collected.

Many other facts have been reported in such a way as to be relevant to one discipline but merely frustrating to others. This frustration arises sometimes from the mode or terminology of the report, more often from the failure to report precisely those related contextual facts that would have given the fact itself wider, cross-disciplinary significance. The reader of the following chapters is likely to gain the impression that, while there is no dearth of appreciation of what other disciplines are doing, there is an even stronger appreciation for what they might have done or might do to increase their usefulness. The text reveals many instances in which information from other disciplines has in fact been useful; it also reveals many instances in which information from other disciplines is clearly necessary but apparently not yet available in usable forms.

The problems of cross-disciplinary communications are, of course, complex. Between disciplines there stand at least the low barriers of specialised vocabularies,

which interrupt the easy flow of information.   But similar interference is encountered even within disciplines, between subdisciplines, for example, and between
different theoretical and methodological traditions.   The emergence of behaviour-
ally oriented research in many disciplines is accompanied by the emergence of new
terminologies designed to identify aspects of a social situation previously unper-
ceived or unexplored.   The interest in general, systemic theory, and the construction of new classifications and typologies introduce unfamiliar words and neologisms.

Such problems of vocabulary, however greatly they inhibit immediate communication, are not insoluble problems; they are solved by learning the language.
And the language is more precise and adequate when different phenomena or
different aspects of a phenomenon are differently symbolised.   Greater difficulties
arise when, with reference to quite different phenomena, the identical term is
used by different disciplines or by different traditions of research within a single
discipline.   The same is true when different disciplines or traditions use different
terms for identical phenomena.   And the greatest difficulties arise when terms are
used with reference to phenomena that have not been observed at all, or have been
only partially observed and partially inferred or only partially reported.

Fact-finding and fact-communication problems such as these are ordinarily
solved by the use of operational definitions.   These consist essentially of descriptions of observed relationships symbolised by the terms and accompanied by a set
of instructions that, if followed, should enable any observer to perceive the same
relationships.   Each of the disciplines and fields of knowledge engaged in African
research must have many 'facts', useful to the others, which lie dormant or obscured
by faulty communications and which, properly described, could help meet the
elemental need for data.

Almost parenthetically, it may here briefly be noted that two other sources of
data, at both the 'fact' and 'idea' levels, appear to be underemployed.   One is the
bodies of material published in languages (and to a lesser extent in countries)
foreign to the scholar.   In this book, of course, these are non-English sources.
The other potentially greater source of information is the literature of the applied
scientist, the development planner and engineer, the experienced colonial and
post-colonial administrator, and the field technician.   This truly enormous reservoir of facts, frequently collected by perceptive observers of social behaviour over
long periods of time, has been insufficiently tapped.

Still another aspect of the fact-communication problem lies in quite a different
quarter: the professional status system and the culture of academic publishing.   A
report of the Publications Policy Committee of the American Anthropological
Association, *Some Foundations for Publication Policy* (1964), analyses this aspect
with reference to the discipline of anthropology.   The report deals in part with
the scarcity of that kind of information which consists of field data (or other
primary, raw data) presented in some of the recognised categories ordinarily
employed in the discipline.   'Materials organized to this extent may be utilized
by other workers in another field without much qualification by the author.   They
can be employed in comparative studies planned in terms of a variety of theoretical
problems, some of which may not have occurred to the original observer.   They
may be purely descriptive, but they constitute descriptions in terms which professionals in the subdiscipline have found relevant to a variety of problems.'

According to the Committee, its study supports the conclusion that materials
of this sort are inadequately distributed in large part because of the professional

status system.   'Prestige and position in the profession are based to a very large
extent upon the individual's performance in the communications system.'   This
system requires that publication be cast in the form of contributions to the development of the theoretical framework of the science, a form, incidentally, which is
also less painful and time-consuming for the author.   There is no scarcity of
publications of this 'idea' variety.   Despite the abundance of published material,
however, the scholar is faced with what amounts to 'an information crisis'.   'Ideally,
the scholar should be free to process his data in accordance with its intellectual
demands, to inform others about his progress at any step of the way, and to be
professionally rewarded when he performs these functions properly.   Today we
are far from the ideal.   We have inadequate documentation, an information crisis,
the forcing of data to fit theoretical interpretations, and rewards for only one type
of communications: the scholarly book or article in letterpress.'

These excerpts from the report are set in a context that delineates a program
for solving a communications problem within a single discipline, but Africanists
will recognise a situation not totally unfamiliar to them.   Predominantly interpretative rather than descriptive data are pre-eminently publishable.   Truly stag-
gering quantities of African 'raw data' must be stored in boxes from which they
either never emerge or emerge only to strengthen the classroom discussion of the
individual researcher-teacher.   Although 'raw facts' ordinarily are not useful to
others, their availability in at least a minimally conceptualised form appropriate to
the discipline and predominantly descriptive in nature might do much to reduce the
apparent gap between desired information and available information.   If the studies
in this volume do not solve the communication problems, they nonetheless may contribute to an awareness of the existence and location of materials already available
and of the need for more materials to be made available in this factual form.

Whatever the reasons, shortages of basic and usable information inhibit the
achievement of understanding.   Among the more serious effects of these shortages
is the difficulty they impose on cross-disciplinary and cross-cultural comparison and
on the comparative analysis of change through time in any 'before-after' formulation.
Regrets about the paucity of data readily available for comparative analysis, however,
need not obscure the significance of the attempts to engage in it.   The methodology
is fundamental to science, to the construction of theory, and to the understanding
of man in Africa.   The contributors to this book are unanimous in their desire to
extend the use of this basic tool and its related techniques of research.   All
recognise the difficulties which occur both before and beyond the collection of
bits of data.   The attractions of Africa's diversity are diminished by the distractions
of diversity.   Africa's social units—the subjects of social research—are diverse, for
example, in scale; there are small groups and local groups and territorial groups
and national groups and regional groups and continental groups, to name several
along merely one kind of simple continuum.   For any variable there are problems
of identification of an appropriate group and problems of collecting reliable and
valid data from the members of a group once it has been identified.   The nature
and relative significance of variables change with time.   Africans are on the move,
literally and figuratively.   Some disciplines engaged in exciting research must deal
with time-spans that are enormous and that clearly require the intuition and logic
of the sleuth as well as the rigorous logic of the scientist.   Sampling procedures are
infrequently used or fully described.   Quantified data is far more rare than qualitatively examined data, and replication of research is practically nonexistent.   Yet

there is a widespread optimism that social research in Africa stands on the threshold of considerable achievement in the use of comparative analyses.

This optimism, like the general atmosphere of expectancy that permeates the studies in this book, seems justified on several grounds. In several disciplines there is considerable satisfaction that deficiencies of information are being, or are on the verge of being, significantly reduced and that methodologies are well-founded or that promising new ones are imminent. Several of the social science disciplines, furthermore, seem to be converging in certain of their theoretical, methodological and problem-definitional interests, and in the terminologies with which they express them. Without losing their identity, several of them are redrawing the maps of knowledge in such a way as to share intellectual territory with previously more distinct disciplines. Problems are being defined in a less grand manner; the canons of evidence are being more rigorously applied. There is a narrowing of the scale of social units or groups selected for study and a narrowing of the scope of problems selected for more intensive analysis. If many of the disciplines engage but little in statistical analysis of carefully drawn samples, there is at least a growing feeling that such analysis ought to be undertaken, or that problems ought to be defined in such a way as to make it possible. All of these are affectively neutral, cross-disciplinary, scientific grounds for optimism.

But there are other grounds as well. One is the increased presence of professionally trained African scholars. In comparatively small numbers, these have long contributed to knowledge about the continent. Now their numbers are growing, and research and training programs are under way that will accelerate the pace at which they participate in social research in Africa and elsewhere. African governments tend to state their present training needs in terms of planners, engineers, administrators and practical men of action, equipped to solve the more immediate and pressing social problems of rapid, multi-faceted development. It may even be that, for a time at least, some governments will tend to discourage the creation of corps of intellectuals engaged primarily in basic or 'pure' research in the sciences and humanities. They may also tend to discourage the presence of non-African scholars engaged in 'impractical' or 'backward-looking' research, possibly into what are thought to be 'delicate' situations or institutions, or other 'irrelevant' and 'personal' intellectual pursuits. These are attitudes that, if they do come to be held, can readily be understood. Nor are they attitudes that need be deplored. Although they represent differences in emphasis, 'applied research' into 'problems of development' and 'pure research' into 'intellectual' or 'basic' problems essentially are or can be complementary. Certain chapters in this book specifically deal with 'applied research', but all others also demonstrate their relevance to the understanding, development and enjoyment of the 'real world'. Regardless of their research frames of reference, African and non-African scholars ultimately are engaged in a single enterprise.

The final basis for optimism is non-scientific and non-disciplinary; it is frankly sentimental. Most researchers seem to acquire an affection for Africa. The sources of this emotion are many and may have nothing whatsoever to do with Africa *per se*. And yet the area elicits a considerable degree of personal commitment from its students, non-African and African alike. The preoccupations of their profession, of their disciplines, of science, or of the pursuit of knowledge or happiness may be paramount for them; for some, these are undoubtedly the sole preoccupations. Viewed in one way, science is essentially an elaborate structure

designed ideally to eliminate the feelings and biases and other non-rational deficiencies of the human observer, and social researchers guard against the instrusion of
these factors into their work.   Like students of other world regions, most students
of Africa, nonetheless, genuinely like the area in which they are intellectually
involved.   They respect its past, they appreciate its present, and they wish it well
in the future.   The intellectual commitment to social research reported in this
book and the affective commitment to the continent and its people that in some
measure motivates the researcher bode well for the future of African areal studies.

HISTORICAL AND SOCIO-CULTURAL
STUDIES

1

Prehistory   J. Desmond Clark

I INTRODUCTION*

1. THE HISTORICAL BACKGROUND

AFRICA IS THE continent to which man must turn for his knowledge of the earliest stages of his own biological and cultural development. Because there are many regions for which little more than one hundred years of historical record exist, archaeological studies provide many of the most important sources of evidence for reconstructing the past history of the present-day races and populations. The realisation of its importance and the unique finds of the past twenty years have stimulated more active prehistoric research in most parts of the African continent than had ever previously been conducted. This modern, disciplined research grew from the interest of amateurs living on the spot during the second half of the last century and the first twenty years of this.

Western Europe in the 1850s was arguing the validity of the claim of Boucher de Perthes that the flaked stone tools he was finding in association with the bones of elephants and other extinct mammals in the gravels of some of the rivers of northern France were, in fact, contemporary with these creatures. At the same time miners, farmers and soldiers were searching the eroded terraces of South African rivers and finding similar artifacts worked by man, the earliest recorded discovery of stone implements in the continent being in 1858 from the mouth of the Fish River in the eastern Cape Province. The extreme richness of Africa in cultural remains of all ages, more especially from the Pleistocene, and sometimes associated with the remains of extinct faunas, so aroused and encouraged interest that, from the beginning of the present century, the search for prehistoric remains on an extensive scale was carried out in the Maghreb, South Africa and the Nile Valley. Research in other regions, such as East Africa and Rhodesia, was later in beginning, but the pioneer workers there had the advantage of coming fresh into the field and of being in possession of the latest knowledge and techniques. A vast quantity of material was collected during this period, but little was known of the age or relationships of the different types of tool assemblages, which in South Africa, for example, were described either as 'Palaeolithic' or 'Bushman', and for long defied any systematic classification.

* Notes and Bibliography for this chapter will be found on page 493.

Much of this early work was carried out by the amateurs. Indeed, like that of Europe, African prehistory has always benefited from the work of the informed layman, and this is as true today as it was at the beginning of the century. Uninformed enthusiasm, of course, is to be discouraged, but in most parts of the continent the richness of the prehistoric field has inspired the amateur scholar to obtain the necessary training, and he has often become as good as many professionals. In fact, not a few of the more important discoveries and advances in prehistory are due to the informed amateur, some of whom, like van Riet Lowe, later became leading professionals. The trained professional archaeologist has always been thin on the ground, and a recent estimate indicates that in Africa each worker could have more than 10,000 square miles of country for his operations.

By the 1920s the pioneer period of prehistoric research in Africa may be considered to have come to an end and the formative stage to have begun. By this time one or two professional archaeologists had begun to appear on the continent. Mainly trained in Europe, these men had the advantage of knowing both the European and the African fields. It early became apparent that their first task was twofold: to construct a firm chronology within which could be fitted the evolving stages of the more imperishable remains of man's material culture being eroded from the river gravels, lake silts, aeolian sands and marine terraces which had preserved them; and, for the southern parts of the continent, to build up a local African terminology, because the rigid de Mortillet scheme of typological evolution for western Europe could not be fitted into an African context. At the Pretoria meeting of the South African Association for the Advancement of Science in 1929, A. J. H. Goodwin and C. van Riet Lowe were responsible for instituting such a new terminology. In the first instance it was applied only within the borders of South Africa, but it was fairly soon extended to East Africa by Leakey and to Rhodesia by Neville Jones. Minor alterations were introduced by the First and Third Pan-African Congresses on Prehistory in 1947 and 1955 respectively, but, with a few amendments, it is still universally used today throughout sub-Saharan Africa.

In North Africa, however, the prehistoric cultures of the Mediterranean littoral have been shown to be related more closely to southern Europe and south-western Asia than with tropical Africa, and Mediterranean terminology, therefore, was retained for this region. The two terminologies may be compared in Table I (pp. 20-21).

The establishment of a chronological framework for the dating of archaeological finds occupied African prehistorians throughout the continent, and, up to the second world war, their primary interest lay in this task. If the different kinds of assemblages were to be compared among themselves and to the European succession, it was essential for each worker to be able to establish a relative chronology into which to fit the cultural succession in the locality where he was working. Considerable emphasis was also placed on the study of typology and, to a lesser extent, of the technology of the various artifact classes. Although this great importance was attached to the lithic content of prehistoric cultures and to pottery wares in the few regions where proto-historic research was being carried out, little or no attempt was made to interpret the ethnography of these remains or the associations under which they were excavated. Indeed, where Stone Age cultures were concerned, and outside the East African Rift Valley and certain localities in northern and southern Africa where artifacts occurred in association with fossil fauna, it was generally conceded that nothing more imperishable than stone had survived. The cultural assemblages were thus treated in the same way as the geologist looks upon palaeontological material: as type fossils in a time horizon. This primary chronological and typological interest was mainly responsible for directing attention to localities where thick, or morphologically good, successions of Quaternary sediments could be found, notwithstanding that most of the cultural assemblages they contained were disturbed and not in their original or primary context. Cave sites were excavated with the same aims in view, and, although in this case the assemblages were usually in their primary contexts, excavation techniques left much to be desired, and it was rarely possible to distinguish successive individual living floors.

This essential preoccupation with chronology and typology during the formative stage of African prehistory did foster, where circumstances permitted, close co-operation between prehistorian, geologist and palaeontologsit. Such was the case in French North Africa, in South and East Africa, the Nile Valley and some other regions. Often the prehistorian and geologist were merged in the same individual, as in the case of J. P. Johnston in South Africa. All too frequently, however, the prehistorian was a lone worker and had no opportunity to obtain geological assistance, because there was no geologist working in his area. Nor did he always have the benefit of the relative dating supplied by the palaeontologist from fossil fauna assemblages, because the acid soil of so much of tropical Africa does not preserve bones.

In spite of these handicaps, however, satisfactory progress was made, and by 1939 the culture history of large parts of the continent had been set into a relative framework of changing climates, and attempts had been made to correlate the successions in the widely separated regions and even to correlate African and European sequences. The most substantial body of this evidence comes from French North Africa, the East African Rift, and the Republic of South Africa, but brilliant results have also been obtained by individual scholars in other areas.

If the pioneer period of African archaeology can be considered to have ended in the 1920s, the modern period is to be regarded as having begun after the end of the second world war. This thirty-year interval, which has here been called the formative period, saw a gradual but striking change in the outlook of the prehistorians working in Africa. This was the period when some of the most significant discoveries were made and when a coherent picture of African archaeology first began to emerge.

French prehistorians were investigating the culture history of Pleistocene man in north-west Africa in relation to the marine sediments of the Mediterranean and Atlantic coasts and were laying the basis for the fine stratigraphic studies of Biberson (1961) and others. The research in Morocco provided what is probably the most complete cultural succession in relation to changing sea levels of anywhere in the world. At the same time, investigations of sites on the interior plateau of Algeria and Tunisia revealed the richness of certain localities in fossil faunas and cultural remains of Pleistocene man. When some of these were re-examined after the second world war by Arambourg, Balout (1955b) and others, they gave us the first knowledge that the makers of the Handaxe Culture, in that part of the continent at least, belonged to the same stock as Pithecanthropus (*Homo erectus*) of the Far East. Prehistoric studies in the Maghreb up to 1939 had provided extensive knowledge of the evolving culture stages of the specialised Upper Pleistocene tanged-point culture (the Aterian), of the blade and burin peoples of the coastal and plateau shell-mounds and rock-shelters, and of the rich rock art and Neolithic cultures of the Sahara, though their relationships with the Nile Valley still had to be determined.

The same activity characterised investigations in South Africa. Visits by European archaeologists and anthropologists such as Burkitt and Breuil, Keith and Haddon, and the detailed studies by South African prehistorians of cave sites and river valley stratigraphy led to the publication of the book *The Stone Age Cultures of South Africa* (Goodwin and Lowe 1929), which laid the foundations for all future work there. Neville Jones had by this time extended investigations to Rhodesia, and in 1926 Colette was engaged in the first excavations in the Congo — at Kalina Point, Leopoldville. In 1924 Leakey (1936, 1951, 1961) started systematic field-work in East Africa. His long-continued and meticulously conducted excavations there have made the prehistory of this region probably better known than that of any other part of the continent. These studies showed the undoubtedly funda-mental importance of the East African tectonic region for understanding the evolution of culture and for providing the basis for establishing a relative chronology for the various stages.

It was in 1924 that Dart provided the first knowledge of the Australopithecine stage of human evolution with his description of the Taung child. He also started a controversy that was settled only in 1935 by Broom's discovery of the first adult Australopithecine from Sterkfontein in the Transvaal. Today the Australopithe-cines are represented by remains of well over 300 individuals, practically all of them from Africa, and their association with tool-making is proved beyond question.

2. SUMMARY OF RESULTS OBTAINED DURING THE FORMATIVE PERIOD

The formative stage of African archaeology was one in which the archaeologist frequently had to work alone, and his main emphasis was on the taxonomy of the surviving material culture, which he strove to fit into as accurate a relative chrono-logical framework as he was able with the inadequate means at his disposal. Since the second world war he has come more and more to use the methods and help of other disciplines; he is no longer — or should not be — a lone worker. His chief aim is no longer taxonomic; he now engages in the attempt to reconstruct the economic and social life of the prehistoric group he is studying and to interpret the rate and mechanics of social change in prehistoric times. Apparent as yet only in the work of a small group of prehistorians, this important trend is gaining momen-tum and is finding expression in the broadened extent of the observations made in the field and in the methods of analysis that are coming to be much more widely adopted. As a result it is today possible to summarise the history of man in the African continent with greater precision and accuracy than ever before. The chronological tables, which are discussed in broad outline below, are an attempt to set out what is now known of man's cultural achievements in Africa.

Sometime during the Lower Pleistocene, bipedal hominids, using their hands for manipulating tools, turned to working stone. Quantities of worked stone are found in association with broken bone with Australopithecine remains on the living floors in Bed I at the Olduvai Gorge. No hominid more advanced than the Australopithecines is known to have been present anywhere in the world at that time level, so that it may be inferred that they were the earliest tool-makers.[1] The Bed I camp floors at Olduvai have been dated to between 1·8 and 1·0 million years by the latest potassium argon results, and they provide unique evidence of hominid behaviour at this early stage.

The continued importance of the African tropical environment during the Middle Pleistocene is demonstrated by the richness of the cultural evidence from these times, and the Olduvai and other habitation sites provide a clear record of steady progress towards ever more efficient equipment and control of natural resources. From about 50,000 BC onwards, even the relatively unspecialised technology of the Middle and Later Stone Age inhabitants rendered it comparatively easy for the hunting-gathering populations to gain a livelihood. The continued richness of the tropical environment was undoubtedly a factor in the passing of cultural initiative from Africa to those regions adjacent to the Upper Pleistocene glaciers in the northern hemisphere. The main technical advances kept pace with those in Europe and Asia, yet the steady improvements to be seen in the African cultures appear now to be the result of innovations and contacts from outside the continent rather than of inventions from within Africa itself. This can best be seen from a study of the origin of food production in Africa and the spread of metallurgy there. There are still many gaps in our knowledge of this subject, but it would seem that the practice of cereal crop cultivation and stock breeding was diffused to Africa from south-west Asia in the late 6th or early 5th millennium BC. Once the idea was adopted, the versatility of African culture was such that it evolved its own characteristic food plants, though it never succeeded in domesticating any of the larger mammals, except the ass.

By 3000 BC Neolithic culture had spread to the Sudan and the Upper Nile and throughout the Sahara. It is to be supposed that the contacts between Africa north and south of the Sahara enabled the Negro population to spread to the northern confines of the desert. These contacts probably also resulted in extensive experimentation with food plants by the specialised hunting and 'vege-cultural' peoples of the West African rainforest and savannah. By 1000 BC an eastern and a western Neolithic complex can be recognised, and it was mainly the movement of populations southwards from the western complex, probably from the southern Sudan, that brought about the economic revolution from food-collecting to food-producing in the subcontinent. The 500-year period which bridges the previous and the present era was a time when effective iron-working techniques spread from Meroe and across the Sahara. It was also during this period that Malaysian influences spread to the East African coast and introduced tropical Asiatic food plants, of which the yam and the banana were the most important.

Central and southern Africa now began to feel the influence of Negroid cultivators and mixed farmers who can probably be identified as the spearhead of the more extensive Bantu movements of later centuries. The present-day interest in proto-historic studies in Africa has developed only within the last few years, but as early as 1939 it was evident that the richness of the indigenous cultures of Benin, the Kasai, and Zimbabwe belied the belief that African culture was incapable of rising above that of the simple village farming community.

II *THE ESTABLISHMENT OF THE CHRONOLOGICAL AND CLIMATIC FRAMEWORK*

The prehistorian has several methods and techniques by means of which he is seeking, with increasing success, to fill in the outline picture of the evolution and history of man in Africa. The first necessity is still that of establishing a chronological framework into which past events in the continent can be fitted and correlated with other areas. One of the chief sources of evidence on which this chronology is being based is that of stratigraphy and the study of the faunal assemblages contained in geological deposits.

1. THE USE OF STRATIGRAPHY AND FAUNA IN ESTABLISHING CHRONOLOGY

Pleistocene archaeology and geology have always been closely linked, so that it is hardly surprising to find that geologists are responsible for not a few archaeological studies. In this connection the pioneer work of E. J. Wayland (1934) stands out. His interpretation of the sedimentary succession and the tectonic history of the Victoria Basin and the Western Rift contributed to the development of the important 'pluvial/interpluvial' hypothesis. Three main 'pluvials' (periods of increased rainfall) were identified, separated by periods of drier climate (or 'interpluvials'). The geological succession of deposits was thus used as a basis on which to reconstruct Pleistocene climatic history.

Both Leakey and Nilsson (1932), working independently in the Gregory Rift, also found evidence contributing to this pluvial/interpluvial theory, and the existence of two post-Pleistocene wet phases — the Makalian and the Nakuran — was also established. Later the Middle Pleistocene pluvial was subdivided, and the four pluvials were named Kageran, Kamasian, Kanjeran and Gamblian; during the interpluvials volcanic activity and tectonic movements were manifest. Leakey was able to correlate the pluvials with the rich cultural history of the region, where two parallel evolving tool traditions — a typical Middle Stone Age, based on the prepared core and faceted flake, and a true blade culture called the Kenya Capsian — had existed since the Gamblian. In the Albertine Rift recent work by Bishop (1963) on the Uganda side and de Heinzelin (1961) on the Congo side has resulted in a better appreciation of the tectonic history and the sedimentary series with their fossil content. As a consequence of these studies, it appears that the human cultures of this region have more in common with those of the Congo Basin than with those of East Africa.

The Eastern Rift contains a number of earlier fossil-bearing deposits of Middle Pleistocene age, and the two most important of these sites yielding artifacts are Kariandusi and Olorgesailie. Both contain many magnificent Acheulian tools that lie on several temporary land surfaces within a general lacustrine sequence. Far and away the most important series of deposits, however, are of Earlier Pleistocene age and are contained in the Olduvai Gorge in northern Tanganyika. Here some 300 feet of stratified sediments provide a unique succession of cultural and faunal stages. These beds and their contents have been investigated by Leakey since 1931 and, because of modern excavation techniques, are providing a knowledge of the behaviour patterns of Lower and Middle Pleistocene man never before considered possible. It is thus in Africa that prehistorians are gaining the most complete knowledge of the biological evolution of the earliest tool-makers and of the very slow development of their culture. Although Olduvai is the most important Earlier Pleistocene site, several other living-sites of this time in North, South and East Africa have also yielded evidence of man's evolving skills, of increasing specialisation, and of the movement towards more complete exploitation of the natural resources of the environment. This type of site has largely been destroyed in temperate Europe where glacial conditions, absent in Africa, caused the imperishable remains of the earliest cultures to be redeposited in some fluviatile gravel or sand.

The Laetolil Beds, south of Olduvai, are another important source of fossil fauna, and the main series there is believed to be contemporary with Olduvai Bed I. Pebble tools have been recovered from these beds together with a hominid fragment related by Robinson (1962) to the Australopithecine *Australopithecus africanus*. Since 1924, when Dart described the Taung child, numerous discoveries of this physical type have been made, and it is clear that it was widely distributed throughout the continent during Lower Pleistocene times. This hominid is particularly well known, however, from the finds in the Transvaal cave breccias in South Africa and, more recently, from finds in the Olduvai Gorge. Darwin's belief that man originated in the tropics, probably in Africa, has thus been vindicated by the discovery there of the Australopithecine stage of his ancestry. On the East African living-floors the bones of these man-apes have now been found in indisputable association with culture, and from their anatomical features there can be no doubt that these hominids were fully competent to make and use the clumsy stone tools found with them. Africa has now provided the earliest known evidence of human culture, and it is apparent that there was a remarkably rapid spread of tool-making techniques from there into Europe and Asia at the end of the Lower Pleistocene.

Other localities in East Africa yielding important stratified sections, sometimes with cultural remains, are the Kanam, Rawi and Kanjera Beds of the Kavirondo Gulf region of Lake Victoria; these represent a long sedimentary series of Lower and Middle Pleistocene age.[2] The first has yielded a human jaw fragment[3] in association with primitive pebble tools and a Lower Pleistocene fauna, and the last, of Late Middle or Early Upper Pleistocene age, contains some fragmentary cranial material with Acheulian forms of handaxe. The very rich fauna recovered by Arambourg and others from the Omo lacustrine series of beds at the north end of Lake Rudolph in Ethiopia is late Villafranchian, and a recent investigation by Howell (1959) shows that primitive flaked pebbles may also be associated.

The study of all this and other faunal material enabled palaeontologists to establish the presence of four faunal stages and to reach formal agreement about them at the Third Pan-African Congress in 1955. These stages, which have been correlated with the pluvials, are known as Omo-Kanam,[4] Lower and Upper Olduvan, and Gamblian or post Olduvan and are distinguished by a steadily decreasing percentage of the archaic forms and the increasing importance of the modern species that they contain.

This chronology, based on climatic interpretation, appeared to provide a firm framework into which the cultural succession could be fitted. With varying degrees of success, attempts were made to correlate it with the stratigraphy and climatic interpretations obtained in other regions. Where the palaeontological evidence was good, such correlations were usually successful; where the evidence was lacking, the results were less certain, because they were based on inferred climatic interpretation and on cultural fossils. The last word, however, has by no means been said.

As long ago as 1937 the validity of this East African scheme had been challenged by Solomon (1959). In 1957 Cooke and, in the following year, Flint (1959a) showed that, because of the instability of the East African region, it was generally impossible to rule out tectonic phenomena as having been responsible for the lacustrine/terrestrial succession of deposits for those periods anterior to the Gamblian. Although the validity of the climatic sequence for the earlier periods is, therefore, in doubt, this does not mean that the sequence is necessarily incorrect.

There is good evidence in support of it from other regions, notably from southern and central Africa, where there has been little or no earth movement since the beginning of the Pleistocene. The succession of events in a wide number of river systems and the redistributions of the aeolian Kalahari Sand indicate that climate was indeed the chief factor behind the morphological history of the river valleys in these regions.

Flint (1959b) has admirably summed up the present position in regard to the climatic chronology scheme: 'I conclude that climate as a primary basis of any stratigraphic scheme is unreliable. This conclusion . . . does not constitute an attack on the reality of climatic change in East Africa, for such change seems truly to have occurred. It seeks only to re-establish climate in the secondary position in which it properly belongs in any stratigraphic scheme. . . The three entities concerned — rock units, faunal zones and cultural materials — constitute, as a group, a reasonable basis from which can emerge broad correlation that will inspire confidence. . .'

Field research is now proceeding along the lines indicated by Flint with some very satisfactory results. Undoubtedly the most important is the Leakeys' work at the Olduvai Gorge, which is yielding a vastly increased knowledge of the Earlier Pleistocene faunas and cultural stages and of the environmental conditions with which these are associated. Work is now being actively undertaken at several sites in Uganda by Bishop and Posnansky and in the Albertine Rift by de Heinzelin; this research has modified Wayland's earlier scheme. Arambourg's work on the Tunisian and Algerian plateau and Biberson's in Morocco have similarly considerably extended knowledge of the fauna and cultures of the Lower and Middle Pleistocene. At the Kalambo Falls in Rhodesia, Bond, Haldemann and Clark have been able to correlate the well stratified and very rich cultural succession with events since the early part of the Upper Pleistocene, and the sequence in the Vaal basin in South Africa is being reinvestigated by Mason (1957, 1962).

2. OTHER RELATIVE METHODS OF ESTABLISHING AGE

This reassessment of the previously accepted chronological and faunal framework into which the cultural succession is fitted will doubtless yield interesting and even exciting results. There are other methods, however, used successfully for the relative dating of both archaeological and faunal material; which are comparatively new. After the last war a number of chemical methods of assessing the relative age of bone were developed. The first of these was Oakley's technique for comparing the percentage of fluorine present in bone from different horizons at the same site. This is particularly valuable for determining whether human skeletal material present in a deposit is of the same age as the other fossil material with which it may be associated. This method was directly responsible for detecting the Piltdown hoax, and, as a result of the exposure of this fraud, several additional tests have been developed. These serve as a check on the fluorine method or as a technique to be used when the latter is not applicable.

One of these tests is the calculation of the uranium fixation in bone, and both it and the fluorine test have been used to prove the conclusive association of the Saldanha skull with the fossil fauna. Another, using nitrogen analysis, has given conclusive evidence of the contemporaneity of the Fish Hoek skull with bone in the Magosian horizon in which it was found. The same test, on the other hand, indicates that the Cape Flats skull belongs to the Later rather than to the Middle

CHRONOLOGY OF AFRICAN PLEISTOCENE CULTURES

KEY TO TABLE I, PAGES 20-21

THE MAIN HOMINID FOSSILS FROM AFRICA

(1)   Yayo, Chad. *Australopithecus robustus* or *Homo habilis?*
(2)   Ternifine jaws and parietal. *Atlanthropus mauretanicus.*
(3)   Rabat mandible and maxilla. *Atlanthropus sp.*
(4)   Temara mandible. *Atlanthropus sp.*
(5)   Sidi Abderrahman mandible fragment. *Atlanthropus sp.*
(6)   Haua Fteah mandible fragment. *Homo neanderthalensis?*
(7)   Jebel Irhoud skulls. *Homo neanderthalensis?*
(8)   Mugharet el Aliyia maxilla fragment and tooth. *Homo neanderthalenis?*
(9)   *Homo sapiens* burials with Capsian and Oranian.
(10)   Kanam mandible fragment now considered to be probably Upper Pleistocene.
(11)   Pre-Zinjanthropus mandible, parietals, hand, foot, etc. (now *Homo habilis*).
(12)   *Zinjanthropus boisei* skull.
(13)   Chellian III skull. *Homo erectus?*
(14)   Kanjera cranial fragments. *Homo sapiens?*
(15)   Eyasi cranial fragments. *Homo rhodesiensis?*
(16)   Dire Dawa mandible fragment. *Homo neanderthalensis?*
(17)   Singa skull. *Homo sapiens.*
(18)   Gambles Cave, Afro-Mediterranean burials. *Homo sapiens.*
(19)   Taungs child skull. *Australopithecus africanus.*
(20)   Sterkfontein main site—*Australopithecus africanus* fossils.
(21)   Makapan Limeworks Cave: *Australopithecus africanus* fossils.
(22a) Swartkrans: *Australopithecus robustus* fossils.
(22b) Swartkrans (*Telanthropus*): *Homo erectus.*
(23)   Kromdraai: *Australopithecus robustus* fossils.
(24)   Cave of Hearths mandible fragment. *Homo rhodesiensis?*
(25)   Elandsfontein Saldanha cranium. *Homo rhodesiensis.*
(26)   Broken Hill *Homo rhodesiensis.*
(27)   Florisbad *Homo Helmei.*
(28)   Boskop cranium and mandible fragment. *Homo sapiens.*
(29)   Mumbwa Caves Bush-Boskopoid fossils. *Homo sapiens.*
(30)   Matjes River, Oakhurst, etc.   Bush-Hottentot burials.

CLASSIFICATION OF THE MAIN HOMINID FOSSILS FROM AFRICA

Hominines.   Homo
- *sapiens* — (9) (14) (17) (18) (27?) (28) (29) (30)
- *neanderthalensis* — (6) (7) (8) (10?) (16)
- *rhodesiensis* — (15) (24?) (25) (26)
- *erectus* — (2) (3) (4) (5) (13) (22b)
- *habilis* — (1?), (11?)

Australopithecines.   Australopithecus
- *robustus* (Paranthropus) (12) (22a) (23)
- *africanus* (Australopithecus) (19) (20) (21)

TABLE I. CHRONOLOGY OF THE AFRICAN PLEISTOCENE CULTURES

Main Pleistocene Divisions	Climatic Divisions (now disused)	MAIN LOCALITIES	
		NORTH AFRICA	EAST AFRICA
Post Pleistocene	Nakuran		
	Makalian Drier	El Mekta La Mouillah, etc. (9) Haua Fteah	Njoro, etc. Ishango, Naivasha
Upper Pleistocene	Gamblian	Taforalt (9)	Magosi Gambles Cave (18)?
		Berard	Enderit Drift Malewa Gorge
		Dar es Soltan Mugharet el Aliyia (8)	Olduvai Bed V
		Sidi Mansur	
		Kharga Oasis	Singa (17)
		Wadi Gan	Dire Dawa (16)
		El Guettar	
		Ain Fritissa	Eyasi Beds (15)
		Jebel Irhoud (7) Haua Fteah (6) Hajj Creiem	
		Sidi Zin Sidi Abderrahman	Nsongezi (M/N Horizo
	Drier		Isimila
	Kanjeran	Lac Karar Tihodaine Adrar Bous	Olorgesailie Kariandusi Kanjera (14) Olduvai Bed IV
		(5)	
	Drier?	Temara (4)	Olduvai Bed III?
		Rabat (3)	
Middle Pleistocene	Kamasian	Ternifine (2)	
		Sidi Abderrahman	Olduvai Bed II (13)
Lower Pleistocene	Drier?		Olduvai Bed I (11) (12
	Kageran	Ain Hanech Yayo (1)	Laetolil Omo
		Ain Boucherit Ain Brimba	Kaiso Kanam (10

		CULTURES		ABSOLUTE DATES	
SOUTH AFRICA		NORTH AFRICA	SUB-SAHARAN AFRICA	B.P.	B.C.
atjes River (30), Oakhurst, etc.	Epi-Palaeolithic		Late Stone Age	Wilton, Smithfield, Tshitolian. Elmenteitan		
ve of Hearths Kalambo Falls		Capsian, Later Oranian, etc.	Second Inter-mediate			
Rose Cottage Cave Howieson's Poort		Oranian Et Tera		Magosian, Lupembo-Tshitolian	10,000	8,000
				? Kenya Capsian		
Mumbwa (29)	Upper Palaeolithic	Aterian	Middle Stone Age	Lupemban, Pietersburg		
Bambata Mufo		and		Stillbay, Mazelspoort	20,000	18,000
Boskop (28)		Levalloisian				
		Dabba Blade Culture			30,000	28,000
Florisbad (27)						
Broken Hill (26)	Middle Palaeolithic	Levallois-Mousterian	First Intermediate	Sangoan and	40,000	38,000
Hopefield (25)		and Acheulio-Levallois		Fauresmith		
(24) Montagu						
Kalambo Falls ve of Hearths					50,000	48,000
		Late Acheulian		Later Acheulian Stage		
rnelia						
l Younger Gravels						
	Lower Palaeolithic	'Middle' Acheulian	Earlier Stone Age	Earlier Acheulian Stage		
mdraai (23) artkrans (22a and b) rkfontein Extension		'Early Acheulian' (Clacto-Abbevillian)			490,000	
pplaatdrif				Chellian Stage		
al Older Gravels kapan (21) rkfontein (20) ngs (19)		Oldowan		Oldowan	1,230,000 1,850,000	

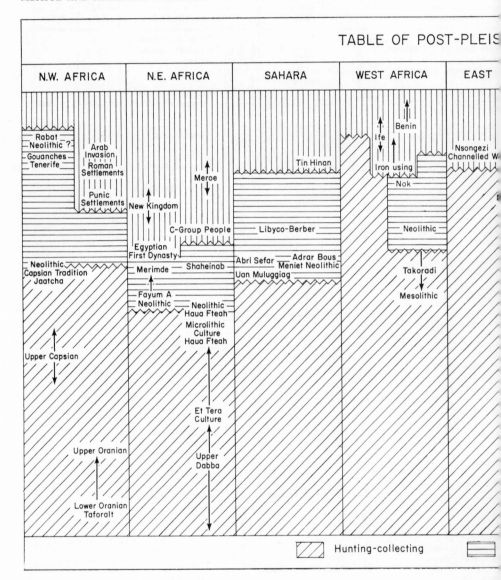

TABLE OF POST-PLEIS

N.W. AFRICA	N.E. AFRICA	SAHARA	WEST AFRICA	EAST

Rabat
Neolithic ?
Gouanches
Tenerife

Arab Invasion
Roman Settlements

Punic Settlements

New Kingdom

Meroe

Tin Hinan

Benin
Ife

Iron using

Nok

Nsongezi
Channelled W

C-Group People

Libyco-Berber

Neolithic

Egyptian First Dynasty

Neolithic
Capsian Tradition
Jaatcha

Merimde — Shaheinab

Abri Sefar — Adrar Bous
Meniet Neolithic
Uan Muluggiag

Takoradi

Fayum A
Neolithic — Neolithic
Haua Fteah

Mesolithic

Microlithic Culture
Haua Fteah

Upper Capsian

Et Tera Culture

Upper Oranian

Upper Dabba

Lower Oranian
Taforalt

Hunting-collecting

CULTURES IN AFRICA

CENTRAL AFRICA	SOUTH AFRICA		B.P.	

Kisalian Culture

Iron Age Feti

Iron Culture Furi I

Mt. Amba Forest clearance

Mufo Tshitolian

Mt. Gafula Tshitolian

Ishango Mesolithic

Mufo Lupembo-Tshitolian

Lusitu
Isamu Pate
Zimbabwe Acropolis

Zimbabwe Q walling
Channelled Ware Kalambo
Channelled Ware Kalambo Machili

Mapungubwe Bambandyanalo

Late Smithfield Waterberg
Magabengberg Late Smithfield

Late Wilton Lusu

Amadzimba Wilton
Lochinvar Wilton

Matjes River Wilton — Nachikufan I Solwezi

Late Magosian Kalambo

Matjes River Smithfield A

B.P.
1000 — 1000 A.D.
2000 — 0
3000 — 1000 B.C.
4000 — 2000
5000 — 3000
6000 — 4000
7000 — 5000
8000 — 6000
9000 — 7000
10,000 — 8000
11,000 — 9000
12,000 — 10,000

||||| Metal using

34. Twin Rivers Kopje
35. Mumbwa Caves
36. Broken Hill
37. Solwezi
38. Kamoa

1. Hangklip
2. Matjes River Shelter
3. Montagu Cave
4. Hopefield (Elandsfontein)
5. Howieson's Poort

10. Pneil
11. Taungs
12. Cornelia
13. Border Cave
14. Klipplaatdrif
15. Sterkfontein, Swartkrans, Kromdraai
16. Wonderboompoort
17. Boskop
18. Makapan Valley (Limeworks; Cave of Hearths)
19. Kalkbank
20. Magabengberg
21. Bambandyanalo
22. Mapungubwe
23. Bambata Cave
24. Amadzimba Cave
25. Khami
26. Zimbabwe
27. Lochard
28. Inyanga
29. Lusitu
30. Kalomo; Isamu Pate
31. Lusu
32. Machili
33. Lochinvar

43. Lake Kisale
44. Mufo; Furi
45. Leopoldville; Mt. Amba; Mt. Gafula
46. Eyasi
47. Laetolil
48. Olduvai Gorge
49. Olorgesailie
50. Kariandusi; Kinangop
51. Melawa Gorge
52. 'Nderit Drift
53. Gamble's Cave; Lanet
54. Njoro
55. Kanam
56. Nyabusoro
57. Nsongezi
58. Bigo
59. Ishango
60. Kaiso
61. Cherangani Hills
62. Magosi
63. Omo
64. Cameroon Mt.
65. Benin
66. Takoradi
67. Ife
68. Old Oyo

73. Abri Sefar
74. Kharga Oasis
75. Fayum
76. Adrar Bous
77. Erg Tihodaine
78. Tassili
79. Uan Muhuggiag
80. Meniet
81. Sidi Abderrahman
82. Dar-es-Soltan
83. Temara
84. Rabat
85. Mugharet el Aliya
86. Taforalt
87. La Mouillah
88. Lac Kerar
89. Ternifine
90. Bérard
91. Ain Hanech; Ain Boucherit
92. Sidi Zin
93. El Mekta
94. Sidi Mansour
95. El Guettar; Ain Brimba
96. Wadi Gan
97. Haua Fteah
98. Hajj Creiem

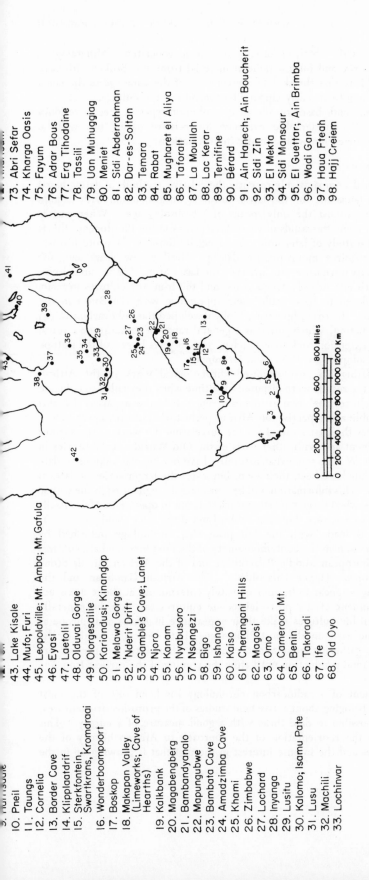

Stone Age horizon with which it usually has been associated. Mineralogical analysis of bone, matrix and human skeletal material from the Broken Hill cave indicates the probability that the skeletal remains are of the same age as the fauna and artifacts and belong to an Early Upper Pleistocene stage of culture.

Certain other methods based on the analysis of grain types in breccia residues and colluvium provide stratigraphic evidence for relative dating but will be considered later in connection with climatic interpretations.

3. ABSOLUTE CHRONOLOGIES

(i) *Radiocarbon*: Until comparatively recently the relative methods of dating based on stratigraphy and fauna or, for the latest cultures, on association with datable exotic material were almost the only means of establishing age. When one is dealing in periods of many thousands of years duration, as in the Pleistocene, this is not a handicap. The study of later cultures, especially those of the proto-historic period, however, requires more precise dating. Until a few years ago, for example, prehistorians were uncertain whether the Later Stone Age in sub-Saharan Africa lasted some 10,000 or only 2,000 years, and the Iron Age cultures in many regions were considered to have made their appearance with the Bantu in the sixteenth century AD! In 1950, however, Libby developed the radiocarbon (C14) method of absolute dating, which now has a general range of some 40,000 years, with possibilities of extension back to as much as 70,000 years by use of the isotope enrichment method adopted by de Vries at Groningen.

Radiocarbon dating has revolutionised chronological work in the African continent, although the results were disputed for a time when they failed to coincide with the African prehistorians' own estimates of age. It is now apparent that this method makes possible a perspective on African prehistoric cultures never before achieved and provides the best method yet for correlating the work in the various regions of the continent and with other parts of the Old World. Laboratories in Europe and the New World, somewhat naturally, have not been as anxious to date African samples as they have been their own, but a steadily larger series of dates is becoming available. This information will be considerably augmented in the course of the next few years when three new laboratories[5] begin to operate in Africa itself.

The results up to 1959 are shown in Tables I and II (pp. 20-21 and pp. 22-23). When comparison is made with the European C14 chronology published by Movius (1959), they confirm the contemporaneity of the First Intermediate cultures in Africa with the European Middle Palaeolithic and of the African Middle Stone Age with the European Upper Palaeolithic. The African Gamblian and the European Würm stages appear to be approximately coterminous at about 8000 BC. The rate of development of the post-Pleistocene cultures can now be generally determined. Mesolithic cultures make their appearance in Africa and Europe at about the same time early in the post-Pleistocene, but, especially south of the Sahara, the hunting-gathering populations continued often into the present era and did not turn to food production until after the coming of the earliest Iron Age immigrants.

The establishment of a radiocarbon chronology has been one of the most important factors in bringing about active field studies of the proto-historic cultures, because it is now possible to date these with a good measure of accuracy. This fact, together with the reorientation of the approach to African history of the historians themselves and the intense interest in the past that is growing up in the newly independent states, is leading to a new understanding of the prehistoric cultural background of the present-day African races and peoples that would not have been possible ten years ago.

(ii) *Potassium Argon:* The other chief method of determining absolute age, the potassium argon (K/A) method, was developed by Evernden and Curtis (1961) in California.   From the prehistorian's point of view it is best suited for dating the Earlier Pleistocene deposits, but its usefulness is restricted to volcanic-derived sediments, which are rich in potassium.   It is thus well suited to the East African region, and dates have been obtained from samples associated with the human fossils recovered from Beds I and II at Olduvai which suggest that man was present in East Africa nearly two million years ago, approximately double the previous estimates.   The Heidelberg laboratory has cast doubt on the validity of the results, but Evernden and Curtis claim that modification of procedure has now eliminated errors induced by contamination of some of the earlier dated samples, and confirm that all the data available agree with an age of approximately two million years for the Lower Pleistocene and the Australopithecine *Zinjanthropus.*   The significance of these K/A dates has been summarised by Howell (1962) and it seems that, in spite of the immediate setbacks, this method remains one of the most promising for the dating of Earlier Pleistocene cultures.

(iii) *Other Absolute Dating Methods:* Attempts have been made to date some of the Kenya obsidians, but the method used is limited as yet in its value, and in any case the relative weathering rates for the East African climatic region have first to be established.   To the writer's knowledge one date has so far been released — that of 33,000 years for an early Kenya Stillbay industry — which seems reasonable.

The Pleistocene sediments of the Kenya Rift lakes sometimes contain thicknesses of varved clays representing annual sedimentation over a period of years. One such section was studied by Nilsson and de Geer in the 1930s, and attempts were made to match the sequence against that obtained for post-glacial times in northern Europe.   Needless to say, no accuracy can be attached to the result, but, in cases where the sediments studied are cores drilled from the bottoms of existing lakes, it might in time be possible to link the chronology with the pollen succession.

III *DETERMINATION OF ENVIRONMENT AND CLIMATIC CHANGE*

The need to reconstruct past environment has long been considered an essential part of Quaternary archaeology in Africa and, indeed, preoccupation with this problem contributed to the production of the climatic correlation scheme.   Because the accepted interpretation of the mechanics of sedimentation and erosion has been called in question, however, it has become necessary to use other methods.   If the material remains of the culture of early man are to be correctly evaluated, all interpretation must be based, in the first instance, on a sound reconstruction of environment: of the habitat and biome.   Knowledge of the palaeo-ecology is particularly important in Africa where ecological zones are often sharply defined and have given rise to very significant differences in the social and economic structures they support.

Studies have shown that there is reason to think that the existing regimen of summer and winter rainfall zones also persisted throughout the Quaternary, and the degree of change, therefore, is probably much smaller than was at first thought.

The effects of rainfall and temperature change in the past must have been limited to a shifting of the vegetation and faunal zones and to changes in surface water supplies rather than drastic and complete replacement of one ecological system by another.   These conditions must be regarded as having affected the distribution of the human population by producing gradual adaptation and specialisation under favourable circumstances and stimulating increased experiment and population movement at unfavourable times.   The drier conditions pertaining at the close of the Pleistocene, for example, were responsible for general population movements and so indirectly provided the basis for freer interchange of improved techniques, especially in regard to food getting.   More favourable environments, such as those existing during much of the Gamblian pluvial, can be expected to have had a stabilising effect on population.   The specialisation and variation present in the cultures of the continent at this time may be interpreted as the outcome of increased exploitation of the environment made possible by the new techniques which had appeared in the Early Upper Pleistocene.   These in turn permitted better adaptation to each region, thus reducing population movement and producing partial regional isolation.

For most environmental studies the prehistorian relies on his colleagues in the natural sciences, and they reciprocally are making increased use of prehistory in an attempt to estimate the rate and degree of constancy at which changes in organisms have come about.   As a result there is today a growing number of studies based on collaboration of this kind and, indeed, most of the methods now available to the archaeologists are the direct outcome of such co-operation.

I. SEDIMENTATION STUDIES

One of the essentials for the prehistorian and palaeo-ecologist is to know the maximum degree to which climates changed in the past.   The basic problem is to determine what were the maximum decreases and increases in rainfall and temperature that can be expected to have occurred in any given locality and to state them in terms of percentages of the present-day figures.   Few attempts have as yet been made to solve this problem, but there are two important studies which show considerable promise.

The first is Brain's study (1958) of the breccias containing the Australopithecine and faunal assemblage of Lower and Middle Pleistocene age in the limestone caves of the Transvaal and northern Cape.   This is based upon a direct comparison of the characteristics of the sandy fractions of the deposits with those of the modern hillside soils.   The sandy portion of the modern dolomitic limestone soils is found to consist of grains of quartz and chert.   Since it can be shown that most of the quartz grains in these breccia residues result from aeolian action, any increase in the proportion of quartz in the deposits over the observed variation from the modern soils would indicate drier conditions; a very low percentage of quartz would point to wetter conditions.   By this means, Brain has been able to show that the Australopithecines lived in the Transvaal at a time when, to begin with, the rainfall was similar to or slightly less than that of the present day but was increasing towards the end.   He has also shown that the maximum and minimum variations in rainfall did not go beyond 50 per cent of the present mean annual rainfall.

The second group of studies is by Bond (1957a, 1957b, 1963), who used the prehistoric succession at Khami, Southern Rhodesia, in an attempt to establish the transporting power of colluvial action in terms of rainfall for much of the Upper

Pleistocene. This is based on the amount of weathering of feldspar at the time of accumulation and shows results very similar to those obtained by Brain from the much older deposits. Bond has also attempted to determine rainfall for an Acheulian site at Lochard on the Zambezi/Limpopo watershed. A close comparison and laboratory examination of the Lochard sediments with those from present-day dambos (shallow, swampy valleys) in Central Africa demonstrates the similarity of the two series of sediments. Dambos do not exist in the 30-inch rainfall zone which today covers much of Southern Rhodesia, but they are present in Northern Rhodesia and Nyasaland where the rainfall is usually over 40 inches. It is inferred, therefore, that the conditions at Lochard were similar to those of the two northern territories today.

Bond's studies of the surface texture of sand grains from the Zambezi and from the Kalahari Sands provide good evidence for deciding which are due to aeolian and which to fluviatile aggradation, while Poldevaart's (1957) heavy mineral analysis of aeolian sand samples from the Kalahari in Bechuanaland provides an indication of the general directions of the winds prevailing when the different series of dune formations were accumulated.

Other studies of the chemical alteration of fossil soils have been used to provide estimates of rainfall intensity. Degrees of calcification and of ferruginisation have been shown to be indicators of drier and wetter conditions respectively. That calcification is not taking place today in areas where rainfall exceeds 18 to 20 inches, or ferruginisation where it is less than 40 inches, indicates something of the magnitude of the changes over a wide area. Local factors, however, may produce exceptions, as Mason and his colleagues have pointed out for South Africa.

2. FOSSIL FAUNAS AND DISCONTINUOUS DISTRIBUTIONS

Many of the larger mammals can live in a very wide range of different habitats, so when they occur as fossils, they are of very little use in determining the climate of the region at the time they lived in it. Elephants will live in moist forest or near-desert scrub; hippos will exist both in the humid lowland rivers and estuaries or in the East African high mountains in water close to the snowline; leopards will occupy all types of country from the snowline downwards. Other forms, however, are less adaptable: the gazelle, oryx and white rhinoceros are restricted essentially to drier, more open country; the okapi, on the other hand, frequents only dense forest. When found as fossils, therefore, such animals are much more certain indicators of past climate. The distribution of fossil gazelle forms in central and southern Africa, for example, indicates that drier climatic conditions at one or more times in the past permitted these creatures to penetrate country that today is far beyond their arid and semi-arid habitats.

Microfaunas are even better indicators of climate than are the larger animals. Although the study of these is as yet only beginning in Africa, work on the fossil rodents of the Transvaal caves has already produced some interesting results which confirm Brain's climatic reconstruction for the area.

Unfortunately fossil fauna is not well preserved in many tropical regions. It is particularly abundant, however, in the volcanic region of East Africa, and there are good assemblages from South and North Africa. These provide sufficient information to permit the compilation of distribution maps which show the spread of certain selected species at particular stages of human culture and help in reconstructing past environments. The existence today of certain species in what are now widely separated habitats is a further indication that at more favourable times in the past they were able to spread out and populate some of the intervening country now environmentally unsuitable. The distribution of certain desert or grassland forms in South West and East Africa — the oryx, white rhinoceros, giraffe and ostrich are typical examples — and, in a few cases, isolated pockets of these specimens — giraffe in the Luangwa valley and ostrich in the Rukwa Rift — confirm this. Similarly, the distribution of blue monkey or yellow-backed duiker in relict patches of forest far distant from the main habitat of denser vegetation are indications of forest expansion at one or more times in the past. Studies of the montane avifauna, restricted essentially to forest on the high mountain ridges, have been carried out by Moreau (1963) who has found that twenty of the forms existing on Cameroon Mountain also occur on the mountains on the eastern side of the Congo basin some 1,300 miles away. There are also similar associations between forms in south-western Angola and in montane forests some 1,500 miles to the east. This and other similar studies lead to the belief that lowered temperatures and increased rainfall in the not too distant past must have been responsible for permitting these migrations to take place. Pollen evidence supported by C_{14} from north-eastern Angola, Kalambo Falls and Cherangani suggests that conditions favourable for such a spread probably existed as recently as the later part of the Upper Pleistocene, up to some 12,000 years ago.

3. PALAEO-BOTANY, RAINFALL AND VEGETATION

Palynology is likely to be perhaps the most important means at the prehistorian's disposal for the reconstruction of past environments, and at present the best source of information comes from macroscopic remains and fossil pollens. For a long time it was considered that African deposits preserved no pollens, but this has since been shown to be incorrect. Under certain conditions pollens have survived, and important studies of samples from selected sites are in progress today. The pioneer work was carried out in South and East Africa by van Zinderen Bakker (1963) and in the Sahara by Quezel (1962) and others from Paris; Osmaston and his colleagues in East Africa are working on pollens from the East African mountains; Lawton has studied pollen spectra from Lake Bangweulu; and D. Livingston carried out an extensive field collection of cores from lake basins in East and Central Africa which are now being investigated. The earliest studies conducted by van Zinderen Bakker on samples from the Florisbad site have been supplemented by his work on the pollens from the Kalambo Falls, north-eastern Angola, and the Cherangani Hills in East Africa. Macroscopic identifications from the Kalambo Falls by Chalk and White supplement the pollen evidence.

These studies are important, because, with the exception of the Cherangani profile, good cultural assemblages are associated with the pollens, and radiocarbon dates are also available. Reconstructions more exact than before can now be made of the prevailing vegetation patterns, and it can be shown that important changes took place both in temperature and in rainfall intensity. Perhaps the most significant changes in vegetation are those which occurred in the Sahara during the Late Acheulian and Aterian times. Pollen analysis there has shown that a Mediterranean flora invaded the desert up to its southern confines, indicating by its composition more temperate conditions and a rainfall of at least 25 inches in an area that is today true desert.

With the aid of the botanist, attempts have also been made to reconstruct hypothetical rainfall and vegetation patterns at the maxima of pluvial and interpluvial conditions. These were first done by Clark and Summers for Northern and Southern Rhodesia and, more recently, by Cooke (1963) for the whole of southern Africa. The latter is based upon the rainfall fluctuation limits indicated by the work of Brain and Bond and so is likely to be more accurate than the earlier estimates. Cooke's maps are based on the assumption that the temperature factor remained unaltered, but, as is now known from the work of the palynologists, the temperature at more than one period in the past ranged to some 5-6°C. lower than at the present time. This will need to be taken into account when compiling other maps of this kind. Although for obvious reasons such maps must be considered as purely tentative reconstructions until a detailed series of pollen investigations provides verification, they do serve as a useful working basis against which to interpret cultural variation.

IV THE ARCHAEOLOGICAL METHODS — RECOVERY, INTERPRETATION AND RECONSTRUCTION

1. EXCAVATION AND FIELD STUDIES

When what may be called the purely cultural side of prehistory is considered, the most striking single factor is the enormous quantity of archaeological material exposed by the extensive erosion that is a feature of the drier parts of the continent. Uninformed and selective collecting from these surface exposures not infrequently has been responsible for the complete disappearance of much material without any record's having been kept. Publications have often included inaccurate or misleading descriptions of cultural compositions. Although African archaeologists early recognised the need to excavate stratified assemblages, except in rare instances it was not until some fifteen years ago that the finds were treated other than taxonomically. In addition, much of the investigation prior to the end of the second world war was done by individual amateurs working discontinuously and as opportunity offered, so that many of the excavations were on a small scale and only in the nature of 'soundings'. Exceptions were the field investigations made by expeditions from overseas institutions, such as the Frobenius Expedition to West and South Africa and the researches carried out by Caton-Thompson (1943, 1952) in the Fayum, at Kharga Oasis and at Zimbabwe.

Since the second world war, however, larger excavation programs have been possible, mainly because of the growing number of professional prehistorians working in the continent, the greater interest generally in African prehistory, and the resulting increase in financial support. These projects, sometimes spread over several years, have been on a scale resembling that which has been the rule in Egypt since before the first world war. In sub-Saharan Africa, however, most of the work has been done by professionals based in the country rather than by foreign expeditions. A notable exception has been the study of the Isimila site in central Tanganyika by Clark Howell and his team from Chicago (1962). Probably the largest project carried out by a professional living in Africa is Leakey's Olduvai Gorge program, financed by the National Geographic Society, Washington, DC, and stretching over several years on a scale previously impossible. The study of the Kalambo Falls site in Rhodesia has been conducted on a smaller though similar scale.

In the proto-historic field a three-year investigation by Fagan of the Iron Age archaeology of a part of Northern Rhodesia, financed by the Nuffield Foundation, has recently been completed. Public support within the territory enabled Summers and Robinson to carry out their survey of the prehistory of the Inyanga district of Southern Rhodesia (Summers 1958), and the national museums, antiquities departments or monuments commissions also sponsor and finance much of this kind of work. Examples are the studies on the Khami (Robinson 1959) and Zimbabwe ruins (Summers, Robinson and Whitty 1961) in Southern Rhodesia, at Benin and Old Oyo in Nigeria, and Davies' work in Ghana. These researchers have usually had as their objectives not only the establishment of the chronological succession but also the more specific investigation of the economic levels, settlement and behaviour patterns. Considerable success is being achieved by the employment of new field techniques.

Important advances have been made at the Palaeolithic level in particular. Realisation that Africa preserves a unique record of living floors on open sites dating back to the beginning of tool-making has resulted in the excavation of these sealed floors as units. Doing so enables the archaeologist to recover the distribution pattern which provides him with evidence hitherto completely lacking for this cultural level. The excavations in Bed I at Olduvai and similar studies elsewhere have shown that considerable variation exists in the size and nature of the occupation units and in the tool assemblages. Concentrations of tools, factory waste and broken bones with *Zinjanthropus* show that the tool-using and bone-bashing activities were intimately connected; the piling up of stones, their arrangement in a regular pattern, or the presence of shallow, stone-filled depressions, suggest the possibility of structures and at least of specialised activities. Activity differences are also apparent from the grouping of one or more classes of tool, and, when studied in relation to the factory waste, these can show whether the process of tool manufacture took place at more than one place. At the Kalambo Falls site, for example, there is evidence that the initial roughing out of handaxes and cleavers by the Acheulian inhabitants had taken place elsewhere, and only the final shaping or resharpening was done on the living site. Excavation of cave sites can be carried out in similar manner, but it is here more difficult to separate undisturbed living floors; this has not yet been attempted in Africa. From detailed association studies of this kind it should be possible to determine extent and perhaps length of occupation as well as the range of activities of a group.

The problems are not so difficult for later prehistoric sites, because there has been less natural disturbance; less of the midden debris has had time to disappear; there is ethnographic evidence to help interpretation; and, because the sites lie close to or on the surface, no costly excavation is necessary to remove the sterile overlying beds. Statistical analysis of artifact concentrations from grid excavation is a simple method of determining the number, structure and population density on Iron Age sites. Calculations based on the numbers of storage pits, concentrations of daga, grindstones, or hut floors can be used to compute the size of a Neolithic or Iron Age population. Nevertheless, very few studies of this kind have as yet been attempted in Africa south of the Sahara, where research has hitherto been concentrated upon the recovery of successions of artifact assemblages which can then be compared.

Probably less is known of the Metal Age than of Stone Age settlements of Africa. These sites are often of a confined and built-up nature, as in the case of the Rhodesian ruins; they are sometimes buried under modern towns, as at Benin, Ife and Axum; elsewhere the wide extent of the site may preclude excavation of all but a small part of it, even where this would be permitted. In Europe the use of the proton magnetometer has been of the greatest assistance in recovering settlement patterns which can then be checked by excavation, and it is hoped that the use of this instrument will resolve the problem posed by this type of site in Africa.

2. MIDDEN ANALYSIS

Much useful information regarding subsistence patterns, duration and density of occupation, and technical ability can be learned from analysis of midden composition. The method for doing so was first evolved in the United States (Heizer 1960). Little attempt has been made thus far to apply it to African sites, but it is being adapted by Fagan to his study of the Iron Age cultures of the Kalomo/Choma districts in Northern Rhodesia, particularly in regard to the fauna, which shows a change from predominantly wild forms to largely domestic stock in the later part of the twelfth century 'Mound Culture'. Inferences can be made about dietary preferences, average consumption of meat, habits in connection with the distribution of the proceeds of the hunt, and the location of the main hunting preserves. Figures for computing the 'concentration index' of the middens at different periods can also be determined. Proportions of the various species of animals and of juveniles to adults are being used to determine whether occupation of the settlement area was seasonal; this can be deduced from the age at which young animals were killed. It can also be determined whether the occupants were stock-breeders and whether hunting was chiefly practised by groups or individuals. Caves on the south coast of South Africa contain very thick (30 feet or more) occupation middens which have accumulated since the end of the Pleistocene, and analysis of this debris has revealed, through deduction, important dietary changes which occurred when it became necessary to rely on sea foods; it has also revealed the methods employed to obtain them, such as the hook and line and the fish trap. Analysis of the content of shell middens on the Natal coast has also shown important differences between Stone Age and Bantu peoples with regard, for example, to the periodicity of occupation and to their fishing practices.

Evidence of the existence of agriculture is less easy to obtain in Africa, but it has been successfully proved by the recovery of carbonised seeds and grains at sites in Southern Rhodesia and the Katanga in addition, of course, to the Neolithic Egyptian sites. Identification of cereal plants or weeds associated with different types of cultivation has not yet been attempted in sub-Saharan Africa, mainly because the necessary pollen evidence has survived but rarely. This would certainly be a fruitful field of study.

3. ASSEMBLAGE ANALYSIS

Up to ten years ago archaeologists were concerned mainly with qualitative rather than quantitative assemblages. Sites were selectively excavated; the formalised tools were preserved; but the waste products were discarded except for a few pieces considered to be helpful in determining the manufacturing processes and techniques. The resulting taxonomic classification was too rigid to be of much value for comparative purposes, and it was only a little over a decade ago that exact quantitative analysis, following the methods employed by Bordes and others in Europe, began to be used in Africa. Such analysis is concerned with all the cultural material and not just with selected specimens found on a site. Through use of these methods trends or modes can be determined and used certainly to express chronological and spatial differences. An example of this is the demonstration of significant differences between the chronological stages of the Middle Stone Age in the Transvaal, as revealed in the nature of the primary artifact classes at the Cave of Hearths (Mason, 1957). Isolated individual industries of the same age can be accurately compared, as Kleindienst (1961, 1962) has done for the Acheulian in East and Central Africa. By statistical analysis of the secondary classes of tools, she has shown that considerable variability in the lithic industries was already present at this early time. Further studies of the Albertine Rift cultures, of those from north-eastern Angola, and, more generally, from the continent as a whole have provided a basis for valid comparison of the lithic cultures from the Acheulian upwards. By this method changes in the proportions of the artifacts and the appearance and distribution of forms can be directly linked with environmental changes where these can be established by pollen analysis.

Most analyses of this kind for the later prehistoric and for proto-historic times have not yet been published. There are those, however, on the pottery wares at Inyanga, Khami and Zimbabwe by Summers (1958) and Robinson (1959, 1961) and the study of Mapungubwe by Gardner. Addison's analysis of the finds from the Jebel Moya excavations is a good example of studies in culture trends where stratigraphical evidence is largely absent.

Studies of raw materials used for artifacts and of their distribution in relation to the sources of origin show the extent of culture contacts or trade and have for long been used to good purpose by prehistorians working in Europe and Asia. In Africa, where such studies have been used to a limited extent on Pleistocene sites, it seems that at times stone was carried up to a hundred miles; even wider contacts between the coast and the interior plateau can be proved for the Later Stone Age by inland finds of coastal imports. Ceramic composition and temper on 'Mound Culture' sites in Northern Rhodesia are being used to distinguish imported pottery wares. Spectographic analysis of manufactured metal objects detects the source area of the ore and is at present being undertaken in respect of gold from a fifteenth-century site in the Zambezi valley. So little is known about the main ore-bearing areas themselves, however, that it will be some time before effective use can be made of such analyses. The best prospects are those for gold and copper.

4. DISTRIBUTIONS

The strikingly different ecological divisions of the continent have forced African prehistorians to work in a geographical isolation that renders it difficult to make comparisons between the main regions and to appreciate the relationships between culture and the varying ecology. Attempts have been made to collate cultural evidence for limited areas — for example, in the former French West African territories, Ghana, the Horn, the Rhodesias and South West Africa — and in some cases these have been related to fluctuations in rainfall and vegetation zones. Such regional distributions are as yet only of limited value by reason of the patchy nature of the fieldwork and the lack of precision in cultural determinations, but they represent an important beginning. A scheme to correlate these regional distributions by the compilation of an Atlas of Prehistory for Africa is at present under way. This seeks to set out the distribution of the main prehistoric cultures prior to the Metal Age against background maps showing the environment. Even allowing for its obvious shortcomings, this atlas will considerably increase knowledge of what were the favourable and unfavourable habitats in prehistoric times and of the economic causes underlying population movements. The incompleteness of the present knowledge of Iron Age cultures makes it impossible at this stage to plot their distributions on a continent-wide basis.

V ETHNO-HISTORICAL METHODS

Just as the historian makes use of source material of an ethno-historical and archaeological nature, so does the prehistorian use this material and that of historical record to help in his reconstructions. Such source material is, of course, of maximum use for the proto-historic cultures, but the conservative nature of African culture has preserved until today not a few practices that in origin may stretch back almost to the beginning of culture itself. If used critically, this evidence can be of great value to the Pleistocene archaeologist as well as to the investigator of later cultural levels.

Because only material remains have survived, the prehistorian is particularly concerned with the study of the material culture and the production techniques of modern populations as an aid to the reconstruction of those of his prehistoric groups. Valid reconstructions of behaviour patterns in Later Stone Age times have been attempted for South Africa by comparing the contents and nature of the sites with observed livelihood patterns among Bush-Hottentot peoples. In this connection the rich prehistoric rock art provides a unique link between ethnography on the one hand and prehistory on the other. The content of the art in the Sahara, the Horn, and in East and South Africa, when critically examined, gives clues to the social and economic life and the magico-religious beliefs that substantially fill out the evidence from the material culture itself. Such studies have been made by Lhote from the Tassili, van Riet Lowe and Willcox from the South African, and Goodall and Cooke from the Rhodesian paintings. It is only to be expected that little direct ethnographic data still exists in connection with the working of stone, but there are indications that a considerable amount of evidence of this kind is likely to be recovered if it is looked for in time. For instance, the punch technique for making gun-flints, recently studied by Clark in Angola, and the observation that has been made of the use of stone and bottle glass for smoothing bow staves on the Northern Rhodesia/Tanganyika border provide a knowledge of the Late Pleistocene and more recent techniques of flaking that could never have been otherwise obtained.

It is in reconstructing the life of the Early Iron Age village farmers that ethnography can play so important a part. The careful application to archaeological remains of house forms, food storage methods, settlement patterns, defence organisation, stone building, metal-working techniques, pottery wares and the use of ritual and religious objects, for example, can provide the firm reconstructions which must be the basis of any record of the earlier history of the existing populations. Such evidence is usually employed in conjunction with any written descriptions that may be available and with the traditional oral history of the present population. The superbly graphic descriptions of the indigenous populations of the south-east African coast, preserved in the accounts of Portuguese travellers of the sixteenth and seventeenth centuries, or reconstructions such as that of the history of the BaKuba peoples by Vansina, can all be used to advantage by the prehistorian. The success of reconstructions based on critical use of such source material in conjunction with radiocarbon dating and strictly disciplined excavation techniques can be seen in reports such as those of the 1929 and 1957 excavations at Zimbabwe and of the Khami ruins or Bigo earthworks.

The prehistorian is also coming to use inferences which can be drawn from the linguistic groupings in Africa. He is perhaps less enthusiastic about these, because they are more liable to undetected errors than the first-mentioned sources. The difficulty of reconciling Greenberg's and Guthrie's schemes of classification and the discrepancies in their chronologies for such phenomena as Bantu origins and movements leave him uncertain of the validity of such reconstructions. Similar uncertainties exist with reference to ethno-botanic evidence; while it does seem to indicate a history of several millennia for agriculture in sub-Saharan Africa, the same evidence has been less convincingly used to hypothecate several independent centres of domestication there.

Blood group studies which determine the gene frequencies in a population and the significant variations of these charted in the distribution maps are also claiming the attention of prehistorians. Although little has yet been done in this direction, such studies should provide evidence of racial origins and the relationships between present-day people and prehistoric populations through the medium of comparison of somatic characteristics and culture features.

VI FUTURE NEEDS AND PROBLEMS

It is obvious that during the past decade there have been many significant advances in African prehistory, and the new approach to prehistoric studies within the discipline itself has resulted in closer and more profitable co-operation between prehistorians and their fellow scientists. Outside Egypt and Nubia, however, there is still much to be done before knowledge about prehistory in Africa is comparable to that available for Europe and Meso-America. The way is now open for a much more intensive application of the new methods on a continent-wide basis, for it seems certain that it is only through them that solutions will be found for the general problems of chronology and reconstruction. Because there are still all too few professional archaeologists in Africa and because funds, though becoming more easily available, are still strictly limited, it is essential that future collaboration be even closer and that more team studies be undertaken at sites carefully selected for their potential value to the solution of both the specific and the general problems.

Absolute chronology and environmental reconstructions are still very incomplete, and a number of systematic studies of wet and dry sediments containing pollens and carbon for dating are needed throughout the continent. Within the limits of the radiocarbon method, a chronology as firm as that supplied by writing for the early literate civilisations will probably be available in a few years for those parts of Africa lacking historical records. C14 laboratories have been set up in Dakar, Leopoldville and Salisbury, and a flow of new dates may be expected from now onwards. For dating the earlier periods the potassium argon technique holds out the best promise of successful absolute correlation. Palaeobotanical studies for reconstruction of habitats are providing the clearest evidence yet available for the interpretation of rainfall, temperature and vegetation changes. The moist basins of the Equatorial lakes and rivers and the high mountain massifs of East Africa lend themselves to these studies and can provide a means of direct correlation with the Later Pleistocene climates in the high latitudes through the medium of radiocarbon.

If settlement and behaviour patterns are to be recovered, variations identified, and activities interpreted, it is necessary that the new field techniques and analytical methods being used by a few African prehistorians be more generally adopted. In addition, those prehistorians who now statistically analyse their cultural assemblages tend to employ methods of their own devising, with the result that comparison between findings is usually difficult and sometimes impossible. It is important, therefore, that agreement be reached on standard methods of presentation and that these new quantitative methods be universally employed in the description of all excavated cultural material from Africa.

One of the prehistorian's most pressing needs is some means of determining how long a site was inhabited. Was it a temporary occupation of a day or a week? Was the site seasonally reoccupied, or was it permanently inhabited for a period of years? For proto-historic times, midden analysis can do much to resolve this problem, but for earlier times no satisfactory method has yet been developed. This is a particularly vital question for the Palaeolithic archaeologist, because it must affect the interpretations based upon his quantitative analyses. The problem strikes at the root of archaeological reconstruction, and it is unlikely that any immediate or quick answer will be found to it, but it is equally certain that it is not beyond solution. Until it is known whether the 150 handaxes and cleavers recovered from an Acheulian living floor represent the activities of a few hours or a number of years, it is impossible to estimate the numbers of individuals involved or the relative importance of these particular tools in the total equipment of Acheulian man. It is probable that the weathering of organic materials associated with stone implements is important in this regard, because the intensity of chemical and mechanical weathering of bone and wood can be determined microscopically. Where this is done the amount of variation shown by these materials on a single floor can indicate how long they had been exposed to differential surface weathering before burial. Help of this kind, combined with the results of quantitative analysis of relationships between tools and other associated human occupation material, will give a much more precise knowledge of the time values involved. This knowledge will in turn provide a more accurate basis for interpreting livelihood patterns and band size from the assemblages and for using the zoological and anthropological data more critically than is now possible.

The primate behaviour studies carried out by biologists and anthropologists are supplying considerable data to the prehistorian and helping him to appreciate better the factors involved in reconstructing the way of life of the Australopithecine tool-makers. Similar studies of the dietary and subsistence habits, seasonal movements, band size variability, and settlement patterns of existing hunter-gatherers living under different ecological conditions could permit direct comparison with prehistoric populations. This kind of detailed information is only very rarely collected by the ethnographer and calls for special investigation by anthropologists and zoologists trained to make such observations.

There are many other problems that require investigation and one can do no more than mention two or three of the most important here. How, for example, does one determine the time level at which prehistoric studies should begin? Some consider that tool-making developed very slowly, others that it made a sudden appearance. It would certainly seem now that the origins go back into the Middle or Lower Villafranchian or perhaps even earlier, so that this question can only be resolved by studying the habits of the tool-using hominids of Pliocene times. It is thus becoming more and more apparent that the prehistorian must push his investigations back before the Pleistocene and, since there appear to be few, if any, Pliocene sediments in Africa which can provide this information, it may possibly be in southern Asia that the answer to the question will be learned. Again, the apparent rapidity of man's physical and intellectual development during the Middle Pleistocene would seem to have been possible only by reason of his ability to make tools. The changes this tool-making activity enabled him to bring about, both in his own way of life and in his environment, could have provided just the enriched conditions necessary for the increased rate of human evolution. These changes in genetic evolution and culture cannot be separated. They are in a feed-back relationship to each other which will only be understood after co-ordinated studies establish more exactly the importance of environmental factors in accelerating or retarding cultural advance at different time levels and in affecting the genetic composition of the indigenous African races.

There are, in addition, other specific problems which are more essentially within the province of the archaeologist. Among these are the origin of the Blade Cultures of Africa and their relationship to the 'proto-Hamitic' stock; the origin and spread of food-production in sub-Saharan Africa; the degree of continuity between present populations of the sub-continent and those Mesolithic hunter-gatherers who successfully adapted to the new economy; and the centre of origin and rate of dispersal of the Bantu peoples. These and many more problems have important implications for the anthropologist, the serologist, agronomist and historian, and they all can be resolved only with the assistance of prehistorians.

The realisation of the importance of Africa for understanding man's evolutionary development from a tool-using Pliocene ancestor has lent new impetus to prehistory. Interest in this field has been maintained at an international level even while its ideological importance to the new African states has become fully appreciated. In the hands of the archaeologist and historian, the prehistoric record is being made to recount the history of the indigenous peoples and so to forge the direct links between past and present that have been largely lacking up to now. Knowledge of such links can stimulate natural interest and pride in cultural origins and can do much to bring populations to modify tribal conservatism and think in terms of a larger unity.

There must be few, if any, of the independent states which do not possess cultural institutions where prehistoric and ethnographic studies are being actively pursued. Indeed, the scale of such work in Nigeria and Ghana is unsurpassed on the continent. Research facilities in Africa may be expected, therefore, to be considerably increased during the coming decade. Established research organisations such as the Institut Français d'Afrique Noire in Senegal, the British Institute of History and Archaeology in East Africa, and the Archaeological Survey Unit in Johannesburg now work in collaboration with new centres such as the Centre Tchadien pour les Sciences Humaines at Fort Lamy and the Institut de Recherches Scientifiques au Congo at Brazzaville. Training of personnel is beginning effectively to be carried out by the museums' associations of southern and middle Africa, by the field training courses organised by institutions such as the Rhodes-Livingstone Museum in Northern Rhodesia, by the establishment of university courses in archaeology, and by the activities of the various antiquities departments and monuments commissions. Though these last exercise necessary control over excavation in the interests of preservation, they are often most active in promoting field research and publication.

Machinery for the co-ordination of archaeological research, moreover, has been in effective operation for several years. Since 1947 the Pan-African Congress on Prehistory, meeting every four years, has played a unique part in bringing together prehistorians from all parts of the continent. Continuity is maintained by societies such as the South African Archaeological Society with its excellent bulletin and by periodic regional conferences. Interdisciplinary collaboration is being effected through such international bodies as the Scientific Council for Africa (CCTA/CSA) and UNESCO and by conferences such as the three organised by the School of Oriental and African Studies (London) on African History and Archaeology. Other useful meetings include the Leverhulme History Conference held in Salisbury, Southern Rhodesia, in 1960, the Conference of Ethno-historians at Dakar in 1961, and the symposium on Early Man in Africa organised by the Wenner-Gren Foundation, also in 1961.

It is encouraging to see the increasing use that natural scientists are making of prehistory to assist them in assessing rates of spread or evolution of biological organisms, speciation rates, vegetation trends, the spread of diseases such as tripanosomiasis or malaria. It is not only the prehistorian, therefore, who derives the benefit from collaboration and team studies, and it is certain that, with the adoption of ever more precise methods of estimating time and change mechanisms, prehistory will become more firmly established as an indispensable part of every African research program.

2

History   J. D. Fage

I INTRODUCTION*

HISTORICAL WRITING ON Africa is as old as the writing of history itself. Herodotus included within the scope of his *History* those parts of the continent that were known to the world of his time, and other classical authors followed his example. This tradition was maintained by the historians of the Islamic civilisation, which succeeded to that of the classical world and which possessed a considerably more extensive knowledge of Africa. Thus the noblest of the Arabic historians, Ibn Khaldun (1332–1406), included a section on the Negro kingdoms of the western Sudan in his great work which was essentially focused on his own North African homeland. Arabic writing on Africa and its history merges naturally with a reawakening of interest in the continent by Europeans, who, from the fifteenth century onwards, were developing a growing traffic with its coasts and on occasion braving its interior. Indeed one of the last great Arab writers on Africa, known as Leo Africanus, wrote his *History and description of Africa* (c. 1520) for a European public. This was not unique; for example, al-Idrisi's *Geography* was written (c. 1150) for Roger of Sicily. The earliest of the new European writings on Africa, such as Zurara's *Chronicle of the discovery and conquest of Guinea* (c. 1454), may have been primarily concerned with European exploits there, but it was not long before Europeans were writing and publishing accounts of the African territories and peoples with which they had come in contact. Many of these contain unique historical material: for example, the books of Marees (1602) and Bosman (1705) on the Guinea coastlands, the accounts of the Congo by Lopes (1591) and Battell (1625), or the *History of Ethiopia* by Ludolf (1681). This line of writing extends ultimately to the works of the explorers of the late eighteenth and the nineteenth century, among which are such monumental works as James Bruce's *Travels to discover the source of the Nile* (1790) and Heinrich Barth's *Travels and discoveries in north and central Africa* (1857–58), which remain to this day fundamental historical source books for the areas they cover.

By the seventeenth century, works of this kind were being gathered together in collections of *Voyages*. They were also being used for the compilation of synthetic accounts of Africa, of which the most famous is probably Dapper's

*Bibliography for this chapter will be found on page 496.

Description of Africa (1668).   As Dapper's title indicates, the character of these was
geographical and ethnographical rather than historical.   But there were also European travellers to Africa who paid specific attention to the history of the peoples
they came across, while the encyclopaedic spirit of the eighteenth century induced
some stay-at-home professional writers to use all materials that came to hand to
compile general histories of Africa.   These last are little regarded today, often
for the very good reason that they do not indicate their sources, so that the reliability of their material cannot be evaluated.   But the histories of particular peoples,
such as Dalzel's *History of Dahomey* (1793) or the histories of Ashanti contained in
the books of Bowdich (1819) and Dupuis (1824), often based on oral sources
which can no longer be approached, are now themselves primary sources for the
historian.

Towards the end of the nineteenth century, however, the situation with
regard to the writing of African history began to deteriorate.   In the first place,
the nature of historical writing was itself changing.   It was becoming less an art
of compiling chronological narratives and more a technique of trying to reconstruct
and analyse the past from the results of meticulous and critical research in original
records.   For the Western countries which first developed this concept of the
historical method, the original records were for the most part inscriptions and
documents.   But sub-Saharan Africa seemed to offer very little written evidence of
its past.   North Africa was much better off, but even so the study of its past
became somewhat eccentric to the mainstream of historical studies.   It was the
preserve of classicists, whose main field of interest lay on the other, European
side of the Mediterranean, and of Arabists, who preferred (except in Spain and to
some extent in France) to concentrate on the centres of Muslim civilisation in the
Near East.   Both groups, moreover, were specialists writing for a rather different
and rather smaller public than were historians generally.   The *Cambridge Ancient
History* (1923–39) and the *Cambridge Medieval History* (1911–36), outstanding
achievements of the new historiography introduced into Britain by Lord Acton,
both have remarkably little to say even about North Africa.   The reader of the
Cambridge Modern History, which Acton himself planned in 1896 just before his
death, is hardly even aware that Africa existed, despite the fact that in modern times
almost the whole continent had come under European rule.

II *AFRICA'S PLACE IN HISTORICAL STUDIES c.* 1900–*c.* 1948

The European historian's view of African history was cogently expressed in 1923
by Professor A. P. Newton, who, as a professor of imperial history, was probably
more aware of the world outside Europe than many of his colleagues.   Addressing
the African Society in London on 'Africa and historical research', he stated bluntly
that Africa south of the Sahara had 'no history before the coming of the Europeans. . .
History only begins when men take to writing' (Newton, 1923: 267).

Newton does not appear to have been claiming that historians could work *only*
from written records.   It seems that he would have agreed, for example, that the
writing of the remoter periods of European history necessitated some recourse to
archaeological evidence, and also perhaps that historians of contemporary or near
contemporary times might sometimes make use of oral testimony, for he admitted
that in Africa information about the pre-colonial past could be found in 'material
remains' and 'in language and primitive custom'.   But in Newton's view such

evidence was essentially the concern not of the historian but of the archaeologist, the linguist and the anthropologist. The historian could only make 'subsidiary use' of these kinds of evidence.

This, unfortunately, was not simply a technical judgment. It is important to remember that Newton belonged to an age in which Europeans had succeeded in conquering or dominating the world to an extent and in a manner quite unparalleled in previous human experience. They were, therefore, apt to regard their own culture as vastly superior to all others. Sub-Saharan Africa was especially vulnerable here. As well as lacking writing — one of the principal distinctions between 'civilisation' and 'barbarism' — its people had for half a millennium appeared in world history principally in the role of slave labourers for the aggressive, expansive Europeans. If African societies and cultures were to be studied, they were to be studied as primitive survivals. They were thus not a field for the historian — nor for that matter for the economist or the political scientist — but for the ethnographer and the archaeologist. The point was not merely that the particular province of the historian was the investigation of written records and that Africa was singularly deficient in these. It was believed that, lacking written records, African peoples were incapable of making the same cumulative advances from past experience that literate peoples could. Until the Europeans (or in a few cases, Semites) came and gave them writing, therefore, Africans could have no history worthy of study.

This leads to a further point, which was not explicit in what Newton said, but which is implicit in the man himself, namely that he was a professor of colonial history. While the writing of African history was no longer a proper professional activity, colonial history had become an accepted, if junior, branch of historical studies. To the extent that Africa had been brought within the sphere of European activities, colonial history tended to be a substitute for African history. It followed not only that what had happened in pre-colonial Africa was of minor account, but also that, within the colonial period itself, what counted was not what the Africans were doing or had inherited from their past, but what the Europeans were doing and what they had brought to Africa. The units of Africa's history thus became not its own peoples and cultures, but first the spheres of influence and then the colonies and empires established by Europeans in Africa. The subjects of study were thus not the kingdom of Monomotapa, but the Portuguese era in south-east Africa; not the adjustments of the Akan-speaking peoples to British rule, but the development of British administration or of the legislative council on the Gold Coast. Furthermore, interest in African territories tended to be proportional to the extent of European influence or control. Most attention was given to those territories in which European settlement had taken firm hold. Thus the history of the white settlement colonies in South Africa received a volume to itself in the *Cambridge History of the British Empire* (1929–59). The rest of British Africa was dealt with through occasional chapters in the first three volumes, and these were interspersed with chapters on such subjects as British trade or emigration or defence, or on the West Indies or colonial North America. In a sense, this distinction was correct, for, from the time of Theal (1888–1919) and Cory (1910–1930) onwards, South Africa had developed its own distinct school of historians, which came to concentrate almost entirely on the history of the settler communities.

For some sixty years from about the 1880s onwards, professional historians had little or no contact with the African past. Its study was but little advanced by workers in other disciplines. What now may be called 'African studies' hardly began to be recognised until after the foundation of the International African Institute in 1926. Moreover, perhaps because African studies were so largely concerned with non-literate societies, there was a tendency to regard them as a junior and poor relation of oriental studies. In London University, the School of Oriental Studies became the School of Oriental and African Studies only in 1938. There was a certain practical value, for instance, to the study of Zulu or of Twi, but from the academic point of view it was manifestly inferior to the study of languages like Arabic or Chinese. It is true that during the early years of the twentieth century the new discipline of social anthropology was being developed, and this was destined to have a very close contact with Africa. But it is sometimes forgotten that an appreciable time elapsed before social anthropologists actively engaged in original field research. C. G. Seligman was perhaps the first social anthropologist to engage in African fieldwork (in the Sudan in 1909–10), but in some respects it can be argued that Seligman was also part of the older tradition of ethnography. The newer generation of anthropologists who went into the African field from the 1920s onwards were at first little concerned with the past of the societies they were exploring.

Such a statement is a generalisation that calls for some qualification. It is most obviously true of the British school of functional anthropologists that stemmed from the inspired teaching of Malinowski and Radcliffe-Brown. But it would seem also to apply (if in rather different ways) to French anthropology, since Durkheim and Levy-Bruhl were French teachers who exerted a profound influence on the English school. It would seem far less appropriate to the Germans and Scandinavians, who tended to remain ethnographers, or to the Americans, who tended to be diffusionists. To the ethnographer and the diffusionist, explanations of culture and of social structure in terms of the past remained significant. But, for obvious political reasons, most of the new anthropological fieldwork in Africa tended to be undertaken by Britons and Frenchmen. At least two of the reasons why these men were little concerned with history are relevant to this survey.

In the first place, it so happened that the pioneers of functionalism and of fieldwork learnt their trade by studying very small primitive communities: Malinowski in the Trobriands, Radcliffe-Brown in the Andaman Islands. For most practical purposes, very little history was involved here. If social structures needed any diachronic illumination, three generations — indeed, a life span — would generally suffice. This was especially so because political functions (which might otherwise have induced more historical research) were of necessity limited and therefore unremarkable. Thus investigation tended to become concentrated on other fields: for example, kinship, magic and religion (Firth, 1957: 21, 240–3). Such interests continued, it would seem, to dominate the attentions of anthropologists until quite recent times, when more of them — and particularly perhaps in Africa — turned to consider much larger societies. More attention was then paid to political functions and also to history. The larger a single coherent society is, the more complex the political functions within it are apt to be, and the more history it is apt to require. (To the historian, indeed, a functional relationship would seem to be involved here.) Certainly the anthropologists who have studied large political groupings in Africa have made extensive use of historical data and of the diachronic method for their functional analyses (e.g., Barnes, 1954; Evans-Pritchard, 1950, 1961; Smith, 1960).

Secondly, the functionalists were less against history than against the conjectural history in which many of the ethnographers had engaged. In their search for explanations of primitive societies, the latter had often lacked historical data. They had therefore reconstructed what 'history' they thought would have been necessary to explain the situations they were examining. Such a process is, of course, as obnoxious to the historian as it is to the social anthropologist, albeit for different reasons. The reconstruction is useless to the social anthropologist because, being conjectural, it cannot be a sure guide to the understanding of a present situation. To the historian, conjectural reconstruction of the past is simply wrong. Because it is not based on the critical analysis of historical data, it is not history.

Although Seligman has an honoured place in the history of social anthropology, he would seem to have had a marked leaning towards conjectural history. It is for this reason that it has earlier been suggested that he also belongs to the older tradition of ethnography. Seligman's little handbook *The Races of Africa* seems to be based on the premise that distinctions between major groupings of peoples in Africa are explicable because 'the civilisations of Africa are the civilisations of the Hamites; its history the record of these people and of their interaction with the two more primitive African stocks, the Negro and the Bushmen' (1930: 96). Thus the Hottentots become 'Hamiticised Bushmen', and the Bantu 'Hamiticised Negroes'.

If it may be doubted whether such judgments were helpful to social anthropologists concerned with the analysis and interpretation of functions within Bantu (or Hottentot) societies, it can be stated with certainty that they were positively misleading to historians. Their interpretations of such historical data as were known to them were almost bound to be coloured by such a pronouncement of a leading authority on African anthropology. This may not be self-evident. It must be remembered (see below pp. 52–54) that historical data are not absolute. They result both from the actions and from the recorded observations of specific human beings. If, as may often be the case in Africa, the historical data are scanty or little understood, then more account is apt to be taken of the general qualities of the human beings concerned in them. It was unfortunate that Seligman ascribed specific social and historical qualities to a group ('Hamites') which is really identifiable only in linguistic and not in social or in historical terms. It is not obvious, for example, in what ways such Hamitic-speaking peoples as the Tuareg or the Galla were more 'civilised' (or less 'primitive') than, say, the Mande or the Baganda.

Seligman's influence on historians was the greater because his judgments tended to run parallel to existing prejudices: the qualities 'white' and 'conquering', which Seligman had unfortunately applied to his Hamites, were in Africa even more characteristic of the people to which most of the historians belonged. The final destruction of this astygmatising 'Hamitic myth' was in very large measure due to Joseph H. Greenberg's demonstration (1955) that it did not accord with ascertainable facts, especially in language. Ironically enough, Malcolm Guthrie (1962: 273) has now suggested that the anthropologist G. P. Murdock (1959) may be in danger of creating new historical myths through uncritical acceptance of some of Greenberg's constructive suggestions for the classification of African languages.

The example of Seligman might seem to suggest that, in so far as anthropologists did concern themselves with African history before about the 1940s, their work has proved as much a hindrance as a help to its proper understanding.   Luckily, this was by no means so.   In the older, predominantly north European, field of ethnography, some useful work was done during this period.   One might mention, for example, the work that led to the production of such scholarly syntheses or compendia as Baumann's *Völkerkunde von Afrika* (1943) or Westermann's *Geschichte Afrikas* (1952), or the work of men like Schebesta (1926) or Krieger (1943), which has provided important stimuli to further research and speculation.   There were also men who engaged in detailed fieldwork of the new type who were not unconcerned with historical data: for example, Rattray (1923–32) in Ghana and Meek (1926) in Nigeria.   But it is interesting to note that men like these often did not begin their careers as anthropologists.   They were administrators or missionaries who came (or were brought) into the new discipline to achieve a fuller understanding of peoples with whom they had been working.   But while their concern with these peoples and their distance from the academic mainstream was such that they tended to record and publish historical data, they were usually sufficiently part of their discipline not to engage in historical reconstruction.   If they were tempted in this way — as, for example, was Talbot (1926) in Nigeria — then they were apt to rival the worst excesses of the older conjectural ethnographers.

If the anthropologists who touched on history did so in part because they retained, at least initially, something of the joys of amateur status, amateurism was far more characteristic of those whose more deliberate intent it was during this period to recover African history.   With professional historians having no contact with Africa, the way was open for the writing of African history by anyone whose work did bring him into touch with the continent and its peoples.   The historians of Africa were therefore explorers, administrators, missionaries, educators, even journalists.   Some of these did such outstanding work that it might seem quite inappropriate to call them 'amateurs'.   But in relation to history (or to any other single discipline) they were so, though in the finest sense of the word.   It was, indeed, the activities of men like Sir Harry Johnston, Maurice Delafosse and Henri Labouret, men of a highly enquiring turn of mind coming to Africa at a time when so little was known about it, and doing so much in so many fields, that pioneered the concept of 'African studies'.

So long as men of this kind confined their historical work to the more or less direct recording of such historical data as they could find for such peoples (and in such languages) as they knew well, their contribution to African history could be very important.   Delafosse's *Haut-Sénégal-Niger* (1912), for example, is as essential as Barth's *Travels* as a source-book for the history of the western Sudan.   But when such men tried to stand back from their own first-hand knowledge and tried to generalise, the results were less happy.   Their sense of historical discipline, often instinctive when they were dealing only with peoples whom they knew intimately, was usually inadequate to the task.   The many short general accounts of the history of Africa or of the Negroes that were produced by Frenchmen from the 1920s to the 1940s — for example, by Delafosse (1922), Labouret (1946), and Georges Hardy (1922) — are now little remembered.   Johnston, for example, was able (cf. Seligman) to see the total history of Africa only in terms of its colonisation by 'alien races' (1899).   Even in their own original work, these men sometimes did not sufficiently distinguish between recording and interpretation and were thus apt to confuse fact and speculation.   This is occasionally true even of Delafosse.   It certainly tends to vitiate a considerable part of the contribution of so meticulous an enquirer as H. R. Palmer (1928), and it remains a stumbling block to the recognition of even so recent a worker as Mrs Meyerowitz (1952; cf. Goody 1959).

A much more straightforward contribution to historical knowledge was apt to result from the work of educated Africans, such as C. C. Reindorf (1895) or Samuel Johnson (1921), whose aim was essentially the limited one of setting down what they could recover about the past of their own ethnic groups.   Other useful contributions were the work of men whose main concern was to ensure that African schools could have textbooks from which some African history could be taught: for example, J. L. Monod (1926), S. J. Hogben (1930) or C. R. Niven (1937), although, as the example of W. T. Balmer (1925) shows, some educators were also happy to indulge in wide speculations.

The examples given so far are of individuals whom circumstances had placed in positions particularly favourable for the recovery of indigenous African tradition. There were other amateurs who wrote histories primarily from written (usually European) sources, though, because they had actually lived and worked in particular colonial territories, they were usually much more alive to the existence and activities of the African peoples than were the professional historians in Europe. In this category one might mention Flora Shaw's (Lady Lugard) *Story of a Tropical Dependency* (1905), the numerous excellent historical summaries in works by Sir Harry Johnston, or the *History of the Gold Coast and Ashanti* by W. W. Claridge (1915).   Some later practitioners of this kind, for example Sir John Gray, with his monumental *History of the Gambia* (1940) and numerous learned articles on East African history, or W. E. F. Ward in his *History of the Gold Coast* (1948), sometimes combined both written records and tradition in such a scholarly manner that they were amateurs only in name.   They were, in fact, among the forerunners of the new school of African historians which began to emerge towards the end of the 1940s.

III   THE REVOLUTION IN AFRICAN HISTORICAL STUDIES

The origins of this modern school of African history are to be found within the great changes that began to impinge on Africa during and after the second world war.   Politically, economically and socially, both the conditions governing opinion within Africa and the opinions held of Africa from outside were radically altered during the 1940s and 1950s and were of themselves bound to affect the climate in which African history came to be written.   The emergence of new African states on to the world stage obviously required new appraisals of their own histories and of the history of the Negro peoples.   But this need was often first felt (among outsiders as well as among Africans themselves) at the levels of journalism or political ideology rather than at the level of original historical enquiry.   Books like Cheikh Anta Diop's *Nations Nègres et Culture* (1955) or even, perhaps, J. C. de Graft Johnson's *African Glory* (1954), sometimes seem as much concerned to establish new Afro-centric myths about the African past as to try to establish what that past really was.   Myth-making, however, is an essential human activity which the historian must recognise just as much as the anthropologist, and in any case not all the new general reappraisals of African history were of this kind.   There was, for example, Basil Davidson's *Old Africa Rediscovered* (1959), a triumphant essay of the type pioneered perhaps by Lady Lugard, that affords a perceptive reinterpretation of Africa's pre-colonial history.   What differentiated Davidson's book from those of Diop and de Graft Johnson was not that he was a European and not an African, but that he had thoroughly steeped himself in the results of the scholarly research into the African past that had been undertaken in the previous ten years or so.

The stimulus for this research was less a result of the general changes that were sweeping Africa than a consequence of a specific development in the field of African education.   If the first involved a vital alteration in the climate in which African history was to be *written*, it was the latter which produced a new situation in which the past of Africa was for the first time to be *studied* by academic historians in the same way and on much the same scale as the past of most of the rest of the world had been studied.

The key event here was the establishment by the colonial powers of university institutions in tropical Africa with a standing equivalent to that of the universities in their own lands.   Before 1948 there was no institution of unequivocal university rank anywhere in Africa between Cairo and Johannesburg.   In 1943–45, as part of Britain's wartime reappraisal of her relations with her colonies, the Asquith and Elliott commissions had determined that there should be universities in the British colonies; from 1948 onwards these began to come into being.   Today they exist in a quantity and a quality (both ever-increasing) that would certainly have astonished the original planners, for what may have started as a scheme to meet the practical needs and the moral obligations of the British in Africa was quickly developed as a categorical imperative of the Africans themselves.   The British example was followed by the Belgians and the French.   The new universities all possessed departments of history.   Some of them included departments of archaeology also, though often the need for these was less apparent, perhaps because both the general and educational revolutions in Africa had tended to engender separate governmental antiquities services.   But the point is that, almost for the first time, men whose sole professional activity was the elucidation of the historical past began, in appreciable numbers, to live and work in Africa.

This is not to forget the teachers of history in the schools in the African colonies: schools which, if usually too few, were sometimes excellent.   Although some of the school teachers (Ward is perhaps an outstanding example) were pioneers in the ways which the university teachers were to develop, they usually differed from the latter in two important respects.   In the first place, they did not have the same obligation to engage in research.   Secondly, they were operating within educational systems that tended to be almost exact replicas of the relevant European systems.   Thus most of the history that was taught in the schools was not African but European history — often, indeed, little more than the history of Britain or of France.   British schools in Africa were perhaps more liberal (i.e. more locally orientated) in their outlook than those of the French or Belgians, but essentially their aim was not so very different.   It was to train Africans who could supplement (and perhaps eventually replace) Europeans in their self-conceived civilising mission in Africa.   More specifically, perhaps, should these Africans be given the opportunity of further education, their early training was such that they would fit directly into the metropolitan educational patterns.

Although initially the purpose of the new universities was often conceived as little more than an extension of the longer-established school systems, their history teachers were faced with questions rarely permitted to the school teachers: what history were they to teach? What history was appropriate to the circumstances in which they found themselves?   They all tended towards the conclusion that they must teach some *African* history.   The speed with which they arrived at this answer and, indeed, the degree to which they accepted it were not, of course, uniform. French-speaking universities, more rigidly controlled from home, tended to have much more difficulty in coming to this decision and reached it less confidently and clearly than English-speaking universities. There were also varying degrees of commitment to the idea of African history among the latter. Nevertheless, all the universities in the African colonies began to introduce some courses in the history of Africa into their teaching. This naturally involved their history teachers in finding out, by their own efforts and research, what African history there was which could be taught.

This took them not only into the field in Africa, but also into the great libraries and record offices of Europe to see how much African history might lie concealed there. The School of Oriental and African Studies in the University of London first specifically turned its attention to African history when it appointed Dr Roland Oliver to its department of history in 1948. By 1953 there was sufficient coming and going between Africa and Europe to suggest to Dr Oliver that a useful service might be done by holding a conference of historians and archaeologists concerned with Africa to discuss current research and the state of knowledge about the African past. The conference was a great success, becoming the first. of a four-yearly series, the most recent of which (1961) drew an attendance of some 180 persons (School of Oriental and African Studies 1955, 1959, 1962). These conferences gave birth to a journal, *The Journal of African History*, which quickly became the continental (and international) complement to the local historical journals, such as the *Transactions of the Historical Society of Ghana* (1952–) and the *Journal of the Nigerian Historical Society* (1954–), which history departments in the African universities in Ghana and at Ibadan had already established. (It should be noted that some other territories had for long had journals which, while not exclusively historical, commonly printed historical articles, e.g. *The Uganda Journal*, *Tanganyika Notes and Records*, and, for French territories, *Bulletin de l'Institut Français d'Afrique Noire* and the local series of *Études*.)

The subject of African history soon came to be recognised even more widely. Thus history took a large part in the Africanists' section of the twenty-fifth Congress of Orientalists (Moscow 1960), and in 1961 the International African Institute brought together both historians and anthropologists to discuss some of the problems of African ethno-history at an international seminar at Dàkar.

Thus from about 1948 onwards, African history began to be recognised as a serious subject for academic study, not only in Africa itself but also in European and American universities, and the number of professional historians working on it began to grow to respectable proportions. Because initially these historians — Africans as well as Europeans or Americans — had of necessity gained their training in the history of the European or Western world, most of them first tended to approach the history of Africa from written sources.

IV WRITTEN SOURCES

It quickly became apparent that the amount of written evidence of the African past was very much greater than historians of Newton's generation or outlook had imagined. In the first place, the growth of interest in African history has been a great stimulus to the formation and maintenance by African governments of public archives. In at least one case, that of the Federation of Nigeria, the setting up of a proper, modern archives service was directly due to the initiative and drive of an African university historian, Dr K. Onwuka Dike (1954). Such archives are, of course, primarily concerned to preserve and to make available for inspection the records of the governments that have brought them into being. Since these were for the most part either colonial governments or their successors, their holdings of official records rarely extend much beyond about 1880 or, at the best, the earlier nineteenth century. Most of these public archives, however, also endeavour to collect unofficial records: the papers of trading companies, missionary societies, private individuals, etc. — and in this way their scope tends to be lengthened as well as broadened (Baxter 1959; Curtin 1960).

The existence of African public archives and sometimes also of important private collections of local material — for example, in the libraries of the new universities — means that for the period from about 1880 onwards at least, the historians of African territories have available to them very much the same kind of resources as are available to their colleagues working on European or American history. For Africa, these records may be supplemented from the archives and collections in the colonising countries. These, indeed, are often of the first importance for the modern period, though, in comparison with the local archives, they tend to be concerned more with the doings of Europeans in Africa and thus to possess less of the kinds of detailed information about the Africans themselves that can be found in local court files or administrators' reports.

For times before about the middle of the nineteenth century, the main deposits of written records for Africa are to be found in these archives and libraries outside the continent, principally in Europe (though it is by no means evident to what extent the resources in some Muslim lands have been properly explored). The extent of the material relating to Africa in European collections is enormous. Both the Portuguese and the Vatican archives, for example, contain large collections of documents dealing with western, middle and north-eastern Africa in the fifteenth and sixteenth centuries. If worked on at all before about 1948, documents of this kind for the most part have been used as source material for European activities in Africa. But they also provide valuable information about African peoples: a fact perhaps first demonstrated on any significant scale by Dr Dike. When most of his contemporaries would have used the records relating to Britain's connection with the Niger delta in the nineteenth century to write on British activities in, or British policy towards, the delta, Dike combined these records with local material to offer an overall picture of *Trade and Politics in the Niger Delta, 1830–1885* (1956). More recently the use of what are essentially European records to illuminate the *African* past has been taken much further. To give but one example: Priestley and Wilks (1960), working essentially from the records of eighteenth-century European traders on the Gold Coast, have been able to indicate that one of the kings of Ashanti has been eliminated from the tradition of that nation.

A useful start has been made in providing guides to the mass of European records that deal with Africa in the work of the West African Guides Committee sponsored by the Institute of Historical Research of the University of London. A volume setting out the materials that exist for West African history in the archives of Belgium and the Netherlands has already been published (Carson 1962), and further volumes are being prepared for the archives of the Vatican, France, Portugal, Scandinavia, etc. It is to be hoped that eventually the scope of the series will not be limited to West Africa.

Apart from the strictly record material, it must not be forgotten that Europe and Asia have been producing literature referring to Africa for something like two and a half thousand years. Scholarly analysis of this literature can offer many revealing clues to African history. As has been seen, descriptions and histories in modern European languages are available for those parts of Africa known to Europeans; such materials date back to the beginnings of European expansion in the fifteenth century. European classical languages provide information for a period of some eight or nine centuries beginning at about the fifth century BC. These works are not confined only to North Africa. The *Periplus of the Erythraean Sea* (1912) and the 'Christian Topography' of Cosmos Indicopleustes (Winstedt 1909), for example, are primary sources for the history of the East African coast around the beginning of the Christian era.

The chronological gap between the classical and the modern European literature is virtually filled by comparable literary sources in Semitic languages. Arabic authors provide information of increasing value over an increasingly large area from about the eighth to the fifteenth centuries, and for north-east Africa, of course, there is an important literature in Ge'ez and Amharic. Some of these sources are well known, but just as the European sources have been examined in the past mainly from a European viewpoint, so the Arabic and other non-European literature relating to Africa has been exploited and published for the most part by people concerned with the history and culture of Asia rather than of Africa. Much of this material needs to be examined afresh from an African standpoint. A most useful guide to the early literature relating to Africa is to be found in Yusuf Kamal's *Monumenta Cartographica Africae et Aegypti* (1926–38), which gives extensive selections from almost all the available texts, together with a parallel French translation, from the earliest times to the fifteenth century.

The Arabic sources for the history of Africa are not only external. Some eight centuries before Negro Africans began to make use of European languages, some of them had begun to adopt Arabic as an international literacy for matters of religion, trade, diplomacy, justice and administration. The Arabic script, furthermore, was adopted for the writing of such major African languages as Hausa and Swahili. From such documents as the *Tarikhs* written at Timbuctu by Mahmoud Kati and Abderrahman as-Sadi, we know that, by the sixteenth and seventeenth centuries at least, Negro Africans were employing their Arabic literacy to write important historical chronicles. Logically, archival materials in Arabic or in Arabic script could also have survived from such times. So far, however, the efforts of interested bodies such as Ibadan University and the Nigeria Federal Antiquities Service seem to indicate that in tropical Africa both climatic and political circumstances have combined to prevent the preservation of many such records from times earlier than about the beginning of the nineteenth century. On the other hand, interesting results may come from the investigation of the Arabic archives of Mediterranean Africa, notably perhaps in Egypt and Morocco, by enquirers well grounded in the history of the lands across the Sahara. Some idea of the Arabic documentation available for one West African territory may be gained from Kensdale (1955–56) and from the notes by H. F. C. Smith in recent issues of the *Bulletin of the Nigerian Historical Society*.

V   UNWRITTEN SOURCES: THEIR NATURE AND PROBLEMS

Arabic writings are a very useful complement to the European sources for African history in that, in addition to helping fill in a chronological gap in the European literature, they represent the results of a penetration which was essentially continental and from the north, while that from Europe was for the most part coastal and sub-Saharan. Nevertheless, there still remain large areas of Africa and long periods of its past for which the historian can command few or no written sources. They are lacking, for example, for the whole of Africa south of the Muslim frontier, which began to emerge in the Sudan in the tenth century, until the establishment of the European frontiers on the coasts in the fifteenth and sixteenth centuries. The Guinea forestlands, until about the eighteenth century, and the interior of large parts of Bantu Africa, until about the middle of the nineteenth century, have also failed as yet to yield written records.

The natural first recourse of historians seeking to bridge these gaps is probably to the allied discipline of archaeology. In Africa the division of the past into chronologically more or less neat periods of pre-history (recovered from archaeological data), proto-history (in which some written evidence is available to supplement the archaeological data), and history (essentially reconstructed from written sources) is almost meaningless. In a sense most African history before the colonial period is proto-history, for any archaeological evidence is of necessity a valuable supplement to evidence gained by other means. This is true, for instance, even for comparatively recent — eighteenth and nineteenth century — history of the Guinea forest states, whose oral traditions are good, and for which the European records and literature are relatively abundant.

Luckily the advantages of co-operation between historians and archaeologists in Africa are well recognised on both sides: a fact that has been clearly exemplified by the conferences organised by the School of Oriental and African Studies. The proper reconstruction of the history of the Iron Age in Africa largely depends on such co-operation, and much is already being done in this respect, most notably perhaps in central Africa. But there are two major difficulties facing the historian here.

In the first place, archaeological knowledge of Africa is still in its infancy. It is only very recently that archaeologists have begun to work in sub-Saharan Africa; the area involved is vast and the conditions are often difficult and, in relation to the tasks confronting them, the archaeologists are still very few. There are still extensive — and historically important — regions of the continent (for example, the lands between Lake Chad and the Nile) which archaeologists have as yet hardly surveyed. Even in areas where many of the sites are known, there is usually an enormous amount of work still to be done, not only in digging them but also in assessing the results and correlating them one with another. Only after this has been done can the archaeologists confidently present a firm picture of the archaeological record. Furthermore, it must be remembered that the Iron Age, which alone really concerns historians, is for archaeologists as a whole a small and sometimes minor aspect of their field. Secondly, even where the archaeological picture is most advanced — as, for example, in Central Africa, where archaeological research has been longer and more consistently supported, and where professionals have succeeded in mobilising useful amateur assistance — the evidence and interpretations of the archaeologist must mainly relate to material cultures. Even where skeletal material has been recovered and has been analysed, as at Mapungubwe, the equation of these cultures with peoples, who are known to and are the concern of the historian, is often a matter of some difficulty.

With the exception of Central Africa, and some parts of East Africa (notably Uganda) and West Africa (especially perhaps Nigeria), therefore, the fruits of co-operation between historians and archaeologists have so far tended to be small. In the circumstances, historians have tended to make much of such clues as they can find in work done in such esoteric fields as physical anthropology, comparative and analytical linguistics, social anthropology, and even ethno-botany and ethno-musicology. The extent and the value of this can be seen from such publications as the special number of the *Journal of African History* (III, 2, 1962) devoted to the third London conference on History and Archaeology in Africa, or the forthcoming record of the Royal Anthropological Institute's 1962 colloquium on 'Music and History'. It must be recognised, nevertheless, that here necessity has driven the historians to dangerous ground.

It is obvious that such contemporary features and characteristics of African peoples as their blood-groupings, the inter-relationships between their languages, their place-names and their loan words, their social, religious and political structures, their crops and their methods of cultivation, their musical traits and instruments, are all the results of historical processes. But for the most part these things are studied and analysed by specialists who are not primarily concerned with history, and rarely is it possible for an historian to master their especial disciplines. He has therefore the invidious task of distinguishing between what the general body of their practitioners is prepared to accept as concrete *data* and what some of them at least are willing to consider as tenable *hypotheses*, either as to the facts or as to their historical explanation. Furthermore, if the historian needs, or is tempted, to extrapolate or to speculate from the data provided by such specialists, he must do so within limits which they alone can really determine. However, the fact that these rules are difficult to observe, and often in fact have not been observed (see, for example, Goody 1959), does not vitiate the value to the historian of evidence from linguistics, social anthropology, and the like. It merely serves to indicate the need for the closest co-operation and mutual understanding between the historian and the practitioners of these disciplines as well as with the archaeologists.

At the present time, the most fruitful source from which historians are seeking to supplement the written evidence for African history is undoubtedly the oral traditions of the African peoples. It is probably in this field of work on oral tradition that the historians of Africa are making their most important contribution to historiography generally, for Africa possesses some of the most highly developed of the non-literate cultures that have survived into recent times.

Practical fieldwork with oral tradition and its theoretical analysis — its general nature and its specific forms, its relation to reality, and the problems involved in ascertaining, testing and using it — have been furthest developed by Professor Jan Vansina. His writings on the subject merit very close study (especially 1961, which contains a comprehensive bibliography). Here there is space to do little more than to comment on Vansina's work. Few historians who have worked with African oral traditions would quarrel with his basic thesis that, as raw materials for historical analysis and synthesis, they are in general terms not so very different from written sources.

Written evidence, even written *records* of the past, are not *inherently* more reliable than oral traditions of the past. Both begin with a human individual's observation of a fact or an event. This observation may be more or less accurate according to whether it is direct (first-hand) or indirect (second-hand), and according to the observer's degree of perception and understanding. If this observation is to be transmitted through time, the transmission is apt to have a purpose behind it, and this purpose may well colour both the original observation and its transmitted form. Whether the mode of transmission is by writing or orally, other (later) individuals are usually concerned. Each of these must have his own particular motivation, degree of accuracy, and capacity for prejudice or bias: all of which may distort the form in which the observation finally becomes available to historical analysis and interpretation. Errors, colourings and divergencies *may* be greater when the mode of transmission is by oral memory rather than by writing. But this is not inherent in the medium, at least not before the introduction of printing. The historian using oral tradition is not in a vitally different position from, say, an historian using a medieval European or Arabic chronicle, which has been preserved for him by the efforts of generations of copyists of varying degrees of literacy, competence and intellectual honesty. He can, indeed he must, subject it to the same fundamental methods of historical criticism to establish its reliability: Where did it originate? Was its first author (or authors) in a good position to ascertain the facts or events purported to be recorded? Did he have any special prejudice or bias to colour his recording or his desire for its perpetuation? How many hands has the observation passed through subsequently? What bias or prejudice may these transmitters have possessed? How does the observation on record square with other observations by other individuals of what purports to be or could possibly be the same fact or event? Is it consistent with other kinds of evidence? For it is not sufficient to check one oral tradition with others; whenever possible, it is necessary to check all relevant traditions with such written, or archaeological, or linguistic, or sociological evidence as may be available.

Approached in this way, oral tradition is just as much the raw material of history as any other kind of evidence. To Vansina, indeed, anything that has been orally transmitted from the past can provide historical information (just as modern historians of literate societies may take as evidence any kind of writing that has survived: the novels of Jane Austen just as much as the despatches of Napoleon). Among the categories of oral tradition he considers are titles and formulas, judicial precedents and explanatory comments, poetry and myths, as well as what are expressly remembered as historical traditions.

This is a perfectly correct approach, but so far most of the other historians who have made much use of African oral traditions — for example, Roland Oliver (1955, 1959) or D. P. Abraham (1959) — seem to have contented themselves with the use of explicitly historical traditions. These exist at a number of levels, social as well as political. Thus there can be family tradition, clan tradition or class tradition (e.g., the tradition of smiths or of drummers); and there can be the traditions of political institutions, such as states and of the units — regional, class or functional — within states. To some extent these two categories overlap. It would seem, nevertheless, that a distinction can be made between the traditions of states and their component political institutions and those of groups of individuals who are organised on a kinship rather than a political basis. The political institution, just because it is an artificial creation of man and not a consequence of natural biology, has a greater need of historical memory. Indeed, a coherent and chronologically progressive concept of its past is necessary to maintain its continuing identity.

Both in East and West Africa, work on the oral traditions of states which were still in effective being at the beginning of the colonial period has produced results which are both intelligible and reasonable in the light of such written or archaeological evidence as is available for as long as some five centuries, indeed as far back as the origins of the states in question (Oliver 1955, 1959; Fage 1956). Such results cannot be obtained for weaker political units, whose tradition is often compressed. Nor can they be secured for areas where once-powerful states have vanished or have been absorbed in other units. The state and its concrete sense of history go together; the need for the latter disappears when the state which has called it into being disappears. Where new states have arisen on old foundations, traditions which are discordant to the new reality are expunged from the record or to a greater or lesser extent rephrased to meet the new situation. Finally, where there is little or no concept of statehood at all, traditions, though often providing useful historical colouring, are usually very difficult to anchor in time or place. Ultimately the enquirer may be left with no more than a minimal family concept of the past, continually sliding through time with a maximum depth of no more than three or four generations: a concept and a depth adequate enough to determine most issues (e.g., marriage or inheritance) which arise within a small kinship group.

A historian's understanding of oral traditions will not be complete, and the use he makes of them may be grossly misleading, unless he is thoroughly at home in the society and the language of the people whose traditions they are. This of course is a truism: a European historian who was not thoroughly conversant with France and the French language would hardly essay the writing of French history, for example. But for the reconstruction of African history from oral traditions, this truism would seem to have especial importance. The traditions which are not purposely historical, for example myths and folk-tales, may not be historically meaningful at all outside their particular social and linguistic contexts. It is also the case that the explicitly historical state traditions are what they are because it is the state that needs them, and so they are necessarily moulded by the particular society that has given rise to the state.

Assessment of the social and linguistic factors involved in African oral traditions can lead to serious practical difficulties. This is not only because so far so many of the practitioners of African history have been Europeans originating wholly outside the societies and languages with which they are working. The problem arises basically from the great number and variety of the social and linguistic units in Africa. For example, even in a territory as small as Ghana, which is no larger than the British Isles, something like fifty separate languages can be recognised, and this is not exceptional. Such a situation would in theory seem to impose an impossible task on any historian wishing to recreate the precolonial history of the peoples of Ghana correctly and in its entirety. Even if he is a native-born Ghanaian, he is unlikely to be thoroughly at home in the languages and societies of more than perhaps two or three of the constituent groups of the population. To acquire an equivalent understanding of any other group may well involve him in a year or two's work. For the social anthropologist or sociologist, such an effort is worthwhile — indeed it is essential — since his concern is with the society as a whole. But the historian is faced with this considerable labour merely to enable him to acquire and to evaluate in its context the society's tradition (Vansina 1960).

Furthermore, because a large part of the history he is seeking to recreate may lie less within each individual social and linguistic group than in its inter-relation with its neighbours, once he has succeeded with one group he will have to pass on and begin the whole laborious process all over again — and not once, but many times. Thus even the native-born historian of such a major unit as the Mande needs to know not only the various Mande dialects, but also a good deal of the society and language of the many other peoples with whom Mande history is interwoven — Fulani, Hausa, Songhai, Tucolor, Tuareg, Mossi and so forth.

Ultimately this difficulty may be less pressing, since so many detailed studies of particular groups will have been made — often by members of these groups themselves — and will have been made public in languages which are widely comprehended, that inter-relationship and synthesis will be much easier (though even then the particular monographists may need deeper knowledge of adjacent peoples and languages than they may normally possess). At the present juncture the only working solution in many cases would seem to be a close working partnership between the historian and those several anthropologists and linguists who are especially knowledgeable about the groups with which the historian is concerned (Fage 1956).

VI CONCLUSION

It cannot be too much stressed, indeed, that at the present time, the unravelling of the African past must to a great extent be an interdisciplinary undertaking. One of the great needs for the better understanding of this past is the establishment of overall syntheses within as absolute a chronological frame as it is possible to achieve. Archaeology can provide absolute dates (by the carbon-14 and other processes) and much else besides in areas and for periods which the historian's techniques cannot touch. Social and physical anthropologists, linguists, botanists, musicologists and so forth, can provide both general illumination and specific historical data beyond the reach of the average historian. This was first formally recognised, perhaps, with the Benin Scheme in Nigeria. Here the initiative of Dr Dike led to a comprehensive enquiry into the Benin past involving full-time research and co-operation from a social anthropologist (Dr R. E. Bradbury), an anthropologist specialising in art and material culture (Dr P. J. C. Dark), and a historian (Dr A. F. C. Ryder). In this instance the historian could concentrate on the rich European documentation available from Portuguese times in the fifteenth century onwards. In the absence of such documentation, the aid of other disciplines is all the more necessary. Without it such elusive historical themes as, for instance, the legends of Kisra in the Nigerian region, or of the Bachwezi in Uganda can hardly be pinned down and given substance.

But the historian in Africa is not merely a synthesiser and a borrower. It is not only that, together with the archaeologist, he brings to Africa the particular purpose of recovering and making meaningful the past that the workers in the other disciplines do not have. In addition he brings a particular discipline and a particular set of skills for the recovery and assessment of data relating to the past. His discipline and skills may be in some respects analogous to those of the archaeologist, but essentially they are both different from and complementary to these. Furthermore, they result from many years of cumulative experience in historical research and exposition throughout the world. It may be that some of the first generation of professional modern historians to work in and on Africa were not as well equipped to deal with its history as they might have been. They tended for the most part to come to Africa *via* colonial history and thus to have specialised in modern history, whereas often both the evidence available for and the problems of African history, even for quite recent periods, more closely resemble those of medieval or ancient history in other parts of the world. But this will be remedied, both in future training and with more practical experience. Even now, however, there are certain things relating to the understanding of the African past that only the historians are really trained to do. One is the preparation of scholarly new editions of the many important historical texts which the non-Africa-orientated historians of the past have either neglected or have used essentially for purposes unconcerned with Africa (SOAS conference on History and Archaeology in Africa 1961; *Journal of African History*, 1962, 2: 192). Another is the careful sifting of historical and para-historical evidence to produce the detailed historical monographs which are all too often lacking for African peoples and lands. This does not always involve new research. There is much historical information still unassessed in the published writings of travellers, missionaries, administrators and the like (not to mention anthropologists, linguists and their like), though in so far as these monographs also incorporate fruits of original and first-hand research, their subjects may be the better understood and illuminated.

A very great deal needs to be done before the public equipment available to the historians of Africa begins to approach in volume and depth that available to the historians of other continents. At the moment it is possible to talk simply and generally of 'African history', because historians have really only just begun to piece together the most basic narratives. Very few historians have yet ventured to provide economic histories of particular African regions or peoples, let alone social, religious or art histories. In the circumstances, the overall synthetic outlines (the need for which has already been mentioned) are quite essential, not only because otherwise such few detailed studies as have been published cannot be seen in any perspective, but also because without these syntheses it cannot be seen where detailed investigation is both most urgent and most feasible. Ultimately, of course, the whole cannot be made until the parts have been produced. The outlines must be subject to continual adjustment so that they fit the parts. And not until we have many more detailed historical investigations — and many more historians at work — can we begin to understand the African past to the extent to which we understand the past of other parts of the world and as it deserves to be understood.

3

Anthropology   P. H. Gulliver

I   INTRODUCTION*

ANTHROPOLOGY IN AFRICA is not, of course, a self-contained intellectual
discipline; it is necessarily a part of the total field of anthropological studies
with its world-wide range.   All Africanist anthropologists must inevitably be concerned with and influenced by data, methodologies and hypotheses coming from
anthropological research and thought in other continents.   With relatively few
exceptions, Africanist anthropologists work in university departments or in
museums where they are in close and constant contact with colleagues who have
non-African specialisations.   It also happens that the acknowledged masters and
innovators in this century have not been Africanists; the major theoretical stimulus
for those who themselves are Africanists has come, therefore, from outside the
continent.   This has been a mixed blessing.   In the English-speaking world, Boas
and Kroeber in North America, and Malinowski and Radcliffe-Brown in Britain
have been the chief figures.   This non-African influence has been particularly strong
among American anthropologists, for they have only fairly recently turned to Africa
as a major region of study.   The British have been specialising there for more than
three decades — long enough, in fact, to produce a number of leading teachers and
theorists who are also primarily Africanists (e.g., Evans-Pritchard and Nadel).

A second feature which keeps Africanist anthropology firmly within the total
discipline is the fact that the range and variety of anthropological data in Africa
are so great that there is really very little which can be considered especially
peculiar to it or which might give it a kind of autonomous status.   That is to say,
there is no distinctive quality or characteristic interest in Africanist anthropology
(comparable, say, to the ubiquitous caste system of the Indian sub-continent) which
gives it a common focus essentially different from that of anthropology elsewhere.
Africanist anthropology is merely a convenient segment of the discipline defined in
geographical terms.   On the other hand, as will be shown later in this chapter,
there have been certain theoretical interests and developments which, though not
peculiar to Africa, have been particularly dependent on African data: the analysis
of indigenous political systems and types of authority, and the study of unilateral
descent groups and segmentary lineage systems, have both been largely developed in
this way (see below pages 93–95).

* Bibliography for this chapter will be found on page 499.

In anthropological studies generally there are two major approaches which are in some vital ways quite distinct, and which will continue, as in the past, to foster markedly different interests, techniques and results. It is of great importance that other social scientists should have some appreciation of the nature of these two approaches, for they should be aware of the basic theoretical orientation which informs any particular work that may be consulted. These two approaches are the sociological (social anthropology) and the cultural (cultural anthropology) respectively. To date, the social anthropologists have been dominant in Africa. This is largely because social anthropology has been the field of specialisation favoured by the British; and it has been British anthropologists who have formed the most important single coherent group at work in Africa. Clearly, the social anthropologists obtained invaluable stimulus from the theoretical sociologists of both Europe and America: especially Durkheim, the French sociologist, whose work much influenced the leading British theoretical exponent of social anthropology, Radcliffe-Brown. But in its contemporary development, social anthropology has become an international discipline, and work in Africa has been more involved in its history than work in any other continent. Today, however, there are distinct signs of the increasing incorporation into social anthropology of much of the cultural approach.

Before discussing the significance of these two different approaches, it is necessary to distinguish both from what is usually called 'ethnography': that is, descriptive accounts of the social and cultural lives of peoples, with little or no attempt at interpretation or 'understanding', as distinct from mere 'knowing'. Ethnography is essential, of course, for it supplies the raw data for analysis, cross-cultural comparison, or other theoretical treatment. All anthropologists are therefore ethnographers, both in their field of research and in their writing. Some are content just to record and much of the non-professional literature is principally ethnography. It has been said, with undoubted truth, that no person can investigate and describe, say, the life and events in an African village or at a chief's court, or the chronology and details of a complex of rituals, without some general (i.e., theoretical) ideas and assumptions; whether he is aware of them or not, these orient his interests and affect the recording of those phenomena. There is a legitimate sense, nevertheless, in which we may say that, within limits, an observer describes what he sees and hears without intruding his interpretation. As has often been the case in Africa, he may not be consciously aware of any need or ability to interpret and therefore to understand; perhaps, too, he may feel that he is describing unique matters (as many historians have held) which are scarcely comparable with conditions and events elsewhere. Anthropologists as social scientists believe that they can do more than describe, more even than aim at objective validity in their research and recording of empirical data. They believe that they can interpret. They aim to develop analyses of particular sets of data relating to a single people. More than that, they seek to improve understanding of human behaviour and human interaction at a more general level. Comparable situations are to be found in every discipline. A political scientist cannot be content to describe the formal principles and rules of a country's constitution, nor yet to record authentically the observed operation of, say, the legislature or a department of state. He desires to go further and to understand how the politico-administrative system actually works, what relations really exist between the legislature and department of state, and what are the limitations of authority and

action resulting from them.   Similarly, an anthropologist has the main goal of
seeking to understand the deeper significance of his data: e.g., the village, chief's
court, system of rituals, etc.

Anthropological publications, therefore, may be in effect ethnographic only,
or they may be both ethnographic and interpretative.   The best work attempts not
to allow the latter to colour the former.   When interpretation is involved, then
of course the theoretical predisposition of the anthropologist is most important:
it affects his choice of data and the relative weight he gives to different kinds of
data.   Above all, it will affect the kind of interpretation he attempts to make.

Social anthropologists have been primarily concerned with the scientific study of
human societies — or, more precisely, the social structure of societies.   By social
structure is meant, in brief, the system of persistent relationships between people
and between groups of people, and the principles of organisation which unite the
component parts of the system.   Social anthropologists seek to abstract from the
raw data of human behaviour and to construct 'a model of the social reality.   The
model represents in effect the anthropologist's hypothesis about "how the society
works" ' (Leach 1954: 8).   The basic interest is in the pattern of relationships
between people and groups, and it can be compared with others relatively independently of the actual content of the relationships.

Radcliffe-Brown wrote that 'the units of social structure are *persons*, and a
person is a human being considered not as an organism but as occupying a position
in a social structure'.   Relations between people are not haphazard, but are
regularised by the accepted and established modes of behaviour, i.e., social institutions.   An institution, he taught, has a function by 'the part it plays in the social
life as a whole, and therefore the contribution it makes to the maintenance of
structural continuity' (Radcliffe-Brown 1952: 9–10, 180).   In reality, even for the
small, simpler society, the social anthropologist can scarcely abstract, describe
and analyse either the total social structure or the function of particular relationships and institutions within that whole structure.   The task would be too complex
at more than a superficial level.   Usually, therefore, the anthropologist is content
to deal with some particular part of the structure, with some particular institutional
complex or sub-system: corporate kin-groups, perhaps, or religious institutions.

In line with Radcliffe-Brown's exposition (stemming from Durkheim) and at
least partly as an uncritical act of convenience, it used to be assumed that all parts
of a society were necessarily and intimately interconnected, whereby it was, or
tended to be, in a state of equilibrium.   This extreme view is not now generally
accepted, for it is empirically obvious that inconsistencies do occur, that societies
continue to operate despite this, and that equilibrium (if it ever exists) must be a
rare condition in a system of human relationships.   Now it is assumed that the
elements of any social system, be it that of a whole community or that of some
institutional complex (say, the kinship system) are inter-related in some degree
and in some ways are interdependent, without positing any essential equilibrium or
presupposing the particular kind and scope of interaction.   Indeed, to study and
take into account the areas of conflict and tension, to understand how far objective
inconsistencies are actually accommodated, and to determine how far they are
productive of change — these are some of the major tasks of current anthropology.
Also among these tasks is the need to study the connections between the abstract
structure, the model system of inter-related roles, and the body of values, ideas

and sentiments which they embody and serve in the ongoing lives of people living together.

Cultural anthropologists claim to take the social structure of a people as but a part of their field of study, for they are concerned with culture rather than society. Culture 'refers to the way of life of a people, to their traditional behaviour, in a broad sense, including their ideas, acts and artifacts . . . (and) it is generally agreed that these ways of thinking and acting are patterned so that behaviour in any society is not random or haphazard' (Herskovits and Bascom 1959: 1). Cultural anthropologists abstract these patterns from the human behaviour of every kind which they witness and record.

Thus both kinds of anthropologist are dealing with much the same kinds of data — the lives, behaviour and ideas of a particular group of people — though the breadth of interest of the cultural anthropologist is greater. But they deal with these data in their rather different ways and therefore produce rather different kinds of accounts of the people. The precise difference in effect is not always easy to see for it lies as much in the degree of emphasis given as in the choice of data. Social anthropologists emphasise relations between people and especially relations between groups, whilst cultural anthropologists emphasise institutions or modes of behaviour.

Evans-Pritchard (a notable British social anthropologist) explained the differences as follows:

> When a social anthropologist describes a primitive society the distinction between society and culture is obscured by the fact that he describes the reality, the raw behaviour, in which both are contained. He tells you, for example, the precise manner in which a man shows respect to his ancestors; but when he comes to interpret the behaviour he has to make abstractions from it in the light of the particular problems he is investigating. If these are problems of social structure he pays attention to the social relationships of the persons concerned in the whole procedure rather than to the details of its cultural expression.

> Thus one, or a partial, interpretation of ancestor worship might be to show how it is consistent with family or kinship structure. The cultural, or customary, actions which a man performs when showing respect to his ancestors, the facts, for instance, that he makes a sacrifice and that what he sacrifices is a cow or ox require a different kind of interpretation. . . One is not making a distinction between different kinds of things — society and culture as entities — but between different kinds of abstraction. (Evans-Pritchard 1951b: 17–18.)

These different kinds of abstraction produce distinctive interpretations and understanding.

A. L. Kroeber and Talcott Parsons have pointed out that there is no cause to assume that either kind of anthropology is superior. These writers suggested that it would be 'often profitable to hold constant either cultural or societal aspects of the same concrete phenomena while addressing attention to the other'. And, they continued, 'we may in time expect to learn in which area each type of conceptualisation is the more applicable and productive' (Kroeber and Parsons 1958).

Melville Herskovits and William Bascom have observed that the sociological approach in Africanist anthropology gives 'precision in method and a sharper definition of problems . . . through concentration on a particular phase of social activity' (Bascom and Herskovits 1959: 6). This is certainly one of the justifications of their specific methodology which social anthropologists claim. The two cultural anthropologists continued: 'Yet this inescapably involves a narrower view of human behavior, a more restricted approach to the institutions, beliefs, customs and traditions which man transmits through learning from one generation to another; and a disregard of the features which in essence differentiate human behavior from that of animals' (loc. cit.).

These two approaches stem from long-standing differences in the study of human beings and their social behaviour, and the respective exponents have not always found it easy to understand and appreciate each other's point of view and achievements. An important Africanist social anthropologist wrote some years ago that although 'notable advances have been made in the theory of social structure . . . theories about culture are unsystematic and unco-ordinated' (Fortes 1953: 39). This is doubtless an over-statement at least, although no more so than the counter-accusation that social anthropologists dehumanise mankind by concentrating on social structure and social systems, which certain non-humans also possess. There is no point in following the debate here; it is sufficient for present purposes to note its existence and to suggest that exaggeration has occurred on either side.

Certainly, in connection with African studies, the alleged and real differences have become less important, and for two reasons. One is the overwhelming preponderance of social anthropology. This is the result partly of the relatively large numbers of British and Commonwealth social anthropologists who have been working in Africa and producing a notable body of publications; and partly it is because many of the other anthropologists who are active in both research and publication have been strongly influenced by the sociological approach: e.g., Bohannan (1957, etc.), Colson (1958, etc.), Fallers (1956) in the United States; Balandier (1955) and Mercier in France. Cultural anthropologists, in the tradition established in American Indian studies, have been relatively few so far in Africa and those who have worked in the continent have tended to remain content with ethnographic reporting.

The second reason for the relative unimportance of the distinctions between sociological and cultural is that, in effect, in African studies at least, they appear to be diminishing on either side as each absorbs many of the advantages of the other. Social anthropologists have often claimed unconcern for purely cultural aspects in order to give added emphasis to their peculiarly sociological contribution to anthropological thought; there is need no longer for this kind of over-insistence. It is true that at one period there was much concentration on 'pure' social structure, and upon patterns of relationships abstractly described through the construction of ideal models (e.g., Evans-Pritchard 1940, Fortes 1945). But social anthropologists have always been strongly aware of the cultural features in the social system; among earlier works, for example, are Evans-Pritchard's classic account of Azande witch-craft and magic (1937), and Nadel's study of the political and economic organisation of the Nupe Emirate (1942): the field research for which were carried out in the late 1920s and middle 1930s respectively. Publications during the last decade show an increasingly self-conscious concern for cultural factors (Gulliver 1955, Evans-Pritchard 1956, Lienhardt 1961, etc.), indicating clearly that social anthropologists have moved beyond the abstractions of ideal patterns and models. They have taken into account the values and ideas of the people which inform their social relationships and their social groupings, giving them meaning and utility.   It is highly doubtful if the claims of some cultural anthropologists to a monopoly in the study of ideas and values was ever true; at any event, it no longer is.

Partly as a result of the language barrier, but also partly because of diverging interests, ethnographic and anthropological writings in French have been unduly neglected by English-speaking social scientists, except when quite specific information is sought in French sources.   It is likely, and of course much to be hoped, that this period of separation is coming to an end.   For one thing, English-speaking anthropologists are increasingly alert to their need to learn from French results and ideas; and the new interest of American anthropologists in Africa is less limited to the English-speaking countries than is the case with their British colleagues.   No less important, however, is the fact that younger French anthropologists are absorbing and adding to social anthropology: that is, they are embracing the predominant anthropological approach of socio-cultural analysis in Africa.

In the past, French anthropology in Africa, and elsewhere, has been somewhat dominated by 'the prestige of philosophy as an academic discipline and the philosophical training of many scholars has left alive in French sociology and anthropology a strong desire for intellectually satisfying syntheses of as holistic a nature as possible' (Mendelson 1958: 254). 'Social philosophy' and 'brute empiricism' have tended to be kept well apart (UNESCO 1954), and too often interest in one has not been able to benefit from the other.   The dominating influence in the past has been the history of race and societies rather than analysis or interpretation of social systems, cultural patterns or human behaviour.   The post-war development of Levi-Strauss's work in general anthropology, and of work by a number of specifically Africanist anthropologists, has already gone far to revitalise and reorient French studies (Mendelson 1958: 261).

The largest single body of work — a single, vast project really — and gaining its stimulus from both older and recent lines of thought, is that inspired and led by the late M. Griaule among the Dogon, Bambara and neighbouring peoples in West Africa.   Here, following considerable general investigations in social organisation (Paulme 1940), linguistics, etc., the emphasis was placed on ideological and symbolic systems, including myth and cosmology.   The results of this work, occurring with breaks during the period between 1933 and 1957, still remain incompletely published, and certainly they are insufficiently appreciated by English-speaking scholars.   Neither British nor American studies have yet aimed at so large and prolonged an enterprise in Africa (cf. Tait 1950, Dieterlen 1951, Griaule and Dieterlen 1954).

There exists a large amount of ethnographic work published on the former French territories, some of it in great detail in certain matters (e.g., material culture in north-west Africa), and some of it markedly deficient in the kind of empirical data required for analysis in the Anglo-American mode.   Both in French and in the lesser amounts published in German and Italian there are few analytic, interpretative works which possess a coherent theoretical framework, such as that provided by social anthropology in Britain.

In this chapter (an outline intended primarily for non-anthropological Africanists), the principal concerns are with the development of anthropological theory and methodology, with the nature and scope of analysis, and with the contribution of anthropologists to the understanding of the *social* lives of African peoples. This one takes to be the more significant part of anthropology in reference to the interests and needs of other social scientists. For the reasons already stated, the contributions of the social anthropologists are necessarily given the most prominence; but it is only fair to note that the writer is a social anthropologist and is, therefore, likely to show bias in the choice of topics and emphasis, even though effort is made to avoid this.

As a result of accepted editorial policy, a number of interests which commonly come within the field of anthropology are not touched on here. They are given separate treatment in other parts of this book. Thus the apparent neglect of such topics as human ecology or esthetics does not at all mean that anthropologists have no contribution to make to their study in Africa.

II *THE DEVELOPMENT OF ANTHROPOLOGY IN AFRICA*

Anthropology has by far the longest history of all the social sciences concerned with Africa; partly because of this and partly because of its holistic nature, it has established a tradition of embracing a very wide range of interests covering virtually all of the study of man. Cultural anthropologists in particular explicitly seek to maintain this range but even the social anthropologists, whose declared area of interest is much narrower, have generally been inclined to collect and make available whatever data they could concerning the particular people they studied. The reason for this is clear: as the continent was invaded, conquered and pacified, and as established government was instituted in the newly demarcated colonial territories, one of the major facts presented to the Western world was the multiplicity and great diversity of indigenous societies and cultures. Although this had been somewhat dimly recognised before, as a result of long coastal contacts, it was made quite obvious during the early part of the twentieth century. More than this: the conditions were also established under which more or less intensive and prolonged enquiries could be made among these exotic peoples. Not only was the personal security of the anthropologist assured, where before there had seemed to be little or none unless he were an armed traveller, but also communications and supplies became increasingly dependable. At the same time the Western world developed a growing intellectual and moral interest in such peoples. It is significant, for example, that in 1908 Sir James Frazer became the first Professor of Social Anthropology in Britain. Various evolutionary and diffusionist theories were exciting public attention and demanding the newly available data to confirm or controvert them. The sketchy accounts of travellers and explorers, of missionaries, traders and administrators aroused much interest in how African peoples lived, what were their laws and customs and their beliefs. For sundry other reasons also — political, philosophical, religious, economic, administrative — there was a demand for more information, and a stimulus, therefore, to obtaining it with increased efficiency.

The dominant feature about these newly revealed and accessible societies was their non-Western nature. This brought them immediately within the domain of anthropology and for a long time excluded them from the concern of other social scientists. Such disciplines as political science or economics, for example, have been firmly rooted in the culture of the scholars themselves, and to a great extent this remains the case. Political scientists really become interested in Africa and its peoples when political institutions and ideas of a demonstrably Western, state-like kind become evident.   It is probably true that, even now, no economist has made a full study at first hand of a subsistence or near-subsistence economy in Africa; many do not consider it their task to do any such thing.   Significantly, the field studies which have been made by economists recently have occurred in areas with especially flourishing cash-crop economies (Ghanaian cocoa farmers, Uganda cotton and coffee producers, for example).   Similarly, psychology seems to be markedly ethnocentric, apart from such very rare exceptions as Dr Field's study in Ghana (1960).   Both the theory and the methodology of anthropology have developed specifically for the scientific study of non-Western peoples.

The earlier anthropologists were primarily concerned with the collation and analysis of data coming from various sources and with the intellectual development of hypotheses about mankind.   It was only gradually that the professionals became concerned with the quality and validity of those data and that they perceived the importance of directly controlling investigation with a vigorous field methodology. They also came to value the personal experience in depth with non-Western peoples. But, despite the possibilities for anthropological research, both money and practical opportunity remained scarce.   For a time, therefore, the 'amateur anthropologist' held the field in Africa: the man who was already there in some other capacity but who found time and interest to investigate and record the indigenous life around him.   Some missionaries and administrators were so zealous and conscientious that they produced what by any standards remain classic studies of the people among whom they lived.   Perhaps the most famous of these, because so exhaustive and reliable, is that of the Thonga of South Africa made by Henri Junod of the Swiss Romande Mission (first edition, 1913).   Other well-known examples are the accounts of the Ila of Northern Rhodesia by Smith and Dale (1920), of various Uganda peoples by Roscoe (1911, 1923), etc.   These are but a few of the highlights from a wealth of information of variable reliability which has come from similar sources.   In total it remains an invaluable, if sometimes tantalising, body of literature.

Perhaps the earliest professional anthropologists to engage actively in field research in Africa were C. G. and B. Z. Seligman, who (at the direct invitation of the Sudan government) made their first trip to the southern Sudan in 1909.   This trip and its successors, however, took the nature of extensive surveys over a large, heterogeneous and unknown region.   Stimulated by the example and teaching of Malinowski (based on his Melanesian experience), anthropologists began to require not only more and better data, but they desired to undertake highly intensive research themselves.   Without attempting any exhaustive catalogue, it can be noted here briefly that Evans-Pritchard made his first field trip in 1926, Schapera in 1929, Richards in 1930, and Herskovits, Mair, and Monica Wilson in 1931. M. Griaule began his great work in the French Soudan in 1933, and the Italians, Conto-Rossi and Grottanelli, had previously been at work.   They and their contemporary colleagues established the professional pattern of anthropological investigations and analysis well before the second world war.   Non-professional studies continued, of course, and they found encouragement both from the examples and from the demands of the professionals.   The dominant pre-war group of anthropologists was British, inspired by the teaching of Malinowski and Radcliffe-Brown; but French workers were also busy at the necessary tasks of recording and classifying.   For workers from both countries, a major incentive was the imperative of their colonial commitments.

The post-war increase in the number of anthropologists at work in Africa and on African materials has coincided with the incursion of other social scientists in growing numbers and expertise.   It has coincided also with the rapid development of nation states, national economies, and other new and large-scale configurations of peoples and activities, which are scarcely susceptible to the established and characteristic methodology of anthropology. Anthropologists have therefore yielded up their near-monopoly of social science in the continent; but they continue to remain pre-eminent, as always, in the study of relatively small communities.   It is a fair claim that on the whole anthropologists, because of the small-scale and intensive nature of their work, continue to enjoy a most intimate and often deep association with the people they study.

III   THE TRIBE AS THE UNIT OF ANTHROPOLOGICAL STUDY

The 'natural' unit of study for the anthropologist in Africa has been the tribe, for this is the unit of marked differentiation in socio-cultural terms.   Although it is so fundamental a group, and generally quite an empirically obvious one both to its members and outsiders, it is not always easy to give a 'tribe' a precise and universal definition.   Unfortunately, anthropologists have sometimes used it in different ways.   In general, however, a tribe is a named group of people distinguished from neighbouring groups in a number of ways: the group occupies and exploits a more or less defined territory, usually to the exclusion of other groups; the people are recognised, and recognise themselves, as being different from others by virtue of their common possession of and adherence to a particular way of life or culture, and by their involvement in a coherent social system.   This common way of life includes institutional modes of behaviour (subjectively held to be 'right conduct'), accepted values and ideas, artifacts and language: such way of life, together with the corpus of myth and tradition which informs and supports it, is considered by the people to be their heritage.   The people of a tribe may be linked together within a single social system embracing the whole group, or the distinctive system may be repeated more or less similarly, and with varying degrees of overlapping, in each autonomous section of the tribe.   Thus, where a tribe has (or recently had) political unity under one centralised authority, there is in a real sense a single social system, even though the structures of different kinds of social relations (e.g., kinship, economic) may well be similar to those in other tribes.   In a tribe composed of a number of small separate chiefdoms or some other kind of autonomous groups, between which there is little or no co-operation and interaction, similar social systems exist in each section.

The general definition of tribe has purposely been made in rather vague terms. Often there need be no confusion: one tribe is easily and clearly distinguished from its neighbours, because socio-cultural differences between them are so pronounced. On the other hand, two or more tribes may have some or even many characteristics in common — perhaps being linked in some way through a single superstructure, by symbiosis in trade, by intermarriage, by ritual co-operation, etc.   Yet these common features are in total less significant than the differences between the tribes, whether they are objectively viewed from outside or subjectively conceived by the peoples themselves.   Similarly, the sections of a tribe may be operationally autonomous of one another; they may even be hostile to one another; members of one section may not know of people in other sections nor be directly affected by their actions; and there may in some ways be important differences between sections (e.g., in the means of livelihood). But the over-riding factors are the major parts of their culture which they share and are roughly aware of sharing, and the similar social system in which they severally live.

There is, then, a series of cultures and sub-cultures and of social systems and sub-systems, ranging from the smallest semi-autonomous group (perhaps an extended family hamlet, or a village governed by its own headman and council, etc.) to the widest limits within which there is recognisable cultural similarity and social inter-action. In one sense it is somewhat arbitrary to select one level in the total series, to label it 'tribe', and to insist on its peculiar significance. The 'tribe', nonethe-less, has reality in the subjective conceptions of virtually all African peoples, and it remains useful to distinguish between variations on a common theme and different though related themes; there is thus a quite valid procedure in recognising and isolating the tribe for study. The anthropologist may empirically concentrate his research at some sub-level, but his description applies *mutatis mutandis* to the tribe as a whole. That portions of his account, and especially his analysis, apply to a wider range of human beings — and in some sense, perhaps, to all human beings — does not spoil this classificatory procedure nor deny its validity.

The tribe in Africa is a convenient unit of anthropological study for other cogent reasons. With relatively few exceptions, the geographical size of tribal territories and the numerical size of tribal populations are small enough to permit the anthropologist to obtain at least some knowledge of all parts of the tribe he studies. In addition the degree of complexity and heterogeneity usually is not so great that the anthropologist is unable to encompass the total socio-cultural system. It may be his intention to give a description covering the whole tribe, identifying the major areas of homogeneity and the range of sub-varieties; or it may be his intent only to establish the general outline before proceeding to the intensive study of those aspects which are peculiarly significant or in which he has special interest. In either case he can relate his particular findings — limited by geographical area or topic — to the wider system. Were the distinctive socio-cultural units larger or more complex (as they are now tending to become), the anthropologists would have had to adopt other methods of approach, as the sociologists have done in Western societies.

An appreciation of this fact is important to the understanding of anthropology in Africa, because it underlies the typically holistic view taken by the discipline. This is revealed in two ways. First, anthropologists of all kinds assume their competence to study all aspects of a tribal society — its technology and artifacts, its cosmology, child-bearing practices, legal system, etc. And, not altogether with a partisan attitude, it is fair to say that anthropologists have demonstrated their competence to do this. Secondly, some anthropologists have held the theoretical view that all parts of a social system are intimately inter-related, so that each affects all the others — rather like a gigantic mobile. Although this conception is no longer dominant, it is clear, nevertheless, that many parts of the system are rather delicately interconnected. The possibility of encompassing the whole system enables the anthropologist to perceive the pattern of interconnections in a tribal society in a way which is denied to social scientists studying larger and more complex units.

In saying this, there is no need to ignore the fact that many African tribes do have rather complex social systems which are by no means so simple and unsophisticated as ethnocentric Westerners often tend to assume. With very few exceptions, and despite anthropologists' pretensions, the ideally holistic aim has seldom been realised: a fact which can quickly be verified in the published literature. The complexity and richness of detail in an African tribal system, however, do not reach those of, say, republican Rome, medieval Britain, or modern Canada. It must also be noted that the great majority of the many hundreds of African tribes number rather less than a quarter of a million people each, and many are much smaller than that. To be sure, there are today some fifteen to twenty groups with populations over one million, and the conventional approach of anthropologists would seem to be inadequate in these instances. But the fact is that none of these larger groups consists of a single social system; their regional diversity is so great that in any case anthropologists are compelled to concentrate on major sub-sections. This they have done profitably, as in studies of the Hausa, Ibo or Somali. Recognising the semantic problems, some anthropologists have written of the larger group as a 'nation', reserving the term 'tribe' for the major sections of the nation.

It must be emphasised that in Africa the degree of socio-cultural differentiation is very great, probably more so than in other parts of the world, relative to size and population. Although characteristics and patterns may extend beyond tribal boundaries, it should not be thought that differences are merely of the order of the well-known regional differences of North America or even of the national differences in Europe. They are, in Africa, more numerous, affect smaller groups of people, and are much more radical than that; so that quite commonly some or all of the neighbours of a tribe have a decisively different social system, and mutual comprehension and co-operation are extremely difficult. That is to say: an anthropologist is virtually compelled by the nature of his data to adopt the tribe as the basic unit of study.

Because of this, the major works (though not the only ones) in Africanist anthropology have related to a single tribe. The monograph is the typical publication of anthropologists. Some of these, and particularly the earlier ones, are mainly descriptive accounts of the cultural and social system of a tribe. They attempt to give an overall account, and the emphases are on inclusiveness rather than on interpretation and analysis, and on generalisation applicable to the whole tribe rather than on detailed empirical examination. There are many examples of this type of monograph, but its nature can be illustrated by one of the fullest and best-known, Melville Herskovits' *Dahomey: an ancient West African kingdom* (1938). In this two-volume work (containing over 800 pages) major parts deal successively with 'The people and their setting', 'Economic life', 'Social organisation' (mainly kinship and the ancestral cult), 'The life-cycle of the individual', 'Political organisation', 'Religious life', and 'Art'. Each part contains several specialist chapters: for example, 'Economic life' is subdivided under the heads of production, distribution, the co-operative element, property, socio-economic classes and fiscal policy. This is, then, a thorough description of the life of the people of the old Dahomey state. Even so, and doubtless inevitably, it is not exhaustive; for instance, neither the human ecology nor judicial processes is adequately covered, at least by the standards of a later generation.

More commonly, and especially so in the post-war era, anthropological monographs, whilst still essentially 'tribal' in their orientation, have been devoted to the investigation of particular problems or sets of problems, to the development of specific lines of analysis, or to the examination of certain hypotheses. Indeed

it is now rare, and is generally considered inadequate, for a research worker to go
to Africa merely to study the social life and culture of a given people; he is expected
to have some focal interest or concern.   Anthropologists have thus come to concentrate on theoretical analysis and argument in the light of a body of data which
they have collected for a single tribe.   Although eschewing exhaustive coverage in
a monograph, the aspect of specialisation, nevertheless, is firmly examined in its
tribal setting.   Some well-known examples will illustrate the nature of these
monographs: Evans-Pritchard's analysis of Azande witchcraft and magic (1937);
the analysis of judicial processes among the Lozi (Gluckman 1955) and among the
Tiv (Bohannan 1957); the study of myths, symbols and religion among the Dogon
(Griaule and Dieterlen 1954); accounts of political change among the Soga (Fallers
1956) and among the Hausa (Smith 1961).   It must be emphasised again that these
are essentially tribal monographs.   Theoretical development is most commonly
implicit rather than explicit in the general exposition; although insight and
stimulus are gained from the work of other anthropologists, these also are left
largely implicit.   The problems of direct comparative study are neglected in these
writings, however large they may loom in the minds of anthropologists themselves,
who remain fundamentally concerned with the treatment of a highly specific body
of material.

The reason for this concentration on certain aspects within the setting of a
tribal system, rather than on the system itself, is of course intimately linked with
theoretical development and sophistication in anthropology.   The amounts of
attention and space required to elucidate the nature of the government of an
African kingdom, or the social relations involved in an ancestor cult, are so great
that it is no longer possible to attempt anything approaching exhaustive coverage
of a total tribal system.   The amount of data collected and the depth of analysis
involved require several monographs: for example, the works of Schapera on the
Bechuana peoples, and of the Wilsons on the Nyakyusa of Tanganyika (1952; 1957;
1959).   More than that: increasingly lengthy periods of field research are required
such as even the generosity of contemporary foundations scarcely permits.   There
has been an imperative need to specialise in this way.   In order to obtain the wealth
of data now desired, the degree of intimacy with and depth of knowledge of the
people under study have become so great that anthropologists are increasingly
finding it necessary to restrict the range of their investigations both in terms of topic
and problem and in terms of the size of the group studied.   There must be a choice
between extensive and intensive research, and recently intensive work has pre-
dominated because of the richness of empirical data and anthropological insight it
gives.   This trend has coincided with a growing awareness of the problem of making
valid generalisations for the tribe as a whole.   Generalisation still remains possible
and desirable, but the more intensive the investigation, the more it is revealed that
the socio-cultural system (or parts of it) varies in an infinite number of ways, from
area to area, from sub-chiefdom to sub-chiefdom, and from community to community.   And it is precisely in some of these variable characteristics that the full
understanding of the sub-chiefdom or of the community lies.

For reasons such as these, anthropologists are inclined now to give less attention to total tribal systems (though not ignoring them completely) and have often
deliberately chosen to concentrate on a 'sub-tribal' study.   In this case, the anthropologist selects a single community, or perhaps two or three contrasting communities, so as to obtain a degree of control in a pseudo-experimental situation.   He

then spends many months with this small group of people, and he is able to relate the orthodox anthropological data to this particular cluster of individuals. The empirical validity of what are claimed to be, or what appear to be, norms of behaviour, institutions and kinds of social situations can then be checked and examined with a thoroughness and sureness not possible at the wider levels.

This kind of research procedure is not particularly concerned with the selection of a typical or sample section of the total tribe. With a more or less unknown population, and because of the relative crudity of techniques, the idea of an authentic sample is inappropriate. Anthropologists, furthermore, are sceptical of the validity of any sample. In any case, what is important is not to examine a sample of something larger, but to study the smaller group for its own sake and as a working system. On this matter Elizabeth Colson has written:

> Whether or not my material for the area studied is in any way representative of the Tonga people [of Northern Rhodesia] as a whole, I do not know. This is a problem which may be of some concern to the administration and to the technical assistants who are trying to deal with the Tonga as though they were a single unit. I do not think that it is a problem which needs to concern the anthropologist who is trying to make a study of the inter-relations of the social factors in a single social system. After all, each area studied does represent a unit in which the people are in close social relations with each other. The factors which exist within that set of relations can be dealt with as though one were dealing with an isolated society. The anthropologist certainly has a duty to outline his method and the area to which his information applies, and furthermore he ought to be able to give some indications of the variations over the general area which might affect his analysis and make it inapplicable or applicable elsewhere. This seems to be about the limit to which he can go, with the time, the assistance, and the resources at his disposal. I see no reason why information collected on particular small units within a larger area which bears the tribal name should not be used for comparison with information drawn from similar small units within other large areas which bear different tribal names. The result of the intensive study of small units may not make for the best description in the style of the standard ethnography, but it is most likely to provide us with the type of information we need for testing hypotheses and for formulating new research into the relations between various social factors. (Colson 1954: 58–9.)

The best recent examples of this methodology are Turner's study of an Ndembu village in Northern Rhodesia (Turner 1957) and Middleton's study of a local lineage among the Lugbara of Uganda (Middleton 1960). This kind of research, by reason of both practical necessity and theoretical inclination, is not entirely new. Faced with the knowledge that among the Ibo of south-eastern Nigeria there was a tremendous diversity of social life — its extent not being known — Margaret Green in 1934 chose to concentrate much of her fieldwork in a single village-group. She made no claim that the selected group was typical of anything (Green 1947). Every anthropologist concerned with a tribe of more than a few thousand people has had to make some selection for more intensive study — whether he specifically reveals this or not — unless he is concerned only with the general superstructure of that tribe. The more recent development, however, is the result of quite deliberate methodological choice, and it is much

more than a practical solution to a particular research problem.   It is an attempt
to get away from over-generalisation and from the tendency to deify abstractions,
and is motivated by the desire to understand how actual people behave, how they
are motivated and make choices in the given social context, how earlier choices
affect subsequent ones, and how previous interaction affects later relationships.
The reintensification of field research thus combines with a return to the active
study of actual people in a kind of reaction to the abstract argument and pattern or
model-making of anthropology just after the second world war.   This development
will be referred to again in the discussion of future trends and problems at the
conclusion of this chapter.

IV   *METHODS OF ANTHROPOLOGICAL STUDY*

Whilst anthropology in Africa was primarily the monopoly of interested amateurs,
giving as much of their time and energy to enquiries about the esoteric life around
them as their primary occupation permitted, there was little that could be described
as an established methodology of research.   Facts and assumed facts were collected,
but their precise validity was not really known.   Much of this earlier anthropology
proved invaluable, nevertheless, not merely because it produced the earliest
records now available, but also because some of these more or less casual workers
were remarkably conscientious.   Some like Junod (1913) or Hollis (1905)
explained how and from whom they had obtained their information, and it is clear
that in general there was a heavy dependence on just one or two informants with
whom the enquirer was friendly.   In most cases enquiries were made through an
interpreter, or at least with the assistance of one, and all the problems of indirect
contact with the people, of mistranslation, interpreter's bias and the like, were
scarcely appreciated.   But even if they were, there was little that could be done
about it, because such enquirers could not afford the time to do much more.

The coming of professional anthropologists did not necessarily involve a
radical change in this rather unsatisfactory practice.   It is true that academic
training, including both wide reading about non-Western peoples and the conscious
formulation of interests and problems, enabled the anthropologist to refine his
approach of formal observation and interview, to be more precise and searching in
his questions, and to be more technical in his enquiries and more sophisticated in
the treatment of data.   The survey work of the Seligmans in the southern Sudan
between 1909 and 1922, and the study of Dahomey by Herskovits (1938) are two
different examples of this kind of earlier professional approach.

Outside Africa, however, anthropologists in both Europe and America were
expounding new research techniques, which eventually became known as participant observation.   The prime exponent of this and the one who (through his
students) most influenced Africanist research, was Bronislaw Malinowski.   As a
result of his fieldwork in Melanesia, Malinowski established quite new standards of
research and reporting.   In brief, his example and teaching established the following major principles, which, with subsequent elaboration, have become the basis of
all acceptable field research.   He asserted the necessity for the anthropologist to
learn and work through the language of the people being studied.   This allows
direct relations between him and the people; it allows him to engage in gossip, to
hear spontaneous conversation, and to make his own understanding and translation
of both significant words and phrases and general semantic patterns.   Secondly,

Malinowski proved the inestimable value to the fieldworker of living among the people, sharing as much of their life as possible (without any facile assumptions of 'being just like one of them'!), joining in dances, funerals, feasts, leisure pursuits, serious discussions, watching both everyday and unusual events, getting to know members of the community as individuals, and in general establishing an intimate rapport and mutual trust. Formal interviews with particular informants are still valuable, but after a time they are mostly replaced by long conversations with reliable friends in the light of direct, detailed observation of ongoing life. Thirdly, Malinowski insisted on the vital importance of gathering many actual case examples, by personal observation wherever possible, of institutional behaviour and aberrant behaviour in all kinds of context. The anthropologist must actually witness people behaving in the circumstances and must do so in more than a single instance. He must record what they do, what they say at the time, the reactions and remarks of others, and the precise context in which the events occur. He must relate particular events to the total configurations of roles and relations. He must distinguish and document differences between the norms of behaviour claimed by the people and their actual behaviour in concrete situations (Kaberry 1957).

This kind of work requires a lengthy period of field research and a readiness by the anthropologist to meet the practical difficulties of living in an exotic community. It involves, too, the real problem of retaining an adequately detached viewpoint whilst yet participating in community life and acquiring a status and probably a set of obligations and responsibilities. It requires meticulous note-taking, diary-keeping, continual alertness. As anthropologists will agree, it is a stimulating experience of the highest consequence for the understanding of an African people: an understanding, as it were, from the inside as well as objectively from the outside.

This over-brief summary of modern research methods may be sufficient to indicate what anthropologists feel to be one of the most distinctive characteristics of their discipline: that is, its intimate connection with the people under study and its necessary concentration, therefore, on relatively small-scale communities. It is not possible to deal with societies containing millions of people; indeed it is only possible to deal with those of tens of thousands of people by selecting a few communities where, within the framework of the general social system, actual social life can be observed and recorded. Most anthropologists feel happiest when limited to such small communities, and many feel that in fact they can scarcely attempt any more than to study these small groups, and then attempt rather crudely to show how far they are illustrative of the larger society.

The degree of intensity of participant observation varies a good deal according to the personality of the anthropologist, the particular problems in which he is interested, and the nature of the people he is studying. It can be rather frustrating to be allocated a status equivalent to a member of the ruling class when one is primarily interested in the economic life of commoners, but in some cases that designation has been unavoidable. The present author remembers the difficulties in one tribe in getting the older men to take him seriously, because he had the status of young man-warrior; later in another tribe, where he had deliberately assumed the age-status of an elder, he found his contact with young men restricted. Yet, unless he chose to remain a purely external, distant observer — an object, therefore of suspicion — it was necessary to adopt some such specific role which the people would recognise in the flow of social activities. He had also to avoid the usual role ascribed to a white man, the official or missionary. Despite the difficulties raised, the author was able to profit tremendously in both his adopted roles because of the genuine rapport they made possible.

The length of time required for anthropological research is necessarily often rather longer than for projects by other social scientists: two periods of nine to twelve months each, separated by an interval of several months as a release from pressure and as an opportunity to make an interim assessment of the work. Not a few anthropologists have spent longer than that with a single tribe; conversely, because of lack of funds, other commitments, illness, etc., many have had perforce to work for much shorter periods. An experienced and notably able fieldworker such as Evans-Pritchard produced one of the most outstanding sets of publications on a single tribe in Africa after a total of some twelve months spent intermittently among the Nuer of the southern Sudan (Evans-Pritchard 1940, 1951a, 1956). Despite his skill he could not have produced detailed studies such as those of, say, Wilson on the Nyakyusa (1952, 1957, 1959, etc.) or Colson on the Tonga (1958, 1960, 1962, etc.).

In the post-war era there has been much development in the use of planned questionnaires and of statistical techniques as supplements and aids to these highly intensive field methods. As in the social sciences generally, this has occasionally led to excesses in the quest for figures for their own sake, and to an over-concentration on things that can be treated quantitatively. In some studies there has been a neglect of those less precise, but ultimately more important, qualitative character-istics of human society. On the whole, and probably because of the intimate nature of their research, anthropologists probably have sinned less than some other social scientists in this respect. For the same reason, anthropologists have concen-trated their statistical enquiries firmly upon empirical facts and events rather than upon what people say or believe about events or ideal norms.

Statistical techniques, though likely to remain of secondary importance, have acquired increasing significance in the refinement of research and in reducing the risks of unwarranted conclusions and hypotheses whose applicability is severely limited. Firstly, these techniques permit the objective testing of the conclusions reached in the small communities where intensive research is carried out. For example, the detailed records and case materials concerning marriage and divorce can be both checked and augmented by carefully ascertaining the facts for all adult members of a range of communities. The anthropologist might wish to know if in fact divorce is as uncommon as the people say and his own months of residence among them suggest: has he accidentally struck a quiet period, was it different a decade ago, etc.? Although this may seem an elementary procedure, it has not always been followed in the past, with the result that earlier studies may be partly vitiated. One reads that divorce is 'frequent' or 'not very frequent', or that 'most men live near their father's home after marriage', and it is impossible to discover the real meaning of these statements without statistics.

Secondly, the anthropologist often wishes to test in the wider society the degree and range of applicability of the conclusions he has reached in his selected communities. For example, he may wish to discover if the direct ratio between the proportion of labour migrants and the amount of arable land is generally valid, and what happens when new variables are introduced (e.g., more or less contact with the outside world, different costs of transporting produce, different kinds of crops grown, etc.). Having isolated the significant factors during intensive research, it is relatively easy to concentrate on these variables in the course of extensive investigations.

Thirdly, anthropologists concerned with research in urban areas and in the new complex societies have necessarily had to give much time to methods using questionnaires. This matter is referred to in the section dealing with urban studies.

V COMPARATIVE AND CROSS-CULTURAL STUDIES

The non-anthropologist justifiably might expect to find in the comparative studies made by anthropologists the clearest statements of their generalisations, conclusions, working hypotheses, and their body of more or less accepted theoretical concepts. In some degree these should be found in all the writings, but they are of special significance in works in which the scholar forsakes his concentration on particular sets of data and research in specific societies and compares his findings with those of his colleagues. Unfortunately this is not the case. In the continually and rapidly growing literature of Africanist anthropology, the proportion concerned directly with comparative and cross-cultural work is still small both in quantity and significance. Some of the most prominent scholars have done little more than deal tentatively with such problems, and quite certainly the most distinguished work has been concerned with accounts of single societies, or parts of them. Anthropologists of whatever theoretical cast much prefer to devote themselves to monographic studies in which they can focus on certain problems of general interest, but specifically in the setting of a particular socio-cultural system.

This inclination follows directly from the special kinds of field research methods characteristic of contemporary anthropology in Africa. It arises, too, from a deep-seated, perhaps over-sensitive, awareness of both the practical and theoretical problems involved in the use of data from differing societies and cultures. Essentially the difficulties emerge from the fact that anthropology deals with data relating to a tremendously wide range of socio-cultural systems, the differences between which are fundamentally significant. For the anthropologist, in addition, an isolated fact is not a fact but merely an abstract 'fiction'. It is possible to discover its real meaning — the significance, say, of a particular role or relationship or pattern of behaviour — only in terms of the social context in which it occurs. Thus, what *prima facie* would appear to be similar and therefore comparable data, turn out to be so conditioned by their social environment as not to be susceptible to treatment on their own.

It is possible, for example, to describe the ideal norms of behaviour between father and son in a particular society. It is possible, further, from detailed investigations to describe the actual kinds of behaviour between such people. But the real significance of the behaviour and of the people's ideas about it tends to be lost if at the same time account is not taken of the status of both father and son *vis-à-vis* other people in all sorts of different connections, such as economic, religious, legal, etc. Or again, the role of village headman in two societies may appear to be roughly comparable. In both cases he may be the ritual leader of the community, the allocator of land, arbiter of disputes, and director of communal activities. But in one case he may be at the apex of a self-contained social system: the village being politically and economically autonomous; in the other case he may occupy the lowest rank in a complex social and political hierarchy.

In the first case, the headman is subject to the social control of his small community and closely dependent on it; in the second, although a member of the community, he is subject to a range of superior authority exerted from outside. In the latter case the headman acts as a cog in a larger machine, and therefore the nature of his authority and leadership, the sanctions on his own activities, and his relations with his fellow-villagers are likely to be markedly different from those of the headman of the autonomous village. To compare the two requires a considerable depth of analysis of each case.

It becomes a most complex operation, therefore, adequately to compare data — bits of behaviour — from different societies; it is not impossible, of course, but highly difficult because it necessitates consideration of complicated inter-connections. Intensely aware of this, anthropologists have commonly chosen to concentrate on the nature of particular relationships or roles within their own specific social milieu. The task of analysis, interpretation and understanding becomes so great that little time or interest remains for the wider comparative enquiry. This preoccupation is most marked among the social anthropologists, but it is not confined to them, for cultural anthropologists too have shown disinclination for comparative work.

Having made this general preliminary explanation, it must be noted that certain kinds of comparative work have been accomplished by Africanist anthropologists. A brief survey of this and of the quality of results obtained is given in this present section.

The ultimate ideal in anthropology might be optimistically described as the establishment of generally applicable statements about human behaviour and social relationships and the discovery of the range and operation of factors which, under varying conditions, affect the application of these generalisations to concrete situations. It is an ideal, however, which anthropologists have either categorically rejected as a pseudo-scientific fiction or reluctantly eschewed as being far beyond their present knowledge and capabilities. Certainly no universally valid 'laws' have been formulated so far: that is, statements of the kind that if a certain factor exists or operates in a certain way, then certain other factors must occur in other ways. On the other hand, anthropologists have made some universalistic state-ments of a descriptive kind which, although perhaps not major achievements, are contrary to, or modifications of, former ideas about human behaviour. For example, earlier beliefs that some peoples do or did practise group marriage or that others recognise no regular form of marriage have been shown to be empirically false. Similarly, the notion that some simpler societies had no form of social control, but that their members instinctively followed custom, has also been refuted. These kinds of conclusions are not in themselves far-reaching, but they have been essential to the clearing away of old prejudices preparatory to more genuine advances in the understanding of mankind.

Although not concerned with the search for laws in the tradition of the physical sciences, anthropologists have attempted more modest comparative tasks. These have taken a number of forms.

Much of the apparently comparative work published in the Africanist field has consisted in effect of collections of rather loosely connected essays by a number of authors on a given topic. The best-known examples are those published by the International African Institute: *African Political Systems* (Evans-Pritchard and Fortes 1940), *African Systems of Kinship and Marriage* (Radcliffe-Brown and Forde 1950) and *African Worlds* (Forde 1954). In like manner are those by Anglo-American groups of anthropologists: *Tribes Without Rulers* (Middleton and Tait 1958) and *Markets in Africa* (Bohannan and Dalton 1963). Excellent as most of the individual contributions are, such books are not true comparative studies nor do the editorial introductions do much to make them so. There is virtually no attempt to provide a sample of the kinds of data under review which is either typical of the variety or representative of the actual distribution in Africa. The contributors submit to minimal editorial control, and each endeavours to give an account — in terms of his own particular interests — of the field data he obtained before the idea of a symposium was suggested. There is little direct effort to draw conclusions from the various contributions considered together. These works are therefore *ad hoc* compilations which indicate the variety in Africa without giving an idea of its extent. They do, however, provide invaluable, organised material for comparative work in the future.

A more truly comparative study is *African Homicide and Suicide*, edited by Paul Bohannan (1959). The editor asked his contributors to collect and present certain kinds of data relevant to the subject. He himself contributed an introductory chapter setting out the state of knowledge and theory in the matter, and explaining the purpose and limits of the new studies. He added a concluding chapter in which he assessed the results and the extent of the contributions in the particular field of social pathology. Clearly the value of the work lies in the close control of the editor and the willing co-operation of his fellow-contributors. The sample of societies was no more than opportunist: those few anthropologists who, at a certain time, happened to be doing research in one part of East Africa were asked to participate. Necessarily limited as the results are, nevertheless here is a clear pointer to the kind of co-operative study that is possible and to the persisting problems that are involved.

Even less common is the case where a single anthropologist performs the comparative analysis. The gains of uniform treatment and singleness of purpose are obvious and extend even beyond those obtained by the close editorial control in Bohannan's study. The best recent example is Schapera's *Government and Politics in Tribal Societies* (1956) in which the author brings together all the available information on indigenous political systems in a single region of Africa. He chose southern Africa (South Africa, South West Africa, High Commission territories) because of his decades of continuous research, reading, teaching and experience there: perhaps an unrivalled regional competence in Africa. Because relatively few new hypotheses and conclusions emerged from the study, some anthropologists characteristically found their suspicions of comparative study merely reinforced. But many anthropologists welcomed the work, both for its own results and for the suggestiveness with respect to methodology. Anthropologists who are not especially conversant with that one region or with that particular topic find that a reliable analytical survey such as this is invaluable and many find it a genuine stimulus to their own work. Non-anthropologists should welcome it and the few similar works (e.g., Mair 1962), for there has been little of comparable value and reliability. Certainly both Schapera and Mair have produced remarkably useful surveys, making it unnecessary for all but the particular specialist to go to the many and varied scattered original sources.

A field of comparative study which has been of much importance is the establishment of typologies, which serve to order particular classes of data and to identify the major factors of differentiation on which, hopefully, more intensive studies can focus. The fact that suggested typologies have not yet achieved widespread acceptance — a preliminary to comparative analysis — indicates the early stages such work has so far reached. Various attempts to set up a typology of political systems illustrate this: the 'Introduction' to Fortes and Evans-Pritchard (1940), Schapera (1956), Eisenstadt (1958), and Middleton and Tait (1958). In order to accomplish this aim, it is necessary to have some agreement about the major features of variation on which a typology can be constructed. Anthropologists have allowed themselves to be overwhelmed by the complexity of the multifold factors involved. When one writer attempts to cut the Gordian knot by asserting the primacy or at least indicator-quality of certain features, his colleagues find ample cause to demur. Kinship systems — relational phenomena of great complexity — have been classified according to residence after marriage, mode of reckoning descent, terminology applied to cousins, etc. None of these criteria has proved pre-eminently superior; none is in itself self-sufficient. Nevertheless, even the attempt to produce typologies has been profitably productive of stimulus to thought, when it has not deteriorated into an intellectual game or into sterile disputation of a semantic kind.

In order to reduce the number and range of variables to be handled comparatively, some anthropologists have suggested concentration on a few historically related peoples whose recent history, current environment and internal development have diverged: for example, studies of the interlacustrine Bantu of western Uganda or of the Akan peoples of the Guinea Coast. The first problem here is to isolate valid clusters of related peoples: a typology problem in different form. Such commonly accepted classifications as the Nilotes or the matrilineal Bantu of Central Africa may not necessarily be suitable for this kind of approach. The range of variables may still be too great or, more practically and likely, information on some members of the group may be wholly inadequate for the purpose. In any case, the number of separate societies concerned is often too large to be handled easily. An alternative is to narrow the choice still further so that the number of societies and the range of variables are both reduced. It has been suggested, for example, that the large grouping of East African peoples conventionally known as the 'Nilo-Hamites' can be divided into a number of 'clusters', each containing some half-dozen tribes which are historically and culturally closely connected and are also territorially adjacent; thus: the Bari, Teso, Nandi, and Masai clusters (Gulliver 1951). This idea has also been applied to the Congo tribes by Merriam (1959). The comparative work following up this establishment of sufficiently small clusters has not yet been properly attempted.

The detailed treatment of a few selected societies can be performed in another way when the nature of the similarity between them is to be found in some common set of factors rather than in historico-cultural affinities. For example, it is profitable to study a group of adjacent peoples all of whom inhabit a region of fairly uniform physical environment, such as the study of shifting cultivation and subsistence economy in the semi-arid bushlands of south-central Africa. It could be useful to examine comparatively the nature of authority and its institutional limitations, or the operation of bureaucracy, in several highly autocratic political systems. Unfortunately it is not possible to refer to definitive studies of this kind: the idea has been raised but remains unfulfilled in anthropological discussions.

It is obvious that, in making comparisons in order to develop generalisations and to test hypotheses, it is of first importance to be sure that the things compared are of the same order. To take a single example: comparison of the conditions and frequency of divorce in relation to kinship and family systems requires at least two kinds of enquiry. It is necessary to know precisely what constitutes divorce rather than separation (which itself may be of various types), and to know precisely what constitutes marriage (which also may be of various types). A couple, for instance, may legitimately be living together and rearing their children, but the marriage wealth transfers may be incomplete. Is this to be regarded as full marriage? If the couple separate permanently, can it be called divorce? Or a Moslem may repudiate his wife: is that divorce when it is accepted that he may take her back without going through a new marriage ceremony? Or is it divorce only when, having repudiated her three times, he cannot regain her until she has been married by another man, has left him, and then undergone a new ceremony with the first husband? Such problems are by no means mere quibbles over details, for they may well involve the essential characteristics of the institutions under examination. Whenever a large number and variety of different socio-cultural systems are involved, it becomes especially necessary to reduce the range of variety by attempting to define factors, institutions, and so forth, fairly rigidly. Too often, however, the rich variety of social phenomena is in some degree unavoidably distorted in this attempt to maintain simplified definitions, and when two sets of data are involved in the comparative study — as divorce and kinship in the hypothetical illustration — the effect of the distortion in both may be such as to give the final result a dubious utility.

If it is possible to avoid that kind of major error, there commonly remains the problem of extracting the kind of data required from the various kinds of ethnographic literature and thereafter of assessing their reliability and significance. How can one compare divorce in one community, where it is reported by an ethnographer to be 'fairly frequent', with that in another community, where it is said to be 'widespread·and common'? Even if more precise data are available, it is necessary to have some appreciation of the biases of the ethnographers, the thoroughness of their field research, the sizes of their samples (if any), the care taken in selecting them, and the time and area in which they were obtained. It cannot be taken for granted that an ethnographic report is a statement of scientific facts; and it must be admitted that too few anthropologists in the past have provided an adequate quantity of data in a reliable form. Many anthropologists deliberately have been more concerned with detecting and describing generalised patterns of social behaviour and have not been concerned, therefore, to provide the detailed empirical evidence which certain types of comparative study require.

When the comparative work attempts to relate the kinship system with divorce (or any other connected factors in a social system), the problem arises as to the range of significant variables which impinges on the relationship. Some of the potential variables may not have received proper attention from the authors who originally wrote about the societies undergoing comparison; among these might be the nature of the economic system, the nature and degree of modern change, the imposition of new legal rules by a colonial or national government, the effect of novel religious ideas and attitudes, and so on. Ideally, in the study of the connection between two sets of social phenomena (such as kinship and divorce), other variables should be kept constant, but this is impossible in the real world investigated by anthropologists. Thus the *prima facie* conclusions of a comparative study might be that with a certain type of kinship system divorce is rare, with another type it is frequent, and so on; and these summary descriptions could perhaps be given statistical values and correlates.   The theoretical suggestiveness of such a study would be valuable, yet the effects of other factors would remain unknown, and the results can be no more than tentative hypotheses, which cannot easily be used in later studies.   Because of considerations such as these, anthropologists have tended to be cautious and have in general preferred the less complicated study of the single society.   On the other hand, the lengthy discussions evoked by Gluckman's comparative study of kinship structure and marriage is good evidence of anthropologists' interests, and a number of theoretical hypotheses have emerged as a result (Gluckman in Radcliffe-Brown and Forde 1950).

Thus far I have been speaking of comparative study in cases for which there is the possibility of some statistical treatment and the phenomena are fairly discreet and explicit.   When the subject of study is less precise than, say, divorce, the problems are likely to be intensified.   For example, a study of the nature of authority and the institutional limitations on it in different kinds of societies allows of no quantitative treatment.   Here comparison must be largely in terms of general patterns and kinds of inter-relationships.   Comparison, in fact, tends to become little more than the establishment of typology and the indication of broad generalisations.

In this brief survey of comparative studies in Africanist anthropology, it has been necessary to give as much space to the description of potential methodologies and tentative explanations as to examples of successful attempts to break out of the concentration on studies of single society.   The situation is still one of possibilities, of hopes and needs, rather than of actual achievement, although there have been a few notable exceptions.   In one way, of course, all anthropologists are constantly and keenly engaged in comparative study, in so far as they seek to gain new insight, stimulus and suggestion from the careful scrutiny of their colleagues' results. Although it may appear to the outsider that anthropologists are working perversely, each in semi-isolation from the others, this is demonstrably incorrect.   Anthropologists most certainly wish to learn from each other, and they give much attention to the possible application of methods, hypotheses and ideas put forward by others.

Viewed from within the discipline and with a historical perspective, it is self-evident that there is a more or less gradual progression in anthropological study.   It is sometimes difficult to perceive the debts which scholars owe to their predecessors but they are generally implicit in their publications.   There is, on the whole, little desire to develop an explicit and coherent corpus of anthropological thought: at least not in print.   This doubtless presents a most difficult problem for the non-anthropologist, because it is not always easy to discover the general principles with which anthropologists are working.   The political scientist wishing to acquaint himself with, and make use of, results reached by anthropologists in the field of indigenous political institutions, for example, must be prepared to read a large number of monographs by separate authors on individual political systems.   If the political scientist has a wider interest — to attempt to learn what he may from anthropologists about social and cultural systems — his task is correspondingly greater.   He will find relatively few general discussions, and even fewer authoritative over-views of the discipline, and these will be widely scattered in the literature.   Nevertheless, it must be insisted that a new analysis of, say, an indigenous African political system by a professional anthropologist will in an important way be a comparative study.

Finally, mention must be made of the pan-African approach in anthropology. Here I refer to the attempt to stand back and review the state of anthropological knowledge and understanding throughout the continent. In effect, there have been only a handful of serious attempts in this field, and of these perhaps three are worth mention. The oldest of the three, *Races of Africa* (Seligman 1957), has appeared in a third edition which had been revised by a panel of social anthropologists; they endeavoured, however, to keep to Seligman's original work as closely as possible. It is a small book which uses a broad classification of African peoples into seven major categories. These are based on historical (sometimes rather conjectural), physical, linguistic and cultural factors, and some (such as 'the Bantu', principally a linguistic category), are scarcely acceptable today except as terms of convenience. Each of these categories is briefly described, with the main attention being given to cultural matters. As an elementary introduction to Africanist anthropology the book has a certain value, but non-anthropologists should not expect it to meet their scholarly demands. There is rather little acknowledgment of modern anthropological theory and recent research.

A similar, but more thorough-going work is *Völkerkunde von Afrika* (Baumann 1940) in which the Germans, Baumann and Westerman, attempt to establish culture areas for the continent. Though now somewhat dated, both in content and methodology, it is superior to Seligman. Unfortunately it contains little recognition of the significant results of social anthropology in Africa.

Murdock's pioneering effort, *Africa: its peoples and their culture history* (1959), attempted to combine two somewhat different interests: the history of African peoples over the last six milennia, and the classification and partial description of the contemporary peoples. Both involved gigantic tasks of scholarship, and both in their scope and detail far surpass anything accomplished before in their fields. In the second and more truly anthropological task, most anthropologists at least reserve judgment or are frankly critical. The vastness of the undertaking was such that attention to detail in each of the forty-five categories of peoples was inadequate, whilst many of the categories themselves are not generally acceptable. Descriptions of the hundreds of different peoples within those categories are by necessity very brief, and they are no substitute for the lengthier ethnographic accounts in the *Ethnographic Survey of Africa* (see below page 92). The work itself has been welcomed (particularly perhaps by those on the periphery of the anthropological discipline) because of the need for an encyclopedic treatment of the whole body of accumulated information on African peoples. Anthropologists themselves on the whole feel much less need for such treatment, but in any case they are much less prepared to accept the avoidable defects when it is attempted. In practice, anthropologists are much more concerned to develop analysis, theoretical understanding and hypothesis-building than to establish encyclopedic surveys. The scope of this sort of enterprise is so great that, in any case, it is probably preferable to restrict it to particular regions of the continent and even to limit the number of topics within such a region. The work of Schapera (1956) is probably more representative of anthropological interest in the whole continent.

VI SYNCHRONIC AND DIACHRONIC STUDIES AND SOCIAL CHANGE

The socio-cultural system operating among a group of people may be more or less unchanging over a period of time, but over a long enough period the system — i.e., its parts and their inter-relations — inevitably undergoes change as the result of internal and external pressures. Anthropologists can choose to concentrate on either synchronic or diachronic accounts of any system they are studying. A synchronic study describes the system as it exists at a particular time and ignores the fact, as far as is possible, that change may be going on at that time; it largely deals with the question of 'how does it work?' at the given time of observation; and it tends to explain particular elements of the system in terms of the system itself. A diachronic account describes a system as it changes over a period of time. By investigating the pattern of development in a system over time and relating the state of affairs to preceding states, it largely deals with the question: 'why is it like it is?' The 'why' usually refers to an explanation of the present in terms of the past, but of course a past state can similarly be investigated (if evidence is available) in terms of its own antecedents.

There has been a dichotomy of interest and endeavour in anthropology based on preferences for either synchronic or diachronic study. Radcliffe-Brown (1952), until recently perhaps the major social anthropological theorist, distinguished specifically between the 'theoretical understanding' and the 'historical explanation' of an institution or a whole society. He and many of his European colleagues and pupils rejected the historical approach partly in reaction against gross abuse of 'pseudo-history': speculative reconstructions of the past and selective interpretations of anthropological data used to demonstrate preconceived hypotheses or grandiose theoretical schema (e.g., those by protagonists of evolutionary or diffusionist theories earlier in this century). Historical explanation was rejected in part because it was believed that information on the past of African (and other pre-literate) peoples was so scanty and inherently unreliable as to be insufficient for scholarly purposes. Indeed, Radcliffe-Brown himself stated categorically that 'in primitive societies that are studied by social anthropologists there are no historical records'.

These anthropologists were deeply impressed by the quantity and the verifiable reliability of the data about the socio-cultural systems which could be obtained on the spot in person, using the modern field techniques developed by Malinowski and others some decades ago. It seemed quite impossible to obtain anything of comparable quality and quantity about the past, and many anthropologists, therefore, were persuaded to concentrate on synchronic analyses. This concentration fitted well with the sociological bias of the large majority of anthropologists working in Africa and with African data, for they (much influenced by the French sociologist, Durkheim) were seeking to gain understanding of institutions and patterns of human relationships in terms of the social systems in which they existed and operated. They assumed, virtually as an axiom, that any feature or element in a social system could be comprehended solely in terms of the functioning of that system and without reference to its origins, real or supposed. The relationship between a man and his mother's brothers, for example, causally may or may not be the result of an earlier matrilineal organisation of that society; but to understand the significance of the relationship at the present time, it is necessary to examine it in its contemporary context of the network of economic, political, religious, kinship and other relationships which a man has in that society. It may be discovered that a man exercises his links with his mother's close kinsmen as a counterweight to heavy demands or tension-loaded relations with his own patrilineal kinsmen. It can be suggested, perhaps, that when patrilineal relationships are easier and more co-operative (for whatever reason), links with maternal kin are much less emphasised; and when they are more difficult, then maternal links become more important. Other hypotheses of a complementary or alternative kind, of course, may also be raised, and none of them need have any reference to past conditions. This is the kind of analysis and understanding attempted by 'social anthropologists'. Beyond this they believed that, in the words of Radcliffe-Brown, 'comparative sociology, of which social anthropology is a branch', could 'provide acceptable generalisations. The theoretical understanding of a particular institution is its interpretation in the light of such generalisations.' That complementary attempts to understand an institution or the working of a social system, and to formulate generalisations, could be made in historical or developmental terms seems to have been overlooked, even when they utilised valid procedures based on adequate information.

The great majority of anthropological accounts of the social life of African peoples consequently are synchronic and often include a specific denial of interest in diachronic possibilities. These synchronic studies are of two principal kinds. There are large numbers of studies of 'traditional' socio-cultural systems, as they are believed to have existed before the advent of colonial conquest and administration and of the new forces from the non-African world. Virtually no anthropologist has in fact been able himself to make an intensive field study of such a pre-colonial system. For several decades no part of Africa has been accessible to anthropologists to which the effects of the Western world have not penetrated. Indeed the anthropologist could scarcely be there were it not for the organisation of communications and facilities and the establishment of supra-tribal government which ensure his reasonable safety. It has frequently seemed possible, nevertheless, to ignore the earliest changes consequent upon colonial intervention and to record what is essentially the pre-colonial essence of a people's life. Even in the second half of the twentieth century, the effects of external forces have been rather slight in the lives of some more remotely placed peoples.

Anthropologists have generally accepted it as an obligation of their discipline to investigate and describe the unique indigenous societies and cultures before they change as a result of contact with the outside world under modern conditions. Whatever they become in the future, the small-scale communities which abound in Africa will at least be different from what they were, and it has been and still is worth while to make a careful record of these indigenous cultures as a contribution to the history and understanding of African peoples. In the introduction to his famous monograph on the Thonga people, Henri Junod tells how he was persuaded of the usefulness of such work by Lord Bryce's encouragement and his remark: 'How thankful we should be, we men of the nineteenth century, if a Roman had taken the trouble fully to investigate the habits of our Celtic forefathers! This work has not been done, and we shall always remain ignorant of things which would have interested us so much' (Junod 1913).

For the benefit of anthropological studies and of the understanding of mankind, the creation of the fullest possible record of the variety of socio-cultural forms is essential. There is no need to assume any facile hypothesis of an Africa untouched prior to modern European colonial intervention. Anthropologists merely see locally evolved patterns of social life gradually disappearing, and they wish to have knowledge of them before they change — that is, vanish — altogether. It had been thought that indigenous cultures would disappear under westernisation far more rapidly than in fact they have, and there was a good deal of concern to record them before it was too late. It is now realised that, even in the areas where the greatest changes have occurred, much of the older culture still persists, often actively, sometimes latently. The first fears, nonetheless, do have some justification; in many cases the indigenous forms have been so radically modified by the 1960s that the precise earlier patterns are difficult, if not impossible, to discern with any degree of certainty.

The second type of synchronic study takes the form of 'snapshot' description of a contemporary socio-cultural system at the particular time of its investigation by the anthropologist. A society is studied purely as a working system; an attempt is made to show how it operates, the inter-relations of its parts, and the forces which sustain it. The presence or absence of change during the colonial era or even at the time of research becomes irrelevant. This approach may involve ignoring a vital factor in the system, namely that it is a system in process of undergoing non-recurrent change. Synchronic analysis, therefore, requires some degree of abstraction. With that limitation, however, and in the awareness that not all African systems are in fact undergoing rapid and radical change, a great deal of intensive work, marked by a notable depth of understanding and empathy, has been accomplished. However the limitations may seem to distort the results, the synchronic method does permit the anthropologist to concentrate on particular aspects of human behaviour in society. It fits well with the practical limitations and requirements of anthropological research: the paucity of records and reliable data prior to the period of research; the relatively brief period of field research (usually one to two years) without much possibility of any follow-up thereafter; and an intensity of research during that short period which can yield a wealth of detailed information without a past or a future, as it were. Many anthropologists, consequently, have frankly admitted their ignorance and, therefore, their lack of concern for conditions much outside that particular period during which their research has been conducted.

It should be emphasised that probably nine out of ten anthropological monographs are synchronic studies of one kind or the other. Whatever the theoretical defects of this general approach, it has allowed intensive concentration on a particular kind of analysis associated with a particular kind of research. It remains a matter of opinion whether the success in depth of penetration has outweighed the concomitant restrictions of perspective and range of problems. At the very least, however, there is no doubt that synchronic studies have provided a much more sophisticated and empirically based understanding of the nature of ongoing societies.

The more culturally inclined anthropologists, and particularly those trained in the American tradition stemming from Amerindian studies, have always been sceptical of the insistence of social anthropologists on synchronic analysis. But they too have been ready to attempt descriptions of the indigenous, pre-colonial systems in an assumed static mode; Herskovits' study of the Dahomey kingdom (Herskovits 1938) is an example of this. Nor have diachronic studies been entirely neglected or derided by social anthropologists at work in Africa, as witnessed, for example, by the study of the South African Mpondo people in *Reaction to Conquest* (Hunter 1936), the study of political development among the Rhodesian Ngoni (Barnes 1954a), and the account of the increasing involvement of nomadic Nigerian Fulani in a Moslem and sedentary political system (Stenning 1959). Indeed, where good historical records have been available, anthropologists have been prepared to investigate the nature of societies through time; among such studies are some of Schapera's on the Bechuana peoples and various works on such well-documented peoples as Zulu, Ganda, Ashanti, Benin, etc.

Until recently, however, social anthropologists in general have persistently maintained the distinction between theoretical (i.e., sociological) understanding and interpretation of an institution or a whole social system on the one hand, and historical explanation on the other. And they have asserted the superiority of the former. Increasingly in the last decade or so there has been a renewed interest in the investigation of change and in the attempt to pose and answer questions of the 'why' kind in theoretical terms. There are a number of reasons for this major development. Many of the present generation of anthropologists have been trained and have gained their experience in an age when the abuses of speculative pseudo-history are no longer emotionally or intellectually important; these anthropologists are able to come back to investigations of history's potential with much less prejudice than their immediate seniors. Some anthropologists have been impressed by the perceived similarity between the nature of their own discipline and that of history, and this too appears to have aroused a certain amount of historical enquiry on their part. The mounting participation of American cultural anthropologists in the African field has been favourable to historical, diachronic investigation. And this general trend is further supported by the beginnings of assistance to be derived from the new incursion of professional historians into Africa, and by the demands of Africans themselves for knowledge of their past.

However, there are two major causes of the growing interest in change and historical process. One is the practical one that, in the second half of the twentieth century, pre-colonial social and cultural systems are remote in time, whilst the dominant fact in the contemporary scene available for research is the rapidity and radical nature of change occurring in them. The other major cause of reorientation is theoretical: anthropologists are less and less content with the limited horizons of synchronic studies, and they see no genuine reason why, with due caution, there should not be a development of the scientific study of change and of processes of change comparable to the study of assumed static systems.

In those areas remote from modern communications, and in the severe physical environments which have not yielded to modern technologies and economies, there still remain African societies in which change has been relatively slight. Even so, it should be mentioned in passing that many anthropologists have probably erred in assuming that change has been slight and theoretically negligible, merely because it was convenient to make that assumption. A nomadic people, which is effectively prevented from intertribal warfare and is restricted within fixed territorial boundaries, must necessarily have had to adapt to a most radical change of circumstances, even though it remains otherwise largely unadministered and economically undeveloped. But in any case, after more than half a century of colonial experience, the large majority of African peoples have undergone changes in their social lives. As the length of time since colonial conquest increases, so does it become less easy and less justifiable per se to attempt to ignore change and to describe 'untouched' indigenous systems. The synchronically orientated anthropologist has already shifted his focus from a construct of indigenous society to the investigation and description of a society as it exists at the time of research. But where change is so rapid and so dominant in the operation of institutions, in the nature of social relationships, and in the minds and attitudes of the people themselves, a simple synchronic conceptualisation becomes more and more abstract, more and more remote from reality. For the field anthropologist, so closely in touch and empathy with the people he studies, it begins to be exceedingly difficult to pretend further that change is not in the essence of the subject-matter he is examining.

An enquiry into the family in a contemporary African community quickly shows that relations between, say, father and son were rather different when the older man himself was in the subordinate position. Every indication points to the fact that when the present sons are fathers, their relationship with their own sons again will be different. And, speculation apart, it is highly significant that the people themselves are aware of the recent and continuing changes, and that they expect further change. To ignore all this is to make an understanding of the family, at least, much less valuable and revealing than it might be.

Because of the degree of change in African societies, the contrast between what was and what is becomes more clearly marked; it demands explanation. This is precisely what Hunter, Barnes and Stenning have attempted to do in the works cited above, and there are increasing numbers of this type of work by Africanist anthropologists: e.g., Fallers (1956), Smith (1960), Southall (1961) and Edwards (1962). The stimulus is particularly strong in those cases where a full anthropological investigation was made earlier and reference can be made to a well documented previous state (Gulliver 1958). It is likely that the number of such analyses will increase in the future.

The theoretical considerations which have stimulated new or renewed interest in the study of social processes through time are founded in growing dissatisfaction with some previously held conceptions. It has been virtually axiomatic among those anthropologists primarily concerned with structural-functional analysis of social systems that every part of a system is interdependent upon all the other parts; the function of each is to be found in its contribution to the maintenance of the whole. Because of this functional unity and the integral necessity of each and every part, furthermore, a system tends to be self-perpetuating, possesses built-in mechanisms to maintain equilibrium or to restore equilibrium when disruptive forces operate. This kind of assumption has underlain a great deal of the synchronic analysis by social anthropologists in Africa. Associated with it has been the idea (not always consciously acknowledged) that before the modern European incursion into Africa most indigenous societies were stable systems in equilibrium, undergoing little or no change. The phrase 'traditional society' (or culture) has commonly been used. It should be added that cultural anthropologists have also tended to assume this same kind of pre-colonial condition, although usually they have been less explicit in their theoretical discussions.

These were convenient assumptions to make, for they simplified the attempt to describe pre-colonial conditions. They may even have been necessary assumptions for the time being, because they allowed anthropologists a period for useful research and for the consolidation of facts and ideas before moving on to a more sophisticated level. The assumptions were also rooted in the rationalisation that African societies were primitive, simple, and geared to a particular environment, and that they had been cut off from external stimulus until rudely invaded from beyond the continent in the nineteenth and early twentieth centuries.

The increase in knowledge of the nature of African societies and of their pre-colonial histories has produced the recognition that, with perhaps just a few exceptions, they were by no means changeless systems.   Even if it is impossible clearly to chart the course of change, it is indisputable that change had been occurring as a result of changing environment, internal evolution and contact with neighbouring groups of peoples.   In some well-known cases (e.g., Zulu, Ngoni, Ganda) innovation and modification were quite radical in the decades immediately preceding the coming of the European.   No longer could it be easily assumed that there had been a 'traditional' or fixed and stable society and culture which began to change only recently.   The attempt to reconstruct and describe such a traditional society was bound to be artificial, and often resulted in a heterogeneous, largely invalid compound of elements collected from periods covering two or three generations.

It may also be a fallacy to assume that all socio-cultural systems are more or less continuously undergoing change, now slowly, now rapidly, but it seems to be less subject to gross error.   In any event anthropologists have become more aware of the probability of divergence from the expected norm, and they now increasingly assume that social systems are changing systems and that neglect of this fact must distort any attempt to understand and describe them.   It has also been perceived empirically that not all parts of a social system are equally and intimately inter-related and that not all parts are equally significant in the whole.   Different institutions and values may even be in conflict, although the conflict can be con-tained and the system enabled to continue to operate.   This sort of conflict in fact serves as a kind of tension-spring in the system, as a vital social force, and as a source of internally stimulated change.

Because of this realisation that change is integral to most social systems, the notion that, even by abstraction, a working system can be isolated at a moment in time (the arbitrary period when field research occurs), is felt to be less satisfactory. So long as the fact of abstraction, of model-building and pattern-making, is quite consciously understood, it may still serve a valuable theoretical purpose.   But it inevitably produces distortion, and the time seems to have come when so high a degree of distortion has been judged to be intolerable.   One line of thought holds that anthropology has gone as far as it can with this kind of synchronic abstraction, and that a return to concrete reality is badly needed.   Another line is that it was an error ever to have departed so far from reality.   The latter criticism seems to be less justifiable, because, just as in economics or psychology, abstract model-building is an essential part of intellectual development in a scientific discipline.   It is the opinion of this writer that synchronic studies will always be important, but that diachronic studies will take first place in the development of the understanding of human behaviour in society.

A further notion now under fire is that which assumes that only synchronic analysis can be scientific, theoretical and sociological, whilst historical perspective can result merely in descriptive explanation of a series of events and conditions. This assumption seems to be based on a misunderstanding of the potentialities of history and perhaps also on an inadequate appreciation of the quantity and quality of historical data which could be made available.   So long as history is conceived of as merely serial description — and some historians have so conceived it — then rightly it will not yield to theoretical analysis.   However, just as one may under-stand and interpret a given institution in terms of its function in the system, one may also understand and interpret the institution in terms of the chronologically preceding conditions under which it developed and operated.   These two are

rather different kinds of interpretation, but they are complementary.   Just as the
advantages of both the sociological and cultural approaches need to be combined,
for the common benefit of the discipline, so 'it will be only in an integrated and
organised study in which historical studies and sociological studies are combined
that we shall be able to reach a real understanding of the development of human
society; and this we have yet to do' (Radcliffe-Brown 1951: 22).   It is ironic that
the very teaching which so greatly inspired the perceptive and intensive synchronic
work in social anthropology should have militated against that integration which
Radcliffe-Brown desired.

In Africanist anthropology — as in the discipline as a whole — the necessity
and the desire to study processes through time and to take into account the vital
quality of change have been fairly well established, but the problems involved have
not yet been overcome or accommodated.   Social anthropologists in particular
regard the difficulties of obtaining and assessing data on the past as a serious obstacle,
for they have long been accustomed to richness and depth of information, combined
with a rigorous observational methodology, in their synchronic studies.   It may
prove necessary to modify the standards of judging evidence in order to develop
diachronic investigation and anthropological studies in general.   On the other
hand, it is at least possible that anthropologists have been hypercritical of data
which they or their colleagues have not themselves collected in the field.   That
they have both a right and obligation to be critical of sources is undisputed, but it is
likely that too little use has been made of some kinds of information.   In saying
this, it must be kept well in mind that neither oral sources of information about
the past — even the not-so-distant past — nor written records can be accepted at
their face value.   The written report of an administrator, missionary or school-
teacher may be as misleading, though in different ways, as the institutionalised
tradition or as the older person's memory of what happened when he was a young
man.   Anthropologists are well aware of the ways in which cultural and personal
assumptions — often not consciously realised — and limitations can colour and
distort accounts of both past and present; they have often shown, too, how history
is manipulated and used to rationalise the present, or to support claims to status
or rights.   It is felt by many anthropologists that historians and other Africanists
still tend to be insufficiently critical of tribal histories and traditions, and that some
of their own colleagues have been no less naïve.   On the other hand, and especially
for some parts of the continent, records are available for periods long enough to
permit adequately documented diachronic studies without involvement on the
thorny ground of pre-literate and pre-colonial conditions.   In some favoured areas
anthropological research was undertaken at an early date, and the results of it can
now be used as a definitive base-line for the study of processes of social change.

There exists, too, the formidable problem of developing a body of theory and
an adequate research methodology to deal with the study of change.   In part,
Africanist anthropologists can draw on the accumulated experience of their colleagues in other continents where historical study has been conducted, and they
are already able to benefit from pioneering works (Redfield 1953; Leach 1954,
1961; Firth 1959).   To date, however, the bulk of the writing on social change in
Africa has been only descriptive, tentative in its methods, and uninformed by a
firm theoretical background.   Much of it, indeed, has come down to the piling
of detail upon detail, with little perspective or perception of the relative significance
of different kinds of evidence and different kinds of inferences made from them.

The raw material is being erratically assembled: it greatly needs to be ordered systematically.

At present there seem to be two main lines of approach, the choice between which is dictated by practical limitations rather than by theoretical inclinations. One is the 'dual synchronic' in which two (or more) synchronic studies of the same society at different times are compared with the intention, first, of describing the changes which have occurred, and second, of discovering the nature and causes of the changes. The other approach is used when it appears to be impossible to reconstruct the earlier stage of the society for comparison with the contemporary, observed condition. The attempt is made to analyse the various forces and processes conducive to change in recent times which bear on the contemporary end product. Factors which seem most likely to produce further change and new directions of change are also considered, not in order to prophesy future conditions, but to increase understanding of the kinds of tensions and tendencies at work in the current circumstances.

A good example of the dual synchronic method is Barnes' study of political change among the Rhodesian Ngoni (Barnes 1954a). His two synchronic times were those of the pre-colonial Ngoni state, prior to its conquest by the British in 1898, and the colonial-dominated Ngoni chiefdom of the late 1940s. Although most illuminating in many ways, this study seems to suffer from two defects almost inherent in this type of treatment. There are inevitable doubts in the reader's mind as to the validity of the account of the earlier period. Is it, in fact, a true synchronic study, or is it at least partly an amalgam of the earlier socio-cultural system as it was emerging over a period of several decades of rapid modification and adaptation? The Mpezeni Ngoni chiefdom was established about 1845 as a mobile conquest state; it migrated over a long distance, eventually settled in one area about 1870, and began rapidly to expand in both territory and population. Its political system had to adapt to these conditions and apparently had insufficient time to reach a stage of consolidation before the British threat and eventual conquest occurred. Before 1898, then, there was no single, established Ngoni political system with which to compare the system in the mid-twentieth century. The attempt at comparison can still be fruitful, but it is necessary to be aware of the possible distortions. This is a problem besetting any such dual study: in the absence of positive evidence, one cannot assume that the pre-colonial system was one of effective stability.

The second defect of the dual synchronic method in the study of socio-cultural change is that too little account is taken of the intervening period. That period cannot *ipso facto* be viewed merely as one of transition between the two selected times. The interim may have a period of continuing change, but there may have been some well-marked and significant stages of relative stability. Change may have been engendered by the operation of forces which, by the time of the second synchronic study, are no longer directly important or even discernible, but which were of crucial significance in the total historical process. The choice of two time periods, after all, may be quite arbitrary.

M. G. Smith's study of political development in one of the Hausa states of northern Nigeria (Smith 1960) attempts to deal with these problems and especially with that of the intervening period. This study contains three successive synchronic analyses: (i) government in the nineteenth-century Hausa state of Abuja, which Smith assumes (rather uncritically) to be the equivalent of Zazzau to the north, whence the Abuja state originated before the Moslem Holy War and the Fulani conquest at the beginning of the century; (ii) government in the Fulani-Hausa state of Zazzau in 1865; and (iii) government in the Emirate of Zaria (chronological successor to Zazzau) in 1950 (the analyses of Abuja and Zazzau depend upon reconstructions by present-day members of the ruling groups). Of his methodology Smith wrote:

> One feature of our analytical method is . . . its inherently comparative character. Our study is really an exercise in the application of the comparative method to the problems of diachronic analysis, despite the fact that the units compared are stages of a single developmental continuum. The application of the comparative method to diachronic analysis presupposes initial study of the units concerned as isolated synchronic systems. The next stage is to make a detailed historical study of the processes of change, and then to develop a single set of categories which will define each of these systems. These categories will then provide the following analyses with a common logic and frame of reference (Smith 1960: 330–1).

Smith thus attempts by 'detailed historical study' to bridge the gap between his selected periods. In this particular case, the available data on the Hausa state permitted the attempt. But data on the Ngoni of Rhodesia were much less adequate, because neither official records nor local memories gave much attention to the earlier part of the interim period.

The length of the transitional period is reduced, of course, when the two times of synchronic study are fairly close together. In my own study of the Nyakyusa of south-western Tanganyika made in 1955 (Gulliver 1958), the research was conducted a little less than twenty years from the time when the anthropologists, Godfrey and Monica Wilson, had made their field investigations. Even so, in the particular topics of interest (land tenure, economics and village life) radical changes had occurred during those two decades, and I did not feel that I had been able to chart the course of events as fully as desirable. Already local memory of events and attitudes was beginning to build up a stereotype in the light of retrospective evaluation.

Although there are weaknesses in the comparative, dual synchronic technique, it is clear, nevertheless, that here is a serious attempt to solve the difficult problems. It seems fair to say that studies of this kind have already begun to demonstrate that sociological and theoretical interpretation is possible in a historical context. They have shown that appreciation of contemporary conditions can be enhanced by taking into account preceding conditions and forces and by accepting change as inherent in the contemporary conditions themselves. They have revealed the weaknesses in the assumptions about natural tendencies to maintain equilibrium. Theoretically it may prove essential to select two or three particular points in time for detailed analysis — thus taking advantage of the highly developed methodology of synchronic treatment — even when fairly full and reliable historical evidence is available. It may also prove possible to develop synchronic analyses so that they deal with whole periods (conveniently relevant to the topic of interest) and enable effective comparison and relating of successive periods without interim passages.

The historical data useful for comparative, dual synchronic work are of various kinds: previous anthropological study, official enquiries and surveys, general administrative reports and records, histories compiled by members of the society itself, and reconstruction on the basis of anthropological research. It is rather unusual for all of these sources to be available for a single society and a single study. Often very little from any source is available, and certainly not enough to allow reliable reconstruction of any earlier period. Yet the recognition of a condition of change remains unavoidable. The anthropologist can then only attempt an assessment of the kinds of factors which have helped to create the present state of affairs and to detect where in the system change is most apparent and functionally most significant.

In such cases many anthropologists have preferred to ignore the whole problem. There is increasing discomfort with such an attitude, however, and many believe it is necessary to make some attempt to grapple with the obviously important problems of change and process, to make some effort to go beyond the purely synchronic study, even though the latter may continue to bulk large in both field research and writing. To illustrate: instead of merely taking for granted the existence of cash-cropping in the condition it happens to be at the time of investigation, an attempt is made to understand how cash-cropping was introduced, against what sorts of opposition, and what were its effects upon, say, the domestic economy, village co-operation, land rights, etc. Questions about such factors as the tensions that may have arisen between father and sons as a result of competition for scarce land or for the proceeds of cash-crop sales can partly be analysed synchronically; but put into the wider time context, the degree of understanding is increased, even when data on the past are poor. Is this tension a new phenomenon in the society, or is it an intensification of earlier patterns? Are people still in the process of trying to adapt to it, or have they a ready-made solution to the problem? (Gulliver 1961). These are typical kinds of questions which ineluctably demand consideration of the time element, and they are questions which must be dealt with if a full analysis of the social situation is to be made, even if information on earlier times is rather meagre.

The trend toward diachronic study and toward the overt and explicit reckoning of the elements of social change and time has been general only for a short time. Anthropologists continue to produce purely synchronic studies, and they will undoubtedly and often justifiably continue to do so in the future. The amounts of theoretically based studies of change and process and even of purely descriptive information on contemporary, changing societies are still small. Any anthropologist who has had to teach students about present-day societies and cultures in Africa is aware of the scarcity of adequate material. Many large and important groups of African peoples are known to the world only by the accounts of them written a couple of decades ago. The state of anthropological knowledge of, say, the Ibo or Nupe of Nigeria, the Kikuyu of Kenya, or the Bemba of Northern Rhodesia (to give only a few random examples) is such that an up-to-date account of them cannot be given, and reliance must be placed on generally deficient sources such as government reports, journalists' accounts and politicians' stereotypes. Many of the standard works of Africanist anthropological literature deal with conditions before the second world war, and ignore most or all factors of change: e.g., Evans-Pritchard's study of Azande witchcraft and magic (1937), or his trilogy on the Nuer of the Sudan (1940, 1951, 1956); Schapera on the Tswana of Bechuanaland (1938); Herskovits on Dahomey (1938); Richards on the Bemba (1939); Fortes on the Tallensi of northern Ghana (1945, 1949).

There are two principal reasons for this marked deficiency in anthropology.

One is the shortage of anthropologists relative to the large number of distinctive socio-cultural systems and the many aspects of study that are relevant to each. The other is the fact that, even in the field research of the last decade or so, anthropologists have been more concerned with synchronic analysis of the specifically indigenous characteristics of the societies than with describing contemporary conditions and recording the course of change. Younger anthropologists starting research in Africa have been motivated to investigate the social life of a people which has not hitherto been well described, and they have continued to be influenced by the older anthropological spirit of seeking especially the non-Western features. Anthropologists still tend quite strongly to seek the exotic: often, no doubt, out of some degree of ennui with their own society and its problems. This single-mindedness is not without its advantages for the future because it will provide a corpus of knowledge, slowly and carefully built up, of great historical value in its own right, and affording reliable base-lines for the developing study of social change.

At the moment, however, anthropological studies of change are few, and many of those which do exist are devoted only to particular aspects of change. In East Africa, for example, one or two anthropologists recently have been studying aspects of social change in Kenya (among the Kipsigis and Kikuyu in particular), but there is almost nothing at all on that country yet published by professional anthropologists. For Uganda the situation is better, largely because of the existence of the East African Institute of Social Research at Kampala. There are Fallers' study of changing governmental organisation among the Soga (1956), and works on the Ganda by Mukwaya (1953), Richards (1955, 1959), and Fallers (1964). By a more or less assiduous searching, a certain amount can be gleaned from anthropologists' writings on other Ugandan peoples, but this is a by-product of their main interests. For Tanganyika there are some brief descriptions of changing political systems, especially the aspect of chieftainship in the Lake Victoria area (Richards 1959), and accounts of the effects of labour migration among the Ngoni (Gulliver 1955b), and of developing land shortage and cash-crop production among the Nyakyusa (Gulliver 1958). For each of these countries, more information can be garnered from shorter articles (some by anthropologists) in specialist and local journals and periodicals. These sources are often excellent, but strictly limited in purpose. Additional information is obtainable from government publications (such as the annual reports of departments) and occasionally from travel books and the like. For Uganda in particular (as a result of the establishment of a college there) the writings of other social scientists are often most useful secondary sources (Low and Pratt 1960; Elkan 1960).

The consequent picture either of change or of contemporary conditions in East Africa is inadequate. Perhaps only for the Ganda does the current degree of knowledge begin to approach desirable standards and even for that people there remain many lacunae. Against this and the other information noted above there obtains an almost complete ignorance in anthropological terms of the nature of change among such major peoples as, say, the Kikuyu or Luhya of Kenya, the Teso of Uganda, and the Sukuma and Chagga of Tanganyika. There is little doubt that substantially the same condition holds for other regions of the continent.

VII   *BRIEF SURVEY OF ANTHROPOLOGICAL COVERAGE IN AFRICA*

The present section will review the state of anthropological research and writings on Africa in terms of geographical coverage and of topics and aspects other than modern social change, which is discussed above.

In geographical terms, anthropologists have achieved considerably less than full coverage of all the social systems on the continent. Using the tribe as the 'natural' unit of study, there are probably over eight hundred and possibly over a thousand such systems, and local variations in the larger units (such as Ibo or Somali) add to the effective number of distinctive systems to be studied and described. It would require a lengthy and profitless investigation to discover what proportion of these units has been described in reasonable detail in all the literature presently available, but probably rather less than one hundred have been described well enough to make possible the construction of a fairly full account of indigenous social life. The number of African peoples for whom there is sufficient information on almost every aspect of their lives is tiny indeed; perhaps only the following qualify: Ashanti, Bemba, Dahomey, Dogon, Ganda, Nuer, Nyakyusa, Tswana and Zulu. Such a list is bound to be somewhat arbitrary, but even were it doubled or trebled, its size gives an indication of the anthropological accomplishment in those terms. There are, of course, excellent studies of particular aspects of many other societies, but none of these provides a total picture.

Conversely, there is a very large number of African peoples about which little is known. Anthropologists still quite commonly go to Africa to study a particular people about which nothing has been written by an anthropologist and which have been the subject of perhaps one or two articles by an administrator or other local person. This point must be stressed, because non-anthropologists (even those with Africanist experience) are much inclined to assume that there is a fair body of knowledge on virtually all African peoples. This is most certainly not the case.

Mozambique and Angola (with the sole exception of the Ovimbundu), South West Africa and Ethiopia are countries for which there is no major anthropological and little other literature. There is information on the material culture, art forms and rituals, but relatively little on the social life of the peoples of North Africa, either Berber or Arab. There are only scattered contributions to an anthropological account of the peoples of Southern Rhodesia, of the northern and western parts of the Republic of the Sudan, and of the Central African republics; probably no single tribe is at all well described in these areas. Many of the major groups of the Congo Republic are little known.

Although French anthropological research has a long history in the former French territories, the degree of coverage is patchy, and much of it remains at a rather unsophisticated level of description. According to one survey of the French work, the institutional organisations established for the purpose 'frequently . . . oblige workers to make only very short fragmentary studies of any given population, though C. Balandier, P. Mercier and some others have, more recently, been able to extend the scope of their projects' (Mendelson 1958: 253). For the French-speaking countries the state of anthropological knowledge is thus generally no more than fair, with certain notable exceptions, such as the Dogon and Bambara areas of the western Sudanic region.

Many of the English-speaking countries have received rather fuller treatment, although those anthropologists who are critical of the British insistence on the study of societies rather than cultures are, of course, also critical of the quality of coverage for those countries. Nevertheless, for Ghana, Nigeria, Uganda, Northern Rhodesia, the High Commission Territories, the South African Republic and for the southern parts of the Republic of the Sudan, there are many major studies and very many supporting publications of a briefer kind on almost all the important peoples. Kenya, Tanganyika, Nyasaland and Sierra Leone have been less adequately treated, and coverage there is comparable to that in most of the former French territories.

Regardless of the quantity and quality of the literature, it cannot be assumed that any one single aspect is fully treated. A good general study of a society may perhaps include an excellent account of political and legal institutions and processes but report very little on religion or economics. Almost every separate people in Uganda has been studied anthropologically, for example, but in only one or two cases is there an adequate account of religious beliefs and practices. Nor is all of the available information of equal value: much, though not all, of the earlier writings, on which Africanists must continue to depend, is not up to the standard required of present-day anthropological work.

To the non-anthropologist this may appear to be a hypercritical survey of the state of anthropological knowledge; or alternatively it may seem that anthropologists, earliest and most numerous of social scientists in Africa, have not been as successful and as enterprising as they might have been. Anthropologists themselves are not seriously perturbed at the apparently large gaps in their knowledge of African peoples and societies, although it is obviously a matter for considerable regret that distinctive, indigenous social systems are changing rapidly before they have been properly recorded. But anthropologists agree that it is preferable to concentrate on a limited number of studies in depth, the result of fairly lengthy and painstaking field research, rather than to aim at a more universal coverage at a superficial level. This is, of course, a matter of opinion and choice of action, but the primary concern of anthropologists has been to develop knowledge and understanding of human behaviour in society, the nature of human interaction and relationships, and the patterns of activities with their concomitant ideas, values and symbols. Because of this, anthropologists have not hesitated in the choice between relatively fewer studies in depth and many more studies in breadth. Anthropological field research is a long-drawn-out enterprise which cannot be hurried or shortened without real risk of impairment of results, and anthropologists naturally have had their own needs and interests principally in mind when planning and developing their work in Africa. This has often meant that they have been less useful to their Africanist colleagues of other disciplines than they might be, at least in the shorter view. On the other hand, the contribution of anthropologists to the study of man is most profitably developed in these ways which they have chosen.

A generally useful summary of the state of factual knowledge of the social and cultural lives of African peoples is to be found in the numerous volumes of the *Ethnographic Survey of Africa*, prepared and published by the International African Institute in London and Paris. This vast, continuing enterprise aims at the assembly of all published information from whatever source, the assessment of its reliability and significance, and the production of a standard, descriptive, essentially ethnographic summary for each of the defined categories of peoples. Although some of the volumes contain a certain amount of theoretical analysis, this is certainly not the principal object of the Survey, and it does not pretend to be a synopsis of Africanist anthropology. Because of the variety of compilers employed in the Survey (ranging from inexperienced students to teachers and scholars of repute), the quality of the volumes varies a good deal, although they all follow a general pattern. The earlier ones (publication began in 1950) have in some cases already begun to be out of date as subsequent major publications relevant to their areas have appeared. On the whole, however, they do provide a fair account in brief form of the available factual knowledge, and the state of knowledge thus revealed bears out the general observations made earlier in this section.

As pointed out at the beginning of this chapter, Africanist anthropology finds its distinctiveness primarily in geographical terms. In general interests and ideas and in its theoretical framework, anthropology admits of no such continental division. Africanists both learn from and contribute to the gradual development of the discipline in a world context. On the other hand, Africanist anthropology has certain characteristics which give it an identity of its own. The first of these, perhaps, is the particular significance of social anthropology in Africa. Despite the participation of anthropologists from many countries and traditions in the collection and recording of ethnographic data, the more analytical and theoretical aspects have been dominated for more than a quarter of a century by the social anthropologists, with their source of inspiration mainly in Britain. In the post-war era, several of the more important non-British anthropologists, whose names have been cited earlier in this chapter, have been strongly influenced by the British social anthropologists; they often have studied and taught in Britain. Like the British anthropologists, they have received great sociological stimulus both from earlier writers, such as Durkheim and Weber, and also from contemporary theorists, such as Parsons in the United States and Levi-Strauss in France. Rich contributions have been made by other anthropologists with different approaches and aims — for example, Herskovits and his pupils, from Northwestern University — but the mainstream of development has been more largely in the area of social anthropology. As has already been noted, a gradual change is discernible in the character of social anthropology itself, as experience and ideas have accumulated and been critically tested, and as increasing attention has been directed towards the study of the systems of ideas, beliefs and values which inform social behaviour and social relationships.

Another of the marked features of Africanist anthropology has been the out-standing work done on indigenous political systems. More attention has probably been given to this than to any other single field, including even that field of perennial interest and concern, kinship. This interest in political systems was undoubtedly greatly stimulated by the needs of colonial administration — especially in the British territories under some kind of 'indirect rule' — and by the fact of the continued existence of these systems in more or less working order at a time when comparable systems were disappearing from other parts of the world. The concern of African anthropologists with social structures has also been conducive to the study of political systems: an aspect of society to which cultural anthropologists have seldom given great attention, as is shown by the dearth of political studies of Amerindian peoples. This Africanist interest has produced some notable studies of small-scale states which are important contributions to political science. Perhaps more importantly, it has resulted in the detailed examination of the nature of government and politics in those kinds of society which have few or no specialised institutions and roles of a political kind, such as chiefs, courts or councils, centralised authority, or indeed much formal public authority on sanctions. At first, such problems tended to be studied in terms of the question of whether such societies had any systems of government and politics at all comparable to that of an African kingdom or a modern nation-state. But soon different kinds of questions were raised: What are the essential tasks of government, and how are they performed in those societies? How are law and order or security from external attack maintained? How are problems discussed and decisions reached on matters relating to a whole community or to a large part of it? Empirically, who are the leaders, and what is the nature of leadership, influence and authority? And what is the nature of consent when specific political and administrative roles do not exist? These sorts of questions were given marked prominence by the publication of *African political systems* (Evans-Pritchard and Fortes 1940); and, although they were not original then, they have been of major interest ever since. This is not the place to attempt a bibliography of this field, but by way of illustration the following may be noted: Evans-Pritchard's *The Nuer* (1940); Bohannan's *Justice and judgment among the Tiv* (1957); *Tribes without rulers* (Middleton and Tait 1958); Lewis's *A pastoral democracy* (1961); *Social control in an African society* (Gulliver 1963); and parts of more general works such as those by Schapera (1956) and Mair (1962).

Another characteristic feature of Africanist anthropology, and one which is closely connected with some aspects of the interest in government in stateless societies, is the development of the study of unilateral descent and lineage systems. This interest concerns the nature and operation of corporate groups which are recruited by the principle of descent in either the male or female line. These groups, or lineages, are each comprised of the descendants of a given male or female ancestor; sub-groups, or lineages of lesser genealogical depth, comprise the descendants of the sons, grandsons or other descendants of the founder. Varying according to the society, lineages of a certain genealogical depth are important in one social context, e.g., the administration of farm land and cattle, or joint responsibility for injuries committed by one of their number; and deeper or shallower ones are significant in other contexts, e.g., propitiation of the ancestors, common residence, economic co-operation, etc. Thus, people who co-operate at one level may be in opposition to each other at a different level. The lineage which, say, forms a local community may be divided into a number of lesser lineages which compete with each other for land rights but which co-operate together *vis-à-vis* other local communities. The dynamics of such a system, the segments of which are lineages of various orders of genealogical depth, have been described and analysed in great detail for many African societies, in which they are a major feature of the social structure. And these analyses have referred especially, though not exclusively, to those societies which have little organised government (Evans-Pritchard 1940, Fortes 1945, Mayer 1949, L. Bohannan 1952, Middleton and Tait 1958, Middleton 1960, etc.).

This interest has been deeply rooted in the fundamental concepts of social anthropology, especially the nature of social structure and the relation between theoretical models and concrete reality. A number of critics, mainly from outside Africanist ranks, have come to feel that there has been a distorting over-concentration upon unilateral descent to the detriment of other kinds of descent and kinship systems. There is doubtless much truth in this; but even so, the special work done on unilineal descent, and in particular on segmentary lineage systems, continues to be both anthropologically valuable and characteristically Africanist. And although the bulk of this work has been done synchronically, it has prepared the way for diachronic study because of its emphasis on the *processes* of fusion, fission and growth of these unilineal groups as responses both to internal developments and external pressures.

In both of these matters, African conditions have been conducive to this special concentration and achievement. Working, indigenous political systems of a wide range of variety have been numerous and easily observed in Africa; and there appears to be something intrinsic in the frequent occurrence and emphasis on unilineal descent among African peoples. Other features of social and cultural life are less distinctive in this way. That is to say, the variety of forms and patterns has not given rise to any peculiarly Africanist development in anthropology. The normal range of anthropological enquiry has been covered with varying degrees of effectiveness, taking into account what has already been said about the incompleteness of the geographical coverage of African socio-cultural systems. Thus, there have been both descriptive ethnographies and theoretical analyses of kinship and family organisation, marriage and divorce; domestic and community economies; indigenous religions, supernatural beliefs and practices; law and judicial processes; forms of association other than those based on kinship and descent; human ecology; material culture and technology; child-rearing and socialisation.

Such a list is bound to be both rather arbitrary and unduly compartmentalised, and other writers might apply a different set of descriptive labels to the topics of interest to anthropologists. It must be repeated that there are also other matters often studied by anthropologists with which this chapter has no concern. The intention here is merely to indicate the general range of anthropological interests. It is probably no less arbitrary to attempt to assess the degree and the success with which these topics have been treated. Nevertheless, probably no Africanist anthropologist would disagree with the statement that, in view of the great range of diversity of African societies, one cannot feel satisfied either with the amount of information available or with the level of understanding on any single aspect of the social lives of African peoples. Because of their focal position in virtually all African societies, and therefore their importance in anthropological terms, family and kinship and their concomitants are the most fully studied. A decade ago, one might have said that the least adequately treated area was religion and the supernatural, particularly in terms of values and ideas rather than activities. As a result of a number of recent publications in this field, this is no longer the case (Dieterlen 1951; Griaule and Dieterlen 1954; Forde 1954; Nadel 1954; Evans-Pritchard 1956; Wilson 1957, 1959; Middleton 1960; Lienhardt 1961; and others).

Whether his interest is in a general understanding of African social and cultural life, in knowledge of a particular people, or in an appreciation of the anthropological contribution in a particular field, the non-anthropologist must be prepared to find what may seem to him to be a rather unsatisfactory state of affairs. Anthropologists are often unwilling to generalise, and they much prefer to concentrate on the study of particular aspects of a single society. When, in addition, only a small proportion of African societies has been well described, the non-anthropologist may conclude that his anthropological requirements, of whatever kind, are often not likely to be met. It has sometimes been suggested that broad anthropological surveys should be made in order to produce areal and topical information which is not now available. This mechanistic and necessarily superficial method could do little more than obtain heterogeneous collections of certain kinds of facts; and even collections of facts which are objectively valid — a quality difficult to obtain — are anthropologically almost useless unless they can be related together and given perspective and significance in their social contexts. This, the most important task of anthropologists, cannot be accomplished by any method of rapid research.

VIII   THE ANTHROPOLOGICAL STUDY OF COMPLEX, URBAN SOCIETIES

With their interests and efforts firmly directed towards the large number and variety of indigenous social systems, almost all of which are intrinsically rural in character, anthropologists have been tardy in coming to the study of the entirely new, complex and as yet amorphous societies in Africa which are predominantly urban in character. Here there has been a marked lack of general interest in, and even wilful neglect of, socio-cultural change. Two early studies by non-anthropologists (Orde-Browne 1933; Davis 1933) aroused little more than casual interest. Significantly, anthropologists began to be really concerned with urban developments and these newly forming societies because of the growing migration of men to employment away from the rural, tribal societies. It was the effects of migration in the areas of more orthodox anthropological enquiry which caught attention, particularly in the eastern and southern regions of the continent where industry was being introduced by European enterprise. As a result, a body of literature has accumulated which is valuable not only to the understanding of contemporary rural communities but also to an appreciation of the conditions of labour, its supply and its instability in employment. This literature has also provided some clues for understanding the reactions, conditions and problems of Africans in urban and other wage-employment areas. In this field, some of the important works are by Read (1942), Schapera (1947), Gulliver (1955b), and Watson (1958).

Only in the last decade have anthropologists begun seriously to investigate conditions in the new towns, and the bulk of their published work is still concerned with attempts to map out the ethnography and other empirical data of these communities. Confronted by situations quite novel to anthropological research, in which many of the routine assumptions about rural life and tribal society have been inapplicable, anthropologists slowly and painfully have had to try to develop both practical research techniques and clearer ideas of the kinds of phenomena they were seeking to describe and understand. Anthropologists have become accustomed to studying relatively self-contained communities in which there is a high degree of concentration of multiplex activities, interests and relationships within a single group. The limits of kinship in a tribal community often are congruent with the boundaries of economic, political, religious and leisure activities and co-operation; one's kinsman is also one's neighbour, a member of the same economic team, the same religious congregation, and so on. Furthermore, these multiplex relationships and cultural patterns of behaviour are more or less enduring. In the new towns, a man's workmate is likely to be quite different from his neighbour, who is neither his kinsman nor his leisure-time companion, etc.; people change their occupations, their residence and their allegiances rather frequently. Above all, the towns contain people (with a distorting preponderance of young adult males) from a wide variety of tribal — i.e., socio-cultural — backgrounds; new and as yet unstable social categories related to income, occupation and social class further complicate the apparent confusion.

In the view of some people, it might have been preferable had the anthropologist left the study of these complex, urban communities to the sociologists, who were thought to be more fitted to undertake it because of their experience in industrial, urban societies in Western countries. There were, and unfortunately still are, too few sociologists available, and both practical and theoretical problems demanded attention. More important than this, however, anthropologists not only were available and increasingly desirous to undertake research, but (unlike most sociologists) they were already knowledgeable about the rural, tribal areas in which the overwhelming majority of African urban workers had been raised and to which periodically and ultimately they returned. Although urban conditions impose new necessities and limitations and also offer new opportunities and values, yet patterns of thought and action are brought to the town from the country by the migrants; and many persist to motivate action and to generate loyalties and ties. The anthropological experience was, therefore, essential. Beyond that, anthropologists were not prepared to accept the proposition that they can study only *certain* kinds of social system, either in Africa or elsewhere.

Ethnographically, some anthropologists conducted their research in urban areas in much the same way as they had done in rural areas; that is, they selected one or more small communities in which they carried out intensive investigations, paying relatively little attention to the connections between their samples or to the larger connurbation in which they were situated. An early example is Hellman's study of a single slum-yard (population 376) in Johannesburg (Hellman 1948); a more recent case is *Townsmen in the making* (Southall and Gutkind 1957): a study conducted in Kampala, Uganda, in which each author concentrated on a single section of the town (populations 2,154 and 1,339 respectively), because they believed it impossible to obtain the kind of data they wanted on any larger scale. Although these and other similar studies were conducted with great empathy, mainly or wholly in the people's own language, it was not possible for them to be of the kind of highly intimate, participant-observation project which has become the hallmark of most rural research. It was impracticable, it was personally unsafe, and it was often disallowed by the local authorities. In any case, urban complexity, the absence of well-established cultural patterns and social structure, even the absence of a single language, made such intensive methodology unprofitable if not actually impossible. By necessity, recourse was had to extensive questionnaire techniques and statistical treatment with their obviously impersonal flavour, to the employment of numbers of field assistants who, despite their real worth, intruded between anthropologist and people in a way to which he was unaccustomed. Facts and figures which could be collected and quantified began to take precedence over attempts to assess qualitatively more critical, but less readily observable, phenomena: the number of people per house and their formal links, if any, rather than the actual state of relations between co-residents of a house, and the norms of behaviour they followed; the number of times a man shifts his residence, rather than the nature of relations between neighbours or the possible persistence of friendly relations with former neighbours; what a man says he does, or did, or would do (in reply to a questionnaire) rather than what he actually does or did in respect of, say, his kinship obligations or the trade union.

Some anthropologists, at least initially, have made no attempt to imitate orthodox anthropological methods when they study urban areas. Following sociological techniques, they conduct extensive enquiries into such matters as tribal origins, length of time in town, kinds of job, marital status, and the like. Attempts have been made to assess men's attitudes to members of all the other tribes with whom they came into contact in town; to assess what kinds of men comprise a person's range of intimates, friends, companions, acquaintances, casual encounters; and to construct the career-histories of samples of town-dwellers with reference to their places and periods of employment and residence in town, visits to and contacts with the rural areas, marital and extra-marital experiences, etc. The work on the Copper Belt of Northern Rhodesia, conducted by the Rhodes-Livingstone Institute and largely directed by Clyde Mitchell during the earlier 1950s, is a good example of this (Mitchell 1954a, 1954b, 1956). McCulloch (1956) has investigated another part of Northern Rhodesia. Similar studies from elsewhere in Africa are Banton's on Freetown, Sierra Leone (1957), the survey of Sekondi-Takoradi (Busia 1950), and much of the work in Brazzaville by Balandier's team (Balandier 1955).

These modifications in research techniques and in the kinds of data obtained have brought complementary modifications in the kinds of accounts written by anthropologists and in the interests they sustain. Many anthropologists continue to be chary of involvement in urban studies because they are disinclined either to embrace these new interests or to accept the diminution of contact and rapport between themselves and the people they study. It is not at all certain in which direction anthropological research and interest will eventually move in this field. It cannot be denied that fact-finding, the rather impersonal and extensive data collecting and measuring, and the examining of the social skeleton of these unformed communities, is essential. Both anthropologist and sociologist are faced with research into a novel situation in Africa. But anthropologists especially seem to be uncomfortably aware of what appears to be a lapse, as it were, back to a kind of old-fashioned ethnography, and they are dissatisfied with the state of their urban studies to date. They are seeking new theoretical ideas, hypotheses, kinds of approach and methodologies, which will help to take them beyond description and statistical correlation to the means of deeper understanding and interpretation. As a result, social anthropologists have attempted a number of experimental approaches, which, although not necessarily proved, have begun to lead to significant contributions to this whole field.

Max Gluckman (Southall 1961) asserts that the starting point for the understanding and analysis of urban society in Africa must be a specifically urban system of relationships in which tribal origins and tribal patterns are but one, and not necessarily the most important, element. The urban-dweller, be he ever so temporary, encounters a variety of restrictions and opportunities which are all intrinsically urban and which, moreover, have features common to urban-dwellers everywhere in the world: e.g., the wage-earning pattern, fixed routine of work, the factors of employers and fellow-employees; new residence patterns, mobility and heterogeneity of people; the absence of factors of social control and co-operation typical of tribal life; the urban classes; the routine and flow of urban life as compared with that of rural life with its seasonal calendar; etc. We must not, says Gluckman, attempt to think of the town-dweller as a tribesman in town. Because of the lack of an immediately obvious structure of social relations, sets of commonly accepted norms, etc., there is no need to despair that any pattern or structure exists. He suggests the technique of studying critical points in the urban life where disturbance, conflict and difficulty provide obvious situations in which patterns of behaviour, alignment of relationships, and evocation of standards can be studied. This suggestion is not new: Gluckman himself advocated something like it twenty years previously (Gluckman 1942), and both Balandier (1955) and

Little (1955) have put forward rather similar ideas. This approach has the value of offering an opportunity to 'get at' something tangible in these rather indistinct, inchoate and unstable social relationships, values and standards, and it creates the opportunity to focus research on specific points rather than generally to try to encompass everything.

Epstein (1958), one of Gluckman's pupils, has shown the advantages to be gained from this kind of 'situational analysis' in his study of the Copper Belt. He examines the social context of a boycott of butchers' shops in one town; the long-drawn-out conflict between government-appointed tribal elders and the people's own representatives drawn from trade union and political party; and the conflicts between various norms which are recurrently demonstrated in the African urban courts. Mitchell (1956), an associate of Gluckman, has brilliantly brought off a similar study centring on competing dance-teams on the Copper Belt. These teams simultaneously remain tribal in composition and loyalty, and exhibit the new, westernised and urban standards of dress, behaviour and class.

It is not clear whether this technique is really more than an expository device of obvious worth, or if it can in fact lead to a new, positive understanding. Mitchell's work on the tribal composition of urban-dwellers, on intertribal attitudes, and on new social classes, did not ultimately depend on his focusing on the dance-teams. On the other hand, and in view of the distressing absence of orientation in many urban studies, one cannot doubt the value of any technique which succeeds in providing some genuine method of concentration.

Balandier (1955) has called for an 'analysis of new social relations, problems of stratification and social classes and the definition of social types emerging in an urban setting'. His research in the city of Brazzaville attempts to do just this.

Epstein (1961) has recently advocated the adoption of the 'network' technique of sociological analysis in African urban studies. This is a method of social analysis used by two social anthropologists outside Africa (Barnes 1954b; Bott 1947), and also advocated by Mitchell. The latter writes that a society should be visualised as a 'reticulation of social relationships in which people are linked and cross-linked by numerous ties and bonds, some operating now to hold people together this way, and some . . . to hold the same people together in a different way' (Mitchell 1960: 30). The reticulation is not uniform, for there are areas of relatively dense linkages where there is a consensus of values and interests and much co-operation, and conversely areas of relatively sparse linkages where there is a marked lack of consensus, little co-operation and much indifference.

Epstein (1961) conceives of the Rhodesian Copper Belt as a single social field in which there are 'different sets of relationships, each of which forms a distinct sub-system'. He sketches the outlines of the various social contacts of a man in a Copper Belt town in terms of (a) degrees of intensity of contacts, from casual and fleeting to regular and integral; and (b) a number of categories, such as neighbourhood and locality, tribe, class and formal associations. He indicates that each person stands at the centre of an ego-focused network of social relations. The people involved in any one such network do not comprise a social group; many do not know or even know of each other. But some of them are closely linked to one another, so that interaction and interdependence are multiplex, frequent and of particular significance. It is through such a network that an individual is in effect related to his urban community. Epstein's contention is that it is necessary to discover the networks of particular individuals in order to understand a person's role and status; to understand how he is subject to social control; and how he becomes exposed to changing attitudes and standards. It is particularly necessary to examine that part of the network where inter-relations are multiplex, with reference both to people and to activities.

This is an even more tentative approach than the others, for it remains to be tested in actual research in Africa. It need not be limited to urban studies, and indeed something very like it has already been attempted in the study of a relatively unchanging, tribal society in eastern Uganda (Gulliver 1955a: chapter 7). In point of fact, the experimental methods being tried out by anthropologists in urban research will be most valuable to their colleagues in other fields of the discipline, particularly as the speed and radical degree of change in some rural areas create similar problems of investigation and analysis. Eventually anthropologists more or less everywhere will have to deal with problems comparable to those which urban research is already defining; and, in this sense, the urban anthropologist may be said to be in the vanguard. Cultural factors, such as ideas and values, will undoubtedly not be neglected, but sociological approaches will become more obviously dominant — as is indeed witnessed by the attraction of the theories of social anthropology to French anthropologists in urban research.

IX CONCLUSION: TRENDS AND PROBLEMS IN ANTHROPOLOGY

Some Africanists, anthropologists and others, have taken the view that, except for antiquarian interests, the era of anthropological study in the continent is coming to an end. In refuting this pessimistic and uninformed judgment, I am not concerned merely to defend the vested interests of my own discipline; much less am I conservatively refusing to recognise the necessity and value of new ideas, new methods and new challenges. Anthropology, unless it be defined in a most narrow and limited way, has definitely not reached a moribund stage. It can continue to contribute to general knowledge and understanding of the peoples of Africa in particular and of man in society in a wider sense. Within the discipline itself there is a multitude of theoretical problems and developments which can be pursued in Africa.

The suspicions about its future seem to be based on the assumption that anthropologists are concerned only with indigenous forms, with autonomous tribes, with essentially non-Western practices and ideas which are summed up in that misleading word, 'traditional'. Africans are rapidly being westernised, it is said; the tribe is disappearing, being replaced by modern nation-states; chiefs have given way to elected politicians and bureaucratic administrators, just as subsistence economies have been abandoned for participation in world markets and a cash economy; and so on. In the past, anthropologists have been predominantly concerned, as I have shown, with the tribe as the unit of study, with established chiefdoms, indigenous religions, primitive technologies, and the like. These were the actual phenomena of the societies and cultures of Africa. But anthropologists are really interested in societies and cultures of small scale, not merely those of a particular variety variously labelled 'traditional', 'primitive' or 'pre-literate', and there they are especially skilled in investigating and describing them. If the tribe vanishes as a culturally distinct social unit — and that is far from being the generally accomplished situation to date — then it will be replaced by some kind of local community which will be a sub-section of a new, large society. When the chief,

his court and subordinates lose their power and obligations and their responsibilities for law and order, then local administration and the opportunities for power
and conflict over policy and its execution will come to reside in some local group
or community within the political state. Anthropologists can study such groups.
People may well adopt new patterns of family life, marriage, leisure activity,
economic co-operation and competition, and achieve new status alignments; but,
whatever patterns and relationships emerge, anthropologsits can study them. With
their typically intensive, small-scale methods, anthropologists have already established useful literatures on peasant communities in Europe, Asia and Latin America,
on highly industrialised and urbanised countries such as the United States and
Britain, and on particular problems the world over. What is being done elsewhere
can readily be undertaken in Africa, and, in the case of urban investigations by
anthropologists, this is already being demonstrated.

Let me be clear in this. Anthropologists may well have rather little to
contribute directly to the study of the new, major social units emerging in Africa.
The political scientist, economist, geographer, historian and others (still retaining
most of the research apparatus derived from the study of their own Western, large-
scale societies) have already assumed a prominent place in the social and humanistic
studies of the new African states. But anthropologists' specialisation in dealing
with micro-structures and sub-systems and with the details of interpersonal, small
group relationships, can continue to produce information and lead to understanding in a way no other discipline can. It must be also emphasised that,
despite many people's hopes (including those of national politicians and administrators) for the emergence of genuine national unity, culture and society, it will
assuredly be a long time yet before the many and deeply rooted socio-cultural
differences between local communities fade away into relative unimportance. In
spite of political development, educational progress and economic improvements,
in many regions of the continent a generation of adults is growing up among whom
the older basic ideas, attitudes and patterns of behaviour and expectancy are well
entrenched. Experience also strongly indicates that African societies and African
cultures are not going to become copies of those of Euro-America. To assume
that they are, and to assume the uselessness of anthropological enquiry and analysis,
is in fact to prejudge the outcome in unnecessarily ethnocentric fashion. Variety
of social and cultural form will persist, even though the particular forms change;
and this variety is obviously susceptible to anthropological study.

It has already been indicated that anthropologists in the post-war era have not
given sufficient attention to socio-cultural change: to its forms and processes and
to its causes and effects. It has also been asserted that anthropologists do not as
yet have an adequate working body of theory to enable them consciously and
intensively to investigate the processes of change. I believe this to be the major
problem to be faced in the immediate future. Synchronic analyses, ethnography,
particular theoretical problems of many kinds — all will continue to be important,
but none is so important to the contemporary African scene as change, its description and interpretation. One may say this both because changing Africa is so
important both to Africans and to outsiders, and also because serious and intensive
study now generally requires that the factor of change be integral to it. The
understanding of process, of social role, of institutions and structures, of systems
and patterns, is likely to be distorted unless it can be related to appreciation of
change. This will involve more open-minded and sophisticated approaches to the

use of historical material; it will certainly require rather different research techniques.   We have to abandon the fiction that we can, as Radcliffe-Brown put it, 'give an account of a form of social life as it exists at a certain time, abstracting as far as possible from changes that may be taking place in its features' (Radcliffe-Brown 1952: 4).   It will doubtless mean that anthropologists must take risks, step out from their cosily entrenched positions established as a result of work during the last few decades, and hazard methods and hypotheses which may or may not be useful.   Anthropologists have only themselves to blame if other social scientists and laymen are inclined to think that they can study only exotic, 'unchanging' tribal societies.   When one protests that this is not really true, it is not always easy to give good examples of work by anthropologists on contemporary, changing societies in Africa.   Against this can be set the fact that many anthropologists have already become acutely aware of the problem.   It is clear that anthropological research, theory and methods can expand to embrace the factor of change.   Its exclusion as a convenient working device is now quite outmoded.

Concomitant with this requirement is the need for anthropologists to take steps to build up as full a historical record as possible of the evolution of African societies and cultures.   It is on such a record that theories and ultimately understanding of social change and resistance to change will depend.   It is particularly important that those societies which have been well described in the past by anthropologists and other writers should have continuous records built up about them. If by unfortunate chance a particular people in Africa was not reasonably well described fairly soon after colonial conquest, there is little that can now be done to rectify that, whatever records may be kept in the future.   But groups which have been well studied provide excellent opportunities for the thorough investigation of change.   These opportunities must not be lost if it can possibly be avoided. Revisits by anthropologists to the peoples whom they have already studied are highly desirable — such as, for example, the revisit of Dr Audrey Richards to the Bemba of Northern Rhodesia in 1955, some twenty years after the completion of her original major research among them.   Too little of this occurs, partly because as anthropologists grow older, they tend to be less enthusiastic to return to the hazards and rigours of the field; but these workers are in an excellent position to study and evaluate the changes which occur.

Alternatively, younger anthropologists should choose to work where their seniors previously worked (Gulliver 1958; Edwards 1962).   Fieldworkers often desire to study a people which has hitherto not been well described: a false, outmoded tradition of pioneering and novelty.   It is admirable that information be obtained for a relatively unknown people, but this tends to lead merely to synchronic or reconstructive and pseudo-'traditional' writing.   Anthropologists have the duty of filling in the many blanks on the ethnographic map; the data often are needed for comparative purposes, and all and any knowledge is potentially useful.   But merely filling up the map is far less important than attempting to close the gaps in knowledge about those peoples which have already been well described.   Where resources (i.e., trained fieldworkers and finances) are relatively scarce, then it seems to me that the best use can be made of them in this way.   Nor should we be content with just a single revisit, perhaps two decades after the first research period.   University departments and programs might very well 'adopt' a number of peoples to which research workers are sent periodically for the collection of adequately filed data, both of a purely factual kind (e.g., the death of an important person, figures of crop production, the making of a new road) and of a more general, diffuse kind (e.g., developing attitudes and ideas, tendencies towards stresses and strains in institutions and relationships, etc.). This would mean the conscious building up of anthropological archives for the selected groups for which the periodic field research reports would be the basic but not the only source. Anthropologists are right when they assert that so often the data on which to base studies of social change are not available. It is up to anthropologists themselves to ensure that these data are now assembled and preserved.

Let me emphasise again the kinds of information and understanding which are required both by anthropologists and others. First, we need to know what are the socio-cultural facts about specific, contemporary, small-scale communities. Secondly, we need to understand how changes occur; what sorts of factors produce change; how susceptible different societies and institutions are to different kinds of forces; where resistance to change occurs and why; how consciously adopted change and unconscious adaptation actually operate; and the nature of the 'chain-reaction' process in which change in one part of the social system foments change in other parts not obviously or directly related. In the light of such research, naïve speculation, more or less based on impression and inadequate data, can be replaced by working hypotheses leading to general principles and the recognition of patterns, based on genuine and ample bodies of knowledge.

Certain of the other, important trends may briefly be summarised in the final paragraphs of this chapter. In one form or another mention of them has previously been made.

Perhaps one of the most distressing characteristics of anthropologists (in the outsider's opinion, at any rate) is their disinclination to take a broad view of their discipline, of the state of knowledge reached, of the general principles and hypotheses which seem to have been reasonably well tested, and of the inter-relation of results obtained in different areas of anthropological enquiry. On the whole this does not worry anthropologists — not as much as it probably should — because of the considerable amount of more or less informal interchange of information and opinion within what is still a relatively small body of professional workers. Monographic single-mindedness (concern for the particular) has undoubtedly advanced anthropological studies a long way and will continue to keep them firmly rooted in empirical evidence and intimate personal experience. There is certainly no substitute for this, and it is altogether unlikely that anthropologists will ever allow themselves to become as isolated from their field of study as were some of their predecessors. Fortunately this monographic concentration has not stifled theoretical development, for all the better works are permeated by general considerations. On the other hand, there might well have been greater progress in the understanding of human behaviour in society had anthropologists been more ready to voice, and their colleagues more prepared sympathetically to attend to, attempts at generalised observations.

The firmly rooted tradition of personal field research and of theoretical development in the context of monographic accounts of social systems and cultures must surely be maintained as the foundation of anthropological studies. Yet more time and interest are definitely required for the assessment of results of the rapidly accumulating mass of data and analyses. A good case could in fact be made to the effect that it is only now that true theoretical synthesis can begin. Many anthropologists feel that, after the long preoccupation with particularist studies, the time has come to move forward.   On the other hand, a word of warning is in order for non-anthropologists: so far it has proved tremendously difficult to devise methods by which to deal scientifically with data from very many, very different cultural contexts.   Conclusions or hypotheses tentatively made about a particular socio-cultural system are not always readily testable in the context of a different system. In some ways it is almost an act of faith by anthropologists to believe that it can be done, so slight has been the progress to date.

Non-anthropologists, nevertheless, need to be informed more directly and succinctly of the experience and interim conclusions of anthropologists.   Conversely, anthropologists need to widen their perspectives by learning from their colleagues in other social sciences.   Attempts at interdisciplinary work of one kind or another are not new, although experience of them has sometimes deterred anthropologists from repeated participation.   Yet with the end of their near-monopoly in Africanist studies, it is also clear that anthropologists need, and feel the need, to learn from others.   In such organisations as the African Studies Association and in many of the research programs in the United States, the trend is towards at least more co-operation.

At a less ambitious level, but related to the need for generalisation and hypothesis-building across the board, is the need for an ethnographic and theoretical assessment of anthropological studies of groups of fairly closely related peoples. The *Ethnographic Survey of Africa* has already prepared the way, and a number of anthropologists have made experimental attempts to do it for selected groups. The work of Schapera (1956) on the peoples of southern Africa is of this kind, and some similar work has been done among the interlacustrine Bantu centred on western Uganda.   It is possible to examine either a group of peoples related historically and culturally (e.g., the interlacustrine Bantu) or a region within which are found groups of rather diverse origins and cultures (e.g., the Guinea Coast). Data for many areas have accumulated in quantity, but they tend to be dispersed over a large number of publications, and there is a danger that some of their potential value may be lost simply because they cannot readily be considered as a whole. Synthesis at more restricted ethnographic and theoretical levels would obviate this danger and provide a great service for other kinds of analysis.

This is a responsibility which anthropologists have towards Africanists in other disciplines.   The requirement is a measure both of the incursion in large numbers of other social scientists into Africa, and of the two-way value of co-operation between anthropologists and other disciplines.   Although anthropologists tend to write most of their results for their colleagues, this is likely to be less marked than it has been in the past, when so few others were directly concerned with the continent.

Another contemporary trend which is most important to anthropologists at the moment is the development of highly intensive, detailed research into small communities.   This is a development of the case-study method for which anthropologists are indebted to Malinowski for his pioneering work.   Such studies hitherto have consisted largely of the close examination of empirical examples of particular aspects, factors and relationships in order to illustrate points of general description or analysis.   These will continue to be invaluable and will serve to keep generalisation anchored to concrete reality.   But more recently some anthropologists have felt that case-studies need not be merely sample illustrations; they can be treated *sui generis*.   Of this Gluckman has written: 'The most fruitful use of cases consists in taking a series of specific incidents affecting the same persons or groups, through a long period of time, and showing how these incidents, these cases, are related to the development and change of social relations among these persons and groups, acting within the framework of their social system and culture' (Gluckman 1961: 10). Some such studies have already been attempted, and their value will encourage more of their kind. For non-anthropologists, this may perhaps seem to show too great a concern for the small scale and to run counter to the need for generalisation and wider synthesis. These micro-studies, however, may make possible an approach to a number of problems, for example, the relation between general norms and particular practice; the concatenation of sets of norms, institutions and relationships when they are brought together in the context of a single small collection of people who can be studied exhaustively; the nature of certain social processes; and methods of diachronic analysis.

A trend certain to continue in Africanist anthropology is the increased study of the growing, complex urban societies. Anthropologists will doubtless be working more and more closely with sociologists, and the results of much of their work will be of direct interest to all others who are concerned with problems of urban development. Apart from its more utilitarian value — keeping scholars informed of events, attitudes and problems in the towns and cities — this kind of research is likely to be of considerable value to anthropologists and other social scientists, in that it may show the way to methods for integrated study both of complex societies and of rural societies which are losing their old qualities of relative stability, self-sufficiency and clear social structures. In any case, many anthropologists believe that the study of rural communities has in fact over-concentrated on formal structures and institutions to the neglect of other aspects. Anthropological experimentation in the investigation and description of urban societies in Africa, therefore, is likely to be instructive and formative in work in other fields of the discipline. It will also probably encourage further the socio-logical element in contemporary anthropology.

There have been several references in this chapter to the need, generally acknowledged but often neglected, to make anthropological data and results available to non-anthropologists concerned with African affairs. One aspect of this is the development of applied anthropology, that is, anthropological enquiry made specifically to assist in the solving of contemporary practical problems of administration, economic development and public planning. Applied anthropology has already had some success in Africa, and one former colonial government, Tanganyika, employed a permanent research staff for this purpose for more than a decade. Many anthropologists dislike the notion of direct applied research, feeling that it may be an injurious non-scientific force in their discipline. They are also sceptical of its effective value. Though properly cautious, others are not so opposed and are willing to participate in planning and policy-making, so long as they need not compromise their scientific integrity. That this can in fact be accomplished has been demonstrated in Tanganyika and elsewhere. Governments, particular departments, planning groups and overseas agencies of many sorts will require various kinds of information which anthropologists can supply. These include both basic information on a given community, people or region and the examination of the possible effects of particular policies, the means of introducing them, and the mitigation of undesirable effects. Applied anthropology does not mean policy-making, which is a political and executive task for which anthropologists *qua* anthropologists are not competent.   They are one of the several kinds of specialist, none the less, who can supply information and informed opinion.

The list of future problems and trends in Africanist anthropology can doubtless be extended, and the contents of any such list will reflect the interests and bias of the compiler.   This concluding section, therefore, is not intended to be definitive, for that is impossible without dogmatism.   The intention is rather to indicate some of the more important factors which will affect the immediate future of anthropological studies.   The non-anthropologist will naturally be more concerned with those features which directly affect his own interests and which may help him to clarify his own problems and understanding.   I have tried, nevertheless, also to indicate the kinds of purely anthropological development which may seem less directly and immediately to concern other Africanists.   This has been done because it is important that other scholars have some appreciation of the problems which engage the attention of anthropologists and because, in due course, the specialist developments within the discipline will affect the whole of the contribution that anthropologists make to African studies.

4

Sociology — Some Aspects of Urban
Plural Societies*   Leo Kuper

I INTRODUCTION†

AFRICA IS AN exciting and unexplored field for the sociologist. Many
phenomena of interest to him are presented under somewhat novel aspects or
are more sharply defined, and many of the processes of change which occurred
earlier in Western industrial society are now taking place in Africa, at a time when
sociologists have some knowledge of the transformation from non-industrial to
industrial society and of the techniques for its study. Urbanisation in Africa offers
a stimulating challenge. The United Nations' *Report on the World Social Situation*
(1957: 114) describes the rapid urban growth of population in Africa from 1·4
million living in cities of 100,000 or more in 1900, to 10·2 million in 1950, and
lists twenty-nine cities in Africa south of the Sahara with a population of 100,000
and over. Some of these have more than doubled their population within a
generation. It seems reasonable to anticipate considerable urbanisation in the
next decades, the present towns and cities representing 'urban islands in a sea of
rurality'.

The towns and cities offer great variety. To stand on a street corner in the
'English' town of Durban, for example, is an introduction to many of the costumes
of the world: modern English, American, Parisian, Italian, the saris of Hindu
women, the fez and the long shirts of Muslim men and the long trousers of their
women, Zulu and Pondo tribal dress, and many variants of it in a process of
modernisation or free experiment. The major world religions are represented —
Hinduism, Islam, Buddhism, Confucianism, Zoroastrianism, Judaism, Christianity
in many denominations and sects, mediated by missionaries from many countries —
as well as syncretisms and ancestral cults. There are indigenous medieval-type
towns and modern Western towns. Kampala combines the traditional African
and the modern Western in a 'twin-town' structure. The agglomeration of

---

* I should like to acknowledge my thanks to my wife, Hilda, and to Professors M. G. Smith and
I. Wallerstein for their comments on this paper. I have not attempted a survey of sociological research
in Africa, but have selected some limited aspects of urban pluralism with special reference to Africans
rather than other population groups. The sociology of independence is now being written. Most of
the research I have analysed relates to the colonial era.
† Bibliography for this chapter will be found on page 502.

Africans in spontaneous or uncontrolled settlements, in shanty towns and *bidon-villes*, provides a similar contrast to the modern towns with which they are loosely linked.   The different cultures of the colonial powers give a different quality to African urbanism, so that one may experience Europe in Africa.   Added to this is the diversity of African cultures, and the possibility of studying the interaction between a particular European society and varied African societies, or varied European societies and the same African society, as, for example, where an African kingdom has been partitioned between two colonial powers.   In many areas there is a wide gulf separating the rural and urban populations, so that urbanisation takes on some of the aspects of immigration.

In race relations, the varied contexts of domination provide rich comparative material on the role of economic factors, systems of government and numbers. Cyclical theories of race relations may here be tested, as may typologies, such as the paternalist and competitive outlined by van den Berghe (1958; 1960), who offers the interesting thesis that social distance tends to be maintained by etiquette under paternalism and by segregation in competitive systems.   The change from subordination to domination, and the corresponding changes in racial attitudes, should yield new insights into the dynamic aspects of race relations and raise new questions about them.   Under certain conditions, the *mores* of the whites, far from being 'deep seated' and rigid, may be highly responsive to changes in the distribution of power, and presumably African racial *mores* may show equal versatility.   As Africans rise rapidly, through a process of racial capillarity, into the vacuum created by the sudden removal of white overlords, is there a tendency to reproduce the racial relations of their former masters or to transform them into class relations with their own people, or to seek the assuaging of past humiliation in a heightened racial intolerance, or to extract from their own suffering more humane patterns of race relations?   Is the extreme racial intolerance of the Afrikaners in South Africa a characteristic of the early stages of emancipation and likely to be reproduced throughout Africa, or is it to be attributed to special circumstances in their social situation?

Some of the unresolved problems of the influence of the religious ethic on race relations may be pursued further.   Actually the basic problem is that of the inter-action of religious and other systems, involving not only the influence of the religious ethic on race relations, but also changes in the religious ethic promoted by the structure of race relations.   There are many mechanisms for reconciling Christianity with race prejudice and race domination, whilst leaving the religious ethic intact, or for modifying the ethic in terms of the political interests of its carriers.   This is not to deny that the religious conscience may transcend social and material conditions and act as an independent factor in race relations, but merely to suggest that, by and large, material interests are a guide to certain expressions of the religious ethic in racially dominated societies.   The relationship between racial interests on the one hand and religious doctrines and organisation on the other has been analysed to some extent in the case of African independent churches — Ethiopian, Zionist and Prophetic — but hardly in the case of the white settler church.   The latter may more or less reproduce the structure of the political system and the same political processes, as is seen, for example, in the device of a junior partnership when the African majority makes a bid for positions of church leadership reserved for whites.   Separatism and syncretism are not exclusively manifestations of the religious movements of subordinate groups.   In the case of the Dutch Reformed

Churches of South Africa — relatively pure types of white settler church — there are trends towards separatism, manifested in increasing detachment from the world community of churches, and towards syncretism in the fusion of Christian ethic with traditional racial beliefs.

The process of restratification, started by colonial domination, industrialisation and urbanisation, continues within the context of nationalism and political independence. The values of traditional societies and of modern Western societies interact. They vary in the emphasis given to particular personal criteria, such as ties of blood and locality, and to universal impersonal criteria, such as qualification and contract, and they vary in their definition of the situations in which particular or universal criteria are perceived as relevant. There are problems of the persistence of traditional bases of association, for example through tribal identification in the towns, and their replacement or modification by new bases of association, class, race, common subordination, religious affiliation, urban residence and purposive voluntary association: problems, that is to say, of old and new bases of cleavage and integration, conflict and consensus. Traditional bonds may seem to have been replaced or to have weakened, when they are only latent and renew themselves under changed conditions. Thus, tribal loyalties may be submerged in national independence movements but become a source of cleavage in the post-independence period, so that analysis should be directed to the conditions which influence persistence or transformation.

Research in Africa provides the opportunity to test theories based on other social contexts and to gain fresh perspectives in the discovery of new societies. In his introduction to *The Politics of the Developing Areas*, the political scientist G. A. Almond (1960) deals with the need to revise concepts derived from a limited sector of experience, primarily in modern complex Western states with differentiated political systems. He attempts to provide a framework for the analysis of political systems differing radically in scale, structure and culture, including societies in which the political structures are intermittent and relatively undifferentiated. In the process, he suggests that the interests of comparative political analysis are served better by a functional than by a structural approach. He rejects the distinction between 'state' and 'non-state' primitive societies: a distinction also under criticism by anthropologists. He questions 'polar' descriptions of society in terms of universalism, achievement and specificity on the one hand, and particularism, ascription and diffuseness on the other, arguing in favour of a cultural 'dualism', that is to say, the mixture of these characteristics in both Western and traditional societies. This again is an argument known to sociologists. But the point is that, for purposes of comparative analysis, the political scientist is obliged to sharpen the concepts provided not only by his own discipline but also by related disciplines, to raise critical questions in regard to accepted theory, and to dissolve the boundaries between the disciplines themselves. He thus tries to effect some integration of political, anthropological and sociological thought.

There is a powerful stimulus for interdisciplinary research in Africa and much convergence of interest among social scientists. Indeed, other academicians are currently laying the basis for the sociological exploration of Africa. The interests of the geographer overlap those of the sociologist, while the interests of the anthropologist are theoretically much the same, the differences lying mainly in the fields and methods of study. In Africa, anthropologists have extended their research into the cities, generally the preserve of the sociologist; presumably under the impact of urbanisation and migrant labour, the traditional societies can hardly be conceived as complete entities.   In their approach to urban sociology, however, their point of reference has tended to be the traditional society, and hence they have interested themselves in such aspects as the migrant worker in the town, detribalisation, stabilisation, family 'disorganisation', and tribal bases of urban association. The sociologist would tend to take the urban structures as far as possible in their own right, though this can hardly be claimed as the specifically sociological approach in contrast to the anthropological.   The anthropologist Max Gluckman (1961: 69), attacking the 'tribalistic' tradition in urban African anthropology, argues for an approach to 'Africans in urban areas as acting primarily within a field whose structure is determined by the urban, industrial setting'.   And the political scientist Thomas Hodgkin (1957: 63) attempts to balance the two viewpoints when he writes:

> The point is often made that the new towns of Africa act as solvents, weakening traditional social ties and loosening the hold of traditional beliefs and values.   This is partly true: but the positive function of towns is no less important . . . African towns have this twofold aspect: seen from one standpoint, they lead to a degradation of African civilisation and ethic; seen from another, they contain the germs of a new, more interesting and diversified, civilisation, with possibilities of greater liberty.

Political scientists have added their valuable contribution to the sociological exploration of Africa.   Hodgkin comments that his book on nationalism is a study in politics, not in sociology.   Yet it is also a study in sociology, with discussion of the new towns, new associations and new social strata.   The emphasis is on the role of these new structures in the development of African nationalism, and the need for their analysis arises in part from Hodgkin's concept of nationalism, which he defines broadly to include any organisation or group that explicitly asserts the rights, claims and aspirations of a given African society in opposition to European authority, whatever its institutional forms and objectives.   In 'The Politics of Sub-Saharan Africa', James Coleman (1960) draws a series of systematic hypotheses as to the social consequences of different patterns of urbanisation, economic development, religious affiliation and educational policy: all topics of interest to sociologists.

This convergence between sociology and political science is a reflection in part of a trend in political science away from legal, formal and normative interests towards an integrated approach, involving analysis of the psychological and sociological dimensions of political behaviour.   It is also a reflection of the African situation.   Under conditions of rapid change involving societies not highly differentiated, the boundaries are less easily drawn between institutions, and there may be much overlapping and ready interchange of functions between social structures.   Thus a lineage, in which membership is defined by birth, may take on some of the forms of a voluntary association, and fulfil some of the functions of a political party branch; or religious 'extremism', instead of being an alternative form for political 'extremism', may be its actual vehicle.   The political consequences of the colonial situation, the reaction of nationalism, and the politics of independence cannot be understood without analysis of the changing structures and cultures of the society.

Against this background of interest and challenge, it is perhaps surprising that sociologists should have held aloof from research in Africa. The colonial era, now virtually closed, attracted little professional attention from them. The reason cannot be an aversion for area studies, since much of sociology consists of area studies, though in the sociologist's homeland. Nor can it be an aversion for description or pure empiricism, which abound in sociological literature; in any event, theoretical interests can be pursued in 'underdeveloped' areas as well as in 'overdeveloped' areas. Perhaps the explanation is quite mundane. Africa has few schools of sociology, and the indigenous research is negligible. Only the United States of America trains really large numbers of sociologists, sufficient for export, but there is a strong local demand for them. There is probably nothing intrinsic to the subject which would drive those who profess it to remote parts of the world, as is the case with the small band of anthropologists. Motivation and recruitment of sociologists may be a factor: in particular, the kindred subjects of anthropology and sociology perhaps draw their students from the same universe, with the more adventurous entering anthropology. Or the scientific emphasis in sociology, supported by the mechanisation of research, may give rise to anxiety as to the validity of findings in a situation where the infrastructures of community inventories, samples, censuses, basic research findings, and trained personnel are inadequate; underdeveloped areas may be regarded as more appropriate fields for less 'scientific' disciplines.

Certainly, the difficulties in the way of scientific research are considerable. The sociologist cannot easily play the role of research administrator and analyst; he is almost inevitably obliged to become a fieldworker. He may have to gather for himself background data of a type publicly available in Western industrialised countries and draw his own sample under conditions in which it is difficult to define the universe with any precision: as, for example, the highly mobile population of a chaotic and protean shanty town. If he wishes to analyse the milieu of an occupational category such as that of African clergymen, there will be few, if any, studies of the churches to which they belong, and the sociologist will be obliged to undertake a series of preliminary investigations into the history, structure and dogma of the churches: an immense task. The population itself is not yet trained and docile to his techniques, and group conflicts may affect rapport. Thus, when a social survey of Jinja, Uganda, was carried out in 1950–51, Africans and Indians, identifying the sociologists with government, projected on to the survey their different fears — that land might be taken away from Africans, or that special measures might be contemplated against Asians — while the dominant Europeans reacted often with surprise and sometimes with resentment at their inclusion in the study (C. and R. Sofer 1955). The tendency has been to study the subordinate groups, no doubt for reasons of interest in cultural difference, the needs of government and administration, and perhaps the tacit assumption that subjection to sociological investigation is a mark of subordinate status. Rounded studies of urban populations are very rare.

In most of the cities and towns of Africa, the sociologist normally will be confronted with great diversity: racial, tribal and cultural. This may present no great difficulty at the level of the purely descriptive survey. Where interest is in the structure of social relationships, however, and tribal and ethnic identities are a significant basis for association, the social scientist may feel the need for a knowledge of the social anthropology of an entire territory — as Banton (1957) seems to have found in his study of Freetown — and indeed of the overseas society of the colonial power. Moreover, the student cannot make the easy assumption that any strand he picks up will lead him to the core of the society: an assumption he might make in studies of small, homogeneous societies. There may be sharp cleavages, so that social relationships do not extend, or become highly attenuated, beyond the boundaries of tribally or ethnically defined groups. If the student favours the intensive analysis of social situations as a method of research, then he may need a representative sample of social situations. He is confronted, in other words, with the research problems of the plural society.

The sociologist's conditioning by his own training in a subject developed within the context of Western industrial society may introduce further difficulties. He is likely to perceive in categories structured by his discipline and his culture. No doubt it was part of the colonial situation that social science research should be carried out mostly by strangers belonging to the dominant or related societies, and the social investigation by strangers still largely persists. There is thus the challenge of enthnocentric perspectives. Much as the Portuguese or French, in their 'assimilado' or 'evolué' policies, were recognising themselves in the African and not any quality of African culture or personality, so too the social scientist may discover mostly himself, and not the new perspectives offered by the study of a strange society. The scholar's own society may serve him as the basic point of reference, more particularly because colonial domination has created phenomena which he knows well — industrialisation, occupational diversity and consequent differentiation in style of life — and because he can move readily from the familiar core, tracing similarities and dissimilarities.

There may be a temptation to frame problems in terms of specific Western developments, as, for example, in the series of studies into the African middle class, sponsored by the International Institute of Differing Civilisations (1956); or in such research hypotheses as that increasing industrialisation, urbanisation, wealth, literacy and mass communication will be associated with democratic forms of representation or with a competitive or participant society, as it is variously phrased. Nor are new perspectives necessarily introduced by indigenous social scientists, since they are also moulded in the Western tradition. The Egyptian sociologist El-Saaty (1957), for example, employs a demographic approach to social class in Egypt which offers essentially a perspective from the London School of Economics. And finally, rapid generalisations, inspired by the urgent need for an overall view of African developments, may shape perceptions and empirical findings rather than the reverse. The volume of available research on which generalisations can be based is small, and the generalisations usually bear the stamp of specialised knowledge of a particular area, which then bestrides Africa (as is no doubt the case in this present discussion). They are valuable in terms of broad perspectives and guides for research, but their effect, combined with cultural conditioning, may be to crystallise knowledge of Africa in premature patterns. Sometimes it seems as if the generalisations are carrying out their own research for the supporting evidence.

Certainly there are many difficulties in the study of the rapidly changing and little-known African societies. But there is also much to attract the sociologist. Chosen for discussion here, as of special interest, is the analysis of pluralism, which is so characteristic of most African societies. Attention will first be focused upon the nature of plural society, then on some manifestations of pluralism in the cities, and finally upon problems of cleavage and integration in terms of race, tribe, class and voluntary association.

II *THE PLURAL SOCIETY*

The concept of the plural society seems theoretically useful and stimulating. Almost all the societies in Africa were plural in the sense in which that term is used below.   The concept has reference to pronounced cleavages between social units. If the cleavages were complete, the social units would constitute distinct societies. A plural society thus implies that the units maintain at least a minimum of relations with each other, that there is a measure of integration, or binding together, even if mainly by governmental regulation and constraint.   Plural societies vary in the extent and nature of the cleavages, and in the mode of their integration.   Some are more plural than others.

In his essay on 'Social and Cultural Pluralism', M. G. Smith (1960) distinguishes the plural society from homogeneous and heterogeneous societies on the basis of the type of institutional participation.   In the socially and culturally homogeneous society, all the members share a single system of institutions; the heterogeneous society also has one basic institutional system, but it operates in a number of styles or with alternatives and specialities, while the plural society is marked by the coexistence of, and participation in, incompatible institutions. Smith restricts the concept to the situation in which a minority exercises domination over a society containing groups practising different and incompatible forms of institutional systems.   Since his definition of institution includes culture and structure, the practice of different institutional forms involves both cultural and social pluralism.   Smith points out that the groups themselves need not be distinguished by racial criteria, since there are racially diversified societies which are not plural, and plural societies in which the divisions are not racial : in other words, though modern plural societies by and large are multiracial, pluralism and multi-racialism vary independently.

Pluralism can be conceived as involving differentiation at three levels.   First, at the base, there are the units of cleavage however they may be defined (racial, tribal, ethnic as the case may be); then associated with these cleavages, there are cultural pluralism, or diversity in basic patterns of behaviour, and social pluralism, or separation in social organisation.   The South African government's policy of apartheid is a theoretical model of the principles of pluralism logically developed. All major aspects of life are regulated in terms of racial and tribal definition, and policy is directed at enhancing the cultural diversity of the racial and tribal groups, and at establishing social boundaries on the basis of race and tribe, so that social relationships are culturally, racially and tribally circumscribed.   Cleavage would be maintained and heightened by exclusive sentiments derived from the narrow social containment and cultural difference.   The power of the state would hold these segments together in separation, as would certain key institutions, such as Bantu Education and Bantu Authorities, which are tribal institutions created by whites and, at the same time, institutions of the white ruling bureaucracy.

The study of plural societies thus involves the study of the component units and their inter-relations.   Since there are sharp conflicts, the research worker may find difficulty in relating himself to the different units, and the research team is likely to become identified with the dominant section.   Because of discontinuities in values and in the chain of social relationships, the use of accepted techniques may raise problems. Smith (1960) suggests that assumptions of cultural unity underlie the community study and sampling techniques. Gluckman's (1961) proposal, that the specifically anthropological contribution to urban sociology should be the interpretation of detailed records of complex social situations, would seem valuable provided selection is made on the basis of a general knowledge of the structure of the groups within the city and their inter-relations. So, too, the intensive analysis of a network of social relationships will certainly contribute to knowledge of urban African life, but it may only be knowledge of a fragment in the mosaic. The very fact of pluralism implies discontinuities in social relationships, and hence imposes the need for more extensive study on the basis of which a series of networks might be selected.

Cultural and social pluralism are never complete. Smith (1960: 772) writes that even in a plural society, institutional diversity does not include differing systems of government. 'Given the fundamental differences of belief, value, and organization that connote pluralism, the monopoly of power by one cultural section is the essential precondition for the maintenance of the total society in its current form.' He comments also that it sometimes happens that some members of different cultural sections associate more regularly with one another than with the sections to which they belong, in which case the social and cultural sections have somewhat different boundaries, and their margins may be dynamic. Plural societies are held together not only by force and regulation. Inevitably there are interdependence, transcending the basic divisions, and some bonds of cultural homogeneity and common association. In the very process of establishing the plural society, sections draw together culturally and socially, either formally or informally. The culture of the dominant group is modified and acquired in varying degrees by the subordinate groups, and many stable relationships develop across the group barriers. Cross-pressures, conflicts of loyalty, and some common values offer a counterpoise to the cleavages. Mitchell (1960: 28) regards 'the relative lack of counterbalancing cleavages across the component ethnic groups as one of the significant features of the plural society'. This would seem the accurate description: the 'relative lack' rather than the complete absence. And he distinguishes the 'unitary' from the plural in terms of common rituals and common values.

For analytical purposes it is useful to separate the social and cultural aspects of pluralism and to analyse their inter-relations. Some of the acute conflicts in colonial society arise precisely from an imbalance between these elements, as for example, social rejection by the white group of educated Westernised Africans: a situation of cultural similarity or homogeneity and social pluralism. Of course, this type of tension is not specific to plural societies but also characterises class societies. The reverse situation, of common association and social mobility in a context of cultural pluralism, is likely to be a major source of conflict in the early phases of independence.

Plural societies have still to be analysed and classified. In Africa they were almost entirely of a type involving what Balandier (1955a) describes as the 'colonial situation', referring to a complex of conditions: domination imposed by a foreign minority of different race and culture over an indigenous majority; justification of domination in terms of racial (or ethnic) and cultural superiority; a relationship between heterogeneous civilisations of contrasted rhythms, economic thrust, material development and religion; antagonism resulting from the instrumental role of the colonised society; and the need for the colonisers to rely not only on force but on a combination of rationalisations and stereotyped behaviour.   He emphasises an approach to the 'colonial situation' as a system and to the colony as a global society, inter-relating colonisers and colonised; he criticises anthropological studies of indigenous societies in abstraction from the colonial context as involving a partial approach.   In much the same vein as Gluckman, and from the point of view of comprehensive interpretation in the context of historical change, he also suggests the desirability of studying 'crisis' situations involving a challenge to domination.

Considering the great variability of the elements in the colonial situation, it is remarkable how many uniform consequences have been reported.   The variations seem almost infinite.   There are the variations in the traditional societies — scale, degree of centralisation, system of stratification, mode of subsistence — all of which may be expected to produce varied consequences.   Then there are the variations in the contact situation — whether initiated by missionaries or traders, established by treaty or conquest, how affected by particular events and the historic developments specific to given areas.   Added to these are the differences between the metropolitan colonial powers and in their policies: direct or indirect rule, assimilation or ultimate transfer of power, economic rather than political development, and so on.   Since the elements are inter-related in particular colonial situations, it would seem improbable that even the same strand, such as French assimilationist policy, could promote the same reaction, say a concern with *négritude*, in different territories.   Colonial policies are variables in the situation, not determinants. One has only to observe the many patterns of response to evangelisation by a single missionary among the members of a single tribal group to be on guard against generalisations about the colonial situations of Africa.   Yet the testimony as to uniformities can hardly be doubted.   Knowledge of one colonial situation is in some measure an introduction to colonial society.   And a major task of sociological research in Africa is to sift the generalisations and to establish valid propositions in regard to colonial interaction and the conditions and modes of variation.

     White settler society is often mentioned as a specific type of plural society in Africa.   The line between the colonial and white settler situations, however, should not be drawn too sharply.   Algeria combined a numerous and tenacious white settler minority with colonial status, while independent South Africa, with the largest white settler population on the continent, seeks to create through its policies of Bantustans and indirect rule what is virtually a colonial situation. Wallerstein's (1961: 31) definition of the colonial situation as the imposition by strangers of a new and increasingly pervasive government institution applies equally to white settler society.   And similar social phenomena may be found.   Jahoda (1961: 54–6), in his analysis of the attitudes of Africans to Europeans in Ghana during the transitional period before independence, reports hostile verbal responses not unlike those which might have been given by Africans under the South African system of apartheid; for example, the following categories of reply to the question how whites feel about Africans (given by four-fifths of the informants): 'animals, not human'; 'inferior, to be looked down on, not respected'; 'low, stupid, backward'; 'slaves, here to serve them, to be kept down'; and 'they dislike us, don't mean well, just pretend to be nice'.   It is important, however, to distinguish white settler society from colonial societies as involving greater interaction and interdependence between the racial groups, with more social relationships across racial divisions and hence competing loyalties and cross-pressures; sharper conflict as a result of the closer relationship, the immediacy of the involvement, and the threat to many small vested interests; the obsessive quality of race conflict; and finally the absence of a directing external colonial power.

Plural societies are in constant danger of splitting asunder or they are threatened by revolutionary change. John Rex (1959: 116), discussing 'The Plural Society in Sociological Theory', refers to Furnivall's (1948) four 'resolutions' of the plural society to be found in Indonesian history, namely: Caste, The Rule of Law, Nationalist Democracy and Federalism. Presumably Caste and Federalism involve a balancing of the plural and unitary principles, while the Rule of Law and Nationalist Democracy involve a strengthening of the unitary principle by the introduction of common norms and of common loyalty and involvement (though nationalism can be a particularly threatening situation for plural societies). Totalitarian trends in plural societies, as elsewhere, express attempts by one segment to impose its rule on the plurality; but perhaps plural societies, because of the greater threat of disruptive conflicts, or because of the sharp antagonisms between segments, are more prone to 'totalitarian' forms of government.

III   THE URBAN CONTEXT OF PLURALISM

Pluralism is strongly manifested in the cities of Africa, and its characteristics may, with advantage, be studied there. The cities of Africa also offer scope for testing the findings of urban sociology which have been developed largely in the context of the Western industrial city.

Though sociologists are careful to distinguish between ideal types and empirical realities, there does seem to have been some confounding of the two in urban sociology, and an abstract model of the Western industrial city has tended to become descriptive of all cities. An article by Louis Wirth exercised considerable influence on sociological thought. He defined a city, for sociological purposes, as a relatively large, dense and permanent settlement of heterogeneous individuals, and derived from these characteristics the distinctive features of the urban way of life.

> Large numbers account for individual variability, the relative absence of intimate personal acquaintanceship, the segmentalization of human relations which are largely anonymous, superficial and transitory, and associated characteristics. Density involves diversification and specialization, the coincidence of close physical contact and distant social relations, glaring contrasts, a complex pattern of segregation, the predominance of formal social control, and accentuated friction, among other phenomena. Heterogeneity tends to break down rigid social structures and to produce increased mobility, instability, and insecurity, and the affiliation of the individuals with a variety of intersecting and tangential social groups with a high rate of membership turnover (Wirth 1938: 1).

Urbanism is basically conceived by Wirth (1938: 20–1) in the familiar terms of classical sociological theory as Gesellschaft, or organic solidarity, or the prevalence of secondary structures. He writes: 'The distinctive features of the urban mode of life have often been described sociologically as consisting of the substitution of secondary for primary contacts, the weakening of bonds of kinship, and the declining social significance of the family, the disappearance of the neighbourhood, and the undermining of the traditional basis of social solidarity. All these phenomena can be substantially verified through objective indices.'

This conception of urbanism is now being subjected to critical testing. Demonstrations of the strength of family ties in the city of London, for example, give a new perspective of the relations between primary and secondary structures in cities. And revision is likely to be in the direction, first, of greater emphasis on the role of primary groups and of diffuse personal relationships, and second, of distinctions between different types of urbanism or of cities. Certainly very different modes of life may be associated with large numbers of heterogeneous people living close together, as is shown strikingly in the new and the old cities of Africa. The concept of heterogeneity itself causes some difficulty. Bascom (1955) raises a question as to what diversity constitutes heterogeneity. He establishes a high degree of urbanisation among the Yoruba, shows that urbanisation is a traditional pattern and not an outgrowth of European acculturation, and demonstrates the importance of kinship ties, lineage, clan, in the organisation of urban life. Ethnically the inhabitants are homogeneous, but they are diversified in terms of specialisation and social strata. Is this heterogeneity? Probably there is nothing to be gained by giving a precise measure of heterogeneity. And in any event, is it to be defined objectively from the outside by the sociologist, or is it to be defined in terms of the subjective reactions of the urban dwellers themselves? And is it to be regarded as a constant or relative to particular situations? At one level, tribal groups may be sharply differentiated, and at another, they may be drawn together.

Sjoberg (1955) distinguishes between the industrial and the pre-industrial city, terms which suggest that the process of evolution is towards the industrial city and that the key variable is industrialisation, as he makes quite explicit. The essence of the distinction is the use of inanimate sources of power in the industrial city and of animate sources in the pre-industrial. Each, the inanimate and animate, has its characteristic forms. The inanimate is associated with extensive industrialisation, rationality and centralisation; economic recruitment and a system of mass education emphasise universalism rather than particularism; the class system stresses achievement rather than ascription; the kinship system is small and flexible. This is more or less similar to *Gesellschaft*, the complex of 'secondary traits', but this time as a characteristic of industrialism, not urbanism, since the 'animated' pre-industrial city has quite different forms, as demonstrated in the work of Roger Le Tourneau (1949, 1957, 1961) on the traditional towns and cities of North Africa.

Le Tourneau shows how the ground plan of the city reflects the values of its townsmen and the principles of its organisation: the main mosque and the most important shops are always in the centre, and sometimes also the abode of the prince or his delegate, representing the three pillars of the Muslim city of North Africa: business, spirituality and authority (where it is the case). The urban way of life is sacred, not secular; urbanism is informed by the religious ethic of Islam, and its rhythm is regulated by the rhythm of prayer and sacred festival. The term *industrial* can hardly be denied some of the large cities such as Tunis and Fez, in which almost half the population lived from industrial occupations, even if it was 'animated' industry, or handicraft industry, organised into guilds. The scale of organisation might be considerable. Thus in Fez, in the sixteenth century, there were more than 500 ateliers of weavers, employing up to 20,000 persons. The basis of social organisation here is not the atomised individual, the largely anonymous, superficial and transitory relationship, the specialised interest group, and the formal system of control. The units are social groups: cells of 'tenacious particularism' defined by religion — with separation of Muslims, Christians and Jews — ethnic origin, guild or occupational corporation, and quarters (distinguished both technically, in terms of the type of life led there, and ethnically, in terms of the origins of the inhabitants). The relative lack of public buildings and civic centres in the ground plan and of common civic organisation in the social plan reflects partly a tradition different from that of the Greek and Roman civilisations, which emphasised the expanding development of municipal life, and partly an organisation based on the particularism of different cells. The quarters could be more or less self-contained and regulated on the pattern of small-scale societies, with close mutual acquaintance of the members.

The persistent force of origins is remarkable. The Muslim towns do not seem to have acted as a 'melting pot' of ethnic diversity, or at any rate certain diversities have resisted fusion for long periods. Le Tourneau (1957: 27–33) describes the ethnic ties among the Berbers, the solidarity of political refugees (Tunisian families of Andalusian origin, for example, still subtly distinguished after three centuries), and groupings with reference to origin beneath the apparent unity of the old citizens, as for example families of the old Turkish aristocracy, or the Kulughli, descendants of the Turks and women of the country. The bonds of sentiment and association in these groupings by origin may be reinforced by a preference for particular occupations. There are thus convergences in ethnic, religious and occupational background, and in grouping by residence and association. Nevertheless, citizenship provides a strong countervailing bond to social and cultural pluralism, and probably the cultural differences are less marked than in many of the cities of sub-Saharan Africa.

The contrast between these societies and the sociological image of the city is sharp. Clearly the typology of cities must include also the non-industrial, or pre-industrial or handicraft industrial. Aidan Southall (1961), dealing with sub-Saharan Africa, distinguishes between the old-established, slowly growing towns, and the new towns with populations of mushroom growth. His distinctions are at a middle level, not in terms of abstract poles of *Gemeinschaft* and *Gesellschaft*, but close to description and empirical research. This is probably a valuable emphasis which may counter the too rapid filing of societies in convenient pigeon-holes. The old towns are characterised by a more or less indigenous population-core of considerable homogeneity; predominantly clerical and commercial occupations rather than industrial, with some contribution from subsistence agriculture; numerous independent entrepreneurs and small working groups; uncontrolled residential patterns; permissive housing policies; and sufficient flexibility for some tribal or kinship concentration. New towns are characterised in the extreme case by a totally immigrant African population; close administrative control which appears to the immigrants to be exercised entirely by a dominant ethnic group of foreign origin and markedly different race; an occupational structure based on clear distinctions between clerical, skilled and unskilled workers, dominated by relatively few but large foreign organisations, and virtually excluding the subsistence basis of rural life; and by controlled housing and difficulties in the way of tribal and kinship concentration. Some centres, Southall comments, conform closely to one or other of the types outlined, but most probably show mixed features. Daryll Forde, in an earlier work (UNESCO 1956: 49) suggested that a relatively complex typology and a series of scales were needed for the sociological analysis of industrial activity and urban life in Africa, so as to take into account such variables as intensity of migration and degree of inter-racial, occupational and cultural complexity and of group solidarity.

The study of the traditional cities of Africa — the old towns — should be specially significant for urban sociological theory. Some combine large numbers, dense settlement and relative heterogeneity with forms of urbanism different from those described by Wirth and often regarded as characteristic of cities. Wirth's paper does not give any precise measure of the size, density or heterogeneity which define the city. But clearly, large numbers are compatible with considerable kinship concentration and primary relationships; density is only one of the influences towards differentiation and specialisation; and heterogeneity may be a basis for tribal, racial and occupational grouping and not necessarily a stimulus towards mobility and fusion. It would seem that some of the accepted characteristics of the urban way of life may be partly consequences of large-scale industrialisation, and partly an expression of certain common elements in Western culture.

The continuous observation of traditional African cities in process of change may help to define the social consequences of industrialisation as distinct from the consequences implicit in dense concentrations of large numbers. It may yield insight into the viability of such particularist ties as extended kinship or tribe, and into the compatibility of primary relationships and pervasive religious sanctions with industrial urban life. These problems may also be analysed in the context of the new cities of Africa, and it is particularly in the new cities that the plural aspects of African societies and the attendant problems of cleavage and integration are most sharply presented.

IV   CLEAVAGE AND INTEGRATION

The problem of cleavage and integration, in the context of the new cities of Africa, may be conceived in terms of the extent to which tribe and race, as bases of cleavage, are counteracted by, or dissolved in, urban forms of association promoted by common interests — class, political, religious and educational; or in terms of the extent to which urban forms of association reinforce racial and tribal cleavage.

1.   TRIBAL OR ETHNIC CLEAVAGE AND INTEGRATION

Tribe and Race are (or were) primary bases of pluralism in most of the societies of Africa. The two interact, exerting a reciprocal influence on each other. Thus, in the colonial situation, the policies of the colonial power may have been directed towards assimilation and hence, theoretically, to the ultimate fusion of tribal and racial groups; or towards the maintenance of the tribal unit, through such mechanisms as indirect rule, segregation of tribal groups in the work and urban situation, and support of the tribal authorities. This does not imply any necessary coincidence between the direction of colonial policy and its results. Support for the tribal authorities and their incorporation into the colonial system of government may serve to undermine the tribal authority, and the very imposition of tribal categories of organisation by a foreign dominating minority may provoke an opposite reaction. Moreover, the needs of the colonial society in education, administration, commerce and industry provide other bases of association than the tribal, whatever the policy, while a common subordination may link tribes together or accentuate the divisions between them.

The effects of a common subordination and hostility are related in a complex way with the total situation, as Georg Simmel has shown in his essays on Domination and Subordination, and on Conflict. Prior to independence, the hostility tribesmen felt for their Western overlords must have been great enough to overcome any repugnance for each other and, in many areas, a united front must have been perceived as offering better prospects of power than tribal division. With independence, or for that matter on the threshold of independence, neither of these conditions necessarily applies, and one of the major problems in many of the new states is the maintenance of a unity temporarily achieved under quite different conditions, or the establishment in other ways of viable relationships between the tribal groups. The tribally based conflicts for power and the varied political solutions attempted provide valuable data for the analysis of the social processes of cleavage and integration.

In a somewhat different form, the same processes may be observed within the Indian community of South Africa. Caste divisions could hardly be maintained, and some of their functions are fulfilled by cultural and linguistic divisions, which are now the main endogamous units. In this respect, there are unifying tendencies at work. But they have not been strengthened, as one might have expected, by the deterioration of Indian rights under apartheid. On the contrary, the divisions between the linguistic and cultural groups, and between Hindu and Muslim, seem if anything more sharp, partly no doubt in consequence of the establishment of the states of Pakistan and Andhra, and a corresponding feeling of separate identities in the South African Indian population. Added to these divisions are fundamental political cleavages, partly class based, between those whose response to a common subordination is to identify with Africans and Coloureds (Eur-Africans) and those who seek alignment with the dominant white group. Thus while the Indian community is drawing closer to other groups within the society, intense discrimination and common subordination within the Indian community itself foster disunity. Perhaps marginal groups are more likely to break apart under pressure.

In their interpretation of exclusive modes of social organisation, Marxists seek out the material interests conserved by these forms. This is certainly a most valuable key to the analysis of the colonial situation. Furnivall (1948: 312) suggests that there is a more complete expression of the capitalist spirit and structure in the colonies than in the capitalist countries. But there are some aspects of tribal sentiment and identification and of the persistence of tribe as a basis of urban organisation which cannot be explained by class interest theory.

Anthropologists have been particularly interested in urban tribalism and three recent studies by Epstein (1958), Banton (1957) and Mayer (1961) illuminate different aspects of it. The urban settings are strongly contrasted. The Copperbelt Town (Epstein) and West African City (Banton) have a great variety of tribal groups, and the latter also a Creole population, while in the South African Town (Mayer) the tribesmen belong predominantly to the Xhosa-speaking group. Both East London and Luanshya are (were) in settler dominated territories, with appreciable industrialisation, while Sierra Leone was not far from achieving independence at the time Banton carried out his study and the territory is little industrialised.

Epstein's study provides a corrective for the point of view that tribalism is a unitary phenomenon, in the sense that tribal loyalties act with the same strength over the total field of social relations in which the urban African is involved. He emphasises instead the principle of situational selection as operating within a developing system marked by the continuing conflict of different principles of social organisation. Presumably situational selection is a general characteristic of all societies, and not a new principle of behaviour evolved by Africans in a Copper-belt town. The change is rather that in particular situations, such as work on the mine, and their relations to white people, Africans have developed new forms of leadership and organisation, while in domestic situations there is a greater tendency to associate on the basis of tribal affinity and tribal custom. As Mayer points out, the antithesis of 'urban-tribal' is developed in terms of situations or sets of relations, rather than in terms of people.

Mayer deals with the tribesmen as people, analysing the structural aspects, in which he studies the town- or country-rootedness of the individual through his network of social relationships, and the cultural aspects, again town or country, as reflected in domestic, kinship and leisure life, and selected values. He explains that there are no different tribes to be transcended, for almost all the large labour force is drawn from the solidly Xhosa-speaking Reserves in the hinterland, and he directs his analysis to the 'sealed-off' areas of intimate life and leisure. Of the work situation he writes (p. xiv): 'Rather than form important new relations at work, the East London workers might be said merely to undergo common experiences there. If they are conscious of common interests they do not express these, except verbally.' And he excludes trade union and political life as evoking little participation. In other words, Mayer excludes those areas in which, in other situations, one would expect to find non-tribal bases of association and non-tribal modes of behaviour more highly developed. The significance of the study lies in a different aspect, however, not simply in situational selection in terms of tribal or urban norms, nor in the substitution of non-tribal for tribal forms of association, but in the persistence of distinctive and contrasted patterns, the 'Red' and the 'School', rooted in the rural societies themselves, and carried over into the town. The contrast is in terms of culture contact: the School groups opened themselves to Christianity and Westernisation, while the Red groups are traditional and conservative. Some migrants, particularly the Red, have resisted urbanisation, whether in structural or cultural terms, even after long periods of urban residence. In other words the cleavages are within the tribe itself, representing different cultural responses to the long periods of war with the white settlers, and encouraging or inhibiting integration in the wider community.

Banton (1957), in his study of a West African city, deals with a relatively recent migration of a variety of tribesmen to the small commercial and administrative centre of Freetown. The account is interesting for its portrayal of persistent and voluntary tribal grouping in the town. Social and cultural cleavages reinforce tribal sentiment and encourage the persistence of tribal groupings. No very clear measures of these cleavages are available. Thus an index of tribal residential segregation is not provided, but there appear to be substantial tribal concentrations. So too — at any rate for certain of the tribes — there is an occupational specialisation. Tribal affiliation and sentiment are strengthened by such structures as tribal headmen, mosques, schools, officials, associations. Again, the balance between the separate structures and the urban integrative is not easily drawn. Banton comments that Freetown has a relative unity, a character that the newcomer has to accept; that the very heterogeneity of tribesmen encourages the growth of mutual understanding, for where there are numerous small groups there is not the tension created by competition between two or three big units; that the European observer may be struck most by the relative weakness of communal as opposed to sectional interests; but that comparison should be made with other African cities (Chapter 5).

In any event the tribe emerges as a basis for urban grouping. It is no doubt for this reason that Banton poses the phenomenon of migration in terms of the adaptation of the tribal system. The issue is not simply that tribesmen come into the town with certain ideas about the ordering of social life and attempt to establish in the towns the familiar social patterns, but rather that they either bring with them a social system or attempt to recreate a social system. Banton distinguishes the integrative problem and the adaptive problem. The integrative problem is that of urban institutions satisfying particular needs and reintegrating the life of immigrants round non-tribal foci, as a result of which the tribal system tends to become a secondary system and may dissolve. The adaptive problem is that of the tribal social system maintaining its distinctive character while adapting its institutions to the demands of the new urban environment (as the Temne did through modernised voluntary associations). Banton's emphasis on the adaptation of the tribal system is unusual, since the more general assumption is that the tribal system cannot be recreated in, or adapted to, the towns and that it merely stamps the migrant with tendencies towards tribally exclusive association and other tribally distinctive behaviour. Presumably Banton was led to this approach by the strength of tribal pluralism in Freetown, though he does write (p. 134) that 'differences between tribes, especially jealousy of one another, are strong enough to inhibit common action in many matters, yet the consciousness of common descent in the case of a single tribe is not so strong as to form a really effective basis of organisation in the urban milieu'. He also confirms Balandier's comment that 'tribal kinship is a factor more effective in rejecting the stranger than in stimulating the organisation of a grouping; it operates more on the level of sociability than on the level of social structure'.

Among the supports of tribal cleavage in the town were: first, the custom of appointing tribal headmen (this is perhaps a recognised pattern since Banton reports, for example, that in the 1850s the Fula, Mandinka and Serakule elected a joint headman, because they wanted to have someone with authority to arrange for the reception of trading caravans); second, the building of tribal structures round this initial nucleus; third, the character of the town, based on government administration, the port, rather minor commerce and small working groups (a character which stands in contrast to the monolithic structure of the mining company on the Rhodesian Copperbelt); and fourth, the role of the Creoles, rejecting the tribesmen, preserving their own privileges, and monopolising municipal government (although this might be expected to unite the tribesmen in opposition to Creole privilege). Of the integrative factors — class and religion — Banton writes that the pattern of stratification is changing from one in which closed ethnic classes were ordered hierarchically to one showing a series of economic strata of uneven thickness split by several vertical faults which follow ethnic lines; and he comments on Islam, that the more any two tribes are Islamised, the less is the likelihood of any antagonism arising between them.

2. RACE

In the past, racial domination was virtually ubiquitous in the plural societies of Africa. The Asio-African Conference at Bandung in April 1955, declared that over and above the questions of colonialism and political liberty, 'we are all interested in racial equality . . . the touchstone for those who are here assembled and the people they represent. There has not been, nor is there now any Western colonial regime, although they differ in their systems and methods, that has not inflicted, on a larger or lesser scale, on the population they dominate the doctrine of their racial inferiority' (International Institute of Differing Civilisations 1957: 498). The sociological interest lies in the consequences for race relations of the interaction of these varied systems of domination with tribal groups of varied culture and structure, under different conditions of economic development, and at different stages in the period from contact to independence. It is conceivable that there are broad regularities in white African race relations, and that the colonial policies — assimilationist or separatist — and the character of the rulers — white migrant bureaucrats or white settlers — are less crucial variables than they would appear. There are, however, few studies of race relations on which to base generalisations, and there is a great need for more precise information. The sociological contribution might be focused at the level of institutions and structures and take the form for the most part of intensive studies rather than broad surveys.

In the field of religion, the African independent churches have attracted particular attention, no doubt because they are exotic and dramatically express tensions and crises of race relations. Hodgkin (1957: 94) comments that in Moslem, as in Christian Africa, religious dissent and political radicalism are often closely related. This relationship is not a peculiarity of African societies. 'The tradition whereby Christian institutions and symbols serve as a form through which men can express their aspirations for social and political change is as ancient as the Church itself.' Nor is separatism necessarily associated with political radicalism: it may express itself in quietism; nor is it necessarily anti-white (Hodgkin 1957: Chapter 3). Wallerstein (1961: 51) links the nativistic, revivalistic and syncretistic movements, quite often clothed in religious garb (such as Kitiwala, Kimbanguism, Alice cult, Mau Mau), with the denial of political expression. 'Where no political outlets for grievances were permitted, at least to the small elite, they or their followers often turned to pseudo-traditional patterns which were, on the one hand, more familiar and easy to handle, and on the other hand, could appeal to a legitimation which even colonial rulers accepted to some extent: religious freedom. In short, political protest did not always or necessarily take a political form.' There are many possible relationships. It might be interesting to test the hypothesis of an inverse relationship between radical political movements and radical or chiliastic religious ethics — a relationship suggested by Lipset (1960) — or between freedom of political association and religious 'separatism'.

Sundkler (1958, 1961), in his study of the African independent churches in South Africa, describes 'separatism' as the African Christian's reaction to racial discrimination in church and state, and links its 'explosive development' with the crisis of the Natives Land Act of 1913, and with the quest for living space and security in terms of ownership of a piece of land. The Ethiopian-type church, with its reaction against white domination in the mission churches, presents an ambivalence: the rejection of the white mission's conquest of the African peoples on the one hand, and a church organisation and bible interpretation largely modelled on the parent (conquering) white churches on the other.

The Zionist and Messianic movements are more consistent: they combine Christian with traditional belief, and they express theologically the reaction against racial discrimination in such doctrines as a reversed colour bar in heaven or identification with the Israelites in their struggle against the land-possessing Philistines and Midianites.   Sundkler comments that the history of native policy was woven into the apocalyptic patterns of Zionist or Bantu Messianic myths.   The difference between the Zionist and Messianic movements revolves round the answers they give to the question: 'Who stands at the Gate? . . .   Is it Jesus Christ of the Scriptures, or is it the Bantu Messiah in the person of Shembe, Khambule, Lekganyane or John Masowe, or some other prophet?'   And the answers are essentially theological solutions to problems of race relations.   At present, Sundkler suggests, there is a trend towards accommodation in education and medicine and government. Hence there is an apparent convergence of interest between some of the prophets of the independent churches and the prophets of apartheid.   The independent churches give spiritual sanction for racial cleavage, either explicitly or implicitly.

There is a need for similar studies of the mission and white settler churches, for objective analysis of their organisation, ritual and dogma as part of a system of race relations within a plural society.   Beliefs may reveal syncretisms of European theologies and white settler *mores*; organisation may reproduce in microcosm the structure of the wider society, or in some respects its antithesis.   The churches may sustain, or they may sometimes contravene, racial domination.   They may integrate the races at different levels of social distance: the maximum perhaps where integration is only at the level of the brotherhood of man, and the minimum perhaps at the level of common worship and communion.   Organisation and theological interpretations, furthermore, may be found to vary in response to changes in the distribution of power between the races.   Inevitably Africans assess the role of the white-dominated churches sometimes with disillusionment and rejection not merely of particular representatives of Christianity but of Christianity itself.   Religious change under independence should illuminate some of the transient relations between power and spirit.

Because of its significance in the colonial situation and under independence, the role of education has attracted particular attention.   That educated Africans tended to pre-empt leadership and to subvert white domination is well established. Much as Marx conceived that capitalism contained within itself the seeds of its own destruction and indeed its own executioners, so too the colonial powers in their need for educated indigenes, are regarded as having nurtured the revolutionary agents of their overthrow.   This colonial 'radicalism' of the African intellectuals is interpreted as a reaction to status deprivation.   They are denied the recognition accorded comparable achievements by members of the white group.   Thus the theodicy of white good fortune and African suffering as justifiably rooted in cultural differences becomes meaningless.   Hopes are frustrated on the threshold of realisation, and the feeling of deprivation is heightened by an incongruity of status, and consequent tension, between the racially dominant white man of modest achievement, such as the *petits-blancs* in French territories, or the lumpen-bureaucracy of the South African government, and the highly accomplished but racially subordinate black man.   Understandably, the intellectuals are encouraged to seek fulfilment in revolution.   Yet the wider effects of education are integrative, providing people of different tribe and race with a common universe of knowledge; and this is probably the case even in South Africa where educational policy is designed to promote cleavage.

The new economic structures bring together the races in co-operative relationships, but at the same time they may sharpen racial cleavages where discrimination follows racial lines.   The race conflict overshadows the class conflict, and Marxism is readily given a racial twist by the identification of whites or non-Africans with the bourgeoisie, and of Africans with the proletariat.   The question of whether to conceptualise the relations between black and white in colonial or white settler societies as caste, class or race, the problem raised by Cox (1948), is of theoretical interest and expresses the close weaving of biological and economic factors into the system of stratification.   As for the relations between tribesmen, their new occupational interests and activities provide bases of association and of class formation transcending tribal affiliation.   The urban class structure may be expected to act as a solvent of some traditional ties by introducing new definitions of the situation, and hence changes in the pattern of situational selection.   Since the balance between traditional and other loyalties is related to the overall social context, it would be affected by changes in that context; for example, the movement from colonial domination to independence might well reactivate traditional ties.

3. CLASS

In analysing the urban class structure, the distinction drawn between restratification and stratification may be useful.   The former would refer to changes effected in an existing system of stratification among the urban dwellers, as in the old cities of Africa, the latter to systems of stratification arising *ab initio* in the new cities among the immigrants.   In these terms the distinction is overdrawn, since also in the new cities, traditional forms of organisation and stratification would inevitably exercise some influence on the urban patterns of stratification.

Restratification in the old cities might take the form of the decomposition of the traditional strata, and the absorption of their members into new strata.   Or it might take the form of the transformation of the old strata in such a way that they still retain in some measure their identity, that is to say, the new class structures are not necessarily solvents of the old.   Sociological interest lies in the factors which encourage dissolution or metamorphosis, much the same sort of problem as is. raised in regard to the. circulation or renewal of elites.   The discussions of restratification in the North African cities by Le Tourneau (1957) and also by the contributors to the XXIXth Session of the International Institute of Differing Civilisations on the development of a middle class in Africa (1956), offer suggestions as to relevant factors.   These are the patterns of tribal migration, as for example the extent to which new arrivals have submerged the traditional urban population; the means to resist 'modernisation' at the disposal of the old strata; and the adaptability of different strata.   Thus the metamorphosis of the traditional merchant into the new capitalist, though involving changes in such social values as the sense of obligation to poorer strata, is more readily accomplished and with less disruption than the transformation into entrepreneurs of handicraft artisans without capital or adequate ideas.   Then there is the extent to which the old elite avails itself of the new means of stratification (education, capitalism, the politics of nationalism), or receives into its ranks through intermarriage the new elites of wealth and education.   The proletariat is a new category, as is also a class to which French writers apply the term *sous-prolétariat*.   It is not very clear what this denotes, but it seems a useful term for an obvious and distinct category of modern stratification in Africa: people in the towns, not trained for, but seeking, industrial employment or other employment, and finding it intermittently; living in the towns but not townsmen; insecure, unstable, surviving by expedients.

Variables affecting stratification along class lines in the new cities, as distinct from restratification in the old, include the structure of the tribal society: the nature and extent of social stratification (for example, a traditional caste structure, and an indeterminate relationship between the old caste superiorities and the new superiorities, reinforcing or negating); the degree of centralisation as a factor influencing individual mobility (the contrast, for example, between the centralised Emirates of Northern Nigeria and the loose equalitarian structure of the Ibo; or between what Jabavu [1962] describes as the 'fossilised claptrap' of the Zulu and the indifference to pomp and ceremonial of the Xhosa); attitudes to social mobility; the range of economic differentiation, including the degree of specialisation, the extent of trade, and forms of property; the structure of the family, the status of women, and the nature of extended kin obligations. Also of importance are the structure of the dominant group, including its occupational distribution and the extent of exposure to competition, and the role of intermediate groups, for example, the Asians, Syrians and Arabs, or the Creoles in Sierra Leone, of whom Sir Richard Burton remarked: 'The men displease me because they kick down the ladder by which they rose' (Banton 1957: 110). This observation draws attention perhaps to a more general phenomenon, of which the Afrikaners in South Africa may be an example. Finally, there is the interaction between these groups and the effects of different policies and types of development.

The analysis of social class in Africa is embryonic, as is perhaps the phenomenon itself among Africans. Some of the interest in African class structure has been directed to questions of nomenclature and classification: whether the term can rightly be applied in societies which acknowledge the ties of extended kinship, or whether it is an attribute of nuclear family systems; what occupational categories are properly included within a particular class, as for example whether policemen or drivers should be counted unto the African middle class; whether there is that degree of class consciousness, and that extension of it, nationally and internationally, which would justify the use of class concepts; and whether the class structure is emerged or emergent. Goldthorpe (1961: 145–58) deals with these types of questions and distinguishes a stage of an elite of individuals intermediate to the formation of a class of families. The label applied to these new forms of differentiating behaviour is, of course, less important than their accurate description and analysis.

Most of the studies rely on general impressions of entire territories, rather than on empirical analysis of narrowly defined urban situations. The difficulty has been the lack of sociological research. Interest is largely confined to the African segment though not in isolation from the total situation. There is discussion of the relationship between different ways of defining the caste line or colour line — evolué, assimilado, apartheid — and the internal stratification of Africans, along the lines of Myrdal's analysis (1944) in The American Dilemma. Inevitably the characteristics of non-African groups — whether administrators, traders, artisans, missionaries, migrant or settler — also emerge as relevant. But little is known of the class structures of the resident non-African groups. African class structure cannot be understood in isolation from the structures of these other groups and their inter-relationship. It is necessary to analyse the interaction of the different class systems within the plural society. What are the effects of particular class structures in the dominant (or intermediate) groups on internal differentiation among the subordinates?   And conversely, what are the effects of the different structures of subordinate groups on the internal structure of domination?   Under what circumstances are classes in the different racial groups likely to find common class interests across the racial barriers?   And between which classes do the most acute tensions arise, sharpening the racial cleavages?

In studies of African class structure, there is a tendency to select the middle class or the elite, terms apparently often used somewhat interchangeably for the same phenomenon, and the class structure as a whole remains shadowy.   Thus education has been a prime mover in the growth of class differentiation among Africans under colonial rule, and one might therefore expect class divisions around the axis of education, comparable to the economic divisions.   There are many indications of this in the literature.   Hodgkin and Schachter (1960) mention the radical opposition offered the established political leadership by the overseas university-trained students.   Apter (1963) refers to the political struggle in Ghana between the 'seventh-form boys' and the university-trained: a struggle between a petite and grande intelligentsia.   Banton (1957: 120) mentions attacks by labouring classes on anyone wearing a collar and tie in the course of riots, and quotes the newspaper West Africa: 'Were we seeing the first signs in West Africa of a revolt of manual workers against domination by clerks?'   Goldthorpe (1961: 156) comments 'that in times of stress such as Mau Mau in Kenya or the 1949 riots in Buganda the group most consistently under attack has been the most Westernised Africans, for whom a fury has been reserved distinctly reminiscent of that against Quislings in German-occupied Europe'.   Such terms as Basenji (savages) and Mindele Ndombe (black-faced Europeans) reflect the same antagonisms.   But we have still to carry out the systematic analysis of this educational dimension of African class structure and of the problems of the recruitment to political power of an intelligentsia divorced from an economic base.

The range of phenomena described in studies of social class among Africans needs to be extended.   The occupational and income structure is generally the core, with some discussion of the style of life, occasional analyses of budgets, references to political role in voluntary associations, friendship patterns.   But there is not much material on the relative weight of kinship and class differences, though frequent references are made to 'family parasitism' as restraining class formation.   The generational depth of class differences is not usually studied, perhaps because of the obvious fluidity of the class structure, though in some of the territories there appear to be well established 'bourgeois' lines in a modern Western idiom.   And, apart from occupational ratings, little is known of the subjective awareness of class differences among Africans, their class consciousness, or the nature of the class distinctions they draw.   Does a racial barrier increase the awareness of class differences in the subordinate group whilst reducing the objective basis for differentiation?   And in what situations are common class interests a bond in opposition to tribal or racial interests?

4. VOLUNTARY ASSOCIATIONS

The voluntary associations organise common interests.   Membership may be racially or tribally exclusive, or inclusive, or a combination of the two.   While exclusive membership would tend to reinforce tribal and racial cleavages, the converse is not equally true, since the different groups may be so related to each other within a single inclusive organisation as to maintain their distinctiveness. From the point of view of cleavage or integration, the issue is not simply that of exclusive or inclusive membership. Nor is it that of the exclusive interests of tribe or race against the more universal interests of religion, occupation, sport and politics. Universal religious ethics may be so reinterpreted or applied as to promote racial domination or tribal aspirations; the occupational distribution may be such that occupational associations follow racial or tribal divisions; and even 'nationalist' political associations may serve the exclusive interests of race or tribe, with the right to organise becoming a focal point in the struggle for power. Nevertheless, the new bases of association in the city may be expected in the long run to dissolve many of the particular ties of tribe and race, though the organisation of the traditional cities of North and West Africa and the continued racial segregation in the cities of the United States are a reminder that racial and tribal bonds, and exclusions, may be remarkably persistent.

The conditions promoting tribal forms of association in the towns are analogous to those which favoured the growth of ethnic associations in American cities: the need for material and psychological security in a foreign and threatening environment, so that members move from the known to the unknown, and a measure of rejection or lack of institutional provision for their incorporation as townsmen. Among the variables affecting tribal association are: the demographic composition of the towns, whether one tribe or many (though in the latter case it is not clear if this is a condition favouring or frustrating tribal association); the situation of the town in relation to the tribal bases (the strength of tribal bonds perhaps decreasing with geographical distance from the tribal location, as suggested in the *Report on the World Social Situation* [United Nations 1957: 164]); official policies encouraging or discouraging tribalism; the potentialities for power in tribal forms of association, either as a technique of fragmentation in the interest of a dominant group, or as a base for political organisation, and the extent to which leaders use these potentialities; the level of mass industrialisation, education, religious conversion, and the manner of organising workers, scholars and devotees. Tribal associations are not necessarily only divisive. They may co-operate in national movements, integration — perhaps temporary and unstable — being achieved on the basis of cleavage. And the tribal associations involve new non-tribal procedures and forms, constituting a common organisational language or culture pattern, which may be expected to facilitate formal intertribal association. Moreover the experience of submission to control in the voluntary organisations is, in some measure, a training in acceptance of broad formal urban controls.

Two common generalisations about African voluntary associations relate to the exuberance of their growth and the diffuseness or protean nature of their objectives. The first generalisation is sometimes linked with the assumption of an African proclivity or proneness for co-operative action, not unlike the assumption of a greater humanity. No doubt the structure of the indigenous societies, rather than any quality of the African personality, explains some of the characteristics of urban African association, more particularly the proliferation of the small mutual aid types of society (such as the 'stock-fair' in South Africa or the 'esusu' in Nigeria) affording some of the security of the wider kinship unit in traditional society. But of at least equal significance is the structure of the urban situation itself. In the colonial or white settler context, the situation may be so structured as to define the areas of legitimate association and to provide a framework of associational activities — for example, statutory residents' associations or parent-teachers' associations. Both the forms and the range of associational life may thus be partly determined. This applies not only to the regulated areas but also to those in which expression is, as it were, by way of reaction, or contradiction, or rebellion. The gulf between educated and uneducated Africans created by restrictive educational policies, as well as limited opportunities for leadership, may encourage oligarchical control of associations by the educated. There may be apathy in the areas of regulated associational life, and proliferation, invention, enthusiasm in the open areas.

Similarly, the diffuse and protean nature of African associational life, if this generalisation is indeed valid, must be related to the conditions both of traditional society and of pluralism. The traditional emphasis on status rather than contract as the bond between persons, and the less differentiated character of social organisation, would encourage diffuse objectives, as would the situation of rapid social change. Associational bonds having been established between persons in the city, they may be used for religious, political, commercial, recreational or welfare ends, or any changing combination of them. The social resource is the bond, rather than the specific interest. Diffuseness and change are also encouraged by the social definitions of plural societies. Racial or ethnic status is interpreted not simply as a matter of origin, but as a diffuse social status. Indeed the social implications may be all-pervasive. Hence specific objectives are not easily segregated.

The areas of racial exclusiveness in associational life are related to the structure of power, and were variously drawn in different colonial and white settler societies, and at different stages of development. No doubt there are well-defined rank orders of discrimination or patterns of associational exclusion linked with particular modes of racial domination. Viewed from an African perspective, associations in the colonial or white settler context may be distinguished, in terms of control, as paternalist and as independent (with partnership as an intermediate type); in terms of membership, as racially exclusive or inter-racial; and in terms of aims, as conservative of the *status quo*, designed to secure change in favour of Africans, or as neutral but with implications for social change.

In the extreme conservative type of white paternalist control of African associations, goals are externally defined, and in consequence the associations tend to be rigid, being maintained under pressure, by repression and change of personnel, while the deliberations may be unrealistic since the major decisions are taken outside the association. Contact between white and African is on a basis of inequality, thus reinforcing the system of racial stratification. Acceptance by African leaders of positions in the associations involves the acceptance of subordinate status and a loss of initiative as a result of the commitment to externally defined goals. An aspect of the personality of the leader is, as it were, detached and utilised under the direction of others, so that the leader may be alienated from himself in the same way as the worker from his labour. This is perhaps an element in the oscillation sometimes observed in this type of association between servility and belligerency; and the intercalary position of the leader, suspended between, and seeking to manipulate two worlds, may have the same consequences.

The initiative for the establishment of inter-racial associations would seem to come from members of the dominant group. In the past, many of these associations were of a paternalist, gradualist, reformist type, with control exercised by whites, though token positions of high prestige but little executive substance might be accorded Africans. Partnership seems to represent a fleeting form of paternalism in a changing structure of power, while association on a basis of equality is recent, relatively untried, and perhaps unlikely to appeal to Africans in the moment of their domination.   It is not very clear to what extent and in what situations inter-racial associations have sharpened or reduced cleavage.

Many of the problems raised in this paper relate to the colonial phase, but the same problems, though in somewhat different forms, are presented in the contemporary context of political independence.   The issues of cleavage and integration may be particularly acute when tribal interests, subordinated to national goals in the liberation movements, reassert themselves on independence, and integration is sought in hero cults, one-party states and legal mechanisms.   Here, one of the contributions of the sociologist would lie in developing different models of the plural society in terms of the basic principles of cleavage between the constituent units, the modes of their inter-relationship or partial integration, and probable behaviour in situations of social change.   The formulation of these models should help to guard the social scientist against ideological inclinations towards larger units — united states, federations — and against sympathetic commitments predisposing him to see a democratic potential in African, but not in other, one-party systems.   And the testing of these models may be a source of enrichment for social theory — enlarging understanding of integrative mechanisms in societies with conflicting value systems — and of cleavages in societies assumed to be integrated by common values: extending concepts and theories to include the phenomena of social and cultural pluralism; and contributing to knowledge of the conditions governing cleavage and integration, and of the functions, containment and resolutions of conflict.

5

Political Science*   Harvey Glickman

I INTRODUCTION: THE SCOPE OF POLITICAL SCIENCE†

1. GENERAL CONCERNS

NO DISCUSSION OF Africa today can avoid the political dimension.[1] Although the ancient Greeks designated the study of politics as 'the queen of the sciences', no people are now more keenly aware of its master role than Africans. All attempts to deal with Africa's numerous problems depend on political conditions, on the results of the political upheaval sweeping the continent. Africa is peculiarly *the* political continent; perhaps nowhere else could masses of people act out the exhortation, 'Seek ye first the political kingdom. . .' Consequently, no group of students is more exhilarated by the prospect of the pursuit of their calling than political scientists in Africa; no group of scholars is, in addition, more aware that their accomplishments must be equal to the great human changes they analyse: the construction of new systems of self-government.

Such a remarkable state of affairs cannot be without its challenges and its burdens. The social institutions of Africa and other underdeveloped areas often appear to be far removed from the customary conceptual environment of political scientists. The 'raw materials' of African politics are not easily analysable in the terms of the grand tradition of political science, a tradition which is rooted in Western European notions of rationalism and the law and bound to Western expressions of political activity. This condition, however, is not without its advantages. African politics, therefore, forces the testing of the appropriateness of categories of analysis which originated with and have been applied to somewhat different situations in Europe and in the United States. In confronting the exotic materials of underdeveloped areas, students of politics have been forced to pay more careful attention to the organising concepts of political science, forced to encompass activity of political relevance which might have been overlooked with categories based solely on Western institutional forms.

This need to comprehend unfamiliar contexts of political activity has enlarged the obvious and time-tested concern of the discipline with the formal structures of

* The author wishes to thank Professor David Apter for his valuable criticism, Mr Robert Bates for his research assistance, and the Haverford College Faculty Research Fund for its support. None of them, of course, is responsible for the views expressed.
† Note and Bibliography for this chapter will be found on page 504.

government. It has also reinforced the trend towards general conceptual intro-
spection which has characterised political studies, particularly in the USA, in the
past fifteen years. This trend has been provoked largely by the proponents of what
has been rather ambiguously called 'the behavioural approach', the aim of which
has been to make political studies more 'scientific'. 'The behavioural approach' —
now labelled a 'mood' rather than a distinctive mode of analysis — attempts to
develop verifiable explanations of political activity which will lead to the construction of theories. It calls for empirical methods which permit replication, for
questions which yield descriptions rather than normative statements, and for
precision and clarity in the definition of concepts and the formulation of hypotheses.
By emphasising the behaviour of individuals and groups it places political research
in a frame of reference common to social psychology, sociology and cultural anthropology (Eulau, Eldersveld, and Janowitz 1956: 3–5; Dahl 1961). Whatever the
specific intent of the behavioural approach, the attention which it focuses on analytical concepts and empirical methods has left an indelible mark on political science
by expanding its conceptual horizons. This development in theoretical political
science occurred as the discipline was extending its research sites and interests into
Africa and other world regions.

It is not altogether clear what kinds of theoretical agreement will emerge from
all these efforts. Recent attempts to take stock of the discipline reveal a wide-
ranging eclecticism (Hyneman 1959; Young 1962). Yet a heightened alertness to
conceptual issues ('scope and method' in the argot of the political science fraternity)
has forced political scientists to adopt an outlook towards their analytical concerns
somewhat more serviceable for the investigation of political problems in Africa.
Strictly speaking, it would not be fair to say that political science has shifted its
essential interest in the process and conditions of governing a community. But
views concerning what constitutes this process, what contributes to these conditions, and what spheres of human activity are relevant to political matters — all
these have undergone some change. It is now clear that the institutions of public
government, particularly in their Western formats, do not include all activities
linked to politics, nor do they lead to comprehending the governmental process in all
types of communities.

Agreement on a statement of what is 'political' often depends upon the
scholarly circles in which one moves, but perhaps the following suffices as a working
definition: political activities deal with making, executing and enforcing decisions;
that is, decisions which apply to everyone in the community. Implicit in this
definition are the basic 'orienting concepts' of the study of politics: 'the allocation
of values' backed up by 'legitimate physical compulsion' (Easton 1950: 90–148;
Almond and Coleman 1960: 5–9). Research focuses on policy — the process and
the outcome of decisions which bind a community — and on power — the resource
for decision-making. As one commentator remarks: 'To understand how policy is
made and put into effect we must know how people are able to control the way
others make and execute decisions' (Easton 1950: 144). To understand how
control is exercised, it is necessary to investigate not only the overt mechanisms of
influence and accountability but the conceptions of authority and purpose which
authenticate those mechanisms.

Formal as well as informal structures are included in this view. It follows,
therefore, that policy encompasses both the declared decision and the manner in
which the decision is implemented in practice. African territorial governments,

for instance, may strip tribal chieftains of their official powers of leadership and adjudication, but deference to chiefly authority in matters of public concern often remains the practice of great numbers of people.   The analysis of policy cannot ignore such matters, as the governments involved usually recognise.   'Official' and 'unofficial' policies constitute politics, because they authorise the allocation of social goods.

There is an important advantage in viewing politics in this manner, for within the same framework it permits analysis of such apparently disperse realms of political activity as international politics and the politics of non-literate societies.   With this conceptual scheme analysis begins not with formal structures but with the process of authoritative settlement of differences; attention is directed less towards political institutions *per se* and more towards the kinds of decisions being made and towards their purposes in any society.   It is impossible to conceive of a society, international or preliterate, that has no 'policy' with regard to satisfying the requirements of collective existence.   There are, therefore, no societies without political systems, although there are a number without centralised authority and administrative institutions.   The connection between African political studies and general advance in political science is evident in that statement, for it is just this point which was clarified largely on the basis of conceptual developments in African anthropology. These developments modified the early dichotomy between 'states' and 'stateless societies', put forward by the anthropologists Meyer Fortes and E. E. Evans-Pritchard (1940: 1–23), and were taken over by students of African politics. Coleman (1960a: 253–4), for example, suggested two sets of variables for the classification of traditional political systems in Africa: the scale and degree of centralised political authority, and the continuity of its operation through specific institutions.   This yields four types of systems.

The main issue here involves the distinguishing characteristics of a political order as opposed to other types of orders.   Since political scientists, with rare exceptions, have not worked in tribal societies, the controversy has been confined largely to anthropologists and sociologists.   The most recent views have established that territoriality and the administration of justice neither define nor form prerequisites for political systems; furthermore, they do not distinguish states from non-states.   The recent summaries by Lucy Mair (1962) and I. Schapera (1956) of politics in a number of traditional societies — apart from providing evidence of political procedures which affect the institutionalisation of political norms at the level of the modern state — show the limitations of the concept of state in describing the early stages of political socialisation in Africa.   In so doing they help eliminate the 'state' as a basic, orienting concept for political studies.   It becomes clear that the analysis of what constitutes new political systems need not be confined to new nations, that it can be extended to include the establishment of new systems of relations between new African nations and between new African nations and the world.

2. RESEARCH PROBLEMS IN POLITICAL SCIENCE

The concern of the discipline with political systems may be ordered under two general headings: policy and power.   Policy is meant to include a concern for the cultural and social basis for decisions; the procedures for making choices which bind a community; the substance and functioning of decisions and practices; the content, distribution and interplay of interests; and the effects of decisions on the political system.   Power is meant to include a concern for the sources and forms of influence and dominance in cultural and social structure, for its organisation (both formal-legal and otherwise), its distribution, its manipulation, and for its operation and transformations.

Although Africa presents several unusual analytical problems, its political problems are not completely divorced from other systems of decision-making. Contemporary analysis is not duplicating the errors of an older approach to African affairs, adopted by European students and politicians, which proved inadequate in comprehending or in responding to a rapid reversal of power relations.   Every community must make the same kinds of basic decisions, i.e., every community embraces a political system, therefore every system must face the same general political problems.   So a review of the subject matter and categories for research must be measured by its ability to illuminate the political problems of all com-munities.   Recognising no necessary precinctual rigidities, then, it is possible to delineate four general problems which must be solved by every political system (Macridis 1955; Apter 1958; Spiro 1962b).   To put it another way, that system which serves to solve the following problems is the political system of any community.

(i) Creating and maintaining legitimate authority, or, in terms of goal achievement, making the system effective.

(ii) Maintaining defence and internal order, or keeping the system stable.

(iii) Resolving conflicts, or integrating the system and making it efficient.

(iv) Providing for welfare, or keeping the system flexible.

These are the general system-problems as defined by the discipline of political science, but each era and each context presents certain inevitable priorities of emphasis and interest.   One writer has summarised the concrete problems of contemporary politics that urgently need study:

. . . the problems of political change, the nature and characteristics of revolu-tion, the institutions of authoritarian systems, the nature and characteristics of political leadership, the relationship between technology and political forms and institutions, the phenomenon of the diffusion of ideologies and the impact of alien ideologies upon particular systems, the relationship between industrial-ization and the growth of bureaucracy, the relationship between specific groups such as labor or the church and the political process, the relationship between the growth of literacy and the performance of the political system, the study of political ideology as an instrument of control (Macridis 1955: 67).

It is remarkable how closely this corresponds to the problems to which political scientists interested in Africa have addressed themselves.

3. RESEARCH PROBLEMS IN AFRICAN POLITICS

The most obvious and most general characteristic of African politics is change.   The main problem, therefore, is political development, and the main task for political science is the description and analysis of the transformation of political institutions and processes.   This emphasis on change and development forces the analyst to consider all the basic problems of political systems.   In Africa, problems which are only latent in firmly established and relatively stabilised political systems are manifest and vital; they are immediate issues in the political process. Legitimacy, stability, adaptation and integration are all in the throes of re-creation because of the disintegration of older social and cultural institutions. In these circumstances the problem of development and the creation of stable, new political orders is most usefully attacked in terms of the requisites of political consensus and of the determinants of an integrated system of values and institutions. Intersecting all dimensions of the problem of development are the issues growing out of the disintegration and reintegration of patterns of interests, patterns of power and patterns of culture.

Among the adjustments that demand examination, perhaps the first are those involving the transformations of authority which have accompanied the Western penetration of Africa and the subsequent overthrow of colonial rule. Fruitful approaches to this gross problem of political development depend on the comprehension of several sets of power relationships. One set, of course, is the colonial system and the conditions of its maintenance; another is the traditional political system. From the standpoint of understanding the rise of national independence movements and the subsequent drive towards national unification, it is useful to present the problem of change in terms of the reciprocal effects of variant forms of colonial rule on variant types of traditional politics.

Although the general political problems, i.e., legitimacy, stability, adaptation and integration, occur in all settings, spatially as well as temporally, their specific definition by the investigator usually depends on the issues they provoke in a particular time and place. The research problems of the politics of colonialism, therefore, have been cast in a form somewhat different from that of the politics of nationalism. In the case of colonialism, the process of establishing colonial authority, the constitutional framework and institutions of colonial rule, the variations in aims and practices of the colonial powers, the forms of administration and operations of the machinery of government and law — these have been (and are) significant areas of inquiry.

The case of nationalism, on the other hand, elicits inquiry into the sources of the challenge to colonial authority, i.e., into the social and cultural impact of the elements of Westernisation and into the conditions and actual process of the devolution of colonial rule. Component problems for investigation include the nature of nationalist demands, the forms of protest, instruments for organising and implementing the aims of nationalism, and the effect of these on colonial institutions. While the latter set of problems emerges from the first, different themes are emphasised.

The process of organising nationalist protest, for example, is part of the movement towards political integration. This relationship grows more obvious with the achievement of independence, as new ruling authorities face the challenge of unifying sentiment and activity around new concrete policies and the institutions of self-government. For the willing political scientist, here is a veritable cornucopia of research problems, all loosely hinged to general political concepts, such as 'state-creation' or 'modernisation', and all of which can be expressed in terms of issues facing African societies. A few examples will suffice:

1. *The ends of government and the purposes of power:* the vital issue of balancing community strength and integrity against individual development is still in the initial stages of explication.

2. *The character of political institutions:* the nature of representation, the forms of deliberation, and the enforcement of public decisions must be explored.

3. *The relationships between formal government and non-governmental political units:* the connections between central party organisations and local governments, between new elites surrounding government and traditional authorities, and between centralised bureaucracies and local political leadership remain to be worked out.

4. *The support and control of political institutions:* popular participation as an instrument of political accountability must be balanced against its uses as an agency of consent and education (Young 1962: 1–5).

Readers familiar with the history of Western political thought will recognise these problems as similar to those which agitated European peoples from the seventeenth to the nineteenth centuries. Interesting hypotheses, therefore, might be devised from an examination of the extent to which African political development is exhibiting a pattern of centralisation of power prior to 'democratisation': a pattern of development characteristic of Western European political history.

Looking at matters from another angle, the problem of democracy is the underlying interest and chief theme of research into Africa's political development: a theme which marries the vocabulary of politicians to the labours of political scientists. Inquiry into the conditions which facilitate democratic practice and the suitability of various forms raises controversial issues for both groups. Stability remains an acceptable goal and criterion, but as a precondition for attaining the purposes of government it merely serves to pose the problem of the acceptable, i.e., legitimate, order. In Africa, it need not be emphasised, there are numerous, enormous obstacles to establishing a stable, integrated, flexible political order, along the lines of the modern state, solely on the basis of popular opinion expressed through elections. Many of the intervening obstacles stem from the desires for 'modernisation' — universal education, a welfare economy, internal social equality, technological progress — and for the qualities of respect and dignity in relationships with other nations. Pressures for modernisation may overcome ideological and cultural commitments to the substance or procedures of democracy, even though modernisation can be achieved within the framework of popular government. But in most new African states, these pressures, coupled with a search for appropriate, indigenous expressions of political action, have served to support the creation of highly centralised, unitary regimes. Viewed in this perspective, consideration of the problem of democracy in Africa may suggest a theory of political development based on the chronology and timing of political integration, national unification and technological advancement.

Thus far, this discussion of research problems in African politics has centred on domestic matters, but the general framework of system development and the problems faced by all systems can be extended to suggest the outlines of problems of interstate relations within Africa and of relations between Africa and the world outside. The character of both sets of relationships is not yet fully defined; it is dependent on several factors, peculiar to Africa, which keep matters in a state of flux. Despite the growth of strong pan-African sentiment and its continuing contribution to further 'decolonisation', the achievement of independence largely within colonial territorial boundaries, the centripetal forces of national integration within each state, and the growth of ideological and territorial rivalries, all contribute to cross-cutting conflicts and fluid alignments. These interstate tensions impinge on the re-formation of Africa's ties with the outside world. The peculiar balance of international relations in a world dominated by two nuclear giants sometimes permits African states to play a role more influential than their measurements on the traditional scale of national power would indicate. The forces impelling a policy of active neutralism, particularly in international organisations, and the economic and cultural forces which continue to pull African states into the orbit of former metropolitan powers require detailed analysis. Consideration of problems of interstate relations in Africa and problems of African relations with the rest of the world ultimately merges with research on problems of modernisation, for the gap between developed and underdeveloped areas represents a general source of world tension.

One central characteristic of African societies is the persistence of traditional political cultures. (The concept of 'political culture' is discussed by Almond [1956], and Beer [1960].) Conceptions of authority and conceptions of the goals of community activity remain profoundly conditioned by the nature and relative strength of ties to the indigenous 'tribal' or ethnic community. The nature of traditional political systems and the manner in which they shape the political perspectives and orientations of the active elites as well as of the masses of people are among the most significant problems for research in Africa. Loyalties to the traditional culture and community and the ethnic divisions which they maintain or help provoke provide the most durable political issues in the new states of Africa, even as political modernisation proceeds. Racial differences are also enormously significant as sources of political tension, sometimes in exacerbating, sometimes in modifying ethnic cleavages.

The elements of 'traditionality' — the great conditioning factor for all political research in Africa — impinge on the investigator in at least three inter-related forms, each demanding analysis. The traditional political system comprises the base, so to speak, for subsequent transformations in its nature and effects. The differential colonial or other impact of the West — its nature, duration, depth of penetration — set in motion forces of fragmentation which continue to affect the role of traditional ties in the modernised milieu and the connections between village and city, elite and mass, etc. Finally, the cultural and political drive towards 're-Africanisation' has selected certain aspects of traditional culture for retention and reformulation; these in turn serve to modify the style and substance of political activity (Coleman 1960b).

In this context it is apparent that mere descriptions of legal governments and considerations of the evolution of constitutions and governmental machinery do not suffice. Political scientists are aware of the cultural dimensions of their problems, although so loosely defined a concept as 'tribalism' requires sharp definition if it is to be useful as a factor in the formation of research problems. It would also be misleading to dismiss constitutional studies as incapable of illuminating matters of significance. The ideologies of the new governing elites, the shape of working compromises among feuding factions, and the formal structure of power, may all be disclosed by close attention to the basic instruments of government. Indeed, changes in these formal instruments can signify broad shifts in the informal distribution of power and alteration in patterns of influence. Concomitantly, and for similar reasons, studies of supporting institutions, such as parties, electoral systems and the civil service, remain important units of study.

Nevertheless, sensitivity to questions of the impact of traditionalism on obviously political institutions may not constitute a sufficient adjustment of the customary perspectives of political science. Flexibility, even adventurousness, in defining what has political relevance and in framing problems for analysis must be steadily encouraged. Compared with other social scientists, political scientists face an unusual problem in this respect in that discussion of politics is not confined to the academic fraternity. The demand for information about relatively remote areas of the world runs far ahead of scholarly resources. During the initial stages of expansion of their interests, students of Africa found themselves dependent on the research of expert journalists. Since political matters today are regarded as everyone's business, the notion that they are also within everyone's easy understanding has gained some currency. Consequently, some studies purporting to describe political changes have only perpetuated research problems which are mere recastings of popular doctrines. Among these are inquiries into the emergence of one-party 'dictatorships' or federalist 'democracies'. A number of students implicitly define political problems in terms of the institutions of constitutional democracy, although the criteria usually adopted — civil liberties, division of powers, more than one political party — are hardly exhaustive or rigorous (Spiro 1962a: 1–11). Sensitivity to the cultural dimension, and especially to the characteristics of African cultures and to their particular significance in African political systems, forces the observer to cast his analytical net more widely and to frame research problems more relevant to the goals and processes of politics in Africa.

II *THEORETICAL CONSIDERATIONS*

1. GENERAL CONCERNS

General political theory constitutes a quarry for gathering relevant theories about African politics, but it does not present a prefabricated edifice. With further effort mutually fruitful relations can be established between the general theoretical accomplishments of political science and the research demands of African politics. Rapid progress may depend, however, on a clearer distinction between empirical and normative emphases in political theory. The confluence of these analytical streams is inevitable, but it has caused some confusion in the past. A recent commentator begins a long survey as follows:

> Imitating the practitioners of many human occupations, political theorists are not agreed among themselves what political theory is or what political theory should be. Some men are inspired by the classical Greek example to attempt construction of a model *polis*, an ideal state, a vision of rational perfection, capable of calling mankind forward into the good life. Others strive to generalize about the governing of men with utter realism, to see into and through all façades, all rationalizations, all ideologies. They would offer the world a glimpse of politics as it really is, possibly with the hope that someone else who knows the good life more intimately than they may use to worthy ends the harsh truth they have revealed. Some think of political theory as a branch of philosophy. Some say it is a field of political science (McDonald 1962: 3).

The writers of 'the Great Books' in political theory were passionately interested in how politics were actually carried on; otherwise they would have had no basis for political prescription.

Somehow in recent years, the mantle of theory slipped from the writers who tried to understand events to scholars who reported, translated, classified and analysed ideas and argued about the ethics of previous writers. Political theory, so embodied, was really a combination of intellectual history and ethics; it had deserted empiricisim for scholasticism (Easton 1950; Hacker 1961).

Interest in the relationship between ideas about politics and behaviour has been sustained by students of ideology. (Ideology may be defined as a set of beliefs critical of the existing state of affairs and containing built-in suggestions for change towards a more desirable state.) Based largely on an interest in mass movements, the study of ideology restores an important link between political life and generalisations about it. The explication of ideologies, however, is not the same thing as the construction of theories of political activity. The former codifies beliefs about politics — it makes no difference whether they can be adjudged 'accurate' or not — and the latter proposes statements about political relationships and about the investigation of those relationships.

Scattered throughout the literature of political science, and not least in the 'Great Books' of political theory, is a variety of hypotheses about the terms and conditions of political activity. They are posed either as propositions of what ought to be or as assertions — sometimes so interesting as to be characterised as 'shrewd insights' — largely accompanied by systematically assembled supporting evidence. The nature of such propositions may be clarified by an example: the problem of legitimacy may be approached by observing that the most effective standard of obligation is based on popular consent, or it may be noted that people should obey only in cases in which they have demonstrated consent. Only the first statement can be empirically investigated and lead to empirical theory; the second cannot, although it has served as the subject of a great deal of normative theory.

The body of political theory contains many propositions which immediately may serve African studies: 'Agreement on "the rules of the game" is necessary in order for a political system to sustain conflict'; or 'A strong middle class tends to insure stability and/or the growth of restraints on government'; or 'Economic development and political stability — or political competition — tend to reinforce one another'. Each of these statements has been the subject of controversy for some time, and perhaps only the last one has been the subject of rigorous inquiry and a preliminary survey of evidential support (Lipset 1959; Coleman 1960a: 536–44).

Carried on with prudence and a sense of proportion, the construction or development of theories of politics in the African context need not decline into sterile model-building or shrink from policy recommendations or even moral judgments. Standards and techniques for verification of hypotheses, indeed for the generation of hypotheses, have developed considerably in recent years. Both the circumstances of Africa and the state of political analysis encourage renewed efforts with old theories as well as the development of new theories to explain political life. Perhaps it can be said that African problems, the character of which is alien to the recent traditions of political inquiry, have already responded in a preliminary way to systematic analytical methods and have served to evoke some promising theoretical beginnings.

2. POLITICAL THEORY AND AFRICAN RESEARCH: TRENDS AND ACCOMPLISHMENTS

In the face of the problems defined by political analysis in Africa what sorts of theories seem applicable? What existing theories have been utilised and what departures in theory has research in Africa sponsored?

Theories designed to aid the understanding of African political problems must deal with traditional political cultures and their effects on political development, with the processes of social and economic change and factors in their instigation, with the stages and types of colonial rule and their governmental expressions and, finally, with the ideological manifestations of conflict engendered by these several dimensions of social transformation. The ensuing discussion will focus on the application of political theory in general to the theory which is emerging from the study of African politics.

African politics are transitional politics. The most useful theories, therefore, will stem from an interest in change and development rather than in stability. This is an obvious point, but it is important to emphasise it, because most political theories deal with stable situations, i.e., nation-running rather than nation-building. One widely accepted theory emphasises competition between social groups both as an explanatory concept and as a desirable state of affairs. When basic political ideals and institutions, comparatively speaking, are undergirded by a broad area of consensus and are no longer sources of fundamental disagreement, this can be a useful explanation (Truman 1951). When ideals and institutions themselves are in process of being defined and developed, other types of explanations may be more apt.

Theories which attempt to relate Western experience to contemporary African circumstances may be derived from analyses of the struggles of Europe to create centralised monarchies in the seventeenth and eighteenth centuries. If this be the case, it would follow that the anti-feudalist writers of early modern times offer more appropriate clues to comprehending the manner and direction of African politics than do the liberal writers to whom most current political scientists trace their ancestry; one should look to Machiavelli and Hobbes rather than to Locke and Mill. Immanuel Wallerstein (1961, 1962b) has emphasised this perspective. On the other hand, African politics also spring from revolutionary democratic impulses as well as from centralising and unifying tendencies. Hence there are good grounds for going back to writers like Rousseau and Marx: theorists who have been noted by Thomas Hodgkin (1961).

As a matter of course, a political scientist first turns to the already formulated explanations of basic political transformations, i.e., to theories of revolution. A number of guidelines for understanding certain conditions of revolt can be established from previous studies of 'classic' revolutions, e.g., the French, the Russian and the American, and from writers on revolution from the seventeenth to the nineteenth centuries: economic grievances, the emergence of new social groups claiming political participation, the spread of ideas to create a 'climate of opinion' which justifies political reorganisation, the growth of non-official political movements, the presence and justification of violence, etc. These lead to a general hypothesis of 'frustrated aspirations', which offers some descriptive help in the African context.

Marxism represents a coherent synthetic theory of revolution (as well as a systematic theory of political change), but its dependence on the maturing of capitalism and class warfare makes it inapplicable to the African situation. The Leninist modifications, embodied in the theory of imperialism, identify capitalism with the nation-state and transform the internal conflict into an international conflict between capitalist-colonialist powers and proletarian colonial peoples. The latter has great significance in explaining some of the ideological apparatus of the African revolution, but it loses the theoretical coherence and elegance of Marxism by destroying the connections between the state of technology and the development of classes (Woddis 1960, 1961). The Marxian view of colonialism as a generator of social conflict, nevertheless, brings into focus the class character of some aspects of the reallocation of power evoked by Western penetration of Africa. This has been ably presented by Thomas Hodgkin (1953, 1956a: 63–92, 115–38) and Martin L. Kilson, Jr. (1960).

Although the orthodox Marxist propensity to characterise traditional societies as feudal is misleading in most African settings, the Marxian interest in the nature of social relationships as basically explanatory of politics provides a clue for the kind of theorising that is necessary. Variations in political adaptation can be related to varying forms of social solidarity and types of authority. The Weberian theory of the development of authority relationships — traditional, charismatic and rational-legal; Tonnies' characterisation of types of solidarity — organic and associational; and Durkheim's theory of the development of 'mechanical solidarity' into 'organic solidarity', have been reservoirs for elements of a theory of African political change (Apter 1955, 1961; Wallerstein 1960, 1961; Sklar 1961). Political adaptation can also be related to colonial policies and to the experiences of traditional systems under colonial rule as well as to the indigenous political cultures.

Investigation of the problem of political development under colonialism has depended largely upon two bodies of theory: the first concerned with planned political change; the second with colonial nationalism. Theories about planned political change have grown out of the interest of anthropologists in culture contact, the interest of political analysts and colonial administrators in orderly government, and in what David E. Apter (1955) has called 'institutional transfer'. Theories of colonial nationalism have drawn upon explanations of nationalist development in other areas of the world, and in so doing have contributed to the delineation of general patterns of nationalism, unification and modernisation in the developing areas (Coleman 1958a, 1960a).

The study of planned political change has focused upon what happens when one type of authority system is imposed on another. Implicitly or explicitly, investigators have utilised models of traditional and modern systems. Anthropologists by and large have defined their problems in terms of the social strains of the role of traditional leadership in the face of the demands of different types of colonial administration (Busia 1951; Fallers 1956; Smith 1960). Political scientists, on the other hand, have engaged primarily in assessing the effectiveness of political institutions and have analysed the issues involved in getting one authority system established in circumstances dominated by another (Hailey 1950–55; Cowan 1958). But the interest is in the same phenomena: the effect of conflicting demands on political structures and activities and the forms and conditions of political reintegration (Liebenow 1956, 1961). Two theoretical developments have emerged from the confluence of approaches grounded in different disciplines. One indicates that the concept of role conflict may be more useful than that of group conflict as a tool of analysis for cases in which the same persons regard both opposing authority systems as desirable in some respects. The theoretical synthesis by Lloyd Fallers (1956) holds that instability results from the institutionalisation of two types of authority in the political process; integration can result only when one gives way to the other. This theory has been complemented by Apter's (1955) suggestion that charisma can serve as the vehicle for the transfer of legitimacy from traditional to secular political structures. These propositions, of course, can be tested in situations involving different types of traditional systems, different colonial policies, or different colonial legacies.

Patterns of modern politics can be revealed by the study of the adaptations of traditional systems to the demands of different types of colonial programs of planned political change, such as indirect or direct rule or policies of identity or of differentiation (whether conducted by a single colonial power or by several). The patterns can also be revealed by analysis of the nature of nationalism as it emerges from the interaction of variant types of traditional systems under different colonial policies. Coleman (1954, 1960a) discusses these processes of social change in terms of the secularisation of culture, restratification and expansion of the scale of the political community, and of the inequality, frustration and economic discontent associated with colonial rule. Why sentiment should crystallise around the concept of 'nationhood' may be generally explained by Karl Deutsch's (1953a, 1953b, 1961) theory of social communication. This maintains that perceptions of territorial association are supported and ties to 'national' entities made operational (i.e., 'mobilised') by universal processes of social change (e.g., urbanisation, commercialisation) and by a consequent pattern of enhanced social communication.

Political science is rich in the elements of theories which try to account for the development of different forms of government, and many of them suggest hypotheses which could be tested in African politics. For example, the theory of constitutionalism developed by Carl Friedrich (1950) holds that centralisation of power usually precedes the institutionalisation of regularised, effective restraints and, further, that such restraints are made most effective when they are related to interests vested in and widely distributed about the particular society (Spiro 1962a: 150–6). Scholars interested in the developing structures of governmental authority (regimes or 'constitutions' in the classic sense) might attempt to relate the outstanding political issues to inherited values and procedures and thereby arrive at some possible classifications of African political systems.

In one promising beginning, David Apter and Carl G. Rosberg (1960) have proposed models of political change — 'mobilisation, reconciliation, modernising autocracy' — which appear applicable to African experience. These correspond to types of emergent national societies and serve to link authority structures, values and institutional manifestations. They seem particularly useful in explaining the different patterns of nationalism and political development in states harbouring dominant traditional political systems of different major types. Apter (1960) is able, for example, to contrast the mobilisation pattern with the modernising autocracy pattern. The former emerges from the clash of nationalism with a traditional system have consummatory values and pyramidal authority (Ashanti); the latter grows out of a system characterised by instrumental values and hierarchical authority (Buganda). The possibilities for theoretical development seem plentiful, for predictions about the types of national authority structures can be based on an analysis of types of traditional authority systems, although these must also be related to other analytical dimensions such as 'institutional factors, stages of colonialism, cycles of perceptions' (Apter 1961: 438).

Other predictions with normative implications can also be attempted. Apter

(1961 : 476) has proposed, for example, that 'the degree of autocracy which emerges after independence is in virtual proportion to the degree of antagonism the government shows to tradition'. (This has been contested as generally unverified by Kilson [1963].) Obviously this hypothesis is an extension of the theory of constitutionalism. Certain restraints on arbitrary power were built into the deliberative procedures of traditional African systems (Schapera 1956; Lambert 1956; Bohannan 1960), and these may penetrate the caucus-type functioning of parties and legislatures in new African governments. Despite these restraints, African constitutionalism may depend on varieties of 'reconciliational' practice, ranging from loose alliances of ideal and material interests to formal federal instruments of government (Carter 1962: 149–236, 272–90, 444–68).

The theory of constitutionalism may also serve as a framework for another line of exploration, beginning with the problem of national unification. On both historical and theoretical grounds it might be expected that the first stage of political development would be characterised by tendencies towards centralisation. An explanation of the form and operation of African political institutions, therefore, might focus only on the pragmatic responses to the immediate threat of disintegration. Immanuel Wallerstein's (1961) characterisation of African political change, for example, lays stress on 'the situation of the new nation' and on the forging of instruments of integration as the key to explaining the political process in new African states. Political parties, political leaders and ideologies may be understood primarily in these terms, although traditional elements of constitutionalism and the modern element of competitive trans-territorial allegiances serve to modify overall generalisations.

The issues involved in constructing a theory of political integration in Africa have also been explored by James Coleman (1955a, 1960a), who proposes this generalisation: Political systems in Africa are characterised by centralising proclivities and executive-bureaucratic dominated governments because of the need to overcome tendencies towards malintegration. These tendencies result from the persistence of traditional cultural, economic and political practices, are conditioned and supported by the divisive results of Western economic and social penetration, and are shaped by the differential effects of alien rule and other external forces.

The foregoing discussion has sketched some theoretical considerations and contributions in three of the four subject-areas significant for a theory of African political development: traditional culture; social change; and colonial government. But African politics is also a fertile ground for the study of the nature and impact of African ideologies and of the stages of their growth. From the standpoint of political sociology, ideology is viewed as both a product and a rationalisation of a particular historical set of social conditions. As such, ideologies can be related to the social institutions which serve to maintain or undercut certain groups in privileged positions. Studies on these lines in Africa have barely begun, although some of the way has been prepared. Hodgkin (1961) and Wallerstein (1961) have each noted the connections between African ideologies, the conditions of revolution, and the demands of political integration. A psycho-social dimension is suggested by A. L. Epstein's (1958) proposal that new political demands arise from conflicting sets of social relations which give rise to new 'social personalities'.

Political science can also provide micro-theories for the analyst of particular institutions. The nature, function and operating conditions of parties, bureaucracies or elections require theories that relate them to the major goals of the emergent African systems. Informal lines of communication and non-official links of authority have been emphasised for some time in organisation theory. The role of elections as devices for mass education, agitation and public identification with the official policies of government has been stressed by theories of totalitarian rule.

It is the central institution of the political party, however, which has received most attention in the African context. Thomas Hodgkin (1962: 166–9) and Ruth Schachter (1961) have contributed to a classification of African parties based on their structure, ideology and type of activity, and have related the consequent types of party systems to the form and direction of different political systems. African conditions and problems give rise to 'one-party dominance', but there are important differences between systems dominated by elite or patron parties and those dominated by mass parties. The theoretical issues revolve around the contribution of the dominant mass party to political stability and to popular government. Events and investigations have not gone very far as yet, but the proposition seems to be emerging that dominant mass parties tend to integrate the functions of politics and government. In so doing they bring popular demands and supports into congruence with official policies and vice versa. Depending on the scale and vigour of internal discussion, these parties seem to be agents of 'democratisation' as well as of control.

New theories of international behaviour are also emerging as a result of obvious changes in the conduct of international relations and of the new approaches of political analysis. The main impetus comes from dissatisfaction with the core-concept of the national 'interests defined as power'. This concept does not adequately reflect the nature of the international community, nor does it permit adequate assessment of the growth of new restraints and premises which inform political action across territorial boundaries. The international activity of African states and political movements has been an exercise in influence despite the absence of power as it is usually conceived. The prime importance of the United Nations, the singular and controversial role of pan-African movements and conferences, and the significance of traditional political systems having no relationship to territorial boundaries all combine to undermine the customary explanations of politics among nation-states (Spiro 1962a: 12–33). The thrust of these developments in world politics lays the basis for explaining the relationship of African states to each other and to the world more in terms of the resonance of opinions and perceived complementarity of interests which cut across state boundaries, and less in terms of state sovereignty, territorial integrity and national power. African leadership, in other words, may be delineating and operating within different sorts of international communities from the ones which suit the widely accepted theories of international relations (Chidzero 1961).

Implications for normative theory are apparent throughout this survey. They do not as yet constitute an African philosophy of politics, but they do suggest the beginnings of one. On questions such as the nature of legitimacy in new political systems, the proper scope and manner of the deliberative process, the scope and manner of control of government, or the aims and uses of public power, something resembling a consensus may be emerging. Most of the writers cited for their contributions to empirical theory remain extremely interested in normative questions. In general, the lesson that African politics ought to be judged on the basis of indigenous conditions, experiences and problems has not been lost on Africa's analysts, and nearly all of them view political modernisation as a desirable and realisable goal of African politics.

This agreement among scholars today reverses a somewhat less broadly based agreement among the analysts of colonialism, such as R. L. Buell (1928), a generation ago. Leaving aside the open justifications of official colonial policies, most research concerned with political development did not conceive of territorial nationalism and the building of states based on European models as desirable or even feasible. Some normative theory of political development in Africa included a concept of Euro-African association, while some was stated in terms of 'good government' and perhaps independence for Africans. The timing in the latter case may have been somewhat ambiguous, but the predicted forms of development were based on Africa's natural and traditional groupings — what the British called Native Authorities (Delavignette 1950). One set of goals of planned political change, most clearly enunciated in the doctrine of indirect rule, involved the strengthening of traditional authorities and their adaptation to the problems of modern government and administration (Perham 1960). Supported by the ideology of the 'dual mandate' and 'the civilising mission', Lord Hailey (1957: 540) sums up the spirit of these views.

> . . . the distinctive feature of the Native Authority system did not lie merely in its use of the traditional authorities as subordinate agencies of rule, nor in their integration into the machinery of government. It lay in the endeavour to encourage them to utilize the influence derived from their traditional position as a means of promoting objects such as the maintenance of order, the administration of justice, or the provision of local services for the benefit of those who by custom fell within the range of their authority.

Efforts to develop empirical theory usually reflect some normative frame of reference. The 'colonial theory of development' led to investigations of the utilisation, modification and adaptation of traditional leadership in cultivating a political life which met the standards of European government. The 'post-colonial theory of development' now fosters studies of national unification and political modernisation, though the norms of political modernity reflect 'Africanised' variations on familiar political forms. But the major issue which integrates normative and empirical emphases, namely the achievement of democratic systems in Africa, has already opened up an area of disagreement that promises to get more fundamental as African systems face more critical times. Specifically, the issue concerns the kind of system which best serves the development of constitutional democracy in Africa. The most cogent statement of the democratic potential of systems based on mass parties of integration is by Immanuel Wallerstein (1961: 161, 163, 164).

> . . . The effective choice for the newly-independent states is between a one-party (or one-dominant party) system, which allows for some real popular participation in, and control over, the government, or anarchy, which means that power reverts to local princelings and patrons, remote from the intellectual contact and stimulation which infuses the modernizing elite of the national structures . . . structural guarantees (of democratic practices) will not be acceptable as long as they threaten the preservation of the state. The build-up of loyalty to the nation, combined with the economic differentiation that development will bring, plus the resulting creation of nationwide interest groups will create a situation in which the institution of structural guarantees will no longer threaten the preservation of the state.

David Apter (1961: 474–7) has taken a somewhat different view.

> The mobilization system and the modernizing autocracy are better prepared
> for rapid economic development, particularly by governmental means, than
> political development.   It is the consociational [reconciliation] type of system
> which hold out the greatest prospects for immediate democracy in most
> instances . . . those systems that make use of tradition and render it meaningful
> and pervasive while not adhering slavishly to old forms and formulas have the
> greatest prospects of immediate democracy.

In general, analysts must be alert to African practices which give new meaning
to customary conceptions of the 'right' forms of political institutions and governmental activities.   Ideologies based on notions such as 'African socialism', 'negritude', or 'communocracy' raise interesting problems for the evaluation of the
accomplishments of African politics in serving the needs and demands of African
peoples.   Just as the problems arising from the development of technology and the
evolution of economic systems forced European political systems into new moulds
and Western political theory into new emphases, the problems of African politics
will undoubtedly make their impact upon theories of the good society and upon the
theories of political systems.

III   METHODOLOGICAL CONSIDERATIONS

1. GENERAL CONCERNS

Although this is not the place to examine issues of the methodology of political
science, methods of political research in Africa cannot be fully understood without
some attention to the discussions that have been going on within the discipline.
Until recently, political science has not been very self-conscious about its methods of
analysis or techniques of gathering data.   Descriptions of political activity based on
constitutional and institutional categories were usually deemed adequate to explain
the real world and, even when they did not quite suffice, there seemed to be enough
agreement about the characteristics of culture and social structure in the areas under
investigation — mainly Western Europe and the United States — to permit acceptable explanations of political action.   It was this state of affairs that 'the behavioural approach' challenged as *ad hoc* and unproductive of theory applicable to a wider
range of circumstances.
    The introduction of new categories of analysis and new techniques of data-
gathering — principally quantitative — has not been accompanied by the universal
conviction that older methods can be replaced.   Any survey of interests in the
discipline would reveal considerable support for the view that too much concern
with refining methods of research is misleading, since political studies will never
achieve the rigour and precision of the physical sciences.   The methods of
'behaviouralism' may modify or tighten up some propositions about certain of the
more quantifiable aspects of political life, such as voting behaviour but, in any case,
the consequent generalisations pertain only to a small portion of the stuff of politics
(Truman 1955; Friedrich 1950; Heckscher 1957: 13–38).   Finally, it is frequently
felt that the emphasis on precision and measurability could lead to a concern with
what is quantifiable instead of what is important, resulting in research which proves
the trivial, labours the obvious, or just substitutes an unfamiliar vocabulary for a
thoroughly serviceable one.

Despite the critique of new departures in method (largely in the context of American political studies), the investigators of politics in 'developing areas' have had to depart from their customary methods of analysis in order to comprehend the processes involved. An informed and sensitive intuition could apply 'common sense' and a rough and ready 'knowledge of human nature' to political problems with the aid of concepts such as 'the powers of government', 'offices', 'institutions' and 'public opinion', and achieve what book reviewers call 'insights'. It implies no denigration of research intelligence to observe that accurate explanation based on these concepts is limited to the particular form of political system which they describe and to societies which have quite differentiated and clearly visible political structures. In other cases, however, experimentation with 'common sense' in the form of unfamiliar frameworks for analysis seems necessary.

Recent contributions to social theory have helped to make political scientists more sensitive to the concept of 'system' implicit in their work and more aware of the interdependence of the elements of political activity revealed through multi-factor analysis. Studies have demonstrated that changes in one aspect of the political process produce changes in other aspects, changes which ultimately influence the initial stimuli as well as the whole process itself. The advent of pressure groups, for example, begets changes in parties, the growth of executive bureaucracy begets legislative and pressure group bureaucracies, technological advances in communications beget changes in electoral behaviour. The utility of more self-conscious attention to the implications of the concept of system seems apparent in studies of African political problems in which new sets of interdependent factors are the main issues. Indeed, the first analysts of African politics — the social anthropologists, who exposed the lineaments of 'primitive government' — have worked with the concept of system as the foundation for the study of societies for some time.

Political scientists as a rule have not pursued the systemic qualities of their subject matter. Although they have been concerned with the description and analysis of political structures — a fundamental aspect of a theory of political systems — their categories and procedures have resulted primarily in statements about the history of phenomena or about the resolution of public policy issues, either foreign or domestic.

The urge to experiment with new methods of analysis in African politics has stemmed largely from ferment within the area of political science loosely called 'comparative government'. Although the oldest theories of politics sprang from the comparison of whole systems of institutions in different contexts (e.g., in the work of Aristotle, Machiavelli or Montesquieu), the study of comparative government declined some time ago into the exposition of foreign governments. More recently students in this area turned to neighbouring disciplines in an attempt to reappraise their efforts. Several points of agreement stand out: a desire for generality and for systematic theory; a willingness to use simplified conceptual models; a desire to broaden the subject matter and conceptions of what was relevant to politics; a willingness to consider new conceptions of the components of politics (roles, actors) and new types of hypotheses (functional); a willingness to consider the integration of theories and methods of politics with other social sciences (SSRC 1953: 641–73; Macridis 1955; Easton 1957; Beer 1960; Almond and Coleman 1960: 3–64). The results of these agreements have become evident in studies of African politics. Descriptions based on institutional concepts have been supplemented by functional approaches, and the concern for single entities has been influenced by the desire to provide recognisable avenues for comparison. At every stage of theory construction — in defining problems and formulating and testing hypotheses — the comparison of political units and political actions offers a means for experimentation without actual manipulation of the units or actors themselves. It is likely that the most illuminating studies of African and other politics will be those which utilise systematic comparisons.

2. RESEARCH METHODS IN AFRICAN POLITICAL STUDIES: TRENDS AND ACCOMPLISHMENTS

The challenge of African political phenomena to customary political science methods, coupled with the opportunities for experimentation emerging from methodological developments in social science, provides the theme for this section. In this discussion use will be made of two working distinctions: institutional approaches and functional approaches; and documentary techniques and behavioural techniques. These are not meant as rigid demarcations, for approaches and techniques usually interpenetrate; but they do signify different emphases each of which is capable of making its distinctive contribution to the comprehension of African political affairs.

Most political analyses are institutional in nature. They range from analyses of governmental-institutional categories to those of movements and groups which are acutely sensitive to the psychological, economic and social factors that shape power relations. In general, problems tend to be defined in terms of conflict between groups concerned with the formal-legal institutions of the society. Such an approach is alert to questions arising out of differences in status and power, to the interests and ideas of groups, and to the results of their interplay. The cutting edge of this approach is historical, and in Africa it illuminates the grand trends of colonialism, nationalism and nation-building. The results have been eminently successful in providing an anatomy of the forces making for political development. African studies are blessed with the materials for the 'natural history' of decolonisation and the early stages of nation-building (Coleman 1958a; Carter 1958; Leys 1959a; Pratt 1960; Emerson 1960).

The most prevalent interest of the institutional approach is illuminated by the discussions of government or of the groups that are customarily 'political' in their orientation. Scholars have written of the development of the provisions of the colonial constitutions and new African constitutions and have compared their emphases (Wiseman 1956, 1957; Buchmann 1960; Franck 1960; Ezera 1960; Rubin and Murray 1961; Cowen 1961; Robinson 1961). They have described the conduct of elections (Dvorin 1954; MacKenzie and Robinson 1960; Bennett and Rosberg 1961). They have traced the organisation and activities of parties and pressure groups (Coleman 1955b; Lloyd 1955; Rezette 1955; Ashford 1960; Lowenkopf 1961; Hodgkin 1962). They have looked into the organisation of selected executive departments and legislatures (Austin 1958; Cole 1960; Binet 1961; Usborne 1961). While it is difficult to discern a unifying analytical scheme in so wide a range of studies, it is possible to observe the emergence of a general analytical issue: how to handle political conflict in circumstances where the structural units 'usually' involved in government do not accomplish their 'usual' tasks. At all points it is agreed that the political process is punctuated by the forces of 'tribalism' and traditionalism.

The question of how structures operate — what they do and how they change

— does not pose special methodological difficulties when the structures more or less perform their 'expected' functions. A legislature that makes the community's laws or a pressure group that organises interests and exerts pressure on a government are units whose forms are sufficiently specialised, whose activities are sufficiently specific, and whose goals are sufficiently precise. An analysis of their operations is a description of political processes. In non-Western societies, however, political structures are not so clearly recognisable and are changing in form. Analysts, therefore, are forced to ask basic questions about the requirements of coherence in a system, to inquire into the contribution of political structures to the larger social system. In order to do this, students of politics have turned to general sociological theory: to the 'action' framework, to the use of 'roles' as structural units, and to framing problems in functional terms.

The functional approach, derived from systems theory and the structural-functional tradition in sociology and anthropology, turns institutional analysis on its head. Instead of beginning with structural categories such as parties, legislatures, pressure groups or classes, analysis begins with categories such as political roles and the performance of political functions. Whatever the specific research problem, whether it be the transfer of parliamentary institutions or the comparison of the processes of political integration in several systems, the conclusions appear to offer more refined explanations of the differences between the various political cultures, sharper delineation of the multifunctions of political structures, and greater understanding of the varied styles of political action. In addition they seem to indicate the possibility of progress towards a theory of political integration which is consistent with general social theory. Finally, if the principal general problem for political analysis in Africa today is that of the integration of political structures, the functional approach may suggest ways to evaluate the viability of the emergent African political systems. In the process it can also expose the underlying discontinuities of political structures and can suggest possibilities for new patterns of change (Apter 1955, 1961; Fallers 1956; Eisenstadt 1959; Coleman 1960a).

The creation of new grounds for legitimacy and the transformation of authority relationships form the basis for one set of functional studies (Balandier 1955a, 1959; Fallers 1956; Epstein 1958: 224–43). Fallers (1956: 5–20) has shown that the difficulties attending the establishment of local governing units in an administrative hierarchy in Uganda are largely dependent on the conflicting roles in which indigenous local leaders find themselves. His method for discovering situations of conflict is to search for situations where two or more institutions claim the adherence of the same groups or persons; situations of harmony are found where institutions bring different groups or persons together by defining overlapping fields of interest. The assessment of conflict or harmony is based upon an analysis of the types of authority structures represented by the traditional and the modern political system (represented by colonial administration at different levels) and upon an evaluation of the claims of each in the same situation. Fallers focuses on leadership within the traditional system. Apter (1955: 273–334; Apter and Lystad 1958) utilises a similar analytical model in investigating institutional transfer at the territorial level in the Gold Coast. In elaborating on the functional requisites of traditional and secular political structures, he has shown that the requirements of legitimation may be met by charismatic leadership, which is the functional equivalent of tribal chieftainship. The unstable balance of forces involved in transplanting the machinery of parliamentary government is summarised as the accomplishment of 'procedural integration' of secular roles, while 'substantive integration' around 'the norms and structures of secular democracy' remains to be achieved.

Other authors have suggested a functional approach to the problem of national integration. Wallerstein (1960) has examined ethnicity in this way, and Douglas E. Ashford (1961c: 3–24) has briefly sketched the types of role relationships that intermesh and conflict in the process of bringing people into national politics. The most ambitious utilisation of a functional approach is the effort by Coleman (1960a) to cast a survey of 'the politics of sub-Saharan Africa' in those terms. Based on the analytical framework constructed by Gabriel Almond, Coleman's survey makes use of the category 'political groups' to discuss the structure of parties and associational and institutional interest groups. The primary burden for illuminating 'the dynamic forces of change that are eroding old systems and conditioning the character of new political systems' falls on a set of universal functional categories: 'interest articulation, interest aggregation, political socialization and recruitment, political communication' (political or input functions) and 'rule-making, rule application and rule adjudication' (authoritative or output functions). These categories prove a great help in revealing more precisely the scope and manner of penetration of all political structures by sub-territorial, parochial, solidary interests: tribe, race, region, communal group.

Probably the most ambitious case-study of political modernisation is Apter's work on Buganda (1961). Methodologically it spans the functional and institutional approaches, although the concepts which contribute to the general models of political authority owe much to work within the systems theory framework. The overall scheme is designed to connect social structure to political systems and to explain variations in the process of political adaptation. 'Role patterns' is the concept which permits the examination of the behavioural consequences of different authority systems; the latter are set up as ideal types. Whereas political change in the Gold Coast is characterised by Apter as the operation of charismatic authority through the roles required by British-style parliamentary government — and revealed by the use of models of secular and traditional authority — political change in Buganda is represented as operating within one of three universal types of authority systems: the modernising autocracy. The critical variables are descriptive of traditional systems of authority, i.e., the structure of power and the values attached to it, and are meant to discriminate more precisely among variant patterns of adaptation.

Africa also provides an intriguing set of problems for experimenting with techniques of gathering data. The most reliable technique in political science remains documentary exegesis, the analysis of 'primary' documents, such as constitutions, statutes, judicial decisions, official minutes and official reports of governmental proceedings, verbatim accounts of speeches and debates, and the literature issued by unofficial groups involved in political activities. To this the analyst usually adds what he can elicit from the published observation and commentary of others. Obvious difficulties attend the use of this technique in African political studies. Documents have increased in quantity with the spread of Western-style political structures, but those dealing with the rise of nationalist parties have proved quite fugitive; in any case, they cover only a part of what is political. To get at the precise nature of political relationships field techniques, such as those employed by anthropologists, are required, but numerous and unfamiliar languages and exotic social circumstances combine to daunt the investigator at the outset.

Despite these formidable obstacles, several interesting starts have been made by supplementing documentary with behavioural techniques. Influenced in part by work in other disciplines, in part by the so-called behavioural studies of political opinions and attitudes, field research is now common in political studies of Africa. Except for techniques of depth interviewing, observational procedures have not been codified, but the influence of the anthropologists has been marked. An effort to comprehend local culture and social structure is mandatory, and the recommended procedure usually involves 'immersion' in a total situation.

Experience in the Middle East and in studies of racial tension suggests that survey techniques might be utilised to advantage (Lerner 1958; Franck 1960: 236–47; Rogers and Frantz 1962). Several interesting, if inconclusive beginnings have been made in election surveys by Birmingham and Jahoda (1955), and in relating cultural and political attitudes to the goal of political modernisation by Ashford (1961a, 1961b). In addition, the study by Jahoda (1961) of the attitudes of Ghanaians to white people holds some promise for work on political ideology. The barriers, of course, remain high. The costs are great, and cultural factors, such as unfamiliarity with questionnaires or hostility to interviews, make the results of massive projects somewhat uncertain. Nevertheless, research in other underdeveloped areas, such as the Middle East and South-East Asia, indicates that survey and field techniques can be applied with profit when investigators are fully cognisant of the historical and cultural peculiarities of the milieu.

IV THE RESULTS OF RESEARCH IN AFRICAN POLITICS

I. A CHRONOLOGY OF CONCERNS

The development of research concerns in Africa reflects the pattern of interests in the West. The earliest studies corresponded to the needs and curiosities characteristic of the viewpoint of Western colonialism, and research problems focused on the effect of African colonialism on European international politics. Accounts of the diplomacy of imperialism eventually gave way to evaluations of the role of colonialism in generating world tensions (Harris 1911; Woolf 1920; Moon 1930). Africa was viewed as an arena for European politics rather than as a participant in the game. There was another side to 'the colonial problem', however, and that reflected a concern with political institutions in Africa and with the problems of colonial administration (Mair 1936). The purposes of colonial rule and the appropriate methods of administration were questions that produced a number of 'classic' studies. The works of Buell (1928), Lugard (1929), Perham (1937) and Hailey (1957), are unparalleled in their detailed analysis of why and how colonies in Africa were run the way they were. Through the interwar years it was accepted that African politics held very little intrinsic interest, except as they represented European initiatives and adaptation to European institutions. The great issues of the period, and in part of the post-war period, were whether colonies 'pay' or whether 'indirect rule' or 'assimilation' was appropriate (Royal Institute of International Affairs 1939, 1947; The Colstone Papers 1950; Kimble 1960, 2: 223–392). International politics aside, the label the British used to describe their colonial operations in Africa indicates the focus of most political studies: native administration.

There remains a rich vein of discussion of the problems of colonial administration, i.e., the constitutional and institutional requisites of orderly and efficient government in a dependency.   Years of inquiry into these problems developed a literature on a set of issues familiar to the colonial civil servant who had to struggle with questions of on-the-spot application.   The era of colonial administration also permitted anthropologists to compile an impressive array of ethnological mono-graphs on a wide range of traditional societies, including their political systems.   A concern for African political institutions *per se* also emerges in the anthropological literature, in isolated instances of writings about the few African independent states, and in studies of the politics of European settler colonies and the Union of South Africa (Bryce *et al.* 1900; Ellis 1911; Rolin 1913; Rattray 1929; Macmillan 1929; Kennedy and Schlosberg 1935; Dilley 1937).

During this period, 'political development' connoted the socialisation of tradi-tionally sanctioned leadership and the recruitment of elements from those small groups which were benefiting from Western commercialisation and education into subaltern positions in colonial administration.   It also meant the refashioning of tribal authority structures so that they would eventually complement and support colonial rule.   The actual programs and style of 'development' naturally conformed to the variations in colonial policy.   But despite the differences in official practice, those interested in colonial administration were concerned to learn something about the extent and the effects of the European intrusion on traditional societies.   In the interstices of official and unofficial studies of culture contact and social change are to be found materials for research on the rise of nationalism.

The post-war era saw shifts in colonial policy which were naturally reflected in changes in the focus of political studies.   A certain 'nationalisation' of interests followed revisions in constitutional schemes and plans for development of the colonies.   Constitutional changes which permitted greater African participation in organs of territorial government were followed by analyses of the relative success of the different programs of the colonial powers (Wight 1947; Royal Institute of International Affairs 1947; Colstone Papers 1950; Wheare 1950; Robinson 1955a, 1955b, 1958).   At the local level, the fundamental change of political direction was symbolised first by the British, when they transformed 'native authorities' into 'local governments' (Cowan 1958; Young and Fosbrooke 1960).   By the mid-1950s the growth of nationalist protest movements in North Africa and West Africa reversed the focus altogether.   African nationalism, rather than colonial government, emerged as the object of political inquiry.   By 1956 Coleman (1954) and Hodgkin (1956a) had constructed frameworks for the study of the social background and the forms of nationalism.   Coupled with Apter's (1955) case-study of 'institutional transfer', these works helped to arm scholars with some of the materials and tools with which to examine new forms of political expression and the process of state-creation.

The development of political studies of eastern and southern Africa in the post-war years was dominated by the race question — as were politics in these areas. Until the late 1950s it was not clear that the settler colonies would follow in the mainstream of African political evolution.   Research in these areas, as exemplified by Dvorin (1958) and Rosberg (1958) reflects the greater durability of British-type parliamentary institutions, the concomitant underdevelopment of African nation-alist movements, and the complicated connections to policy debates in Britain.   In South Africa the race problem has cast the political system in a reasonably predict-able mould to such a degree that an astute observer like R. L. Buell (1928) could state the issues in 1927 in a form remarkably similar to the way they appeared over twenty years later to Gwendolen Carter (1958).

2. SUBJECT AREAS OF POLITICAL STUDIES: ACHIEVEMENTS AND GAPS

The global process of political transformation has been viewed as the disintegration or adaptation of one set of authority structures and the consolidation of new ones. In the past decade analysts have been working with an implicit historical conception of revolution and reintegration. The impact of the West — chiefly in the form of colonial rule — upon alien and diverse non-literate societies generated numerous processes of social conflict and, inevitably, of social change. At the same time the pressure towards modernisation exerted by colonialism served to awaken aspirations, to mobilise the discontents attending social conflict, and eventually to call into question the legitimacy of colonialism itself. The ensuing process of evolution towards independence and the reorganisation of political institutions around new demands, new goals and new loyalties continue at the levels of the national state and beyond.

This conception of development in African politics makes a muted appearance in studies of international relations. But perhaps a sharper delineation is to be found in a general model of the process of political modernisation advanced by S. N. Eisenstadt (1962): (1) the development of specific political roles and institutions and differentiated political structures, centralisation and unification of the polity; development of specific political goals and orientations; (2) extension of the scope of centralised political activities and their permeation into all spheres of the society; (3) the continuous spread of political power to a wider circle of groups in the society and eventually its extension to all capable of participating in political life; (4) the weakening of traditional elites and patterns of legitimation and the establishment of ideological and institutional accountability of the rulers.

Description and analyses of these processes in Africa have not followed the form suggested by the model, although the findings requisite to putting flesh on its skeleton can be developed from the literature and from future analyses which use methods appropriate to the variables posited. Political studies of emergent African states and their relations at this stage can do little more than suggest tendencies appearing in the character of politics and propose broad hypotheses designed to explain these tendencies. It is hoped that the ensuing discussion of research areas will also suggest types of hypotheses which can be fitted into a general model of political modernisation.

(i) *Adaptation and effects of traditional systems:* Coleman (1960a: 258) has noted that 'traditional political systems have largely shaped the political perspectives, orientation to politics and attitudes towards authority of all but a small fraction . . . of Africans involved in modern political activity'. Discussion of the differential responses of traditional systems and their effects on modern politics begins with the effort to classify and characterise these systems. Modification of the early dichotomy of states and stateless societies by Coleman has resulted in four types distinguished on the bases of scale, the degree of centralisation of political authority, and the degree of continuous operation of political authority through explicit political institutions: (1) large-scale states; (2) centralised chiefdoms; (3) dispersed tribal societies; (4) small autonomous local communities. Analysis of the political processes in these variant systems leads to hypotheses about the extent and nature of tribal support for different forms of change and for 'modernised' authorities, e.g., colonial administration or political parties (Albert 1960; Lewis 1961).

Apter (1961: 84–107, 435–78) has distinguished three types of traditional systems, distinguished on the bases of structure of authority and value system, although he has concentrated on the use of two types and four possible authority-value combinations.   The different patterns of adaptation demonstrated by the different type-combinations lead to hypotheses about patterns of modernisation, e.g., about the course of nationalism, the structure of political parties, and ideological orientation.   For purposes of comprehending present tendencies in political transformation, the issues to be explored in the separate systems are the absorption of innovation; the nature, course and effects of internal divisions; the nature of competition for affiliation between modernist and traditionalist tendencies; and the nature of conflicts over legitimacy.   Authority structures and value systems provide the analytical focus.

Existing studies of traditional systems can be re-examined for their potential contribution to explanations of variant forms of 'tribal' influence on behaviour in the modernised political sector.   'Tribalism' is perhaps the most utilised and least precisely defined aspect of the subject of traditionalism in modern African politics. Connections can be established between different types of traditional systems and different foci of nationalist sentiments — between tribal nationalism and territorial nationalism, for example — but much remains to be done in establishing the connections between such structures as tribal federations and national politics or between tribes of various sizes and scales and support for different policy positions on basic constitutional matters.   On the latter problem, for example, Mary Douglas and Daniel Biebuyck (1961: 26–43) have suggested that a wide dispersion of membership or numerous small tribes can support unitary nationalism.

Entry into the problem of tribalism in modern politics has been considerably eased by distinctions suggested by Sklar (1960) and Wallerstein (1960) and based on the types of values that tribal allegiances represent — e.g., communal or associational; political, social or kinship (Epstein 1958: 231 ff.; Gluckman 1960; 55–70). An aspect that could bear further scrutiny is the relationship between newer forms of political representation and social stratification at the local level.   The need here is for community studies at the village level which try to relate tribalism to emerging practices.   The precise relationships between traditional elites or deposed traditional elites and nationalist movements and modern government also need exploration.   There are areas in which the field techniques of anthropologists and the survey techniques of social psychologists might profitably be adapted by political scientists.

(ii) *Construction and reconstruction of governmental institutions:* In the construction of hypotheses about the extension of the scope of centralised government and the spread of power to newly claimant groups, political scientists can turn for suggestions to numerous studies of the establishment and refashioning of governmental institutions.   Hypotheses about the responses of traditional political systems and about the patterns of decline of traditional elites require assessment of the effects of colonial policies on traditional systems as well as analysis of their operations.   The classic distinction between 'direct' and 'indirect rule' has been reformulated by Coleman (1960a: 257) on a basis more cognisant of actual practice with respect to African elites.   He contrasts the policy of 'differentiation' (British) with a policy of 'identity' (French, Belgian and Portuguese).   The variant levels of success achieved by these policies have been subjected unevenly to analysis, the French studies concentrating largely on legal and administrative matters, the British — in line with the eclecticism of their administrative practices — combining 'applied anthropology' with organisational description. Hypotheses connecting traditional systems with types of colonial policy or with types of modern political movements must relate the strength of tribal institutions to their differential treatment under colonialism. For example, a policy of differentiation applied to large-scale states hinders subsequent efforts to achieve territorial unification and centralisation of government.

Hypotheses about the formative stages of modern politics in Africa require a classification of territories based on the nature of the political structures which shaped the contact of the West. It is possible to distinguish between 'the dual polities' of settled alien oligarchies and territories ruled by colonial bureaucracies. In one case, political reconstruction depends on intra-oligarchic politics; in the other, it is determined by different colonial policies. Analysis of the issues involved in colonial government and of the problems of governmental reconstruction which endure after independence may also utilise three additional variables: (a) the mode of tribal administration; (b) the roles prescribed for the new African elite (e.g., ranging from exclusion to assimilation); and (c) the degree of freedom permitted for political activity (Coleman 1960a: 257). For instance, the strength of pressure for federal structures, evidence of tension between traditionalist and modernist elements in the population, and pressure towards a multiplicity of parties are all directly proportional to the effectiveness of an administration based on principles of indirect rule. Another hypothesis, by Hodgkin (1956a: 93–114) would relate the incidence of violence and sublimation of political demands in messianic religious movements to the amount of participation and freedom permitted for African groups.

Political scientists have expended a great deal of effort in studies of the process of constitutional change and of the operation of colonial governmental institutions in the light of proposed or supposed policy objectives. This endeavour is continuing, as scholars such as Jean Buchmann (1960, 1962), Quermonne (1961), Gonidec (1961–62) classify and describe constitutions and types of political systems in the independent African states.

Many problems involving traditional African procedures and conceptions of authority and their relation to the forms taken by new African constitutions remain to be explored. The 'latent constitutionalism' of traditional systems and the theme of consensualism in tribal deliberations have been mentioned by Spiro (1960), but their precise significance has not been demonstrated. The same may be said of the putative links between the nature and operation of territorially centralised governmental institutions and the nature of political loyalties and sentiments. Hypotheses dealing with the growth of constitutions, e.g., whether federal or unitary, etc., to some extent suggested by Donald Rothchild (1960) lead in several directions: towards studies of traditional societies, towards studies of colonial government and towards studies of modern political movements.

The areas subject to greatest constitutional conflict have attracted the greatest interest: Central African and South African problems have yielded the largest number of constitutional studies (Clegg 1960; Gray 1960; Mason 1960; Wood 1960; Bennett and Rosberg 1961; cf. Bretton 1958). Although there are significant policy questions to be illuminated by studies of the government of settler colonies, the fragility of constitutional edifices tends to reduce their long-term value for hypothesis and theory construction. Analysis of the procedures involved in transferring power and redesigning constitutional structures, nevertheless, does aid identification of the durable political issues and styles.

Research 'snap-shots', which capture and record the activity surrounding the transition from colony to independent state in other than formal legal terms, would also help to indicate the kinds of institutions African leaders are constructing and the use that will be made of them. This kind of study has been less fully explored in non-English-speaking territories, although the two encyclopaedic surveys of colonial institutions in former French West Africa and French Equatorial Africa by Virginia Thompson and Richard Adloff (1958, 1960), the spate of investigations directed towards finding 'the reason why' in the international crisis following independence in the former Belgian Congo (Van Langenhove 1960; Merriam 1961), and the recent natural surge of interest in rebellion in the Portuguese colonies (Harris 1958; Duffy 1959; Institute of Race Relations 1962), have combined to fill part of a great gap.

Studies of elections represent an obvious format for connecting structures of government to political movements. Nothing on the scale or the level of sophistication of American voting studies has yet been attempted, nor is it wise to think in these terms until greater quantities of accurate supporting data are available. For purposes of demonstrating the function of elections in Africa, the kinds of descriptive studies which have appeared after each national election in Britain since the second world war seem adequate. W. J. M. Mackenzie and Kenneth Robinson (1960), in the only comparative study thus far attempted, have demonstrated the significance of electoral systems in shaping the early development of parties and legislatures under colonial rule. Although elections as a device for political control or political choice have diminished in importance in new African states, there remains some point in comparing electoral systems in order to relate them to the character of political systems. The very decline of national elections in many independent states serves to underline the importance of investigating governmental institutions as consent-seeking mechanisms as well as authoritative structures. Despite a certain loss in explanatory power, studies of elections can still fulfil an important role as research 'snap-shots', for they compress the life of a political system into a small space in time. Perhaps most important, however, elections can act as agencies of political development by enlisting participation and enhancing the spread of communications; they therefore provide occasions for testing general hypotheses about the course of political development (Leys 1959b; Austin and Tordoff 1960; Austin 1961).

(iii) *Mobilisation of political movements:* The scope and pace of governmental reconstruction is regulated by the objectives and strength of political movements. Indeed the concern for political transformation in Africa among scholars might be translated as a great effort to describe and analyse political mobilisation. This topic has already been tackled from several standpoints.

Some of the processes of social change which have exercised great influence in the rise and subsequent character of nationalism are urbanism, Western education and religion, and commercialisation. Pioneering surveys and comprehensive studies of the evolution of nationalist movements in specific territories have elicited interesting connections between patterns of urban development and modern politics. Tribal unions, for example, form an important base for political parties, and old town residents hold a special position in rising movements. Patterns of economic development also affect modern politics, and it has been found useful to measure the relative importance of labour leaders in relation to the distribution of wage earners. There have been relatively few specific studies of the links among all these

phenomena, but here is an area obviously deserving inquiry.   Perhaps most important of these social factors is the effect of Western education upon processes of social
restratification and secularisation.   Hypotheses can be constructed which relate
the incidence of group tensions to areal variations in the acquisition of Western
education, or which relate shifts in power relationships between historic tribal
antagonists to opportunities for higher education under colonialism and to the size
and type of new African elites.   As might be expected, the connections between
politics and these factors of social change have not all been studied by political
scientists; the range of relevant work extends into sociology and history (Shepperson
1953, 1954; Balandier 1955b; Mercier 1960; Smythe and Smythe 1960).
    Another mode of analysis is that which focuses on the reintegration of roles
around changing authority structures.   Apter's (1955, 1961) work on political
change in Ghana and Uganda suggests polar types of nationalist movements, charismatic and bureaucratic, which are intricately related to the type of traditional background, the subsequent pattern of change, and the consequent trends towards
variant types of political systems.   These movements have operated as the chief
agencies of political reintegration before and after independence.   Because of this
and because a major issue in post-colonial Africa is national integration, a strong case
can be made for the concentration of research on the organisation, leadership, social
basis and ideology of Africa's nationalist political parties.
    It has become evident that the study of nationalist movements merges with the
study of parties, since the dominant parties of Africa in most cases are heirs to comprehensive nationalist movements — and it is the objectives and experiences of
nationalist movements that shape the character of emergent national and international systems.   Classifications of African states by type of party system, however,
have limited utility, because 'no-party' systems, single-party systems, and competitive party systems are all in transition.   A more durable classification may be found
in the trichotomy suggested by Apter and Rosberg (1960) and demonstrated to
some extent in several studies by Apter: the mobilisation system, the reconciliation system, and the modernising autocracy.   These are based on several systemic
variables — the most notable being the distribution of power, the structure of
authority, and ideology — but they also reflect the type and position of parties within
the system.   Apter's categories suggest hypotheses connecting types of parties with
social modernisation.   If parties are distinguished on the basis of distribution of
power, degree of continuity in the operation of authority through their organs and
ranks, scale and type of support, and ideology, then it may be predicted that modernisation will occur at the slowest pace in reconciliation systems.   Similar variables
utilised by Hodgkin and Schachter classify parties into mass-type and patron-type,
with modernisation proceeding fastest in situations of mass party dominance.
    At this stage, an interest in party development cannot be separated from
studies of governmental reconstruction.   The most recent studies reflect the
merging of the functions of 'party' and 'government' as African territories cross the
threshold of independence (Carter 1962).   In this respect the conduct of African
politics reflects the centralising tendency previously identified in the model of
political development (Eisenstadt 1962).   At another level it suggests the possibility
of interesting comparisons of linkages between African parties and governments with
those between parties and parliamentary institutions in Western Europe and between
parties and governments in totalitarian states.
    Wallerstein's (1961) discussion of the role of parties in emerging Africa is

representative of the interests of a number of students of the development of African parties. By centring on the integrating functions of parties (and party leaders), it is possible to connect the organisation of parties with their type of leadership and with their ideology and policies when in power. When parties are viewed as primary instruments of national integration, then hypotheses which link their circumstances and activities seem to go farthest towards explaining the patterns of political development. By the same token, diversities in patterns of development may be explained by assessments of the relative effectiveness of parties in overcoming cultural and institutional obstacles to the unification of loyalties and activities.

As the customary boundaries between political institutions grow more obscure, the utility of the functional approach grows more evident. Comprehension of 'party politics' in countries controlled by European oligarchies is facilitated by considering the function that parties perform in the overall system. When such parties are analysed as instruments of European dominance (Leys 1959a: 131–89), aberrations from party practices in Europe become less significant, although they remain interesting variants on standard behaviour. Studies of political parties in multiracial territories necessarily tend to be diffuse. The importance of the European-dominated arena, the concomitant fluidity of African political expression, and the almost continuous pressure for constitutional change divide the attentions of investigators. Except in South Africa, political groups in these countries have taken on a kaleidoscopic quality; it is possible, nevertheless, to draw up hypotheses about the development of African nationalist strength and about the changing nature and extent of control exercised by European oligarchies.

The South African situation reflects a special set of circumstances in which the presence of a majority of disenfranchised Africans remains the omnipresent political issue. But the parties are divided by cultural nationalism and operate in institutional circumstances, which, but for their African setting, resemble the political forms of the 'old Dominions' of the British Commonwealth. Hypotheses about the rigid course of party development in South Africa set forth by Charles Nixon (1958) and Gwendolen Carter (1958) will probably remain viable long after a fundamental shift in the basis of party politics in East and Central Africa.

The concern for interest groups, customarily allied to the study of parties, also benefits from a functional approach. Except for scattered trade unions and economic associations, especially in European-oligarchic states, interest group activity has largely been studied in the context of governmental institutions or of tribal associations (Balandier 1955b; Ottenberg 1955; Leys 1959a: 98–130; Warmington 1961). Coleman (1955c) has commented on the significance of tribal associations, which play the role of pressure groups in early phases of nationalism and provide the infrastructure for political parties. He also notes the importance of distinguishing between the effects of tribal associations and of the institutions of traditionalism, for in some cases they run directly counter to one another. As economic development proceeds, interest differentiation will probably grow more apparent, although it is clear that the expression and aggregation of interests in modernising African states will remain 'executive-dominant' for some time. Hypotheses about the role of the 'vested interests' await further study, but the influence of institutional interest groups has not gone completely unnoticed, as a few brief studies of the political role of the Christian and Islamic churches and of the armed services and the civil services in selected countries will attest (Hodgkin 1956b; Carter 1958; 272–81; Hahn 1960; Lewis 1961).

The final aspect of studies of political mobilisation which contribute to a theory of political modernisation in Africa is that of ideology. All studies of nationalism have commented on the ideology of the African revolt in terms of the demands made on colonial rulers. The contents of this ideology of nationalism have been subject to close scrutiny, however, only in rare cases. Hodgkin (1961, 1962: 161–5) has compared the statements of many leaders and organisational manifestoes and noted the similarity to popular democratic attitudes and beliefs in revolutionary situations elsewhere. His short pioneering effort has highlighted the lines of further inquiry, and his theme — that fundamental political problems give rise to certain universal ways of thinking about them — has been echoed in other studies. The theme enables students to unify certain apparently disparate aspects of African nationalist ideology, such as pan-Africanism and 're-Africanisation', egalitarianism and modernisation, populism and strong leadership.

Studies of African nationalism emphasise its eclecticism. Although original connections to Marxism are evident, strong contradicting forces are also apparent. The few studies of ideology in practice by Walter Laqueur (1962) and others (Fischer 1959; Shepperson 1960) underline this point. The connections between ideology and political behaviour, however, have not been studied in any great detail. Ashford's (1961b) use of questionnaires to elicit attitudes expressing the influence of Islam on political goals suggests minimum significance for highly abstract concepts: a conclusion worth testing and amplifying in other contexts and for other notions, such as 'Negritude' and 'the African personality'. Distinctions between types of political systems harbour ideological connotations. In place of the usual dichotomy of radical and conservative ideological expressions, Apter (1961: 20–7) has suggested forms of ideological expression which help to describe the three types of systems. The mobilisation system is described as ideologically specialised but fundamentally opportunistic, with the common organisational affiliation rather than a set of principles as the basis of commitment. A reconciliation system is described as ideologically diffuse but seeking a common set of symbols and beliefs. Finally, a modernising autocracy is neo-traditional or revivalist in ideological orientation, emphasising a set of symbols which can be invested with concrete meanings adaptable to new situations.

The process of developing specific political goals and patterns of legitimation and accountability is obviously affected by ideological forms. Except for a concern for the links between apartheid and racial separation in South Africa (Dvorin 1952) and between 'partnership' in theory and practice (Mason 1960: 51–69), there have been few attempts such as Henry Bretton's (1958) to assess the interconnections of ideology and actual policy (Pienaar and Sampson 1960; Leys and Pratt 1960; Mason 1960). In this area, Robert Good's (1961) study of policy-making on international issues surrounding the Congo crisis in the UN points the way for future studies of the influence of ideology in concrete cases and for studies of the impact of political issues on ideological development. His exposition of the positions of new African states on a set of issues that affected them immediately and directly indicates a preliminary way of measuring the role of ideology (by explanations and votes in the UN). Perhaps more important, the discussion of 'neutralism' in action illustrates the close relationship between international and domestic politics.

(iv) *International and trans-territorial relations:* The concern for political development usually stops with the boundaries of states, but there is intrinsic reason why this should not be so.   A significant aspect of modernisation is the growth of new ties between states and territories.   A process similar to the development of nationhood inside new states is also occurring between new states and between African political units and the world outside.   A system of trans-territorial contacts and connections is emerging which adds the ancient practices and formal ties of diplomacy to an existing network of regional and continental ties.   The fact that African states now participate in the customary arenas of international politics is not in itself a sign of political modernisation, although the change from dependence to independence in practice usually follows the development of nationalist sentiments and groups, which is part of the modernisation process.   The point is that the political emergence of Africa accompanies and, to some extent, fosters the general transformation of international relations from one type of system to another. It might even be argued that the formal independence of African states, coupled with their burden of numerous dependency relationships with the outside world, confirms the development of a pattern of 'permanent', negotiated intervention by some states in the affairs of other states.   Research in African international politics, therefore, contributes to a comprehension of global political development in this dimension.

These studies, quite naturally, have been influenced by the expansion of relations that has accompanied the process of decolonisation.   Until the beginnings of nationalism in Africa, students of 'the colonial problem' were interested less in African politics *per se* than in European policy and administration.   Because of their presumed special problems of weakness and underdevelopment, African territories did attract the interest of a few scholars (Buell 1927, 1928) during the interwar years, and special international attention was suggested.   An interest in the fortunes of that new form of international administration, the Mandate System, drew a few historians (Logan 1948) to consideration of the fate of African Mandated territories under pressures generated by conflicts among the Great Powers.   Directly descended from this interest are studies of the effects of Trusteeship in several African territories.   In general, their conclusion is that certain practices innovated by Trusteeship, such as Special Visiting Missions, contributed to the growth of nationalism and hence to more rapid progress towards independence, but that Trust Territories were subject to treatment similar to colonies at the hands of the colonial powers.   The knotty problems involved in 'self-determination', the pace of progress, the form of political development, and the ultimate disposition of the territories, therefore, were not 'solved' by Trust status (Bates 1955; Coleman 1956; McKay 1957; Castagno 1959; Goldblatt 1961).   Indeed, they were further complicated by the objectives of the different administering powers and their reactions to international criticism.

The progress of decolonisation in Africa has contributed nothing special to resolving 'the great issues of nationalism and self-determination', although it has shunted them aside, as Rupert Emerson (1960) has shown in the only study thus far which attempts to assess the significance of decolonisation for international relations.   The international politics of new states initially operate within the framework established by colonial partitions, but existing fragmentary studies of trans-territorial political activity yield support for tentative hypotheses about the emergence of new patterns.

Certain students have followed the growth of non-official contacts and conferences that have contributed to the development of the spirit of 'pan-Africanism'.

The cultural dimensions — e.g., 'Negritude' — and its ideological reflection in the politics of new African states — e.g., 'communocratic government', or 'a United States of Africa' — have been the subject of much curiosity and comment (Padmore 1956; Henry 1959; Decraene 1961; Wallerstein 1961; 103–35; Legum 1962). The scope and precise nature of the impact of organisations emerging from the All-Africa Peoples Conferences and the Afro-Asian Solidarity Conference — to take just two examples — remain difficult to evaluate, although it is clear that they play an important role in stimulating the growth of nationalism in colonial territories. Tracing the evolution of non-official associations into official organisations and classifying the myriad forms of functional and territorial federations, confederations and blocs have become nearly full-time undertakings for students of African politics (Hodgkin and Schachter 1960; Legum 1962; 133–278; Kloman 1962; Marcum 1962). Impressive rosters of types of formal co-operative organisations have been compiled, and discussions of the 'politics of blocs' take account of differences among African leaders about the scope and strength of their respective organs of co-operation. Other issues, however, also arise, and analyses must give weight to differing territorial ambitions — often based on the artificial partition of tribal lands — and differing notions of the nature and proper pace of modernisation.

Assessment of the full significance of pan-African ties awaits further research — and further stabilisation of relations. At this point it is possible to build an impressive case for the 'success' of nationalist parochialism as analyses of growing 'irredentisms' in various parts of Africa (Merle 1959; Castagno 1960) attest. Consequently, there remain differences of opinion on the role of pan-Africanism in the process of political modernisation. Wallerstein (1961: 118–9) has concluded that political pan-Africanism correlates with tendencies towards radical nationalism, centralisation of power and modernisation. Apter and Coleman (1960: 16–25) have argued somewhat differently: the imperatives of nation-building and some of the very sentiments which support pan-Africanism — i.e., democracy and socialism — tend to reinforce national separateness when applied concretely within state boundaries. In addition, it is possible to show that some recent efforts to achieve political unity may be dysfunctional to complete political and economic independence — e.g., federation in Central Africa and the functional ties between the members of the 'Brazzaville group' and between those states and France. These differences should not be exaggerated, but they suggest a great need for further classification of types and levels of pan-Africanism and analysis of its political expressions in action before general hypotheses can be elaborated and tested.

The final area of studies of African international relations is that of political responses to the pressures of world politics. There has been much discussion of the policy of African states with respect to issues of 'the Cold War'. In common with most of the underdeveloped world, African states have adopted a posture of 'neutralism' or 'non-alignment'. Assessments of the meaning of neutralism as an overall policy and in particular situations form an essential part of all investigations of foreign policy and international politics today, but no clear picture has emerged. The Congo crisis of 1960–61 provided the first opportunity for close observation of the way African states advanced their basic interests, and conclusions about the evolution of 'blocs' reflect positions taken at the height of tension. Inspection of the dynamics of neutralism has led to a general hypothesis about the connections between foreign and domestic politics in the new African states (Good 1961; Wallerstein 1961: 147–51, 1962a; Glickman 1961). Neutralism, pan-Africanism,

African socialism and radical nationalism — as ideas and as institutions — are seen as closely related to one another.   Although their precise connections remain unclear and therefore, fertile areas for exploration, 'positive neutralism', militant pan-Africanism, and mass parties of integration also seem to be related concepts.

The interest in neutralism is matched by an interest in certain other aspects of African international relations.   The course of African political development obviously will be deeply affected by the influence of Marxism, communist penetration, the influence of smaller powers such as Israel and Egypt in the affairs of individual states, the evolution of economic and cultural ties between the developed world and Africa, and the defence and security arrangements African states make for themselves (McKay 1954; Marcum 1957; Cattell 1959; Morrison 1961; Laqueur 1961; Rivkin 1962).   In fact, all the issues of African international politics may be seen as resulting from the Africans' continuing search for grounds on which to manoeuvre more freely in the face of numerous persistent dependency relationships. In this realm the diversification of dependency ties reinforces a doctrinal commitment to 'neutralism'.   Evidence for the effectiveness of African responses to their perceived interests may be culled from the behaviour of African delegations at the UN.   Thomas Hovet (1962) has indicated the peculiar significance of the UN as the prime arena for inter-African contact and as a ready-made forum for the views of small states (Spencer 1962).

Much remains to be done if the study of African international politics is to meet the challenge of the development and diversification of relationships.   The issues of decolonisation and national integration serve to force new African states into a variety of unstable positions and alignments, and analysis which is too closely concerned with current policy can mistake tactical moves for permanent trends. Although the historical perspective necessary for judgment is still lacking, there may be a process of 'phasing' of issues at work; the alignments between several states which are based on their shared demand for national liberation may not coincide with other emergent alignments which are based on similar interpretations of the problem of internal civil liberties.   This possibility suggests that the analytical models utilised in studying the development of territorial political systems may be adapted to the study of the development of trans-territorial systems, since conflict may be involved in the roles assumed by leaders of contemporary 'blocs' in Africa as well as in the leadership roles assumed within a single state.   The main point, however, is that African international politics are developing in ways and circumstances different from those which have prevailed in other regions and in previous eras.   New restraints operate, and new opportunities for exerting influence exist. The politics of neutralism and the mounting importance of the UN symbolise a new significance for Africa in international politics, but, more important, they may also symbolise Africa's contribution to a changing system of world politics.   Although future analysis must not ignore the customary artifacts of international politics inside Africa, it must be alert to the use of new instruments and techniques of international contact and pressure.

V   THE FUTURE OF RESEARCH IN AFRICAN POLITICS

1. SOME CAVEATS

Despite the trans-territorial strength of the forces shaping the transfers of power and the politics of modernisation in Africa, the lack of reliable data and the fluidity of relations within and between territorial units have limited the claims and the acceptance of the validity of most studies to specific circumstances.   The most useful studies are those which can delineate the structure of emerging political relationships in terms which transcend the particular case.   At this stage, however, no two case studies with these pretensions have been conducted in the same terms or with the same analytical model.   In order to cope with the highly transitional nature of African politics, a number of students have worked at the other end of the spectrum and produced several brief but extremely suggestive surveys of global trends in African politics.   But these have not been closely related to research on particular cases.   Except for rough, descriptive comparisons, the surveys which promise explanatory power have not been linked to the case studies of the same nature, although there are signs of more scientific co-operation in the character of extant research projects — if not in their individual products up to now.

As the colonial territories receive their independence, there is some danger that political scientists may permit the legal forms of government to dictate their interests and analytical frameworks.   The pressing need for information about structures of government and political issues within the new states creates great pressure to make only slight adjustments in the way their political processes are analysed.   This only postpones evaluation of the new states with categories more representative of their institutions or with frameworks more revealing of their styles of politics.

Despite these difficulties, political study of Africa does require at least a rough inventory of governments, their primary structural components and recent political histories.   In fact, a rapid multiplication of configurative studies with this con-glomerate focus is in the offing.   Until now there have been few attempts to analyse the transfer of power in the separate territories as a process which involves the influence of colonial policy, the cultural and social structure of the territory, and international pressures.   In the same vein, case studies which illuminate the precise nature and extent of dependency relationships with the former metropole or with other powers, the relationships between political organisation and particular ethnic configurations, and the relationship between constitutional formalities and govern-mental practices, would be welcome; they are in fact prerequisite to reliable generalisations in the future.   A full-length study of every legal political entity in Africa will not solve students' analytical problems, and in any case is quixotic.   It is likely, nevertheless, that Africa-wide generalisations will require modification as variations in economic, geographic and ideological factors find expression in concrete political systems.

Comparative analysis and theory construction, on the other hand, do not await the completion of depth-probings into a large number of new African states.   A number of research schemes and preliminary surveys already provide the grounds for generalisations about the forms and functions of African political systems, parties, the growth of nationalism, pan-Africanism, and the role of Africa in world politics.   Available also are variations of institutional and functional approaches, which offer some general means for connecting configurative to comparative studies.

2. SOME SUGGESTIONS

Africanists in political science face their future tasks in a buoyant mood.   The 'first generation' of analysts of the African revolution has succeeded in providing a map of the general lines of political development in an astonishingly short time.   The main political forces which have swept over a whole continent have been met head-on by investigators, and it would seem fair to say that at this stage preliminary conclusions about the evolution of decolonisation, the growth of nationalism, and the main problems of national unification will serve to frame future projects designed to fill in the gaps in particular sectors.   Not only are the descriptive frameworks remarkably comprehensive, but the analytical models, centring on concepts such as social mobilisation and role conflict, have demonstrated preliminary results which suggest wider applications.   In common with other under-developed areas, the politics of Africa seem amenable to a functional approach, which in turn may suggest certain conclusions about the process of political develop-ment in any place and time.

The map that is available, however, represents only the results of the first observations of the terrain.   The markings remain vague, especially if they are supposed to identify specific features.   It is important to continue to compile more evidence of political structures and political processes in local situations, so that more refined classifications and hypotheses may be attempted.   Sufficiently sug-gestive models already exist for the analysis of macropolitics, and further evidence of institutional development could be related in a more cumulative fashion.   The existent models also suggest certain other general lines of inquiry.   The analysis of modernisation, for example, requires somewhat more refined concepts for the discussion of such processes as political acculturation, i.e., the development of a civil consciousness crystallising around a national unit.   The psychology of what used to be called 'citizenship education' is a research area that has had some atten-tion in Europe and the United States; perhaps the concept of 'reference groups' deserves more use in the African setting.

To take another example from the analysis of modernisation: a distinction might be made between social and political modernisation and industrialisation. Many of the institutional aspects of modern society can be developed in Africa without being co-ordinated with an advancing industrialisation. Expanding modernisation in this respect need not even accompany expanding 'rationalisation' of the political process.   Research in this area would require a closer look at political and economic planning: its goals, its effectiveness, and its specific impact on the sort of economic and political development that actually takes place.

Modernisation may also take on distinctive 'styles', arising from the cultural and institutional opportunities available to the emergent elites and peculiar to the type and circumstances of stewardship prior to independence.   Hence the expres-sion of issues and the manner in which political business is conducted may some-times relate more directly to the politics of Britain or France than to the problems of Africa.   Similarly, the analysis of 'plural societies' might derive some benefit from comparisons with non-African territories beset by communal divisions, such as Malaya or the Caribbean states.

Future research might also be improved by some shrinkage in the scope of individual efforts.   The influence of ideas of property and land ownership has long been recognised as extremely important in the process of modernisation.   Litiga-tion over land rights, for example, remains an important source of political tension. Indeed the whole question of the role of traditional loyalties can be attacked through consideration of the problem of the individual's relation to the land worked by his family or fellow-villagers.   Roland Young (1962) has emphasised the signi-ficance for political studies of the fact that political systems have been related to control over the environment.   The nature of the land shapes the form and the functions of traditional systems, and it is clear that progress in developing the economies of many of the new states is heavily dependent on reorganisation of political privileges associated with the land.   Several purposes might therefore be served by more research on the politics of land use at the village level.   The impact of the establishment of bureaucratic governmental structures, the nature of political adaptation, and the process of communicating the objectives and procedures of a national political community to groups only intermittently participant in its mechanisms, can all be assessed.

Finally, certain topics have been unduly neglected up to now.   It has often been observed that African leadership is quite young compared to that in other regions.   Yet the contributions of youth as a group to the process of modernisation in Africa have not been analysed, nor have the problems of the short span between first and second generation political elites been given more than passing attention. The role of youth and student groups in formal as well as categorical associations might be singled out for special treatment because of the obvious influence they already wield as the carriers of the ideals of national reconstruction.   In another realm, guerrilla warfare and the control of violence would seem to be increasingly prominent factors in determining the leadership of territories still seeking independence from colonialism.   It is not yet clear how this will affect the type of political systems that emerge, nor what precise significance this will have on ties between nations and groups proffering and receiving military assistance.   The military factor, however, deserves extended treatment (Coleman and Brice 1962), not only because of its present broadening role but also because of its prominence in the process of modernisation in other underdeveloped areas.

The optimism here expressed about the future course of studies of African politics stems from the evidence of fruitful communication between political science and its neighbouring disciplines.   Analytical concepts have been freely borrowed from models utilised in sociological and anthropological studies.   Some political scientists would even maintain that progress in all political studies depends upon a discriminating use of concepts and techniques utilised in the 'behavioural sciences'. Continued advance in the study of socialisation and of communication, for example, would directly benefit the analytical work of political science in Africa.   An understanding of African political development — the most pressing demand on political science at present — will only come about through the continued readiness of political scientists to make use of the work of their fellow social scientists.   This has been amply demonstrated in comprehending the problems of nationalism and will be fully borne out as research proceeds on problems of modernisation.

6

Law   A. Arthur Schiller

I LEGAL PLURALISM *

1. INTRODUCTION

A SURVEY OF RESEARCH in the field of law throughout the continent of
Africa would seem at first sight to require separate treatment of the independent
states, of the emerging states, and of the remaining colonial possessions of European
nations.   In the case of a few states, such as the United Arab Republic or the
Republic of South Africa, separate treatment might well be preferable.   But in line
with the other contributions to this volume, it seems best to frame this discussion
in light of a common factor pervading the legal structure throughout the continent,
namely, legal pluralism.

The presence of a number of legal systems within a given area is a phenomenon
not unique to Africa.   The resolution of the problems arising from the interaction
and the integration of distinct legal systems within the territories of Africa takes
prime place in a study of the legal structure of that continent.   In the region termed
'south of the Sahara' the recurring component elements are indigenous legal systems
existing alongside the non-indigenous Western-oriented law.   Generally there are
a number of indigenous legal systems within the area, corresponding to the various
tribal units.   The non-indigenous law derives from that country which occupied
the territory.   In this survey reference will be made primarily to research available
on the English-speaking areas.   This research does not necessarily cover the same
ground as studies on the former French or Belgian territories, or upon the Portuguese or Spanish provinces in Africa, but the English research is typical of the effort
devoted to the field of African law.   Bibliographical reference to studies in the
other areas must suffice for further coverage.

In some of the stretches in Africa just south of the Sahara, a third legal system
finds its place, the Islamic law.   The Islamic law practised by the native population
largely replaces the indigenous law, with the result that a doctrinaire application of
Islamic law is normally precluded.   Refashioned Islamic law, substituting for or
existing alongside indigenous law is found in combination with the Western-derived
system in most of the states *d'expression française*, in the former British possessions
of West Africa, in Sudan and Somalia, and in East Africa.

* Notes for this chapter will be found on page 512, and Bibliography on page 522.

The legal pluralism of tropical and southern Africa contrasts sharply with that found in North Africa.   In North Africa, Islam has practically displaced the indigenous law of the Berbers, and thus the plurality derives from the introduction of Western law into the local Islamic scene.   The interaction of the two systems has been the subject of intensive study for decades, particularly in Algeria and in the former French protectorates, though such study has been divorced from any tie with comparable situations south of the Sahara.   In this chapter major attention will be given: (1) to the delineation of the component elements of the law south of the Sahara (indigenous, non-indigenous, and Islamic law); (2) to the legal policy, forms and techniques which have been or will in the future be adopted to establish national legal systems; (3) to the organisation of the courts and the administration of justice of African territories; and (4) to a survey of the primary research in the substance of the law.   North African law will be treated occasionally in excursus, inasmuch as the legal situation in those states is not truly comparable to that of the remainder of the continent.   In this sphere the reader is again advised to consult other bibliographical aids.

2. INDIGENOUS LAW

The first component element of the pluralistic legal systems found in Africa is the law of the indigenous population.   This is frequently termed 'African customary law' or, in British legislative parlance, 'native law and custom'.   Though it may be argued that the common characteristic, namely, pluralism, which affords a tie in the legal sphere and leads to a general 'African law', is over-emphasised, most scholars recognise common elements in African indigenous law.   Evidence in support of this unity in African customary law has been offered by Allott.[1]   Certainly variations in habitat, economic activity, social organisation and the rest, lead to diversity in legal institutions and legal rules, as they do in all other facets of society.   Still, common features in the indigenous law prevail.   Customary law is not professional law.   It is not taught in law schools nor is it practised by advocates.   It is unwritten law tracing back to the habits and usages of the people.   In these respects there is nothing peculiarly 'African' about the indigenous law, for there are other peoples who have no written legal system—as for example, the indigenous population of Indonesia.[2]   But certain distinctive features, attitudes and procedures do characterise the indigenous law of Africa.   Here the role of the court or arbiter serves to promote settlement as well as to educate the assembled spectators and parties in the legal norms of the society.   Here the supernatural is invoked in a whole gamut of legal institutions.   And in African law the presence of the community or communal action is involved in connection with individual rights and duties.   In contrast to the unity of African indigenous law, it might be suggested that distinct law circles, law areas and law families are also to be found on the continent. This line of research was pioneered by van Vollenhoven in Indonesian adat (customary) law.[3]

What was possibly a first attempt at synthesis of African customary law in the ideology of the indigenous population itself was the work of Possoz, a Belgian scholar.[4]   To Possoz, it appeared that the body of rules comprising indigenous customary law stemmed from philosophical concepts wholly foreign to our view of life.   The idea that 'paternity is law, law is paternity', seems fundamental.   The patriarch, the chief, the living representative of the common ancestor of the members of the clan or tribe, is the holder of all rights.   Members of the paternal group exercise rights solely at the will of this 'pater'. To Possoz, the notion of paternity, that is, *inequality*, is basic to all African customary law. The Belgian missionary, Father Tempels, also attempted to describe the position of customary law as seen by the Bantu.[5] Bantu philosophy centres around the idea of *muntu*: living force. Life is force, capable of being reinforced. This living force is the centre of all humanity. As such, it is the norm of natural law as well as of positive law. From the Bantu point of view, all customary law is inspired, animated and justified by reason of the idea of the vital force; its values and its strength are based on this and other integrally related philosophical ideas.

Discussions in English of the nature of the African indigenous law have come from social anthropologists. Among the earlier students of the African field, law — reinforced by religious and social sanctions — was viewed as embracing the totality of the rules of conduct regulating the behaviour of society.[6] In contrast, Radcliffe-Brown adopted a definition of law, attributed to the jurist Pound, in which law is 'social control through the systematic application of the force of politically organized society'. Hence, he maintained that the field of law was coterminous with that of organised legal sanctions and thus obligations imposed where there were no legal sanctions were matters of custom but not of law.[7] Fortes and Evans-Pritchard adopted this view in distinguishing between those indigenous societies of Africa (Group A) 'which have centralized authority, administrative machinery, and judicial institutions — in short, a government', and those (Group B) which lack such authority, machinery and constituted judicial institutions.[8] Evans-Pritchard can thus state, in oft-quoted words: 'In the strict sense of the word, the Nuer have no law. There is no one with legislative or judicial functions. There are conventional payments considered due . . . but these do not make a legal system, for there is no constituted and impartial authority who decides on the rights and wrongs of a dispute and there is no external power to enforce such a decision were it given.'[9]

In a recent collection of anthropological studies, Tait notes that he omitted discussion of law among the Konkomba of northern Ghana inasmuch as 'there are no patterns for formal legislation or for judicial decisions, nor are there law enforcement officers of any kind'.[10] Thus in the Radcliffe-Brown sense there is no law; there are merely standards of behaviour for the breach of which the individual offended or the group involved may take action in retribution against the offender, such action being approved by Konkomba society as a whole. Tait would term these 'jural activities' — Fortes had spoken of 'jural relations' — punitive acts with moral backing, but not law. Goldschmidt has recently argued that, in the distinction between tribal societies and states, emphasis should be placed on the structure that is to be found.[11] Government is distinguished from law; law may be found in tribal societies which are without government. It is in the state social system that the governmental structure has the function of maintaining order, and accordingly has a monopoly on the legitimate use of force: that is, on the institution and procedures of adjudication. It is the absence of the exercise of such powers by a third party or group in the settlement of disputes and not the absence of law, that distinguishes tribal society from a state.

Other anthropologists concerned with the nature of African law have been influenced by those jurists who have emphasised the role of the courts in the fashioning of the law. Salmond has defined law as the 'body of principles recognised and applied by the state in the administration of justice'.[12] Schapera reflects this view in describing Tswana law when he notes that certain rules of conduct were enforced by tribal courts though others were not.[13]   Hence, for him, law is any rule of conduct likely to be enforced by the courts if and when it is brought before them.   Gluckman offers an elaborate discussion of the nature of indigenous law as embodied in the decisions of the native courts.[14]   Law consists, first, of the body of general rules (*corpus juris*) to which people ought to conform and which the courts ought to enforce, and second, of a series of specific judgments in particular disputes (adjudication).   Gluckman calls attention to the rational processes employed by Lozi judges — reminiscent of Western judicial processes — in handling general principles and particular rules in an attempt to achieve justice.   For instance, the Lozi judge places considerable weight on the concept of the 'reasonable man'.[15] Gluckman concludes his illuminating study with a consideration of the implications of the Lozi judicial process for jurisprudential problems of universal interest.

Sharply contrasted to Gluckman's approach is that of Bohannon.[16]   In a description of the manner in which the Tiv people of central Nigeria resolve disputes without the use of formal courts or agencies to enforce decisions, this anthropologist deplores the attempt to translate the Tiv folk-system into categories and concepts of another society.   In order to understand Tiv law, he suggests it is necessary to present the ideas and the processes involved in the ways the Tiv think of them rathern than in Western terms.   Some anthropologists have quarrelled with this approach to African customary law.[17]   Gluckman notes the fact that terms like 'law' have many meanings and there are many defensible definitions.[18]   To select a particular sense of the word and then to force a whole range of diverse phenomena within this single connotation leads to distortion of the evidence.   Equally erroneous, says Gluckman, is the failure to distinguish verbally between entirely different processes of social control, such as the court trial, the Eskimo song-contest, or the Ndembu divinatory séance.   But acceptance of the idea that it is improper to describe the 'folk-system' of one people in the categories of another would sterilise research in tribal law.   Gluckman concludes that disagreement often arises because authorities apply different intrinsic meanings of multivocal words such as 'law' to different ranges of facts.   He suggests employing different words and phrases from the wealth of the English language to cover different phenomena.

The social anthropologists have provided exhaustive studies of many African societies.   They have described the nature and extent of the indigenous law, or at least the jural relations of these societies.   Account is seldom taken, however, of the possible impact of Western institutions upon the indigenous systems.[19]   But the lawyer interested in African law and seeking to determine the nature of indigenous law cannot disregard the roles of the Western legislative and judicial organs.   The colonial power has usually provided that, subject to certain limitations, indigenous law is to be applied in the disputes heard before the native courts.   In the British territories such law is generally described as 'native law and custom', but other terms like 'native law' or 'customary law' or a particular system, such as 'Buganda law', are also to be found.   Though there appears to be no judicial determination, the consensus of opinion is that whatever word or phrase is employed, the same concept is intended.[20]   Lawyers, like anthropologists, differ in their opinions of the nature of 'native law and custom', or customary law.   Hannigan states that the phrase may connote, first, custom, which must be proved; and second, native law, which is derived from judicial decisions and needs no proving.[21]   This stems from the fact that — if Salmond's definition of law is employed — unless and until a rule of native custom is judicially noticed it cannot be treated as law. This view is set forth as dictum in a case before the Judicial Committee of the Privy Council:

> As is the case with all customary law, it has to be proved in the first instance by calling witnesses acquainted with the native customs until the particular customs have by frequent proof in the courts become so notorious that the courts will take judicial notice of them. [22]

Hence, to Hannigan, native custom does not fall within the category known in English law as 'legal custom', but it is to be considered 'conventional custom' and thus constitutes a matter of fact capable of being varied by the courts until it has been accepted by judicial notice.

Criticism of this point of view has been expressed by Read, who states that it is too narrow a view of 'native law and custom'. [23] The customary rules which form the basis of decisions by native courts are certainly valid legal rules, even if they do not have the approval of non-native courts. On the other hand, there is no need for the assent of the community — as there is for 'conventional custom' — before a native custom may be said to exist; the decision of a court or a decree by a tribal chief is sufficient. Perhaps the difficulty may be resolved by distinguishing, as Allott does, between native customary law as a question of fact, and native customary law as a matter of law. [24] In this way, habits, customs, manners of common or general knowledge can be judicially noticed as notorious fact, while customary law, known to the judges or the courts concerned with its administration, can be noticed as law, whether the parties to the litigation are aware of its existence or not.

It does seem valuable to differentiate custom from law, though not necessarily so decisively as in the formulation 'law is what is enforced, custom is what is not enforced'. [25] In their book on Haya customary law, [26] Cory and Hartnoll note that some paragraphs deal not with customary law but with custom. The reason for this is that, although such custom has legal consequences, no penalty is imposed for its disregard. It serves merely as the background for cases litigated before the courts. Some of the legal textbooks devoted to a treatment of 'native law' likewise seek to differentiate between those habits and usages which form the background upon which disputes are laid and those customary norms utilised by native courts in arriving at their decisions. [27]

When the idea prevailed that custom completely guided the lives and actions of the members of primitive societies, it might have been proper to denominate as customary law a system in which the rules of law traced back to the habits and usages of the people and remained completely unwritten. [28] Even so, the indigenous law of primitive peoples seems to have had little in common with the external expression of the popular consciousness of the particular society — the German people — to which the term 'customary law' (Gewohnheitsrecht) was first applied. [29] In any event, in recent years 'African customary law' has been used to describe legal systems in which the unwritten law has been significantly replaced by legislative enactment, by executive and administrative declarations and, above all, by a host of judicial decisions. [30] At a recent conference in London, many of the participants deplored the use of the term, preferring the designation 'native law' or even 'local law'. [31] Neither of these is wholly satisfactory. The former has unpleasant overtones, while the latter is not truly descriptive of the content. So long as one keeps in mind that African customary law or indigenous law is one of the major component elements of African law, and hence derives from a variety of sources in addition to 'custom', and will continue to play a significant role in the future, then little harm is done, whatever the term used.

Legislation, both the traditional and the Western in form, together with decisions of the local courts (native courts, African courts) and of the ordinary courts (primarily administering non-indigenous law), have supplemented the unwritten legal rules. In some areas it has been said that 'native law and custom' which derives from non-native administration or judicial decision surpasses in extent the customary law which flows from the traditional sources.[32] This raises the question: how do the judges obtain knowledge of the rules of customary law to be applied in deciding cases brought before them? A distinction must be made between judges of the native courts and those of the ordinary courts.

The primary source of legal rulings for the native courts is tribal custom, the usual practice. This is generally acceptable, if certain and established, and related to the class of person involved in the controversy. A second source of law might be either statutes of the governing power or the enactments of the tribal rulers, if such existed in a given society. Decisions of superior courts and earlier decisions of their own native court or courts could be called upon, but as illustrations of customary practice or indicative of moral principles rather than as binding or even persuasive precedents. Moral principles and ethics, the regular processes of nature and of human behaviour: these complete the list of sources to which Lozi judges turned, according to the observations of Gluckman.[33] The analysis of the manner in which sources of law are called upon by judges in Tswana tribal courts affirms the practice of the Lozi judges, save that reliance upon tribal legislation is somewhat exceptional.[34] The problem of the ascertainment of customary law was one of the topics discussed at the London conference.[35] It was suggested that the notion of uncertainty in the indigenous law was in the minds of foreigners rather than of those subject to its rules. It was admitted that in some areas the younger generation was not learning the traditional custom. Uncertainty might arise about which customary law to apply if there were gaps in the law but, for the most part, the native courts were developing ways of dealing with present-day conditions.

In the non-native (ordinary) courts, at times concerned with indigenous law in first instance as well as on appeal or revision, customary law has to be pleaded and proven.[36] The proof is normally provided by witnesses. Sometimes the court may call upon assessors (experts in the customary law) to advise on questions of custom.[37] Referees (chiefs or other persons with specialised knowledge of the customary law) in some areas take the place of assessors, their opinions constituting evidence presumed correct rather than mere advice given to the judge. In addition, authoritative textbooks and judicial decisions may provide evidence of indigenous law. The decision of a native court on customary law is a determination of a question of fact as far as the appellate or revisional non-native court is concerned, and hence should not lightly be departed from unless an erroneous view would thus be established.

The indigenous law, however, may be a question of law rather than of fact to the superior non-native court. As stated above, when rules of indigenous law have become notorious by reason of frequent decisions the court takes judicial notice of such rules. When the stamp of authority is thus placed on such legal principles, further proof is not required. In addition, the doctrines of case law and precedent — English legal techniques in an African setting — then come to play a role in the development of the customary law.[38]

Indigenous law can be readily ascertained by the courts if it has been reduced to writing under governmental auspices. But there has been only one instance of comprehensive enactment of customary law by a central legislature, namely, the Natal Code of Native Law. Opinions differ as to the value of this codification and it is significant that this example has not been followed.[39] Some of the tribal societies in the past resorted to their own legislative formalities to alter or modify the traditional law, and there are compilations made by various native organs which are generally accepted as authoritative.[40] At present there is statutory provision in many territories for declaration by local authorities of what customary law is applicable in the area and of the statutory power to modify the indigenous law and to limit its application.[41]

Customary law has long been recognised as the law generally applicable to the indigenous population.[42] But there are two circumstances in which it is excluded: first, if it is inconsistent with existing legislation, and second, if it is repugnant to natural justice, equity or good conscience.[43] Little difficulty arises with respect to the interpretation of the first of these limitations. There appears to be no restriction on the local (colonial) legislature from over-riding the indigenous customary law, and there certainly can be no curtailment of the sovereign power of an independent state in this regard. The determination of what constitutes repugnancy — a determination to be made by the courts — has proved more difficult. The application of the doctrine has conclusively brought about the rejection of barbarous customs and harmful practices as offensive to 'good conscience' or 'morality'.[44] But the judges have not applied strict English standards or ideas of Christian ethics to reject customary law. 'Natural justice' has been interpreted to comprehend many of the basic human rights that have become recognised in the rule of law, while 'equity', in the general sense of the term, imparts that degree of fairness which calls for the disregard of substantive rules of law when these produce unfair results. To one writer, the equitable principles which stem from technical English 'equity' have played a major role in the modification of the indigenous law.[45] In many systems the elimination of portions of the customary law held 'repugnant to natural justice, equity and good conscience' has provided the means by which the indigenous law can be adapted to meet the new social and economic needs of Africa.

Indigenous law is far from being a static body of rules even though it is based on oral tradition. It responds slowly to social and economic and political change, but like all other aspects of indigenous African culture, the tempo currently has steadily quickened. Customary law is the dynamic factor in the slogan: 'changing law in a changing Africa'.[46]

3. NON-INDIGENOUS LAW

The other major element in the law of the plural societies of Africa is the non-indigenous law. Normally this is based upon the law of the colonial power which occupied the territory, though occasionally it may either wholly or in part be a foreign legal system voluntarily chosen by an African state. In the British possessions in Africa, English law was introduced by express enactment.[47] In many cases there was a general reception of the English law, namely, 'the common law, the doctrines of equity and the statutes of general application which were then in force in England'; that is, at the time the colony or protectorate was established. There has been little question as to the nature of the common law or the doctrines of equity. As for statutes of general application, these must be determined in the individual case. A test often employed for this determination is to consider by what courts the statute was applied in England, and to what classes of the community it was applied. There has also been general reception of the English law outside the purely British dependencies, as in the Sudan,[48] and, through the medium of the American law, in Liberia.[49]

English common law, doctrines of equity, and statutes of general application thus provide the residual law of the territory: the source of law in the absence of other legal rule. This raises an important question as to the authority of the decisions of English courts in the African courts, since the content of the common law and equity as well as the interpretation of statutes depends on the decisions of the courts in the Anglo-American legal system.[50] It appears that decisions on common law and equity handed down by English courts prior to the date of the reception of English law in the territory are binding upon colonial courts, while those subsequent in date are not binding but are entitled to the highest respect, unless the English law itself has been changed. Decisions of English courts on statutes of general application in force in a territory are binding on the local courts if handed down before the date of reception, and of persuasive authority if thereafter. Where there are colonial statutes similar to English statutes (*pari materia*), decisions of English courts upon the English statutes are not binding upon the colonial courts, but persuasive to an extent which depends upon the rank of the court rendering the decision, the force of the decision as precedent in England, and whether it was given before or after the date of the colonial statute. Decisions of the Judicial Committee of the Privy Council stand upon a different footing, since the decisions of this court are binding upon all inferior colonial tribunals.[51]

The development of the non-indigenous law within the colony or protectorate has taken on added importance in the years preceding independence. English law which had been received might be modified by reason of its conflict with pre-existing systems of law, whether or not indigenous.[52] Further, the courts of the colony may, by statute, be called upon to exclude an English rule of law when it would be manifestly inapplicable by reason of the local circumstances. Finally, in accord with the case-law system which flourishes in the British possessions, the local courts may modify and substantially alter the rules of the common law, doctrines of equity, or statutory enactment which have ultimately derived from the English source. Colonial legislatures have been set up, and in the course of years the enactments of these bodies have largely replaced the English statutes of general application as well as other British legislation introduced into the African territories.[53] It is clear, though not always recognised, that the non-indigenous law of the African territory is not identical with the law of the mother country.[54]

The territories of other colonial powers reflect similar adoption and adaptation of the law of the mother country.[55] Reference to the decisions of the courts of the homeland is not generally found, due to the different concept of the role of courts in continental legal systems. But, as with the British, the metropolitan law has been modified and adapted to local circumstances, by local legislation and by the decisions of colonial courts. As an example of the extent to which a legal system has been provided for the non-African elements of the society, attention may be directed to the description of the non-indigenous law of the Belgian Congo just before independence.[56] Increasing autonomy and eventual independence may well loosen the bonds with the non-indigenous law inherited from the mother country, both in non-British and in British colonies and protectorates. The excellent study of the private law of Tunisia by Jambu-Merlin portrays the shift in the legal system of the former French protectorate.[57] Comparable studies of many of the former British possessions should appear in the near future.

Obviously the reception of the law of the homeland accounts for the type of non-indigenous law found in most of Africa. But there are instances which depart from the general picture. Roman-Dutch law, derived from Holland in the seventeenth and eighteenth centuries, persists in South Africa, and has been introduced into Southern Rhodesia and the High Commission Territories.[58] English law was early received in the Sudan but at present it is applicable only in the civil division courts, if it be the 'custom' (personal law) of the parties concerned.[59] The adoption of Western law wholly foreign to an African state is evidenced in Ethiopia where a series of codes is in the process of being promulgated.[60]

The non-indigenous law in the African territories has served as a most essential complement to indigenous law by satisfying the needs of a population entering into the modern world. It has exerted considerable force in the total development of the legal systems of the various territories. The techniques which have grown up in the Western homelands have been taken over in the colonial possessions to good purpose. Legislative devices and judicial doctrines have served as unifying forces in the evolution of the law of the African lands.[61] Thus the reception of non-indigenous law has provided much of the substance of the legal rules and has introduced a dynamic element into the establishment of the legal systems of Africa.

4. ISLAMIC LAW

Many of the plural legal systems in Africa possess a special cachet by reason of the intrusion of Islamic law into the complex of indigenous African law and non-indigenous Western law. In contrast to the relatively uniform juxtaposition of the latter two elements in most of tropical and southern Africa, the reception of Islamic law displays two distinct forms. In North Africa, Islamic law has almost completely displaced indigenous customary law. Different schools of Islamic law prevail in the various states of North Africa. Actually, the role of Islamic law in this part of the continent differs little from that accorded it in the Near and Middle East. *Sharia* (the divine law of Islam) has been challenged in the past century by legislative enactments derived from European law and more recently by reform legislation of Islamic character.[62] Inasmuch as the contrast between Islamic law and legislative enactment in North Africa is not the typical African dichotomy, and since this contrast has been largely the subject of study by a group of scholars with no concern for the legal systems of Africa south of the Sahara, it has little relation to the remainder of the subject matter of this chapter. The present status of Islamic law in the 'Arab' states is a subject of its own.

Attention may be drawn to a single recent study which indicates the trend of legal development in the Islamic law of North Africa. In one of a series of volumes devoted to contemporary legal systems, Jambu-Merlin offers a most illuminating study of the private law of Tunisia.[63] He points out that prior to the French Protectorate, Moslem courts applied Islamic law in controversies involving Moslems, rabbinical courts heard cases concerning Jewish residents, while consular tribunals judged their nationals according to their own laws. With the establishment of the Protectorate in Tunisia, French courts gained competence over all cases concerning foreigners, applying French codes of civil and criminal procedure and the laws and

ordinances then in force in Algeria.   In the course of the following decades French
law gave way to local (Tunisian) legislation.   Gradually civil courts took over from
the religious courts, though the law applied in matters of personal status and family
continued to be the personal (religious) law of the parties.   The enactment of the
Code of Personal Status in 1956 put an end to questions of internal conflict of laws,
that is, the choice of law when the personal status of the parties differed.   The
French courts were suppressed in 1957 and today there exists a single hierarchy of
courts.   Though the Code of Personal Status is a modern rendition of principles of
Islamic law in the field of persons, family and succession, its interpretation is in the
hands of civil rather than of religious judges.   The idea that the law depends upon
the status of the person (principle of personality) has been displaced.   Thus the
plurality of legal systems in Tunisia is a thing of the past.   There is today a single
legal system composed of a fusion of French and Tunisian — in part based on
Islamic — legal rules.

Throughout a broad belt stretching across Africa south of the Sahara and in
eastern Africa Islamic law occupies a very different position from that held in North
Africa.   In some places it virtually replaces the indigenous law, but more frequently
it constitutes the particular law of a segment of the society, a part of the 'native law
and custom'.[64]   In the latter situation, it regulates matters of personal status,
marriage and divorce, and occasionally succession, among the Moslem members of
the group.   The status of Islamic law differs considerably from area to area, and it is
particularly fortunate that there exists a detailed exposition of the place and nature
of Islamic law in the present and former British possessions in Africa.[65]   Among the
other areas of Africa where Islam has penetrated, the same diverse reception is
encountered.   In the Sudan, Islamic law is the indigenous law for the Moslem
population.[66]   To the east, in Eritrea, the Moslem population lives according to an
admixture of Islamic and customary norms.[67]   In Ethiopia proper, only the Moslem
population around Harrar is subject to Islamic law,[68] with the proviso that this may
be altered by reason of the enactment of the Civil Code.   In British Somaliland,
Islamic law prevailed as 'native law and custom' for the indigenous inhabitants, and
as the 'law of the defendant' in the case of immigrant Moslems.   For practical
purposes *Sharia* law of the Shafei school was applied in the subordinate courts.[69]   In
present-day Somalia, customary law and Islamic law undoubtedly share as the residual
law of the state, upon which are superimposed the accepted legislative enactments
of the previous regimes and the legislation of the independent state.[70]   In the states
d'expression française of West Africa the same relative impact of Islamic law is found,
from a virtual take-over as indigenous law in Mauretania to the particular law for
personal relations of the Moslem population in Guinea.

In the states of North Africa, where Islam reigns supreme, an ever-expanding
effort to codify the Islamic law is pursued.   In the course of such codification
modernisation of the law takes place, as for example, in Morocco with the Code of
Personal Status and Inheritance.[71]   Moroccan jurists of the Malikite school of
Islam have accepted the idea of codification, and a selection of opinions drawn from
the different schools and a variety of Islamic jurists form the basis of the rules laid
down.   The principle of selection appears to have been the public interest rather
than the merits of the arguments upon which the particular opinion was based.
Libya and Egypt are endeavouring to follow the path taken by Tunisia and Morocco.

In Africa south of the Sahara the future of Islamic law is more limited.
Anderson has competently told the story of the manner in which Islamic criminal

law was voluntarily given up in Northern Nigeria, to be replaced by a criminal code derived from the Anglo-Indian through the Sudan Penal Code.[72] In the Sudanic belt of Africa, Islamic law will ultimately be limited to the law of persons and of family, the law of succession and *waqf* (charitable foundation). Even the personal law of African Moslems needs reform.[73] Islamic law does not lend itself to judicial development; recourse would best be had to legislation, and it may well be wise to follow the practice employed in the North African codifications.[74] Where reform is needed (it does not seem advisable to displace Islamic law completely), machinery must be devised to provide authoritative judicial instructions — on the advice of Moslem jurists — that some more suitable rule be drawn from another recognised school of Islamic law or from some variant opinion in the same school. This substitution of another rule has already found support in the practice of the French courts in Algeria and in the machinery regularly used in the Sudan and in a series of laws promulgated in the independent Moslem countries of the Near and Middle East.

II *LEGAL POLICY AND ITS IMPLEMENTATION*

The swift current of political events in Africa affects the legal as it does all phases of social life. It is repetitive to emphasise the rapidity with which African society is moving into the world scene. But this does not necessarily imply a departure from policies and trends which have been followed in past decades. As a matter of fact, as far as law is concerned, there is little direct enunciation of policy aims and objectives in the new states of the African continent. Examination of trends in the development of the law and in the reorganisation of the administration of justice, however, clearly shows that the pluralistic legal structure, so characteristic of most of Africa, may not be the ultimate expression of the law of the African states. In this section an attempt will be made to present the policies which possibly will be followed in the immediate future and to outline means of implementation of policies chosen.

I. LEGAL POLICY

Granted the existence of a plurality of legal systems in most of the territories of Africa, the side-by-side presence of one or more indigenous legal systems (with or without intrusion of portions of the Islamic law), and of a non-indigenous legal system accommodated to local circumstances, there are three major possibilities for the course of legal development. *First*, the pluralism of law may continue, either purposely adopted by the authorities or simply persisting in the absence of any change of policy; *second*, a new state may select one of the component elements of a plural legal structure to the exclusion of the others; and *third*, there may occur a fusion of the elements of the plural legal system into a single national legal system, a process which would normally call for the directed evolution of the indigenous law in order to integrate it with the non-indigenous law into a modern legal structure.[1]

Most colonial powers, and certainly the new states, appear to have renounced the idea that a plurality of legal systems can exist side by side in the new Africa. The Germans seem never to have considered that the Africans of their colonial possessions would voluntarily give up, or that the governing power would alter, their way of life.[2] If the Spanish and Portuguese once intended to perpetuate the distinction between the indigenous law and the Spanish or Portuguese law — on the assumption that the great mass of African population would be unable to 'immatriculate' into the Western legal systems — the official position in recent years is certainly to the contrary.[3] The few statements by French and Belgian writers favouring the creation of a special regime of indigenous custom and European law for the semi-civilised, leaving the mass to their own indigenous law, have been repudiated.[4]

Today only the Republic of South Africa proposes to continue the plurality of legal systems. Explicit policy statements along these lines are not yet available, but logically the creation of Bantustans and the transference of autonomy to these units, seem to intensify the cleavage between native law and common (Roman-Dutch) law. It is idle to speculate what the next few years will bring, but possibilities include codification of the indigenous legal systems (Xhosa, Zulu, Venda, etc.), substitution of indigenous appeal courts for (government) Native Appeal Courts, and expansion of the indigenous law by means of native legislation to cover all areas of the law. Elsewhere in Africa, there seems to be temporary acceptance of the plurality of legal systems. The so-called 'aborigines' of Liberia, comprising the majority of the population, are to live according to their own native law and custom, while the educated part of the population is to be governed by the enactments collected in the recent code.[5] The disputes within minority groups in the Sudan involving the law of persons, the family and succession, are decided according to the 'custom' applicable to the parties concerned: that is, canon law or English law or the customary law of the pagan natives.[6] But in these and similar situations[7] the exceptions will eventually be integrated into the general picture. There will then be little to distinguish such states' legal systems from those which will be described later as the third possibility for the law of the future.

A second possible policy is the selection of one of the component elements of the plural system to the exclusion of the other. This might be the non-indigenous law — or some other foreign legal system — on the one hand, or the selection of one or more of the indigenous legal systems on the other. Though some support has been given for the adoption of English law — as modified by colonial legislation and practice — to the exclusion of the indigenous law in one or more of the British territories,[8] there is no indication that any of the emerging states will adopt this policy. Indeed no state which has achieved independence has taken such a position. There was a time when it seemed that the French government favoured the replacement of the customary law in its territories by French legislation.[9] It was then (1946) that the inhabitants of the overseas possessions were subjected to the jurisdiction of French courts and French law — as decreed for the overseas territories — in criminal cases.[10] Similarly, a later decree (1952) extended French labour law to all the population of the African territories.[11] These were single efforts, and by and large, pluralism of law and diversity of courts continued to the date of independence of the states d'expression française.[12] Any tendency to displace customary law, possibly contemplated in some states such as Senegal or Gabon, has not yet been realised.

Only the Empire of Ethiopia seems embarked on a policy looking towards the total adoption of Western-based law — and here the introduction of Western legislation dates back many decades.[13] It was first used to supplement the 'Law of Kings' (Fetha Negast)[14] and the customary law applicable to the various ethnic groups of the Ethiopian population.[15] Then, in 1954, the emperor set up a Codification Commission, entrusting the compilation of a series of codes to encompass the fields of civil and criminal law and procedure to the continental European members of the Commission.[16] Though the emperor called for a legal system that 'would respond and be adapted to the genius of Ethiopian traditions and institutions', [17] an examination of the two codes published to date reveals very little especially characteristic of Ethiopia. [18]   Indeed, these projects embody the most modern ideas and principles devised by outstanding academic scholars of European continental law.   The provisions of the codes are drawn from various sources and reflect the newest ideas of Western authorities.   It is questionable whether these rules of law will actually be put into effect in much of Ethiopia within the near future. [19]

Apart from Ethiopia — and including the atypical states of North Africa — no other state has attempted to adopt a foreign, Western system of law. [20]   The overseas provinces of the Portuguese are now — under steadily refined legislation — being more closely incorporated into the structure of the metropolitan state.   In the Portuguese provinces of Guinea, Angola and Mozambique, continued recognition of native customs for the indigenous population is viewed as the exceptional occurrence of local custom within the scope of Portuguese common law.   According to Portuguese policy, this local customary law will gradually be replaced, as indeed it has already been in the Portuguese provinces of São Tomé, Principe and Timor.   Portuguese common law will eventually be applicable to all the inhabitants. [21]   With regard to the four Spanish provinces of Africa: Ifni and Sahara seem to be incorporated in the metropolitan state and subject to the same laws and decrees as the rest of the national territory.   Temporarily, the provinces of Fernando Poo and Rio Muni are administered under the fundamental laws and national legislation, subject to the proviso that enactments in the area of substantive as well as procedural law shall not derogate from the traditional customary norms valid in these provinces. [22]

The other side of the coin would be the adoption of an indigenous legal system. This is hardly likely in view of the present desire of the African states rapidly to enter the modern world.   It is generally recognised that the indigenous systems of law in Africa are deficient in the areas of commerce, finance, labour and social welfare.   Further, the indigenous law is considered inadequate in the field of obligations and property and in most aspects of public law.   It is interesting to note, however, that at least one anthropologist, Rattray, has suggested the possibility of developing an indigenous legal system (the Ashanti) into a legal structure satisfactory for a nation in the modern world. [23]

In the view of most students, the future African legal systems will most likely — and properly so — combine Western-derived legal principles with indigenous legal doctrines so modified and developed as to fit changing needs of society.   A modern state with a centrally organised government requires a general law to regulate the business and financial efforts of the population and to afford it internal security.   The colonial powers introduced Western legal institutions in the fields of commerce, banking, security, criminal law and procedure.   These will continue to serve and be continuously expanded to meet the growing needs of the new state. [24]   At the same time, it seemed to be the consensus of experts at a conference on the future of customary law in Africa that indigenous law would and should continue to govern family relations, succession and land under customary tenure for some time to come. [25]   But even within these limited areas the indigenous institutions cannot meet the needs of African society without undergoing substantial adaptation.   Here the experts were in accord. [26]   A directed evolution of the institutions of indigenous law is necessary if fusion of this element with the advanced legal doctrine of Western hue is intended to constitute a national legal system. [27]

Lines of development in the past have demonstrated the potentialities of African customary law for the future.[28]   At the London Conference on the Future of Law in Africa, during December 1959 and January 1960, it was pointed out that, while economic development would be fostered if brought under one unified general system of law for a country, the law established should have full regard for the traditions, family and personal law.   It was stressed that 'questions of family relations, marriage, divorce, wills and succession are so essentially personal that they must in large part continue to be governed by the customary law of the community to which the person belongs'.[29]   Outside the British areas the fusion of the non-indigenous law with principles deriving from the directed evolution of the indigenous law is likewise the ultimate objective.[30]   Indeed, it is asserted that unification of the modern law and the traditional law has been achieved in Guinea.[31] It may be stated, therefore, that the third possibility — the fusion of indigenous and non-indigenous law — is the guiding policy, expressed or unexpressed, for most of the emerging states of Africa.[32]

2. IMPLEMENTATION OF THE POLICY

Obviously the integration of the non-indigenous with the indigenous law depends on the continued existence of the customary (indigenous) law.   This by no means follows, for there have been indications pointing to a total eclipse of the indigenous law.   During the age of colonial occupation much of the existing customary law became obsolete, and some of it was excluded for reasons of repugnancy, by the operation of desuetude, or by the enactment of contrary legislation.[33]   Today those systems with application to a limited group of persons tend to give way to those with wider applicability.   Ajayi, for instance, holds that the division of Nigeria into autonomous regions will make it less easy for the customary law of the individual regions to resist the encroachment of English law.[34]   Clearly, extensive legislation or codification along Western lines weakens the hold of indigenous law.[35]   Even the avowed permanent nature of many of the rules and institutions of the customary law may be insufficient to withstand the forces of change which lean towards favouring the non-indigenous law.[36]

The future of the African indigenous law depends upon a variety of social and legal factors.   What form will the African family take in the future?   Will the father's position in the family be reduced?   With what speed will traditional life lose its sacral character and dependence upon the supernatural?   Is there more than a possibility that certain institutions will give way to the pressures of Western economic life, as for instance, matrilineal succession and matrilocal residence to patrilineal succession and residence with the husband?   Is there a possibility that informal, proverbial guides of a way of life may become transformed into a formal, juridical system of legal rules?   The answers to these and many, many more questions will determine the eventual role of the indigenous law in the total national legal system.[37]   We have evidence that in the past customary law responded constructively to accelerated change.   This has come about because change itself is inherent in the nature of the indigenous law.   As Allott has demonstrated, every native legal system has undergone constant change throughout the whole of any colonial period.[38]   Then towards the end of the colonial period and in the days of independence there has been further centralisation of the administration, and with this centralisation legal reforms tend to be pushed through, even if doubtfully acceptable to the mass of the population.   Attempts to stifle development of the customary law have been overcome.[39]   Eventually, through a modification of the indigenous law at both the central and the local level, together with the requisite amount of legislation along Western lines, the new states will arrive at a balance between the general (Western-oriented) and the special (indigenous) law.[40]

The fields which for the time being seem best left to the domain of the indigenous law have often been outlined.   This was done at the Amsterdam Conference (1955) when the proper field of customary law was said to be restricted to family relations, succession and immovable property in so far as such property continues to be held under customary forms of tenure.   It was felt, furthermore, that the application of customary law should be limited to matters in which customary law would only constitute a supplementary body of law and would not involve a dualism of laws by overlapping with the general law in the same sphere of operation.[41]   Individual participants in this conference along with other persons have made similar suggestions in various works.[42]   The conditions under which indigenous law should apply have recently been formulated in the following manner: if native custom is not conducive to the safety of a modern state or endangers its economic development, then Western-type law should be used, as in criminal law or with respect to commercial matters; where a substantive change is desired by the population and preparations have been taken for the change, as in land tenure, there indigenous law may not be satisfactory; but where the retention of the native law does not affect the development or the safety of the state, there the indigenous law should be employed as modified to fit present-day needs.[43]

3. MEASURES FOR THE DIRECTED EVOLUTION OF THE LAW

In recent years students of African law have given thoughtful attention to the measures and techniques to be employed in adapting the plural legal systems — and particularly the indigenous law element thereof — to the ever-changing needs of the times.   Today such consideration is of unique value since new nations are rapidly fashioning national legal systems out of the heritage of the past and from constructive suggestions of current legal thought.   Several devices have been favoured, including legislative enactment and semi-legislative declaration, codification and restatement of the ·customary law, development by court decisions, and reliance upon legal or paralegal textbooks.   Certainly there are other ways by which the law can be advanced, but these methods are among those more thoroughly canvassed.

With the granting of greater autonomy to the British possessions in Africa prior to independence, colonial legislatures considerably enlarged the field of statutory enactment in the individual territories.[44]   English common law, doctrines of equity, and statutes of general application have gradually been replaced by a host of acts and ordinances covering all areas of the law save those firmly entrenched within the sphere of the indigenous (customary) law.   At times this legislation has been pretty much an effort to bring the Western (English) law up to date, as in the case of the Property and Conveyancing Act, 1959, of Western Nigeria.[45]   In other cases there has been the desire to improve upon the present status of the English law and to modify it so that it is better suited to the needs of the African nation; an example of this is the Company Law and Partnership Law drafted at the request of the government of Ghana by a leading English scholar in these fields.[46]   Not only the central governments of the present and former British possessions but also those regional units possessing a measure of autonomy have resorted to legislation in order to

supplement both the customary law and the previous acts of the central government.[47] It is to be expected, therefore, that the new states will continue to
employ the legislative organs of the state to supplement, modify and alter the
extensive statutory heritage of colonial times.   A similar pattern may occur in the
former French and Belgian possessions.[48]

A different question may be raised about the wisdom of resorting to legislation
in order to fill the gaps which exist in those fields of law generally considered to lie
within the scope of the indigenous law.   Legislation was conceded a prominent
role in this respect by the participants of the recent London Conference, but with
the proviso that customary law principles should be taken into account when framing
the legislation.[49]   Legislation may also be resorted to in clarifying the status of the
customary law.   Allott looks to legislative enactment to preserve an indigenous
form of arbitration in Ghana, so that the identification of this type of arbitration
with English arbitration by the courts could be prevented.[50]   The urge to reduce
much of the indigenous law to written form may be met by the expanded use of
legislative enactment.[51]

Opinions have long differed about the question of whether legislation is the
superior way of modifying or amending the customary law.   Phillips, an early
English scholar in African law, favoured legislation over decision by the courts
(case-law) as a means of advancing the customary law in Kenya.[52]   There have also
been strenuous advocates of case-law over legislation as the means by which to
develop the customary law.[53]   Comments made by some critics suggest that efforts
to replace customary law with legislation in former French and Belgian possessions
have not brought results which would recommend its unrestricted use in the new
Africa.[54]   Evidently case-law and legislation each play a role in the modification
of the customary law.   The courts must recognise in their decisions those changes
which have taken place, and the legislature must propose those changes for which
the populace seems ready.[55]

Turning once more to the Amsterdam Symposium on the Future of the Customary Law, the role of legislation with respect to native law and custom was
qualified as follows:

> In matters of legislation the principal role should be assigned to local legisla-
> tive bodies where such exist, and particularly to traditional and tribal bodies,
> the intervention of any superior legislature remaining the exception.[56]

It may be surmised that past experience demonstrated the greater merit of local
legislation, more particularly tribal legislation.   Surprisingly, there is only one
reference to tribal legislation in recent times, though this single instance is cited
frequently.[57]   This is the case in which there was use of legislation by Tswana
chiefs in council to introduce changes in the customary law of many of the Tswana
tribes.[58]   Apart from this instance, there seems to be no legislation beneath the
regional level.[59]

A more significant means of developing customary law may derive from the
grant of power by the central government to local authorities to state the substance
of native law and custom on any subject.   Such declaration is coupled with the
power to prohibit, restrict or regulate matters within the compass of indigenous
law.[60]   The so-called Laws of Lerotholi were given the stamp of approval by
various native authorities in Basutoland, and yet, according to Duncan, they have no
validity unless they reflect immemorial custom.[61]   The issuing of declarations of

the customary law by native authorities is a practice of long standing[62] and has been recommended by a number of conferences.[63] The practice is gaining ground, and the future may well see a substantial increase in this method of modifying the customary law.[64] Under other enactments the power to state the customary law has been conferred on private or semi-official bodies, harking back to the traditional authorities of earlier days. According to the Chiefs Law of Western Nigeria, the traditional members of the local government councils have the right to make declarations of the customary law respecting chieftaincy matters.[65] The Kiambu Law Panel has set forth rules concerning the adoption of children among the Kikuyu.[66] There are other instances, and the chances are that 'declarations of customary law' may become a regular practice in many of the new states.

If codification is suggested as a possible measure to aid in the formation of a national legal system, it should be noted that it normally has reference to codification of the customary law, that is, primarily the indigenous law of the family, of succession and of land under customary tenure. Codes in other fields of law applicable to the whole of the population are by no means unknown in the African territories. Those best known are the penal codes and the codes of criminal procedure. Many of these are modelled upon earlier codes drafted by colonial officials for use in India and Australia.[67] Other fields of the Western law have also been encompassed within a single legislative act, comprehending the whole of the rules of a given legal institution.[68] The continental European powers also transported codes to the colonies; indeed, much of the colonial law based on that of the mother country was promulgated in code form.[69] At the present time a series of codes is being prepared for the Kingdom of Ethiopia.[70] The American-flavoured legislation in Liberia, from the establishment of that state to the present time, has been revised and compiled to form the Liberian Code of Laws of 1956 and is perhaps the basis of a new code.[71] There will undoubtedly be substantial revision, amendment and further codification of the non-indigenous law of the various African states, but this is not the type of codification pertinent to the question of the directed evolution of the law.

Is it feasible to codify the customary law, and if so, would this be desirable? The majority of writers answer both parts of this question negatively.[72] Some say we do not have sufficient knowledge of the principles of the indigenous law to attempt codification for most ethnic groups in Africa. The point is made, too, that within most states the homogeneous population is not sufficiently large nor the territory occupied sufficiently extensive to warrant codification.[73] There are so many preliminary steps to be taken in collecting and assessing the customary law that codification is still a long way off. Many hold that even if feasible a code of customary law is undesirable.[74] The only instance of such codification in Africa is the Natal Code of Native Law. This has generally been unfavourably received at the hands of the scholars, though for many decades it has been the basis of much of the indigenous law in Natal (Zululand).[75] Arguments against codification and against this code in particular have been expounded by Kerr.[76] Because opinions frequently differ about a rule of law for a given situation, a code does put undue emphasis upon the rule selected to the prejudice of variants which may have been guiding in particular areas of the land. If at all detailed, a code brings rigidity to the law difficult to overcome. Errors which may creep into the compilation often cause more harm than do mistakes handed down in individual judicial decisions. Omissions, too, raise a difficult question: did the codification commission know-

ingly omit the matter at issue in order that it be not considered within the scope of
the customary law? These are among the factors which seem to outweigh the
possible advantages to be gained from the certainty and completeness of coverage:
the two asserted benefits of a code. Kerr, as do others, prefers forms of written
exposition of customary law other than codification.[77]

There continue to be proponents of codification. Pogucki, for example, sees
no reason for not codifying customary land law of the Gold Coast, and he has
strongly urged that this task be carried out.[78] A proposal to codify the customary
law of French West Africa was made in 1953, but this effort was later altered and
became a plea for a restatement of the indigenous law.[79] Quite recently the
codification of the *coutume* of Rwanda and of Burundi has been urged, largely to offset
such deterioration as has resulted from the political disturbances, but also to put
these countries on a par with their neighbours in the legal field.[80] Finally, a commission has been appointed to undertake the preparation of a Code Civil Malgache,
in order to bring about unification of Malgache customary law with modern Western
law under the French regime.[81] In the states with British background the likelihood
of codification of the indigenous law seems remote, even though the matter may be
reconsidered.[82]

Because codification of indigenous law is not presently favoured, attention has
been turned to the restatement of the customary law as the most significant step in
preparing for a national legal system. Only in exceptional cases has restatement
been undertaken by members of the indigenous population itself. Recent instances
are represented in the collections made by various peoples of the plateau regions of
northern Ethiopia and Eritrea.[83] Western scholars have usually served as guiding
hands in preparation of restatements of African customary law. Cory, the Government Sociologist in Tanganyika, furnishes two typical post-war examples in the
restatement of the customary law of the Haya tribe and of the Sukuma Federation.
That of the Haya was compiled after consultation with native court assessors, discussion with further court assessors and chiefs, and finally published as a collection
of some twelve hundred legal rules illustrated with over two hundred cases.[84] A
more elaborate method was employed in obtaining a restatement of the tribal laws
of the chiefdoms of the Sukuma Federation. An assembly of well-informed elders
representing various chiefdoms met four times in month-long sessions with the
purpose of drafting a statement of rules acceptable to the majority. Results were
submitted to councils of chiefs, clerks and assessors. Divergency of opinion was
largely settled by compromise positions, and the whole was eventually published
as the statement of the customary law of the member chiefdoms of the Sukuma
Federation.[85]

Difficulties involved in preparing a restatement of the indigenous law of the
African territories are apparent.[86] This sphere of the law is by no means static,
and any compilation must therefore admit the possibility of further directed evolution. Even though work is undertaken under Western auspices, a restatement must
eliminate the occidental point of view and classification. Some half-dozen methods
of procedure in collecting and presenting customary materials have been employed
in the past. The views of Allott, who is serving as director of the current project
to restate the customary law of the indigenous peoples within the bounds of the
former British possessions, illustrate the methods and objectives of this project.[87]
The first step is the collection of information already available in written form.
Bibliographies of materials relating to marriage, the family, land tenure and

succession in West Africa, East Africa and Central-Southern Africa will be under-taken.[88]   The gaps can then be filled by means of research in the field.   Regional restatements will be prepared in a form resting between the Restatements of the American Law Institute and the Digests of the Customary Law of the Punjab.[89]   The Restatement Project has completed four years of its first seven-year term.[90]

The systematic recording and restatement of the indigenous law in Africa serve many purposes.   Allott, for example, points out the manner in which it reveals the existing materials and indicates the extent of the similarities and differences to be found in the customary law of diverse localities and distinct ethnic groups; it can assist the courts in discovering and applying the appropriate rules, especially when they have had no previous experience in the administration of the indigenous law; and it provides information aiding African governments in the modernisation and the unification of their laws.[91]   The scientific inventory of indigenous customs is required before it will be possible to proceed with adequate codification.   The restatement of the law will of itself lend considerable drive to the directed evolution of the law and aid in the fusion of the indigenous and non-indigenous law in the African states.

An Anglo-American lawyer would attribute a primary role to the courts in the development of a legal system.   Judicial decisions became the source of the common law; the doctrines of equity were forged by the courts of chancery; and statutes were given their full meaning as a result of judicial interpretation.   What could be more natural than that this heritage of the English law be handed on to the courts of the British colonial possessions in Africa?[92]   It is to be expected that the courts of the emerging states will continue to fashion the non-indigenous law along lines typical of those employed by other courts within the Anglo-American legal tradition, by case-law, precedent, judicial interpretation and construction.   Some students possibly feel that the future evolution of the indigenous law might best be entrusted to judicial action.[93]   Care must be taken, on the one hand, that the precedent of a single case does not prevent the evolution of a legal rule, and, on the other hand, that the courts do not engage in unrestricted judicial legislation.   A proper balance between the two must be maintained.[94]   But the courts, particularly the superior courts, have a duty to recognise judicially changes in customs and not to perpetuate erroneous interpretation of the customary law.[95]   Lawyers, particu-larly those trained in the civil law tradition, warn against usurpation of the legislative function by the judiciary, but even they stress the role of the courts in fashioning the new trends in the indigenous law.[96]

Native courts, including the African and local courts, have not been too well prepared to rely upon case-law and precedent as possible measures for the directed evolution of the law.   Much needs to be done to lay the foundations for such judicial action.   The nature of the judicial process operating in many of the native courts and the ulterior motives which frequently influence decisions do not always lead to adequate recognition of changes in custom.[97]   A number of instances, neverthe-less, clearly indicate that native courts may be as fully prepared as some superior courts to take account of new economic and social conditions in the administration of justice.   Knowles has shown how native courts in Nyanza (Kenya) have enter-tained divorce suits instigated by the wife instead of the wife's father or guardian.[98] Equitable principles protect a *bona fide* purchaser of property among the Yoruba (Nigeria) where the conveyance lacks the consent of the family and thus would be void *ab initio* under the customary law.[99]   A number of new principles, constituting considerable departure from the traditional rules of land tenure, have recently been developed among the Basoga (Uganda) by the District Native Courts.[100]   Most striking perhaps is the notice that the decisions of native courts with appellate jurisdiction among the Tiv of central Nigeria have tended to be accepted by the lower courts as establishing principles of general application.   Though these decisions do not have the force of binding precedent, the result has been a growing tendency towards uniformity.[101]   Judicial decisions of the European as well as of the native courts — or of the integrated hierarchy of courts of the new nations — will emphasise the role of case-law and precedent as a technique for the evolution of a national legal system: the fusion of the indigenous and the non-indigenous law.

Finally, reliance upon legal and para-legal textbooks has been another means suggested to further the development of the legal structure in Africa.   The use of textbooks, French *doctrine*, is a device that is most familiar to students of African law who come to it from the continental European civil law background.   A number of monographs have attempted to portray the nature of an institution or an area of the indigenous or non-indigenous law.[102]   But common opinion seems to be that the time has not arrived for the definitive treatise which would serve as the point of departure for the further development of the law.[103]   Social anthropologists have written monographs dealing with particular institutions or a whole legal system.   Many of these have come to be accepted as authoritative sources of the law and are utilised by legal experts and referred to by the courts as authentic statements of the law.[104]   But it seems questionable that they are particularly fitted to serve as tools for the further evolution of the law.   Perhaps the role of legal scholar should be to provide textbooks, whether these are to aid the administration and the courts or to assist in the development of the law.[105]   A legal text can, as Elias says,

> . . . promote the unification of diverse bodies of customary law better than a code; it is also the best method of relating customary law to the enacted law of the country concerned, and so helps in producing the synthesis and harmonious relationship between the two, which is so vital to African societies today.[106]

The legal textbook takes its significant place alongside judicial decision, codification and restatement, legislation and directive.   It offers a variety of means, given proper human guidance, for helping to build African systems of law capable of meeting the needs of present-day society.

4. CULTURAL AND GEOGRAPHICAL CONSIDERATIONS

In the previous pages attention has been directed to technical devices which might be employed to further the directed evolution of the law, though techniques alone cannot provide the structure of future African legal systems.   Techniques which attempt to foist novel institutions upon a reluctant populace lead to disastrous results.   A government must weigh carefully the effects of the introduction or, conversely, the perpetuation of particular legal devices and conceptions.   On the other hand, religious conversion, urbanisation and industrialisation may cause a severe dislocation to a part of the citizenry.   What new measures are then required in the legal as well as social spheres of a changing African society?   A few of the instances which introduce cultural considerations — as I have termed these factors — are noted here, in the hope that they will give an indication of the tremendous significance of policy decision to legal development.

It is a commonplace that polygyny is widespread throughout the continent of Africa. This practice is largely governed by the rules of the indigenous law.[1] The colonial powers everywhere introduced legislation to provide for monogamous union, and almost always permitted African converts to Christianity to choose this form of marriage. Thus two forms of matrimony (with Islamic marriage often a third) existed side by side.[2] The new states sooner or later must take a stand upon the question. Will the plural marriage system be continued? When the Criminal Code of 1960 rephrased the Ghanaian law respecting bigamy, the impression gained circulation that polygyny was to be abolished. As a result the government issued a White Paper reaffirming the liberty of a man under the Ghanaian customary marriage system 'to have one or more wives according to his choice'.[3] Legislation was introduced permitting the registration of one wife who would in fact be the successor to the widow's share of the husband's estate if he died intestate. Reaction to the existence of a dual system of marriage led to a strong bill virtually abolishing the statutory monogamous marriage as a separate institution in Ghana.[4] In contrast to this action a conference of representative African women held at Conakry (Guinea) recommended the abolition of polygyny.[5] Miss Colson presents a further instance in which social pressures are affecting legal institutions in the law of the family. She suggests possible repercussions from granting the Tonga of Northern Rhodesia the opportunity of making wills.[6] Knowles discusses the right of the African wife to institute divorce proceedings without having recourse to the father or guardian to bring the suit.[7] Allott says: 'It is obvious that the more radical governments will not be content to leave the personal law of their countries just as they received it.'[8]

Reform in land tenure for purposes of economic development may also have profound effect upon the evolution of a legal system. The traditional communal right of disposal of the land gave the individual member of the community the right to work it only during his lifetime. No individual title, a growing fragmentation and lack of permanence in holdings, and no right of alienation led Kenya, for example, to radical change. Farmers were urged to exchange parcels in order to consolidate their lands. Where the idea of individual holding had emerged and where the community was willing, a local committee, chosen from among the elders, made a listing of persons whose rights should be recognised as constituting full ownership. Registration by these parties converted this recognition to title. In this way legislation provided the opportunity, and individuals made a start towards private ownership of land. Sale of land to non-Africans was prevented by granting district committees control over alienation of such individually held property. Until wills of Africans are recognised as valid instruments for conveying real property, the customary law of succession continues to apply, but the number of heirs recognised as co-heirs of land is limited to five.[9] On the face of it, this change in the indigenous law seems squarely to meet economic needs and to satisfy individual desires. But the sociological effect of the sweeping change may preclude its general acceptance elsewhere in Africa. Drastic change of land law changes a community way of life. The small leaseholder enters the labour market, causing flight to the urban areas and increasing unemployment. The new buildings may not be economically viable.[10] Other governments may well turn to instances of the development of individual land tenure in the indigenous law of such peoples as the Chagga or Kikuyu to evolve a modern scheme.[11] To a West African scholar acquainted with the rules of land tenure of many indigenous legal systems, 'individual ownership is conceivable in any system where alienation by an accredited owner is possible'.[12]   One can conclude that for land reform, policy determinants which are non-legal in nature will dictate the choice between models taken from the indigenous law and models chosen from those offered by the non-indigenous law.

The last instance reviewed is illustrative of the changes wrought by urbanisation, specifically by creation of the mining towns in the Copper Belt of Northern Rhodesia.   Most of the African immigrants to the area come as bachelors for a few years' labour in the minefields.   They then return to their rural homes, though some marry and settle in the urban settlements.   The individuals come from distinct ethnic groups, each of which has its own system of law.   Because disputes in the urban areas could not be settled by distant native courts, the Northern Rhodesian government established urban courts having limited civil jurisdiction and minor criminal competence.   The judges were chosen by the Native Authorities in the rural areas of the major ethnic groups from which the mine workers came.   Thus there was generally available an expert on the particular customary law to be applied to the litigant or litigants.   But a panel of judges rendered the decision, and so before long an urban native law was being developed.   This was not Bemba law nor Lozi law nor any other indigenous legal system, nor indeed Western non-indigenous law.   The law was one peculiarly suited to a social group which had temporarily broken the kinship ties and substituted bonds of a local territorial and economic nature.[13]   There has been a warning that urban native courts 'must not be left to create a law that is neither native nor western [Roman-Dutch] law, that is, just their common sense — a rather rare commodity'.[14]   But it is doubtful whether such a view would be particularly compelling to the African state which inherited a large migrant African population in the urban areas.   All the factors involved in such a social-political situation dictate the course of development of the law for the urban citizens.

There may be other considerations which will affect the direction of the evolution of a national legal system.   There is the problem of unification of the law within the state, of reconciliation of diverse legal systems between regional units of a federation, of concessions to be made in the light of participation in larger unions, or by reason of international relations.   These may be termed geographical considerations.

The indigenous law is the law applicable to the African of a given tribal group, generally without regard to his residence or domicile.   But behind that, the indigenous law of a given group is tied to a certain geographical locale.   The differences between the legal systems of neighbouring African tribes are striking.   When, however, there is concerted effort to eliminate much of this distinction between ethnically related groups within a given state, a considerable degree of unification of the customary law can be achieved.   Earlier, reference was made to the method followed by Cory in drafting his restatement of the law of the Sukuma chiefdoms which make up the Sukuma Federation, in order to eliminate the differences which may have existed.   In the more ambitious undertaking to unify the customary law throughout Tanganyika, Cory had reached general agreement on the customary law rules in the law of persons and of family among most of the tribes of the western regions, including the Sukuma, the Nyamwezi, the Ha, the Gogo and the Haya.[15]   But Cotran has pointed to grave reasons why such unification of the customary law might be no more than agreement on paper.   Tanganyika comprises so many tribal groups with diametrically opposed kinship structures, distinct means of livelihood and religious tenets, to mention only the most obvious factors, that it is unlikely that the views of so-called 'experts' will be accepted.[16]

In the past, some superior courts brought about a certain unification in the customary law by utilising precedents from one indigenous legal system in deciding similar questions in another legal system, without any real attempt to establish that the two legal systems were comparable.[17]   The courts of the Gold Coast, for instance, were prone to treat native customary law as a single body of rules throughout the colony, in spite of the complete contrast between the legal systems of the tribal groups, and the variants within the subdivisions of a group.[18]   Even more, in a decision of the West African Court of Appeal, Verity, cj, said:

> Although the principles of native law and custom to which we have referred are, in the specific instances cited, applicable expressly to the law and custom of the Gold Coast, they are nevertheless equally applicable as general principles to the law and custom of Nigeria, a departure from which can only be justified if it is established by evidence that the native law and custom in any particular area differs from the general principle.[19]

Coker is in accord that the general principles of the concept of family property are identical throughout West Africa, but a case note maintains that this dictum establishes a doctrine harmful to the future development of the indigenous law.[20]

In this respect one might call attention to a phase in the study of the indigenous law (adat) of Indonesia, namely, the determination of law families, law areas within a law family, law tribes within a law area, etc.[21]   This type of classification provides for the identification of generally homogeneous legal systems, with variations in particulars not sufficiently diverse to warrant exclusion from the larger group. Only a start has been made in the classification of law areas within the Middle-African law family.[22]   Further study along these lines will provide another tool looking towards the unification of the indigenous law.   It may well be that the new states will attempt unification of diverse legal systems within their bounds, but the courts will probably be less liable to ascribe similarity to legal institutions in two different sovereign states — even though the indigenous population be ethnically related — and accordingly less prone to attribute the force of precedent to the decisions of foreign courts.[23]

The colonial heritage will undoubtedly affect the techniques of development of the national legal systems.   What if the circumstances should bring together two different heritages, as in Cameroon or Somalia?   The unification of the indigenous law may be readily accomplished, but the Western non-indigenous laws will be quite distinct, and — perhaps even more significant — there will exist two dissimilar sets of means to be used in forging a single national legal system.   A further 'geographical' factor will arise in the case of federal states.   It has been argued that regionalisation will bring — or continue — an emphasis on the differences in the legal structure, so much so that customary law may give way to Western-influenced statutory enactment.[24]   The course of the evolution in federal states will depend to a considerable extent on the powers of the federal legislature and the functions of the federal supreme court.

The broadest geographical implications for the directed evolution of the law will arise from the obligations which derive from entrance into an economic or political union with other states, or from bilateral or multilateral treaties with other nations.   Problems of common market or of international relations are not, of course, unique to African countries. The national legal systems of European nations are undergoing alterations in the structure of the private law to adjust to the new groupings. African legal systems will have to do the same. The creation of adequate national legal systems in Africa, however, places the international aspects of the private law in the background for the time being.

5. LEGAL EDUCATION AND THE LEGAL PROFESSION

The strength of a modern legal system and the effective administration of justice depend to a considerable extent upon the government personnel trained in the law and, as far as desired, a proficient legal profession. The colonial powers made little effort to provide legal education on the spot. The British universities — and occasionally those elsewhere in the Commonwealth — and the Inns of Court in London provided the legal personnel. Under these circumstances, the lack of financial means prevented most Africans from obtaining legal education sufficient to qualify for the higher legal posts or to act as practitioners in the superior courts. In parts of British West Africa, however, there was a fairly large bar made up of African lawyers.[25] Posts for Africans in the government service requiring legal skills, such as judges in the native courts, clerks, etc., were filled by persons without formal legal training. A similar situation prevailed in the French and Belgian territories of Africa.

Following the second world war, two conferences were held with judicial advisers from many of the territories. Attention was called to the necessity of training representative government personnel in the law in order to fill many posts in the administration of justice.[26] But only later, at the London Conference in the winter of 1959–60, was the legal education of Africans treated as a problem of prime importance. The new governments sought Africanisation in the judiciary as well as in other legal posts, and the resources of training abroad were clearly not adequate. For positions requiring only basic legal knowledge, the education imparted indirectly by appellate and reviewing instances to the personnel of the lower tribunals might be supplemented by formal instruction at training schools for civil servants and by on-the-spot teaching by judicial advisers.[27] Allott suggested that legal education should be locally provided at an elementary level sufficient to the taking of Part I of the Bar Examination. Successful candidates could be recruited as clerks or even as members of African courts.[28] The Commission to Study Legal Education, with Lord Denning as chairman, called for revision of legal education in England in order better to suit the needs of African students, and recommended that institutes for basic legal training be set up in each African territory. These institutes are to prepare judges, staff and advisers of African courts, and students for Part I of the Bar Examination. A limited number of Faculties of Law and Schools of Law for practical training should be established in Africa.[29]

Legal education in Africa is presently making a tremendous surge, but even with instructors from abroad there are insufficient law teachers to supply the needs.[30] In January 1962, the first conference on legal education was held on African soil. Here co-operation between all interested African states was envisaged as being helpful in solving the difficulties in the field of legal education.[31]

The curricula of the law faculties which have been established at the universities in British areas normally combine courses in the basic subjects of the English Common Law (with the particular local overtones added), an introduction to the indigenous law, and elective study of the more complex Western law topics and further training in customary and Islamic law. In the law schools, practice, procedure, conveyancing and the like are stressed.[32] The method of legal instruction follows the English model, though case-method and problem seminars reflect the influence of law instruction from the United States. It has been suggested that a combined faculty of law and political science conducted along continental European lines is particularly well suited to Africa.[33] Though the British universities and Inns of Court will continue to train numbers of African law students — financed largely by government grants — it seems likely that the law schools of the United States and eventually law teaching in British universities may serve as graduate instruction for the African law student who has completed his primary legal education in his own country. The teaching of African law in the United States will advantageously introduce American law students and other American trained social scientists to the nature of the legal structure of the African nations in the modern world.[34]

The judiciary in the British colonial possessions has a deservedly high reputation. Recently, however, the independence of the colonial judge has been at issue because of uncertainty about the method of removal of judges.[35] It is unfortunate that at this moment of transfer of sovereignty it should be suggested that the judiciary serves at the whim of the executive or legislative. At the Lagos Conference of the International Commission of Jurists on the Rule of Law, the position of the judiciary was reinforced, as follows: 'In a free society practising the Rule of Law, it is essential that the absolute independence of the Judiciary be guaranteed.'[36]

It has been indicated above that Africans are gradually replacing the colonial judiciary in the superior courts and replacing colonial civil servants in the highest legal posts of the new states. Many of these Africans have been trained in England, so there is no severe dislocation in this area of the administration of justice. But the situation with respect to the members and the staff of the native or African courts has become crucial. At the Judicial Advisers' Conferences of 1953 and 1956 emphasis was placed on the necessity of separating the executive from the judiciary in the lower courts: the chief should not be judge.[37] This is clearly an innovation in traditional African culture, and has often resulted in the chief's loss of prestige and his inability or reluctance to maintain law and order. It is, nevertheless, a necessary step in the provision of modern local courts with wide competence in matters both of indigenous and non-indigenous law.[38] The attempt to provide the requisite number of African or local courts with enough court members and assistance by trained clerks and other personnel is one of the most pressing concerns of the new states.

A professional bar has long existed in most of the African territories. This bar comprises Europeans, Africans (particularly in West Africa) and Indians (in East Africa).[39] The training of further practitioners can be accomplished in the law faculties and law schools in Africa and by education abroad. The problem to be resolved, however, is the determination of the kinds of courts in which these lawyers may practise. Partly as a result of abuses in the early days, legislation in the individual British territories excluded legal practitioners from appearing on behalf of clients before the native and lower subordinate courts.[40] The husband or wife or other duly authorised relative of a litigant could act as representative in certain cases before the native courts, but care was taken to see that such representatives did not become 'bush-lawyers' and spend most of their effort in obtaining cases in return for the fees involved.[41] In the course of time, it may be possible to permit attorneys in Native Appeal Courts, as has been the case in South Africa for some time.[42]   Up to the present, however, it appears that the new states are not yet prepared to admit legal practitioners to the local courts.[43]   Barristers and solicitors qualified to practise before the superior courts of Britain and the Commonwealth are now qualified to practise before the superior courts of the former British possessions. It is anticipated that graduates of the new law faculties will also be admitted to practise upon successful completion of local bar examinations.[44]

Research into African law must supplement the effort to provide an adequate bench and bar.   As indicated earlier, a number of attempts have been made to restate the customary law of various areas.   A beginning was made towards the recording of the customary laws of the ethnic groups of Tanganyika, but this effort was temporarily halted by the death of the Government Sociologist, Cory.[45] The need for further study of the indigenous law in all African states is generally recognised.[46]   Without such study one of the most important sources of material may be irretrievably lost.   The unpublished records of cases in the subordinate courts and, more particularly, in native courts of appeal and of first instance are in the files of administrative officers throughout the former British territories in Africa.   Principles derived from research on these cases could be tested against other sources of customary law.   Case-law is thoroughly familiar to the superior courts in African states, and extension of this method to the decisions of the courts primarily concerned with the indigenous law would be readily accepted.[47]   Though there has been call for such action, even today very few of the territories afford digests of the more important cases on customary law.[48]   The principal exception to this has been the Belgian Congo, in which the decisions of the tribunals dealing with the indigenous law have long been reported and in relatively large numbers.   A recent subject-matter index to this *jurisprudence* offers a rather full guide to the indigenous legal institutions of some two hundred tribal units within the former Belgian Congo and Ruanda-Urundi.[49]   As a source of case-law for research in the indigenous law, mention should also be made of the files of the social anthropologists who have been able to utilise only a limited number of cases they have observed in their published works.

Not only the indigenous law but all elements of African law are sorely in need of considerable research.[50] We find too few treatises depicting the law of the individual states.   The relation of the fields of indigenous law to those of non-indigenous law have not been worked out.   The nature of the judicial process, practice and procedure is not fully comprehended.   It will be necessary to put handbooks and other materials into the hands of the new judiciary, because they will have to concern themselves, in part, with entirely new fields of law.   The legal scholar in Africa and abroad can assist in the preparation of materials for African use.   Scholars abroad can delve into the many legal problems facing the legislatures of the African states, because library facilities and trained personnel with leisure for research are generally unavailable in Africa.   The English and the French universities offer opportunities for Africans as well as Westerners for studying the intricacies of African law.   Law library facilities are inadequate in most places in the United States or elsewhere in Europe.   It is hoped that very soon the law of each African state will be better known and that academicians may co-operate with the legal profession and legislative drafting bureaux in furthering the development of the African law.

III *ORGANISATION OF THE COURTS AND THE ADMINISTRATION OF JUSTICE*

The establishment of national legal systems will stem both from an implementation of policies which fuse existing plural legal systems into a single unit and from the reorganisation of existing court structures in such a way that an integrated hierarchy of tribunals will afford a uniform administration of justice. In the previous sections the problems of fusing indigenous and non-indigenous law have been somewhat extensively treated. It is not necessary to elaborate upon the questions involved in fashioning an integrated court system. Treatment may be briefer due to the fact that there has already been fairly extensive study of the organisation of the courts — at least in the British colonial possessions — and the whole situation has been adequately described in a recent publication.[1] It will suffice here to present the broad outlines of the development of the court systems, with illustrations which indicate the primary problems faced in various areas.

British administration of justice during the early years was solely concerned with the preservation of law and order in the territories under British control and with the settlement of disputes of the merchants and settlers in these outposts of imperial rule. Special courts and commissions to handle particular situations gradually gave way to a fairly uniform hierarchy of tribunals based on English models and culminating in a supreme court or high court, with appeal to the Judicial Committee of the Privy Council. More recently, an intermediate instance has been provided in the West African and East African Court of Appeal.[2] French and Belgian colonial governments likewise evolved simplified systems of the administration of justice, based on the metropolitan models and intended to cope with the cases involving persons of European origin.[3]

The British did not begin to exercise real control over indigenous administration of justice until the last years of the nineteenth century. Then a host of different kinds of existing native tribunals were recognised, and new ones were created where traditional tribunals had not existed or had disappeared. Under supervision of the colonial administration these native courts were encouraged to administer native law and custom to the members of the indigenous population.[4] During the first decades of this century, the administration of native justice was usually under the guidance of the departments of native affairs, and not of justice. There was very little contact between the native tribunals and the British courts.[5] By the 1930s two distinct types of organisation — with some intermediate forms — were recognisable. One type of court organisation may be termed the 'parallel' pattern, the other the 'integrated' pattern.[6] In the first there existed no tie between the two sides of the administration of justice. In native courts and British courts there was a hierarchy of appellate instances, with no right of appeal of any significance from one to the other. In the integrated pattern there was a chain of appellate rights integrating the highest grade of native court with the subordinate and eventually the high court.

Tanganyika was perhaps the ideal instance of the parallel pattern.[7] Native courts were under the control of the provincial commissioners, with appeal provided from native court to a superior native court, thence to the district officer, to the provincial commissioner, and finally to the governor's Appeal Board. The whole was an administrative system of appeal and revision. Severance from contact with the Tanganyika High Court was virtually complete.[8] Until 1930 the native tribunals of Kenya were integrated into the judicial system insofar as appeal lay to the magistrate's court and thence to the Supreme Court. But in that year the parallel system was adopted. Reforms were subsequently made which led to the creation of the Court of Review, and this replaced the appellate jurisdiction of the provincial commissioner.[9] The Gold Coast was a colony that displayed a typical integrated system to the end of British rule. Issues relating to land under customary tenure went from native court and native court of appeal to a land court, a division of the High Court, and thence to the West African Court of Appeal on matters of law. Personal suits could be appealed from the native court of appeal to a magistrate's court, and thence to a division of the High Court.[10] In Nigeria, until independence, there was what might be called an intermediate pattern. Normally, full control of native courts was vested in an administrative official who had power to transfer cases from one court to another, to revise, confirm or set aside native court judgments. Appeal lay from the native court of appeal to district and provincial administrative officers and eventually to the governor. Where the warrants of the court provided, appeal could be had to a magistrate's court or to the High Court.[11]

Dissatisfaction with the operation of the native courts and desire to re-examine the nature of control exercised over them, with special reference to questions of appeal or revision,[12] led to a great number of surveys within individual territories as well as conferences of representatives of various areas.[13] The principle was established that integration of the two branches of the administration of justice was a *sine qua non* to further development of a national legal system, and even more, that the local court, whatever its composition, should have unrestricted jurisdiction as to persons. A first step was presaged by one of the resolutions of the Amsterdam Conference in 1955 which declared that customary law should not be regarded as solely the function of native courts.[14] In the decade since 1951, when the Court of Review was established, there have been trends towards the integration of the courts in Kenya, with the African courts taking over some of the functions of the magistrate courts.[15] In 1957 Western Nigeria eliminated administrative supervision of what were now called Customary Courts, and established a means of appeal to the superior courts. Instead of the native law and custom of the region a common procedure for all Customary Courts was decreed.[16] The final step was reached in the 1958 Local Courts Act of Ghana. This gave the local court which had competence over the subject matter unrestricted jurisdiction as to parties.[17]

The integration of the courts of Ghana and Tanganyika dramatically illustrates the direction in which policy is moving in the new states with respect to the administration of justice. The Ghana Courts Act 1960, enacted just prior to the date of the inauguration of the republic, remodels the previous system of courts. The constitution and powers of the superior and circuit courts and of district and juvenile courts are set forth at length. One part of this Act establishes local courts which have unrestricted jurisdiction as to persons, except over public officials. They have civil competence in matters of customary law where debt, damage or demand does not exceed £Gh.100, and they entertain criminal causes of a minor nature. The local court is thus the ordinary court of first instance, with appeal to district court for all but land and succession cases. The latter go to the circuit court of appeal. Hence, the local courts replace both magistrate and native courts. There is but one integrated court system administering both customary and common law as called for in a particular case.[18] The new state of Tanganyika has also brought about integration of the local courts system into a general framework set forth in the Ordinance of 1961. The parallel pattern had remained steadfast in

Tanganyika.   A 1951 law had replaced native courts with local courts and had established a Central Court of Appeal in place of the governor's Appeal Board.   The fact that a High Court judge acted as president did not mean the integration of local courts into the judicial structure.   Under the law of 1961 appeals from the local court go to the local court of appeal and thence to a district commissioner.   Instead of the next step of appeal from district commissioner to Central Court of Appeal with leave of the provincial commissioner, appeal now lies from the district commissioner to High Court with leave of the Local Courts Appeal Officer.   The parallel pattern has been replaced by the integrated structure.   In addition, by the same Act, local courts gain concurrent jurisdiction over the administration of decedents' estates where administrators are required.   Gradually the single system of administration of justice is being forged, though subordinate magistrate courts still exist alongside local courts.[19]

The new states of Africa, both the former British territories and the states d'expression française, have moved towards the integration of their court systems into a single hierarchy for the administration of justice.   As a matter of fact, several of the latter have already realised complete integration of the administration of droit moderne and droit traditionel.[20]   The stage is set for judicial participation in the forging of a national legal system.   The organisation of the court structure permits the formation of case-law to complement legislative action in bringing about the development of national systems of law.   What is to be the substance, the content of these new African legal systems?   What efforts have already been made in the study of the substantive and procedural law of the colonial possessions and young states to provide a solid foundation for further evolution of the law?

IV   THE SUBSTANCE OF AFRICAN LAW

In the previous pages an attempt has been made to outline the discussion which concerns the nature of African law, the lines of its development, and the structure of the judicial systems by which it has been administered.   It seems proper to conclude with a summary of the efforts to describe the substance of the law itself. Manifestly such a survey cannot do more than indicate the major contributions of the secondary literature to our understanding of the content of African law.   The primary sources, that is, the statutes, judicial decisions and government reports, are readily found in the official publications.   The gaps in knowledge will be apparent to the reader, and it will serve no purpose to particularise the major areas in which enlightenment is urgently needed.   Research and writing would be very welcome in almost any legal field, and the work of recent years indicates that the students of African law are responding admirably to the pressing need of governments and administrators for more extensive knowledge of the rules and practices of the law.

Reference has repeatedly been made to the handbooks of the social anthropologists devoted to an exposition of the law and custom of particular ethnic groups. These portray the status of the indigenous law of the family and of marriage, of succession and inheritance within the ethnic group concerned, without giving much attention to the modifications wrought by legislation.   Occasionally they consider the rights respecting land held under customary tenure.   In spite of the absence of a lawyer's slant, these descriptive works are among the major sources of our information.   They range from comprehensive expositions of the legal rules of a single tribe, such as Cory and Hartnoll for the Haya, or Van Warmelo and Phophi for the Venda, to summary treatment of the ethnic groups of the whole country, as Fenton for the native law of Sierra Leone, and the pamphlets on native customs in Nyasaland.[1]

Very few texts attempt to describe the non-indigenous law and the indigenous law as reflected in the decisions of the superior courts. Elias' treatment of Nigerian law and, more recently, his survey of Ghanaian and Sierra Leone law, are notable instances of such endeavour.[2] So also, for a region within a new state, is Haydon's treatment of the law of Buganda.[3] Treatises on the whole of the law in South Africa, in the Congo, in the states of North Africa, are generally not studies of plural legal systems, but rather of the Western or Islamic element in the African law.[4]

The time has not yet come for all-inclusive coverage. The preliminary task is monographic treatment of fields of the law or of single legal institutions. Personal status in both its private and public law aspects has received some attention from French and Belgian scholars,[5] but in the English-speaking African territories, study has been largely devoted to the question of what constitutes a native or an African.[6] A good beginning has been made with the related question of internal conflict of laws, that is, the determination of the law to be applied depending on the personal status (racial or religious group) of the parties.[7] The types of conflict problems which may arise have been elucidated, and several studies in depth have provided insight into the complexity of inter-racial internal conflict of laws.[8] Choice of law in this connection ties up with choice of court, though the newest legislation has tended to eliminate the latter factor.[9] The choice-of-law questions which stem from the multiplicity of tribal laws in a single territory, intertribal or interlocal conflict of laws, are sometimes raised before local or African courts. There have been a few studies on this problem; more await research of court files.[10]

In the area of the law of the family, a few studies deal with guardianship and adoption and with general matters within the scope of domestic relations,[11] but the topic of marriage has received chief attention. There is a superb fundamental study, *Survey of African Marriage and Family Life*, which must be the point of departure for all future research in this field.[12] This study offers three approaches, social, legal and ecclesiastical. So far as the legal section is concerned, the study deals with all problems encountered in customary marriage throughout Africa south of the Sahara, in Moslem marriage, and in statutory marriage. There also exist many special studies of more recent date. These stress the peculiarities of customary marriage, the role of polygyny, the frequency of divorce and the factors of marriage stability, reforms in Islamic law, etc. — all of which should be considered within the framework of the basic study.[13] There is no sharp line drawn between the institutions of the law of the family and the law relating to testate and intestate succession. There is available a range of articles and monographic studies describing various aspects of this part of the private law. But there is no basic text comparable to that on marriage, and the coverage is still far from complete.

Several studies provide access to details of the law of inheritance among peoples of the states *d'expression française*, among ethnic groups within the former British possessions, and among the peoples of the Congo and Ruanda-Urundi.[14] Cory has a chapter on succession among the Sukuma of Tanganyika; Lloyd, one on that of the Yoruba of Western Nigeria.[15] The peculiarities of testamentary succession serve as the subject matter of studies by Matson, Colson and J. Sohier.[16] The new legislation on administration of estates in Ghana gets a brief notice.[17]

There is no field of African law which has been so extensively studied as that relating to land held under customary tenure.   The subject has been the topic of discussion at a number of international congresses, including that held at Lovanium University, Elizabethville, in 1963.[18]   Scores of articles touch upon all phases of the topic.   In order to give some idea of the breadth of discussion, a few of the more recent are noted.   Allott indicates modern changes in the concept of land tenure in Africa south of the Sahara.[19]   A report by a working party on progress in land consolidation and registration of title was submitted to the government of Kenya.[20] Another group studied the Kenya and Uganda developments to determine possible application of these measures in Northern Rhodesia.[21]   Simmance treats of land redemption among the Fort Hall Kikuyu.[22]   In another study Allott discusses the relation of the use of writing to title to land.[23]   The novel legislation on land in Guinea and Mali is reported in the overseas French law review.[24]   The legislation on land affecting Africans in Southern Rhodesia is treated in the Federation law journal.[25]

More extensive monographs devoted to land usage and land tenure have been prepared for many of the territories of Africa.   For Nigeria alone, one can turn to the general studies of Elias and Meek,[26] to that restricted to the customary institution of family property among the Yorubas largely as revealed by decisions of the superior courts,[27] and to the treatise on Yoruba customary land law as seen by native and district courts.[28]   For Ghana the series of reports prepared by Pogucki and the treatise by Ollennu can be compared with the forthcoming study by Bentsi-Enchill.[29]   There is a study of Kenya land law by Sonius, a Dutch scholar.[30]   There are several monographs on land usage in various districts in Northern Rhodesia[31] and an excellent comprehensive treatment of land tenure among the indigenes of the Congo,[32] in addition to reports on the individual ethnic groups of that country.[33]

There is, indeed, a mass of information relating to the law of real property. The policy-making forces in the new states will have the opportunity of canvassing the experience of neighbouring nations, in addition to studying the plans derived from non-indigenous legal systems, when they set about drafting legislation to fashion a system of land tenure geared to meet commercial and industrial requirements.   In contrast to the discussion of property in land, only the barest mention of personal property is to be found in the secondary literature.[34]

The law respecting contractual obligations, commercial law and law relating to industry and finance, is, as would be expected, largely non-indigenous in nature. Only a few institutions in the indigenous law can serve mercantile purposes, and hence there are only a few treatments of such topics as secured loans, mortgages of land, and the simpler types of contracts and forms of business organisation possible within the indigenous legal structure.[35]   In some of the textbooks a chapter or two is devoted to the subject.[36]   The great mass of legal rules in this broad field is still to be found in the statute books and occasionally construed and interpreted in the decisions of the courts, but not analysed in the commentaries of the legal scholars.   A few manuals on 'how to do business in', some trade-mark or tax services, an article here or there on commercial law, insolvency, the development corporation and labour law, are to be found,[37] but save in established world-trade nations, like the Republic of South Africa or Southern Rhodesia, there are no monographs in this most significant field of the modern law.

There is also little concerning the field of tort liability,[38] though much has been written on criminal responsibility.   The allegedly close connection between civil and criminal liability in 'primitive' law has been re-examined,[39] and literature is

available on some of the extraordinary criminal offences of customary law.[40]   Most
effort, however, has been directed to analysis of the various penal codes introduced
into the territories of tropical Africa.[41]   There are a few studies devoted to practice
and procedure in the criminal courts.[42]   An interesting report of recent date
attempts to restate the nature of local customary offences in Kenya.[43]   As this brief
statement would indicate, much remains to be done in presenting the substance of
criminal law and procedure—as well as criminology[44] — to the administrative and
legislative arms of African governments as well as to social scientists generally.

This brief survey may be concluded with a summary of the contributions at the
secondary level in the field of civil procedure.   In this field a clear distinction must
be made between customary procedure and Western procedure.   Many of the most
significant contributions of social anthropologists in recent years have been devoted
to the judicial process of the indigenous tribunals of African society.[45]   The lawyers
have also undertaken to analyse the various types of customary procedure, and at
some conferences the question of the adaptation of the customary process to modern
needs has been discussed.[46]   Most frequently, however, Western process has come
to supplant customary procedure.[47]   It may at one time have been necessary carefully to distinguish appeal from revision,[48] but as the court structure tends more and
more to be an integrated rather than a parallel one, the need for review of the
determination of native African courts by administrative officers will cease to exist.
Revision will give way completely to appeal.   In the former British territories there
have recently appeared full handbooks on procedure, practice and evidence.[49]   In
the ex-French and Belgian territories there are fairly comprehensive textbooks on
these subjects.[50]   Within a few years one may expect a more scholarly approach to
the topic in the former British colonies — from a comparative point of view, it is to
be hoped.   Civil procedure like criminal law and procedure, and a good part of
commercial law, will probably not depend to any considerable extent upon the
indigenous law base.   The non-indigenous British law background should provide
a certain uniformity in civil procedure and in other fields of Western influence in the
African states *d'expression anglaise*.

V   AFRICAN LAW STUDIES IN THE UNITED STATES

Interest in and attention to African law in the United States arise on many sides.[51]
Mention has been made of the effort of a number of American law schools to supply
teachers for the burgeoning law schools and departments of law in the universities
of Africa.   Clearly, the American law professors are equipped to offer instruction
only in those areas of law related to the non-indigenous spheres of law in the former
British territories of Africa.   There is great need for supplementary aid, but it is
obvious that the American-trained law teacher can be of assistance only in a very
small segment of the total requirement.   Reference has also been made to the
education of the African law student in the United States.   This will most likely be
on the graduate level and will again be primarily in those fields of the law in which
the American legal system most closely parallels the non-indigenous law of the
former British possessions.   Actually, then, these two aspects of American competence touch upon matters dealt with only in passing in this chapter.

Some of the universities and a few of the law schools in the United States possess
excellent library facilities for research in African law, not only of the former British,
but of the French and Belgian colonial territories also.   More institutions are

turning to the subject at the present time.   There is excellent opportunity to
provide sorely needed studies of legal institutions for practically all the emerging
states of Africa.   Up to this time there have been few students in this country
seriously devoted to African law.   The number is certain to increase, partly as a
result of the interest of the American legal profession in the commercial and
financial areas of the law.   From interest in these areas it is not difficult to turn to
the areas of contract, tort, and even to land tenure, succession and the law of the
family.   The resources are at hand, and the field is practically untilled.   African
law affords a fertile ground for American legal research.

Perhaps the most vital effort in African law study in the United States is to
provide the other social sciences with current developments in the field of law.   In
the past the anthropologist partially met this need, but with the law now entering a
more technical stage, other kinds of contributions are necessary.   The anthropologist, the sociologist, the political scientist, the economist: all are necessarily
interested in the newest legal developments, but clearly these specialists can devote
only a small part of their effort to gaining this information.   An African law centre
in the United States seems imperative.   Such a centre must provide interested
lawyers as well as experts outside the law with the necessary data.   Timely
presentation of significant developments in the field should be made.   An African
law centre must have library holdings for the colonial epoch which are virtually
complete, current accessions which are comprehensive, and a librarian qualified to
direct a continuing and specialised African law collection.   The centre must be
provided with competent staff to digest and review legislative enactments, judicial
decisions and secondary legal literature.   Ideally there must be in such a centre a
processing department for the preparation of microfilm or Xerox materials.
Scholars and institutions will then be able to obtain the full text of documents briefly
presented in the periodical survey.   Such an African law centre must be established
in the near future.   Law plays a vigorous and important role in the total evolution
of African society.   It is essential that facilities be easily available to gain insight into
the course of the development of African law in the new African states.

7

Education   David Scanlon

I   INTRODUCTION*

EDUCATION IN AFRICA is a phrase used to cover everything from the highly developed medical studies offered in some African universities to the slow and laborious literacy campaigns run in the most remote villages. It can conjure to mind the secondary schoolboy studying Greek, the annual Shakespeare play presented by a school, the barely literate boy who is serving as a carpenter's apprentice, the farmer taking part in a tree-planting project, or a group of chiefs in Uganda receiving instruction in the laws of the new constitution.

Education cuts a broad swath through practically every segment of African society. While there may be pockets of resistance, the general pattern is one of governments racing to build more schools, extending community development, expanding training programs, erecting institutions of higher education and providing an unprecedented number of scholarships for Africans to study abroad.

For the majority in Africa today, education is the keystone for rapid development. For some, it may be viewed as a panacea that will pave the way for a technological society and simultaneously cure social and political tensions. Not since Mexico in the 1920s has so much faith been placed in education. Never in the history of education has expansion taken place so rapidly, and never has there been such a concern to accelerate even faster the educational framework.

The acceleration in African education started after the second world war and has been moving at a rapid rate during the past decade. From the few classes organised by Portuguese missionaries four centuries ago, Western education proceeded at a casual rate until the second world war. A few landmarks had been established, such as Fourah Bay College (1827) in Sierra Leone, and in East Africa an outstanding secondary school, Makerere (1921), that was destined to become the University College of East Africa. But the distribution of educational facilities throughout sub-Saharan Africa was uneven and spotty. In West Africa, the coastal regions almost always had better opportunities for students than the interiors. Missionaries, who had accepted the responsibility for the education of the Africans, had established more permanent centres near the coast. Difficulties of transportation and communication helped to reinforce the establishment of schools near the coastal cities.

* Bibliography for this chapter will be found on page 525.

In addition, the Muslim populations were ordinarily found in greater numbers in the northern areas of such countries as Ghana and Nigeria.   The difficulties of converting Muslims to Christianity resulted in most missionaries' concentrating their efforts on areas that appeared to hold greater possibilities for co-operation and conversion. When missionaries did open schools, there was a natural reluctance on the part of Muslim parents to send their children to a school where conversion was possible.

In East Africa, it was the larger communities in the interior that became the centres for educational development.   Royal College and Alliance High School in Nairobi, Makerere in Uganda, and Tabora in Tanganyika — all located hundreds of miles from the coast — became the educational centres.   Again, it was the heavy Muslim population of the coastal areas that encouraged early missionaries to forsake the old cities of Mombasa, Zanzibar and Dar-es-Salaam, and bear the inconvenience of the long overland journey in order to work among people, such as the Ganda and Kikuyu, who were more receptive to working with missionary societies.

The heavy reliance by governments on the work of the missionary societies and voluntary agencies led, in East Africa, to a proliferation of educational systems. There were the broad religious and racial divisions, such as Protestant, Catholic, Arab, Indian and European; but within each division there were additional sub-divisions.   Thus, in addition to government schools for Europeans, there were boarding schools for Catholics and Protestants.   What in the past were labelled Indian schools and now Asian schools could be divided into government schools (non-denominational), Muslim, Hindu and Sikh.   The Muslims, Hindus and Sikhs, however, had each also split into two major religious divisions, and each maintained its own system.   In Uganda two groups of Muslims maintained separate school systems, as did two sects of Hindus and two sects of Sikhs.   This has remained as an aspect of the basic system until today.

In the Congo and in Central Africa, the pattern followed that of other sectors. Missionaries established centres where there was a possibility of co-operation or, at least, of no violent opposition on the part of the indigenous people.   From these mission stations came the first experiments in Western education in Africa.

A pattern thus began to emerge by the close of the first world war.   Schools existed where missionaries found a physical and social climate in which it was possible to establish a mission station.   Almost invariably, literacy became either mandatory among Protestant groups or desired among Catholic groups for conversion to the faith.   From this foundation came the schools.

The unevenness of distribution of schools was well illustrated in West Africa. As recently as 1954, eleven of the thirteen secondary schools in Sierra Leone were located in the colony and only two in the protectorate.   In former French West Africa, 'the percentages of children of school age actually attending primary schools in 1955 ranged from a low of 2·6 per cent in Niger to 24·3 per cent in Dahomey' (Thompson and Adloff 1957: 523).   This condition continues today as reported in the Conference of African States on the Development of Education in Africa held by UNESCO in 1961.   While some African states reported 60 per cent of the school age children in school, others reported only 2 per cent (UNESCO 1961: 3).

The thrust in higher education since the second world war has been one of the most spectacular developments in African education.   Of the twenty-eight universities serving Africa throughout the continent, twenty-three have been opened since 1945, thirteen within the last decade.   On the basis of present plans there appears every likelihood that this expansion will continue rapidly.

While the growth of education since 1945 has been remarkable, it is but the beginning. 'In the majority of cases [countries] the proportion of children out of school exceeds 80 per cent of the school age population' (UNESCO 1961: 3). Emphasis on education has been expansion of present systems. Effort has been directed primarily towards meeting the demands of villagers for more schools, of youths for more education, and of businesses and governments for trained personnel. The general approach throughout most of Africa, therefore, has been to expand the existing structure under the pressure of the need to produce more trained personnel for the country.

There is an increasing demand in every country that the curriculum of the schools be Africanised. This fact was emphasised at the Addis Ababa Conference and is a topic of discussion at every meeting of educators concerned with African education. The basic problem, again emphasised at all meetings, is the paucity of research in the field. For over twenty-five years there have been discussions on the need for an African Educational Research Centre or, as a minimum, a Documentation Centre where the few depth studies being undertaken in education could be distributed to other African states. There has been no appreciable degree of the blending of social science disciplines with education that is found in the United States and is being developed in Europe. While Americans may think of the social sciences as being the foundation of education, the emphasis in Africa has been upon methodology, and too often it has been a methodology imported from the former colonial power. The basic studies relating the social sciences to education have for the most part been ignored. And yet studies relating anthropology, sociology, economics and psychology to education should constitute the basis for development of a successful African curriculum.

In view of the requests from African educational leaders, the basic studies needed for change in curriculum will undoubtedly be developed, and promising beginnings are being made. Until this research is concluded, however, the basic pattern of education found throughout Africa will be the pattern introduced and developed by the metropolitan power. The orthodoxy of the metropolitan system varies from area to area, but it constitutes the basic foundation of education in Africa today. Throughout former British Africa and French Africa, the path to the university is still the secondary school examination. In East Africa, the Cambridge Syndicate sets the examinations. In those western African countries that were formerly British territories, the West African Examinations Council sets the examinations, but they are closely allied to the Cambridge Syndicate. In former French Africa the usual pattern is to have the baccalaureate degree controlled by one of the French universities that historically has been closely associated with a given country. Examinations for higher education in the Congo have remained relatively unchanged despite the political upheaval. The educational ties between the metropole and those areas that are or were under French control have been so close as to permit few radical departures.

In most cases the fact of independence has done little to change examination systems — and examinations that are given at the end of the secondary school are the keys in educational systems where the emphasis is on academic preparation rather than on a comprehensive secondary school education. The secondary school examination not only determines who will go on to the university, but also determines the acceptability of the individual for employment by the government or private industry. The great importance placed on the secondary-school-leaving examination has meant that preparation for the examination has dominated the curriculum not only of the secondary school but also of the elementary school. A parallel can be drawn with the concern shown by parents in the United States for their children to begin their preparation for college in the elementary school and continue it in college preparatory classes in the high school. In Africa the over-riding concern for the examination has made it difficult to introduce alternative courses of study.

The rapid expansion of education has even served to strengthen adherence to the examination system, for many African educators have been concerned to guarantee that the established standards shall be maintained in the expansion process. There is a nearly universal fear that, in the educational revolution that is taking place, the quality of education will decline. The provision of enough qualified secondary school teachers to replace expatriate teachers is an acute problem in itself. To produce the teachers for the continuing expansion of education while maintaining standards will certainly require imaginative and bold programs.

Any examination of the educational system in Africa today must take into account the broad educational policies adopted by the metropolitan powers. In most cases, the metropolitan system remains the foundation, and innovations that may occur are still based on the structure established within the past four decades. It is for this reason that understanding of the historical development of education assumes such great importance. The hoped-for studies in the methodology of education, and the even more important studies that will relate education to the social sciences and give greater depth to the entire educational process in Africa, will of necessity have to include inspection of the roots of the established system.

II THE FOUNDATION OF AFRICAN EDUCATION

The past decade can be considered the take-off period in African education — the era of the great expansion of the educational systems — but the beginning of govern-ment interest on the part of the metropolitan powers began shortly after the first world war.

The publication of the Phelps-Stokes reports in 1922 and 1928, which severely criticised the organisation and content of education in Africa, came at an auspicious time. African exports were beginning to bring in revenues, and, under the stimulation of the first world war, there was organised concern in some of the metropolitan powers for the development of greater social services in the colonies.

1. BRITISH AFRICA

In Britain, the Phelps-Stokes reports were particularly influential, and in November 1923 the Secretary of State for the colonies appointed an Advisory Committee on Native Education in the British Tropical African Dependencies to serve in an advisory capacity to the Secretary. From this period until the mid-1950s the Advisory Committee periodically issued policy statements. These represented the view of distinguished British educators and civil servants. How they were inter-preted within various colonies depended upon the interests of the governors and the inclinations of local officers. Nevertheless, they constituted a framework, a structure that gave form to the development of education in those areas under British control. The first paper published by the Committee, *Memorandum on Education Policy in British Tropical Africa* (Advisory Committee . . . 1925), set forth the broad principles under which education was to be developed. They are interesting from an historical point of view, for they parallel many of the recommendations made at the recent Conference of African States on the Development of Education in Africa held in Addis Ababa in 1961. The memorandum stated: (1) governments control educational policy and will co-operate with other educational agencies; (2) religion and character training are of the greatest importance; (3) the educational service should attract the best men from Britain; (4) voluntary schools which meet basic requirements should receive grants; (5) African languages as well as English should be used in education; (6) there should be an adequate teaching staff of Africans properly qualified and they should include women; (7) village schools may be improved by the use of specially trained visiting teachers; (8) inspection and supervision of schools is essential; (9) industrial training of a technical nature is best given in government workshops; (10) vocational training should be carried out in government departments; (11) the education of girls and women is of great importance; (12) an educational system should include primary education, secondary education of varying types, technical and vocational schools, and institutions of university rank for such subjects as teacher education, medicine and agriculture. Adult education was also stressed, and 'the education of the whole community should advance *pari passu*'. One of the most interesting principles stated:

> Education should be adapted to the mentality, aptitudes, occupations and traditions of the various peoples, conserving as far as possible all sound and healthy elements in the fabric of their social life; adapting them where necessary to changed circumstances and progressive ideas, as an agent of natural growth and evaluation. This includes the fostering and the educational use of African arts and culture, and will, it is hoped, narrow the hiatus between the educated class and the rest of the community whether chiefs or peasantry (Advisory Committee . . . 1925: 4).

Many of these principles could easily be applied today, and there is strong evidence to suggest that if these principles had been followed carefully, the present difficulties faced by educators in Africa would indeed be fewer. There are undoubtedly many reasons why these principles were not more fully implemented. There was a shortage of funds, and there was a feeling among many administrators that the academic type of preparation should have precedence in the developing nations. If funds were available, then one could offer the other types of education suggested by the Advisory Committee; in fact little was done to establish secondary schools of 'different types'.

The concept of developing education within the cultural milieu of the people also remains one of the most pressing demands in African education today. There is universal agreement that education in Africa should be developed within an African framework, that it should represent African culture and be based upon African society. However, while this need was recognised nearly forty years ago, virtually nothing could be done to satisfy it until organised research could build a bridge between the society and those responsible for the curriculum and its context in the school. The lack of adequate funds greatly limited the amount of research that could have provided the basic material necessary for the Africanisation of the curriculum. In addition, the reluctance of many Africans to accept any other than an academic education, coupled with the lack of education officers who had any experience other than that of the formal academic approach, further hampered research.

There was little in Britain itself to give assistance to the educational officer who wanted to break with the concept of a single track (academic) educational system. To this was added the assumption that anything except academic education was not really education at all. This is reflected in the very titles, 'training institutions', given to those schools devoted to specialised fields. This distinction between institutions was not lost on the Africans, who quickly preferred to obtain the best 'education' as opposed to mere training.

While the *Memorandum on Educational Policy* (1925) urged that the African teaching staff be adequate, it appeared that little could be done rapidly to increase the number of teachers. Young men and women who had attained the schooling necessary to qualify as teachers could ordinarily find employment in an expanding economy and in the enlarging government services.

It is perhaps for the reasons indicated above and because of other problems, that the majority of the remaining reports by the Advisory Committee were concerned with co-operation between schools and other educational agencies helping to raise the level of village life. The memorandum, *The Education of African Communities* (Advisory Committee . . . 1935), stressed health, agriculture, adult education, co-operative societies, co-ordination of all educational effort, the stimulation of African initiative, and the need for environmental studies. In setting forth the broad outlines for what was to become community development, the committee was making use of the work that had been carried on by the League of Nations in China, the Mexican Cultural Missions (Hughes 1950), and the individual work of such outstanding leaders as James Yen (Scanlon 1960).

The development of education in Africa in the British territories was, in effect, an attempt to apply the principles stated in the memoranda of 1925 and 1935. In various British territories advisory committees were established to develop educational policies in line with the overall concepts stated by the Advisory Committee. The ideas discussed in the 1935 memorandum were reinforced by a third memorandum issued by the Advisory Committee, *Mass Education in African Society* (Advisory Committee . . . 1944). The basic idea of the new memorandum was that the education of the school child should be accompanied by an education of the whole community that would result in a better living for all. The committee viewed as dangerous the education of school children in Western ideas and techniques which would alienate them from the rest of the African society of which they were members.

The fact that the later memoranda stressed principles in community development rather than in the formal type of education is perhaps indicative of the view of the Advisory Committee. The memorandum of 1935 indicated the need for environmental studies, and that of 1944 stressed the danger of creating gulfs and potential conflict between segments of the society. But the successful application of these principles would require a vast amount of research. It is one thing to indicate the need: it is quite a different thing to carry out a viable program. There were few social scientists engaged in the kind of research that would have helped make what was considered educationally desirable educationally and administratively possible. Except for the services of the anthropologist Margaret Read (1956) and a few others, educators had little help in introducing the new approaches that depended particularly upon research in sociology and anthropology.

There was the additional inhibiting fact that, until 1944, British secondary education was restricted to a fraction of the potential school age population. It was overwhelmingly of an academic, pre-university preparatory type. It was only after the passing of the Education Act of 1944 that secondary education in Britain began its large-scale effort to produce education for all in modern, comprehensive schools more specifically designed for the non-academic, non-university student. Education officers sent out to work in the colonies, therefore, had little within their own experience in Britain which could help make viable the broad principles outlined in the memorandum of 1925. The fact must also be considered that in most areas of Africa the actual operation of the schools was in the hands of the missionaries, many of whom were not trained as educators, and who were working in most cases under severe financial and staff shortages.

Despite the handicaps, great efforts were made to develop higher education in order to train the professional and government leaders needed in the territories. In 1943 the Asquith Commission was appointed to advise the government on how to develop universities in the colonies. The commission also desired to secure the co-operation of universities in the United Kingdom for colonial universities and university colleges. The Asquith Commission was assisted in West Africa by the Elliot Commission. As a result of the work of these commissions, the beginnings of the expansion of higher education were made. University colleges were created in the Gold Coast, Nigeria and in Uganda. The staff at the University of London and the staff in Africa collaborated in drawing up the syllabi. The recognition of African degrees by British universities led the African universities and university colleges to adopt a pattern of course offerings similar to that of the British university. The concern of many — British and African — was to guarantee that the associated African university would maintain standards as close as possible to those of the British university. This development led to an African concept of the role of the university or college which is essentially identical with the British concept. It is a concept which had served Britain well over the centuries, and it was and continues to be supported by many African educators (Olubummo and Ferguson 1960). In opposition to it are those who see the university more closely related to the economic development of Africa and who, therefore, are interested in broadening its scope, offerings and degree programs.

2. FRENCH AFRICA

The pride that France took in the educational system of its African territories is apparent to anyone who has travelled in French communities in Africa or discussed education with French Africanists. The most popular saying among French educators in Paris and in the French community is: 'When the Portuguese colonised, they built churches; when the British colonised, they built trading stations; when the French colonised, they built schools'. From the viewpoint of the French and of many African educators, the success of the system was proved by the increasing number of students who passed the baccalaureate. The concern of the majority was not to Africanise the curriculum but to guarantee that the curriculum would be equal to that of metropolitan France. Except in Guinea, there is little evidence that this basic philosophy has changed, and the patterns, structure and philosophies that developed when the present independent countries were colonies remains nearly unchanged.

In 1903 a public school system for French Africa was established. This move represented an effort on the part of the French government to carry out in the colonies the legal separation of church and state that had been enacted in France. Such a movement anticipated the secularisation of the schools in France with a law that forbad all members of the religious orders to teach in any kind of school (Foulquié 1947: 43–7). To enforce the law was virtually impossible in an area where the vast majority of schools were run by missionary groups, and it was never fully applied. The custom of the nineteenth century had been for missionaries to be sent to Africa by their respective societies but under government contract. Efforts to establish public schools were meagre and ordinarily were made in Muslim areas where the missionaries were not operating. The only outstanding public school was that established by Governor Faidherbe in Senegal in 1854 for the sons of chiefs.

As governor-general of French West Africa, Roume established a public system that remained the basic pattern until 1944. For those students who were selected as potential candidates for schools in metropolitan France, a system was created that followed the model of the French schools. For the select, the curriculum, examination system and general requirements paralleled those of the metropolitan power. A high proportion of the school budget was allotted to bringing teachers from France for language instruction, as the mastery of the French language was considered of prime importance. In this respect there was a sharp philosophical difference from the British who taught in the local vernacular for the first few years and then transferred to English. French missionaries had tried teaching in the vernacular in the early decades of the nineteenth century and had termed the results disastrous. Consequently, it became official policy for all instruction to be given in French.

Only a few students were selected for advanced work. For the vast majority who would not go on to advanced work, village schools were created. In the village or town non-academic school, the pupil studied the rudiments of the French language, reading, writing, arithmetic, and whatever might be considered desirable for him to know in order to improve his economic position in the society. As the majority of the schools were in rural areas, agriculture was stressed. Boarding facilities were offered for students who attended advanced technical schools. At the apex of the system within West Africa was the William Ponty School — later renamed Sébikotane, although its graduates continued to be called 'Ponty teachers' — in Senegal; founded in 1903, it prepared teachers for advanced classes, pharmacists and lawyers. Also at the apex was the Dakar Medical School founded in 1918.

The importance of teacher training was stressed from the turn of the century, and the oldest normal school, the William Ponty, was founded in the same year that the West African Federation was formed. While it was originally conceived primarily as a teacher training institution, it soon became a training school for African leaders in government and business. The school seldom produced more than thirty teachers a year, and they were the best prepared in the Federation. Thirty was an infinitesimally small number, however, in terms of the number needed. The result was a dependence on highly qualified overseas expatriates, on the one hand, and on what were referred to as monitors, on the other. Monitors included men and women who held primary school certificates and had been given courses in teacher education. As the number of schools expanded, the monitors were faced with large classes: a condition that would have challenged the most experienced and highly trained teacher. The problem became acute in the 1930s, and three additional normal schools were opened. In the Soudan a school was founded that graduated agricultural supervisors; in the Ivory Coast a school was started that stressed preparation in the practical aspects of the curriculum; in Rufisque a normal school was opened for the training of the much needed women teachers.

On the eve of the second world war, there were few schools; '. . . there existed in 1935 only three hundred-odd village schools [French West Africa] throughout the Federation with a total of 29,294 pupils and about eighty regional schools attended by 23,321 children' (Thompson and Adloff 1957: 518). While the policy of gallicisation of the elite by educating a select group in France was severely criticised by foreign observers, it did produce an educated group capable of assuming leadership. If there was a criticism of the educational system by African leaders, it generally was that the system did not go far enough in following the example of metropolitan France. The emphasis on agriculture and crafts in the village schools, so highly praised by visiting educators, did not receive strong support from African leaders. Buell's observation: 'Despite the use of the French language, the French educational system had adapted courses of instruction to the needs of the African much more successfully than has been done in any other territory in Africa . . . texts and courses have been designed to fit native needs' (Buell 1928: II: 61), would have received scant support by the educated African in the French territories.

Although the role of education was not a major consideration at the Brazzaville Conference of 1944, there was agreement among the educators present that primary education should be expanded rapidly. The enormity of the problem can be grasped in the agreement of the educators: 'By advocating the building of a school in every village having at least fifty children of school age, the men of Brazzaville optimistically envisaged universal primary education for all French Black Africa by 1995' (Thompson and Adloff 1957: 521).

The sharp dichotomy in philosophy between what the French educators thought desirable for Africa and what the Africans themselves thought is illustrated in the plans for education developed in the overseas portion of the Plan for Modernisation and Equipment in 1946. At the planning sessions for the scheme, African educators pressed for expansion of secondary and technical education. This was in sharp contrast to the proposed expansion of primary education made two years earlier at the Brazzaville Conference. The approach suggested by the Africans was radical in that it ignored the older concept of colonial self-sufficiency and called for the establishment of ten-year development projects for the French dependencies. Through the Fonds d'Investissement pour le Développement Économique et Social (FIDES), some funds were provided for this expansion.

The uneven distribution of schools and the reaction of African parents created unusual problems in the years following the adoption of the FIDES. The abolishment of forced labour in 1946 led some parents, who had sent their children to school only to forestall that threat, to withdraw their children from the schools. Paradoxically, in other areas there was a greater demand than ever before for schools. The result was overcrowded schools in some areas and empty schools in others, severe shortages of teachers in some areas and unemployed teachers in other sections of the Federation.

Although an edict had been passed requiring all primary age children to attend school, there was a realisation that this would be impossible to enforce where schools were not available and where there was such opposition to schools on the part of parents that incidents could occur.   Each territory was granted the freedom to decide when the edict should be enforced, and the edict itself was viewed as a goal rather than a reality.

It was believed that much of the parental opposition to schools would disappear when schools were actually available, and a great effort was made rapidly to build schools throughout the territories.   Because of the haste many buildings were poorly constructed, and it became evident that an increasing amount of the school budget was going into repair costs rather than into equipment and teacher salaries. Control of the problem was sought by requiring approval before a school could be built and establishing basic minimum building regulations.

In an effort to upgrade the quality of teachers, an attempt was made in 1949 to establish the same requirements in African normal schools as in metropolitan France.   Because of low pay and low status, many students used the normal schools for the same purposes for which students have used teacher training colleges in many sections of the world: that is, as a stepping stone to more promising careers in government and business.   The lack of qualified teachers in the secondary schools is illustrated by the fact that in 1954 there were only twenty Africans on the staff of the Federation's secondary schools.   The enrolment in the normal schools continued to increase and in some areas, such as the Soudan, the production of primary school and lower form teachers was ahead of actual school construction, so that it was necessary for such teachers to seek employment in other areas of the Federation.

The strengthening of the lycées helped many of them to reach the level of those operating in metropolitan France, and the upgrading actually meant a closer adherence to the curriculum of the metropolitan lycée.   The increase in the number of lycées and the identity of the academic curricula led to a decrease in the number of students sent to France.

In the field of higher education, a University Institute had been established in Dakar in 1948.   The objective in establishing the Institute was to broaden the offerings in advanced studies which, until the second world war, had been confined to the School of Medicine and Pharmacy at Dakar.   In order to grant prestige to the new institution and rapidly to raise and maintain high standards, the new institute was placed under the direction of the universities of Paris and Bordeaux, and its management was assumed by the federal director-general of education and a council of leading educators and laymen.   During its early stages, nevertheless, the institute was not considered to be on the same academic level as the metropolitan universities.   This provoked the criticism by some African leaders that the institute was offering second-rate education.   Two years after its founding and as a result of increasing criticism by French as well as African leaders, an Institute of Advanced Studies was established.   This institute offered courses in medicine, law, letters and natural science, and, though the offerings were approximately the equivalent of those at the metropolitan universities, they still were not equal to the courses at Paris or Bordeaux.   This factor, together with what the Africans viewed as unnecessary political control, produced increased complaints against the Institute of Advanced Studies.   Some Africans saw its very establishment as a political move to block Africans from going to France for studies.   Others resented the inclusion of African studies in higher education; this was viewed as a dilution of the offerings and of the funds which could have been used to better effect in other departments of the institute.   What many Africans wanted was both an African university that paralleled the course offerings of the French universities and the continuation of the plan to send more students to France.

Dissatisfaction with the Institute led students in 1953 to send a petition to the Grand Council urging that the Institute be abolished and that all students be sent to France for higher education.   The French were reluctant to continue the expensive plan of sending large numbers of African students to France and attempted to meet the criticism by improving and expanding the institute.   Libraries and laboratories were expanded, student stipends were increased, and every effort was made to attract students.   In 1955 a School of Pedagogy was established to strengthen teacher-education.   In 1957 the Institute became the University of Dakar.

With independence, there have been few radical changes in the educational systems of those countries that were formerly part of French West and Equatorial Africa.   There is almost universal evidence of the high regard for education and of the concern to find the most expeditious way to expand educational opportunity. Throughout the countries, community development schemes have been enlarged, village schools expanded, and, at great sacrifice, secondary education developed. As in other African countries, this last aspect — secondary education — is especially viewed as the key to economic development.   With the exception of Guinea, however, the pattern of academic secondary education remains basically the same. In the Cameroun, for example, the examination for the baccalaureate is still controlled by the University of Bordeaux.   The University of Dakar approximates as much as possible the universities of Paris and Bordeaux.   In the secondary examination system and the offerings of the university, there is a close parallel to the examination system and university structure in the former British territories.

3. CONGO

Educational policy in the former Belgian Congo was based on two foundations.   The first was an emphasis on developing and expanding primary education.   From 1878 until 1948 there was created a vast system of urban and village schools which offered language instruction in one of the selected local African languages, arithmetic, writing, religious instruction, and some practical instruction, e.g., agriculture, that was considered essential to people living in a specific area.   In 1948 token secondary education was introduced.   What had primarily been labelled secondary education had actually been post-primary education for the training of tradesmen and artisans.

The second foundation of the educational policy was the dependence of the system upon mission schools, particularly Roman Catholic schools.   A secular school system was not started until 1954, and what had been regarded as the state system from 1884–1954 was in effect a mission system.   The success of the missions in operating the schools was such that in 1959–60, five years after the inauguration of the secular system, 97 per cent of students in school were still enrolled in mission schools.

Before the formation of the International Association of the Congo by King Leopold, education was primarily the work of Protestant missionaries.   Under Leopold, Catholic missionaries were encouraged to open missions and take over the management of 'school colonies' which in effect were orphanages that had been opened in a few areas.   The Catholic missions were strengthened by a convention concluded between the Independent State of the Congo and the Holy See in 1906. According to this convention, each missionary establishment agreed to create a school, to adopt a curriculum determined by the mission and the governor-general, and to include instruction in agriculture, forestry and manual occupations. Instruction in one of the two national languages of Belgium was obligatory, and schools were to be subject to periodic inspections by the government. In exchange for their educational services, the missions received free concessions of 100 to 200 hectares of land.

The first world war interrupted the development of the system which had already come under increasing criticism. In 1922 the Minister for the Colonies appointed a commission to review education in the Congo. The commission published its report in 1924 (Ministre des Colonies . . . 1924) and included the following among its recommendations:

(i) *Adaptation to Native Environment:* The school should offer knowledge that will be helpful to the child in his daily life. The program of instruction should be conceived in terms of the native environment. The teacher in the Congo should have a knowledge of the local language and the customs of the people. European programs in history and geography should be disregarded, and lessons should be drawn from the local environment. Hygiene, along with agriculture and the arts and crafts, should be stressed.

(ii) *Instruction and Training:* The first concern of the school should be with the development of character and moral discipline. Instruction may be helpful or harmful but training is essential. Children need a new moral framework to replace the discarded African imperatives, and Christian morality will meet this need. As experience in other colonies has shown the danger of a bookish type of instruction, there should be ample opportunity for manual and agricultural training.

(iii) *Language of Instruction:* Instruction should be given in native languages [this was a reversal of the policy under the Convention of 1906]. French will not be taught in the villages; in the urban centre, it may be one of the subjects studied but will not be the language of instruction. While many Africans want to learn French, it is important that the Africans be taught and trained in their own languages.

(iv) *Co-operation of the Missions:* The Christian religion, which the missionaries propagate, involves an excellent moral training for the natives. Belgian missionaries especially render an important service, for in addition to spreading the gospel, they spread the lore and influence of Europe to all corners of Central Africa. Therefore, it is important for the government to help the missions establish a school system. A public school system would create a serious drain on the treasury.

(v) *Importance of the Normal Schools:* As the expansion of education depends upon the training of local teachers, the creation of normal schools is of great importance.

(vi) *Compulsory Attendance:* It would be impossible to put into effect any compulsory education law because of the lack of facilities and the resistance of some parents to sending their children to school even if offered free meals and clothing, prizes, free medical supplies and post-school benefits for the children.

(vii) *Schools for Girls:* Schools for girls are important in order that educated young Africans may have wives with a similar background. The school program for girls should be modelled after the program for boys, emphasising manual training, home management, hygiene and child care.

As a result of the recommendations of 1924, twenty-year conventions were signed by the government and the Catholic mission societies; they guaranteed subsidies to Catholic mission schools and, in effect, recognised the Catholic mission schools as the state schools for the Congo. These conventions governed the Congo school system until 1948. During this period the missions expanded primary education and opened technical schools primarily for the training of artisans and lower-level administrators. Some schools of the latter type were also opened and operated by the government and private industrial and commercial companies.

In 1948 a modern reform bill was passed which changed the direction of education in the Congo. The school reforms were considered part of the Ten-Year Plan for Economic and Social Development of the Congo, and funds from the regular colonial budget were augmented by allocations from the Native Welfare Fund. This association of education with economic and social development placed added emphasis on technical education, although the need to accelerate the expansion of all education was recognised. Secondary education, on a level equal to that offered in Belgium, was organised for the first time. Protestant missions, which had been operating without government subsidy, were offered financial assistance if they could meet government standards. In an effort to increase the number of schools, the government relaxed the standards required of teachers.

During the next decade, educational policy reflected the shifting political situation in Belgium. In 1954 a governmental commission on education representing an anti-clerical coalition of the Socialist and Liberal parties in Belgium strongly recommended that a secular school system be established. This report was adopted, and the establishment of a state, non-religious school system was undertaken (Ministre des Colonies . . . 1954). The commission was particularly concerned with the poor quality of instruction in the Congo and alarmed by the fact that so many teachers were not qualified to teach. The commission recommended the creation of sections in the senior high schools for the training of teachers for the upper grades of the elementary schools; it also recommended the formation of high schools in urban centres for the training of assistant elementary teachers. The elections of 1958 in Belgium, however, reversed the emphasis on building a secular education system in the Congo.

Although a beginning had been made in 1948, secondary school development was slow. On the eve of independence, there were only 850 high school graduates in the Congo.

The Reforms of 1948 had urged the development of higher education, and the following year the Centre Universitaire Congolais Lovanium was established. In 1954 Lovanium University was established in Leopoldville, and two years later Katanga State University was founded as the Official University of the Belgian Congo and Ruanda-Urundi. At Usumbura in Ruanda-Urundi the Jesuits organised the University Centre in 1960. Entrance requirements are identical with those of universities in Belgium — a secondary school background with majors in language and literature or mathematics — and the universities are modelled after the Belgian university. Since independence, the seven institutes that offered advanced training at pre-university levels have been reduced to two: the Teacher Training Institute and the Higher Technical Institute for Social Welfare. Both institutes offer a two- or three-year specialised course.

III *AREAS OF NEEDED RESEARCH*

Western education in Africa may be said to have started in the 1920s.   Although mission schools had been established as early as the sixteenth century, it was only in the period following the first world war that governments assumed an increasing responsibility in financially assisting and supervising education.   France, England and Belgium began then to issue series of policy statements on the direction that education should take in the African territories.

Plans for the development of education in all colonies were interrupted by the depression and by the second world war.   Following the war, England, France and Belgium inaugurated plans for the rapid expansion of education.   With funds provided under Colonial and Development Welfare Funds in the British territories, FIDES in the French areas, the Ten-Year Plan in the Congo, and with the high priority given to education in such newly independent countries as Ghana, the scale and scope of education increased more in the decade of the 1950s than it had in the entire past history of the continent.   The results have been remarkable, and yet it must be remembered that, while educational conditions vary from state to state, 'in the majority of cases, the proportion of children out of school exceeds 80 per cent'.

The growth of education that did occur was primarily an extension of what had existed previously.   The movement was concerned with bringing greater numbers of children into schools that followed the traditional curriculum.   This was particularly true on the secondary level, where the existence of external examinations, controlled to a large extent by the European country, determined the content of the course offerings.

Few educators in Africa were trained in an academic discipline that could be applied to problems of educational reform.   Planning on the secondary level, therefore, consisted primarily of building a curriculum that followed the curriculum of the European country, with only slight variations allowed for local conditions. There was a great fear that in the expansion of schooling the standards would be weakened.   With limited funds, little could be done in the way of basic research that would relate the social sciences to education.   A few specialists attempted to bridge the gap between the social sciences and education, but there is little evidence to suggest that the approach was common in the African territories.   For many educators serving in Africa, such studies seemed unnecessary and were considered as frills or luxuries irrelevant to getting on with the task of expanding education.   The European countries themselves had failed to bridge this gap, and as a result there was no precedence for its being done overseas.

England, France and Belgium did introduce basic educational reforms, during and after the second world war, which broadened the offerings on the secondary level and introduced courses alternate to those of the traditional grammar school. The enlargement of education to provide for the many rather than for the few who had traditionally gone to the secondary school also stimulated research that represented a fusion of the social sciences and education.   In the territories and newly independent countries, however, expansion was of the traditional grammar or academic type and hardly influenced by the European reforms; the results of the growing research in the social, political and philosophical foundations of education failed to penetrate Africa.   On the university level the system established in the former territories remained basically the same as that introduced by the European power.

The opportunity for the development of social research related to education in Africa has thus been limited. The publications of such centres as the East African Institute of Social Research are now occasionally being used in the study of education, but such cases are unusual. The need for research is inherent in the Phelps-Stokes Reports of the 1920s and was emphasised in papers submitted to the Addis Ababa Conference (UNESCO 1961). Research into more pressing problems that require the joint efforts of educators and social scientists may be classified in two categories. The first includes studies of the problems of adapting the curriculum to its African environment; such studies directly relate education to nearly all the social sciences and will lay the foundations upon which adaptation may take place. The second includes studies of those problems that appear to be only educational in nature but which, nevertheless, involve the social sciences; in this category are such problems that range from the teaching of English as a second language to experimental programs in teacher training.

Some of the priorities in these two categories are: Africanisation of the curriculum; human growth and development; citizenship training; aptitude testing; teaching of English as a second language; and acceleration of teacher-training programs.

I. AFRICANISATION OF THE CURRICULUM

Few topics have been discussed as thoroughly as the need to Africanise the curriculum. For some, this has meant an attempt to clothe in respectability a system that was obviously designed to prevent the African from advancing. Since the Phelps-Stokes Reports, however, for the vast majority of educators it has meant the attempt to adapt the curriculum to the needs of the African environment. It is a striving for a system that will present those universals needed by an educated person in the world and yet relate them to the local and African setting. It is an attempt to strip the imported cultural baggage from the curriculum, retain the core of knowledge, skills and attitudes, and surround it with an African setting. Few challenge the need for such a movement: its various aspects have been considered by educators for forty years, and yet little appreciable headway has been made.

Africanisation of the curriculum would require extended research in the history, geography, natural sciences, folklore and folk music of the areas. Attempts have been made by some teachers to gather data on local history and geography. Such amateur efforts are well meaning and undoubtedly have been helpful, but the need is for studies conducted by specialists trained in a discipline.

Africans of all nations are greatly interested in learning more about their own country and about their neighbours' as well. School children in Sierra Leone should know their neighbour, Guinea, as children in Uganda should know the Congo; but material is scarce, information scant and libraries limited.

Africanisation will depend, therefore, on the production of studies in the subject areas, the countries and the continent. Once the studies have been made, it will become the task of textbook writers and curriculum experts to determine how the content can be built into the elementary and secondary school. There is little doubt that many countries are ready to proceed with this program, but the scarcity of material has consistently blocked the most enthusiastic textbook writer and educational specialist.

There is an additional and related need to train educators who can apply the findings of the social sciences to education. Recognition of the relationship of the social sciences to education has been primarily an American phenomenon. The idea that education has its roots in the social, philosophical, historical and psychological foundations of the society itself, has been investigated by social scientists and educators in close co-operation since the turn of the century. The results of such study have been reflected not only in the content of the curriculum but also in the actual methodology of teaching and have led to the development of graduate study programs for individuals who are first trained in a discipline and then apply the discipline to education. This fusion of interests has not been achieved to any degree in the great majority of African countries. Such an approach is necessary, however, if the Africanisation of the curriculum is correctly understood as a continual process. At present, the inclination of the institutes of education is to concentrate on methodology. The institutes are attached to universities but operate in comparative isolation from the rest of the university. Few would question the great need for the development of more efficient teaching methods, but the success of the methodology depends in many instances on the framework of the society in which it is being taught.

2. HUMAN GROWTH AND DEVELOPMENT

Studies of African children have for the most part been concerned with *rites de passage*, traditional practices, isolated rural communities or tribal education. Such studies have been valuable to the educators, but of even greater importance are the studies which need to be made of contemporary African children who today are passing through a difficult period of social and cultural change. What are the characteristics of children in the elementary and secondary schools? In most European countries such studies have only recently been started, principally because the relative stability of the culture, the long precedence for educational development, the child's knowledge of his place in the society, and the close ties of the school with the general culture of the area minimised the need for such studies. The present expansion of secondary education in Europe, however, has stimulated an increasing interest in knowledge about the kind of student that is entering school, for the knowledge about the students of past centuries is no longer valid. The new secondary school student — the young man or woman who is not going on to the university — is quite a different individual from the wealthy, upper class student who traditionally attended the secondary school.

After the turn of the century, when secondary education was expanded to include the majority of the relevant age groups, and when the influence of psychology was being brought to bear on education, Americans recognised the need to study secondary students. The common denominators of culture found in European schools and societies did not exist in the United States, and educators were forced to enlist the aid of psychologists and sociologists in gaining an understanding about the nature of their students. But the influence of child study and research into human growth and development was not confined to the secondary level. The acceptance of the century-old principle of national school education for all contributed to a growing interest in the maturation of children at all levels, and child study became an integral part of the entire education system in the United States.

Studies of human growth and development and in the psychology of learning have assumed great importance for the methodology of teaching. A teacher must be aware of the processes by which people learn, must understand the different modes of learning, be able to solve the technical problems of learning and frame the subject matter within a logical ongoing process. For any teacher, a knowledge of behaviour changes in learning is helpful in understanding the learning process. Problems of how one learns to reason, to develop concepts and generalisations, to acquire skills, form attitudes, and create aesthetic products, are all part of the overall term: the 'learning process'. Of equal importance to comprehension of the 'learning process' are investigations into retention, transfer and motivation.

Schematic presentation of this area of knowledge being developed by educators and social scientists generally includes the following: the general nature of learning, processes of behavioural change, and learning functions and problems. 'Processes of behavioural change' include such areas as reasoning; aesthetic creativity or the application of creative thought in aesthetic production; conceptual learning or the interpretation of situations, signs and symbols and their meaning in terms of definitions, generalisations and qualities; skill learning, involving the co-ordination of sensory and perceptual functions in motor performance; attitudinal learning and group learning. 'Learning functions and problems' includes such critical functions as motivation, retention and transfer.

Underlying all of the studies in the learning process is the assumption that various developmental levels of children and youth are known, and that — though the developmental level may vary from person to person — there are common grids that can be used as guidelines. In the case of African students, the developmental studies have not as yet been done. A beginning has been made in a few centres, such as the Institute of Education at the University of Ghana, which has published *Child Training in Ghana* by Barrington Kaye (1960). This study is one of the first to attempt an impressionistic description of the backgrounds of Ghanaian children. Other studies have been planned, but as yet few have been produced.

Studies in human development mean little unless they are part of the larger studies of the society; the study of children cannot be done in a vacuum. It is not yet clear, furthermore, how much of the studies concerned with the learning process in one culture can be transferred to other cultures. There are basic principles that appear to be universal, but so much is related to the developmental levels that extended investigation will have to be undertaken before the present resources, studies and surveys can be safely applied, cross-culturally. This fact once more suggests the need for the combined efforts of social science disciplines and education in the scientific study of human growth and development within an African framework.

3. CITIZENSHIP TRAINING

The use of the school as an agent in promoting nationalism is well known to the student of history. Carried to an extreme, it can be perverted, as it was in Nazi Germany. But some extreme examples should not negate appreciation of the positive force the school can exert in uniting a nation. In the United States the immigration of Europeans that began in the 1830s and 1840s caused many Americans, conscious of their own American nationalism, to support the idea of a common school which would have the responsibility of inculcating the newcomers with those values vital to participation in the American community. The common school would provide a meeting place where the children of immigrants and of the native population could meet, and some who undoubtedly would not have supported the concept of a system of public education did accept the idea of a common school where the children of immigrants would become 'Americanised'.

Although other possible agents of nationalism — radio, press and television — have expanded rapidly in recent decades, the school remains one of the most effective means of strengthening the concept of nationhood. Most African countries still face in varying degrees the persistent problem of bringing together people who have traditionally thought in terms of ethnic units smaller than that of the nation. Citizenship training in the school could be an important aid in nation-building. In some countries, such as Ghana, and in regions of Nigeria such a program is being developed; but throughout much of Africa, it is ignored or presented in an academic manner that is focused more on the structure of government than on the interaction of the groups within the nation.

This is another area in which there is a need for close co-operation between social scientists and educators who can direct the findings of the sciences into the curriculum of the school. Part of the necessary research undoubtedly would be concerned with history and government, but there is also a need for the social psychologist who can measure the degrees and sources of hostility between groups and work with textbook writers and curriculum specialists to break down narrow parochialism and help in nation-building.

There are few elements in the curriculum that could not be used for this purpose. Geography, if approached from the standpoint of human geography, could make valuable contributions as could the studies of folk art, folk music and folk crafts. Studies of the larger groups found within countries could become units of study within the history and geography courses. Oral histories of the various groups could be exchanged and recorded, and comparative studies of religion could be introduced.

Such an approach is not directed towards the destruction of local history and culture; rather, it is an attempt to search for the common denominators between people. It would identify the role of the local group within the structure of the nation. It would encourage the individual student to maintain pride in his local culture while integrating his knowledge with that of others within the larger framework of the country itself.

Citizenship training of this kind also facilitates presentation of the needs of the country with respect to manpower, occupations and fields essential to economic development. A curriculum which follows this pattern, furthermore, can emphasise the role and responsibility of citizenship without degenerating into narrow jingoism, dedicated to one man. The direction it will take will be determined by the state, but there would appear to be less danger of this happening if the efforts are directed by competent social scientists and educators.

4. APTITUDE TESTING

The one aspect of African education that has been explored in more detail than any other has been the relationship of education to economic development. *Investment in Education* (Ashby *et al*. 1960), *Education and Economic Development in Sierra Leone* (Harris, Hoad, and Hartie 1961), and the *Final Report of the Conference of African States on the Development of Education in Africa* (UNESCO 1961) are examples of the increasing interest in education and economic development.

The conclusion reached by all reports is similar: manpower situations will remain critical for some time. Facilities for training individuals in the needed areas are limited. Qualified instructors in all areas are scarce. There has been a realisation that increases are required not only in the quantity but also in the quality of training, if the mounting needs are to be met.

Until it is possible to establish training schools in the variety of areas in which they are needed, it will be necessary to make maximum use of existing institutions and concentrate on improving the quality of instruction.   To make maximum use of existing facilities and to produce the best technicians places a great obligation on those educators reponsible for the selection of students.   The failure to find students with aptitudes for the technical training has particularly damaging consequences in societies where manpower shortages are so critical.

Unfortunately, few suitable procedures for the screening of applicants have been developed anywhere in Africa.   The available techniques and methods almost exclusively relate to the United States and Europe and reflect to a large extent the culture of these regions.   The cultural limitations and problems of language inherent in the present aptitude tests make them inappropriate for an African environment.

An additional limitation on the use of American and European tests is the cost of administering them.   Because openings in many of the technical training programs are limited, there may be hundreds of applicants for a single opening, and unless an aptitude test can be produced cheaply and administered simply, it is doubtful that it could be used.   To meet the existing emergency, it will also be necessary to devise tests which can be administered by individuals who have not had the training in the psychology of testing.   Obviously this area is one that requires the joint effort of psychologists, anthropologists, sociologists, linguists, personnel administrators and educators.

Preliminary work in this area had been completed by the American Institute for Research for the Agency for International Development (Schwarz 1961).   On the basis of principles established by the team engaged in the research, twelve instruments were constructed to measure the aptitude of the examinees.   While the centre for the research was Nigeria, limited try-outs were also made in Uganda and Kenya.   On the basis of this preliminary work, it was found that the general level of abilities in the Nigerian population is higher than has been supposed, that there is much variability in individual aptitudes, and that the number of people with identifiable high aptitudes may be doubled if adequate selection techniques are made (Schwarz 1961 : 84).   The research undertaken by the Institute is an indication of the kind of study that can make more realistic the fusion of education and economic development.

5. TEACHING OF ENGLISH AS A SECOND LANGUAGE

Throughout those countries that were former British protectorates and colonies, the problem of teaching English as a second language has been recognised as one of the most difficult problems in expanding education on the elementary level and producing competent English-speaking students for the equivalent of the British sixth form and the universities.   Unlike the French, who began language instruction when the child entered school, the British favoured a system in which the child was taught in one of the selected local languages for the first few years with a transfer to English in the later years.   In Tanganyika, all children learn Swahili in the earlier grades and gradually move to English.   Liberia has chosen to emphasise English from the earliest grades.   But in the other English-speaking areas, a variety of African languages have been used.

There is little satisfaction on the part of educators with the manner in which

English is now being taught as a second language. In many areas, the English examination in the Cambridge syndicate examination becomes the greatest stumbling block for students; the number of cases of students who have done well in all parts of the examination except English is legion. Under the present arrangement in most countries, the student who does not make an appropriate score on the English examination is barred from university work despite his apparent ability in other areas. In many cases the failure of the student is the result of inadequate instruction in the language. As indicated earlier, one of the major problems is the great number of teachers who, though unqualified, are teaching because of the acute teacher shortage.

Although many of the current problems lie in the area of general and applied linguistics, there are also many that may be considered social and psychological. Studies relating to these problems are imperative, if the studies in linguistics are to have meaning and be used efficiently in the learning process. Thus far speculation has abounded about the effect of a second language on the child's learning in school, but no definitive studies have yet been made. Still another problem area is that of the motivation of the student in learning English as a second language. Why does he want to learn the language? What does he expect to gain as a result of mastering English? In addition to the needs and demands of the learner, the needs and demands of the community should also be studied from the viewpoint of practical bilingualism.

The question of when English should be introduced into the school has provoked much discussions, but little research substantiates the opinions of various groups. It has been assumed that the transition from the local African language to English should take place in the fourth to the sixth grade, but this opinion lacks support based on methodical investigation. There is no agreement on how the process should take place nor on what subjects should be taught in English. From the viewpoint of most experts in the field, one of the most efficient techniques for increasing the ability of the student to read in English is to have reading materials based on the local culture. The assumption underlying this proposal is that such material provides a ready point of contact with the second culture. However, though the merits of this approach have gained recognition, little has been done to produce appropriate materials.

Finally, there is the vast new, untouched area of research into the influence of the English medium on the failure of students in subjects other than English. The importance of language study as the foundation for the entire process of learning has long been realised, but its direct relationship to success and failure in mathematics, history, science, geography and other subjects has not been scientifically examined.

6. ACCELERATION OF TEACHER TRAINING PROGRAMS

The requests from Africa for large numbers of secondary teachers from the Peace Corps and private recruiting agencies — such as the African-American Institute, the Teachers for East Africa Program operated by the Teachers' College at Columbia University and numerous other programs — are indicative of the rapid expansion of secondary education in many African countries. The use of expatriates is viewed as a stop-gap measure until such time as the countries can produce enough secondary teachers to meet their needs. Unfortunately, at the present time the demand for educated young Africans is manifest in all of the non-teaching areas of rapidly expanding economies and governments. Opportunities appear more rewarding in occupations other than teaching, and as a result the institutes of education attached to colleges and the institutes of pedagogy are not producing a fraction of the teachers needed to achieve self-sufficiency. The low percentage of African teachers on the secondary level in the French community has been described in an earlier part of this chapter. In East Africa the overwhelming majority of secondary school teachers are expatriates.

There has been an increasing concern that, in the rapid expansion of education, standards will be lowered and the education system weakened. This concern is shared by most educators, and yet there remains the practical problem of how to increase rapidly the number of secondary school teachers. Unless there are alternate plans for teacher education, it would appear that secondary education will be dominated by expatriate teachers for many years.

The African ministries face a difficult decision. If the traditional secondary grammar school continues as the principal type of secondary education, the staffing of the schools by Africans will certainly be in the distant future. If, however, the development of secondary education is in the direction of more technical and agricultural education, or if the modern type of high school recently introduced in Britain or the American pattern of secondary education gain acceptance, the problem can be solved. The staffing of the traditional school is bound by the content of the internal and external examinations. It is particularly the latter that have so structured the system that deviation is virtually impossible. A new type of school, with high standards but with a content determined by the specific goals of the ministry rather than by external examinations would be free to conduct the kinds of experimentation needed to extend secondary education to the various groups other than those which hope to go on to the university.

Manpower needs are so great that there has been a reluctance to break with the traditional approach to teacher training and try experimental methods. Today, however, there is an increasing realisation that unless new techniques are devised and a new methodology introduced, the possibility of expanding secondary education will continue to depend upon the expatriates. The planning for experimental work should be the task of educators and the social scientists. Experimentation will permit a re-examination of the content of teacher training as well as of the content of the curriculum, and the situation requires the co-operation of all these related disciplines.

IV   CONCLUSION

The expansion of education during the past decade in Africa has been unmatched in history. While the pattern varies from country to country, it reflects a universal concern for education and a realisation that education is a vital part of economic and social development. The growth of education, however, with few exceptions has represented an expansion of the system introduced by the colonial powers. The need for Africanisation of the curriculum, the examination of curriculum patterns, and the studies of the relationship of education to economic development, all provide ample evidence that a modification of the system is desirable. In order to achieve this and to reach the goals set by African educators at the Addis Ababa Conference, close collaboration between the social scientists and educators is necessary. The areas of research discussed in this chapter are but a few needing exploration in African education today.   Urbanisation, school drop-outs, the effects of local concepts of natural phenomena on the teaching and learning of science, the value structures of secondary and college graduates, the position of overseas educated Africans upon their return home — and many other questions demand attention. Moreover, it can be seen from the nature of these problems that there are few problems in African education today that are purely pedagogical.

8

Economics and Economic Development

Andrew Martin Kamarck

I INTRODUCTION*

THERE IS NO African 'personality' in economics. There is no 'African' economic theory as such that has been developed for and is applicable only to Africa. Most of the writing on economics and economic development problems and theory is usually presented in general terms applicable to all the world or to all of the underdeveloped world. Much of this is relevant to Africa and often has been the result of research on Africa but the conclusions are generalised into theory which is not limited to Africa alone. However, there are aspects of economic problems which are especially applicable to Africa, as well as specifically African manifestations of general economic phenomena.

The economics most significant for Africa is the economics of development, i.e., the economics of a society that is transforming itself, rather than the economics of a society where the fundamental structure remains unchanged. Consequently, consciously or unconsciously, economists working on African economic problems tend to be much less narrowly specialised and to be more interested in problems related to other disciplines than is generally true of economists who work on industrialised societies. It is no accident that S. H. Frankel — a pioneer in work on African economic problems, who wrote the classic *Capital Investment* (1938) in Africa before the second world war — is also the author of *The Economic Impact on Underdeveloped Societies* (1953). The former work concentrated on the flow of capital into Africa; the latter emphasises that capital can do nothing except in the hands of people who know how to use it, maintain it, replace it, and consume its products. The lesson of the second work, in short, is that economic development on any scale whatsoever is inseparably social and political transformation. In the same way, even the analysis of quite technical subjects such as the level of wages, agricultural productivity, etc., must go deep into the structure of African society.

Probably one of the biggest gaps in economic work on Africa so far has been the paucity of studies on the history of economic development in the continent. What is needed are not collections of curious historical facts, but an analytical history of

* Bibliography for this chapter will be found on page 525.

why an economy developed the way it did.   Apart from a handful of studies such as those of C. W. de Kiewiet (1941) on South Africa, N. A. Cox-George (1961) and David Carney (1961) on Sierra Leone, and the series being edited by David Walker on East Africa, the shelves are quite bare.

In addition to the emphasis on transformation of the economy, there are a number of other economic characteristics which are present in an especially accentuated form in Africa and therefore especially differentiate the economic work on it from most other areas.   The African economies, other than South Africa, are pre-eminently 'dependent' economies.   They are dependent on the rest of the world not only for a major part of the supply of their total capital investment (at least half of the total) but also for a major part of their entrepreneurs, technicians and other key personnel.   They are pre-eminently export-oriented.   The dependence of Africa's income on exports is greater than that of Latin America or Asia. In addition to being highly dependent on export income, the exports of the African countries consist in the main of one or a few primary products.   (The impact of these factors is discussed later on in the section on Economic Dependence.)

A strong point in the economic development of Africa is that Africans in most areas have shown an exceptional willingness and ability to adapt or change their institutions to the requirements of economic development.   There are, of course, many specific exceptions to this generalisation but, in the main, the African openness to innovation is comparable perhaps only to the Japanese and Americans in the past.   Herbert J. Spiro, in his The New Africa in Politics, has made this point even more strongly:

> . . . Africans are the most present-minded people on earth. . .   Without significant exceptions, all African leaders . . . share the passionate desire to acquire all the good things which western civilization has produced in the two millenia of its history.   They want especially to get the technological blessings of American civilization, and to do so as quickly as possible.   The lack of historical consciousness of their peoples gives the African leaders a great advantage in moving rapidly toward this goal of modernization.   They are not encumbered by written traditions, or by the visible and tangible physical presence of the ruins of their own 'civilized' past — as most Asians have been. Therefore, they do not have to reconcile every innovation with the different practices of their past. (1962: 5–6).

There has also been an exceptional mobility of labour within and across national boundaries in response to economic demands.   At the same time, the subsistence economy has continued to be a pervasive factor that influences economic behaviour even in the most monetised African sectors.

A striking difference between Africa and most of the rest of the underdeveloped world has been, until recently, the absence of indigenous inflations and their accompanying balance of payments problems.   This has been largely due to the monetary and banking systems of the colonial era which, whatever defects they may have had, were primarily designed to provide a sound currency and were run by experienced technicians.   There also has been absence of any latifundia and land-lord-tenant problem in agriculture.   This is, however, offset in Africa by the peculiar importance of the various kinds of communal or tribal land tenure arrangements which have dominated much of the agricultural economic policy and which according to some views have been so important in retarding economic progress.

Finally, the fact that Africa is pre-eminently the continent of the tropics, about which man knows least, has given an exceptional economic importance to research on tropical diseases, pests and agricultural techniques.

II POLICY ISSUES

I. DEFINING AND MEASURING THE STRUCTURE OF AFRICAN ECONOMIES

The first step in making any useful economic policy decisions in or about a country is to have some idea of what you are talking about.   That is, the economist should have as accurate an idea as possible of what the economy actually is.   One of the most useful ways of describing an economy is the preparation of what is called a system of national or social accounts.   These give a systematic presentation of the major economic flows within the framework of a comprehensive accounting system. A fairly complete system of such accounts for a country presents information on the total value and the main categories of the goods and services produced during the year.   It shows how the national income represented by those goods and services was divided by major economic groups.   It tells how big a share of national income was consumed and how much was invested in future growth.   It tells how important the role of government was and how much of the national income was used for governmental services.   One part of the accounts presents the balance of payments showing the main economic relationships of the country with the rest of the world. Over a period of years, the national accounts show how fast the economy was growing in real terms and whether the standard of living of the average person was growing and how fast.   National accounts in short can provide a kind of economic X-ray of the economy.

Most of the industrialised countries have only begun calculating national accounts regularly since the second world war.   In Africa even partial accounts for a single year do not exist for all countries, but considerable progress is being made. More than twenty-five African countries have at one time or another published simplified or partial national accounts for a single year and about ten now produce regular annual accounts.   South Africa has estimates from 1918 on, the former Federation of Rhodesia and Nyasaland has a series for Southern Rhodesia beginning from 1939, for Northern Rhodesia from 1945, and for the Federation from 1950.

Apart from the incompleteness of the national accounts now prepared in Africa, they differ from those of industrialised countries also in significance.   The national accounts describe best a monetary economy (although economists are also aware of pitfalls even there).   In a country with a large subsistence sector, the significance of the accounts is quite different.   The problem is that it is impossible to ignore the subsistence activities, but it is almost equally impossible to bring them into the accounts in a meaningful way.   How do you value something in money terms when its essence is that it is non-monetary?   The pioneer work on this problem was done by Phyllis Deane in her *Colonial Social Accounting* (1953).   What she, and everyone since then, had to do was first to decide where to draw the line between non-economic and economic subsistence activities.   The former (e.g., the passage of goods at the time of betrothal or marriage) could be neglected, while the latter had to have a price tag put on if the goods and services involved were not exchanged for money but were used directly by their producers.   But the process of putting a price tag on subsistence output is in itself difficult to justify logically.   As Phyllis Deane said: 'Where the bulk of goods in a given category are traded, it does not greatly strain the conceptual framework to impute a value to the remainder. Where the bulk are *not* traded, it is obviously a highly artificial process which bears no direct relation to the physical facts of the case. The figure for subsistence output can never be more than a token figure.'

Besides the problems of valuation, at present there is no general agreement on what should be valued in subsistence activities and included in the national accounts. A meeting of a working party on this subject at the Economic Commission for Africa in 1960 agreed that all countries should include subsistence activities in agriculture, forestry, fishing, building, construction and land works by households. It was left to the individual countries to decide whether to include processing, storage, transport and distribution of own primary output; home processing of goods purchased; and other services such as collection of firewood and fetching of water.

The general practice today is to include a figure for subsistence in the national accounts, but this quite clearly is not of the same validity as the rest of the figures. With time, of course, the increased monetisation of Africa will give more and more meaning to the prices used to evalue subsistence output. In the meantime, we have to make do with the figures we have. But it is important to remember that the significance of what appear to be similar figures is not the same in most of Africa as in more economically developed countries. (In fact, the statistical data are not good enough even for making very meaningful per capita comparisons or comparisons of composition of output or income between any two African countries.) For example: when after making the usual allowances for subsistence production one finds that the per capita income in a particular country is, say, equivalent to $50 per year, this should not be interpreted as having the same significance as $50 would have in the United States. A per capita income of $50 a year in the United States means death by starvation, whereas in Africa many populations continue to live and to grow on this low income level.

Another problem in the meaning of the national accounts that are prepared for African countries arises from the great economic importance in many countries of the expatriates and foreign investment. There are two conventional ways of presenting national accounts in this connection: one is to compute them on a territorial basis, taking into the accounts what happens within the territorial boundaries of a country and paying no attention to national ownership of assets or nationality of the income-receiver. In countries that have a large foreign enclave, this, of course, exaggerates the real income and well-being of the permanent residents of the country. Another method is to exclude the enclaves, but this understates the economic position of the country, since after all the country does derive some benefit from the expatriates present and the enclave investments. Jo Saxe (1961) has suggested that a compromise should be affected under which the accounts presented would 'show clearly and in detail what part of the expenditure by expatriate individuals and which of the investments by foreign-owned firms have an affect on the incomes of the indigenous inhabitants'. This important refinement will probably have to wait until much more progress has been made in compiling even the usual conventional accounts.

A somewhat different approach is represented in Barber's *The Economy of British Central Africa* (1961). The non-African element in the economy of British Central Africa is so large and so important that it would be misleading to treat it purely as an enclave. Barber believes that economies like the one he discusses (i.e., the settler countries) should be considered as dual economies.   That is, rather than considering a country as having a 'money' sector and a 'subsistence' sector in a single economy, the two parts, though connected, are sufficiently independent and autonomous to justify calling them two economies.   He makes the point that traditional agriculture functions according to its own peculiar set of rules that differentiate its economic processes from the remainder of the economic system.   The unique properties of this traditional economic system may have a crucial influence on the course of economic change (as will be discussed later on).   In the money economy, production and exchange are well-organised, largely financed and administered by Europeans, and heavily dependent on external trade and investments.   Members of the indigenous people may derive part of their livelihood from both economies simultaneously or they may move between them at different times.

One important implication of the 'dual economy' approach is that the usual simple test of economic development — increase in real income per capita — is not enough.   One might get this by an increase in European immigration into the country, while the incomes of the Africans remained unchanged.   The test consequently must be whether (a) income per capita increases in real terms for the economy as a whole, and (b) the per capita real income of the indigenous population also improves.

At the present time, there are two systems of national accounts being used in Africa: the UN 'Standardised System' which is used in the non-French-speaking countries and in Congo (Leopoldville), Ruanda and Burundi; and the 'French System' used in most of the French-speaking countries.   The difference between the two systems is mainly one of approach.   The UN system stresses the final destination of the main flows resulting from production and presents these final destinations in product, income and expenditure tables.   The French system also presents the intermediate calculations whereby the final economic data can be arrived at from the basic data.

All of the difficulties in the preparation and interpretation of the national accounts in Africa have suggested to some economists that some alternative approach be adopted.   Dudley Seers (1952–53) recommended that instead of trying to build up national accounts for a country, priority should be given to securing statistics on specific important aspects of the economy.   Along this line, William O. Jones and Christian Merat (1962) have made an attempt at providing an indicator of economic well-being and of economic progress other than through construction of national accounts.   They have done this by using the data on physical imports consumed directly by the indigenous inhabitants of ten African countries.   The data they have presented do achieve their objective: Ghana, for example, clearly comes out with a much higher per capita economic well-being than the Ivory Coast in 1955–57 or any of the other African countries represented in the data.   As a means of reconstructing the development of the African countries in the past, when essentially only trade statistics are available, the Jones-Merat approach undoubtedly has considerable value.   As a substitute for national accounts now and for the future, it is more dubious because less comprehensive and less flexible in its coverage of rapidly changing economies.

2. ECONOMIC RATIONALITY

One of the early fundamental problems that economists encountered in Africa was the belief expressed by 'old hands' that the general laws of economics do not apply to Africa because Africans do not behave in an economically rational fashion. Of course, there are very few people anywhere in the world who behave in a completely economically rational fashion. The question really is whether Africans, like other people, are sufficiently motivated by economic considerations to make economic analysis meaningful. The answer by economists has been unanimous: 'Yes'. In general, it has been found that whenever the African's economic behaviour has seemed to be irrational, it has been because there has been insufficient understanding of the major forces in his environment influencing his behaviour. This has often been because of the lack of real understanding by the observer of the African environment. (As a matter of fact, some agricultural schemes and some industrial incentives in industry have failed because the Africans affected worked out what would pay them best more accurately than the people who set up the scheme.)

The accusation of economic irrationality has usually come in the form of a statement of the premise that a higher price for produce or higher pay does not result in greater effort or more regular work: that higher prices or pay, in fact, may result in less work. (The truth of this as regards farmers will be discussed later on; at this point our remarks will apply mainly to wage-earners.)

3. LABOUR SUPPLY AND WAGES

In actual fact, this phenomenon of the 'target' worker (or the worker who is working to acquire a given sum of money to buy a given set of goods and is not interested in earning more) is not new. It was first identified in Western Europe when the European countries were beginning their industrialisation. Max Weber, in *The Protestant Ethic and the Spirit of Capitalism* describes it as follows:

> . . . a peculiar difficulty has been met with surprising frequency: raising the piece-rates has often had the result that not more but less has been accomplished in the same time, because the worker reacted to the increase not by increasing but by decreasing the amount of his work. . .[the worker] did not ask: how much can I earn in a day if I do as much work as possible? but: how much must I work in order to earn the wage, $2\frac{1}{2}$ marks, which I earned before and which takes care of my traditional needs?

This phenomenon, in economic terms, is described as a backward-bending supply curve for labour, i.e., the supply of labour called forth by a higher price at a certain point, instead of increasing with an increase in wages, bends backwards and decreases. Such behaviour is completely economically rational. When wants that can be met by purchases with money are limited and are satisfied, and the demand for holding money, or saving, for unknown needs in the future is either still unknown or satisfied, the rational economic behaviour quite understandably can be to prefer leisure to higher earnings when the rate of pay goes up. And, in fact, this happens quite frequently in highly developed societies when people's incomes for some reason shoot up more rapidly than their wants for goods can grow.

The second question that flows from this discussion is: how important today is such behaviour in Africa? Or to put it more precisely: is the aggregate supply curve for African labour backward-bending for any significant range of wages? Elliot J. Berg (1961) has done the definitive study on this quite recently. There are several forces operating: the level of income an African can get by remaining on the land; his own particular supply curve of labour (e.g., at what wages can he be induced to leave the land, and what wages are his target income?); and the number of individuals affected by these forces.   As far as the individual African worker is concerned, the quantity of wage labour he is willing to do tends to be inversely related to changes in village income and to changes in wage-rates in the exchange sector.   This relationship was quite definite in the early years when migrants tended to be reluctant target workers whose elasticity of demand for income, once their target income was achieved, approached zero for everything except leisure; that is, once a worker got the sum of money he wanted, he quit.   Nowadays, the target income is getting more and more remote as wants increase in size and flexibility.   It has little significance for the 'committed' workers in the urban areas who no longer move back and forth between the land and wage-employment.

The shape of the aggregate labour supply curve — giving the total labour supply that will be forthcoming at each level of wage-rates — depends on the net outcome of two contrary changes that follow a wage-rise: changes in the number of people from the land that are induced into work for wages, and changes in the average time each man spends at work.   In early days, the curve probably tended quite soon to be backward-sloping; a rise in wages induced few new men into employment while it encouraged many of those in paid employment to cut short their stay.   In present-day Africa this is no longer true: a wage-rate stimulates many more men to emigrate to paid jobs and leads far fewer to reduce their time in paid employment.   And, broadly speaking, when account is taken of the peculiar international character of African labour markets, it is most unlikely that for any given country for any long length of time the aggregate supply of labour was ever negatively elastic with respect to wage-rates.

Wilbert E. Moore (1951) has pointed out that an important factor in increasing the supply of labour in many areas has been the push from the rural areas resulting from the decline of alternative opportunities more in keeping with the traditional order of things.   This may be due to the pressure of population on the land with the given levels of techniques and organisation in agriculture.   In some parts of southern and eastern Africa this has been accentuated by the forcible restriction of African agriculture to confined areas while the pressure has been accentuated by the persistence of the 'cattle culture' which leads to over-grazing and growing poverty.

Now that economists have decided that Africans going into wage-labour are behaving rationally, the next question is: what are the main forces particularly important in the African environment that affect the level of African wages?   We have touched on some of these already, of course, in our discussion of 'target' incomes.   There are two special aspects of supply of labour in Africa which are present in some other parts of the world but are so important in Africa as to seem peculiarly African.   The first is the infinite elasticity of supply of labour or, more simply, the unlimited supply of labour.   That is, the developing enclaves in Africa are still so small in relation to the sea of subsistence activities which surround them, and the mobility of labour — nationally and internationally — is so great, that within a reasonable range of wages the supply of labour can be considered practically unlimited.   What then determines the level of wages of unskilled labour?

This problem has been worked on for a number of years.   Ida Greaves (1935) concluded that wages paid to an unskilled worker had to be high enough to overcome the strength of the tradition that binds him to customary tribal practices.   (Wages, therefore, could be used by an anthropologist to measure the strength of tribal tradition.)   W. Arthur Lewis (1954) went further.   He concluded that the floor, or the minimum level of wages paid, was set by the subsistence income the African could earn on the land while the ceiling was set by this income plus the necessary incentive to go into wage-labour. William Barber (1961) accepted this theory for the permanent labour force and went on to explain the forces influencing migrant labour. This is the second distinguishing characteristic of the labour position in Africa compared to most other continents: the great importance of short-term labour migration within the whole supply of labour. While the measurement of this is very difficult, it is quite clear that in most countries in sub-Saharan Africa the percentage of permanent African wage-earners in the total labour force is still very small.

In explaining migrant labour, Barber points out that a man will seek wage-income when it serves to maximise the real income of his family. In much of Africa, he can take on temporary work during his time of periodic underempolyment. Since a man's function in subsistence agriculture often is to clear new land every two or three years for his wife to cultivate, in between he can go to work for wages and so maximise his family's income. This is what I have named 'sociological underemployment', i.e., underemployment of men due to the peculiar division of labour between the sexes as laid down by society. Migrant labour, then, makes good economic sense for the African engaging in it.

There are other aspects of this problem that have been analysed by Walter Elkan (1960). An important point that comes out is the fact that the English experience during the beginning of the industrial revolution has not been a precedent for Africa. The people from the countryside in England who settled in the cities as the new proletariat were not farmers but agricultural labourers who had no property stake left in the countryside. This has not been true of most of the African wage-earners and their economic calculus is consequently different. In most of Africa, the existing land tenure and market arrangements do not give land as such a money value. The only way a man can secure benefit from his claim to land is by keeping his family on it to work it. Land provides social security against unemployment, sickness and old age, but the individual cannot use it for these purposes if he does not preserve his claim to it. Thus, he himself will have a constant incentive to quit his industrial job for longer or shorter periods to return to his family and land.

Given the prevalence of migrant labour, industries that must rely on semi-skilled or skilled African labour find it difficult to become efficient. In other words, this analysis shows that progress in industrialisation like agricultural advance (as I discuss below) may be closely related to the slow processes of change in land tenure and of the relationship of men to the land. It should also be said that the implications of the economic analysis just presented are not always fully appreciated by non-economists in their considerations of the policies that should be followed to achieve permanent urban settlement of Africans.

There has been very little work done on some of the implications of this analysis. For example: what happens if wage-rates are raised — by minimum wage legislation, union action or other influences — above the wage 'ceiling' for unskilled labour? Clearly the wage will keep on attracting labour from the subsistence economy into the urban areas even after there is no longer any need for more workers. The results may be that the unemployed will keep on increasing until the average real income of wage-workers in town is reduced below Lewis' 'ceiling' by their having to support some of their unemployed tribal brothers, or until the capacity of the town to hold the unemployed is reached (housing limita-tions, police action, petty jobs available, etc.). Given the forces which keep up nominal wages, the level of unemployment then would be like a pressure gauge. It would always show some unemployment, and the exact level would be set by the pressure of the movement of people from the land into towns against the counter-pressure of the absorptive capacity of the towns for the number of unemployed.

Without passing judgment on the merits of policies of governments to bar foreign Africans and to expel those who have been living there for years, it is quite clear that such action would help raise the average level of the unskilled wages in the countries concerned by putting definite limits on the number of workers available to work for wages, even though these policies may retard the general growth of the economy otherwise.

A new situation in some countries results from educational efforts which turn out large numbers of school-leavers in excess of the jobs currently available. These school-leavers, as Callaway's research (1962) is showing, have economic attitudes towards the land quite different from those of their fathers; in short, the English industrial revolution may be becoming more of a precedent now.

4. LAND AND AGRICULTURE

Since in Africa most people still make their living in agriculture, the economic problems of agriculture are central. The first item to dispose of is the question of the economic rationality of African farmers. In general, the remarks we have made about target income in the case of wage-labour apply: that is, if income from farming (due to rapidly rising prices or extraordinarily good crops) rises more rapidly than the farmer acquires new wants, the supply curve of his labour will become backward-bending at some point. Normally, however, with the passage of time and the spread of education — formal and informal — in Africa, this point at which the curve becomes backward-bending will become less and less relevant. In the mean-time, however, and certainly in many areas, the backward-bending supply curve may still be very relevant to economic policy. It will also still be true in most areas that the lack of adequate knowledge of precisely where the bending point is will be a handicap in forming agricultural policy.

S. D. Neumark (1958) has commented that often the economic reasons for an apparent lack of response by farmers to higher prices for a commodity are not evident to a casual observer, and yet these reasons may fully justify the farmers' behaviour: they may not increase output of a commodity whose price has gone up, for example, because the relative prices of other crops may still make these a more profitable opportunity than the crop whose price has increased. Often the lack of response is misunderstood because it is due to circumstances over which the individual farmer has no control. These may consist of institutional and tribal deterrents, such as systems of communal land holdings or lack of transport and marketing facilities. John Raeburn (1959) has also emphasised the factor of uncer-tainty as a force that explains what otherwise appears to be irrational behaviour. The answer, in short, may lie in other economic factors or in sociological or institu-tional factors which prevent the economic forces from operating.

While there is still not unanimity on this point, Johnston and Mellors (1961) conclude that most of those who have given careful study to the problems of peasant agriculture would endorse the view that '. . . the peasant farms his land as ration-ally as possible under the social and economic conditions affecting him and within the limit of his opportunities as regard labour, land, markets, capital, knowledge and managerial skill'. Of course, the much greater relative importance of the constraint put on the farmer by the social conditions affecting him constitutes a significant difference between Africa and more developed areas.

Of these social conditions, the economist would consider as among the most important the system of land tenure affecting the farmer. Probably in this regard the economist comes most directly in opposition to the anthropologist. The strongest position here is taken by Frankel who believes the indigenous systems of land tenure are the main obstacle to economic development in Africa. As he put it in *The Tyranny of Economic Paternalism in Africa* (1960):

> . . . it is clear that the root cause of the economic backwardness of various African territories, as well as of the native areas in the Union, lies in the failure to modify customary control of land occupation and tenure, which has prevented the emergence of land use and ownership compatible with modern forms of commercialized production in a money economy. The failure to make of the land a viable economic factor of production has condemned the peoples on it to eke out a precarious subsistence.

Nearly all economists would agree that development in agriculture would be accelerated if conditions were such that African farms were held on some sort of individual freehold tenure. The basis for this belief is that the communal system of land tenure does not provide incentive towards the best use and conservation of land. The responsibility felt by the community is less than that felt by the individual towards his own land. Once the farmer has a secure title to his land, he can invest in it, since he knows that he and his family will benefit from this. He has thus every incentive to improve his farm and increase his production from it. The title to land, when land is scarce, is valuable and is the best collateral for borrowing capital to improve the farm. The best system of land tenure is that which provides the greatest incentive for the farm family to exploit its own labour. Under the communal system those able and willing to undertake new ways of production often cannot obtain farms large enough to do so which are protected against alienation and so ensure to the farmer the undisturbed reward of his labour for himself and his children.

The economist's bias does not, of course, mean that every economist believes an immediate shift from communal tenure is always desirable and possible. The World Bank's Economic Survey Mission report on *The Economic Development of Uganda* (1962), for example, advocates a policy of moving to individual land tenure. But it recognises that this is a costly process to achieve and that benefits are slow in maturing. It also points out that certain preconditions must exist: a relatively high density of population, use of land to grow cash crops and thus the imputation of money value to land, and a growing rate of litigation over land rights (showing that these are acquiring growing value). In addition, it is important that the program should not be imposed against the wishes of the local population affected.

Most farming in Africa is still subsistence farming. Perhaps the most important economic change taking place in Africa today is the transition from subsistence to market agriculture. Subsistence production is, of course, production for the direct use of the procers and their families. Montague Yudelman in *Africans on the Land* (1964) has divided the transition from subsistence to market agriculture into four stages. The first stage comprises areas where production is used entirely for subsistence and which are completely self-contained; this is already very rare — perhaps it exists only in the Kalahari desert. There are still many communities in the second stage where, although some sales or barter transactions take place, the production of a small surplus above immediate subsistence requirements is largely unintentional and the result of an occasional particularly favourable season. The third stage in the transition is where the regular production of a marketable surplus is deliberately sought but the main emphasis is still on subsistence production. In the fourth stage, production for the market predominates over subsistence. The bulk of the African producers in South, Central and East Africa are in the second and third categories. The cocoa farmers in Ghana and in the Western Region of Nigeria and the coffee producers of Buganda have probably now reached the last stage mentioned above. More than half of the total agricultural production of Africa south of the Sahara is for subsistence, and this means that the average farm family produces food enough only to feed itself and less than one other family off the farm. In some of the developed agricultural countries elsewhere in the world the average farm family may produce enough to feed itself and some ten to twenty non-farm families as well.

Subsistence production has a number of important economic effects. Subsistence producers tend to be isolated from the economic influences of the outside world. This means that the action of the price mechanism and the inflow of innovations and ideas is accordingly greatly limited. Specialisation, which is the important means of growth in productivity, is strongly inhibited. Specialisation can develop only to the extent that exchange takes place.

Very roughly, almost all of the increase in agricultural output in Africa that has occurred so far in modern times has come from an increase in the number of acres farmed. Where yields per farmer have increased, it has come mostly from an increase in the number of acres farmed per farmer. There has been very little increase in yield per acre, which is, on the other hand, a main element in agricultural progress in most of the rest of the world.

A practical set of decisions on investment policy in agriculture that often confronts governments is the choice between putting resources into large-scale agricultural projects, such as resettlement or irrigation schemes, or concentrating on and trying to increase production within the existing areas of agricultural production. There is no easy answer to this, although theoretically it is just a matter of comparing the yield of investment in alternative projects (including both private and social costs and benefits in the calculation). There is a tendency for governments to prefer the large schemes. This is in part because they are more spectacular and in part because it is easier in these schemes to calculate and to demonstrate the benefits coming from governmental action than it is when the benefits are scattered over the mass of a farming population which tends to impute all the credit for increased output to its own efforts. It was for reasons such as this that the British government took the decision to launch the ill-fated scheme in Tanganyika to increase the supply of groundnuts rather than to help the Nigerian farmers to produce more and get their groundnuts to market. It is obvious in hindsight that, if a small fraction of the money wasted on the groundnut scheme had been used in Nigeria to improve transport, there would have been great beneficial results. The Tanganyika scheme is, of course, only the most notorious of a number of project failures of this kind in various parts of Africa.

There are cases, as in the Gezira scheme, in which investment in a large-scale project clearly has paid off. But, in general, the conclusions of Johnston and

Mellors (1961) would be accepted by most economists with broad experience in Africa: the most practical and economic approach to achieving a sizable increase in agricultural productivity and output in most of Africa at present lies in enhancing the efficiency of the existing agricultural economy.

Programs to increase agricultural output in the existing agricultural economy, as Yudelman has shown, can be divided into two main categories: exogenous or endogenous.   That is to say, there are (a) programs that change the infrastructure and environment in which the farmer operates, or (b) programs that require change in the way the farmer himself operates.   Instances of the first would include: the provision of roads and water supplies; control of locust breeding places and of locust swarms; spraying of crops by government; rigid control over and provision only of selected seed; etc.   These are all actions that can be performed by the government or other organisation without calling on the farmer to improve his own management techniques.   They do not require the individual to show initiative and enterprise or to change his age-old method of farming.   This first category of program is still much more manageable and successful in Africa than the second category, in large part because of the lack of adequate technical knowledge of the latter case.

It is in planning this second category of programs that the points discussed in the first part of this section become most relevant.   That is: just how do price and other monetary incentives affect a particular group of farmers?   What are the cultural and tribal restraints that prevent economic incentives from being most effective?   What is the most effective way of getting adopted a change in techniques and getting it spread through a group?   These are, of course, questions for which the economist must find the answers, but it may be that other disciplines have better tools than economists to find the right answers more quickly.

The answer at which the economists have arrived (as exemplified in *The Economic Development of Uganda*) as the best way to secure changes in the farmer himself, is to pick out individual farmers who have shown themselves innovators, or appear to have the potential to be such, and to give them special help, credit facilities and other services to enable them to forge ahead.   This is almost par excellence an economist's approach: using the scarce resources available to the government where they will produce the highest returns most quickly.

This conclusion poses a number of practical difficulties, however.   It means spending money on agricultural research, education and extension services.   It may also mean subsidising the provision of implements, ploughs, oxen, sprayers and other equipment to farmers in order to encourage them to improve their techniques. But, unfortunately, it is very difficult, practically impossible at the present time in Africa, to forecast the increase in output or cut in costs that will result from a given expenditure on research or extension workers.   In addition, because these expenditures are not on conventional capital equipment, they are usually regarded as 'recurrent' rather than investment expenditures and cannot be financed by loans. The Uganda Survey Mission recommended the inclusion of such items in the investment program in Uganda, but it is not yet clear that financing for them can be found.

III *OTHER KEY POLICY ISSUES IN ECONOMIC DEVELOPMENT*

Most economists would agree that the purpose of research on the economic problems of Africa is to get sufficient understanding to make it possible to take intelligent action to deal with those problems. The main economic objective of most of the African countries is economic development; or more simply, they want to feed, clothe and house their people better, and to give them the chance to live healthier and longer lives.

One technique of trying to achieve this end is economic planning. Nearly all of the African countries have done some economic planning in the post-war period. Even South Africa, which made no pretence of having an economic plan, set up a national economic advisory council several years ago. Until recently, however, very few of the economic plans properly deserve the name, being in most cases little more than collections of disparate projects with little co-ordination of policy and objective. The main exceptions to this have been the development plans suggested by the World Bank economic survey missions (Nigeria, Tanganyika, Libya, Uganda and Kenya), the development plans of the Federation of Rhodesia and Nyasaland during C. H. Thompson's tenure as Economic Adviser to the Prime Minister, and the 1961–64 Four-Year Plan of Senegal prepared by Père Lebret and his collaborators. Nigeria, the Sudan and Tunisia have also recently announced plans which will be valuable instruments in their economic development.

The central motive of economic development has already come out in the discussion on economists' attitudes towards land tenure where differences among economists are mainly on the question of timing and degree of the pace of change from communal to individual land tenure, and in the discussion on land and agriculture. In fact, it is very difficult to consider any economic subject concerning Africa without policy issues connected with economic development playing a central role or at least being very much present in the background. This discussion will have to focus, therefore, on some of the other issues that have been or are of most interest.

I. ECONOMIC DEPENDENCE

Among these there is the problem of dependence on the outside world or specialisation which was mentioned at the beginning of the chapter. Walter A. Chudson (1962) has pointed out that, because of the heavy dependence of African countries on exports, an appraisal of their export prospects is fundamental to any attempt to estimate their capacity to provide from their own efforts the savings and the foreign exchange resources required to finance their economic development. 'In the coming decade, at least, trends in the national product of most countries of the region are likely to continue to be dominated or strongly influenced by the evolution of export proceeds; indeed, in some cases the transition from subsistence to commercial production may increase the degree of dependence.' By the same token, an appraisal of export prospects is basic to an estimate of the African countries' requirements for external financial assistance and capital inflow generally and, indeed, of their capacity to obtain capital from abroad rather than aid in the form of grants or soft loans.

As Pierre Moussa has shown in Les Nations Proletaires (1959), the dependence of the African countries on a few primary product exports is a source of great difficulty to them because these products are subject to wide price and supply fluctuations. This dependence makes a greater demand on the ability of the African governments to cope with wide swings in export income, national income and government revenues than do the cyclical problems facing the governments of most developed countries. (It must be said, however, that the situation is better now than before the second world war when the industrialised countries were unable to avoid severe depressions.) It has also become increasingly evident in recent years that world demand for primary products does not, and is not likely to, keep pace with the growth of world income for a number of reasons: the development of synthetics; the fact that much of the increase in income in industrialised countries is spent in the form of greater fabrication of industrial commodities without an increase in the raw material content; and the greater consumption of services as individual incomes increase. This means that primary producers as a whole have an increasingly difficult task just to keep up with the rate of growth of income in industry and it is much more difficult to close the gap of the existing absolute differences between the industralised and underdeveloped countries.

These remarks, it should be noted, apply to primary producers as a whole. As far as primary producers in Africa are concerned, there are several mitigating factors. First, not all primary producers are in underdeveloped countries; the United States, for example, is still a much larger primary producer for its own consumption and export than it is an importer of primary products. Especially in the case of minerals, many of the developed countries are or have been important producers. Minerals are a wasting asset. By taking over a larger share of a growing market, therefore, the developing countries may be able to keep up with or surpass the rate of growth of the economies of the industrialised countries.

Especially in Africa, minerals have been of great importance in sparking off economic growth. The modern development of South Africa began with the diamonds in 1867 and gold in 1886. The development of Northern Rhodesia and the Congo (Leopoldville) began with copper. And, in recent years, iron ore and bauxite mining have become propulsive sectors in a number of countries (Mauretania, Guinea, Liberia, Gabon, Swaziland).

The countries producing tropical agricultural products do not have the same type of opportunities as the mineral producers. An FAO projection for 1970 of agricultural exports produced by underdeveloped countries forecasts only a slow growth in demand with the bulk of this being in Western Europe, the Sino-Soviet bloc and Japan. For the political scientist, this may well have important implications both within Africa and for its relations with the rest of the world. If the African countries producing agricultural products for export wish to secure a faster rate of growth than the projections would indicate, they must rely on securing a growing share of the total market.

One conclusion that most economists do *not* draw from the consideration of the problems resulting from reliance on export of primary products is that the development of the export of the primary products was a mistake. On the other hand, probably a large number of non-economists do draw this conclusion. Most economists instead would agree with S. H. Frankel and Cyril Ehrlich that the initiation and growth of the export of these primary products was a most important factor in achieving the degree of economic development that the African countries have attained and that it still is a most important engine of economic development. It is well to remember in this connection that it was the growth of export income that was a powerful force in getting the economy growing of countries like the United Kingdom, United States and Japan, and so started them on their way to industrialisation. The existence of export markets for minerals or the agricultural products that Africa can produce provides a ready means of securing a money income for the individual and the country. It makes it possible for the government of the area to secure sufficient revenues to provide the necessary minimum of law and order and to begin to make the investment in building up the human capabilities necessary for progress.   Consequently, in prescribing policies to quicken the economic growth of an African country, the majority of economists almost instinctively look first to an investigation of the possibilities of increasing the income from existing export commodities and of finding new possibilities for export.

In this connection, Chudson (1962) has pointed out that from 1950 to 1960 the value of exports from tropical Africa rose by about 70 per cent.   This was an impressive performance, particularly in comparison with the sluggish growth of exports from Asia outside of Japan and the virtual stagnation of Latin America's exports as a whole.   This growth of exports helped to make possible the more rapid economic growth of Africa compared with the other major underdeveloped regions. Africa's economic performance also may not be unrelated to the rapid development of demands for political independence that occurred during the 1950s.   The FAO projection of possible deterioration in the prices of some of the major African agricultural products over the remainder of the 1960s may also have political implications, if this is allowed to occur.

Another important facet of the commodity problem is the difficult decision confronting African countries at the present time in the negotiations on international action to stabilise the prices of some of their export commodities.   The African countries, for example, are clearly low-cost producers of coffee, and their long-range interest is in getting a bigger share of the world market.   On the other hand, they are also interested in higher prices at present and in preventing a further drop in prices.   But, in order to keep prices up through international agreement they have to agree to hold down expansion in their output.

2. INDUSTRIALISATION

In view of the sober prospects for primary products, a natural sequence is to consider the possibilities of industrialisation in Africa.   The majority of economists, following on from their positions as just given, emphasise the approach from the market side.   In general, it is fair to say that while there are many obstacles to industrialisation in African countries — lack of entrepreneurs, managers, technicians, etc. — in most cases a ruling constraint is the size of the market to be supplied.   The size of the market primarily depends on the incomes of the overwhelming mass of the population, that is, of the farmers.   Economists consequently go on to draw conclusions such as those of the Uganda Economic Development Committee in 1958, influenced by W. T. Newlyn and David Walker: 'The Committee conclude therefore that the most effective steps which can be taken to secure development of manufacturing industry in Uganda, paradoxical though it may seem, are steps which will have the effect of increasing agricultural production.   The committee *recommended* [italics in the original] that Government's economic strategy should be determined accordingly.'

In the World Bank's report on *The Economic Development of Uganda* (1962) there was a subtle change in emphasis, but the essence of the policy recommendations remained the same.   This report recommended that 'everything that is administratively and economically feasible be done in the next five years to increase output in manufacturing, mining and agriculture. . .   It is quite obvious, however, that in spite of doing everything possible in manufacturing and mining, the main opportunities for economic growth in Uganda in the next five years are in agriculture.'

To some extent, of course, the forces also run the other way.   As manufacturing and towns grow, the internal market for agricultural products grows, and the internal market can provide more and more of the propulsive impulse that export markets originally provided in Africa.

At the current stage of development of the African economies, this relationship between development of agriculture and development of manufacturing also appears in another form. Elkan's previously noted research on migrant labour also found that in Africa south of the Sahara one of the important motives for Africans to go to work in towns is to save as much money as possible to buy the necessary tools for increasing production on their farms. This seems to be almost a peculiarly African manifestation of the general proposition that economic growth is self-reinforcing; i.e., that not only does growth of manufacturing depend on the growth of the market due to higher incomes of farmers, but growth of manufacturing and of towns helps in the growth of agriculture. It also follows from this that as agriculture progresses and becomes more specialised and more capitalised the possibility for Africans to move back and forth between agriculture and towns will become less and less. In other words, they will begin to become either more efficient farmers because specialised, or more efficient industrial workers because specialised. This pioneering work of Elkan's has consequently given us new insights into the process of economic development in Africa; but it still needs to be tested in other areas and to be followed up as Africa's economic development goes on.

3. MARKET FORCES V. GOVERNMENT ACTION

An important policy issue in Africa which takes many forms is the extent to which there should be reliance on market forces to bring about economic development and the extent to which direct governmental or administrative action in the economy should be relied on. It would be practically impossible nowadays to find any economist who would subscribe to the economic philosophy, dominant before the second world war, of a very narrow restricted role for government in this regard. The earlier approach was perhaps most succinctly phrased by Adam Smith in his *Wealth of Nations* (1776): 'Little else is requisite to carry a state to the highest degree of opulence from the lowest barbarism but peace, easy taxes and a tolerable administration of justice; all the rest being brought about by the natural course of things'.

Even in the communist sphere, however, there would not be unanimity on the proposition that the state should do everything. Most economists, therefore, believe that there should be some mixture of governmental and market forces in the economy as a whole. The disputes arise on the amount of each ingredient needed in particular sectors. Some of these disputes arise from neglect of the fact that there is no absolute in this field: a particular policy may be more relevant to one stage of development than it is to the next. What at one time may be a desirable degree of government action in helping the economy to grow may be a fetter on the economy at a subsequent stage after entrepreneurs have developed.

One of the most important and most acute of these disputes has been over the marketing and division of the proceeds of some of the main export commodities since the war. In view of the central importance given to exports in the economic development in Africa, this question is clearly crucial. Briefly, in a number of countries marketing boards or *caisses de stabilisation* were set up to handle the marketing of some of the export crops. There were various reasons for doing so, some of which were not completely formulated, and some of which may even have been quite contradictory. The important point for this discussion is that, as world prices in the post-war period went up, the prices received by the growers of the crops — particularly in the English-speaking countries — did not follow suit all the way. Some of the difference between the world market prices and the prices paid to the farmers by the marketing boards was set aside in price reserve funds, and part of this was later taken over or borrowed by the governments for their development plans. Some part of the export proceeds was also directly taken by the governments in the form of export taxes and used to finance capital and current expenditures.

For the early portion of the post-war period, some justification of the policy of building up large price reserve funds is essentially uncontroversial, in that the supply of commodities the farmers could buy was limited anyway, and giving them extra money would simply have resulted in their bidding up prices against themselves. But once this first period of scarcities was over, the issue was clearly joined. The East African Royal Commission (Walker and Ehrlich: 1955) criticised the policy in East Africa, and Bauer and Paish (1952) criticised the policy in West Africa. The point they made is essentially that, if the African peasants had received the full benefit of the higher prices, economic development would have progressed faster than it did with the government's use of the money. This was on the grounds that: (a) the higher prices would have called forth greater output of the commodities concerned by the farmers' putting forth greater efforts; (b) the African farmers would have saved more and used the funds to develop, improve and even transform their farms; (c) the higher purchasing power in the rural areas would have stimulated other forms of economic development — African traders and back-yard industry; (d) the farmer was insulated from world market prices; this hindered the development of an entrepreneurial sense and led the farmer to believe that the way to cure low prices is to put pressure on the government; (e) government expenditures, both current and capital, were enabled to grow rapidly through the higher availability of funds to the government. Much of this money went into assets, such as education and research, which have a very slow yield, and, with abundant funds available to the government, probably much was used for extravagance and waste.

This is a formidable indictment. Unfortunately, no thorough research on the ground has been done either to prove or to disprove these points. There is perhaps some possibility of research to throw light on the main point of whether higher incomes for farmers do have the beneficial results claimed for them. This might be done through a study comparing the results obtained in Ghana, which follows the policy of taxing cocoa producers quite heavily (and quite justifiably, because they are a relatively prosperous part of the economy), with the results obtained in some of the French-speaking territories in which France has made available a part of her aid by paying prices to the producers of some crops above what would be justified by world market prices.

Not all economists agreed or agree with the main weight of the criticisms of the marketing board policies as given above. In view of the lack of any real data on which to base decisions, attitudes towards the accomplishments or deficiencies of marketing board policies are largely matters of judgment. After making as thorough an assessment as they could of the policies and their results, the World Bank Economic Survey missions to Nigeria and Uganda have come to the conclusion that, on balance, the way the export proceeds had been used did contribute effectively to the development of their countries. Of Nigeria the mission said: 'On the whole, the operations of the marketing boards have benefited the producers of the controlled crops and the Nigerian economy in general'. It pointed out that under any stabilisation scheme, a period of rising prices is the time for the formation of reserves. The setting of relatively low producer prices greatly mitigated the severity of inflationary pressures at a time when no other machinery for anti-inflationary action existed. The accumulated stabilisation reserves were large enough not only to assure producers the direct benefit of reasonable and relatively stable prices for many years, but also to enable the boards to lend large sums to the government for development purposes.

In Uganda, the mission felt that the marketing boards and export tax arrangements had made a useful contribution in financing a large growth of the infrastructure and of most of Uganda's modern economy outside of agriculture. The mission went on to point out that, in view of the very high cotton and coffee prices that prevailed, and the predominant position of these two crops in the Uganda economy, together with the fact that Africans were exempt from income tax, the government had no choice but to tap this tax source. It is also true, however, that the export tax introduced an element of inequality: cotton and coffee growers became subject to a rather heavy tax burden, while the producers of other crops and livestock paid no similar tax.

Johnston and Mellors (1961) come to a similar practical economic policy conclusion:

> An underdeveloped country that is making determined efforts to achieve economic progress faces formidable requirements for capital to finance the creation and expansion of manufacturing and mining enterprise, for overhead investment in transportation and utilities, and in the revenue needed for recurrent expenditure for expansion of education and developmental services. These requirements are certain to outstrip the supply of funds available except in those countries which have large earnings from petroleum or mineral exports or particularly favorable access to foreign capital. The sheer size of the agricultural sector as the only major existing industry points to its importance as a source of capital for overall economic growth.

By now it is generally agreed that marketing boards and *caisses de stabilisation* should be regarded as multipurpose institutions, not merely as stabilisation devices. They perform useful technical and commercial services for the small farmers and protect them against collusive buying by middlemen. They often finance technical aids to production which have frequently been very effective. In general, as David Walker (1960) has emphasised, the stabilisation that is sought is stabilisation of national income, not necessarily stabilisation of the price paid to producers. In some cases it is possible to act to stabilise the national income by using the resources of the marketing board elsewhere rather than by increasing prices to producers.

4. TRADE

Most economists are in agreement in their attitudes towards trade in Africa and in their strong opposition to many of the governmental policies on trade and traders. As Peter Bauer (1954) has so well brought out, trade is an effective instrument for the development of resources and for fostering their growth. Traders penetrating to every part of an African country are among the most potent agents for change and for the awakening of economic incentives. In brief, the economist's attitude is to encourage and facilitate the work of the trader.

Unfortunately, in almost every African country people of non-African origin are prominent or predominant in trade outside the subsistence sector. This, combined with the lack of economic training of most administrators and with their fondness for neatness and direct administrative action, has often led to restrictions on the activity of traders and to attempts to fit them into an 'orderly' structure of trade. Where the economist would rely on encouragement of traders and on increasing the number of competitors in order to avoid abuses, governments often tend instead to rely on restrictions and controls. The result is that the costs of procuring and distributing goods are raised, and the leavening effect of the trader on the economy is reduced. (It might also be mentioned in passing that the over-regulation of road transport is also often another area of misguided paternalism in some African countries.)

5. FEDERATIONS AND COMMON MARKETS

An important group of economic policy questions arises from the formation of or the proposals for federations or common markets among the African states. Economists have done considerable work on these questions in Africa, especially in the last ten years, and have, in the main, agreed on several important conclusions. The import of these may be rather surprising to some non-economists; it is that the economic benefits of a federation or a common market for a particular individual country may be slight or even nugatory. The particular circumstances of the country have to be investigated before a definite conclusion on this point is reached.

Economists agree in general that a tariff area as a whole may gain from protection. An infant industry may be protected until it can stand on its own feet; a market, which initially may be too small to permit an industry to develop, may remain small until the industry does develop. Protection may allow that industry to grow and so enlarge the size of its market as to justify the original decision to organise a new industry. The social benefits from establishing a new industry in the way of training workers and entrepreneurs and shaking up the indigenous economy may also be large enough to warrant putting on a tariff to make it possible for the industry to run at a private profit.

But the gain from tariffs may be unevenly distributed. A customs union between a relatively developed country and a relatively undeveloped country will benefit the former because it will give it bigger markets, but it may not benefit or may even hurt the latter. In his authoritative work on customs unions, Jacob Viner (1950) in fact regarded the common market in East Africa as a good example of how the establishment of a customs union works to the detriment of the less developed part of the union.

The point is that a customs union or common market will help the area, all other things being equal, if the area covered is regarded as a single unit. The larger the market created, the greater the economic benefits possible. But if the focus of interest on the area as a whole is narrowed to a particular region or country within the area, the balance of advantages may shift quite considerably. In a common market, a more advanced Country A has considerable advantages over Country B in attracting further investment and industry. Some of this might not have come into the area at all had it not been for the larger market provided by the common market. But some of this investment might well have gone to the less developed Country B in order to meet the needs of that country, if the common market did not exist. Country B, in addition, could have erected a tariff to protect the industry from the competition of Country A, which in the common market is not possible.

The East African Fiscal Commission (Raisman Commission), which reported in February 1961, and the World Bank's Survey mission to Uganda both examined the East African common market from this standpoint. They agreed on the general economic analysis applicable but disagreed on some of the particulars as regards Uganda. The Raisman Commission and the Uganda mission agreed the common market had resulted in special benefits to Kenya along the lines of the discussion above. To offset this, some special compensation should be paid to Kenya's partners in the common market. The Raisman Commission felt, however, that Uganda and Tanganyika had gained some benefits from the overspill of Nairobi's development, and these reduced the size of needed compensation. On the other hand, the Uganda mission was not able to find any such benefits, pointing out that any increase in demand for Uganda's agricultural products in Kenya that might have come from the higher income in Kenya resulting from industrialisation was prevented from resulting in higher Uganda sales in Kenya by various impediments that Kenya put in the way. In the longer run, Uganda might gain from a demand for Uganda labour in Nairobi, but this had not yet occurred. In addition, Uganda was hurt by having to pay more when a protective tariff led to a shift in Uganda's purchases from imported goods to goods manufactured in Kenya. In this last instance, furthermore, whether the import was costly or not, Uganda lost the revenue from the import duty.

The Uganda mission, nevertheless, did not recommend abandoning the common market. If this were to be done, customs barriers would have to be erected which would be costly and hard to police. In the longer run, Uganda may get more benefits from interterritorial trade as Kenya removes some of the impediments to Uganda sales of agricultural products in Kenya. A unilateral attack on the common market would put in jeopardy the common services from which Uganda gains much. Finally, the mission pointed out that Uganda will find it difficult to share equitably in the gains of economic integration without a substantial degree of political integration which would make it possible more equitably to share the benefits of a large economic unit.

Unlike East Africa, the Federation of Rhodesia and Nyasaland created both a customs union and a political federation. The economic benefits of this governmental unit have been investigated most notably by Hazlewood and Henderson (1960). They found that, while the extent to which the Federation contributed to the economic development of the three territories could not be ascertained exactly, it did make some positive contribution; this, however, was not as great as most discussions on the matter imply. The contribution it did make was mainly due to to the fact that government current expenditure and investment was higher than it would have been without federation. This stemmed from the fact that tax revenues from the Copperbelt in Northern Rhodesia could be used for the Federation, whereas without federation the revenues would have reduced or eliminated the need to borrow by the Northern Rhodesian government.

The bulk of the advantage of having a customs union and a common tariff for the three territories fell to Southern Rhodesia, which, as the region most attractive to investors, may have drawn industry that without the common market might have gone to Nyasaland or Northern Rhodesia. In addition, tariff changes were made that were to the detriment of Nyasaland consumers but in the interests of industry in Southern Rhodesia. Because Nyasaland was not able to set tariffs to protect industry from Southern Rhodesian competition, industry may also have been prevented from developing in Nyasaland. This could have been offset by a deliberate policy of offering other inducements to industry, but such steps were not taken.

The main benefits that Nyasaland got from federation were an increase in government revenues at the expense of Northern Rhodesia and an increase in employment opportunities for Nyasas in the Rhodesias.

The lessons to be drawn from the foregoing discussion would be somewhat as follows: it cannot be taken for granted that a particular country will or will not benefit from participating in a common market, customs union or federation. The answer must depend on an economic analysis within the framework of the political and constitutional decisions that determine how the economic benefits can be distributed. In other words, the political scientist cannot get a general judgment from the economist that a federation or customs union is desirable per se for Country X until he can tell the economist how the distribution of political power will influence economic decisions.

What should be noted here, especially, is that the economist may look at the problem of federation from two different levels. From the vantage point of a particular country, he may conclude that a proposed federation may be quite against its interests. On the other hand, from the vantage point of the development of Africa or of the particular portion of Africa involved, he can also quite legitimately conclude that the proposed federation is economically advantageous. Similarly, in any consideration of the allocation of revenues and expenditures within a federation, an economist advising a constituent part of the federation could legitimately propose a transference of revenues from the richer to the poorer sections, while from the federal level, he could conclude that the national economic interest lay in getting the most rapid growth of gross national product by concentrating on the development of the already richer section. This also applies, of course, to multiracial countries; there is no necessary coincidence between policies that result in the most rapid national growth and those that most rapidly raise the standard of living of a particular race.

This whole class of problems is particularly hard to handle because political considerations are so dominant. No economist has yet ventured far into this field. J. W. Garmany, in the South African Journal of Economics, March 1962, suggested that some attempt should be made on an economic basis to work out a guiding principle for the allocation of funds between governments in a federation and for the allocation of funds by governments between different forms of investment. As a beginning, he suggested that attempts be made to measure the inputs and the outputs concerned. The chances are, however, that political scientists will have to decide these questions without any appreciable help from the economists.

II

PHYSICO-BIOLOGICAL STUDIES

9

Geography   Benjamin E. Thomas

I INTRODUCTION: THE NATURE AND SCOPE OF GEOGRAPHY*

GEOGRAPHY MAY BE defined as: 'the study of the distributions or patterns of the physical and human elements of the earth's surface, both past and present, and their inter-relationships'. A shorter definition, still inclusive enough to cover the many branches of the subject, would be: 'the study of areal differentiation of phenomena on the earth's surface'. Geography provides for the mapping and description of these elements or phenomena, develops theories about the patterns that are discovered, and explains their relations to other patterns.

The discipline is both a physical and a social science, but the former will be discussed here only when it has a bearing on social research. The work of geographers who deal exclusively with physical or non-human topics (for example, the patterns of landform features, their causes, and relations to climates, drainage, soils and vegetation) will be omitted unless associated with research on aspects of human geography like settlement and agriculture; and consideration of map-making or cartography — a long-established branch of geography — will be restricted primarily to the mapping of human features like population, roads and farming areas.

The discipline of geography includes the discovery and statement of those principles which explain recurrent conditions, distributions and relationships on the earth's surface; the identification, and measurement if possible, of regional similarities, differences and movements; and the recognition of change, whether rapid or slow, past or present. It is often divided into physical, human and regional geography for purposes of giving instruction or classifying publications.

The generally accepted limits of the discipline of geography are so broad that in practice geographers with special research interests tend to form 'schools of thought' or to identify themselves with branches of the field. Examples from physical geography are: (1) cartography, (2) climatology, (3) landforms geography or geomorphology, and (4) biogeography (plant and animal geography).

Many geographers with interests in the cultural aspects of their field focus their attention on the development of a general theory and method of studying human geography. Examples are: the culture history approach (cultural geography); the ecological approach or the study of the relations of man to his natural

* Bibliography for this chapter will be found on page 527.

environment (possibilism and environmental determinism); the study of material, man-made features of the earth's surface (landscape purism); the study of the physical earth and man's use of it (land-use mapping and geography); and others. A second focus is on systematic topics, or particular types of features of the earth's surface (cities, agriculture, trade routes, etc.), and the subjects can be identified as urban geography, agricultural geography, transportation geography, and so on. A third focus is regional; the geographer considers many types of systematic features (physical, cultural, or — most commonly — both) of a part of the earth's surface, such as the Nile Delta, or southern Africa.

Most geographers have an interest in several aspects of the field, so that one may be an economic geographer or climatologist as well as a regional specialist on Nigeria. This overlapping of interests, together with the common background of training in cartography and in both physical and human geography, added to a general concern for the history and philosophy of the discipline, prevents the field from becoming permanently divided into several parts. Because geography is one of the oldest of academic disciplines and has many branches, the history and philosophy of the subject and the literature available upon many topics are extraordinarily diverse and complicated. Philosophical questions can be given only minor attention here. For those interested in the story of the development of different schools of thought, Hartshorne's well-known works are recommended (Hartshorne 1959, 1961).

The total amount of geographical material that has been published is large and reflects the discipline's many technical branches. In Germany alone, more than 300 geographical serials have been published. The number of serial publications in the world (numbered journals, monographs, reviews and research notes, etc., either current or closed) which are primarily geographic in content total more than 1,600 published in thirty-seven languages (Harris and Fellman 1960). A single geographer or even an entire department of geography, therefore, concentrates on the major themes or principles of the subject, on the use of a few languages, and on a few specialties, with no attempt to consider all the details of the various branches.

The school that comes closest to attempting extensive and intensive work on most fields is Moscow State University in the Soviet Union. It has a Geography Faculty under a dean, with fifteen departments for separate subjects like economic geography, cartography and climatology. Each department has from a few to a dozen geographers of professorial rank, and in 1961 there were eighteen research laboratories in operation at Moscow and twenty-six expeditions in the field. The total staff for the Faculty of Geography is estimated at about 560 (Harris 1961).

II   AFRICAN GEOGRAPHY

The study of the geography of Africa, as of most other places, has advanced faster and reached a level more mature in the systematic than in the regional fields. The major reasons for this are the support given to systematic geography by recent studies in related subjects, and the comparative ease of exchanging information across disciplinary boundaries when similar phenomena are studied. Two examples may illustrate this exchange between related subjects.

A physical geographer or climatologist who wishes to prepare a climatic map of all or part of Africa and to provide a text to explain the causes and effects of the climatic differences, may use data from weather stations, information on the atmosphere from meteorology and on ocean currents from oceanography, new ideas from geophysical studies, etc. He must still convert the data into usable forms and make his own maps and interpretations, but the advances in methodology, concepts, and data collecting in related sciences are of great value to him. In similar fashion the economic geographer who is studying and mapping the patterns of mineral production and export in Africa can obtain both data and ideas from government reports and from the subjects of economic geology, economics, international relations and foreign trade, as well as from his own discipline.

There is considerable emphasis in geography on fieldwork and the collection of new data from the earth itself by observation, aerial photography, mapping, and other techniques. In the above examples, for small areas a physical geographer could collect some of the climatic data with his own instruments, and the economic geographer might compile original maps from previously unpublished field data and local information. But even in these cases the systematic approach has advantages: the geographical techniques obviously benefit from the experience of meteorology in the first case and from mineral surveying in the second, and one can become skilled at collecting, mapping and understanding one kind of information on the basis of experience in related fields.

Regional geography has been able to benefit much less than systematic geography from the data and techniques of other disciplines. If one attempts to map, describe and analyse all aspects of geography for a river basin or a territory in Africa, data on many factors are likely to be either unobtainable or unavailable in a form useful to the geographer. No other subject is primarily concerned with the total complex of natural and human features that characterise a portion of the earth's surface, so geography has had to develop many of its own techniques for the recording, mapping and analysing of inter-related features.

The culture of man and the details of the earth's surface vary so much from place to place that the regional geographer, like the ethnologist, must devote years of study to a people and their area before he can thoroughly understand them and present a reasonably complete picture. It is true perhaps that neither the ethnologist nor the regional geographer is really able to comprehend the totality of his subject for an area of even moderate size, but he can accomplish much of value in working towards this ideal. In geography, it is sometimes said that the systematic fields are sciences of the order of the natural or social types, but that regional geography is an art.

In the sections below, selected topics of the systematic geography of Africa will be considered. These will be followed by a discussion of integrating subjects like historical, cultural and regional geography, and by a brief summary of major trends in geographical research.

I. THE EXPLORATION OF AFRICA

The desire for geographical knowledge, in one form or another, arose in all the early civilisations. Ancient Egypt, the Assyrian Empire and Phoenicia used maps of a sort, and had an interest in both the physical aspects and the people of northern Africa (Dickinson and Howarth 1933). Geography, history, natural science, religion, philosophy and other subjects were usually studied, with no attempt to divide knowledge into distinct branches. The information collected about the earth, however, might be listed in three categories: beliefs as to the nature of the physical earth and its place in the universe; measurement of the earth and its parts; and data and ideas about the inhabited world.

The study of the earth and the universe later became physical geography, astronomy, natural science of several kinds, and philosophy; measurement became mathematical geography, cartography, surveying and geometry; and studies on the inhabited world became human geography, history and social science. Geography developed along with all three categories, but the origins of human geography and its earliest contribution to 'social research in Africa' are probably to be found in the third category: 'data and ideas about the inhabited world'. These consisted largely of information about the coasts and coastal peoples of Africa; exploration was necessary before the geography of the interior could be studied.

Many of the famous Greek philosphers and historians made contributions to knowledge about the physical earth and its measurement as well as about man and his activities on the earth's surface. Only the latter subjects are of direct concern here, and it may be sufficient to note that Herodotus (c. 484–25 BC), provided descriptions and ideas on the human geography of northern Africa which geographers, anthropologists and historians still find worthy of study. Alexander the Great (356–23 BC) led campaigns in south-west Asia and Egypt which resulted in geographical exploration as well as conquest. Some of these were in north-eastern Africa, and the observations were recorded by Alexander's non-military aides. When Alexander's empire was divided, Ptolemy acquired Egypt, and the city of Alexandria became a centre of Greek learning with a world-famous library. Geographical study was extended to most parts of north-eastern Africa.

The rise of Rome occurred at the same time as that of Alexandria, and, after the alliance of Rome with Egypt in 273 BC, there was an exchange of geographical information through visits of scholars between the two centres. Rome was especially interested in north-western Africa and made contributions through both the collection of topographical information and the improvement of survey and measurement techniques for military and road-making purposes. Descriptive geographies of Roman provinces during the second and first centuries BC included both physical and human elements in order to facilitate administration and trade, but there was little in the way of analysis or explanation.

Strabo (c. 64 BC–AD 20), a historian and geographer, is especially noteworthy for his *Geography*, because it is one of the few ancient works which survives nearly intact. Only one of the seventeen books, however, deals with Africa, and that only with the northern fringe. Another book by an unknown author of about the same period, the *Periplus of the Erythraean Sea*, contains information on north-eastern and coastal East Africa.

Geographike Syntaxis, written by Claudius Ptolemaeus (Ptolemy) of Alexandria about AD 150, was another noted geography. The maps and descriptions included the northern half of Africa, but much vague information had apparently been obtained by hearsay from travellers and was plotted by inaccurate methods. Interior lakes and rivers were shown, but only the Nile system bore a reasonable resemblance to actuality. It is hard to determine whether some of the interior rivers reflected knowledge of the Senegal and the Niger or were merely errors in plotting other streams. This work, with its combination of gross omissions and crude errors mixed with useful representations of African geography, was the high point in recording the results of exploration before the Dark Ages.

The early Christian period and the Middle Ages in Europe provided little new knowledge of Africa, and the Vandals in North Africa wrote no geographies. After the Arab conquests, however, there were at least a dozen noted Muslim scholars who studied the records of the past, explored and described North Africa, and gave increased attention to both physical and human geography. Ibn Haukal, for example, travelled widely and wrote his *Book of Roads and Kingdoms* in 977. Ibn Batuta of Tangier (1304–78) is estimated to have travelled 75,000 miles, and he wrote accurate geographical descriptions which were unknown in Europe until centuries after his death. Ibn Khaldun of Tunis (1332–1406) not only recorded the results of study and explorations but also did able work on the human geography of nomadic societies and oases of North Africa and on geographical history. Leo Africanus, born in Spain about 1495, lived in Morocco, travelled in West Africa, and described the great Negro and North African empires of his time. Arab geographies of North Africa often surpassed those of previous periods in both completeness and sophistication.

A renaissance in European geography overlapped the last part of the period of Muslim geography, and a combination of new conditions led to the well-known explorations of the coasts of Africa and the New World. The exploration of Africa proceeded, after a long hesitation at the margins, to the nineteenth-century search for the sources of rivers and then to a more rapid investigation of the remaining unknown interior areas. The story of John Speke, Livingstone, Stanley and the other African explorers is so familiar to most Africanists that it should be sufficient here merely to comment upon the parts of the process which might be assigned to history or to geography and upon trends which had a bearing upon social research.

The story of the men and the events of exploration form a part of European and African history, whereas the results of explorations — as recorded on maps and in descriptions, and as evidenced by new ideas about the earth's surface — are geographical in nature. There are several methods of combining history and geography which will be discussed later under 'historical geography and geographical history'. But in the last analysis, any developmental sequence in geographical or other knowledge can be included in history as a part of the history of sciences or of the history of civilisations.

The exploration period for Africa was about over by the first decade of this century. There are still a few unexplored sites, such as certain swamps and mountain peaks, but travels by explorers have given way to scientific investigations by geologists, geographers, biologists and anthropologists. Heinrich Barth, who was professor of geography at the University of Berlin and made notable explorations between 1845 and 1855, probably represents the beginning of the transition from geographical exploration to geographical fieldwork in the modern sense. Geographical field studies are now under way in almost every country in Africa, and even the geographers and geologists who recently helped to fill in the knowledge of glaciated peaks of the Ruwenzori Mountains were doing 'fieldwork' rather than 'exploring'.

Exploration was important in substituting locational facts for ignorance, but on the whole the explorers of Africa made useful contributions to ideas on geographical social research in only a few isolated periods, such as the enlightened ones of Greek and Arab scholarship. A few explorers had some insight into the attitudes and cultures of African peoples and made a start on sympathetic interpretations of the associations of culture and environment. But most explorers were mainly interested in routes, resources and locations, and wrote prejudiced and unenlightened descriptions of 'natives' which centred on oddities and barbarism. It may even be said that the total result of their work for social research was in some ways more negative than positive. Much of the recent effort of anthropologists, historians, geographers, sociologists and others has been expended in an attempt to correct the misinformation on the human aspects of the former Dark Continent.

2. GENERAL MAPPING

Mapping has been an important part of exploration as well as a technique in other forms of geographical research. At first almost all mapping was done in connection with the discipline of geography, but now the mapping of rock types, for example, is done by geologists and has become 'geological mapping'. The shape of surface forms and the indication of cultural (man-made) features like roads and houses has become 'topographic' or 'geographic' mapping, and is done by survey departments and geographic or mapping institutes. The preparation of atlases for general use is also regarded as a type of geographic work. Cartography or map-making is usually associated with the physical science part of geography, and in this essay, therefore, a summary of the status of mapping in Africa and its implications for research on social topics should be sufficient.

Great advances were made in the techniques for surveying and map-making in Europe during the seventeenth and eighteenth centuries, and these enabled mapping to follow closely upon the heels of exploration in Africa. It is true that the European powers did not have sufficiently accurate maps for determining all the details of boundaries during the partition of Africa during the 1880s, but the major features of Africa were known and were indicated on maps of many types (Bartholomew 1890). Following the partition of the continent, the colonial powers undertook surveys to provide more detailed topographic maps, and before the first world war, reconnaissance or approximate survey maps of medium scale were available for all of Africa except a few desert and mountain areas (Finsterwalder and Hueber 1943). By the second world war the millionth map, requiring 130 sheets to show all of Africa, was about complete, and since that time the progress on detailed mapping has been more rapid than ever before. Many accurate general maps are available for all of Africa, and the largest remaining areas without detailed (large-scale) topographic maps are the Sahara, Ethiopia and Angola.

The implications for social research are that maps of dams and power lines, roads, the distribution of houses, and many other human features, can often be compiled from available topographic maps and aerial photographs. Topographic sheets can also provide the base maps and some of the data for economic and agricultural plans, population censuses, and sociological and land use analysis. As a striking example, the great contrasts between the scattered huts and winding paths of the pre-Mau Mau settlements in the Kikuyu country of Kenya and the large villages, schools and motor roads after the villagisation program, are shown on the old and new topographic sheets of the Kenya survey. Further information on the uses and availability of maps and aerial photographs may be found in the survey by Dahlberg and Thomas (1962a).

A number of general atlases of Africa and more detailed atlases of individual African countries have been produced since the second world war. Many of these are the products of survey departments and geographical publishing companies, but university geography departments have also participated. Probably the best known example is the atlas prepared by Talbot and Talbot (1960).

3. PHYSICAL GEOGRAPHY

The study of the geography of landforms, climates, soils and vegetation differs in its viewpoints and objectives from those of geology, biology and other sciences in that the geographical purpose is to map distributions and to explain their origins, associations with other distributions, and their importance to regional character and to the life of man. For the most part, these elements of physical geography will be considered here only when they are appropriate to the interests of human geography.

Many studies in physical geography, however, have general human implications which do not fit into specific categories. An example of a classic, now largely outdated by the rapid advance of science, is *Vegetation and Soils of Africa* (Shantz and Marbut 1923). It outlined the broad zones of soils and vegetation for Africa and discussed their importance to man and the effect of man upon them. Many years later, Shantz returned to the sites he had studied earlier in order to note the changes and assess the importance of natural and human influences on vegetation (Shantz and Turner 1958). It should also be noted that the soils map by Marbut was the first to apply the new knowledge of inter-relationships between climates, vegetation and soils in such a way as to show the broad soil zones for Africa. Garnier has worked on several studies of the delimitation of the humid tropics and on the measurement of the effects of rainfall amounts and of the seasons on the adequacy or deficiency of soil moisture for agriculture (Garnier 1956).

Investigations of the landforms of Africa, as a physical science in its own right, have been carried on in many parts of the continent, especially by German and English physical geographers. The results of these studies and their human implications have been included in many regional studies which will be considered later. A few studies for large portions of the continent, however, have been published separately (King 1951).

From the viewpoint of human subsistence, the study of water resources is an especially important part of earth science. This is a field of interest for hydrologists, engineers and geologists, as well as for physical geographers. Debenham has written a number of regional and popular books on Africa, and his well-known report on water resources and their uses surveyed conditions for a large area (Debenham 1948).

Another very helpful type of study is the total physical-regional analysis. A monograph on the Central Namib Desert (Logan 1960) places major emphasis upon climates and landforms. These are then correlated with the patterns of vegetation and animal life and analysed with reference to the people's use of their total resources.

For Africa as a whole, geographers have probably given about as much attention to human as to physical aspects of their subject. The foregoing are representative examples of the implications of physical geography for human geography, but it is the latter to which further consideration must now be given.

4. POPULATION AND SETTLEMENT GEOGRAPHY

Every social science is interested in at least certain aspects of the distribution and characteristics of population, and the discipline of demography focuses on all of the problems related to population. Some of the problems, such as the construction of population pyramids and the compiling of statistics on fertility, are rarely dealt with by geographers, but others, such as the population distribution map, are of vital importance to the human geographer.

By separating geographical aspects from other features of population and by combining them with elements from certain other segments of the discipline, the 'population and settlement' branch of geography has been formed.   The relations of this branch to other social sciences obviously are intimate and complicated.   It is concerned essentially with the distribution and movements of population and with their relationship to settlement forms and physical and economic environments.   A complete analysis of the sub-field would require separate consideration of the phases dealing with population and with settlement, respectively, but in this outline of research results, the two will be considered together.   Geographical research on population and settlements principally consists of: (1) the collection and analysis of census data; (2) the mapping and explanation of population distributions; (3) the mapping and analysis of population types and movements; (4) studies of the possibilities and problems of settlement; and (5) the analysis of settlement forms and patterns.

Geographers have been called upon in many countries during the past century to assist in the preparation of maps of census enumeration areas, the planning of fieldwork in collecting census data, the computation of areas and population densities, the preparation of census atlases, and other work related to cartography and area analysis.   In the United States, geographic assistance started with the census of 1880.   In tropical Africa, few countries have even had a regular census, and Ghana has been the first to employ professional geographers (Boateng 1960). Countries in northern and southern Africa have had some form of census taking for many decades, but the incomplete and fragmentary nature of census data for tropical Africa has posed a problem for many kinds of research.   This has led to geographical studies which would provide the basis for population maps.

Through analyses of settlements on topographic sheets, regional studies and scattered data on population, it is sometimes possible to construct population maps for pre-census periods or for areas with fragmentary census data.   An example of this may be found in a geographical analysis of Ashanti which includes a population distribution map compiled from general maps; this map is far superior to those which can be made from the census data alone (Steel 1948).   In another study, tropical Africa was selected as a test case in an attempt to provide the best maps possible under conditions of sub-standard population census data (Trewartha and Zelinsky 1954).   These maps have been widely used by Africanists.

After finding the data and solving the cartographic problems of making dot, isopleth or other types of maps, the population geographer begins to pursue his main objective: to discover the reasons for the population patterns and densities. There have been many such studies in Africa (Baker 1937; Dixey 1928; Gillman 1936; Gourou 1953; Hilton 1960), and there are numerous theories as to the relative importance of soils, climates, agricultural techniques, and historical conflicts and migrations in determining population patterns.   The gross features can be explained, but much more information is needed on physical geography, agriculture, demography, and African culture and history before some of the important variations in densities can be interpreted satisfactorily.

The third kind of study, the mapping and analysis of population types and movements, suffers even more from a lack of basic data than studies dealing with population distribution and density; and the concepts and techniques are still undeveloped.   Anthropologists are working on the identification of African tribes and their locations, but there are many complex problems yet to be solved: the definition of the tribal concept; the identification of different groups mixed together in various relationships in the same area; the development of methods of enumerating and mapping ethnic groups; and so on.   Tribal maps have now been compiled for the entire continent, but only on the elementary and non-quantitative level at which tribes are indicated by names spread over the approximate location of the tribe or by estimated boundaries enclosing tribal areas.   The bringing of our knowledge of African peoples up to the level where it is possible to make such maps has been a very substantial contribution of anthropologists during the last few decades.

Mapping techniques and analysis, however, have far outrun the collection of data in Africa.   It may be noted, for example, that the contour line was used to show depths in the English Channel in 1737, and that population maps showing distribution and densities by numerically graduated dots and tones of shading were in use by the 1830s.   In contrast, the first quantitative cartographic representation of African tribal groups (by percentages of groups in different areas) to come to the writer's attention was published in January 1962 (Prothero 1962), although there are other examples of geographers who have done considerable work on population types and migrations in Africa (Barbour and Prothero 1961).   Employment, food and other features of African areas are related to population distribution and migration, and several of these have been examined in a symposium of the International Geographical Union held at Makerere College, Kampala, Uganda, in September 1955 (Stamp 1956a).   General routes of migrant workers and major pastoral groups have been discovered and roughly mapped for most parts of Africa (Mather 1956).   In general, however, and despite encouraging progress, it must be said that the existing knowledge of such aspects of African population as distribution and density mapping and analysis is elementary.

The possibilities of African areas as places for European settlement, especially from the standpoints of economic potentialities and health conditions, was a topic widely investigated by geographers and others during the colonial period.   The trend has been steadily towards a greater emphasis upon the possibilities of increased African population and settlement until, in current studies, the latter emphasis predominates.   The period studied, therefore, has had a great bearing upon the kinds of questions for which answers have been sought as well as upon the kinds of data which are now available.   Knowledge about such physical features as soils and climates and of agricultural potentialities, marketing conditions, and the attitudes and desires of African peoples has gradually increased.   Several examples of studies which contribute to the knowledge of 'possibilities of settlement' are available (Gillman 1942; Marinelli 1913; Price 1939; Troll 1936; and Wellington 1937).

The weight given to different elements in the examination of settlement possibilities for indigenous peoples varies greatly from place to place in Africa, because both the natural environment and the technical skills and culture of the people constitute variables.   Studies by geographers which demonstrate these differences are those of Deshler (1960) on Uganda, Despois (1946) on the Fezzan, and Steel (1955) on British tropical Africa.

Settlement can also be studied as a process, with emphasis being placed upon changes resulting from the introduction of new domesticated plants and new farming techniques, upon conflicts between settlers and original inhabitants, upon the economic geography of the settled areas, or upon the conversion of a natural into a cultivated landscape by settlement.   The geographical study of settlement thus incorporates much of the material relevant to the analysis of the colonisation process. France, with a dozen universities or institutes in which colonial geography has been a subject of instruction or research, has been the leader in this field, but some scholars from England and Germany have also taken this broad view of settlement or colonisation geography (Church 1951; Demangeon 1923; Hardy 1933; Salvadori 1938; Weigt 1955).

The purposes of studying forms of rural settlement, such as houses and farm-steads and their relations to roads and natural features, are both practical and theoretical. Practical applications lie in the construction of population maps and in regional planning. Settlements are of theoretical interest for the light they throw on the origins and historical sequences of man-made earth features and for the insight they give into regional character and functional relations. The absence of recent detailed topographic maps or of series of maps at different dates, and the incomplete nature of anthropological or geographical field studies for many tribal areas, usually preclude the advanced types of studies which are possible for western Europe. Studies of indigenous settlements in several parts of Africa have, never-theless, been made. French geographers have studied settlements in northern Africa for many decades (Bernard 1921), and one of the most interesting of recent studies has been made by a Belgian (Annaert 1960). The latter considers not only the patterns of settlements but also the living conditions of the Africans and such things as their preference for small warm huts to the large cold, brick buildings sponsored by the government. Since the second world war, American geographers have conducted field investigations of indigenous settlements in several parts of Africa (Brooke 1959; Houk 1958; Mikesell 1958; Urquhart 1961).

The trends and gaps in research have been suggested above for each phase of population and settlement geography, but a comparative estimate of national contributions may be interesting. Several dozen geographers have done research on population distribution and problems of settlement in Africa, and all the European colonial powers, as well as South Africa, Algeria and the United States, are repre-sented among the scholars. The study of the cultural aspects of settlement and colonisation has received most attention from the French school of human geography, but recent population mapping in tropical Africa has been conducted in greater degree by British geographers in former British areas than by the French in their former territories. Despite the loss of colonies, the German tradition of thorough work on settlement and settlement forms has continued. In recent years a few American studies have been made in almost every category.

5. MEDICAL GEOGRAPHY AND PHYSIOLOGICAL CLIMATOLOGY

When the early explorers and geographers investigated Africa, their reports included observations on (1) the prevalence of fever in swampy areas and of sleeping sickness in the tropical bush, and (2) the debilitating effects of heat and humidity in equatorial regions and the refreshing effects of less warm breezes from the ocean or of dry air from the Sahara. These two aspects of geographical lore, under the influence of modern medicine, physiology and climatology, have become the research fields of medical geography and physiological climatology. Although often considered along with the systematic topics of geography, they are normally classified as associated fields rather than as integral parts of the discipline. Their relationships with other aspects of geography are, however, worthy of attention.

Medical geography may be defined as: 'the study of the areal distribution of disease and its relationship to the environment'. Although the viewpoint and organising themes are geographic, most of the content is substantially medical. A major problem of the field has been to replace a collection of unverified impressions and shaky hypotheses about the relations of diseases to their environment with theories which can be tested in the light of reliable data. The line of research usually runs from the diseases themselves to the organisms which cause them and on to the environmental circumstances which affect the organisms. Research involves the mapping of diseases and the determination of causative agents, vectors, intermediate hosts, and reservoirs for the disease. These may be related to the environment in either obvious or obscure ways.

Most of the important discoveries in medical geography have come from sciences like bacteriology, biology and entomology, and the disciplines of medicine and geography have benefited greatly from this knowledge. Geography has provided assistance on the natural environment and on mapping diseases. Dr Jacques May, head of the Department of Medical Geography of the American Geographical Society of New York, is in charge of a project on the mapping of diseases which is especially helpful for places like Africa where areal knowledge is incomplete. Maps of malaria vectors, the distribution of dengue and yellow fever, etc., are published periodically as plates for the Society's *Atlas of Disease* (also May 1958).

Physiological climatology is the study of the effect of atmospheric conditions on the functioning of the normal human body. The effect of climate on man has been a favourite topic for geographers, often in connection with theories of environmental determinism, but only a part of the earlier ideas has been substantiated by modern research. Physiological climatology was established as a new field during and following the second world war, primarily by scientists in the United States and Canada. Climatologists, physicists, physiologists and geographers contribute to the field.

The heat balance of the human body forms the focus for quantitative study. Physiologists study and measure the effects of thermal conditions on this heat balance along with the adaptations made by the normal body to meet these conditions. Thermal stress is calculated for the conditions of physical activity and type of clothing worn, as well as for temperature, humidity, air movement and radiation. These last four items bring in climatologists or physical geographers to assist on measurement and mapping. Practical applications lie in the planning of work regimes, clothing and housing for tropical areas like Africa (Adolf 1947; Lee and Lemons 1949; Winslow and Herrington 1949).

6. LAND UTILISATION AND LAND-USE SURVEYS

The study of how man uses the land in serving his social and economic needs is one of the central themes in geography. Some human geographers employ the concept as the basis for their philosophy: those things concerning the natural environment, mapping and the ways of mankind which help one to understand how and why man uses and changes the face of the earth, are of interest. In some cases this approach is the reverse of studying the effect of the environment on man; the emphasis may be upon the effect of man on his environment.

When interest centres on the social, historical or economic processes involved, a study may be as close to the concepts of certain anthropologists, historians, sociologists, biologists, conservationists and economists as it is to those of geographers.   An illustration was the interdisciplinary 'international symposium on man's role in changing the face of the earth' with seventy-six participants which was held in New York in 1955 under the co-chairmanship of Carl O. Sauer, Marston Bates and Lewis Mumford.   About fifteen of the participants were geographers, of whom two made contributions on Africa (Huzayyin 1956; Gourou 1956).

Each of the elements of geography, both physical and cultural, is involved in the total analysis of the changing picture of land-use.   These elements, such as soils, irrigated land, railways and population, and their relations to land utilisation, have been studied for many scattered areas in Africa (Stamp 1938; Nicolai and Jacques 1955; Crary 1949a; Lebon 1958; Willimott and Clarke 1960).

Another type of study is one in which land-use patterns are mapped and explained as a central feature of regional or economic geography.   These studies have been carried out in South Africa by well-known geographers (Wellington 1932, 1955a; Talbot 1947).   An especially helpful device is the map of present patterns of land-use : farm land of various types, land used for villages and pasturages, and so on.   Such land-use maps provide basic areal data for the theoretical study of the cultural landscapes and man-land relationships.   They are also of prime importance in planning improvements in land utilisation, or agricultural and settlement schemes; it is obviously very difficult to plan the use of the land for the future without knowing the situation at the present.   In places like Britain and the United States, land-use surveys have been a part of the planning process during the last several decades.

The International Geographical Union has a program for world-wide land-use mapping.   One of the methodological problems of land-use mapping in Africa, especially in tropical areas, is that classifications and viewpoints adapted to the European scene do not meet African needs.   Considerable progress has been made, however, especially in former British and French territories, with new concepts developed by local university geography staffs, survey departments and research institutes.   Several territories are now covered by general land-use maps.   Data are obtained from topographic sheets, air photographs, and field methods such as plane-table mapping, traverse sketching and the recording of information on maps by numerical code systems.   Several reports on progress and problems were made at the symposium of the International Geographical Union at Makerere College, Kampala, Uganda, in September 1955 (Stamp 1956b; Wills 1956; Toupet 1956; Lebon 1956).

The making of 'land capability' maps for tropical Africa lies mostly in the future.   Such maps go a step beyond the recording of present land-use to the mapping of the potentialities of the land, or the best use, according to given conditions of physical requirements, agricultural techniques, transportation costs, and the general social and economic situation.   In technically advanced countries such maps are commonly used in regional planning, with a trend towards preparation based upon team research by scientists from several fields.   New discoveries in Africa by soil scientists on the physical side, or by anthropologists or economists on the cultural side, can upset the assumptions upon which such maps are made. The difficulties in producing these very helpful studies are aptly summarised by the oft-quoted remark of J. Russell Smith: 'In the weighing of lands to determine their value to man, the geographer has had to change his scales every time science has put into his hands a new set of weights'.

7. ECONOMIC GEOGRAPHY: AGRICULTURE AND MINERALS

The preceding sections on population and settlements, medical geography, and part of the one on land utilisation, were largely about 'social' or 'human' phases of geography. The present section on agriculture and minerals as well as the following ones on transportation, trade and industrial geography, belong to the 'economic geography' category. Economic geography deals with the regional differences and relational aspects of how man makes a living from the earth, but there are so many branches of the field that an individual geographer or research project rarely deals with all of them.

Agricultural geography and the geography of mineral production are separate fields which will be combined here for purposes of brevity. The associated features of the earth's surface are different, however, for the two subjects. Agriculture is closely related to such physical conditions as rainfall, temperature, soils and drainage, and to cultural features like food habits, agricultural techniques and systems, handicrafts, and social organisation. Mining, on the other hand, if it is of the large-scale commercial variety, is largely dependent upon geological structure on the physical side and is related to a different set of cultural conditions, such as the needs for power, geological and engineering skills, and mine labour. In the development of transport lines and seaports and in the dependence of commercial exports upon world market conditions, however, there are similarities in the requirements for research on economic and political affairs.

In the geographical study of agricultural and mineral products there is also a similarity in that two general approaches are possible: (1) topical or commodity studies, and (2) regional investigations. The commodity approach was especially developed by the British, perhaps because of their interest in world production and trade in raw materials for their industries. The regional approach was given more attention in continental European countries, where there was an emphasis upon the better utilisation of local agricultural and mineral resources. At present, however, geographers in all the major nations use both approaches.

Commodity studies are undertaken by economists as well as geographers. There is a great deal of overlap, but the economic studies usually give more emphasis to economic theory, market conditions and financial aspects, whereas the geographic investigations place more emphasis on regional associations and differences, the relations with natural and cultural conditions, and the patterns of production and trade. When agricultural economists include the natural conditions which are related to production, they sometimes closely approach the geographic viewpoint.

Local geographic studies of particular agricultural products are sometimes so thorough and consider so many of the associations with other regional conditions that they become almost a complete physical, historical and economic geography of the region. An example is the study of grape production in Algeria (Isnard 1951). More typical, however, are shorter geographical studies of agricultural commodities for the purpose of determining the reasons for the localisation of the product in specific areas, the relations to cultural and natural conditions, the problems, nature of changes and importance of the product to the region (Dresch 1949; Hiernaux 1948; Kline 1956).

Minerals can be studied by the same geographic methods, but as noted above, the locational factors are comparatively free of associations with soil fertility and climate and are closely associated with geology. The related fields are economics and, more particularly, economic geology. Geologists often give more emphasis to rock structure and mining techniques, whereas the geographer is more interested in areal relations and the importance of minerals in giving individuality to particular regions.   In Africa, geologists have done by far the greatest amount of work on mineral products, but — especially in South Africa — geographers have also been involved (Scott 1951a, 1951b).

A typical methodological problem for the geographer dealing with agricultural products or minerals, or both, is the search for uniform criteria: a system for showing many products on the same map and for analysing them as items which give different characteristics to different regions.   This goal — to show regional differences in Africa — has been sought for by almost every economic geographer who has worked on major portions of the continent.   The use on maps of non-quantitative symbols for different products, along with written analyses of the distributions, is an example of a traditional but elementary method.   Quantitative symbols, such as graduated circles and bar graphs on maps, can be used where statistics or reliable estimates are available; these permit more advanced types of analyses.   A recent study maps both agricultural and mineral products on a uniform basis (as percentages of total production) and provides a new view of the salient features of commercial production in tropical Africa (Hance, Kotschar, and Peterec 1961).

In countries where adequate census data are available, geographers and agricultural economists have been able to construct maps showing quantities and ratios per unit area.   Type examples are: the percentage of land in various crops for different areas; the number of animals per square mile; and the ratio of the value of vegetables to the value of farm animals.   Such maps permit the quantitative analysis of differences from place to place, but for most parts of Africa they are merely possibilities for the future.

Probably every commodity of importance in Africa has been studied to some extent by geographers as well as by economists.   Regional geographical studies of economic products have also been made, in one form or another, for every territory in Africa.   Most of these studies have been done by the geographers of the former colonial power and often include treatments of related features like climate and transport (Suret-Canale 1948; Tenreiro 1949; Manshard 1961b).

More general studies of natural resources and of the geographical aspects of economic development have been made for most of the territories of Africa and for the continent as a whole.   These have been published in all the major European languages (Carvalho and Vasconcellos 1921; Green and Fair 1962; Massi 1941; Waibel 1937).   American geographers have also made major contributions along the same lines (Hance 1958a; Kimble 1960; Lee 1957; Randall 1956; Shantz 1940, 1941, 1942, 1943).

Despite the quantity of published material on the economic geography of Africa, there are large and important gaps.   The most thorough investigations have been made on areas of European activity and for places where commercial exports have been developed by Africans.   The study of the subsistence economies of inland areas, however, has merely been started, although there is now a trend in this direction, especially among British geographers (McMaster 1962a; Morgan 1959; White 1958).

Co-operation among the several interested disciplines on the geography of commercial production has taken place through the exchange of quantitative data and of ideas.   A geographer, for example, can often convert the areal statistics of the economist or economic geologist to cartographic purposes, and the ideas on production are useful in regional analysis. The climatic and other maps of the geographer are similarly useful to the agricultural economist, as are his estimates of the effects of irregular rainfall on agriculture. Quantitative data on production in the remote areas of subsistence agriculture, however, is often lacking; anthropologists, agricultural advisers and geographers may have made only scattered investigations at different dates, and the techniques and viewpoints developed in areas of commercial production may not be readily applicable to the areas of subsistence production.

8. THE GEOGRAPHY OF TRANSPORTATION AND TRADE

Africa, from the first, has been a continent where the natural obstacles or hindrances of strong surf, lack of natural harbours, muddy deltas and mangrove swamps, cataract-interrupted rivers, dense forests, tropical climates and diseases, and the broad expanse of the Sahara, have been recognised as some of the factors in the slow penetration of the 'Dark Continent'. It is not surprising, therefore, that geographers and others have written on these topics and even more on the related subjects of trade and transportation, for these were intimately associated with exploration and with the partition of Africa among the colonial powers. These nations, as well as the present independent African states, have given considerable attention to the problems of developing harbours, railways and roads, and of stimulating trade. For many areas in Africa the information on the geography of transportation is more complete than that on other topics, but many gaps remain.

A major purpose of transportation geography is to describe the nature of transportation as a feature of the earth's surface and to explain *why* it occurs in a give place, time and manner. The three major methods of working towards this objective emphasise, respectively: (1) the means of transportation, such as the types of animals or vehicles employed; (2) the nature of the goods carried; and (3) the routes followed by the various types of transportation and the resulting patterns on the earth's surface. All three methods are used in attempting to answer the question of why transportation occurs. In moving towards the common goal of description, analysis and explanation, however, it may be observed that concentration on the means of transportation stresses *how* and why, studying the nature of the traffic stresses *what* and why, and focusing on routes and patterns stresses *where* and why, goods and people are transported.

Each of the three methods may eventually consider much of the same material and use many of the same concepts: for example, climatic and cultural differences are basic factors in trade and transportation; and land routes usually converge at mountain passes and on important trade centres. These three, however, serve somewhat different purposes: the 'how' method may give more insight into cultural or human phases of the subject; the 'what' method may provide more of practical value for economic or commercial purposes; and the 'where' method may best outline certain regional differences and relationships.

Investigators of *circulation* within the French school of *géographie humaine* have provided some of the best examples of the use of the first method. Robert Capot-Rey (1946) has shown the way people travel and transport goods in various parts of Africa and elsewhere, and has demonstrated the reasons for and the consequences of the differences. The American school of cultural geography (to be discussed in more detail in a later section) is also more interested in the means of transportation than in such factors as economic traffic flow, and often places an emphasis on origins and diffusion (Mikesell 1955; Bennett 1957).

Scholars in European countries with African colonies have had a strong interest in the second method: the study of goods carried over trade routes, especially exports and imports. The British school of commercial geography, the German *Verkehrsgeographie*, and economic geographers in France, Spain, Italy and Portugal, have produced literally hundreds of such studies. These are often included with larger publications on economic and regional geography, in handbooks on the colonies, and in scattered articles in geographic, economic and colonial journals. The purpose usually has been to provide practical information about all the major products. It is sometimes hard to separate the geographic aspects of traffic flow in these publications from the statistical and economic aspects, and many planners and scholars have been frankly less concerned with providing a study that fits into the recognised limits of a particular discipline than to record useful data and give helpful explanations. In recent decades there has been a trend for geographers to combine statistics of traffic flow with studies of the routes themselves.

The third method — the mapping and analysis of the patterns of trade routes in Africa — has been more closely identified than the other two with the discipline of geography. This is a logical development because of the close relationship of this method to cartography and to other systematic fields of geography, and because its objective is more narrowly geographic: that is, to answer the questions of where and why transportation lines have been developed and of how they affect the character of the earth's surface. There are many of these studies for Africa because the subject is of prime importance in regional analysis, and the basic data is more readily available than for some other topics (Church 1949b, 1956b; Köhler 1956; Lartilleux 1949, 1950; B. E. Thomas 1953, 1957a). Transportation on inland lakes and rivers has also been studied, especially for the places where traffic is of importance to the regional economy and where a good deal of the shipping is by power vessels (Ford 1955).

It is possible to combine studies of commercial production with analyses of transportation routes, seaports and traffic movements. The longest and most complete recent investigations of this type have been made by Hance and Van Dongen. Individually, or in joint publications, these two scholars have provided dozens of papers which cover most parts of tropical Africa (Hance 1958b; Hance and Van Dongen 1958a, 1958b; Van Dongen 1954, 1960). These studies utilise both the second and third methods of transportation geography through the use of traffic flow charts and other devices. In the United States there is a strong recent trend for economic geographers to accomplish somewhat the same ends by using the statistical and other quantitative techniques of regional science, including the comparison of theoretical models of traffic flow (based upon distance, population density, etc.) with actual regional examples. Some of these techniques have been used in the study of transport in Ghana and Nigeria (Gould 1960, 1961).

Another objective of transportation geography is to show the effects of African climates and other natural conditions upon the problems of transportation. This has often been done in studies in historical geography, to be considered later, and a few geographers have applied the viewpoint to the modern scene (Church 1949a; B. E. Thomas 1960).

Information on the transportation geography of Africa is most complete for railways and ports, because maps and records are always compiled, in one form or another, during the planning, construction and operating stages. Airlines and mechanised inland water transportation systems also have records. Road information is less complete, and there are gaps in the available knowledge of such things as traffic flow and the relations of roads to local geography, economic development and social change. There are few studies which show the effects of seasonal variations in climate and drainage upon road and water transport. Scattered and diverse information is available on animal and canoe transport, but objectives and methods for geographical study of this kind are still in the early stages of development.

9. URBAN AND INDUSTRIAL GEOGRAPHY

The subject matter of urban geography developed during the last century around two themes: (1) the investigation of geographical factors in the location and rise of cities; and (2) the study of urban settlement forms and patterns as a separate phase of settlement geography. These are now combined in a field which may be defined as the study of the forms and patterns of urbanised areas, the reasons for their development, and their relations to other features of the earth's surface, both physical and cultural. Among the major research problems of this field are: the site and situation of cities; their internal forms, patterns and functions; the relations with other areas; and the size and distribution of cities. Some of these problems are also of great interest to other disciplines, but its orientation around areal features, both internal and external, gives the field of urban geography more coherence than many other branches of the discipline.

Industrial or manufacturing geography is normally considered a separate field, but it will be discussed here for reasons of convenience and brevity. The subject deals with the locations and patterns of industrial districts; the complex inter-relationships between individual manufacturing establishments or industrial areas and the local community; and the areal relations between different kinds of manufacturing and such elements as raw materials, power, labour, markets and transportation. The associations between this branch of geography and economic history are numerous and varied. Much of the content of location theory has come from economists and economic historians, and the economic geographer who works on manufacturing must be trained in economics and statistical methods as well as in geography. Some of the best-known contributions by geographers have been in the field of mapping the distribution and intensity of manufacturing and the flow of raw materials by quantitative cartographic methods.

Urban geography in Africa has progressed further on the study of the location of cities than on any other aspect. The site and situation of every town of moderate or large size has probably been investigated by one or more geographers. Studies of urban site — the location and internal arrangement of a city with respect to the bay, peninsula, hill, flood plain, or other terrain feature upon which it rests — are included in numerous works on economic, regional and urban geography.

The situation of a city refers to its location with respect to regional features such as rivers, trade routes, political areas, mines and agricultural land. Studies of situation vary from historical investigations of the rise and fall of cities, associated with changing regional conditions, to statistical investigations of the economic base, flow of traffic through the city, and the expansion or contraction of the trade area served by the city. These are often combined with studies of urban sites (Hance and Van Dongen 1958a, 1958b; Jarrett 1956; Munger 1951; B. E. Thomas 1955; Whittlesey 1941).

Some of the dominant locations for African cities are: (1) on the coasts at spots where it was possible to find or develop harbours; (2) at inland points on rivers and lakes which are suitable for break of bulk functions; and (3) at the crossroads of interior land routes. It is well known that commercial functions have played a large part in the rise of modern cities. But there are many phases of urbanisation — sociological, anthropological, historical, economic, political and administrative, and geographical — which are still imperfectly known. From the viewpoint of geography, the site and situation for each city is unique, but further study by workers in many fields will no doubt lead to additional generalisations. Some geographers have started to synthesise the available information into regional studies (Church 1959; Dresch 1947; Manshard 1961a; B. E. Thomas 1957b; White 1959).

When the internal geography of a city is considered, the focus can be on the patterns and functions of different districts, the direction of growth, changes in functions of different areas, and so on. This often involves the mapping of land-use and settlement types, the reconstruction of previous conditions, and the analysis of patterns and changes. There have been studies of this type for scattered towns in Africa (de Blij 1962; Larimore 1958), and studies of the general urban geography of a city, including most or all of the above factors, have been made for some of the major cities of Africa (Joly 1948; Lespes 1930, 1938; Walmsley 1957; Whittlesey 1937).

Geographers have taken note of rising industrialisation in the major cities of tropical Africa in connection with economic and urban problems, but special studies of the geography of industrialisation and of particular manufacturing types or districts, as would be expected, have been typical only of the parts of southern and northern Africa where both industries and geographers are more numerous (Capot-Rey 1947; Mountjoy 1952; Scott 1951c).

In summary, only the topic of location — site and situation — among the many aspects of urban and industrial geography has received a moderate degree of attention. But it seems reasonable to expect that the study of other geographical aspects of these subjects will expand as urbanisation and industrialisation increase. This has been the trend in other countries, and it has already started in northern and southern Africa, and at a few spots in tropical Africa.

10. BOUNDARIES AND POLITICAL GEOGRAPHY

There are few topics in geography harder to define to the satisfaction of everyone than political geography. Some aspects, such as the demarcating of boundary lines on the earth's surface, have been studied so often by military, governmental and academic geographers and surveyors that a close association with geography and mapping is probably recognised by all. When the treaties, the maps, and the geographical, historical and political conditions involved in the original establishment of the boundaries are analysed, opinions vary greatly, both within and without the discipline, as to how much of the analysis should be considered as political geography. A study of the natural and other resources of a nation as components of military power can be regarded as political geography, history, political science, economics, international relations, military science, geo-politics, or something else, depending upon the philosophy of the investigator. The attitudes of different schools of geographic thought towards political geography vary from a strong feeling that it is an important and respectable adult member of the family to the view that it is probably a wayward child of doubtful prospects.

One of the reasons for the variation in attitudes towards political geography is the diverse and ill-defined nature of the field.   Another reason is that, in the minds of people who have vaguely heard of 'political geography' and Nazi 'geopolitics', it has been difficult to establish a clear distinction between solid, scholarly work in political geography and the Nazi mixture of facts, prejudice and intellectual dishonesty.

Nazi political and geographical theories and propaganda, under the name of geopolitics, supported the return to Germany of its former German colonies in Africa.   The theories, misuse of facts and distorted reasoning had somewhat the same distasteful flavour to some geographers that Nazi racial theories had to ethnologists and physical anthropologists.   If it were not for these conditions, 'geopolitics' might be a useful term for the study of the geographical aspects of the political relationships in states and between states.   As it is, whereas some geographers have abandoned the term geopolitics, other geographers and some political scientists have attempted to redefine it in terms of the geographical factors in policy-making.   This has led to further confusion because there can be as many policies as there are nations.   There appears, however, to be no great disagreement among the geographers — mostly British or American trained — who have recently worked on the political features of Africa.   Probably most would accept 'the study of the inter-relations of political boundaries, territories and capitals with other human and physical features of the earth's surface', or 'the study of political aspects of the geography of African states and territories', as approximations of the content of political geography.

Two reasons are suggested for this comparative harmony in a field often marked by sharp controversy.   First, national power struggles in Africa, either between European colonial nations or new African states, do not at present have any great influence upon the research interests of political geographers.   The present period of decolonisation tends to focus attention on such things as the effects of new national boundaries on trade and on internal problems of political harmony or economic development.   Secondly, most of the scholars who do research on political geography in Africa have also made investigations into problems characteristic of the fields of economic or regional geography.   Their interests and experience probably incline them towards geographic methods of fieldwork and regional analysis in working on political features, rather than towards political theorising.   When African students and scholars who are now studying political geography start publishing their views on the subject, the interests and the tone may well be different.

Before continuing with the status of present research, a short post-mortem on Nazi geopolitics may be of value for purposes of clarification and contrast.   One assumption of Nazi geopolitical theory was that certain geographical conditions not only justified the expansion of German territory in Europe and Africa but also made the expansion inevitable.   But when the self-same arguments, applied to other areas, suggested the inevitable loss of German territory or the expansion of other powers, the arguments were omitted or twisted to the benefit of Germany. Geopolitics included trickery in map-making and geography.   Colours and symbols were used on maps to give false or exaggerated impressions or to conceal unwanted facts.   Although the Nazi geographer-politicians never published a clear statement about the scope of geopolitics, it might be described as a pseudo-scientific rationalisation based on the application of all kinds of knowledge about areas in such a way as to serve the purposes of the German state.   Dr Arthur Dix was one of the best-known Nazi propagandists who used geopolitical arguments for the return of former African colonies to Germany (Dix, n.d.).

It should be emphasised that respectable and notable work was done by German scholars on political and other types of geography before and after the Nazi period. Even during the Hitler regime, economic, physical and military geographers made accurate maps and scientific studies on transportation, terrain and resources for governmental use, but these are of a different order from that of propagandistic geopolitics.

Recent research in political geography has produced a considerable literature. Whittlesey, a noted scholar in both the political and the regional geography of Africa, has published a study which deals with many facets of historical and political geography (1939).   Completed before the second world war stimulated the move-ment towards independence, the chapter on Africa ended with the prophetic view that Africans would not remain content to serve European purposes in Africa and would force political changes.   Whittlesey studied the origins of African boundaries and their functions or effects in enclosing new political areas, dividing tribes, and changing the patterns of population and trade.   Additional aspects of boundaries on which political geographers often work are delimitation (the determination of a boundary line by agreement and its definition in writing), demarcation (the marking of the boundary on the ground), and the advantages or problems of different types of boundaries (stream channels, surveyed meridians, mountain crests, etc.) for carrying out border functions (Boggs 1940).

The studies of Whittlesey and Boggs on the boundaries of Africa clarified some regional differences and added facts and new thoughts on details, but probably their confirmation of several concepts concerning boundaries is of most interest.   Both believe that the obsolescent practice of classifying boundaries as 'natural' or 'artificial' is of little value, because all boundaries are artificial in the sense of being man-made, because other categories are more meaningful, and because a boundary which follows a natural feature may or may not be a good one depending upon where it is and what it separates.   Boundaries arbitrarily prescribed by distant authorities possessing only incomplete geographical information often cause trouble for both the surveyor and the local people.   Rivers and mountain ridges appear as lines on small-scale maps, but on the ground they are zones through which lines must be run after solving the many problems of interpretation.   All rivers, for example, vary with the seasons and are constantly changing their courses by erosion; they are troublesome as boundaries.   The division of tribes by boundaries is, of course, a widely recognised problem in Africa.

There have been a number of articles by British geographers and surveyors in the *Geographical Journal* of London on the demarcation and functioning of African boundaries (Clifford 1936; L. N. King 1928; Peake 1934).   The Geographer of the US Department of State is publishing a series of studies on individual boundary segments in Africa (Office of the Geographer, US Department of State 1961).   And there have been a few studies of the general problems of boundaries (Church 1956a; Reyner 1961; Whittlesey 1938).   With the addition of map information from survey departments and a study on African treaties and maps (Hertslet 1909), the research that has been done on boundaries exceeds that for other features of political geography.   Thorough field studies of local adjustments of population, trade and other elements to political borders, however, are comparatively rare.

Another aspect of political units is the degree of homogeneity or cohesion within national borders. Because of the mosaic of tribes in most African states, political scientists, anthropologists, historians and administrators have addressed themselves to this matter, but because this social problem can also be considered from the viewpoint of its inter-relations with human or physical areal features, it may also be of interest to the geographer (Brookfield 1957; Buchanan 1953). The political geography of internal patterns of alienated land, tribal land units, forest and game reserves, townships, etc., have also been investigated by geographers in connection with the problems of economic and regional geography (Floyd 1961).

Rivers which cross boundaries require international agreements on their use for transportation, irrigation and other purposes. With reference to these and other geographical and political aspects, the Nile system has been the object of study by many scholars (Crary 1949b; Lebon 1960; Whittlesey 1953).

Only a few geographers have considered the varied aspects of political features of major parts of Africa. The contributions of Whittlesey have been mentioned earlier; Munger (1961) has reported upon many countries in his letters for the American Universities Field Staff written over a period of ten years; and other geographers have discussed some of the salient political features in chapters in books (Buchanan 1956; B. E. Thomas 1959).

The total of these and other similar studies, however, represents merely a beginning on the study of the continent. Among the major branches of the discipline, political geography is probably the one which has the smallest literature on Africa, and the one in which there are the greatest gaps in areas of coverage, as well as in philosophical orientation and depth of perception. With the current great increases in interest in human geography, in Africa and in political affairs, the field is likely to expand considerably in the near future.

11. HISTORICAL GEOGRAPHY AND GEOGRAPHICAL HISTORY

The topic of historical geography is subject to several interpretations among workers in fields related to geography as well as among geographers themselves. Many geographers define 'historical geography' as the study of past geography, or the study of geographical changes on the earth's surface. The point of view which most closely parallels this usage would be that of 'historical geology', which is the study of past geology, including geological periods and geological changes. 'Historical geography' in this interpretation differs from 'history' in that its focus is upon the earth's surface or upon distributions on the earth rather than upon human events. Information on man-made features of the earth's surface may be found in some of the same written records used by the historian, but the historical geography of physical features may require additional climatic, botanical or geological evidence. When studies in historical geography are extended back to the periods before there were written records, some of the materials and methods are similar to those of geology, archaeology, anthropology and prehistory.

Another term, 'geographical history', has unfortunately come to be designated by many other names, including 'historical geography'; it is also referred to, in part, as 'economic history'. This type of study, which will herein be identified as 'geographical history', is concerned with the significance of natural features or areal differentiation for changes in society or for human events. Historical documents and maps provide the data, the methods are similar to those of history, and both geographers and historians have contributed to the store of knowledge.

Geographical history is essentially history which is centred upon geographical themes: the influence of the natural environment upon man; the importance of local economic resources on the development of culture and national policies; the bearing of locations, distances and areal differences in natural and human earth features upon the development of a military campaign, etc.

Works on African geographical history are most numerous for the part of the continent which has the longest written records — the Mediterranean fringe — and well-known volumes exist from every period of civilisation (Khaldun 1925–56; Semple 1931). The histories and geographies of countries like Algeria and the Republic of South Africa contain many paragraphs, sections or whole chapters devoted to geographical history, and numerous journal articles provide additional material. Parts of the volumes of Herodotus (1920) and Strabo (1917–33) deal with the geographical history of Africa. Most military and economic historians take account of geography in their studies.

The major accomplishment of the field of geographical history is that so much has been put into written form, but there are few branches of geography in which the philosophy varies so greatly from scholar to scholar or in which there is so little agreement on principles, scope and method. A number of works, especially earlier ones, placed emphasis upon the influence, or even control, exerted by the environment upon the course of human events. It is difficult, however, to find either a geographer or a historian presently working in the African field who could adequately be described as an 'environmental determinist'. Geographical research strives to discover facts relating to the importance of the environment to man, but it assumes man to be the active agent and recognises the importance of cultural factors. Economic resources, for example, include not only the materials which exist on the earth but also the attitudes, skills and technical equipment of people who may consider the materials to be useful or worthless. It should be re-empha-sised that, of the past geographers and historians who have written on geographical history, only a relative few were environmental determinists. It may be noted further that the influence of the natural environment on man has been only one of several questions investigated in geographical history and that, among those scholars who have been especially interested in environmental influence, the trend in inter-pretation has been away from the extremes of determinism.

Much remains to be done to fill in the gaps on the geographical history of Africa; only a start has been made on the non-Mediterranean and non-colonial aspects of the subject. The geographical study of tropical Africa suffers from the same lack of documentary evidence which hinders the study of history. Funda-mental problems in philosophy remain to be solved. Questions about the major facts and their interpretations even for places like Egypt and the Barbary states have not been answered; for example, the question of whether there has been a decrease in rainfall in North Africa since Roman times is still in dispute (Murphey 1951).

Returning now to historical geography (the study of the geography of the past), one can note some comparisons and contrasts with geographical history. Only a small percentage of geographers would regard either as a speciality or major interest. Most geographers, however, physical and cultural alike, use the methods and viewpoints of historical geography to some extent and include a certain amount of historical geography in their studies. An example should help both to explain the method and to distinguish the field from history.

A geographer may study a highland region in Ethiopia or Kenya and try to visualise the historical geography of landforms — the original nature of the plateau and the subsequent formation of rift valleys by faulting, river valleys by stream erosion, and so on.   He may also try to determine the former natural vegetation and soils and how they have been changed by man or by natural processes.   Observation of a farming area, village and road may lead to questions about when, how and why these features developed into their present patterns.   Field observation, aerial photographs, maps or records might provide the answers.   The information thus elicited might then be used to explain the present patterns of valleys and rivers, or of farms, roads and villages.   The major purpose of such a study in historical geography would be to provide a geographical description and explanation for the present surface of the earth rather than to construct a history of the area.   Several regions of Africa have been thus studied (Gautier 1928).

The methods of historical geography have been especially helpful in furthering work on other aspects of systematic geography, and the results should probably be judged as much on the basis of the steady advance along these lines as by the accumulation of a separate body of literature on historical geography.   In and of itself, development of the field has proceeded much further for Europe and North America than for Africa.

Because historical geography is so often included as a part of other kinds of geography, there are those who subscribe to the view that this type of geography is to be considered more properly as a useful method for solving problems in geography than as a systematic branch of geography.   When the emphasis is upon cultural origins, dispersions and development (culture history), the approach can be regarded as relevant to all human geography.   This theory or method forms one of the bases for the school of thought known as 'cultural geography'.

12. CULTURAL GEOGRAPHY

The term 'cultural geography' has two widely accepted meanings.   It is often used to denote human geography, or 'all geography that is not physical'.   A second and more restricted meaning has been adopted by the school of geography which focuses attention on those elements of material culture which give distinctive character to each area.   It is in this latter sense that the term will be used here.

Cultural geography studies man and his material culture in order to understand his part in modifying the face of the earth (W. L. Thomas 1956).   This viewpoint, it may be noted, is almost the converse of environmentalism or the study of the influence of the natural environment upon man.   One way of expressing the work of the cultural geographer is to say that he studies the transformation of the natural landscape into the cultural landscape by examining the successive cultures in an area, beginning with the earliest and proceeding to the present.   Many of the things in which the cultural geographer is interested, therefore, are also the concern of the archaeologist and the anthropologist, but it should be stressed that the cultural geographer, like others in his discipline, has the ultimate objective of understanding areal differentiation on the earth's surface.

Cultural geographers have studied Africa, along with other continents, partly because the Ethiopian Highland is one of the source regions of certain domesticated plants used by man in transforming the face of the earth (Sauer 1952).   Another interest is in the development of the cultural landscape (Simoons 1960; Spencer and Hale 1961; Mikesell 1961).   The effects of man's religion on the earth's surface in land holdings, religious structures, policies towards various foods and animals, and in other ways have been demonstrated in a study of Southern Rhodesia (Isaac 1961–62). There are also studies by geographers on the spread of individual domesticated plants (McMaster 1962b).

The cultural geography approach, widely used in countries like Germany and the United States, will no doubt be used to a greater extent in Africa in the future. It has obvious utility in the study of indigenous areas, but much research by anthropologists and geographers is necessary for establishing the stages of succession in the development of African cultural landscapes. This is probably the phase of geography which is of most interest to anthropologists and in which the work of the anthropologist is of most direct concern to geography.

13. REGIONAL GEOGRAPHY OF AFRICA

It is obvious from the above analyses of selected topics from systematic geography that the discipline has many schools of thought and many approaches and techniques for solving its problems. It is also apparent that data and techniques from many associated fields can be adapted to the purposes of geography, just as advances in systematic geography can contribute to studies in related disciplines.

Regional geography, as noted earlier, does not have such close associations with other subjects in either methods or viewpoint. If one were to study the geography of Africa using a regional approach, one would proceed from region to region, with each section of the study containing an analysis of all the elements of geography, both physical and human. One possible method of organising such a study would utilise an introduction outlining the distinctive character of Africa as a continent, followed by sections dealing with large regions like the Sahara, the Eastern Highlands or West Africa, and smaller divisions or chapters devoted to countries or areas like the Nile Delta.

There are regional schools of thought which favour the division of subject matter by political units on the pragmatic grounds that data is collected by political units and more people are familiar with them. Other regional geographers seek areal divisions based upon the distinctive character of the earth's surface as modified by man or upon the 'landscapes' produced by combined physical and human processes. Because human or tribal borders in Africa rarely correspond with political frontiers, this approach would yield regional analyses related to regional culture and land use rather than to colonial history. In the parts of the world where geographers have been at work for many decades, there are a number of these regional divisions which have gained a certain amount of general acceptance, e.g., 'Normandy' and 'Brittany' in France. Several such 'combined physical and cultural areas' in Africa have been studied by geographers and accorded regional terms. The Algerian Sahara, for example, has 'the Souf', and 'the Mzab'. This procedure, however, has certain disadvantages. Such studies require many geographers who can gain intimate and detailed knowledge through fieldwork and, after long study, become experts upon particular areas. Furthermore, no particular regional system is suitable for all purposes or acceptable to all geographers. Knowledge of Africa is so elementary that any total regional study for the entire continent, if written rapidly under any system, would probably fail to meet the standards already set by studies conducted in the well-developed parts of the world.

Despite these difficulties, there is a great demand for regional courses and regional geographic information on Africa. Several methods have therefore been devised for gaining some of the end results of regional study — especially a picture of the combined physical and human landscapes of particular areas — while avoiding some of the problems and the slow pace of total local or regional geography.   Three of these methods are widely used.   1. Many regional studies of Africa are frankly less than total regional geography; the topics that are not urgently or immediately necessary, and the unsurveyed topics are omitted.   2. A country may be studied systematically, i.e., by considering climate, economic geography, etc., in separate sections rather than regionally.   This represents an attempt to gain regional results by systematic methods.   3. A study may be part systematic and part regional, with preliminary sections on landforms, climates, and so on, followed by later sections which are areal in nature.   This method, especially with physical geography treated systematically and human features treated regionally, is widely used for textbooks.

There are scores of regional geographies on African areas, and they are probably the geographical publications best known to people outside the field.   Because the emphasis here is on research, rather than on textbooks, the discussion will be restricted largely to regional works based upon field studies or original syntheses.

The French school of regional geography has made notable contributions to the understanding of former French areas in Africa and of other regions; it began its work in the last century and has continued to the present.   Although British and South African geographers worked upon Africa during the same period, their most detailed regional geographies have appeared in the last few decades and especially since the second world war.

For the continent as a whole, there are the three African volumes of the French *Géographie Universelle* (Bernard 1937–39; Maurette 1938), Walter Fitzgerald's *Africa* (1961) and Fritz Jaeger's *Afrika* (1954), as well as other general geographies of the continent in several languages (Stamp 1953; Suggate 1956).

For more detailed studies of major parts of the continent, there are works in both English (Cole 1961; Church 1960; Wellington 1955b) and French (Capot-Rey 1953; Despois 1949; Richard-Molard 1949).   In French there are also volumes by geographers on almost every former French territory (Celerier 1948; Dandouau 1950; Larnaude 1950) and the Italians, Portuguese and Spanish have likewise given attention to their present or former territories (Almagià 1935; Ribeiro 1950; Carvalho e Vasconcellos 1921; Hernandez-Pacheco 1949).   A recent development has been the publication by British-trained geographers who have resided in African areas of volumes which deal with African culture, agriculture and industries in more detail and on a higher level of sophistication than the generalised geographies of past decades (Barbour 1961; Boateng 1959; Buchanan and Pugh 1955; Hickman and Dickins 1960; Jarrett 1962; Varley and White 1958).

III MAJOR TRENDS IN RESEARCH

There have been several notable trends in geographic research in Africa.   In ancient and medieval times, interest in obtaining information on the northern part of the continent, its physical features and its people and products, increased and decreased with the varying fortunes of civilisation in Europe, south-west Asia and northern Africa.   During the fifteenth and sixteenth centuries, when the great discoveries were being made, geographical knowledge of the African coast became more accurate, and map-making reached a transitional stage between the primitive and the modern scientific level.   Gradual progress was made during the seventeenth century in cartography, physical geography, navigation, surveying and human geography.

The advances of the eighteenth century were more impressive, and geography was introduced as a university subject. When Immanuel Kant started lecturing on physical and human geography at the University of Königsberg in 1765, the maps of Africa had an almost perfect outline for the seacoast, northern Africa had been studied for centuries, and there was a general knowledge of scattered coastal areas. The tropical interior was almost unknown, however, and the foundations of modern human geography, in any case, were not laid until the first half of the nineteenth century by men like Alexander von Humboldt and Karl Ritter.

The nineteenth century was noted for the geographical exploration of interior tropical Africa. By the time the continent was partitioned during the 1880s, the main outlines of the physical features were on the map. Exploration and mapping continued, but there was a great increase in investigations of resources, of exports and trade, and of possible routes for railways. Attention turned to economic geography and to the possibilities for settlement and development in the newly acquired colonies. Such studies had already been made before 1900 for places like Egypt, Algeria and South Africa.

During the present century, work on the physical geography of Africa has continued under the direction of scholars in Germany, Britain, France, Italy and other European countries, but interest in economic and human geography has increased until it is now the major branch of the discipline. By the time of the first world war, the general economic and physical geography was known for most parts of Africa, and there was gradual improvement until the second world war. A few American geographers worked on Africa, but by far the greatest amount of research was done by geographers from the colonial powers which controlled the various territories of Africa.

Since the second world war, there have been many new developments. Progress on topographic mapping and on the production of national atlases has been much more rapid than in any previous period of equal length. Approximate general knowledge is being replaced by detailed and accurate knowledge in almost every country. The establishment of a dozen new colleges and universities in tropical Africa, almost all with departments of geography, and the expanded operations of research institutes provide better facilities for geographical studies. The great post-war increase in African trade, the emphasis on economic planning and development, and the appearance of new nations have directed attention to the economic, political and regional geography of the continent.

Among the several dozen American geographers who have done research work on Africa since the second world war, there have been some who were especially interested in physical, political or cultural topics, but most have worked on economic aspects of the discipline. In economic geography the current American contribution to research on Africa probably equals that of some of the European countries, but still lags behind that of Britain, France and Germany.

Within Africa, universities and research institutes in Egypt, Algeria and South Africa have made notable contributions to both physical and human geography. There are groups of geographers in Rabat, Tunis, Dakar, Freetown, Accra, Ibadan, Leopoldville, Kampala, Nairobi, Addis Ababa and Khartoum who have published geographical studies and will probably undertake an increasing proportion of the research work on the continent.

10

Demography

Frank Lorimer, William Brass
and Etienne van de Walle

I INTRODUCTION: THE POPULATION*

THE POPULATION OF Africa is somewhere in the vicinity of 250 million persons. In describing its distribution, official estimates as of mid-year 1959 will be used as they are given in the *United Nations Demographic Yearbook* 1960, with the following modifications: substitution of revised 1959 estimates indicated by the results of subsequent inquiries in Dahomey, Ghana, Morocco, South Africa and Upper Volta; and a figure for the unknown population of Ethiopia that is three million below the official estimate, though much above the figure apparently used in the United Nations estimation of the population in northern Africa. The summary of national figures, many of which (even apart from the quite arbitrary figure for Ethiopia) are subject to considerable error, gives about 247 million as of mid-year 1959. The regional figures given here refer to the same time and should be read in all cases with an implicit 'more or less'.

The Sahara occupies about three-tenths of the continent. A Saharan zone of about nine million square kilometres has about three million inhabitants along its edges and in oases. Excluding this zone, there are some eighty-four million persons in North Africa, the Sudan, Ethiopia and the Somalias. Some estimated mean densities here are: Morocco (excluding a former Spanish zone in the south), twenty-seven persons per square kilometre; northern Algeria, forty-eight per km²; Tunisia, thirty-one per km²; the Nile valley and delta in Egypt, over 700 per km²; Sudan, six per km²; Ethiopia and Eritrea, perhaps sixteen per km²; Somalia three persons per square kilometre.

There are about five million persons in Madagascar, where the average density (nine persons per km²) is only slightly above that for all Africa including the Sahara (about eight persons per km²). Altogether there are about 6·6 million persons on various islands, including Madagascar, separated by a hundred kilometres or more from the mainland. Among these, Mauritius, with over 600,000 inhabitants (over 300 per km²), is the most densely populated.

There are, then, about 154 million persons in continental sub-Saharan Africa: an area of about sixteen million square kilometres. This total includes about four and a half million Europeans and South Asians, leaving approximately 150 million Africans.

* Bibliography for this chapter will be found on page 534.

Nine-tenths of the Europeans live in the southern and south-central part of the region, including the Rhodesias, Angola and Mozambique. According to the census of the Union (now the Republic) of South Africa, there were slightly over three million Europeans there in 1960 (19 per cent of the total, a somewhat smaller proportion than in 1950). There were also 73,000 Europeans in South West Africa (14 per cent of its total). There were about 300,000 Europeans in the Rhodesias and Nyasaland in 1959. They formed 7 per cent of the total in Southern Rhodesia and 3 per cent of the total in Northern Rhodesia. The two large Portuguese territories together have some 150,000 Europeans, more or less; there are no recent official figures on this subject. In 1950, Europeans were 2 per cent of all persons in Angola and eight-tenths of one per cent in Mozambique. So altogether there were about three and a half million Europeans in southern and central Africa in 1959.

There were less than 400,000 Europeans in all other countries south of the Sahara. They are less than one-half of one per cent of population in West Africa, about one-half of one per cent in East Africa as a whole. Proportionately they are most important in Senegal, where, in 1956, 50,000 Europeans were 2 per cent of the total. In absolute number, they were most important in the Belgian Congo, with 114,000 Europeans in 1959 (less than one per cent of the total), and in Kenya with 66,000 Europeans (about one per cent of the total).

There were some 900,000 South Asians in African countries along the Indian Ocean as of 1959. Somewhat over half of these are in South Africa, where they are 3 per cent of the total. Also, nearly 3 per cent of all persons in Kenya are South Asians, but their proportions are lower in all other countries, except off-shore Zanzibar.

The continental sub-Saharan population is distributed by major regions somewhat as follows:

Region	Area (1,000 km²)	Population (1 m. persons)	Persons per km²
West Africa (Coastal countries, Senegal to the the Cameroon Mountain; Upper Volta and parts of Mali and Niger)	3,487	68·5	20
East Africa (Including Rwanda, Burundi and Zanzibar)	1,820	27·1	15
Central Africa (Cameroon, excl. former Br. Cam.; former French and Spanish Equatorial Africa, excl. northern half of Chad; Congo, Angola)	5,920	26·6	4·5
East Central Africa (Mozambique, Nyasaland, the Rhodesias)	2,036	14·4	7
Southern Africa (Including High Commission Territories)			
Arid Zone	2,026	1·8	1
Remainder	780	15·3	20

There are, of course, wide variations of density within major regions. The highest average densities in large political divisions are found in the Eastern Region of Nigeria (106 persons per km²), the Western Region of Nigeria (sixty-one persons per km²), and Rwanda and Burundi (together, eighty-eight persons per km²). The more specific (and more significant) distribution by small areas, considered in relation to resources and economic opportunity, is treated in the chapter on Geographical Research. Some aspects of these relations will be mentioned below in dealing with studies on migration.

Attention is merely called here to the demographic importance of West Africa, which has about forty-four per cent of the total population of continental sub-Saharan Africa. Even outside the coastal and forest zones, it includes rather large concentrations in some interior areas, such as Upper Volta and parts of northern Nigeria. This is the region of ancient agricultural societies. Indigenous agriculture is generally more advanced here than in other sub-Saharan regions, except in parts of East Africa. The formation of its population was also influenced by ancient centres and channels of trade. The comparable density of population in the non-arid parts of southern Africa can be attributed in larger part to the influence of external forces during the last four centuries.

II THE DEVELOPMENT OF DEMOGRAPHIC STATISTICS

For a long time there has been fairly complete information on the European population of most dependent territories in Africa. This information can be treated in accordance with well-established methods. This is only partially true with respect to the information on Asians in Africa. Types of data obtained in censuses of the European population of various countries are usually obtained on Asians where they are numerically important, but the data for Asians may be less reliable. Vital statistics are also generally less complete for Asians than for Europeans in southern, east-central and eastern Africa. Nevertheless, consideration of the development of demographic statistics will be limited to information on Africans because of their numerical predominance and because of the special problems encountered in the development of this information.

The first important and critical investigation of information on the population of Africa was carried out by R. R. Kuczynski. His study on the Cameroons and Togoland (1939) was followed by A Demographic Survey of the British Colonial Empire, of which Volumes I (1948) and II (1949), dealt with British Africa. His findings with respect to the possibility of positive knowledge on the basis of the information then available were largely negative.

Prior to this time, the population of Africa had been treated incidentally by certain scholars — notably G. Riccioli in the seventeenth century and W. Willcox and A. Carr-Saunders in the 1930s — in preparing estimates of the world's population. Willcox followed Riccioli in using the figure 100 million for Africa in 1650 — which was perhaps as near the truth as any other equally round number — and held this as a constant figure up to 1850. Carr-Saunders used the same figure for 1650, but assumed some decline to a low point around 1800 and partial recovery in 1850. For 1933 he used the figure 145 million, obtained by summation of official estimates for the population of African countries published in the Statistical Yearbook of the League of Nations. This series is continued in the United Nations Demographic Yearbook. The agencies responsible for this series warn against interpreting changes in estimates as changes in population. The Secretariat of the United Nations in recent years, however, has presented tentative estimates of fertility, mortality and global population trends in Africa, usually in terms of a range of values. In preparing these estimates, the Secretariat attempts to take available information critically into account, but it has not been in a position to carry out intensive research on the subject.

Censuses of the total population were initiated in Algeria and in Egypt near the middle of the nineteenth century, in Morocco and Tunisia in 1921, and in Libya in 1936. Censuses were taken in the several South African countries in 1904 (prior to the formation of the Union) and in the Union and the High Commission Territories from 1911 on. Prior to 1936, however, the figures for Africans in these 'censuses' were based mainly on estimates by local officials. There were field enumerations of the total population of Uganda in 1931 and of Angola and Mozambique in 1940. Apart from the countries mentioned here, so-called 'censuses' in Africa prior to the second world war were generally limited to the enumeration of non-African minorities, complete censuses of a few cities, islands and other restricted areas, and estimates of African population on the basis of tax registers, local inquiries, etc. A great advance in this respect has been made during the last fifteen years.

The great increase of demographic information on the population of tropical Africa during the last fifteen years is the joint effect of advances along several lines. These include: (1) increased recognition by the governments of African countries of their responsibilities with respect to economic and social conditions; (2) general progress in education and recognition of the importance of relying on African field-workers in large-scale inquiries, along with special provisions for their training; (3) the stimulus towards the development of social statistics by the United Nations and technical assistance by this and other international organisations, by various governments and by private organisations and foundations; (4) advances in methods of collecting and processing quantitative data; and (5) advances in the theory and application of methods of sampling. Censuses or systematic sampling inquiries have been completed within the last fifteen years or are reportedly under way for the whole or major segments of the following African countries (arranged in geographical order): Egypt (1947, 1957); Sudan (1956); Libya (1954); Tunisia (1956); Algeria (1954, 1960); Morocco (1952, 1960); Spanish territories in North and West Africa (1950, 1960); Cape Verde Islands (1950, 1960); Senegal (1960–61); Mali (1960–61); Niger (1960); Portuguese Guinea (1950, 1960); Guinea Republic (1954–55); Liberia (1962); Sierra Leone (1962); Ivory Coast (1957–58); Ghana (1948, 1960); Upper Volta (1960–61); Togo (1958–60, 1961); Dahomey (1961); Nigeria (1952–53, 1963); Cameroon (1960–62); São Tome and Principe (1950, 1960); Central African Republic (1959–60); Gabon (1960–61); Congo (Brazzaville) (1961); Congo (Leopoldville) (1955–57); Ruanda-Urandi (1952–57); Angola (1950, 1960); Bechuanaland, Basutoland, Swaziland (1956); Republic of South Africa (1951, 1960); Southern Rhodesia (1948, 1953, 1962); Northern Rhodesia (1950–51, 1962); Mozambique (1950, 1960); Tanganyika (1948, 1957); Uganda (1948, 1959); Kenya (1948, 1962); Zanzibar and Pemba (1948, 1958); Mauritius (1952).

The results of these undertakings naturally vary greatly in quality, but many of them provide a substantial basis for a critical investigation of population trends. In this respect many of the sampling inquiries — notably the large-scale national or regional demographic inquiries on a sampling basis in countries with French and Belgian administrative traditions — are superior to many of the complete enumerations.   In East Africa and Ghana intensive post-enumeration surveys on a sampling basis have been used to complement the information obtained in a complete enumeration.   There is wide variation in the amount and types of data collected, and in the extent to which these data have been tabulated and published.   The results from some of the recent inquiries have not yet appeared but are forthcoming. Meanwhile similar investigations are being planned and organised in several other countries.

The volume of African demographic data is undergoing rapid expansion, but most of these data are, as yet, undigested.   Their systematic appraisal and analysis is inherently difficult, in the absence of vital statistics or, in most cases, comparable results from successive censuses that are similar in method and coverage.   The data for many countries are still too meagre and erratic to provide a basis for any positive conclusions.   If data are sufficiently bad, they cannot be evaluated — except to note that they lack credibility.   Kuczynski could not make much sense out of most nineteenth-century reports on African population; he could only demonstrate that they were inconsistent.   In order to achieve any substantial results one must have at disposal a considerable body of related information.   The fact is that, for the first time, sets of demographic data for some African countries are now emerging above the threshold of completeness and specificity required for critical evaluation and analysis.

III   METHODS OF COLLECTING DEMOGRAPHIC STATISTICS

The study of demography requires extensive, detailed and accurate statistics.   The collection of material of this kind, in most parts of the world, is a recent development.   It is also expensive, and the costs can only be justified, in economic terms, in a country which can use the results valuably for administrative and social purposes. It is not surprising, therefore, that it is only recently that population statistics of native Africans have achieved sufficient accuracy to justify anything more than the crudest analysis.   It is also clear why a great deal of research effort in Africa has been devoted to the problems of how to collect demographic statistics efficiently that is, how to attain high accuracy at a minimum cost.

1. TYPES OF DEMOGRAPHIC DATA

Demographic data can be classified into two kinds.   One concerns the state of the population in an area at a given point in time, and the other demographic processes, such as birth, death and migration.   These two divisions of data have been called the 'stock' and the 'flow'.   The former gives a profile of the characteristics of the population at the particular moment; the flow shows how this is being modified with time.   Two sets of material can be used to build up a demographic picture of a country as it moves through time; this, in turn, is a starting point for forecasting the future characteristics upon which economic and social planning depends.

Normally data of the stock kind have been collected by census-type inquiries, in which the number of persons in a country is recorded along with their distribution by the major biological, economic and social divisions: sex, age groups, families, occupations, religions, etc.   The counting of events in periods of time in order to measure rates has normally been confined to births, deaths and marriages.

This has traditionally been done through the registration of each occurrence shortly after it took place.   Recording of migration, when attempted, has usually been unsatisfactory and dependent on administrative systems of permits, reporting and statements of intention.   The division of the number of events in a particular category occurring in an appropriate period of time (usually a year) by the number of persons exposed to risk gives the standard measurements of the relative speed at which changes are taking place, e.g., age, specific birth and death rates.

2. SPECIAL PROBLEMS IN AFRICA

The methods of collecting demographic statistics described above are simple, direct and well tried, and there is no reason to doubt that, in the future, the basic population data of Africa will be obtained in these ways.   At present, however, there are special circumstances in most African territories which have made the study and use of alternative procedures necessary and advantageous.   Among these special difficulties are the illiteracy of the majority of the population and vagueness about time periods, particularly ages, the physical and mental difficulties of communications, and cultural factors such as the belief that misfortune may follow the disclosure of certain facts.   There is also resistance to questioning and falsification of results for economic and political reasons, although there is no evidence that this is more prevalent in Africa than in other places.   Awkward problems arise from these causes, but more important are certain factors in the social and technical milieu.   In Europe, the United States and elsewhere the quality of demographic statistics improved slowly in parallel with advances in theory, heightened recognition of administrative needs, and increasing prosperity.   The really distinctive feature of Africa is that the modern standards of accuracy required for useful economic and social planning must be achieved without a fully evolved administrative system and with limited resources.

A census-type inquiry is less subject to these difficulties than are other methods of collecting demographic statistics.   It is important to note that this type of survey has a wider scope than is implied by the word 'census', which is often defined as an inquiry in which the attributes of each individual in the population are recorded separately on household schedules.   Included in census-type inquiries are enumerations in which the data are collected in aggregate form; for example the inhabitants of each village might be gathered together, and the numbers counted in a few categories by sex, broad age-groups, etc.   There have been many surveys of this type — differing greatly in methods and complexity but each providing important information — carried out in Africa, particularly in the past fifteen years.   These inquiries have included full-scale censuses on the Western pattern in several North African countries, e.g., Egypt, and in 1960 in Ghana, aggregate enumerations by household in Kenya, Tanganyika and Uganda in 1948, and composite systems in which the inhabitants of each village were gathered together and then recorded individually, one to a line on a schedule; the latter was done for the Natives of South Africa and in the Portuguese territories of Mozambique, Angola and Guinea in 1950 and 1960.   The introduction of sampling methods has extended the range of the census-type inquiry even further, as will be shown below.   As a result of these surveys, many designed with experimental needs in mind, it has become clear that the census-type inquiry is a very flexible instrument and attractive for use in Africa.   Because it is essentially an isolated project, it is not necessary to establish a permanent organisation on an extensive scale at the outset.   By changes in the methods of census taking, the sizes of aggregate groups, and the extent and complexity of the questions, the amount of resources required for the census-type inquiry can be varied over a wide range. The problems of costs, staff and administration can thus be solved, tentatively and empirically, in terms of current needs.

There have been many attempts to establish vital registration systems in African countries, particularly on an experimental basis in limited areas, but the results have been disappointing. In some parts of Uganda registration started as long ago as 1904 but probably not more than about fifty per cent of the births and deaths are now recorded; in the earlier years coverage was higher. General experience in Africa and elsewhere is that, while it is not too difficult to achieve the registration of a high proportion of vital events for limited areas and periods, the attainment of effectively complete coverage for a whole country is a tremendous task. There is no easy solution to the problems imposed by scattered, isolated groups or reluctance to record children who die within a few days of birth. To achieve and maintain efficient registration close supervision is required. The administrative organisation must be extensive with representatives in quite small population units.

In most countries the recording of vital events is an integral part of the running of a modern state, essential for legal and social security purposes. The completeness of coverage depends mainly on the pressure of these purposes on the individuals of the population. In some areas of Africa registration is improving in accuracy and may be nearing completeness, e.g., in parts of Egypt, and in towns such as Freetown, Bathurst and Nairobi; a high coverage was reached in some areas of Congo (Leopoldville) in the 1950s. It is possible that, in some territories, administrative developments will be so rapid that the achievement of accuracy in the near future will become conceivable. In general, however, this is not a promising source of convincing vital rates at the present time.

The recent developments in principle and practice which make it possible to collect demographic statistics in Africa with good accuracy but lower cost will be discussed under four headings. These are: (1) Sampling; (2) Retrospective recording of events; (3) Cross-checks; (4) and Field experiments. The application of these procedures in African demography has now been given considerable study and the experimental evidence is substantial. Nevertheless, many problems remain untouched and conclusions must be tentative.

(i) *Sampling:* In sampling, a fraction of the population is chosen as representative of the whole. The results from this fraction (sample) are appropriately adjusted to give estimates for the whole population within calculable limits of probable error. The principles of sampling are by no means elementary, and the theory is very extensive. It is only appropriate here to indicate the main implications of the technique for African demography. The first major sample census inquiry in Africa was in Southern Rhodesia in 1948. This was followed by others in Ruanda-Urundi (1952), Northern Rhodesia (1950-51), Sudan (1955–56) and the Belgian Congo (1955–57). The theory and principles of the Rhodesian surveys were fully explained by Shaul (1948). An extensive series of demographic sample inquiries covering most of the former French possessions has been carried out, beginning with Guinea (1954–55); the results of many of these inquiries have not yet been published.

The simple and outstanding conclusion from this work is that statistics of satisfactory accuracy can be obtained for a large population by recording data for a small fraction of the persons in it.   Costs can thus be enormously reduced.   The determination of the numbers required is complicated and depends on many factors, but in general useful information can be obtained even from samples of a few thousand persons.   Most of the surveys in Africa have covered 5 to 10 per cent of the population.   Many of the more important estimates of distributions of the total population among categories (e.g., sex, age, numbers of children) can be made with satisfactory accuracy from inquiries among relatively few but large sampling units, e.g., villages with several hundred inhabitants.

Sampling schemes of this type, however, are not useful for the study of even the most basic statistics (e.g., total numbers) for the small regions of a country. This is because the accuracy of estimation depends mainly on the absolute number of units chosen for inquiry and very little on the sampling fraction.   Since there will be few units in a small region, the estimates of its characteristics will be subject to large errors.   This problem has been overcome in a number of instances by recording the primary data (e.g., total numbers, sex, employment) by means of a complete census-type inquiry and ascertaining the more detailed statistics (ages, fertility, length of residence, literacy) by sampling.   Because the primary data are easier to record, the skills and hence costs of enumerators for the complete inquiry can be much less than if the attempt is made to carry out an orthodox census of European type.   Procedures of this kind have been used in East Africa and were included in plans for the 1962 census of Nigeria.

An advantage of sampling is that it requires a smaller number of enumerators than a complete census.   These can then be more carefully chosen, thoroughly trained and closely supervised.   The inquiry in the enormous area of the Belgian Congo was carried out by three small teams of enumerators who did the fieldwork, region by region, over a period of about two years.   In a number of sample inquiries there seems to have been some misjudgment of the amount of labour required for the processing and analysis of the data.   This is more complex than for a complete census, although the amount of material is less.   In general, tabulation has been rather slow and limited and interpretation sketchy.

(ii) *Retrospective recording:* In vital registration, events are noted as they happen.   It is also possible to record the happenings in a period retrospectively, that is, some time after they have occurred.   In particular, births and deaths in a year or some other convenient time span can be counted at the end of the period.   This is possible if, by suitable questioning, reports on all events can be obtained and if each event is recorded only once.   Under reasonably stable conditions this is, at least in theory, practicable.   During any year, births to the women living in the country at the end of it will differ from the number which ideally could have been registered only because of deaths of mothers of very young children and because of migration. The derived fertility rates could be even more accurate because of the compensating changes in the number of women exposed to the risk of childbearing.   Similarly deaths in the year in still existing households or even in larger population units should not differ much from the registrable total.   Retrospective statistics which fall somewhere between the 'stock' and 'flow' categories are those measuring the outcome of a sequence of events over the previous lifetime, e.g., the total number of children born per woman, or the number of those who have died.   Such data have implications both for states (e.g., distribution of family sizes) and for rates (e.g., specific fertilities and mortalities).

It is, in principle, possible to obtain details both of recent, current vital events and of these retrospective ratios by questions asked in census-type inquiries. This information can be collected, without any of the administrative organisation required for registration, more quickly and at a lower cost. This device has been adopted in many African inquiries of the past fifteen years, although the extent and the nature of the data collected have varied greatly. In Rhodesia and the Sudan recording was mainly of births and deaths in the past year, although some broad information on total children born was also tabulated. In the Portuguese possessions statistics on children born and survived by age of women were compiled, but current births and deaths were not collected; similar data for a small fraction of the population were published in the 1948 census of the Gold Coast (now Ghana). At the sample inquiries in the former French possessions — Guinea, Upper Volta, Dahomey, Mali, Ivory Coast, etc. — statistics both of current births and deaths and of total children born and died were collected in great detail, and both types of information were recorded at the census surveys of Zanzibar (1958) and Uganda (1959).

There are three main difficulties in the use of such retrospective data for the estimation of vital rates. These are attainment of accuracy, selection and the interpretation of results in an unorthodox form. The first raises the most serious problems. To obtain accurate reports of the events in a previous year it is necessary that the prescribed reference period be correctly recognised in the memories of those reporting and that no relevant happenings be omitted. In African surveys an attempt often is made to define the period by some distinctive feature of about a year before. There is conclusive evidence, however, that in many (perhaps all) of these inquiries current births and deaths have been wrongly reported. It is not clear what part of this error is due to a wrong reference period and what to omissions. In some surveys births have been overstated, e.g., in Guinea (1954–55) and parts of the Belgian Congo (1955–57); this may be associated with a tendency to equate the age of weaning with one year when it is, on the average, much higher. In other inquiries (e.g., Zanzibar, 1958), reported births have been far too few. In general deaths seem to be under-reported (in some surveys the data on mortality have been summarily rejected and not published for this reason), but it is not clear how the reporting differs with respect to the ages of persons at death.

Measures which cumulate events up to the time of the inquiry are not subject to errors of time scale, but they are liable to be affected by omissions. In nearly all surveys where the total numbers of children born are recorded by age group of mother it can be demonstrated, by cross-checks of the type described later, that there have been considerable omissions by the older women. In some studies the evidence is strong that the omissions are almost entirely of children already dead — and there is some direct information on this (Schapera 1947) — but it is clear in other studies that many live children have also been forgotten. There has been considerable research into methods for detecting and allowing for these errors; the resulting procedures are outlined in the sections on analysis.

Selection occurs when the persons questioned about previous events are not a proper representation of the group to whom all the events have happened. The older women in a population, for example, are selected by survival from those born in the same period; the fertility and child mortality rates for mothers who have died are not necessarily the same as for those who have survived. Again, bias in estimated mortality at older ages is present because of the dissolution of households consisting of one old person (usually a man in Africa) who died in the year preceding the survey. Studies of migration, particularly when it is a short-term, periodical nature, are particularly subject to difficulties of this kind. At any given moment the persons absent from a population contain a much higher proportion of those who migrate for long periods (in one or frequent trips) than do the residents present in the population. Records of migration (length of stay, previous absences, etc.) of the inhabitants present may give a very false picture. Many of the problems of selection can be overcome or minimised by skilful design of the field inquiries, framing of questions, and analysis. So far little attention has been given to this subject in Africa or elsewhere, and there is wide scope for both theoretical and applied demographic studies along these lines.

The interpretation of rates obtained from retrospective surveys demands care. Mistakes have been very common, particularly in the analysis of data from small African studies. Only an indication can be given of the types of error that may arise. Thus, in the calculation of death rates from retrospective reports of the number of children who died in an age group (say, under one year or one to four years), allowance must be made for the fact that some children who entered the age group are still alive in it and thus have not experienced the full force of mortality over the age interval. Again, division of the number of women in an age group into the number of children born to them in the past year gives an age specific fertility rate. But this rate is for an age interval one half year younger, on average, than that of the women at the time of the survey: the births were spread over a period when the women were zero to one year less in age. The neglect of this time adjustment can lead to considerable error in the reconciliation of estimates of fertility distributions made by different means. There is little guidance on such problems in the standard demographic textbooks. Before any type of data on events is collected by retrospective recording, it is necessary to consider very carefully what measures are to be derived and how this is to be done.

(iii) *Cross-checks*: The only way in which the accuracy of a survey can be assessed and necessary corrections made is by cross-checks between data for which errors are independent or partly independent. The principle of extensive cross-checks is not unique to African demography. In fact its main development has been in countries like the United States with good population statistics. It is particularly important in Africa, however, where errors may be large and of a nature which is not anticipated. It is convenient to distinguish between external checks in which the comparisons are of data obtained from different sources, and internal checks, in which various features of the material collected at the one inquiry are examined. In addition it is useful to make a broad division of checks into 'aggregate' and 'unit'.

The most important external comparisons are of data from two census-type inquiries or of a census-type inquiry against some form of registration. In aggregate checks the two sets of statistics are for effectively the same units, but comparisons are made only for large groups of these units (e.g., districts or villages). For example, the populations of regions estimated from the sample censuses in the former French possessions were compared with the corresponding totals in the administrative registers. These maintain a record of the current state of the population; new persons entering through birth and immigration are added, and those leaving by death or emigration removed. The comparisons revealed, in general, that the administrative registers were very incomplete and the estimates of population made from them too low.   Because of the scarcity and poorness of vital registration in African territories, checks of data so obtained against the results of census-type inquiries have not been common or powerful.   Some use of this procedure has been made in studies of the Congo (Leopoldville) and Ruanda-Urundi. General comparisons of fertility, as indicated by reports of children ever born and by age distributions from census materials on the one hand, and with vital registration on the other, have been made for Egypt by El-Badry (1955).

The most useful procedure for external cross-checks of census-type inquiries in Africa is some form of post-enumeration survey, in which a sample of the population originally covered is investigated more intensively.   This may be used in combination with an original complete census, as in Ghana (1960), or with a sample, as in the Sudan (1955–56).   Checks may be aggregate or by small units, preferably individuals.   Such person-to-person identifications in two independent sets of records can reveal a great deal about types of error through the characteristics of the units which appear in one set but not in the other.   This form of investigation is very laborious and costly and is particularly difficult under African conditions where names are often duplicated or changed.   Nevertheless it was used in Ghana for some areas where the discrepancies between census and post-enumeration results were large, and provided key information about the causes of the discrepancies.

Different aims may be combined if the original enumeration is a complete census-type inquiry with a very limited schedule of questions, and a sample is used both as a means of obtaining detailed records and as a post-enumerative survey. This was done, to a limited extent, in Uganda (1959), Ghana (1960) and was planned for Nigeria (1962).   The amount of possible checking, however, is restricted by the complete census procedure and schedule of questions.   Only comparisons for broad categories of persons (e.g., total populations, numbers by sex) in aggregate groups may be possible.   Whatever the exact process, it is essential that recording at the post-enumeration survey be independent of recording at the census and that it be done with the greatest care and accuracy.   It is much better to reduce the sample to a small size, if this is all that can be dealt with thoroughly, rather than to cover a large number with less reason for confidence in the value of the returns.

The uses of internal checks are less well understood; the subject is complex and is capable of great development.   Some of the most powerful methods involve comparisons of measures calculated from the current births and deaths reported at an inquiry, with retrospective ratios of children born and died by age of mother. More indirect checks arise from the biological and cultural consistencies which form the basis of demographic theory.   Investigation of the inter-relations of fertility, mortality and age distribution has long been a central topic in demography, and work in this field has been considerably advanced in recent years.   This approach is now being applied in the examination of African data.   An account of this will be given in the sections on methods of analysis.   Little study of this kind has been given to nuptiality or migration, although to some extent the same principles apply.

The development of this approach leads to a number of conclusions about the collection of statistics by census-type inquiries.   The primary lesson is that data should be recorded both (1) on events in the previous year (births, deaths, migration, marriages, etc.), and (2) on the cumulated outcomes of these events (children born and died per woman, previous migration history of persons present, marital status).   The combination of information of both types is far more valuable than either set alone. The greater the detail of presentation the stronger the checks.   In particular it is essential that ages be recorded in reasonable detail, whatever the errors and biases involved.   Most of the more recent census-type inquiries in Africa have reported ages by individual years or five-year groups, in contrast to the older system of giving only broad age classes, e.g., children, adults, old people.   The detailed classification is required for any serious demographic studies.

(iv) *Field experiments*: Although the procedures discussed are greatly extending the scope of African demography, there are still many doubtful and unsatisfactory aspects of the subject.   The estimation of specific rates from vital events, and particularly of the mortality of older persons, is subject to great uncertainty.   Pending the establishment of accurate registration, the most fruitful attack on this problem must come from an extension of knowledge of the kinds of error to which the retrospective reporting at census inquiries is subject.   This could be done by field experiments, in particular by the 'continuous observation' survey which has been advocated by Martin (1953) and others, and much discussed at conferences such as the Colloquium on Problems in African Demography (International Union . . . 1960).   In this type of survey, a detailed census is carried out in selected areas.   Following this, births, deaths and migration movements are registered continuously by resident enumerators for at least several years.   At the end of the period there is a check census.   This is the basic pattern, but there can be many variations in detail.   No complete 'continuous observation' survey has yet been undertaken in Africa, although there have been experiments along these lines.

Close comparisons of the census data, e.g., on births, deaths and movements in the previous year, retrospective total numbers of children born and died, ages of living persons, etc., with the registration records of vital events, migration, ages at death and so on, could reveal a great deal about reporting errors.   Coale (1961) has pointed out the great power of unit checks for this purpose.   This knowledge could then be used to devise methods of collecting and analysing statistics so that accurate measures could be obtained quickly and cheaply.   It is important to realise, however, that for success such an experiment would have to be closely controlled and relatively large in scale.   Adequate size is necessary to reduce the uncertainties due to chance and the temporal fluctuations in vital and other events.   A scheme covering about 100,000 person-years (say a population of 25,000 for four years) would be desirable.   This would be a costly project, demanding very competent staff and organisation.   There could be no partial success, for, unless high accuracy was achieved, particularly in registration, the results would be of little value.

There has sometimes been confusion between the ideas of 'continuous observation' surveys and experimental registration areas.   The aim of the latter is to establish or improve vital registration in selected parts of a country by concentrating resources on them rather than spreading the effort widely over the whole territory.   By this means it may be possible to obtain usable statistics more quickly.   Gil (1961) has proposed a scheme for Ghana in which experimental registration areas would be rapidly extended over the whole country.   There have been many plans for such projects in different parts of Africa, but they have not achieved notable results.   It is always doubtful how far such experimental regions are (or can remain) representative of the whole country.

3. DESIGN OF INQUIRIES AND FIELDWORK

The detailed design of demographic inquiries, the precise information to be collected, and the framing of the questions depend so closely on aims and on the particular circumstances of the population concerned that little of a generally useful nature can be said. Only a few miscellaneous remarks will be added here.

In African surveys a greater responsibility is placed on enumerators than is usually required elsewhere. By careful questioning the enumerator has to determine such basic data as age, marriage state and births: facts which are clearly known in more developed territories but are often not known in Africa. For this reason it has been found necessary in census-type inquiries to lay special emphasis on the recruiting and training of enumerators, and a large share of the costs has been allocated to this. In addition, long periods before the census have been required for these preparatory purposes. Because it is difficult to obtain good staff for temporary work and the constant training of new enumerators is wasteful, there are great advantages in maintaining a census organisation with skilled, permanent employees.

Little study has been made of how census questions in Africa should be framed in order to produce the most accurate replies. There are many indications, however, that the more specific the questions, the better the results obtained. An inquiry on the total numbers of children born and died will give poorer accuracy than an orderly, detailed examination of a woman's maternal history. Experiments with types of question in the inquiries in the former French territories have indicated that it is better to ask, 'When did the last deaths in the household happen?' and allocate the relevant ones to the previous year, rather than merely to request the number of deaths in that period. There is need for more research on the wording of questions, on the kind of information which could be obtained by registration or census-type inquiries, and on the kinds of information most useful for economic, social and biological studies. The traditional European preoccupation with such classifications as religion, social class, marriage status, relation to head of household, etc., should not be transferred to Africa without proper assessment.

IV ANALYSIS OF DEMOGRAPHIC TRENDS*

There are several ways in which the analysis of demographic data from African territories differs from the standard procedures. Firstly and probably most importantly, usable vital statistics calculated from registration are hardly anywhere available. One of the main tools of the demographer, therefore, is missing. Secondly, the census inquiry materials, although now extensive geographically, are affected by considerable errors. In many cases the influences of these errors are apparent, but this provides little quantitative guide to the adjustments required. Perhaps the most striking of these errors are related to the determination of time scales and, in particular, to ages. All refined demographic analysis depends heavily on correct age information. Although returns of these statistics are suspect for all underdeveloped areas, the inaccuracy seems to be greater in Africa than elsewhere. Where there is a series of comparable and reasonably complete censuses, some of

* In this section several references are made to analysis techniques developed by the Princeton African Demography Project. The publication of a monograph giving a full account of this work has been planned.

these drawbacks can be overcome. For example, rates of natural increase can be obtained directly from the changes in total populations, and age errors can be corrected by comparisons of reports for the same cohorts at different censuses. In Africa, however, series with the necessary reliability and detail are not yet available anywhere, with the possible exception of some of the North African countries, notably Egypt.

The foremost problem of demographic analysis in Africa is to devise techniques for extracting measures from materials in unusual form, e.g., vital rates from retrospective reports. These measures should be insensitive to the types of error which are known to affect the data. However ingenious the methods developed may be, it is impossible to be sure that the results are not seriously distorted by reporting errors. A further need, therefore, is for the development of cross-checks by which independent or partly independent measures of the same features can be compared. Demographic facts do not stand in isolation. The analysis must lead to a coherent pattern into which each piece of information must fit when allowance has been made for error distortion. The evidence from such a pattern is much more convincing than individual, untested measures.

1. POPULATION MODELS

Among the most useful tools in the analysis of incomplete and deficient data are population models. These have not been developed specifically for this purpose or for use with African data, but some of the more recent work in this field, especially at the Office of Population Research, Princeton University, has been prompted by these needs. Population models are mathematical constructions of demographic processes which rely on the biological and cultural consistencies in human behaviour. The aim is approximately to describe complex and varied quantitative patterns of measurements by a limited set of possibilities. The value of an effective model in the analysis of incomplete and inaccurate data is that the most appropriate pattern from the set may be defined by the best sections of the material. The errors in the remainder of the results are then corrected by reference to the model.

Among the best known and most useful tools of this kind is the series of model life-tables published by the United Nations (1955, 1956). Essentially, these are sets of mortality patterns, separate for males and females, such that there is one life-table for each level of mortality. This level may be defined in a number of ways, e.g., by the expectation of life at birth or at any other age, by infant mortality, etc. Thus, if only one satisfactory measure of the mortality of a population is known, the corresponding United Nations model life-table can be chosen. These patterns were calculated as forms of averages from the tabulated statistics for populations with different levels of mortality.

Despite the value of these tables, it has become clear that there may be considerable variation in the mortality patterns of different populations, even when the level is about the same. Two more refined and complex sets of models have been constructed and used in African studies: regional models and parametric models.

Sets of regional models have been developed by Coale and Demeny. These are based on the same principle as the United Nations tables, although the method of calculation is different. The main distinguishing feature, however, is that there are four sets of life-tables. Each of these is calculated from mortality statistics of acceptable accuracy for the populations in a geographical region, with a few additions of data for countries which do not fall conveniently within the area framework.

The mortality patterns in each of these regions are much more homogeneous than for the world as a whole, but there are distinctive differences between sets. The regions defined are all dominated by the statistics of populations which are European or mainly of European descent because of the small number of accurate life-tables from other countries. There is no *a priori* means of judging which regional set of measures will be most appropriate for Africa.

A parametric model scheme has been produced by Brass. With one average life-table as a standard, sets of mortality patterns are generated by mathematical relations. Any specific pattern is determined by two measurements, one of which can be regarded as defining the level of mortality and the other the rate of change of specific death rates with age for a given level. The standard life-table can be an overall average, e.g., similar to one of the United Nations patterns, or regional, equivalent to a selection from one of the Coale-Demeny sets. These two developments provide a range of more flexible and refined model life-tables which are being used in the analysis of African data.

The stable population theory of Lotka is a cornerstone of the science of demography. Briefly this states that if the specific rates of fertility and mortality in a population remain constant and there is no migration, the natural increase and the proportional age distribution will tend to fixed limits. These limits can be calculated if the fertility and mortality are known. The importance of this in the analysis of demographic statistics of underdeveloped territories is that, in many instances, the conditions hold, approximately. Rates of natural increase and proportional age distributions are, therefore, directly dependent on fertility and mortality. This provides a means for checking estimates of different measures against each other and for obtaining rates indirectly. In African countries this is particularly useful in the examination of reported age distributions in relation to whatever information is available on fertility and mortality. These comparisons provide a powerful means of detecting and correcting errors in all these measures.

More recently, what has been called 'quasi-stable' population theory has been developed, mainly by Coale (1956) and Bourgeois-Pichat (1958). They have shown that age distributions are not very sensitive to changes in mortality and thus can provide information on fertility even if little is known about death rates. This theory has been used, particularly in conjunction with the United Nations model life-tables, to derive demographic measures from very broad age distributions when there is very little additional evidence. Some applications of this kind have been made in Africa, e.g., to the census statistics of the Sudan (1955–56) by Krotki (1961). Of course these procedures are only approximate. They can be made sharper if the material is slightly more complete. In the Princeton African Demography Project this sharpening of procedures has been accomplished by the use of the more flexible model life-table systems described, in conjunction with the detailed study of errors in age reporting.

Models of fertility distributions by age of woman are of less importance, since estimates are not very dependent on the exact way in which specific fertility rates vary with age. For this reason, rather rough approximations are good enough. Accuracy can be improved, however, if there is some knowledge of the mean of the distribution, i.e., the average age of women at births, if the effect of the variation of the numbers in the population with age is eliminated. Models are useful in taking account of this mean and for graduation purposes. Several have been constructed and applied in the analysis of African demographic data (Brass 1960, 1961).

2. SEX AND AGE DISTRIBUTIONS

The proportions of the two sexes in a population are determined by the sex ratio at birth, the differences between male and female mortality, and migration.   All of these factors are difficult to study quantitatively, and the materials for a useful examination of the precise weight to be given to each in any African country are not available.   The sex ratio at birth varies among populations for reasons which are not clearly understood, even when statistics are accurate.   It is particularly subject to reporting error through the wrong inclusion of stillbirths or omission of children who died very young, errors which are complicated by sex differentials in neonatal mortality.   Determination of sex ratios, furthermore, requires that large numbers of births be recorded, before the influence of chance variation becomes unimportant.   There is little indication of misreporting in African countries due to preferences by the parents for children of one sex.   There is, however, considerable evidence that the proportion of males at birth is, in general, rather lower in Africa than in most parts of the world.   A study of nearly 170,000 births of Africans in hospitals in French possessions, 1951–53 (Ministère de la France d'Outre-Mer, Service des Statistiques 1953), gave a sex ratio of just over 103 male births per 100 females.   This seems to be a good central value on the data available but, of course, the possibility of considerable variation among countries is not ruled out.

Information on mortality differentials by sex is meagre, suspect and conflicting. There is acceptable evidence that the pattern of higher male death rates in childhood, prevalent in most high quality mortality data for other parts of the world, operates in some countries, but in others the differential is slight or absent.   The estimates of adult mortality are doubtful and the possibility of differential reporting by sex strong.   The populations of most African countries are affected by migration, but statistics of the volume are missing or unreliable.   It is consequently impossible to study the sex division by means of these components and thus assess the accuracy of census results.

Age distribution tabulations are now being provided in some detail (by single years of five-year groups) from recent African census-type inquiries.   These have been examined by reference to quasi-stable population theory and independent estimates of fertility and mortality.   This has revealed characteristic biases in the recording of ages of females; in particular, there is a tendency to underestimate the ages of children up to about ten years, to under-report numbers in the group ten to nineteen years, to show preference for the central reproductive ages twenty to thirty-nine years, and frequently to overestimate the ages of the old.   The effect of migration on the age distributions of females in Africa is usually small, both because there is usually little movement of women, and because when they move they are more likely to be accompanied by children.   The position is very different for males since their migration is large and strongly age selective.   It is thus much more difficult to determine the biases in the reporting of male ages.   It is clear, however, that the under- and over-estimation respectively of ages of the young and the old also occur for males.   There is less of a tendency for the number aged ten to nineteen years to be too few but, in general, the ratios of males to females in the early and middle adult years are low.   In some countries this latter feature is probably due to migration, but this is not a satisfactory explanation in all cases. Most of these biases are certainly due to wrong age reporting, but underenumeration may also be present, particularly for the mobile adult males.

The standard methods for smoothing and adjusting age distributions by graduation formulae are designed to reduce the effects of fluctuating short-range errors such as those caused by the preference for 'round' ages and particular digits. Such formulae were used for smoothing the age distributions of the province of Buganda in the thorough analysis of the statistics from the 1959 Census of Uganda (Uganda Ministry of Economic Development, Statistics Branch 1961). This did little, however, to remove the long period systematic biases. For the other provinces of Uganda with poorer age data more extreme graphical graduation was adopted. Errors in the reported age distributions of Egypt were corrected by El-Badry through comparisons of the results from the five decennial censuses between 1907 and 1947. He assumed that the age distributions had remained the same because of the stability of conditions, and he was then able to adjust through detailed investigations of variations in sex ratios and age proportions from census to census. An excellent treatment of graphical and other graduation methods with particular reference to census statistics for Egypt is given in a paper by Carrier and Farrag (1959). The procedures suggested, however, depend in some instances on the availability of detailed age distributions from a series of censuses and, in general, on the errors being relatively small. They can be used profitably on data from a few African censuses but are not suitable for adjusting the large, long period, systematic biases which are commonly present.

The most convenient method for adjusting large systematic errors in the age distribution is by the use of quasi-stable population theory. Every stable age distribution is the product of a life-table survivorship function and an exponential of age times the natural rate of increase. Because the form of observed survivorship functions is contained within limits, although rather broad ones, the possible stable age distributions form a fairly well-defined family. From this family the distribution which best fits the data is selected. The decision on the method of fitting must depend on the information available. Knowledge of fertility, of the rate of natural increase, or of exact proportions surviving to certain ages can be used to limit the choice. Any two of these, in conjunction with a set of model-life tables, provide an independent age distribution with which the reported one can be compared. If only the reported age data are available, a graduated distribution which is, in some sense, central to the observed one must be chosen. This requires some judgment about the types of bias in the reporting and the implications of any choice can be considered by an examination of the differences between observed and fitted numbers in each age group. The graduation is not much influenced even by substantial deviations in the selected model life-table from the true set of mortality rates, except for the estimation of numbers at the upper ages where the relative error may be large. This method is valid only if the effect of migration on age distribution is unimportant: a condition which is often true for females in Africa but not always for males. If male migration is appreciable, it must be allowed for, directly or indirectly, by the correction of a distribution estimated from the female results. It may only be possible to do this very approximately.

Quasi-stable population theory has been used in the graduation of age distributions of Tunisia by Seklani (1961), who fitted a model based on the United Nations tables to observations based on a rough knowledge of current death and natural increase rates. Abdel-Aty (1961) calculated a life-table for Egypt by adjusting the reported age distribution of the 1947 census to eliminate the effects of the estimated rate of increase. The results were taken as equivalent to a life-table population apart from the distortions caused by omissions and age errors. From these measures he calculated the expectation of life at age ten years, which largely averages out the error; this age was chosen because of possible underenumeration of children.   The United Nations model table with the same expectation of life at ten years was selected as the estimate, and the graduated age distribution was obtained by reapplying the assumed rate of increase.

3. FERTILITY

Attempts to obtain estimates of fertility from survey reports of total children ever born to women have been made in Africa from early in the present century.   It was believed that such results would be more reliable than guesses based on the scanty birth statistics.   Kuczynski pointed out that, apart from the effects of differential death rates, the mean completed family size of women over the age of reproduction would be the same as the total fertility under stable conditions.   It was soon realised, however, that the reports of children born to the older women were particularly liable to omissions.   Attempts were then made to derive formulae for estimating the total fertility from ratios of total children born to all women or born to women in the reproductive period.   Because many of these births would have occurred to younger women a relatively short time before the survey, the results would be more recent and less subject to omissions.

Shaul (1946) derived a constant factor for multiplying the ratio of children born to women in the reproductive period to give the total fertility.   This gives reasonable values on average but may be very inaccurate for individual populations. More refined procedures, which take into account the effects of the age distributions of women and their specific fertilities and require some rough values of these measures, were produced by Brass (1953) and Myburgh (1954, 1956).   Brass (1954) also developed formulae for obtaining total fertilities from the ratios either of total children born to mothers (instead of to all women) in the reproductive years or of all births to first births in a period.   These formulae have the advantage of being less affected by errors in ages of women, the numbers reporting no children, and the inserted measures of age and fertility distributions; the estimate from the ratio of all to first births does not depend on the time period and can be used with incomplete vital registration data, if omissions do not depend on the order of birth. These procedures were designed for use when age records were in very broad groups or highly inaccurate.   They have been applied in the analysis of the material from the sample censuses of the Rhodesias and of Uganda and also from the maternity records collected by the East African Medical Survey (Laurie et al. 1954).

When age distributions are known in some detail (by five-year groups preferably) and statistics of both retrospective and current births are obtained at a census-type inquiry, more powerful methods of analysis are available.   These have been developed by the Princeton African Demography Project and depend on careful, age-group by age-group, comparisons of the two sets of data.   From the specific fertility rates calculated from current births, with a half-year correction where necessary — as noted in the section on retrospective recording — the corresponding total births per woman at ages twenty, twenty-five years and so on can be found. From these the ratios of children born to women in the standard five-year age groups can be estimated (Series A), either graphically or by a graduation method given by Brass (1960), and compared with the observed retrospective values (Series B).   This is best done by calculating the ratios of B/A for each age group.   If these are all close to one, the two sets of data are consistent.   Experience has shown that when this is not so the *level* of fertility is most accurately given by the retrospective B values for the younger women but that the *pattern* of fertility is better taken from the A series, which is for recent births.   In general, the B/A ratios fall with age because of omissions by the older women, and, moreover, all often differ from one because of time scale or other errors in current reports.   The best estimates of total fertility are then obtained by correcting the reported current specific fertility rates for level from the B/A ratios for the younger women.   It may also be necessary to make some adjustment for errors in the reporting of the number of women in the reproductive period.   This is best done by applying the correction for level directly to the reported birth rate and estimating the total fertility by the use of the quasi-stable population.   These procedures have been applied in the Princeton study to the data from the former French possessions in Africa, Congo (Leopoldville), Uganda, Zanzibar and some other territories.

Useful information on fertility can be obtained from tabulations by age group of the distribution of women by the number of children born.   It is particularly important that there be data on both the number of childless women and the number failing to report.   El-Badry (1961) has shown that in Egyptian and other censuses many childless women have been erroneously tabulated in the second category.   He has presented analytic methods for correcting this.   The reverse may be true in other cases.   Inspection of distributions of women by children born can give some guidance on misreporting, particularly if fertility appears to be low.   In particular, the proportions of women reported to be childless may be inconsistently high in relation to the percentages with one or two children.   If, in addition to this material, there are distributions of births in the past year by order, these can be used to make very precise comparisons between current and retrospective data by procedures similar to the use of the B/A ratios described above.   There is scope for much more research into techniques for making checks of this kind as an aid in the detection and correction of errors.

So far, convincing estimates of fertility are only available for a small number of countries of Africa.   These, however, reveal some interesting features.   Although the general level is high it is by no means extreme.   Many regions have total fertility ratios of five to six children per woman.   There is a tremendous variability among regions.   In some countries or large areas the total fertility probably exceeds seven but there is overwhelming evidence that it is as low as three to four for several tribal groups.   Such areas of low fertility occur in parts of Congo (Leopoldville), Cameroons, Centre-Oubangui, Uganda and Tanganyika; the list might be much longer if data which could be critically evaluated were more extensive.   These groups are characterised by high proportions of childlessness as well as low numbers of children per mother.   In general childbearing begins early in these (as in nearly all) African populations, but the fertility rates of women over twenty-five or thirty years are very low.   There has been some investigation of the causes of these low fertilities, particularly in the Belgian Congo and East Africa, but no very conclusive results have been obtained.   Romaniuk (1961) has suggested that the main cause is venereal disease, and certainly this seems to be prevalent in most of these areas; however, there are other regions with a severe venereal incidence where fertility is relatively high.   Other possible factors stem from the breakdown of the traditional social structure.   This is one of the important problems of applied African demography and more study is needed.

4. MORTALITY

Mortality rates calculated directly from current deaths, registered or reported at a census inquiry, are suspect for all countries of Africa and in many instances clearly wrong. There has been considerable research into methods of checking such rates or making estimates by alternative means. The calculation of mortalities from the age distributions of successive censuses, adjusted for recording errors and migration, is a long-established procedure, e.g., in India and Brazil. The principle of this method is that survivorship proportions and thus specific death rates for different spans of life can be found by relating the numbers in an age group at the later census to the totals for the corresponding group *n* years younger at the earlier one, where *n* is the interval between successive censuses. At present, this has few applications in Africa because of the lack of successive censuses with sufficiently accurate and detailed age distributions.

The main alternative sources of mortality rates are retrospective statistics of the proportions of children dying, as reported by mothers at census-type inquiries, and age distributions, used in conjunction with model life-tables and other measures. A formula for obtaining the life-table survivorship ratio to an age near the end of childhood from the proportion of children dying to mothers of all ages in the reproductive period was developed by Brass (1953). Myburgh (1956) derived methods for estimating the expectation of life at birth from the proportion of children dying to all mothers in the population and applied these to the census statistics from the Rhodesias. These methods take little account of the influence of fertility and age distributions in individual countries, and reports of children dead from older as well as from younger women are included in the proportions. They are suitable for making estimates from very limited materials but allow no critical appraisal of the data.

When there are retrospective statistics of children born and died by age group of mother, more searching techniques can be applied. In a number of reports on the demographic inquiries in the former French African possessions, the proportion of children died for each age group of mother was equated, approximately, with the probability of dying before a given age (France, Ministère de la France d'Outre-Mer, Service des Statistiques 1955). In fact the ages given are somewhat too high for the younger mothers. A more systematic attack on this problem has been made by Brass. In the most recent work, series of multipliers have been developed for application to the proportion of children died for each age group of mother. A set of these multipliers is chosen (one for each age group) by the use of a rough measure (which may be obtained in various ways) of the relation of fertility to age of woman. This measure may be the mean or median age of childbearing or the ratio of total children born per woman of fifteen to nineteen years to the corresponding value for the twenty to twenty-four years age group. The use of the multipliers gives estimates of the probabilities of dying before ages one, two, three, five and then up by five-year steps from the proportion of children dead to mothers aged fifteen to nineteen, twenty to twenty-four years and so on. The multipliers, which are all close to one, were derived by the use of model mortality and fertility distributions. With the exception of the results from the first age group, these estimates are rather insensitive to errors in age reporting or the exact form of the models.

This procedure has been extensively applied to the results of African surveys. Examination of the pattern of derived probabilities of dying has revealed a widespread tendency for these to be too low at the higher ages as compared with the values at ages two, three and five. This effect is certainly due to differential omissions of dead children in the reports of the older mothers. The probabilities at the early ages can be regarded as approximately minimum estimates of child mortality. There may be a little inflation due to the inclusion of stillbirths, but error due to the omission of children who die very young is more likely. In general, the derived child mortalities in African countries have been high or very high (usually between 30 per cent and 45 per cent dead before five years). Almost invariably the child mortalities calculated in this way have been much higher than those found directly from current deaths. Clearly the latter are considerably under-reported.

Most of the data examined have shown a pattern of childhood mortality in which the proportion of the deaths in the first five years — especially between one and four years — is much higher than is usual in published life-tables. In addition there are indications that mortality between five and twenty years is also high relative to that of infancy. This pattern is quite similar to the Northern one of the regional model life-tables. There is a very extensive medical literature on the pattern of very early childhood mortality in Africa, mostly based on records of hospitals and clinics. On the whole the evidence is that the force of mortality is particularly high from six months up to a few years, relative to that of non-African countries with accurate data. This pattern may be due to insect-borne diseases (particularly malaria) and malnutrition following weaning.

Statistics of adult mortality are particularly unsatisfactory, because these can only be obtained from the deaths reported in the year previous to a census inquiry or, in a few cases, from registration. For almost all populations it can be shown that the recorded deaths of children in such sources are too low. Adult deaths may be just as much under-reported, approximately correct, or even overstated, if the time reference period is wrong. Probably the accuracy of reporting varies with the sex and age group of the deceased. If a good estimate of childhood mortality can be made, a model life-table can be selected which is in agreement with this. For example the United Nations model life-tables could be used or, when the evidence of pattern supports this, the Northern regional tables. The adult mortalities implied by the table can then be compared with any observed rates. A method based on a rather similar principle but applied in a different way is given by Gabriel and Ronen (1958). This is an exceedingly blunt weapon, however, since highly varied adult death rates can be associated with the same level of child mortality in different populations. In the Princeton African Demography Project parametric model life-tables, normally with the Northern regional pattern as a standard, have been fitted to the data for many populations; the level of childhood mortality is determined from the retrospective proportions of children died, applying the multiplier technique, and the course of death rates at later ages relative to those in childhood is determined from the current data. Although the use of these methods narrows the margin of error, the resulting estimates cannot be very precise.

If the population is nearly stable and a good estimate of the rate of natural increase can be obtained, e.g., from successive censuses, the age distribution can be adjusted to give a life-table, although this will be distorted by underenumeration and biases in age reporting. This was the technique used by El-Badry (1955) and Abdel-Aty (1961), but the former adjusted the age distribution by comparisons of the series of censuses, and the latter corrected the derived life-table by reference to the United Nations models.

5. POPULATION TRENDS

If the total fertility and childhood mortality are known, it is possible to calculate the resulting age distribution by quasi-stable population theory to a good approximation, except for the proportion of old persons.   Observed age distributions can thus be used to make checks of estimated fertilities and child mortalities, and conversely the latter can reveal underenumeration and biases in age statements. This check is based essentially on the number of children surviving the first year or two of life.   It cannot reveal omissions which are common to births and deaths, e.g., of children who died very young, since these would lead to compensating errors.   While such omissions are important in making a true assessment of the demographic state of the population and, in particular, the scope for change, they have little effect on the calculation of reproduction or natural increase.

On the other hand a close estimate of the rate at which the population is increasing also requires a knowledge of adult mortality at least in the reproductive period; for this purpose death rates at older ages are not so important, unless they are changing rapidly.   Adult mortality and natural increase cannot be effectively checked against age distributions.   A wide range of combinations of these rates can lead to much the same age composition; there are differences in detail, but these cannot be distinguished from the effects of errors and fluctuations in vital indices. It has been pointed out that in most African countries the materials for making good estimates of adult mortality do not exist.   As a consequence, rates of natural increase computed from the estimates of fertility and mortality are subject to considerable uncertainty.   Because the rate of natural increase is the difference between birth and death rates, it may have a large relative error even if the two components are fairly accurate.   For example, an underestimate of 15 per cent in a death rate of, say, forty per thousand with a birth rate correctly estimated at forty-five per thousand would give a calculated natural increase of eleven per thousand, more than twice that of the true rate.   An inaccuracy of this size could seriously distort assessments made for planning purposes.

Direct estimates of natural increase from successive enumerations are not so sensitive to errors, if allowances can be made for migration and a well-organised census procedure has been established.   With the exception of some of the North African countries, problems of improving the accuracy of inquiries and of determining the effects of migration are to be found in all areas in which successive censuses have been taken.   However, the direct estimates for the Republic of South Africa, Uganda, Zanzibar, Angola and Mozambique supply valuable evidence.

It will be clear from this account that very little can be said about population trends in Africa as a whole.   There is certainly a great variability from area to area, with populations of some countries or regions showing a rapid increase of twenty-five per thousand or more (e.g., Uganda) and others remaining almost stationary (as in parts of the Central African Republic and the Cameroons).   Since it is difficult to estimate present tends, it is even more speculative to forecast what will happen in the future in any African country.   There is some evidence that the rate of natural increase is accelerating in a number of countries (e.g., Egypt, Republic of South Africa, Uganda, Ruanda-Urundi and Ghana) because of decreasing mortality.   On the other hand, in most of the areas of low fertility in Africa the old women report larger families than those women who are in or just at the end of the reproductive period.   The argument that there has been a relatively recent fall in fertility in these areas is strong.   The scientific study of population trends in Africa has hardly begun, and there is enormous scope for further surveys, for the detailed investigation of existing statistics, and for analysis of those statistics as yet unpublished, resulting from inquiries which have already been carried out or planned.

6. SPECIAL DEMOGRAPHIC STUDIES

The detection and clarification of the factors influencing demographic measures can often best be done through detailed investigation of cross-tabulated data for small, homogeneous populations.   The material analysed may be part of the results of a countrywide census or, more commonly, collected by a special survey.   In Africa such surveys have, so far, been rare but mention should be made of the pioneering work of the Culwicks (1938, 1939) on the effects of the Maji-Maji rebellion on reproduction in the Ulanga district of Tanganyika, Mitchell's (1949) analysis of the fertility of the Yao of South Nyasaland, and the careful study by Fortes (1954) of the demographic characteristics of an Ashanti population in Ghana.

Even where absolute measures calculated from survey or registration materials are suspect, it may be possible to study differentials; this depends on the knowledge or assumption that the errors for the groups compared have similar effects.   There have been few systematic and extensive investigations of demographic differentials in Africa, although there have been a number of small-scale studies with anthropological and medical aims which have indicated interesting possibilities.   One of the most important fields for further research in fertility — the causes of the low levels in several regions — has already been mentioned.   The study of social and economic differentials has hardly been started.   El-Badry (1956) has made an investigation of fertility differences in Egypt by region and by the occupations of fathers.   The data on maternity histories collected by the East African Medical Survey were analysed by marital status, occupation class of husband, hut size, and certain conditions of the woman indicative of diseases such as malaria and syphilis.   The notable feature of these results was the absence of any signs of appreciable differentials in fertility. In this connection the effects of urbanisation also deserve research; in some countries, e.g., Congo (Leopoldville), fertility may be as high or higher in cities than in rural areas.   There is some evidence that polygyny lowers the rate of child-bearing, and the inter-relations between migrant labour, polygyny and fertility merit careful attention.

Differentials in mortality are more striking, although just as much work is required to confirm these and assess their causes and effects.   There is some puzzling evidence that death rates may be much below the average level in certain African groups.   Infant mortality in many urban areas (e.g., Nairobi and Leopoldville) has undoubtedly fallen greatly.   Brass (1959) has shown that in some communities of East Africa there are large differentials in child mortality by the stability of the marriage experience of the mother, by size of family and by birth spacing; he has demonstrated smaller differences by the occupation class of the husband and the size of the hut.   Census inquiry data which can be used for making analyses of this kind are beginning to be tabulated more extensively, and the stock of information about the demographic characteristics of Africa should rapidly increase.

V   NUPTIALITY

Marriage has been a favourite theme of anthropologists in Africa.   Their interest has been focused mainly on the functional significance of different forms of marriage and on the role of marriage in the social structure of particular African societies. These studies have not generally involved measurement of the frequency of different types of marital behaviour.   Some comparative studies of marriage in different societies, however, have led to statistical investigations.   For example, attempts have been made to apply statistical tests to hypotheses concerning the relation of marital stability to kinship systems.   The work of Barnes (1949, 1951) and of Mitchell (1961a) was developed in this context.   Studies of social change in various situations, notably under the conditions of urban life, have also prompted attempts to measure various aspects of marriage, including fertility.

The collection and analysis of data on marriage in censuses or other large-scale inquiries on people with a variety of cultures, influenced by changing conditions in Africa, involves difficult problems in definition.   The statistician must take account of the work of anthropologists in dealing with these problems and in framing realistic inquiries.   A simple application of Western concepts in this sphere leads to serious confusion.

Marriage is an important institution in all tribal societies, but its definition varies greatly among tribes, and may be quite different even among tribes in the same region.   Two factors have usually been implicit in questions concerning marital status.   These factors are: (1) a rite or formality that involves the legal transfer of the bride to her husband; this rite can be customary, for example, the payment of bride-wealth, or civil or religious; (2) cohabitation of the spouses. Confusion with respect to the first of these criteria results from conflict between civil law and customary law.   Cases in point are in countries (e.g., Congo, and now Ghana) where polygyny has been banned, and in the former French territories, where child marriage was outlawed by the Décret Mandel.   In any case, it is difficult to frame any definition of marriage that fits all societies.   This affects the second factor mentioned above, i.e., cohabitation.   In Ghana neither Ashanti nor Ga spouses ordinarily live together.   Yet this factor was stressed in the Congo inquiry as useful in distinguishing between casual unions and stable consensual unions.   No attempt was made to define the criteria of marriage in the Guinea inquiry.   Instructions on this subject to enumerators in the post-enumeration survey of the Ghana inquiry were rather ambiguous.   They were told that marriage 'means' a union sanctioned by some customary, civil or religious rite, but were also told to report as married all persons who said that they were.

Marriages in Africa are frequently established in stages, involving a series of payments which in many societies are an essential aspect of marriage.   As stated by Radcliffe-Brown (p. 49): 'To understand African marriage we must think of it not as an event or condition but as a developing process.'   This complicates the reporting, because the census or inquiry may intervene at any moment in the development.   Prior to the final and sometimes principal payments, there will have been preliminary exchanges bringing ritual recognition of rights and obligations by the man and woman concerned and/or their kin.   These exchanges often initiate a probatory period of cohabitation, which it seems reasonable in many respects to treat as marriage.   Unions of this stage were classified as consensual unions in the Congo inquiry.

A difficult problem also arises with respect to the classification of concubines and — especially in the mixed population of cities and other areas affected by rapid transition — of unions formed without customary or legal sanctions.   These may range from casual association to generally recognised and enduring consensual unions.   The presence of such relations raises very complex problems in the measurement of nuptiality and its relation to fertility — treated in a different context (the Caribbean region) by Roberts and Braithwaite (1961).   There is no simple solution of the problems thus presented.   An attempt was made in the Congo inquiry to distinguish between concubinages and consensual unions by restricting the latter to those that had endured six months or more.   It has been argued by Barnes (1951) that stability over a number of years transforms a consensual union into a marriage, and that what counts is the type of husband-wife relationship, the relations of their two kinship lineages, and the public attitude.   Among the Ngoni he has studied, the bride-wealth has become obsolete.   A legalisation payment has taken its place, but a sizable portion of the unions occur without any payment. Such changes have been brought about by Western contact in many parts of Africa. Some African states now require, at least in theory, the civil registration of marriages.

Some attempt to classify marriages by type is made in many inquiries.   Quite different schemes of classification are used, however, notably with respect to the distinction between legal and consensual unions.   In the Guinea inquiry consensual unions were included among customary unions without distinction from unions instituted in accord with customary law.   On the other hand, in the Ghana and the Congo inquiries these were treated as separate categories.   It seems desirable that greater effort be made to standardise procedures in this respect.   In any case, it is important that the methods used in any inquiry be taken into account in the treatment of its results.

African women generally marry at fairly early ages, and few women remain permanently single— though the marriage of men may be subject to greater delay, especially where polygyny is frequent.   Yet there are considerable differences among regions and tribes in the usual ages of women at first marriage.   Data on this subject must be used with caution, not only because of ambiguities in the definition of marriage, but also because of the possible influence of errors in the estimation of ages.   As shown in the previous section, there is frequently a deficit in the number of females reported at ages ten to nineteen years and an excess at ages twenty to twenty-nine.   It is highly probable that the errors responsible for this distortion are associated with marriage and fertility.   Enumerators frequently accept, or assign, later ages to married 'women' and mothers than to unmarried 'girls' of equal chronological age.   According to the Congo inquiry, the apparent variation in the proportion of single women at fifteen to nineteen years ranges from 22 per cent in the Maniema district to 86 per cent in the Cataractes district, which is adjacent to Leopoldville.   The latter figure may be influenced by the actual migration of young married women from the district to the city.   It may also, in part, reflect relative freedom from bias in the estimation of ages.   It is the only district in which the reported number of females at age fifteen to nineteen years exceeds the number at age twenty to twenty-four years.   These considerations suggest that special caution must be used in an attempt to derive indices of marriage by age from census data on the proportions of women married at successive ages, such as the estimation of the 'singulate mean age at first marriage' proposed by Hajnal (1953).

Only when the field of marriage has been delimited can one turn to the influence of marital status on fertility.   The concept of legitimacy is of dubious usefulness in the African context, except in particular cases.   It cannot be used without caution in inter-regional comparisons.   From the standpoint of demography,

a broad definition of nuptial fertility seems appropriate.   But here again it is clear
that more attention must be given to questions of concept and definition.   For
purposes of comparison, there is need for standardisation.

Polygyny is recognised in the customary law of most African societies, but
there is great variation among regions and tribes in its frequency and characteristics.
The previous observations concerning the definition and measurement of marriage
apply to polygynous unions.   The large volume of information on this subject,
supplied by census-type inquiries, must be treated with special caution.   For
example, the Congo law withholds recognition from polygynous marriages contracted since 1951.   As a result, recent second marriages had to be considered by
the interviewers of the 1955–57 demographic inquiry as consensual unions, even if
bride-wealth had been supplied.   In a country where one man out of four is a poly-
gynist, the task of interviewers was a formidable one.   Despite the instructions, a
sizable proportion of the girls aged fifteen to nineteen, who were aged ten to fourteen in 1951, was reported as polygynously married.

Considerable attention has been directed to studies on the relation of polygyny
to fertility.   The relation is obviously complex and may vary in net effect under
different conditions.   Most investigators conclude that, in general, polygyny tends
to lower female fertility but that its influence in this respect is moderate.   Even
where a negative relation between polygyny and fertility is observed, the causal
relations may be obscure.   As pointed out by Blanc (1961) and others, the infertility of a first wife is often a major factor in a man's decision to enlarge his household.   It is unlikely that variation in the frequency of polygyny is a major determinant of the observed wide variations of fertility among African populations.

The collection of information on the dissolution of marriages is beset by the
difficulties already discussed in the definition of marriage.   Customary law usually
has definite rules relating to divorce, though in practice there may be many deviations.   Colson (1958 : 177) points out that among the Plateau Tonga a woman who
is separated from her husband may call herself divorced though no formal action has
been taken and, if reconciled, she may return to her husband without ceremony.
The question is also complicated in some regions by the indissolubility of Catholic
marriages.   The concept of 'divorce' is, of course, not properly applicable to the
disruption of consensual unions, and still less to concubinage, or 'free unions'.
Thus the dissolution of conjugal unions, as it concerns demography and many social
issues, may range from a civil action, or return of the bride-wealth under customary
law, to the prolonged absence of a husband who has migrated, or to the separation
of a man and woman who have been living in consensual union.

A question concerning previous marriages has been included in many of the
demographic inquiries planned by French statisticians.   A detailed tabulation of
reports by persons, classified by sex and age, on numbers of previous marriages,
those ended by death of spouse and those ended by divorce or separation, could
supply much useful information.

An elaborate method of measuring the frequency of divorce in African
societies, involving the collection of complete marital histories and the computation of 'marriage duration tables' has been proposed by Barnes (1949), but rarely,
if ever, applied.   A simpler procedure is recommended by Mitchell (1961a) who
gives some illustrations of its application.

It is quite possible that the association of fertility with stability of marriages in
Africa is stronger than with either variation in age at marriage or polygyny.   Using

data from the Guinea inquiry, Blanc (1961) has shown that total fertility decreased with the number of marriages experienced by women past childbearing ages. This relation is ambiguous, however, in that marital stability may have been affected by relative infertility. One of the most intensive studies of marriage and fertility in Africa has been carried out by the Ardeners (1960, 1961) on the Bakweri in the southern Cameroons. The complete returns are not yet available, but they are partially reported in their two publications. The Bakweri are a small tribe strongly influenced by the in-movement of large numbers of workers, many of them men without families, from other regions to plantations in the vicinity of their villages. Many Bakweri women live for varying periods as concubines or prostitutes. In this situation, 63 per cent of all terminated legitimate unions reported by 1,062 village women and 49 per cent of all legitimate unions ever contracted had ended in divorce (Ardener 1961: 93). The Bakweri have distinctly low fertility. The complete report will deal with the relation of marital stability to type of first marriage and other associated conditions and to fertility. The situation treated in this study is abnormal, but somewhat analogous conditions may prevail in various other localities in Africa.

Instability of marriage has often accompanied the disruption of the tribal cohesiveness by Western contact, intercourse between tribes, and work for wages. Urbanisation has created new values and new ways of life. Imbalance in the numbers of men and women in cities has fostered the prevalence of free unions and a high frequency of divorce or separation in urban settings. New legal forms of marriages, the civil and the religious marriage, are becoming increasingly important. The effect of the new marriage patterns on fertility is as yet uncertain. Additional data for the study of changing conditions affecting marriage and fertility in the expanding urban population are provided by censuses and special surveys in cities.

The demographic study of marriage in Africa is a neglected field. Progress in dealing with this very difficult topic requires both more systematic evaluation and analysis of information already at hand and greater attention to the design of inquiries aimed at the provision of needed basic data on various aspects of this subject.

VI DEMOGRAPHIC ASPECTS OF MIGRATION

The measurement of migration in Africa is complicated by the heterogeneity of its patterns, which vary in relative importance between different regions and in the same region at different times. At present the dominant pattern in some regions, notably in South Africa and the Rhodesias, is an oscillation between villages, organised on the basis of subsistence economy, and cities, plantations or commercial farms that offer opportunities for employment for wages — with limited periods of stay by the migrants in the commercial centres. On the other hand, although most West African cities include large transient elements, they also have important cores of permanent residents which are being constantly augmented by the accession of migrants who stay indefinitely, and often permanently, in the urban milieu. These contrasting patterns overlap in many regions, and there is a continuum of intermediate types. The measurement of trends in the periodicity of migration, therefore, is as important in many African situations as is the measurement of its volume.

The movement to opportunities for employment or other forms of temporary gainful work in agriculture, crafts or trade in southern, central and eastern Africa is usually not primarily a seasonal phenomenon; the periods of wage work often extend through one or two years or longer, though they may be somewhat influenced in timing by seasonal conditions. The movements of migratory herdsmen through arid regions are, of course, essentially seasonal and circular. So, too, are movements of farmers between flood plains and higher ground in some regions (e.g., in the southern Sudan). There are also large seasonal movements of farmers between the drier interior zone of West Africa, where cropping is limited to a few months in each year, and its forest and coastal regions. In some cases farmers leave their homes during the off-season to engage in cash cropping elsewhere by renting land or sharing the produce. In other cases they work for wages on commercial farms or in cities. The periods of such employment may be of short duration, or they may lead to indefinite relocation. Finally there is considerable inter-rural resettlement, both within and across national boundaries.

The particular methods most appropriate to the investigation of some types, or some aspects, of migration may be inefficient in the treatment of other situations. Research opportunities, moreover, are necessarily affected by the types of data that happen to be readily available in different countries, or that can be obtained by modifications of research programs already under way. A variety of approaches to the measurement of migration in Africa is, therefore, to be expected under present conditions.

It is important to bear in mind that the results obtained in any study are in part determined by its method. For example, the distribution of migrants by length of absence from home will be quite different in the case of migrants interviewed in an area where they are temporarily employed from that of migrants in transit or of the present and former migrants from an area of origin. At a given time only part of the stay of migrants present in a city or absent from their homes will have been completed at the time of the survey (on the average this is about half of the whole stay but is influenced by the timing of a survey in relation to the flow of migrants). Moreover, the chance of inclusion at all in the survey will be directly proportional to length of stay. These conditions (incompleteness of stay and chances of inclusion) influence the distribution of reported durations of absence in opposite directions, but their effects will have different weight. The same considerations apply to data on absentee migrants from the area of origin, but not to information (if this can be obtained) on all living persons born in an area who have ever been absent.

Census data, or preferably the results of successive censuses, provide the simplest approach to the measurement of the *redistribution* of population by migration. For this purpose in Africa the use of information on persons classified by tribe has one distinct advantage over information on persons by place of birth; classification by tribe also has several more questionable advantages and certain disadvantages. In using tribal data one deals with size of a total migrant stock, including the children born to migrants. In using place-of-birth data one deals with a migrant stock exclusive of children born to the migrants in the new location. The figures in either case are influenced by deaths of migrants in the new location. Neither the effect of deaths among migrants nor the effect of their procreation on population changes can be accurately estimated except on the basis of very detailed information. For many purposes, therefore, measurement of the *net* effect of migration and of the vital trends of the migrant stock on the redistribution of population or on the increase or decrease of a total population, is more satisfactory than is the attempt to measure migration apart from its consequent births and deaths.   The value of information on persons by tribal affiliation is greatly increased if presented with classification by sex and age.   Such classification is even more critically important in data on persons by place of birth.

Unfortunately, statements on tribal affiliation are frequently ambiguous.   One man may name his lineage or chieftainship; his brother may name a more inclusive ethnic group; and a kinsman may refer to the same group by a different name. Conversely, the same name is sometimes used for different tribes.   There are other confusions resulting from intermarriage, serf relations and assimilation. Statements of tribal affiliation, nevertheless, afford a useful index of origin in many situations.   Moreover, although the established homes of some tribes are dispersed through several areas, confusion on this account may often be less, or can be more accurately taken into account, than confusion arising from an attempt to classify persons by origin in different administrative areas.

Southall (1961), analysing the 1948 census in Kenya, two censuses in Tanganyika and two in Uganda, obtained proportions of males and females of various tribes who were living outside their home districts for use as indices of migration.   These indices show significant contrasts in tendencies towards dispersion between tribes in different situations.   Ardener (Ardener and Warmington 1961) combined employment records of the Cameroons Development Corporation with 1953 census data to obtain estimates of the proportions of the 'home population', by district and tribe, employed by the Corporation in 1954.   In this procedure, the use of tribal data from different sources necessitated a reconciliation of differences in classification that could be effected only by a person with intimate knowledge of local conditions.   Tribal data from censuses have been quite widely used in the investigation of the components of various urban populations.   In the case of some widely dispersed ethnic stocks, such as the Fulani, some further classification by region of origin may be important.   For example, the homeland of the Rwanda, many of whom migrate from Ruanda to Uganda, extends across the border into the Kigezi district in Uganda.   It is important, therefore, here to distinguish between those originating east and west of this border.

A two-way classification of persons (1) by region of birth or by place of residence at some previous date, and (2) by location at the time of a census becomes very complex if presented in detail both with respect to origins and present locations.   With the limited resources for statistical investigations in Africa today, general tabulations of this sort must usually be limited to exchanges between major regions.   It is frequently important, however, to obtain information on migration to or from specific localities, for example in studying the relation of migration to economic and social conditions in rural areas or the influence of migration in the formation of urban populations.   Major attention must often be focused on selected areas of either origin or destination, or in some cases, on both areas of an important migratory movement.

In an intensive investigation of a rural area, it is theoretically possible to obtain an account of the movements of all living persons born there, including permanent absentees.   This is a painstaking process, however, that requires close rapport between the investigator and the local community and reliance on retrospective reports, including reports by relatives concerning absentees.   Information of this sort was collected by Gulliver (1955) in a study of the Ngoni and Ndendenli of the Songea district, southern Tanganyika.   Even with the favourable conditions established in this inquiry, the author states that the ten per cent proportion of persons 'lost' as permanent absentees must be viewed as a minimum.

In view of the difficulty of obtaining retrospective information over an indefinite period, an inquiry on migration may be limited to some specified period. For example, in the 1960 demographic inquiry in Upper Volta (a nation characterised by heavy, largely temporary out-migration), a question was asked concerning all persons domiciled there who had been absent more than six months at any time during the previous five years. Detailed questions were then asked about the most recent absence of such persons and (if there was more than one absence) about the first trip. The results of this experimental investigation have not yet been published.

Rather more extensive information about migrants in urban areas has been collected in census-type inquiries and in intensive surveys. A series of studies on many aspects of migration has been carried out by J. Clyde Mitchell in the Copperbelt of Northern Rhodesia and extended to all towns in this territory. Some of the important findings in these studies are reviewed, along with other information, in 'Labour and Population Movements in Central Africa', in the symposium edited by Barbour and Prothero (1961). This article includes a selected bibliography on other relevant studies. Other recent studies on migrants in towns include a study of the Toucouleur in Dakar by Diop (1961) and a study of Usumbura by van de Walle (1961).

Information on streams of *migrants in transit* through key points can complement census-type information on migration in various ways. Continuous records of migrants in transit can be used to show seasonal and annual variations in the volume of migration under different conditions, whereas information on this subject cannot easily be obtained from censuses or other one-time surveys. Such information on fluctuations in migration over time may be useful, even though all the migrants between the regions in question do not pass through the points selected for observation — provided that the effects of any important changes in routes can be taken properly into account in interpreting the results. Information of this sort is used effectively in the study of migration in Buganda edited by Richards (1954: Chapter III and Appendix A). Intensive investigations of migrants in transit have usually been aimed mainly at obtaining detailed information on the characteristics of migrants, their motives and associated conditions. Investigations of this sort are an important part of the comprehensive study of migration to Ghana and the Ivory Coast, directed by Jean Rouch. (The results of this study have not yet been published. The findings of an earlier study in this field were presented by Rouch in 1956.)

The most frequent approach to the investigation of *migration processes* is through the use of information on the characteristics of migrants present in particular areas, or absent from particular areas, at the time of a census or other survey. The implications of such information with respect to the underlying processes are usually indirect, but they may nevertheless be useful. For example, a high ratio of men to women at ages over fifteen years among certain groups born outside a given area (or living elsewhere in the case of absentees) usually indicates a predominance of short-term movements, though it may only indicate the recent arrival of a group of migrants who may or may not remain indefinitely. On the other hand, approximate equality among the men and women of an exogenous group does not in all situations exclude the possibility that many of them are temporary migrants.

Information on the ages of persons originating outside the area under consideration has similar value and limitations.

Retrospective information on the frequency or periodicity of migratory movements can be obtained through specific inquiries on this subject, though, as noted above, the relation of such information to the method of inquiry must always be taken into account. A question on length of stay in the present locality (usually limited to the period since last arrival) has been used in several African censuses and is generally included in intensive studies of migrants in particular situations.

Some of the chracteristics of migrants which throw light on previous processes — apart from information on sex, age, place of birth, number of previous moves and length of stay — are marital status, occupation and conditions of residence. Married persons may also be classified with respect to the presence or absence of the spouse.

There is no method of measuring migration that is both theoretically satisfactory and administratively feasible in Africa at the present time. From a theoretical viewpoint, the ideal is a complete system of population accounting, such as that maintained in the Scandinavian countries and the Netherlands. The African population registers developed under French and Belgian administrations, beginning with registers of taxable males and later extended to the whole population, resemble such an accounting system but have not been, and are not likely to be, maintained with sufficient accuracy to yield reliable demographic statistics. It is possible that complete information of this sort for a few small areas and for limited periods may be obtained in experimental programs of continuous observation of vital events and migration, but such programs cannot be extended widely. Theoretically ideal information on migration might also be obtained from complete retrospective reports on the migration experience of all living persons originating in a given area; this would make possible a systematic development of the information in a form comparable to a life-table. But, as noted above, information of this sort cannot be expected in Africa except perhaps from a few intensive studies in selected areas.

In view of the importance of migration in many aspects of African life, there would seem to be good reason for giving increased attention to this subject in official inquiries. It is possible that, after further experimentation, some standard questions on migration may be recommended by international agencies for inclusion in census-type inquiries in Africa. A question on place of birth and a tabulation to show numbers of persons present in different localities by major region of birth, classified by sex and age, may be expected in most censuses and sampling demographic inquiries. In some cases reports on place of birth may be cross-classified with data on tribal affiliation. Information obtained in this way for African countries would be analogous to that obtained in the United States during the last century on state of birth; though unsatisfactory in many ways and now complemented by more detailed data on place of residence at some previous time, this information has been extremely useful. A question may also be included in many surveys on length of stay in the present location in the case of persons born elsewhere, with tabulation of replies by sex and age. Such information would be useful even though subject to ambiguity in interpretation.

In general, research on the complex processes of migration and population redistribution in Africa, both as demographic phenomena and in their association with other changes, has been pluralistic and experimental. One aspect of this pluralistic approach involves the use of data from census-type surveys (plus other types of mass data from establishment reports on employment, records of frontier crossings, etc.) in conjunction with the results of intensive investigations in particular situations.   Such use of diverse types of information does not lead to neat, precise formulations, except perhaps in particular aspects; but it can be fruitful in the provision of knowledge required in administration, planning and in the development of social theory.   Some studies that illustrate this approach are the investigation of migration into Ghana and the Ivory Coast, directed by Jean Rouch, under the auspices of UNESCO in co-operation with CCTA (1961) and the governments of the countries concerned; the studies on migration in Buganda edited by Richards (1954); studies of social and demographic problems in the southern Cameroons by the Ardeners (1960, 1961); and the research represented in the contributions by Mitchell and Southall to *Essays on African Population*, edited by Barbour and Prothero (1961).   It is also characteristic of the investigation by Prothero (1961), under the auspices of WHO, on migratory movements in Africa in relation to the control of malaria.   There may, indeed, be important contributions in the near future to methods of research on migration appropriate to conditions in Africa.   But it is likely that most work in this field during the next few decades, as in the last, will be experimental and pluralistic and that the interpretation of the results achieved will be mainly synthetic.

VII   CONCLUSION

The volume of basic data on the population of Africa is being rapidly expanded by the results of official surveys.   There is, or soon will be, a fair basis for estimating the size and distribution of population in most African countries.   Ethiopia, which has a large population, concerning which there are widely divergent estimates, is the most glaring exception.   Plans are being made to fill this gap, but at best their execution will take several years.   The reliability of data on the status of population in Africa, though still very imperfect, has been greatly improved during the last two decades by the introduction of more systematic methods of inquiry and better control of field operations.   There is also an increasing tendency to present the results in sufficient detail so that critical evaluation is possible, and the most serious defects can be spotted and in some cases overcome through the use of complementary data.

There has, however, as yet been little critical evaluation and systematic development of the data already collected — particularly with respect to information that can be used to provide reasonable estimates of fertility and, subject to larger reservations, of mortality, natural increase, migration and total population change.   An urgent need at this stage in African demography is, therefore, the systematic evaluation and analysis of the basic data now being produced.   The program of research on African demography at Princeton University has been conceived as a contribution towards meeting this need.   Attention has been centred mainly on the experimental development of methods of appraising and using the kinds of data now forthcoming from censuses and demographic inquiries in Africa.   The possibilities of deriving useful indices of various aspects of population change in Africa and of defining the types of error to which they are subject are, in general, promising.   It is hoped that the preliminary work already completed along this line may provide an impetus to other attempts, both in Africa and elsewhere, to use current information critically and systematically in order to provide knowledge about population trends in different regions and under different conditions.

At the same time that the critical use of available data provides information that is immediately valuable, it reveals sharply those defects that most seriously cripple efforts to attain positive information.   The specific implications of studies already made for the expansion and revision of procedures are reviewed above in the section on Methods of Collecting Demographic Statistics.   The greatest need is for the development of methods of providing more adequate information on births and deaths, especially information on deaths in infancy and at successive stages in later life.   The achievement of real advance along this line will require both large investment of energy and resources and a considerable amount of imaginative experimentation in particular situations.   A second important desideratum is the periodic repetition of census-type inquiries with sufficient constancy in method to yield comparable results.

One encouraging feature in the situation is the increasing exchange of information on technical problems and co-operation among governments, intergovernmental agencies, and scientists.   The organs of the United Nations, including its Economic Commission on Africa, play an important role in this respect.   There are important developments under academic auspices in fields related to the advance of population studies.   One especially notable advance has been the establishment of a program in Demography at the University of Ghana, with the assistance of the Population Council (New York).

There is no comprehensive study of population trends in an African country. This is not surprising because up to this time there has hardly been sufficient information, except perhaps for some North African countries, to warrant such an undertaking.   Some serious attempts to provide expositions of this sort might well be made in the near future.

Finally, there is the need to relate measurements of various aspects and trends of population to investigations in other fields, including medicine, economics and sociology.   Population trends can to some extent be analysed in abstraction, but they are inherently biological and social processes.   An understanding of their determinants and consequences requires the collaboration of demographers and scientists in other fields.   It may be hoped that a review of different contributions to this symposium may suggest new lines of fruitful co-operation in African research.

11

Biological Studies   Neil C. Tappen

I INTRODUCTION*

ANTHROPOLOGY AND PSYCHOLOGY have retained closer ties with biology
than have the other social sciences.   The following discussion is concerned
primarily with the former discipline.   The biological factors in anthropology have
been mainly the concern of physical anthropologists.   The central problem of
physical anthropology is the study of human evolution, even though many physical
anthropologists pursue investigations which have only rather tenuous connections
with this main theme.   Recent years have witnessed a revival of interest in social,
cultural and other behavioural factors which may have contributed to the processes
of human evolution in the past.   This approach has supplemented the application
of more sophisticated principles developed by paleontologists and geneticists for the
study of the evolution of all organisms.

Virtually concurrently, there has been a growing realisation among cultural
anthropologists that many inter-related aspects of human evolution need to be clarified, if general theories concerning the behaviour of present-day man are to have
validity.   Thus, at a time when a vast array of new kinds of biological information
relevant to human evolution becomes available, there is developing an overlap of
interests among cultural and physical anthropologists.   Some of the most significant studies contributing to this unified point of view have been made in Africa or
have used data derived from Africa.   This chapter touches upon a few of these and
attempts to show some of the ways in which fashions in thinking have recently been
changed by such studies.

II FOSSIL AND LIVING RECORDS

1. FOSSIL PRIMATES

In the record of man's evolution from primate ancestors some of the most significant discoveries have been made in Africa, and the pace of recent discovery
suggests that many more are in the offing.   Primates are among the most ancient
of the surviving orders of mammals, the earliest discoveries dating from the Paleocene.   Africa is almost completely unrepresented in this early stage of mammalian

* Bibliography for this chapter will be found on page 537.

evolution. In Paleocene and Eocene formations, primate fossils are abundant and varied in North America and Europe; Simpson (1945) lists more than fifty genera, grouped into at least five separate lines of evolution at the family level, with numerous sub-families. Other genera are still of uncertain position taxonomically.

All of the early primates were small animals whose structural features indicate a wide range of adaptations, but at a prosimian level of organisation. Barth (1953) had called them 'the rats of the Paleocene', and chisel-like incisor teeth, similar to those of rodents, were indeed present in three separate families. Other groups, however, show clear relationships to such living prosimians as the Tarsiers and Lemurs. In the late Eocene and especially the early Oligocene, there is a drastic decrease in primate fossils, and after the early Oligocene the one remaining family disappears from the fossil record. It is clear that a widespread extinction of the early primates occurred during this critical period. Fossils of prosimian primates are very rare from then until the Pleistocene of Madagascar, where several kinds of lemurs have been discovered. This is a gap of approximately thirty million years.

The decline of the early prosimian primates is coincident with the first evidences of the higher primates and with the rise of the true rodents. It has been suggested that the early primates could not compete with rodents and that the near extinction of primate groups followed directly. Furthermore, the evolution of the higher primates from prosimian ancestors may be a result of this rigorous competition. While the situation fostered extinction, it also may have brought about a 'quantum evolution' (Simpson 1944): a major shift in adaptation in a few remaining groups to a more complex level of physical organisation.

(i) *Oligocene:* The Fayum deposits from the early Oligocene of Egypt have provided most of the information on the development of primates during this critical period, but the specimens are quite fragmentary and have supplied new puzzles. *Propliopithecus* from Fayum is the earliest undoubted catarrhine primate. Its affinities with the anthropoid apes rather than with the Old World monkeys are assumed on the basis of part of a mandible with teeth — all that has been recovered. The sequence: prosimian to monkey to ape — which might be expected — is thus not supported by the fossil record. The earliest known Old World monkeys are from the Miocene of Europe and Africa. Recent speculation that Miocene apes may have had quadrupedal locomotion similar to monkeys adds another dimension to the problem of the relationships between these subdivisions of the catarrhine primates.

Other primates from Fayum show evidence of being transitional from prosimian to simian. *Parapithecus* has the same number of teeth as man and all living Old World monkeys and apes, but the individual teeth differ significantly, and the form of the mandible is more like that of the lemurs. *Apidium*, whose status as a primate was for a time doubted by several authorities, shows detailed similarities of the teeth to *Oreopithecus*, in spite of the two forms' being separated by perhaps twenty-five million years. The hominoid status of *Oreopithecus*, found in Europe, has only recently been established, though its relationship to man and anthropoid apes is not clear. A nearly complete frontal bone of a small primate, showing the postorbital closure characteristic of higher primates, was described for the first time by Simons (1959). This specimen was collected at Fayum in 1908.

Delays such as this are not uncommon. It is one thing to dig up a fossil and quite another thing to free it of matrix and describe it. While investigating the early primates, Simons (1960) found that other specimens have also been lying unreported in museums for many years.   There are probably others not yet freed of matrix.   Furthermore, the general experience in primate and human paleontology has been that additional field exploration and collecting in the areas of original discoveries have yielded more and even better fossils, spectacularly so in South Africa, for example.   This probably will prove to be the case in the Oligocene deposits in Egypt, which have by no means been exhausted of fossils.   There is thus promise that Africa will yield much more information on the transitions from lower to higher primates.

(ii) *Miocene:* In the succeeding Miocene several discoveries of anthropoid ape remains have been made in East Africa in recent years.   *Limnopithecus* is related to living gibbons, on the basis of the skull, but has much shorter arms.   *Proconsul* is a larger anthropoid which could have been ancestral to modern apes and to man.   There may have been more than one species of this genus.   Several specimens of it have been recovered, including some limb bones.   The arms are shorter than the legs. Le Gros Clark (1960) believes that it may have been quadrupedal and ancestral to both brachiating anthropoid apes and upright hominids.   The debate over the mechanisms of development of the upright posture in human ancestors has thus been reopened in acute form.   Was brachiation the precursor of human bipedalism? The question has numerous important ramifications, not the least of which concern the time of divergence of human ancestors from those of other living primates; the degree of genetic similarity and genetic divergence between man and those living primates selected for behavioural and learning studies; and theories concerning the evolution of the human cultural adaptation and their application to problems of human behaviour.   Once again the African continent promises to offer much better fossil evidence than is now available on the evolution of human ancestors from a pongid stage.   The recent discovery in Kenya of a fossil assignable to *Sivapithecus* — an anthropoid previously reported only from the Pliocene of India and Europe — is indicative of the rewards awaiting further exploration.

(iii) *Pliocene and Pleistocene:* Exposed Pliocene deposits are virtually unknown in Africa, except possibly at the vague boundary with the succeeding Pleistocene. From this point on, the record is exceedingly rich and highly significant.   The post-war discoveries of large numbers of Australopithecine man-ape remains have changed the prevalent viewpoint about the major features of human evolution during the Pleistocene.   Previously it was generally assumed that the increase in size of the brain either preceded or accompanied the assumption of upright posture.   Several fossil hominid limb and pelvic bones of modern appearance had been found with skulls of primitive structure, but the association was doubted.   Now it appears that fully upright posture preceded any great expansion of the brain beyond the size of the brain of living anthropoid apes.   Much of the record of fossil man in the Pleistocene of other parts of the world has consequently fitted into a meaningful and relatively orderly pattern, in contrast with the chaotic state of human paleontology before the second world war.

Enough details are now known about Australopithecine structure and biotic associations to have stimulated a number of theoretical articles interpreting their fundamental ecology and their bearing upon theories of human evolution.   Bartholomew and Birdsell (1953) point out that the bipedal gait and absence of long canine teeth imply that tools and weapons must have been fundamental to the survival of these open-country creatures, since they would have been too slow to catch or flee from larger animals and could inflict no serious wound with the teeth.   There have also been interpretations of the organisation of their family and social structure (Etkin 1954; Chance and Mead 1952); their presumed predatory habits (Washburn 1957; Dart 1958); and the nature of their tools and whether or not they manu- factured them.   The establishment of some of the major facts about the course of human evolution has thus led to a considerable amount of thinking by investigators interested in problems at the boundaries between biological and social sciences.   It seems probable that studies of human behaviour will make use of this increasing body of knowledge to maintain a balanced development.

The absence of stone tools from most of the deposits led some authorities to doubt Dart's interpretation of many of the bone fragments as purposefully fashioned tools.   He has, however, turned up more and more examples which are very difficult to explain on any basis other than human workmanship, and statistical treat- ment of the large collections of presumed bone tools in comparison with the total number and kind of bone fragments in the deposits supports his position (Dart 1957, 1960).   Presumed evidence for the use of fire (hence the name *Australopi- thecus prometheus*) has not been confirmed by later investigation in the South African deposits.

In the meantime, stone tools have been discovered in deposits of Australo- pithecine age, and the discovery by Leakey (1959) of a man-ape skull in Tanganyika, well to the north of the earlier South African finds, in deposits with a well-estab- lished stone industry, leaves little question that these small-brained creatures possessed at least the beginnings of this cultural adaptation.   Opinions differ about whether or not this implies that symbolic language was also a characteristic at this stage of human evolution.   It is unlikely that existing research methods will be able to settle the question, but it does not appear that formal language could have come much later.

The problems raised by the Australopithecine discoveries are of a lower order of magnitude than the ones they solve.   Robinson (1953a) has shown detailed similarities of the teeth of *Plesianthropus* with those of *Meganthropus* from Java, indicating a wide geographic range of a single genus and probably a single species. Robinson (1953b), however, also believes that there is another genus, *Telanthropus*, among the South African finds.   He indicates that it is directly ancestral to the fossil hominids of the later Pleistocene.   Dart (1955) regards this as being within the range of variability of other Australopithecines, and doubts that the South African forms ever constituted more than a single species at a given time.   Dart is thus breaking with a fine old tradition in human paleontology: that of assigning new genus and species names to each new discovery — a custom most recently exemplified by Leakey's *Zinjanthropus*.   The probability that a large number of contemporaneous fossils will eventually be collected should allow a statistical treatment that will determine ranges of variability and the presence or absence of discontinuities indicating specific or generic distinctions.   Until then, it seems likely that opinion will favour the reduction of number of genera, and perhaps even to think of the group as a single variable interbreeding population evolving through time, even though the generic names may habitually be used out of deference to their dis- coverers.   This would follow a general tendency in paleontology to recognise the theories of population genetics.

Another problem of lesser significance is that of dating the African man-apes. Some authorities place them as far back in time as late Pliocene; others think they are Middle Pleistocene forms. The question is related to that of the status of the discovered fossils: are they to be viewed as direct ancestors of modern man or as collateral relatives remaining at an equivalent stage of evolution? Few authorities now doubt that protohominids were very much like these creatures. The gradual accumulation of the cultural evidence of artifacts is favouring the idea that the African forms are direct ancestors, and that the actual shift into the cultural adaptation was taking place during the very time that the complementary processes of fossilisation and littering were congealing so much information for modern scholars.

Potassium-argon dates on the Olduvai deposits in which Leakey found the man-ape skull indicate a much greater age (c. 1,750,000 years) than has been accepted for the earliest stone artifacts. Some of the controversy that has arisen is reviewed by Howell (1962). The question of the proper sequences of deposits and extent of intrusion can probably be resolved with further exploration. The degree of accuracy of the new potassium-argon dating method for such relatively recent deposits has also been questioned, but it is probable that its reliability will increase as more experience is gained in its technology and methods of application. Absolute dating for many of the African protohominids is thus in sight, and with it the solution to some of the problems of the origins of culture.

The relationships of the man-apes to the later, more definitely hominid African fossils, are obscure. The evolution of man was proceeding rapidly during the Pleistocene — by far the briefest of the geological epochs. The usual estimate for its beginning is about one million years ago, and the majority of recent investigations indicate its duration was even less. With the probability that there was no more than a single hominid species from at least the Middle Pleistocene onward, it may well be that tracing genetic relationships at this level requires precision of information not obtainable from fossil material.

2. LIVING PRIMATES

In addition to the fossil record of the primate order, anthropologists are traditionally interested in living primates for the information they give on taxonomy, structure, locomotor function, diet, social structure, vocalisation and speech, and many other biological and behavioural features that lead to a better understanding of the primate *Homo sapiens*. Africa is one of the world's great primate reservoirs, with several species of prosimians, numerous representatives of the two great subdivisions of the catarrhine monkeys, and two anthropoid apes: the chimpanzee and gorilla. Nearby Madagascar has the greatest variety of prosimians in the world; it is the home of the 'true lemurs', and approximately half the mammal species of the island are representatives of the Lemuroidea. In a sense, then, the equivalents of the historical successions survive without excessive modification, allowing — with due caution — investigations of evolutionary processes in many biological and behavioural systems not revealed by fossil bone.

The distribution of the African primates is known with considerably greater accuracy than is that of the monkeys of South America, another great primate area, but there are gaps in the records of numerous species. Allen (1939) gives the broad outlines of their locations, as well as those of the other mammals of the continent. The distribution and adaptation of the monkeys, though not of the other African primates, has been reviewed in greater detail by Tappen (1960), but the analysis of fundamental ecologies is lacking in all but a few species. Probably more is known about *Cercopithecus ascanius* in the wild state, however, than about any other primate,

thanks to the monograph of Haddow (1952) and to a number of other studies by
Haddow and his colleagues at the East African Virus Research Institute.   This is
the species most clearly implicated in the spread of sylvan yellow fever to man from
a general primate reservoir, and the detailed studies stem from its medical importance.

Field studies which are primarily behavioural in orientation have until recently
been few in number.   Nissen's (1931) pioneer study of the chimpanzee was of very
limited duration.   Others have been largely confined to baboons, which are easy to
observe in open country.   Various field studies are now in progress or have been
completed so recently that only preliminary reports have been made available, but
the thoroughness of the investigations promises a great deal more information in the
near future on chimpanzees, gorillas and a few monkey species.   Studies in the
forests — the heart of primate country — remain distressingly scarce, except for the
gorilla.   This, the largest of living primates, is continuing to receive a dispropor-
tionate share of attention.   One of the latest studies is by a team of Japanese investigators (Kawai and Mizuhara 1959).   There is concern in some quarters that gorillas
are in danger of extinction.   New African governments will probably have to continue policies of protecting these animals in game reserves if they are to survive in
the long run, although fears of their immediate extermination are probably
exaggerated.

The African primate that has contributed most significantly as a laboratory
animal is the chimpanzee.   The Yerkes Laboratories at Orange Park in Florida
established its usefulness as a viable animal which will breed in captivity.   It falls
within the size-range of man, can probably solve more problems than any other non-
human primate, and is more co-operative than other anthropoid apes.   Perhaps
most important in assessing its potential value in problems of social research has been
the demonstration of the extent to which its behaviour is learned rather than
inherited (Nissen 1953).

In recent years baboons and the smaller Cercopithecus aethiops (usually called
'green monkey' by dealers) have seen more use in laboratories.   With the demand
for monkeys beginning to put severe strain on the traditional Asiatic supplies, there
is no doubt that these and other African primates will be used increasingly.   The
trend should be further stimulated by the new Primate Centers being established in
Georgia, Louisiana, Massachusetts, Wisconsin, Washington, Oregon and California,
with long-range support by National Institutes of Health — the research arm of the
United States Public Health Service.   A number of these centres plan to study a
variety of species and have programs which include studies of primate behaviour in
addition to use of these animals in purely medical problems.   There is an emerging
trend to try more closely to relate laboratory and field investigations, and this will
inevitably lead to more fieldwork in Africa.

3. FOSSIL MAN IN THE PLEISTOCENE

Satisfactorily preserved hominid fossils in Africa are rare for the period immediately
after the Australopithecines, but fragmentary finds (called Atlanthropus) in Algeria
and possibly another (called Africanthropus) in Tanganyika indicate that there were
men in Africa at a stage of evolution equivalent to the Asiatic men Pithecanthropus
and Sinanthropus, at a level of advancement intermediate between Australopithecus
and Homo.   It is probable that these four 'genera' actually were representatives of a
single species with a range throughout much of the Old World.   As with the

Australopithecines, it thus appears that claims for particular areas as the place of origin of man are meaningless.

The question of the date and location of the earliest appearance of fossils indistinguishable from modern man remains unsettled.   At one time there was a school of thought, led by Keith, which held that a group of hominids of essentially *Homo sapiens* form was present far back in the Pleistocene, contemporary with much more primitive men.   A lot of the supposed evidence for this point of view has been discounted in recent years, however.   Some of the specimens have been shown to be intrusions into more ancient strata, and other discoveries have suffered from overestimations of the age of their faunal associations.   Others have been shown by further study to be not modern in form at all, or — as in the Piltdown case — actual forgeries (Weiner 1955).   In Africa, the Kanam mandibular fragment discovered by Leakey in Kenya was associated with fossils of other animals of Early Pleistocene age. Although massive, the jaw appeared to have a chin, frequently supposed to be a criterion of modern status.   Analysis of the radioactive uranium accumulated after the death of the individual indicates that it is much less ancient than the associated Early Pleistocene animal fossils.   Further study also indicates that the appearance of a chin was caused by a bone tumour, so the discovery no longer has much relevance to the problem.

The study does illustrate, however, the use of modern technology in the determination of the relative dating of fossils.   Until recently the only way of telling the approximate age of paleontological specimens was by comparing them with specimens with which they were associated and with others from deposits elsewhere. This redundancy was justified by the consistency of the results and the absence of other methods, and such comparisons are still the main reliance of paleontologists. With the development of a variety of techniques for determining the contemporaneity (or lack of it) of the rare hominid fossils with the more abundant remains of other animals, intrusions and frauds need no longer be a major concern.   In fact, the testing of the fluorine relative dating method led to the detection of the Piltdown hoax.

Heizer (1953) and Zeuner (1960) have recently reviewed many of the relative and absolute dating methods now in use or being developed.   They describe the great variety of approaches to dating which have been attempted, of which some have demonstrated their value, and others show great promise.   When additional absolute dating methods are perfected and made generally available, the major features of human evolution in the Pleistocene will have an accurate time scale, and the questions of the relationships of Australopithecines to Hominids, of *Homo sapiens* to more primitive fossil Hominids, and the number of hominid species at any given time should be greatly clarified.

Already the carbon-14 method, which can give absolute dates from about 70,000 years before the present, has shown that forms beyond the range of variability in modern populations were still in existence as recently as 35,000 years ago. In Africa, the skull of Rhodesian Man, one of the most famous and best preserved human fossils in the world, has a close counterpart in the Saldanha skullcap from the Atlantic coast of South Africa.   Also similar are the specimens from Lake Eyasi, Tanganyika.

These specimens differ not only from modern man but also from the roughly contemporary 'classic Neanderthal' skulls clustered in western Europe.   This suggests that processes of race formation were going on during the Pleistocene and may have caused levels of genetic difference greater than those between any present-day human groups.   This information may thus be relevant to the question of the age of contemporary races; it suggests that they formed after an initial spread of *Homo sapiens* forms, because it is not likely that earlier populations which were more divergent would give rise to succeeding populations which became more similar to each other.   However, since it is unlikely that human differences were so great as to cause reproductive isolation, it is probable that previously established populations to some extent interbred with the entering groups and thus contributed some distinctive genes in different areas.

III   RACE CLASSIFICATION AND RELATIONSHIPS

I.   RACE CLASSIFICATION

Students of race have increasingly been forced to come to terms with theories of population genetics as well as with the actual findings of the allelic frequencies of newly demonstrated genes.   This has made racial classification more complex than ever.   In theory, race is equivalent to subspecies and local population, but actually to define human racial groups is difficult when the amount of reproductive isolation between them is unknown.   In a recently published book which grapples with these problems, Garn (1961) emphasises that races may continue to form as a result of local changes of gene frequency.   This continuing process through time makes it unlikely that there were originally only three major races, with smaller subdivisions resulting from migrations and intermixtures.   It also makes racial 'type' an out-moded concept, rejecting, for example, notions that the darkest skin, the most tightly curled hair, and the greatest lip dimensions represent the most 'African' characteristics, diluted by invaders in varying degrees in different populations.   He lists nine 'geographical races', of which one is the African geographical race; it is a collection of his lower taxonomic categories: 'local races' and 'micro-races' indi-genous to Africa 'north of the Sahara' (*sic*) — he clearly means 'south'.

'Local races', Garn's next category in the descending taxonomic hierarchy, are represented in Africa by the following examples: East African, Sudanese, Forest Negro and Bantu.   From the sketchy description and the very vaguely defined location of the East African local race, it appears that he includes the Somalis and Ethiopians among African rather than Mediterranean peoples.   The book does not pretend to give an exhaustive listing of local races or micro-races in Africa or else-where, perhaps in part because of the difficulties of applying the categories to many actual population situations.   It is worth noting that the words 'migration' and 'gene flow' (two different terms for approximately the same concept in population genetics) are not listed in Garn's index, and the possibilities that migrations may blur the clear-cut geographical delimitation of races are not discussed in detail anywhere.

Another way of dealing with the classification of races has been suggested. Livingstone (1962) has advanced the idea that the concept of race has no relationship to the realities of the population situation within a single species.   In this view, since the geographic distribution of one variable characteristic in human populations does not correspond to the distribution of another, and the distribution of these two does not correspond to yet a third, and so on, the arbitrary designation of races is meaningless.   This is in accordance with the findings of population genetics in which allelic frequencies at one locus in a population are usually different from allelic frequencies at another locus in the same population.

This denial of the concept of race as a valid taxonomic category is comparable in its arguments to those of biologists who do not believe the sub-species category corresponds to the facts.   In Livingstone's words:

> Their main argument was that the genetic variation among the local populations of a species was discordant.   Variation is concordant if the geographic variation of the genetic characters is correlated, so that a classification based on one character would reflect the variability in any other.   Such a pattern of variation is almost never found among the local populations of a wide-ranging species, although it is usually found among related relatively allopatric species. Thus, although it is possible to divide a group of related species into discrete units, namely the species, it is impossible to divide a single species into groups larger than the panmictic population (1962: 279).

Discussion of this point of view can involve the species concept itself as well as the highest categories of the Linnæan taxonomic system.   Only two remarks will be made here.   First: the discussion is an extension of realist-nominalist controversies.   The nominalist approach seems to help in avoiding much fruitless discussion by denying that categories have an existence independent of the classifier, and by assuming that categories are imperfect representations of the behaviour of concrete entities such as animals or people.   Thus there are no established criteria for categories in the Linnæan taxonomic hierarchy above the species.   The species category is relatively easy to deal with in its modern form, where it refers to the total population of sexually reproducing organisms able to interbreed.   Even here there are population situations demonstrated in nature which do not fit this criterion, and attempts to define local populations on the same kind of basis naturally run into difficulties.   The non-existence of races is in this sense paralleled by the non-existence of species, genera, families and even kingdoms.   This does not mean, however, that classification is useless, nor that it does not help in projecting meaning into situations occurring in nature.

Secondly, and stemming from the first: the implication is that the geographical variability of *all* genetic characters should be correlated if the subspecies is to be valid taxonomically.   If this is so, then species can no more be demonstrated to be valid than can subspecies.   The species is actually defined on the single basis of reproductive isolation, although in contiguous areas discernible differences have to be present in order to demonstrate that reproductive isolation is actually achieved. Closely related species actually have many genetic characteristics in common, and these characteristics may vary within each species on a geographic basis.

If it is not required that all genetically varying characteristics be correlated, the clustering of 'family likenesses' in localised populations to make discernible differences from neighbours is in many cases actually possible.   This is presumably a result of correlations of some of the variable gene effects.   The clustering is more likely to be produced and maintained in human populations which are partially isolated reproductively from their neighbours, and therefore more easily defined, grouped and named by interested biologists or anthropologists.   The easily distinguishable 'race', Bushmen, is an example of this.   In other populations, the processes controlling gene frequencies — selection, migration, mutation and drift — have operated to leave far less clear-cut distinctions.   The difficulties in grouping people described as 'Bantu' and the amount of speculation as to the causes of their variability and the nature of their kinship to other African peoples arise from the operation of these factors.

2. RELATIONSHIP OF AFRICAN PEOPLES TO OTHER MEN

The peoples of Africa south of the Sahara are generally considered to resemble each other more than they resemble those of the rest of the world. There are, however, some scattered populations elsewhere with characteristics which have been regarded as showing an origin held in common with present African populations. Although all living men neatly fit the modern conception of a species, in that they constitute a population able to interbreed, the supposed distinctiveness of sub-Saharan Africans has been interpreted as indicating that they have been partially isolated from the rest of the world for a long time. Not enough is known of the differences in genetic norms on the different continents to permit any satisfactory conclusions about how long this time may have been. In view of the extent to which genetic accident and selective pressures of an environmental and cultural nature may bring about evolutionary changes (see below), it may well be that this kind of evidence can never give satisfactory answers to the question.

The fossil record may some day yield more definitive answers, but the variability of the human fossils from Africa and the problems of determining their dates have so far prevented any conclusions by other than doctrinaire writers. Some authors (Weidenreich 1947; Livingstone 1961) believe that the racial differences on different continents, for which there is some evidence well back into the Pleistocene, are continued into those of present races. Others (Howell 1952) believe that anatomically modern man spread relatively late in the Pleistocene and replaced indigenous hominids. Presumably the present racial divergences developed after this rapid spread, resulting more from evolution *in situ* than from genetic contributions of the earlier peoples. Either hypothesis can be reconciled with theories of the evolution of populations, and neither is inconsistent with the belief that man has constituted only a single species in the later phases of his evolution.

Some of the people of Melanesia and Papua are similar to those of Africa in skin colour, nose form and hair form. Scattered pygmies in Malaysia show enough similarities to African groups to create questions of their origin which remain unresolved in the minds of many anthropologists. The prevailing belief at one time was that these populations represented remnants of what was once a continuous distribution of Negroid peoples, largely supplanted by other racial groups. The fact that many are located in refuge areas lends some support to this idea. The Bushmen-Hottentot group have characteristics also found in Mongoloids, including high incidence of prominent malars, epicanthic fold and yellowish skin. Some students have suggested that these similarities to peoples elsewhere may be either fortuitous or a function of adaptation to some similar environmental feature. The present trend is to regard this latter explanation as more probable, partly because of the complex movements of people that would be required to bring about the present distribution, partly because there is little archaeological evidence to support the other theory, and partly because genetic studies so far do not show close similarities of African peoples with presumed Negroid peoples elsewhere. Swindler (1955), for example, found no evidence of sickle cell trait in New Britain. However, as with other characters which can at present be used in determining the genetic composition of populations, this is an effect of a gene at or near a single locus. The complex genetic effects causing the more readily observable and measurable similarities could have been retained from a common genetic origin not subsequently modified by evolutionary processes. Since present methods do not allow determination of the genetic control of these characters, this remains speculative.

3. RELATIONSHIPS OF AFRICAN PEOPLES TO EACH OTHER

While the human populations of Africa south of the Sahara generally resemble each other more than they resemble peoples of other continents, the observable differences between some of them are as least as great as the differences found between peoples usually classified, for example, as Caucasoid. The initial identification of several major groupings is relatively undisputed, but attempts at finer subdivisions are perhaps more questionable.

Racial studies generally go beyond naming and classification in trying to determine (1) the degree of relationship between human groups, and (2) the racial history of an area. Those who have tried to tackle these problems in Africa have had to face an almost total lack of knowledge concerning genetics of racial variation, migrations of peoples, amount of interbreeding, time at which separations of populations took place, and the effect of natural selection on the criteria used in classification.

For the most part the classic problems of racial taxonomy are essentially insoluble in the present state of knowledge, and they are likely to remain so for a long time to come. This survey will therefore not attempt any classification of African peoples. It will attempt rather to review some of the approaches which have been made to racial classification and to present some current thinking about African race questions.

The grouping of Africans on linguistic, tribal and even caste grounds is frequently accompanied by reference to certain unmistakable physical differences between groups. The Bushmen differ from surrounding Bantu in their lighter colour, stature, prominent malar structure, epicanthic fold and peppercorn hair form; the differences are so great that a period of effective isolation of the two population at some time is probable. Linguistic and cultural separation helps to maintain the physical distinctions by restricting interbreeding.

Some authors have a tendency to assume historical occurrences in the racial classification of all African peoples, so that the groupings of Seligman (1957) are sometimes made on the basis of linguistics, caste or assumed migrations. At times language and caste coincide rather nicely, as in the case of such herding peoples as the Masai, whose 'Nilo-Hamitic' language differs from surrounding Bantu-speaking peoples, with whom they have a caste-like relationship and from whom they differ physically. In the case of the Batutsi-Bahutu relationship in Ruanda, however, the linguistic difference does not hold up since both groups speak the same Bantu language. Some authors explain that the Batutsi have lost their original language after migrating into the area; but this movement is only assumed. There are marked physical differences between Batutsi and other herding groups which maintain the Nilo-Hamitic language and culture traits. For that matter, there are substantial physical differences between the Masai and other herding tribes just to the north of them, which also speak Nilo-Hamitic languages.

The scattered groups of pygmies in the equatorial forest belt and a few of its outregions seem always to have a caste-like relationship with whatever tribe of larger people they associate with geographically, but pygmies invariably speak the language of their neighbours, be it Bantu or non-Bantu. The physical distinctions, in addition to size, are quite striking, however, and this has led to the assumption that they were the original hunting occupants of the forest zone and that they subsequently became culturally and economically attached to incoming agricultural tribes. This seems plausible, but, as is the case with so many other inferences based on cultural and distributional data, there is no archaeological evidence to support it.

Little research is being done now on the genetic relationships of African groups to each other and to races elsewhere. This is partly because measuring techniques, while analysed with increasingly sophisticated statistical methods (Talbot and Mulhall 1962 is based on data collected mainly in 1922 and 1923), have not yielded conclusive answers to the main problems. Probably more important, however, has been the shift in emphasis to newer methods of determining frequencies of single gene effects in populations. The belief, commonly held at one time, was that many characteristics, such as nose form, hair form and even pigmentation, were adaptively neutral, less readily modifiable by natural selection and consequently more valuable for taxonomic purposes (e.g., Hooton 1931, 1946). More recently, some authors have begun to suggest that these characteristics, which have been used in distinguishing racial groups, are adaptive in nature, and to speculate upon just what their adaptive value might be. Thus Coon, Garn and Birdsell (1950) regard the dark pigmentation of African peoples as being protective against ultraviolet radiation and tightly curled head hair as a possible mechanism for heat regulation. Similarly, the blood group antigens were at one time regarded as being adaptively neutral. The high variability of their allelic frequencies throughout the world and their lack of correspondence to groups distinguishable by measurements, pointed out for the East Africa area by Oschinsky (1959), had been perplexing until more new findings led to a radical change in the climate of thought.

The indications that a variety of genetically controlled aberrant hemoglobins may be involved in resistance to malarial parasites have given support to Fisher's (1930) thesis that non-adaptive genes cannot survive at high frequencies in a population. They have also led to studies of the possible effects of an individual's blood groups on susceptibility to diseases, relative fertility of matings, and other features which may be responsible for a maintenance of different allelic frequencies or which may have caused them at some critical period in the past. The emphasis has thus shifted from classification to basic studies of the causes of the differences of gene frequencies between populations, and thus to processes of small-scale human evolution. This story deserves more detailed examination, because much of the basic research was done in Africa, because it reveals how a few break-throughs can change fashions in evolutionary research, and because it has strong implications for research at the boundaries between biological and social studies. A more detailed account of recent progress in research on hemoglobins in African populations is given in this volume in chapter 13 by Robert F. Gray.

4. STUDIES OF POPULATIONS OF AFRICAN ORIGIN IN OTHER GEOGRAPHIC AREAS

The fact that people of African origin are dispersed in other parts of the world, as recognisable populations whose partial reproductive isolation is maintained by social barriers, makes a close approximation to a laboratory situation. Peoples with different genetic backgrounds are presumably subjected to the same environmental conditions. The idea is implicit in a variety of studies. The experimental procedure has been well controlled in studies such as that of Baker (1958), in which American Negroes and Whites have been subjected to extremes of heat, cold, humidity, air pressure, etc., and mean racial differences in ability to withstand such extremes have indeed been demonstrated. Other studies have attempted to analyse differences in a variety of tests of mental capacity; here the assumption of a common environment has been subjected to much criticism (Klineberg 1935).

Some of the human genetic characteristics of African origin have been discovered in the United States, where elaborate apparatus is available for testing and analysis, and many new procedures have been devised. This kind of information has then aided in medical and social studies in Africa. The abnormal hemoglobins come readily to mind as an example: the sickle cell characteristic was discovered in America and the analysis of the mode of inheritance of sickle cell trait and sickle cell anaemia was first made in studies conducted among American Negro families. The results permitted rational interpretation of the frequency of the characteristic in different parts of Africa and an eventual broad solution to the mystery of their high frequencies.

Genetic studies within the White and Negro segments of the American population similarly promise not only analyses of the processes of interbreeding (Roberts 1955; Pollitzer 1958) but also information on the mechanisms of action of specific genes. In addition, evolutionary processes involving changes in gene frequencies of known alleles can be studied actively in the new environment. This can aid in analysis of the adaptive significance of genes characteristic of African populations. The American frequency of the gene for sickling is consistent with the belief that it is gradually being eliminated from the population. From this time forward, the actual changes in gene frequency can be actively observed.

12

*Agricultural Research** John J. McKelvey, Jr.

I *INTRODUCTION*†

AGRICULTURE IN AFRICA, interpreted broadly to include hunting and pastoral activities, is the social, cultural and economic life of 90 per cent of the continent's inhabitants. Situated astride the equatorial belt and stretching into the southern Mediterranean regions of ancient civilisation and agriculture, Africa embraces an extraordinary range of environmental conditions and of peoples of ancient and often primitive ways of life, who mingle with others of modern outlooks and values.

The continent's diverse whole is composed of areas of apparently uniform ecological conditions, some of which are harsh and monotonous. In any such setting, the inhabitants would seem to have little choice of occupation, but by skilful and often ingenious utilisation of their resources they do, in fact, derive their livings in distinctly different ways. For instance, the semi-arid plains of north-eastern Nigeria, which drain into Lake Chad, afford the nomadic Fulani people grasslands for their cattle. On these same plains, where barely enough rain falls to mature a crop, the sedentary Hausa practise agriculture, in the limited sense of the word, growing their sorghums and millets in well-defined fields. Some wild animals still roam through fields and bush in this region and supply the sustenance for other tribes who eke out their existence by bow and arrow. The diversity of environments, the range of human experience in making a living under difficult ecological conditions, and the potentialities for supplying burgeoning populations with a good livelihood from existing resources make Africa a continent of opportunity and challenge for development.

* Many people have assisted in the preparation of this chapter. Dr Richard Bradfield, Professor Emeritus of Soil Science, Cornell University; Professor Fergus Wilson of the Faculty of Agriculture of Makerere University College; Dr A. H. Moseman, Director for Agricultural Sciences; and Dr J. G. Harrar, President of The Rockefeller Foundation, read the manuscript and offered suggestions which strengthened it. Mr W. C. Cobb, head of the Office of Publications of The Rockefeller Foundation, furnished expert editorial guidance. My wife assisted greatly in reviewing the manuscript critically at several stages during its preparation. Miss Marjorie Kinney, my secretary, the office service staff, and the reference service of the Foundation gave most valuable help. I should like to express especial appreciation to Miss E. A. Widenmann of the Office of Publications, who as research assistant undertook an exhaustive search for literature and worked tirelessly on all other phases of the preparation of the manuscript.
† Notes and bibliography for this chapter will be found on page 539.

A number of excellent treatises have been written on the natural renewable and non-renewable resources of Africa. Lord Hailey, dean of the students of Africa as a whole, an ex-colonial servant who celebrated his ninetieth birthday in 1962, compiled one of the most comprehensive accounts of this kind: *An African Survey* (1956), issued under the auspices of the Royal Institute of International Affairs, which is now in its third edition. Dr E. B. Worthington, a former secretary-general of the Commission for Technical Co-operation in Africa South of the Sahara (CCTA), now deputy director-general of the Nature Conservancy in England, spent some fifteen years in Africa. His text (1958) on science and technology in the development of the continent is one of the basic references in this field. Recently, the United Nations Educational, Scientific and Cultural Organisation (UNESCO) convened a group of specialists in Addis Ababa and published a survey of the natural resources of the continent based on their studies.

Many special-purpose studies are also available to the student of Africa's agricultural and natural resources. The International Bank for Reconstruction and Development (World Bank) has undertaken economic development surveys of several of the new nations of Africa. The National Academy of Sciences of the United States (1959) made a survey of selected areas of Africa south of the Sahara and north of the Union to be used in advising United States aid agencies on program possibilities. The Food and Agriculture Organisation of the United Nations (FAO), jointly with the former International Co-operation Administration (ICA) and also alone, has sponsored a number of specific surveys dealing with agriculture and natural resources (FAO 1961).

This chapter constitutes an attempt to trace several of the main trends in agricultural development in Africa and to identify some of the current problems. It will show, where possible, how the great body of research on crop and animal improvement and on better utilisation of natural resources has influenced the social, economic and cultural life of the people.[1]

II EARLY RESEARCH

Research on agricultural and other natural resources in Africa is deeply rooted in early investigations on taxonomic and economic botany, thus following a course of development parallel to that in Europe and in other parts of the world. A high degree of individualism characterised this early research. Inquisitiveness about the investigator's surroundings, rather than a search for ways in which these could be altered, dominated early research endeavour.

In the plant sciences, much taxonomic work was done on African material from the late 1700s to the middle 1800s. The Sierra Leone Company employed the Swedish botanist, Adam Afzelius — a pupil of Linnæus — to work in the territory from 1792 to 1794. The Royal Botanical Gardens at Kew published a flora of Africa; the botanical work *Flora Capensis* was initiated in 1859, and in 1868 a flora of tropical Africa began to appear. From about 1839 to 1855, a Dr Schimper worked on the flora of Ethiopia.

As the European powers began to scramble for African raw materials, the work of the botanists and zoologists who catalogued African flora and fauna provided focal points for the development of research institutions whose investigations have had far-reaching effect upon the social and economic lives of the people.

In the 1890s, King Leopold II dispatched the Belgian botanist, Emile Laurent, to the Congo specifically to look into the possibilities for the production of economic tropical crops. Laurent made three trips: in 1893, in 1895 and in 1903. He discovered the principal varieties of robusta coffee; he recommended cocoa, cotton and rubber as crops to be grown for profit; he suggested that clean cultivation practices, commonly recommended in Europe in 1900, were unsuitable for use in the tropics. The tropical botanical garden at Eala, in the province of Equateur, was founded on his initiative. Laurent also played a role in creating the agricultural service of the Congo. At Kisantu he established a first-class botanical garden and agronomic centre. These accomplishments preceded the establishment, in 1926, of the oil palm plantations directorate (the Régie des Plantations), and the subsequent development, in 1933, of the network of agricultural experiment stations in the Congo administered by the National Institute for Agricultural Investigations in the Congo (INEAC), with headquarters in Brussels (Stoffels 1956: 1472–3).

In British tropical dependencies, the initial activity in agricultural development is also to be found in the establishment of botanical gardens under superintendents who had some kind of scientific or practical training with plants. In 1887 a botanical garden was started at Lagos, Nigeria. The Royal Niger Company founded a garden for the distribution of plants at Asaba in 1888 and established four other agricultural stations at various locations in Nigeria in 1889 and 1890, for experiments with coffee, cocoa, and other crops. Later came the founding of a botanical station at Calabar in the Oil Rivers Protectorate in 1893 and a model farm at Ibadan in 1899. The botanical station at Calabar and the model farm at Ibadan were the forerunners, respectively, of the interterritorial oil palm research station and of the federal agricultural experiment station, Moor Plantation. A government botanical station was established in the Gold Coast (now Ghana) in 1890.

The Germans in Tanganyika actively sought economic crops for plantation development. In 1893, Dr Richard Hindorf of the German East Africa Company managed to import bulbils of *Agave sisalana* from Florida. These importations formed the basis of the subsequent sisal industry of Tanganyika. The German government founded a research station at Amani in the Usambara Mountains in 1902. The British reopened the station in 1927 as the East African Research Station, the forerunner of the East African Agriculture and Forestry Research Organisation (EAAFRO). The British transferred the herbarium, library and research projects from Amani to Muguga, Kenya, between 1947 and 1950.

Meanwhile the introduction of economic crops new to Africa was exerting profound influences on traditional African agriculture. Peanuts, referred to as groundnuts in Africa, came to Senegal from Central America in 1820. Cocoa was introduced to São Tomé by the Portuguese in 1822. It did not flourish when attempts were made to grow it in the Gold Coast in the early nineteenth century, but after missionaries and government botanists distributed seeds and plants there in the 1880s, cocoa farming quickly became a lucrative commercial enterprise. In the late nineteenth century, production of varieties of Asiatic rice became important in the swamps of Sierra Leone. At an earlier date, around 1840, Arab traders had introduced rice into the Belgian Congo. The Harbour Master and Commissioner of Customs under the Voortrekker Republic persuaded some Durban merchants to import sugar cane to Natal in 1847 from what is now Reunion in the Indian Ocean. By 1861 corn (maize) was being extensively grown in Natal. The catholic missions of Kenya and Uganda were instrumental in establishing coffee as an economic crop in East Africa through the importation of seeds and trees of the arabica variety from Reunion, to which it probably had come from Ethiopia, its home.

Some of the new crops — groundnuts, corn and rice, for example — were food crops, but they were cultivated mainly as cash crops. As such, they materially affected the lives of the African people, whose agriculture was of a subsistence kind, based on the cultivation of indigenous plants. Furthermore, as the new crops spread over large expanses of territory, they were grown under soil, climatic and biotic conditions which were not necessarily optimal. Investigations were necessary to ensure that they would prosper.

The need for research on introduced crops and animals was driven home to a most colourful pioneer in the early days of the development of the European highlands of Kenya. He was Lord Delamere, an Englishman who lived from 1870 to 1931, and who did more than any other single individual of his time for the development of agriculture and agricultural research in these highlands. Lord Delamere made a number of trips to East Africa, particularly to Somaliland, for big game hunting. When he extended his journeys into Kenya, he recognised that the highlands were potentially good farming land. Lord Delamere suffered a serious accident in 1903, and, as he lay recuperating in Nairobi, he decided to make his home permanently in the Kenya highlands. He wanted to prove that Europeans could settle in East Africa and that East Africa could become a true British colony. First, however, he had to show that top-quality stock could be bred there which would give good returns, and that crops could be grown which would lift the people from the level of subsistence farming. He obtained a concession of 100,000 acres at Njoro, on land which the Masai did not use for grazing their animals because it was heavily infested with ticks. The government rented this unoccupied land to him for £200 a year, provided he would spend £5,000 developing it during the next five years.

Lord Delamere faced many setbacks during this first five-year period. The pastures were too rich and too damp for his flock of imported merino ewes: four-fifths of them died. Many of his other sheep succumbed to lung trouble and to intestinal worms. The beef cattle which he imported suffered from a nutritional deficiency. It was not until 1925 that studies at the Rowett Research Institute at Aberdeen indicated that this disease was due to an iron deficiency in the soil.[2] When Delamere started dairy farming his imported livestock were doomed, for the brown tick which carried East Coast Fever abounded on the land. In those days there was no means of safeguarding cattle against ticks and the contraction of the fever.

Lord Delamere's initial efforts to make Equator Ranch a thriving stock farm failed, so he tried to grow wheat and corn. The land had to be ploughed, but no trained oxen were available. He had to build fences to keep out the wild animals. Even after he had overcome these obstacles, his first big crop of wheat failed: the plants were devastated by rust. Delamere would have been ruined had he been unable to raise a mortgage on his estate near Chester in England. But with funds from this and other sources, he survived for the next six years in a windowless, mud-floored building, working to track down a remedy for wheat rust.

From New South Wales, India, Egypt, South Africa and Canada, he imported wheat which he hoped would be resistant to rust. An enthusiastic amateur scientist himself, he engaged a young investigator, G. W. Evans, and built for him a simple laboratory in which to conduct experiments on a rust-resistant variety of wheat. The first distinctive and successful East African wheat, named Equator after the farm, was developed there, and three years later Delamere harvested a very large crop, including wheat of several new varieties (Huxley 1935).

III CROPS IN AFRICA

1. CASH CROPS

During the first half of the twentieth century, business interests enthusiastically promoted the production of crops for export from Africa. Some of these were indigenous crops simply extended in range; most were newly introduced. In West Africa, oil palm, cocoa, groundnuts, cotton, rubber and rice constituted the main crops grown for export. In East Africa, coffee, sisal, tea, cotton, pyrethrum and cloves held a dominant position. In the Rhodesias and Nyasaland, tobacco and corn became the most important export crops.

The founding of commodity research stations followed closely upon the heels of expansion in the production of these crops. Such stations grew in response to the need to improve the crops and to bring about efficient production for export. Any one of the commodity crops could serve as an example of the overwhelming emphasis placed on the development of agriculture aimed at the production of crops for export, but two were of special significance. One of these was the African oil palm, native to the delta of the Niger, which gave name to the former Oil Rivers Protectorate, cradle of the modern nation of Nigeria. The other was Upland cotton from the Americas, which far surpassed the Old World type in yield and in length of staple, virtually replacing it on African soil.

(i) *Palm Oil:* Commerce in oil palm products from Nigeria began under highly propitious conditions. The Industrial Revolution, in full swing in Europe, created a need for lubricating oil for engines, and in those days palm oil satisfied it. Life was becoming dirtier, and the European housewife needed better soap. Chevreul, the French chemist, had discovered that palm oil furnished just the right ingredient to make soap lather well. The British had outlawed the slave trade, and as a consequence the Liverpool merchants who had built a lucrative business on it were looking for other uses for their ships and facilities. The growing oil palm industry fitted their needs perfectly.

Oil palm production did not reach its zenith in Nigeria, because there the people clung to their traditional ways of harvesting and marketing the crop. Many growers with small holdings pressed the oil from seeds of the wild palm, which grew under variable conditions. The ungraded oil then passed to African middlemen, who would never permit European traders to deal directly with African producers. Thus organised, the industry could not provide a sufficiently firm financial basis for the development of an appropriate commodity research institution until a very much later date.

In 1924, Lord Leverhulme, the soap tycoon, advocated the admission of a European-run plantation system to Nigeria, to foster increased production. The governor of Nigeria, following British policy, supported the local systems of land tenure and rebuffed Lord Leverhulme. The Lever organisation then turned to the Belgian Congo, where it had previously obtained large concessions, and planted oil palms in direct competition with the Nigerian peasant. At about the same time, the Belgians founded the Régie des Plantations, which was succeeded by INEAC; there oil palm breeding received major attention. Inspired in part by information and results from an improvement program in Indonesia, the plant breeders of INEAC's Yangambi station crossed two varieties, *dura* and *pisifera*, to create a hybrid which in the first generation yielded twice as much as either parental variety alone.

These results, together with the increasing competition from plantation-produced oil, greatly stimulated the development of research in Nigeria. In 1939, large-scale agronomic and plant breeding experiments on oil palm were undertaken at the Oil Palm Research Station near Benin City. The West African Institute for Oil Palm Research (WAIFOR) was created in 1951. The research of its staff ramified into all aspects of oil palm improvement and production.

(ii) *Cotton*: The cotton industry in Africa received its main impetus after the American Civil War. The cotton famine in Europe caused by the war encouraged Manchester textile merchants and others to co-operate in planting American varieties in Uganda, Nigeria and the Sudan in the decades immediately following. A series of semi-official cotton production and improvement organisations was formed; this trend culminated in the creation of the Empire Cotton Growing Corporation in 1921.

The climate and soils of Uganda were not suitable for the production of cotton of the traditional Egyptian type, of Old World origin. The Uganda Company Limited, which took over the work of the Uganda Industrial Mission of the Church Missionary Society, acquired two and a half tons of seed of the American Upland type, which it distributed to native chiefs in 1904. Later, 'The Company reported with satisfaction that "the great chiefs in Uganda are shareholders in the Company, and that they have all taken up the idea of cotton cultivation with enthusiasm" ' (Masefield 1950: 86).

The availability of a new stock of cotton, the acceptance of this crop by the local people, and the development of a thriving industry enabled the government of Uganda to impose an export tax on cotton in 1919. The first proceeds were earmarked for two cotton experiment stations, at Serere and Bukalasa. Later, the Empire Cotton Growing Corporation developed at Namulonge a high-quality research program on the genetics and physiology of the cotton plant, on cotton crop protection, and on production practices and techniques.

Similar research programs sprang up in other areas where the introduction of cotton had prepared the ground for a cash crop economy. Stations were built at Samaru in Nigeria, and at several places in French-speaking West Africa. A cotton research centre was established in Mozambique. These and other institutions became integral parts of the developing cotton economy of much of Africa. In the Sudan, research on cotton also developed in response to a series of demonstrated needs for the improvement of production. Cotton growing became the major industry of the Sudan soon after the American entrepreneur Leigh Hunt showed that American Upland cotton could be an outstanding success there. An official co-operative development program for the region, based on the cultivation of this crop, was subsequently established: the Gezira Scheme.

Better plant protection techniques seemed to be the first need of the infant industry, and several institutions were soon formed for research in this field. The Wellcome Laboratories, founded in 1902 in Khartoum primarily for the treatment of problems in entomology and chemistry, became linked in 1918 with the Shambat Experimental Farm, founded in 1904, to form the Gezira Research Station and, ultimately, the Agricultural Research Institute. Each in turn played an important role in the success of the scheme. As Dr Frank Crowther, an eminent former director of the institute, so forcefully and correctly stated: 'There has never been any question of their [the Gezira research workers] merely selecting interesting problems for academic study, for the Gezira Scheme has always bristled with problems whose urgency has largely determined the nature and programme of the agricultural research work' (Tothill 1948: 440).

2. DIVERSIFICATION OF RESEARCH

As cotton and other export crops increased in economic importance, their culture involved large numbers of African people, extensive land holdings, and problems in production that went well beyond the scope of initial research objectives. The existing research institutions, devoted to specific crop problems, expanded their programs to meet these broader, more urgent needs: needs which stemmed from the simple fact that African people were dependent on the land and that their ways of life were deeply affected by the introduction of new crops and new techniques.

The Agricultural Research Institute of the Gezira Scheme expanded rapidly. The resident director soon had a staff of scientific workers, among them plant pathologists, botanists, soil chemists, plant breeders and experimental farm managers. Their research made possible the control of two important diseases of cotton: blackarm and leaf curl. The development of strains of cotton resistant to these diseases enabled the producers to attain better yields. The search for cash crops to supplement cotton, a set of experiments on water economy, and the breeding of a dual-purpose herd of indigenous cattle became part of the research program.

The solution of one problem led to the consideration of another. After the plant pathologists bred cotton resistant to blackarm and leaf curl, they had to turn their attention to developing varieties of high quality which could compete favourably on the world market. Leaf-sucking jassid insects crept into the cotton fields in alarming numbers in the northern Gezira in 1940, after three consecutive years of good cotton crops. Experimental spraying with DDT to control the jassids showed that a 40 per cent increase in yield might be obtained through the application of insecticides. Contract spraying from both land and air became a routine operation.

With diseases and pests under control, the fluctuations in yield which still occurred from season to season and from area to area came under scrutiny. Some research workers observed a negative correlation between the yield of the current year and the total quantity of rain which had fallen the preceding year; others saw a positive correlation between heavy rains preceding sowing and high subsequent yields. Exhaustive research reconciled these two phenomena: the depressant effect of the previous year's rains was found to result in large measure from the weeds which grew on the fallow land during the rains. Then it became important to ascertain how the growth of weeds caused the depressant effect; it proved that the removal of both moisture and nutrients from the soil was responsible. Irrigation of fallow and greater use of nitrogenous fertiliser offset this effect, but these measures created practical and social problems. Irrigation out of season encouraged enormously the growth of undesirable seid grass. Expensive ploughing in depth was the only known control. But then a most serious complication arose. Although weeds growing in the off-season were harmful to crops, they were indispensable to the tenants of the scheme as fodder for their animals, which supplied meat and milk in the villages.

Anti-jassid spraying, seid grass control, fallow weeding and fodder conservation

required mechanised operations and management techniques which did not har-
monise with the concept of peasant farmers and their families working by hand
labour.   The social results of the new techniques had to be taken into consideration
as much as their effect on profits.   Questions basic to the objectives of the Gezira
Scheme arose, according to Dr Arthur Gaitskell, from the advanced methods of
agriculture that the research men recommended (Gaitskell 1959: chap. 14).
Should the industrialised methods applied to this scheme be allowed to determine
what type of social organisation the people must adopt?   Or should certain economic gains be sacrificed and a measure of inefficiency be accepted in deference to
the way of life the tenants wished to lead?   These questions plague every country
which seeks to implement advanced methods of farming today.

While the Gezira Institute was developing a program which successfully
covered an increasing number of facets of agricultural research, other business,
governmental and philanthropic organisations realised the need for diversified
research programs and recognised that cash crops were but small pieces of the entire
agricultural puzzle.

In Nigeria the Northern Region Experiment Station, established at Samaru in
1922, gradually amplified its program to include research on sorghum, millets, soil
improvement, animal husbandry and farm mechanisation to complement its main
program of investigations on cotton and groundnuts.

INEAC proliferated into a series of experiment stations which handled the full
array of economic crops of the main ecological zones of the Belgian Congo.   The
central station at Yangambi, overlooking the Congo river, studied the improvement
of oil palm, rubber, robusta coffee, cocoa and horticultural crops, and undertook
forest management in the Guinean forest zone.   The botany division and herbarium
were located there.   The stations at Bambesa and Gandajika stressed research on
cotton in the tropical savannah.   The Keyberg station paid special attention to
horticultural crops and livestock on the copper red soils near Elisabethville in
Katanga.   The Mvuazi station in the west, in tropical Bas-Congo, was mainly concerned with bananas and citrus; the Gimbi and Luki stations, also in the province
of Bas-Congo, concentrated on fibre crops and forest studies; Mulungu in the highlands near Kivu, experimented with arabica coffee, tea, pyrethrum, oil plants and
food crops; and Nioka in the far north dealt with livestock.

The Liberian Institute was established in 1952 with a grant of $325,000 from
Harvey Firestone, Jr, to the American Foundation for Tropical Medicine, Inc.   It
started work in three fields: tropical diseases of man, diseases of domestic animals
which could be a source of food in tropical countries, and development of crops
which could be grown in the tropics as food for man and animals.

In the former Federation of Rhodesia and Nyasaland, more than forty stations
which conduct applied research problems have been developed.   In East Africa,
Tanganyika has four main research stations, each in a distinct ecological zone.   The
station at Arusha on the slopes of Mount Kilimanjaro in northern Tanganyika deals
with coffee investigations.   Two others, one in the southern and the other in the
central region, are concerned with the crops native to the ecological conditions of
these areas.   The fourth, situated at Ukiriguru, emphasises cotton improvement.
Research at Ukiriguru and at Namulonge in Uganda has demonstrated that the
intensity of solar radiation is a factor in the attainment of high yields from cotton
grown on the sunny south-eastern side of Lake Victoria in comparison with yields
on the north-western side, which is subject to cloudier weather.   The difference in

solar radiation may help to explain why the Uganda farmer frequently diversifies his crops, while his counterpart in the Lake Province of Tanganyika depends mainly on cotton for his livelihood.

Through government funds, Uganda supports two and Kenya nine principal research stations equipped to deal with the crop and animal problems of specific regions. In East Africa as a whole, the East Africa High Commission (EAHC) undertook the responsibility for somewhat more fundamental research on problems in agriculture, forestry, veterinary medicine, and marine and fresh water fisheries. The East African Common Services Organisation (EACSO), which superseded the High Commission in 1961, continues to support these stations.

3. NUTRITION

In diversifying their programs, research institutions were responding to an imperative need for more and better food for the African people, who were multiplying in number beyond the capacity of the land to support them under the cultural methods they employed. Diseased and poorly fed, these people could not contribute effectively to the economic growth of the continent. Medical and agricultural specialists began to see the practical and intimate relationships between health, nutrition, work output and education; they began to realise that the introduction of a cash economy in agriculture has often modified diet and changed traditional systems of land use for the worse rather than for the better.

In 1926, the Empire Marketing Board of Great Britain financed a study, now a classic, on the nutrition, physique and health of two tribes in Kenya which were at opposite ends of the nutrition spectrum: the Kikuyu (who subsist mainly on cereals, but also eat roots and fruits), and the Masai (who live on milk, meat, and raw blood). The feeling prevailed then, as it does now, that people in a poor state of health have a low working capacity. Justification for these studies, reported by Lord Boyd Orr and Dr J. L. Gilks, in fact turned on this point. The investigators recognised that ethnic and other considerations might account for the fact that the Masai male was five inches taller and twenty-three pounds heavier, and had muscular strength 50 per cent greater, on the average, than his Kikuyu counterpart; but they presented definite evidence that the incidence of certain diseases might be correlated with diet, and they raised the question, at least, of the extent to which diet may affect physique (Orr and Gilks 1931).

Innumerable published descriptions of the food habits of the people of Africa testify to the diversity of diet from tribe to tribe, and to the influence upon diet of abundance or scarcity of staple food crops and of livestock. But any one ethnic group may be deficient in important components of a balanced diet. Often, food habits carry the sanction of religion and of social acceptance; frequently these habits may not coincide with proper nutrition.

Different points of view regarding the nutritional welfare of the people in West Africa emphasise the need for additional research on the subject. Some nutritionists say that the people in West Africa who occupy the savannah zone south of the Sahara, where sorghum and millet are the dominant cereals, enjoy a diet which is adequate in carbohydrates and proteins; others do not concur. All seem agreed that in the cassava and yam zone near the coast, the people's diet, though adequate in carbohydrates, is deficient in proteins. In both zones, the abundance of carbohydrates as well as of plant proteins disappears when crops fail; then famine conditions ensue.

In certain West African villages hidden by the lush tropical forest the cash crop cocoa may occupy virtually all the good arable land, leaving little room for food crops. Dr W. R. F. Collis, Dr I. Dema, and their co-workers at the Institute of Child Health of the University of Ibadan have conducted studies of the nutritional status of the people who live in villages of diverse agricultural and medical backgrounds in Nigeria. They found that the people in the 'pure cocoa' villages were in worse straits nutritionally and socially than those living where cocoa and food crops were grown in reasonable balance. Villages with 40 per cent of the land planted to cocoa and 60 per cent to food crops showed the best nutrition picture among those they surveyed. Nigerian parents were wealthier in villages devoted principally to cocoa production, but their children suffered a greater incidence of nutritional disorders than those in villages where corn, plantains, cassava and yams formed part of the agricultural system (Collis, Dema and Omololu 1961).

However, the children in all the villages studied were undernourished to an alarming degree, particularly in regard to protein requirements. The village children, when compared with those of well-to-do people at Ibadan (children of university staff members), were six inches shorter at the age of three and a half, and the difference was still widening at eight years. Children of the Hausa and hill tribes north of the cocoa belt were equally undernourished at three and a half, but tended to approach the standard at Ibadan by the age of seven and a half. The diet of the forest children of the cocoa belt consists basically of yam, maize and cassava; that of the Northern plateau children, of millet, guinea corn, maize and some milk; that of the optimum group (children of the university staff) is quite varied.

Dr Collis and his colleagues are conducting their experiments in co-operation with agricultural specialists. The implications of such co-operative exercises extend well beyond the clinical findings. Their experiments may lead to recommendations for altering the present one-crop system of cocoa production. Introduction of poultry husbandry in these villages, better transport of foodstuffs, legal restrictions on land to limit the amount planted to cocoa, introduction of better-yielding clones to enable the farmer to reduce the area planted to cocoa without loss of production, thus freeing land for food crops — these are some of the improvements which could result from these studies. To grow and harvest food crops in the tropics requires a heavier expenditure of labour than that needed to cultivate cocoa and to harvest the bean; consequently, changes such as those mentioned above must certainly be accompanied by investigations on labour.

During the dry season of the year, the inhabitants of northern Nigeria strip the baobab tree of its leaves, which they use to make soup, but in many parts of tropical Africa vast amounts of leaf protein go unused. Non-conventional research may supplement conventional studies aimed at making more and better food available for the people. Dr N. W. Pirie, of the Rothamsted Experimental Station in England, has devised a 'mechanical cow' for manufacturing protein concentrate from green leafy material of all kinds. As one of its projects, the Faculty of Agriculture of Makerere University College may investigate the use of this technique in East Africa to supplement the present protein-deficient diet of many of the people.

The agricultural staff at Makerere pursues a great deal of important conventional research directed towards the health and welfare of the Uganda farmer. Improved breeds of cattle, poultry and swine, better animal management, improved vegetables, cereals and legumes, and modern agricultural techniques adapted for use by the peasant farmer constitute some of the research goals at this primarily academic institution.   Positive results will furnish local farmers with the means for improving their diet, income and standard of living.

4. FOOD CROPS

African soil has furnished the setting for a long-drawn-out drama in which a host of indigenous food crops — teff, neug, sorghums, millets, yams, native rice and certain wheats — have competed for a place in the sun against introduced ones like wheat, Asiatic rice, corn, cassava and groundnuts.   The importance of any one of these in the life of the people depends on a myriad of changing factors: physical, biological, religious and social.   The caprices of the people may also be significant in the acceptance of food crops.   Research on the principal introduced food crops is advanced in comparison with research on the indigenous ones, but investigators have been giving increasing attention to the latter in recent years.

Certain of the local crops have limited geographical range.   Teff and neug, for instance, are cultivated only in the highlands of Ethiopia.   Ensete, a type of banana, is important mainly in tropical places in southern Ethiopia and in parts of the Sudan and Uganda.   The possibility of future expansion of these crops has not yet been ascertained.

Other native crops like sorghum and millet have a wide geographic range. These cereals serve as the dietary mainstay of millions of African people in the semi-arid zone which stretches from Senegal to the Sudan and south to the Republic of South Africa.   They have also become important for food and for feed in India, the United States and other parts of the world.

(i) *Teff*: Most Ethiopians who live on the high plateau where the Blue Nile originates prefer teff to wheat as their basic cereal.   As with corn in Latin America, an entire culture has evolved around the minuscule seeded teff — milling the seed, preparing the sour dough, termed enjera, and cooking the enjera — yet virtually no research is under way on this crop.   The staff at the Imperial Ethiopian College of Agricultural and Mechanical Arts at Alemaya has begun recently to make selections of genetic material and to analyse this grass seed to ascertain its mineral and vitamin content and protein value.[3]

(ii) *Neug*: Neug, which in blossom looks like a miniature sunflower, serves as the main source of vegetable oil for the peasants in Ethiopia, but research on it there has only begun.   Neug (niger seed) also grows in India, and there V. M. Chavans has written a book about it and safflower.   Certain investigations on Ethiopian material are being pursued, in part at the Jimma Agricultural Technical School in southern Ethiopia and in part in the United States.   Studies on the morphologic, genetic and agronomic characteristics of the neug plant itself, and preliminary selection for plants which produce a high yield of good quality seeds and edible oil have just gotten under way.   If neug is to maintain an important place as an oil crop for the Ethiopians, extracting agencies will require a homogeneous neug seed population; this does not exist in the farmers' fields today.

Ethiopia supports twenty-one million inhabitants on teff, neug, ensete, wheat, sorghums, millets, and such livestock production as ecological conditions permit. To what extent will teff, neug and ensete, as compared with wheat, sorghums and millets, continue to provide the Ethiopian people with all or part of their bulk dietary needs? How well can these indigenous crops compete with others?   What will research show regarding their usefulness as basic food crops?   These are questions still to be answered. The answers will depend in part upon sustained research effort to determine the maximum yields and the quality of the foodstuffs which may be obtained from them.

(iii) *Wheat:* One of the most important food crops to watch in the development of the agricultural resources of Africa is wheat, for wheat consumption among European and African populations alike is increasing at a rapid rate. The peculiarities of ecological niches in Ethiopia, disease in Kenya, and too many weeds and poor soil conditions in the Rhodesias constitute major limitations on wheat production and therefore provide the main research problems on the eastern plateaux of Africa.

From its primary centre of origin in the Near East, 28-chromosome 'hard' wheat moved into Ethiopia centuries ago, where, to survive under a wide range of ecological conditions, this and related species underwent great racial and varietal diversification. Italian scientists initiated studies on wheat improvement in Ethiopia during the second world war, but these investigations lapsed. Currently the Department of Plant Breeding of the University of Minnesota is examining selections of Ethiopian wheats in the hope of finding new genetic material useful in breeding wheat resistant to its major pathogens throughout the world.

Temperature and other climatic conditions seem ideal for wheat production in the highlands of Kenya, but as Lord Delamere found out, they have proved equally ideal for the development of three of wheat's major diseases: black stem rust (*Puccinia graminis*), yellow rust (*P. glumarum*), and orange leaf rust (*P. triticina*) (Huxley 1935: I, 170). Ever since Delamere imported wheats from all parts of the world to Kenya in the hope that some would resist disease and yield well, breeding for resistance has constituted the main weapon for combating wheat rust in Kenya as elsewhere.

Successful in keeping the wheat rust organisms at bay, plant breeders at Njoro cannot rest on their laurels. The need to protect the wheat-growing industry in the Kenya highlands is as acute today as it was in 1930, when the government organised the Plant Breeding Station at Njoro. Within the last few years, a super-virulent race of black stem rust, P189, caused a breakdown in resistance of one of the most dependable high-altitude varieties. However, the scientists at Njoro had vast stores of genetic material at their disposal, and they developed alternative varieties which would resist P189. In a personal communication to the author dated February 18, 1961, E. Hainsworth (Acting Chief Research Officer, Ministry of Agriculture, Animal Husbandry and Water Resources, the Government of Kenya) expressed the view that should all agricultural research in Kenya stop, wheat would be the first crop to die out completely.

In addition to enabling farmers in Kenya to continue to make a profit from the production of wheat in the highlands, the research of Njoro has had international impact. Some of the most virulent races of stem rust known to science occur naturally in the region of Njoro. Dr H. C. Thorpe, who for more than twenty years was plant breeder at this experiment station, and his successors, Dr G. E. Dixon and Dr E. J. Guthrie, have tested varieties of wheat from all parts of the world against these races of rust. Strains of wheat with outstanding qualities of rust resistance that have been developed in the Kenya highlands have supplied genetic material for programs of wheat improvement throughout Latin America and the United States, and in other wheat-growing areas. Scientists in Kenya co-operate with those in Ethiopia, the Rhodesias and other centres of wheat production in

Africa, but the need has not been fully met for strong, inter-related, co-operative programs on the improvement of this crop, which is of expanding importance in Africa.

In West Africa the hot temperatures around the southern fringes of the Sahara prevent wheat from assuming major importance as a staple food crop for local consumption. This makes bread a luxury item. However, in spite of unfavourable temperature conditions, wheat is under cultivation in Chad, in parts of Upper Volta, and in several isolated localities of northern Nigeria. In 1960, the federal government of Nigeria strongly urged that the regional experiment station at Samaru, in the Northern Region, initiate investigations on varieties of wheat which might be adapted for commercial production in the *wadis* of the river basins, where residual moisture in the soil might permit a crop to mature during the cool part of the dry season. Grown under these conditions, wheat is not likely to compete favourably with the standard crops, sorghum and millet. The project illustrates, however, the importance the Nigerian government attaches to wheat production. It also indicates a growing realisation among government officials that the research stations which they finance can provide objective information important to any policy the government may formulate on agricultural development.

(iv) *Sorghum:* The future range and importance of sorghum as a basic cereal for the rising populations in semi-arid Africa will depend mainly on finding a control for the damage that weaver birds cause to the maturing grain. These birds (*Quelea* spp.) ravage the fields of sorghum and other small grains in the savannah zone of Africa at the time when the grain is in the milky stage. Flying over extensive areas and appearing in enormous flocks, they defy usual methods of control. The damage these birds cause undoubtedly contributed to the failure of several rice-producing schemes in the Niger and Senegal valleys. It seriously hampered wartime rice production schemes in East Africa and a wheat scheme in Tanganyika. As the intensified production of arable crops continues, these pests will have to be dealt with definitively. They are driving the farmers who traditionally grow sorghum and millet in these regions to substitute maize or cassava, which the birds do not attack.

The weaver birds are so pestiferous that a bird control officer, whose job was to try to exterminate them, was assigned to Bornu Province in northern Nigeria, where the damage they cause is particularly severe. Blasting these birds with dynamite at their nesting sites has proven helpful in their control; application of pesticides to kill them has not been so effective. In Bornu Province, government scouts locate nesting colonies of birds suitable for extermination. They report to the bird control officer, who moves in supplies to lay and explode bombs. The officer strategically places about ten forty-gallon drums filled with petrol over an area of an acre and explodes them by gelignite charges coupled with an instantaneous fuse. In notes, 'Control measures against Quelea', circulated by CCTA/CSA (ref. 4/141–56), an officer of the Ministry of Agriculture of the Northern Region has estimated that one hundred million individual nests were destroyed in this way during the 1961 season. Each nest probably contained two young birds; thus, approximately two hundred million birds were destroyed.

The urgency for bird control has led Dr Hugh Doggett (1962) and his colleagues at EAAFRO to attempt to develop varieties of sorghum resistant to bird attack. Goose-necked heads, large glumes to cover the sorghum seeds, long barbs on the glumes, and curved stems are some of the characteristics they have been trying to incorporate into the commonly used sorghums to make it awkward for the birds to feed upon them.

Dr Doggett harbours no illusion that he can breed sorghum plants resistant to hungry birds who must eat. But weaver birds in Africa have a choice of food, and therefore his program seems a practical one. The birds feed upon sorghum grain because they like it, not because they have to; grass seed constitutes their main source of food. The bird problem is a temporary one according to Doggett. The use of improved farming methods, with larger fields leaving less brush cover for the birds, for example, will go a long way towards effecting their control. Meanwhile sorghum varieties which the birds do not favour will be valuable. Doggett's long-range investigations include breeding sorghum resistant to many diseases and pests, and to the purple-flowered witchweed that feeds upon the roots of sorghum plants. This weed found its way into the United States recently and now poses a threat to the sorghum and corn farming area of the southern states.

An accelerated cereal improvement program based on sorghum and millet is under way at Samaru in northern Nigeria. This program will utilise the best selections of sorghum and millet strains of Africa in combination with material from abroad. The Kolo Agronomy Station in Niger and the Saria Agricultural Station in Upper Volta, which have developed extensive varietal collections of these food crops, are also intensifying their research for improving these cereal grains.

(v) *Rice:* When Asiatic rice (*Oryza sativa*) came to Africa, it met with different degrees of acceptance, owing in part to the social and cultural customs of the people, and in part to the biological and physical conditions under which it had to be grown. As Professor Bruce F. Johnston and other scholars have noted, the rice production zone of West Africa has a fairly definite eastern limit — the Bandama river in the Ivory Coast. The matriarchal societies of the Ivory Coast living east of this boundary traditionally depended on root crops as staple foods, whereas the largely patrilineal societies of the country west of the river had been cultivating African rice (*O. glaberrima*) for centuries before the introduction of Asiatic rice. Those people, already accustomed to growing rice, accepted the Asiatic varieties easily, while those who grew root crops found cassava and corn better suited to their needs (Miège 1954).

For reasons related to the physical environment, Asiatic rice did not spread rapidly. West Africa lacks the fertile deltas and flood plains characteristic of the great rivers of Asia. In the central part of Africa, specifically in the Congo, weak insolation (cloudy weather) during the growing season prevented rice from attaining high yields.

Many social reasons also influenced the acceptance of rice as a main staple for the people. Rice requires more labour to produce than do cassava, sorghum and millet, and labour was not plentiful; Africa was sparsely populated at the time new varieties of rice reached West Africa. Draft animals were lacking, owing to the prevalence of tsetse fly. Political instability and the lack of long-established civilisa-tion also made it difficult for rice to compete advantageously with the existing staples, because continuity in cultural practices year after year is inherent in rice culture. Much effort has been expended on the development of rice as a staple crop for Africa, but agricultural specialists have found invariably that its cultivation cannot be encouraged beyond the willingness of the people, based on their experi-ence, to grow it.

Contemporary research on rice at the West African Rice Research Station in Rokupr, Sierra Leone, and at the Richard-Toll Station in Senegal is designed to make this cereal better adapted to the physical, biological and social conditions of its African environment. These investigations are taking place today under three basically different ecological situations: where rice is grown in tidal mangrove swamps; where it is grown in sedge or grass swamps; and where it is grown as an upland crop. Each situation has its peculiarities regarding soil, water and possible cultivation practices. In the tidal mangrove swamps, problems of soil acidity, caused by the oxidation of sulphur compounds, have to be studied and floating rices of African origin must be compared with those of Asiatic origin.

(vi) *Corn (Maize)*: Corn, like rice, became established in West Africa with some difficulty. Eventually, this crop from the New World took hold along the entire coast of the Gulf of Guinea, but people used it most widely from the Ivory Coast to Nigeria, and came to depend upon it as one of their important staple crops. In 1949, *Puccinia polysora*, which causes a rust on the leaves of the corn plant, arrived in Sierra Leone by unexplained means. It moved eastward and devastated the crop in Ghana and Nigeria, thereby creating famine conditions in those countries. The importance of corn as a staple and the seriousness of this particular disease were the chief factors in the creation of the West African Maize Research Unit with headquarters at Ibadan, Nigeria. Here, plant breeders tested a number of bulk stocks of corn to select varieties resistant to corn rust.

As the corn rust fungus overtook its host and spread from West to East Africa, it also stimulated investigations there on means for its control. Working at EAAFRO, Dr H. H. Storey amassed genetic material from Africa and from Latin America. He and his colleague Dr A. K. Ryland selected strains highly resistant to the disease organism from the 200 lines of corn which they had been growing in their greenhouses. They found that one dominant gene controlled resistance of corn to *P. polysora*, and incorporated this resistance into varieties which could be used commercially. Their research, together with that of scientists working in West Africa, has made further devastations from this disease of corn unlikely in the immediate future. However, as the disease organism itself continues to develop new physiological races, a danger exists that the newly developed resistant corn varieties may become susceptible in the years to come. Were it not for the research undertaken in East and West Africa, corn might not occupy today its prominent position as a basic food for the people of Africa.

Corn breeding in the Rhodesias took a rather sophisticated bent. It began in Salisbury in 1932 on the basis of the research of the scientists who have been in charge of the program since its inception. In 1949, seventeen years after they initiated their experiments, Southern Rhodesia released its first hybrid; it thus became the first country outside the United States to produce hybrid corn commercially. Eighty-four per cent of the European-grown corn in Southern Rhodesia and 73 per cent of that grown in Northern Rhodesia by Europeans is now planted to Salisbury hybrids. E. J. R. Hazelden from Kenya, who recently reported (*Kenya Farmer*, February 1962) on the research on hybrid corn in the Rhodesias, attributes the success of this program to the continuity of the investigations and to the original happy choice of inbred lines with good combining ability for making hybrids.

The production of hybrid corn, so successful in the Rhodesias, may not be the system most suitable for Kenya, Tanganyika, Uganda and Zanzibar. African farmers in these countries may not have access to fertilisers, to better management practices, or to funds for the purchase of new seed every year. Today, only 2 per cent of their total acreage is planted to hybrids. The production of 'synthetics', open-pollinated, improved varieties of corn, may prove to be more satisfactory for them than would the development of hybrids. Whatever the system that plant breeders in East Africa recommend, they must take into consideration the value of introducing large quantities of new genetic material to the stocks immediately around them.

Plant breeders in Africa are beginning to enrich their local stocks with material from germ plasm banks in Latin America that shows promise not simply for disease resistance, but also for the many agronomic characteristics important to the success of corn in lowland tropical and highland temperate regions. In the *Kenya Farmer* of May 1962, Dr M. N. Harrison announced high yield increases from trials of crosses of two Central American corn varieities which he tested in Kenya.

Corn and sorghum compete with one another for position as the dominant cereal crop in certain semi-arid regions of East Africa. Sorghum would yield better than corn but for the damage it suffers from weaver birds. Peasant families used to employ their children to frighten away the birds, but the children now go to school and can no longer do this job. Here the people have to decide whether to continue to grow their traditional crop, sorghum, or to switch to growing corn. Their choice may well rest upon the comparative performance of the drought-resistant corn and the bird-resistant sorghum that the crop scientists who are working on these problems will be able to offer them.

(vii) *Cassava:* When the cassava plant came to Africa, it was poorly received. No one knew how to prepare its long starchy roots as manioc flour. After a method for the preparation of manioc flour was introduced, cassava spread all over tropical Africa. Because cassava has less stringent soil requirements than the native yams, it began to replace yams in areas of low soil fertility. Its general usefulness under a wide variety of conditions, especially as a 'famine insurance' crop, has made it one of the most important staples of Africa. The roots keep well in the soil and may be harvested as needed when most other crops have been consumed.

Two virus diseases of great importance — mosaic and brown streak — attack cassava, but, as in the case of corn, resistant varieties are now available. These varieties are a product of the investigations of H. H. Storey and his colleagues who worked at Amani in Tanganyika. They obtained sevenfold increases in yield from resistant varieties in comparison to susceptible strains where both were planted in experimental plots in the Eastern Province of Uganda. A full-scale administrative campaign was then mounted in eastern Uganda for the complete replacement of the prevalent disease-ridden stock. Orders making it compulsory to pull up all cassava plants showing mosaic symptoms were enforced. Not only were the clean high-yielding varieties quickly multiplied, but the source of heavily infected material was virtually eliminated. The combined effects of basic research and of an applied action program enabled the peasant farmer to realise substantial increases in yield per acre (Storey 1950[?]: 13).

5. LAND TENURE AND LAND USE

The introduction of crops new to African conditions and of the concept of growing crops for revenue had considerable impact on the life of the African people. So did the introduction of foreign ideas of land use and land tenure. On these points the African people and the European settlers had to deal from the very beginning.

The constant pressure upon available resources, on the one hand from European interests in cash crops and on the other from population increase among the Africans, has made land ownership and land use one of the main problems on the continent. It led, for example, to the development of African reserves in Tanganyika in 1896, to the definition of crown land and public land in Kenya in 1901, and to the establishment of native reserves there in 1904.

The existence in Africa of large areas that are still underpopulated and underdeveloped, however, has encouraged governments and private companies to establish numerous development and resettlement schemes. The number of these which have turned out to be successful has been disappointingly small. Those which have succeeded possess two important attributes: they have been planned in areas where the African people clearly desired to participate, and they have been based on constant investigations, research and re-evaluation to make them work. The Zande Scheme in the southern Sudan, the Groundnut Scheme in Tanganyika, and the Niger Agricultural Project in Nigeria lacked one or both of these attributes; the Swynnerton Plan in Kenya possessed them to a remarkable degree.

The Zande Scheme, formulated in 1943, did not evolve in response to any need which the Zande tribes felt for a cash crop like cotton or for an improved standard of living. It developed because expatriates firmly believed that the people ought to want to change their way of life. As a consequence the scheme never got off the ground.

The Groundnut Scheme, conceived in 1946 as a means for turning 20,000 acres of land in Tanganyika into oil crop production to satisfy the needs of the British housewife for vegetable oils, had a remarkable lack of orientation with the realities of the environment at Kongwa in the Central Province of Tanganyika, where it was placed. Alan Wood (1950) describes this economic disaster in his book *The Groundnut Affair*. In his articles in *The Times* (London) of October 2 and 5, 1950, 'The Kongwa experiment', Dr S. Herbert Frankel has also drawn attention to the main reasons why this scheme failed. It suffices here simply to say that evidence abounds to show that lack of investigations on rainfall, soil properties, mechanisation, farm management, and a host of other agricultural problems thought to be unimportant at the time, militated against the success of the scheme.

The Niger Agricultural Project had many objectives in view. It was supposed to lead to increased production of peanuts and sorghum, to demonstrate better methods of farming in northern Nigeria, and to provide for the settlement of farm families in an unoccupied but fertile area. Beginning in 1949, the Colonial Development Corporation financed it as a marginal project not expected to yield any returns until 1958. In 1950, the program was still considered experimental. In 1951, capital development was slowed down. By 1952 real worries set in, and discussions were initiated about the future of the project. In 1954, the company was liquidated and its assets purchased by the government of the Northern Region.

In the mid-1950s Dr K. D. S. Baldwin (1957), agricultural economist, spent nine months analysing the scheme; of his conclusions, two seem especially relevant to the success or failure of this and similar projects. The company paid no attention to the need for research on rotation trials, soil fertility, farm production economics, mechanical cultivation and economic methods of weed control. It assumed that such work was being done by the government of the Northern Region.   The company, in addition, grossly underestimated the importance of the social and practical problems involved in mobilising African settlers to live and work of their own volition under new conditions.   S. Herbert Frankel, in the foreword to Baldwin's book (1957: xi–xii), points out that the Niger project illustrated the twin dangers inherent in all developmental projects — grandiosity and arrogance: the belief that ignorance of the facts of an economic situation can best be met by throwing more men and machines into the fray; the belief that the actions of others which we do not readily understand are irrational.   The African peasants who refused to be drawn into the scheme were neither fools nor knaves and certainly not acting irrationally — they were acting as economic men.

The Swynnerton Plan (Swynnerton 1954), much more comprehensive than many development schemes, had as its purpose the acceleration of the development of agriculture in native areas.   This was to be accomplished by instituting individual ownership of land, by introducing high value cash crops for the African farmer to grow in areas of high agricultural potential, by improving livestock, by developing water supplies in semi-arid pastoral regions, and by instituting grazing management, protective afforestation and tsetse fly control.   The plan went into operation in 1954, and by 1959 it had cost about £8,000,000.   It was sensibly rooted in the active desire of the tribes, the Kikuyu especially, to consolidate their scattered land holdings.   They were tired of haggling incessantly over land disputes and were glad to register land in the name of individual owners.   Each of the main tribes — Suk, Nandi, Kipsigis, Luo and Kikuyu — responded differently to the plan.   Progressive Elgeyo farmers asked for irrigation taps and terraces, and were willing to pay for them.   Designed to raise the agricultural level of production according to the ecological possibilities and tribal peculiarities of each region, the scheme succeeded so well that it tripled African income in the region in three years.   As a consequence, in 1961 Kenya qualified for an $8,400,000 loan from the World Bank to expand the scheme.

The Swynnerton Plan worked because it satisfied three basic conditions: a recognition of the need for a reasonable balance in emphasis between cash crops and subsistence crops; a desire among the tribal people to modernise their methods; and a realisation of the importance of research.   Although the ten-year ALDEV development scheme which preceded the plan was not a research scheme *per se*, many of the research staff members of the Kenya Department of Agriculture participated in it and in devising the Swynnerton Plan.   Elspeth Huxley (1960), in *A New Earth*, vividly portrays the problems which technicians and farmers had to face to make the plan work.

New economic and social forces are also influencing the age-old system of land tenure in Africa, according to Dr H. A. Oluwasanmi (1957), agricultural economist in the Faculty of Agriculture of the University of Ibadan, Nigeria.   Nigeria's traditional pattern is one of communal land ownership.   This type of ownership and the practice of shifting cultivation developed when land was abundant and the population sparse.   The forces working to change this traditional pattern are: the commercialisation of agriculture; the development of cash crops for the export market; the increase of population which has brought about a reduction in the period of bush fallow; and the emergence of new economic and social classes which derive their power and prestige from material wealth and from formal western education.

Oluwasanmi points out that communal tenure has acted as a strong cohesive force in an agrarian society, but that under the pressure of burgeoning populations, soil depletion and excessive fractionation of holdings are rendering the system untenable.   Other students emphasise that traditions of inheritance, influenced by religion or tribal custom by which sons inherit land in equal parcels, aggravate the problem of maintaining land parcels in economically profitable units (Elias 1953). Oluwasanmi suggests that in Nigeria the state should supplant the tribal organisation in control over uncultivated bush land, so that it may foster plantation cultivation or resettlement on the wild domain and discourage further extension of the peasant system of farming with shifting cultivation.   He believes that the settlement schemes sponsored by the Regional Production Board of Western Nigeria will become the instruments for capitalisation of tropical agriculture; in these schemes the tenants have inheritable holdings subject to state control.

New social, cultural and economic forces are not likely to bring about changes in land use and land tenure in time to allow subsistence agriculture to evolve into a balanced, cash crop agriculture and to relieve the land of excessive population pressure where it exists.   The agricultural scientist, therefore, must direct his attention to crop and animal improvement programs which fit current systems of land use and land tenure.   He must consider ways to improve peasant agriculture and subsistence farming, as well as ways to promote increase in production under more ideal conditions.

The Rhodes-Livingstone Institute at Lusaka, Northern Rhodesia, founded in 1937, has supported a series of land use investigations.   Those of Dr William Allan (1949) led to the publication of his study on land usage among the native people of Northern Rhodesia.   His observations and those of subsequent investigators show a remarkable adjustment of people to their land resources.   The Northern Rhodesian tribes which Allan studied practise a kind of subsistence agriculture called the 'chite-mene' system.   They gather the brush from wide areas and concentrate it in small circular gardens where they burn it to supply fertiliser for their crops.

Allan poses the question: How much land does a man require?   No one has answered this question satisfactorily — least of all in Africa — for no one knows the maximum productivity of which any piece of land is capable.   The answer may depend, in part, upon the man's social, economic, educational and technical horizons, and in part upon the broad physical limits to production of the land in his environment.   The agricultural research worker, however, has a responsibility to devise methods for increasing production per unit area in order to accommodate inexorable population increases.

Dr P. H. Nye (1957) describes three major systems of subsistence agriculture in West Africa.   One is continuous cropping, which relies on slow removal of nutrients in relation to the soil's ability to supply them.   Tree crops fit into this system because they feed at greater depths than do annuals and remove nutrients at a slower rate.   A second is one in which the soil is drained of nutrients faster than it can renew them.   This system leads to shifting cultivation, which is nothing more than an alternation of land planted to field crops with land left fallow for a period sufficient for the soil to regenerate.   The third is mixed farming in which cattle grazing over an extensive area provide fertiliser for continuous cropping around the homestead.   Each of these schemes can be employed only in so far as it enables the plants to satisfy their basic nutrient requirements.

In discussing subsistence agriculture, E. B. Worthington (1958: 12) defines two kinds of shifting cultivation: one in which the people live permanently in the same place and cultivate the surrounding plots in rotation, as in the highlands of Rwanda; the other in which the village site is changed every few years, as in the chitemene system in Northern Rhodesia.

Where shifting cultivation is practised under tropical forest conditions, land scarcity occurs in a few areas only. Tropical forest areas of Sierra Leone and of the Eastern Region of Nigeria are, however, experiencing land hunger under the pressure of dense populations. Here, according to Nye, the only way to intensify agriculture, short of resettlement, is to use fertilisers.

In the tropical forests of the Congo, ample land is still available, but even here, signs of maladjustment between land resources and people are beginning to appear. R. de Coene (1956), a former director of INEAC, pointed out that Bantu and Sudanese populations on the southern and northern limits of the tropical forest, whose diet consisted of cereals, had already shortened the fallow period allowing only time for grass to develop, when bush or tree fallow would have been better. Annual fires would soon turn this area into permanent savannah.

European administration of lands in the Congo also gave rise to the destruction of the forest cover. The introduction of crops grown for cash and the necessity of producing food for townspeople led to the working of larger areas. To avoid the hard labour of clearing mature fallows, lush with tropical trees, farmers began to clear them early or to lengthen the cropping period in the cleared area before leaving it to fallow. Shortage of farming land became a factor. Soil deterioration, extension of the cultivated area without a corresponding increase in crop yield, fragmentation of fields resulting from the search for fresh fertile soil, and impoverishment of rural communities ensued. For a variety of reasons the usual European techniques for improving yields and modifying customary methods of cropping proved not to be feasible. Since the prevalence of the tsetse fly in forested areas prevents the raising of cattle, the native farmer could not practise mixed farming. He had neither draft animals, dung nor transport, and the application of imported fertilisers was not a paying venture. The alternative seemed to be to improve the Bantu system, shifting cultivation on a regularised and organised basis (de Coene 1956).

The Belgians recognised the merits of the bush fallow (shifting cultivation) system and were able to mould it into the corridor system. After a study of the most desirable length and shape for the rotational blocks, based on traditional systems of land ownership and on optimum rotation to maintain fertility, the European agronomists recommended two systems. One was the Babua-type settlement in which each man received a farm that cut north and south across the full length of the series of east-west rotational blocks. The other was the Turumba settlement: a semi-communal method in which the individual farmer might receive a different lot each year. These patterns were employed in the settlement schemes known as Paysannats.

Each system had its advantages and disadvantages. The value of both systems, however, lay in grouping small individual fields into large clearings which facilitated the application of modern agronomic techniques, particularly in respect to plant sanitation and the control of crop pests. One hundred and twenty thousand families were settled in the Paysannats of the Congo as of 1955 and the settlement of 450,000 native families out of 2,500,000 was envisaged by 1965 (Huge 1955). The communities created will undoubtedly require public services, such as co-operative stores for buying and selling, water distribution, schools, dispensaries and public buildings. Successful under European direction, these systems initiated some twenty years ago have now to prove themselves under changed conditions.

The corridor system in the Paysannats of the Congo demonstrates exceedingly well that each of two cultures — the African and the European — can contribute to the development of improved management practices for tropical forest land. Much remains to be done, especially on problems of soil fertility, soil management, green manure and cover crops, to ensure that intensive crop production can be practised in the humid tropics without soil depletion. Moreover, the problem of devising a satisfactory mixed farming system in the humid tropics has still to be solved.

IV LIVESTOCK

I. CATTLE

Over vast areas of Africa, in the temperate as well as in tropical areas, cattle are so important to the people that their possession has become an end in itself, transcending any realistic appraisal of the place of livestock in an agricultural system. The prestige value of a herd to its owner, its conspicuousness as a status-symbol and its worth as a self-improvement investment, as well as the role of cattle in the marriage-price and dowry system, have been pointed out by Dr R. A. Hutchinson in his summary of animal husbandry in West Africa (Wills 1962: chap 24) and by others.

The possessive attitude of people towards their cattle may change as increasing population pressures push more inhabitants into the tropical rain forests, and force farmers to shorten the bush fallow period, thus inviting soil depletion. Eventually they may begin to think of cattle or other domesticated animals as factors in rebuilding and renewing the fertility of soil: a realisation which would move them towards a mixed farming system. Some experimentation on the practice of mixed farming under African conditions has already been conducted, notably by animal husbandry specialists in the Northern Region of Nigeria, who began their studies in 1928. Some tribal peoples have spontaneously developed mixed-farming techniques, but this pattern is still very much the exception over most of the continent.

Specialists in animal husbandry and veterinary science who seek to increase the usefulness of cattle in tropical areas must direct their attention to several well-defined problems. Before cattle in tropical areas can serve for milk and meat and contribute to a balanced farming system, research on breeding must create stock adapted for better yield under tropical conditions. Similarly, forage must be improved to give a basis for better nutrition, and a great deal must be done to ensure more effective control of disease.

A number of tropical experiment stations have undertaken cattle breeding programs in West Africa: the experiment station at Bamako, Mali, established in 1922; the Shika Experiment Station in the Northern Region of Nigeria; and stations at Ibadan and Lagos in Nigeria, at Kumasi and Accra in Ghana, and at Harbel near Monrovia in Liberia. Professor K. Twum-Barima and his colleagues in Ghana, among others in West Africa, are upgrading Ndama cattle. Quite apart from the recent experiment station work, in northern Nigeria at least five strains of humped cattle with Indian Zebu blood have evolved under generations of management by Fulani herdsmen.

Dr P. Mahadevan of Makerere University College is studying the upgrading of African cattle with the Indian Sahiwal milch breed. In the Rhodesias, Europeans have crossed local cattle of three strains with Herefords and Aberdeen Angus to get a satisfactory ranch animal. Since 1937, the Matopos experiment station near Bulawayo has conducted a breeding program with pure-bred Hereford, Afrikander and native cattle. These experiments have indicated that exotic European-type cattle deteriorate on the natural veld.

The unsolved question remains: is it better to upgrade the local breeds through selection or to cross-breed local with foreign stock to develop a strain of cattle especially suited to the dry or humid tropics? The answer depends on the environment in which cattle are expected to thrive and the purposes people expect them to serve.

South African and Central African experiment stations have been productive in cataloguing the grasses of the temperate African plateaux and in the elaboration of adequate management techniques. This research has often turned on the use of fire as a tool for eliminating plant refuse on the range. Research in Ghana and Nigeria and in the French-speaking countries of West Africa has complemented such studies. Work in progress in Ibadan at federal and state experiment stations and research by Drs R. J. McIlroy and Desmond Hill of the University of Ibadan, will, it is hoped, yield fruitful information about tropical pastures. Such information should enable cattle herders to make use of immense stretches of tropical grass which lie idle in the derived savannahs bordering the rain forests of West Africa.

Research on cattle improvement and cattle management, important as it is, will have little impact on African agriculture without strong parallel research effort on the control of disease. The continent of Africa serves as host to virtually all the important cattle diseases — rinderpest, bovine pleuropneumonia, foot and mouth disease, East Coast Fever, and nagana (trypanosomiasis), to mention a few. Research on cattle diseases in Africa began when rinderpest gained a foothold on the African continent. Rinderpest reached Egypt from Asia in the 1840s, moved up the Nile to Ethiopia by about 1860, and by 1890 decimated the cattle of the Masai in Kenya and in Tanganyika. These nomadic cattle herders depended exclusively upon their cattle for sustenance. After rinderpest affected their stock, the Masai never regained the dominant position they had previously held in this region. The British posted a Captain Haslam, a veterinarian, to Ukambani at this time to deal with rinder pest, and although he was murdered in Kikuyu land, his work continued. In 1910 the Veterinary Research Laboratory at Kabete in Kenya was opened, and in 1923 the Animal Health Research Centre at Entebbe, Uganda, came into being.

While rinderpest was sweeping the continent, Lord Delamere's stock in the Kenya highlands was also suffering from East Coast Fever. Sir Arnold Theiler in South Africa described East Coast Fever in 1904, but it took decades more to discover the microscopic blood parasite which causes it and to elucidate the intricate relationships between the parasite and its vector, the brown tick. The conditions which had led to the development of high tick populations around Njoro in Kenya and the importance of wild game as a reservoir for the parasite remained a mystery for a long time. The dipping methods used today for disinfecting cattle and killing the ticks are the result of years of research. The veterinary research institute at Onderstepoort, South Africa, and the laboratory at Kabete are among the institutions which tackled these problems.

Rinderpest and East Coast Fever have prevented man from making the best use of the resources around him, but the disease with the most far-reaching consequences is nagana, the animal form of human sleeping sickness, caused by trypanosomes and transmitted by tsetse flies. Mentioned by the Arabs in the fourteenth century as a disease whose human form frequently befell the Mali in West Africa and imputed to be the cause of the loss of many cattle and camels by the Portuguese when they made an expedition into East Africa in the sixteenth century, this zoonosis is thought to be a major reason for the absence of draft animals in the tropics (Scott 1939: 454–5). Nagana is also said to have played an important part in the establishment of Ibadan, Nigeria, the most populous African city on the continent. According to Akin Mabogunje (1962), Ibadan was originally a war encampment, founded by the gregarious Yoruba, who had a propensity for settling in large towns. Between the late eighteenth and early nineteenth centuries, the Fulani, whose military power was based on cavalry, forced the Yoruba south, and Ibadan, among other towns, received them. The Yoruba in Ibadan prospered because the location of the town in a tsetse fly-infested region made further conquest by the Fulani impossible. Their cavalry could not survive in such country. Ibadan also prospered, of course, because it had easy access to the north to derived savannah lands for the cultivation of grains and access to the south to rich tropical forest soils where cocoa became the cash crop of the region.

Twenty-one species of tsetse fly (*Glossina*), have been described, and of these, several are known to transmit trypanosomiasis either to man or to animals. Many different forms of trypanosomes which affect either man or animals have been identified. Prophylactic and therapeutic means of disease control are available as a result of past research. Yet an astounding lack of knowledge about the causal agents persists, and the animal forms of this disease still prevail to block the development of the tropical resources of the continent. Livestock specialists hesitate to use Zebu or European high-yielding, but susceptible, stock for breeding programs in the tsetse fly belt of West Africa. The long-suffering Ndama, a small longhorned cow which gives low milk yield, but which has, apparently, through contact with nagana developed resistance to it, is the dependable cattle stock of this region. Recent knowledge gained by Dr P. Glover of the Kenya Veterinary Department and other investigators of the delicate balance which the vectors of trypanosomiasis maintain with their environment sharpens the controversy, still unsettled: will the tsetse fly as it affects cattle recede naturally with the normal encroachment of agriculture and modern livestock management on wild bush and forest land, or will it be necessary to resort to other, more expensive, means of control?

Wild animals, which contribute so importantly to the economic life of the people, must be considered in the future planning of investigations on nagana of cattle. J. Ford, director of the Department of Tsetse Fly and Trypanosomiasis Control and Reclamation of the Rhodesias, held the view that tsetse flies inhabit those parts of Africa in which man can live only with difficulty and in which human populations are sparse. He conceded that there are occasions when the flies as vectors of trypanosomiasis drive out people, but generalised to say that when an area is evacuated by its population for any cause — failure of water supplies, soil exhaustion or epidemic diseases — the tsetse fly moves in following the reappearance of full natural vegetation and the replacement of man and his domestic stock by wild game (CCTA/CSA 1961: *Document Agr*. R. (61) 3 (a), App. III). E. B. Worthington (1958: 15) points out that one could consider tsetse flies as beneficial insects, for they have prevented the misuse of vast areas of land and the occupation of such land by scrub cattle.

Research on tsetse flies has led to the accumulation of data to show that their control is perfectly feasible in several different ways.   Among these are the destruction of wild game, the application of insecticides, and the manipulation of the environment to make it unattractive to fly survival.   Game destruction to eliminate the wild reservoir of trypanosomiasis has been a successful method of control in the Rhodesias and in Uganda.   Strongly criticised in the past, it deserves to come under even stronger criticism now that wide expanses of wild land have become more accessible to management and alternative methods of control have become practicable.

The experience gained in Zululand on mass application of insecticides which freed 7,000 square miles from *Glossina pallidipes*, the game destruction in Southern Rhodesia which liberated 10,000 square miles of territory from the fly, and the selective clearing processes worked out in Tanganyika in 1945 demonstrate that effective means for the control of tsetse are at hand.   Some of these profoundly influence the way of life of the people in the regions where they are applied.   As Ford pointed out in 1955, the main problem today is to work out the proper development and use of the land freed from tsetse (Worthington 1958: 254).

2. SMALL ANIMALS AND POULTRY

Sheep and goats, pigs and poultry enter into the livestock economy of the continent, but until recently little research was conducted on their improvement.   Subject to Nairobi sheep disease and blue tongue in the highlands of Kenya, sheep did come under some study for the control of these diseases at the East African Veterinary Research Organisation (EAVRO) and at the Kabete laboratories.   The chestnut-fleeced Sokoto goat, best known to Europeans in the form of Morocco leather, has received little research attention.   No one has seriously undertaken an investigation as to why this goat produces higher quality skins in the north-western corner of Nigeria than it does when raised elsewhere.

For the past six years EAVRO has engaged in a co-operative program on the study of African swine fever with members of the United States Department of Agriculture stationed at Muguga near Nairobi, Kenya.   The Ashanti pig in Ghana has been the subject of selection and upgrading.   Apart from these investigations, the breeding, management and disease control of small animals has been woefully inadequate.

In Africa, as elsewhere in the world, the highly efficient protein producer, poultry, has been the basis for an expanding industry.   Urbanisation is also helping to transform this industry from a primitive chicken-by-chicken operation to a modern business of broiler and egg production, which will supply the growing cities with a portion of the animal protein that the people badly need.   The poultry husbandry specialist, Dr A. N. A. Modebe, of the University of Ibadan faculty, is attempting to find a satisfactory poultry feed made from local produce.   He is experimenting with management techniques which will make poultry production attractive and profitable for the small village farmer in the densely populated Western Region of Nigeria.

3. WILD ANIMALS

The absence of a satisfactory draft animal for the African tropics has led people repeatedly to attempt to domesticate species of wildlife which are already adapted to the African environment.   Even in the temperate highlands of Kenya, when Lord Delamere experienced difficulties with his imported stock, he tried to cross donkeys with a zebra — the four foals which he succeeded in breeding were strong enough for his purpose but had vicious natures. His scheme to breed tame elands for draft purposes and for meat also died in its infancy (Huxley 1935: 1, 289–90). The Belgians, who needed beasts of burden in the Congo, found that African elephants were not nearly as tractable under domestication as were those in India. It would undoubtedly take generations, if not centuries, to bring wild animals of the tropics to the level of usefulness of cattle and other domesticated stock, which have been bred to meet the specific requirements human beings have set for them.

Treasured as a resource for the recreational needs of people, the wildlife of Africa has a vastly more important function in the economy of the continent than to serve as a target for gun and camera. Nor should it dwindle to extinction because people use it indiscriminately for food. The wild animal population is rich in species of ruminants which can convert low-quality herbage and bush, on a sustained yield basis, into badly needed animal protein more efficiently under some conditions than can domesticated cattle.

Thane Riney, Raymond Dasmann, and Archie S. Mossman, Fulbright fellows at the National Museum of Bulawayo, Southern Rhodesia, studied the ecology of wildlife on the Wankie Game Reserve and the coexistence of wild animals with cattle on large ranches in Southern Rhodesia. They looked at concepts of wildlife conservation and management from the point of view of the vast size of the wild animal population, its position as virtually sole consumer of the plant food which the savannahs produce, its capacity to reach a 'biomass' (sum total of all species) on poor grazing land as high or almost as high as cattle attain on excellent artificial grazing land, and its potential as a source of food. These concepts were timely. Intensive research which had been carried out over many years in the Albert National Park of the former Belgian Congo and in the network of parks of other parts of Africa was beginning to show that wild animals, free from the predations of man, could increase far in excess of available food sources. Natural balance among animals was not, as previously thought, capable of maintaining the flora and fauna of a region unchanged. In 1961, on a grant from the National Academy of Sciences, Dr Lee Talbot and his wife travelled widely through East Africa to gain precise information on comparative yields per unit area from land devoted to cattle production, to wild animals, or to a combination of domesticated and wild herds. They were able to corroborate the findings of Thane Riney and his colleagues.

Animal physiologists are now considering the mechanisms wild animals employ for water use and conservation, and for heat dissipation. Using new methods for anaesthetising animals in the wild, Dr A. M. Harthoorn and his colleagues in the Department of Veterinary Physiology at Kabete, Kenya, are turning up interesting data on the role that the elephant's ears may play in reducing its body temperature. Dr W. J. A. Payne of EAAFRO is engaged in a comparative study of the weight gains of wild animals, and of different breeds of cattle exposed to conditions of drought. Dr F. Bourlière points out that managing wild animal populations is much easier in theory than it is in practice, but research on new techniques of guiding game to corrals, on immobilisation drugs to make it possible to transport live animals for restocking areas, and on field spraying with antibiotics to help preserve meat, these, among other investigations, may go a long way towards changing the fate of some of the large ungulates of Africa and towards supplying badly needed animal protein for the people (UNESCO Document NS/NR/2 chap. VII).

V   CURRENT AND FUTURE DEVELOPMENTS

1. THE NEW NATIONS AND AGRICULTURAL RESEARCH

By the time 'Uhuru' became the cry in the late 1950s and early 1960s, a sound background of research on some of the most important aspects of the use of agricultural and natural resources had emerged.   Cash crops, food crops, nutrition, pests and diseases, livestock, animal management — work on these and a host of other subjects benefited from the results of research conducted in institutions situated in Africa, and in others abroad dedicated to the problems of Africa.   Co-operative research among territories administered by the same colonial power and even among those of two or more powers, was an important factor in agricultural improvement. These programs continue today, though largely on a residual staff and programming basis: their future hangs in the balance.

The French-speaking areas of Africa still retain a high degree of cohesion in research endeavour.   For 1962 the French government budgeted more than $11,000,000 for scientific research and training in those countries with which France has special relations (McGrew 1962).   The Ministry of Co-operation has the main responsibility for financing this research, the National Centre for Scientific Research takes part in planning, and the Office de la Recherche Scientifique et Technique Outre-Mer (ORSTOM)—a highly centralised organisation with its main laboratories in Bondy, France — will be the main beneficiary.

ORSTOM will undertake fundamental research in tropical agriculture and in animal husbandry, as it has in the past, in the Ivory Coast, Senegal, Togo, the Congo (Brazzaville), the Central African Republic, Chad, Cameroon and the Malagasy Republic.   Its installations at Adiopodoumé, near Abidjan, Ivory Coast, are especially well located and equipped for research in nematology, plant pathology, entomology and soils.   ORSTOM is training about sixty specialists in tropical research annually.   Africans make up less than half of this number (McGrew 1962).

Eight other specialised research organisations which co-operate closely with ORSTOM undertake the applied aspects of agronomic research.   These are the Centre Technique Forestier Tropical (CTFT), with centres in Gabon, the Malagasy Republic and the Congo (Brazzaville); the Institut d'Elevage et de Médecine Vétérinaire des Pays Tropicaux (IEMVT), with a veterinary research laboratory in Chad, a central station and three outlying stations in the Central African Republic, two centres in Senegal, and three in the Malagasy Republic; the Institut de Recherches Agronomiques Tropicales et des Cultures Vivrières (IRAT), for the improvement of tropical food crops; the Institut de Recherches pour les Huiles et les Oléagineux (IRHO), for research on oil-producing plants; the Institut de Recherches du Coton et des Textiles Exotiques (IRCT); the Institut Français du Café, du Cacao et autres Plantes Stimulantes (IFCC); the Institut Français de Recherches Fruitières Outre-Mer (IFAC), which puts main emphasis on bananas and pineapples; and the Institut de Recherches sur le Caoutchouc en Afrique (IRCA) for research on rubber.   In 1962, France was to support more than 400 research scientists in Africa, sixty of them African, and 185 research workers conducting related investigations in France (McGrew 1962).

In English-speaking West Africa, the financing, staffing and equipping of the interterritorial research institutions have come to an impasse.   One, the West African Cocoa Research Institute (WACRI), at Tafo in Ghana, built up an enviable reputation for the excellence of its staff and for its success in solving major regional problems of cocoa, such as swollen shoot disease, capsid damage and black pod disease. The staff of this institute conducted experiments in soil fertility, crop management and crop breeding that pointed the way towards yields of 3,000 pounds of cocoa beans an acre (in contrast to 300 pounds) in Ghana and in neighbouring countries. The future of this institute, financed by Ghana, Nigeria, Sierra Leone, Gambia and the Cameroons, and by the United Kingdom through Colonial Development and Welfare funds, is in doubt.

The government of Ghana recently reviewed the interterritorial research organisation and concluded that it was 'cumbersome and ineffectual in contributing regularly to Ghana's present development plans'. Ghana proposed to replace 'the present West African Research Organisation with a body which would foster close collaboration of as many independent African states as are interested, while making the actual operation of research programs a national responsibility functioning through national institutes or organizations' (Dillon 1962). Internally in Ghana the trend is towards unification of existing educational and research institutions. In 1961, the Kwame Nkrumah University came into being; its Faculty of Agriculture was to consist of the teaching and research facilities of the University of Ghana at Legon, near Accra, and of the School of Agriculture belonging to the former Kumasi College of Technology. In addition it was to take over the extensive experiment station at Kwadaso, near Kumasi, where the Department of Agriculture had its headquarters for research, and where it conducted some very fine studies on soils. The implementation of this comprehensive organisation has still to be carried out.

In Nigeria the trend is also towards merging, where possible, the teaching and research institutions. The newly created University of the North, to be situated at Zaria, will build its faculty of agriculture upon the Samaru and Shika experiment stations, the school of agriculture close by, and the teaching facilities of the former Nigerian College of Arts, Sciences and Technology at Zaria. The federal university located at Ibadan and the federal portion of Moor Plantation may find it convenient, for financial and staffing reasons, to join forces. A federal university grants commission is in the process of being formed to co-ordinate research and to assist with its financing.

In Angola and Mozambique, research initiative stems from three institutions in Portugal: the Estacão Agronómica Nacional, the Instituto Superior de Agronomia, and the Junta de Investigacões do Ultramar (Overseas Research Council). In Angola the Department of Agriculture is responsible for the actual direction of research, but the formulation of plans generally comes from Lisbon.

The Republic of South Africa has an advanced network of modern experiment stations. In a paper submitted for discussion at the CCTA/CSA Symposium on the Organisation of Agricultural Research in 1961, the Department of Agriculture reported a total of 1,090 major research projects under way. These embraced every conceivable problem important to agricultural and livestock improvement under local environmental conditions. This report stated that during the last few years 75 to 90 per cent of the professional posts were occupied and that less than 2 per cent of the posts in the Department of Agricultural Technical Services for non-academically trained technical officers were vacant (CCTA/CSA 1961: Document Agr. R. (61) 3 (d)). Nevertheless, a number of eminent scientists have left South Africa because they have felt isolated from their colleagues elsewhere in the world.

The organisation of research in the Rhodesias and Nyasaland reflects the tenuous structure of the Federation and the racial problems which Central Africa confronts.*

* The comments on the Rhodesias and Nyasaland reflect the situation obtaining *before* the Federation's dissolution at the end of 1963; this left the question of the organisation of agricultural research unresolved.

A series of reports beginning in the late 1940s by Dr J. E. Keyston, Sir Frank Engledow and Dr D. G. Kingwill provided the framework for the federal government's research institutions and for the Agricultural Research Council of the Federation. In Southern Rhodesia, European agriculture and research are federal functions; African agriculture is a territorial function. In Northern Rhodesia the federal government is theoretically responsible for non-African agriculture excepting animal health and tsetse control, and the territorial government for African agriculture. Research is a federal function, but there are also territorial research stations. In Nyasaland, the federal Ministry of Agriculture has not assumed any responsibility for agriculture or agricultural research.

The Monckton Commission considered agricultural development when it made recommendations for possible constitutional changes in the Federation. (Advisory Commission . . . 1960: 60.) The consensus of the Commission was that responsibility for agriculture should not be divided on a racial basis. The Commission felt that agricultural research might become a territorial responsibility in which the federal government might maintain an interest.

In spite of division of responsibility along racial and governmental lines, agricultural development and research have been progressing apace. The Henderson Research Station near Salisbury, the Grasslands Experiment Station at Marandellos and the Matopos Experiment Station at Bulawayo have strong programs on forage crops, grassland improvement and range improvement, respectively. Staff in the Faculty of Sciences at the University College of Rhodesia and Nyasaland are undertaking research on snails, which harbour schistosomiasis, and on tsetse flies, the vectors of trypanosomiasis. These diseases and their vectors more than any others obstruct agricultural development in the Federation. The Agricultural Research Council — an autonomous body organised in 1939 — endeavours to strengthen those federal and territorial research projects which show the most promise. In addition, it has initiated five special studies of its own: a survey of calving rates; a collation of ecological studies; a review of tsetse research; a study of trace elements in the soil; and work with chemical sterilisation of milking equipment (Agricultural Research Council 1961). The role of the Agricultural Research Council could be signal in the co-ordination of the research now under way at the many federal and territorial experiment stations with the investigations at the University College, those supported by industry, and those sponsored by the National Museum of Southern Rhodesia.

Political uncertainties in East Africa, shortage of funds and the departure of expatriates whose posts remain vacant, threaten the continuation of research on crops and animals of fundamental and interterritorial significance. The disparate state of the East African political units in their advancement towards independence made the East Africa High Commission obsolete and brought EACSO into being in 1961. On recommendation of a team of scientists, which included Professor A. C. Frazer and Dr E. G. Cox of the United Kingdom, EACSO will finance the several research organisations that deal with agriculture and forestry, veterinary medicine, trypanosomiasis, and marine and fresh water fisheries, as did its predecessor, the High Commission (East Africa High Commission 1961). But stresses and strains are appearing. The newly created University of East Africa is developing strong programs in agriculture, in veterinary science and in the natural sciences. Sooner or later the university and the Common Services Organisation may find it necessary and desirable to combine their resources. Both have yet to settle into the African milieu and to become truly African institutions.

The former Belgian Congo has experienced the nearly complete disintegration of INEAC, which built near Stanleyville one of the finest tropical agricultural research centres in the world. By the spring of 1962, the parent institution in Brussels still controlled INEAC funds; these were frozen, pending the improvement of conditions in the Congo. Prior to Congolese independence, INEAC employed approximately 450 Belgian scientists and technicians. Of these, 400 left shortly after independence, and the number in the Congo in April 1962, was down to sixteen. One can only hope that the hiatus in research activity is a temporary one.

2. THE NEED FOR REVIEW OF PHYSICAL AND BIOLOGICAL RESOURCES

The establishment of independent economic and political units has created a need for a reassessment of the physical and biological resources of the continent in terms of what each country has at its disposal. The United Nations has helped to meet this need through the work of the Special Fund, the World Bank, UNESCO and FAO. The Special Fund has financed economic development surveys of the Awash River basin in Ethiopia and the Volta River flood plain in Ghana, and of agricultural and water resources of Somalia, the Sudan, Togo and several other countries. The World Bank has conducted economic surveys of Somalia, Nigeria, Libya, Tanganyika, Uganda and Kenya. These surveys have led to the financing of key development projects. FAO is undertaking hydrological studies of the Rufiji river basin in Tanganyika and of the Kafue river basin in Northern Rhodesia.

Population pressure and urbanisation have aggravated the need to reassess the water resources of Africa, which are by no means excessive. Worthington (1958: 124) estimates that currently only 5 per cent of the water that falls on the continent of Africa actually reaches the sea. Water for drinking and for washing, for hydro-electric power and for irrigation is sought after competitively. Its wise use is essential to the welfare of the people living on the continent. Rivers come under close scrutiny because the needs they fill are especially urgent. Even the Nile, with its five dams in Egypt and with the original Aswan Dam raised twice, must respond to expanded demands for water to irrigate crops and for power for cities. The current construction of the High Dam at Aswan, the building of another dam at Roseires in the Sudan and of a weir below Lake Tana in Ethiopia will enable the people along the Nile to make fuller use of this river, every cubic centimetre of whose waters has been counted for millenia.

Over one-seventh of the land area in Uganda consists of swamps. People know little about the basic ecology of these tropical swamps and about the changes that follow drainage. Drainage may not be the best answer for their utilisation. Leaving them water-logged to grow rice might be satisfactory in some instances, in others not. Under the auspices of the Nuffield Foundation, the departments of zoology and botany of Makerere College are looking into the chemical, botanical and entomological characteristics of the swamps of Uganda. This research, of academic as well as practical interest, has the important objective of throwing light upon alternative possibilities for the wisest use of the vast swampy areas of Africa for food production (Farrer-Brown 1960: 207).

Not only the rivers and the swamps, but also the underground water and the run-off, need co-ordinated study as expendable resources which must be husbanded frugally. For several years now, the government of the Northern Region of Nigeria has been successfully tapping an artesian source of water which lies from 600 to 1,000 feet or more below the ground at Maiduguri. Geologists know the general extent of this underground reservoir, which borders Lake Chad in Bornu Province. They do not know at what rate it can be drawn for water for human beings and cattle without exhausting the supply.   This new water source has special significance because it encourages the nomadic Fulani to settle with their cattle when they normally would travel south in search of water and greener pastures.   If this new water supply is depleted through overuse, serious social problems could result.   In the same area, where rain is scanty and the growing season short, the government of the Northern Region and the Empire Cotton Growing Corporation support research on effective use of rainfall.   These investigations range from a search for quickly maturing varieties of sorghum and millet to experiments on soil and water relationships.   Impounding water from flash storms, cultivating land prior to rainfall to permit water to percolate in the soil, and improving drainage techniques where rainfall is momentarily excessive, constitute some of the major projects in progress.

The widening base from which the new nations can draw financial support has stimulated foreign organisations to make surveys to ascertain the potential for development of the physical and biological resources of these nations.   The National Academy of Sciences of the United States undertook such a survey and issued a report entitled *Recommendations for Strengthening Science and Technology in Selected Areas of Africa South of the Sahara* (1959).   Its purpose was to advise ICA, the predecessor of the Agency for International Development (AID), on projects of significance.   In Ghana and Nigeria, the Rockefeller Brothers Fund has made feasibility studies of special opportunities for private enterprise and for government to foster business.

3. CO-OPERATIVE RESEARCH

To make maximum economic and social progress and to protect their people from widespread scourges, the new nations must unite in their efforts to support research on problems which are truly international in scope.   Pests and diseases provide cases in point.   The trypanosomes which the tsetse fly carries, the locusts that swarm over much of semi-arid Africa, and the Quelea bird, pest of sorghum and millet, are pan-African in range; it will take constant international effort to keep them under control.

The human form of sleeping sickness has been present in Africa for at least 600 years; it developed into widespread epidemics, however, only after 1880.   Outbreaks in East Africa resulted from infections introduced from the Congo by travellers and slavers.   West African epidemics followed expansion in travel, commerce and agriculture which accompanied British and French colonisation.   By 1940, large areas of the most fertile and well-watered river valleys of the Volta and the Niger systems were depopulated, whereas in unaffected areas population increased by 10 to 15 per cent in a decade.   West Africa could ill afford nonproductive, depopulated areas (Morris 1960).

Investigations on the biology, ecology and control of tsetse flies and the protozoan trypanosomes which they carry, together with subsequent action programs, led to the lowering of the incidence of human forms of trypanosomiasis to an insignificant figure, but no one knows when a new outbreak of this endemic disease may flare up.   Dr K. R. S. Morris (1960), who has described the campaigns British and French scientists and technicians conducted to eradicate sleeping sickness from the Volta and the Niger river basins, has expressed fear that nationalism may bring a disturbing reversal of the past half-century of progress in the conquest of disease, if the international aspects of disease control are neglected. In several regions where sleeping sickness is endemic in West Africa, it is quiescent today; but increasing populations in areas where man comes into too close and too frequent contact with tsetse flies may create just the right conditions for another decimating epidemic. These regions cut across newly established national boundaries.

The main responsibility for broadly regional research programs formerly fell within the province of the colonial powers. The institutions which these powers created are now subject to crucial readjustments in staffing, financing and programming. For example, the West African Institute for Trypanosomiasis Research (WAITR), with fine laboratories, library and field facilities at Kaduna and Vom in Nigeria, served all English-speaking West Africa as the centre for research on both animal and human aspects of this important disease. It stands today with a skeletal expatriate staff whose members are nervous about continuing their careers at WAITR, fearing possible curtailment of financial support and a consequent reduction in breadth of program. The West African Research Council, under whose aegis WAITR flourished, has broken up. Perhaps the government of Nigeria will provide the entire financial support for this institution as an appendage of the newly created University of the North. Possibly the institute will find security and scope for program development in association with the trypanosomiasis institutions of the adjoining French-speaking countries of West Africa. Other organisations may supplant it. Whatever the fate of WAITR and former interterritorial institutions like it, the problem of conducting regional research on sleeping sickness remains an international one that will require co-operation from all.

Fortunately, the years of research on locusts in Africa have led to action programs for locust control which everyone now accepts as necessary and as requiring financial support from many different sources. The brilliant work that the Russian entomologist B. P. Uvarov did thirty years ago to elucidate the migratory and the sedentary phases of locusts, paved the way for subsequent exhaustive studies in Africa on the biology and control of the three major species: the Red Locust, the Migratory Locust and the Desert Locust. Their breeding grounds are now defined, their activities well known, and their control effective. In October 1961 the third session of the FAO Eastern African Desert Locust Control Subcommittee met in Addis Ababa. It drafted an intergovernmental convention, published in its report (1961), for the control of the desert locust in eastern Africa. Realising the necessity of sustained effort to keep this pest under control, the governments of Ethiopia, French Somaliland, Kenya, the Somali Republic, Sudan, Tanganyika and Uganda agreed to finance co-operatively the control program and to set up headquarters at Dire Dawa in Ethiopia. A small but important part of this program will enable the committee to continue with operational research on locust control.

The Quelea bird of Africa is as serious a pest as the desert locust, as has been emphasised by Dr Nigel Heseltine of FAO in his statement published in *World Crops*, June 1960; international co-operation for its control needs strengthening. Drs P. L. Dekeyser, G. Morel and F. Bourlière have studied the biology and ecology of this weaver bird in French West Africa. P. Ward has been conducting similar studies in Nigeria. International co-operation would assist in bringing their work into concert. It would help in amassing the much-needed information on the migrations and range of this pest and in collating local observations which have been made in scattered areas on its biology, ecology and control.

Outside institutions are assisting the new nations in developing international aspects of research. These include philanthropic institutions, universities from abroad, United Nations agencies, and technical co-operation programs of the countries of Europe and of the United States. Two important institutions devoted specifically to African scientific development are the Commission for Technical Co-operation in Africa (CCTA — 'South of the Sahara' was dropped from the name in the summer of 1962), and its sister organisation, the Scientific Council for Africa South of the Sahara (CSA). Established in 1950, these organisations have sponsored technical conferences on a large number of subjects related to agriculture and natural resources, ranging from trypanosomiasis, rinderpest and conservation of wildlife to the organisation of agricultural research, soil improvement and weed control. They perform an important service by keeping scientists in Africa in touch with one another, and by directing the attention of governments to significant programs which need support.

4. EDUCATION AND RESEARCH

A century of effort has gone into the acquisition of knowledge to make effective and rational use of the continent's physical and biological resources. It stimulated the founding of special institutions and programs which became well established long before universities started to educate African students in agriculture and related sciences.

Today, research in Africa lacks the element most essential to its continuation: a cadre of adequately trained African scientists. Outstanding African scientists and research workers, most of them trained abroad, may be found, but not in the numbers required to man the existing programs, to say nothing of the additional ones which should be instituted. The dearth of African research staff is bound to occasion a drastic cut in the number of institutions presently operating in Africa, a reorientation of those that survive the cut, and a review of priorities with regard to research which ought to receive financial support. Most important of all, it leaves present research programs, institutions and personnel without the rapport they ought to have with laymen and with local sources of finance, both governmental and non-governmental.

Universities in Africa have barely awakened to their responsibility for educating agricultural scientists in numbers. Only one university exists in French-speaking West Africa. Located in Dakar, it trains students in the natural sciences, but it still has no affiliated agricultural school. Agricultural and veterinary students must go to France for their education.

In the former Belgian Congo, six African students have been graduated from Lovanium University near Leopoldville. They have entered other fields. The absence of a corps of successful African career men in agricultural research left these young students without inspirational leadership or the desire to pursue agriculture. No university exists in Angola or Mozambique, although plans call for the founding of one in each territory. As a consequence, no advanced training for students in agriculture is available in these large sectors of Africa.

The Liberian government, the United Nations Special Fund and the University of Liberia have just negotiated a contract for building a faculty of agriculture. This contract ought to enable Liberia to produce sixty graduates in agriculture and forestry annually, within ten years (UNESCO 1962: 58). In Ethiopia, the Imperial Ethiopian College of Agricultural and Mechanical Arts has graduated 146 agricultural students since 1957. Several of these are currently taking post-graduate studies abroad to equip them for teaching posts in the college when they return; the research posts far outnumber the qualified Ethiopian scientists available to fill them.

Five institutions presently or formerly in special relationship with the University of London, in Ghana, Nigeria, the Sudan, the Rhodesias and Nyasaland, and East Africa — all products of the 1950s — have scarcely begun to think in terms of the vast number of students who must be trained in agriculture. The number of graduates in agriculture from these African university colleges totalled 154 for the ten-year period from 1953 to 1962. Many times this number will be required in the near future to meet the needs of these nations in research, extension, teaching and commercial agriculture.

Nigeria, in the throes of building five universities, has the educational resources in the University of Ibadan, the oldest of these centres, for developing post-graduate studies in agriculture. Here, research programs are growing in agricultural chemistry, forage crop improvement, stored grain pest control, farm management, animal husbandry, marketing and production economics, and agronomy. In Nigeria the idea of the university as a teaching and research unit, which should devote some of its resources to applied research, may alter the prevalent concept of a university as a centre for fundamental research only.

The opportunities are bright in East Africa for developing a system of agricultural education uniquely adapted to the needs of this politically and geographically diverse area, with each of several institutions participating to educate African students for careers in agriculture, from the most practical to the most academic. Tanganyika expects to found an agricultural school affiliated with the new University College at Dar-es-Salaam. It will develop teaching and research related to the varied agricultural patterns and the potential of that large new country. Kenya already profits from the presence of Egerton College, founded twenty years ago in the European highlands to train the sons of European farmers in agriculture, which has just opened its doors to students of all races. This institution will specialise in crop and animal husbandry. Uganda is fortunate to have Makerere University College, the senior college of the new University of East Africa, with a faculty of agriculture of high academic attainment, that may also embark upon a post-graduate program of instruction. The University College at Nairobi, Kenya (formerly the Royal College), also a constituent unit of the University of East Africa as is its namesake in Tanganyika, has instituted work in veterinary science at Nairobi and Kabete. In agriculture the university is rapidly becoming the research centre as well as the teaching centre in East Africa for the study of agriculture and the utilisation of other natural resources.

Improvements in primary and secondary school teaching and facilities would be helpful in guiding gifted students to careers in science and research. UNESCO organised a conference at Addis Ababa in May 1961, at which all levels of African education were discussed. The conferees mapped out a program which would provide full elementary schooling for all children, starting at six years of age, and greatly expand facilities for secondary as well as higher education in the newly created states of Africa. The cost of the total program would rise to $1,150 million in 1965 and to $2,600 million in 1980 (UNECA 1962: chap. 4). In an article in *The Times Educational Supplement*, January 5, 1962, Dr T. Balogh, senior economic adviser to the director-general of FAO at the conference, warned that such a program must take into consideration the financial resources these countries possess for implementing it, and the need for a curriculum that would furnish technical knowledge in the agricultural sciences.   He emphasised that agriculture is, after all, the main activity of the people; that it is appallingly primitive and inefficient, and that therefore the people are poor and ill fed; and that, through practical curricula designed to give students the appropriate skills in agriculture, African communities could do much to raise their standard of living.

5. RESEARCH PROBLEMS AND TRENDS

The pattern of agricultural development and the growth of the vast body of research associated with it have been similar in Africa to those in most of the underdeveloped areas of the world.   The most striking characteristic of agriculture in Africa, how-ever, is the range in systems and methods which people employ, from the most primitive to the most advanced.   Encouraging the wide use of modern methods has been an extremely complex task.

Research on agricultural and other natural resources started mainly with the identification and evaluation of native plants, animals and minerals for economic use. Simultaneously, crops and animals new to Africa and of great economic and social significance gained a foothold on the continent.   They required research for adjust-ment to new environmental conditions, and for high production.   Later, a great emphasis on crops to sell on foreign markets guided research in the agricultural sciences towards extremely practical crop improvement.   As people from Europe came into contact with the people of Africa, each had adjustments to make.   The acceptance of new crops of economic importance, the idea of growing crops for revenue, and the concept of individual land ownership were among some of the fundamental ideas with which the African people had to become acquainted.   The Europeans found themselves living and making a living under tropical and other ecological conditions entirely unfamiliar to them.   They had to deal with systems of land tenure, subsistence agricultural practices and shifting agriculture, which their own ancestors had employed generations earlier, but which they found strange and exotic.

The steady population increase, among livestock as well as among human beings, pressed hard against the natural resources of the continent, sharpening the conflict between wild and domesticated animals and between the settlers and the nomadic herders.   All competed for the same physical and biological resources.   Land for crops and for pasture became scarce, and research in crop and pasture improvement resulted from necessity.

By the time a reorganisation of political units became a reality, almost every conceivable problem of research in agriculture and in the utilisation of natural resources had been under study to some extent at some place in Africa.   The critical aspect of this development was the almost complete lack of preparation of African research workers to carry on.   The development of educational institutions lagged far behind that of research institutions, and African investigators had not been trained.

The formation of new nations brought about a new look at the natural resources of the continent.   It occasioned a readjustment in the financing of research institu-tions, in the planning of programs, and in the establishment of priorities with regard to future development.   It stimulated the newly created universities to train students at a pace and at an academic level which strained the very concept of a university as it existed in Africa.

The importance of cash crops to the economy of the new nations will require that research continue on them. The growing population will demand stepped-up programs on cereals and other food crops, and on adequate human nutrition. Shrinking land resources will make research necessary on more efficient use of grazing land for cattle and wild animals, grazing and browsing separately or together; on mixed farming; on animal and plant diseases; and on many such problems which influence the social, cultural and economic well-being of the people.

Sustained effort in such fields as plant breeding, plant protection, soil improvement, better land use, animal management, and disease control is an indispensable attribute of a modern and efficient agriculture. To match the degree of excellence that has characterised past research in these areas in Africa will call for the mobilisation of manpower from foreign and local sources alike. The new nations will experience their greatest opportunity and challenge in educating their own people well enough and in sufficient numbers to man the existing programs and to staff new ones directed towards modern agricultural practices and the wise use of natural resources.

13

Medical Research: Some Anthropological Aspects

Robert F. Gray

I INTRODUCTION*

A DISCUSSION OF medical problems in a book dealing with social research in Africa should require no special justification at this time, for in recent years anthropologists and other social scientists have been concerning themselves increasingly with problems of a medical character. A recent survey of this field of study, limited largely to North America (Polgar 1962), lists over 500 publications. Among medical scientists there has also been a growing awareness of the importance of social and cultural factors in the study of disease, and at almost every conference or symposium on tropical medicine the need for a broad multiple disciplinary approach is stressed (Freeborn et al. 1960). The more usual approach has been to focus on the effects of social factors on medical situations, but it is also true that diseases have had a profound effect upon society and culture throughout human evolution and history. The present study attempts to give consideration to both viewpoints.

Instead of attempting to survey the whole vast field of medical research in Africa, the following pages deal mainly with three topics which in the past have been studied principally by medical science. These topics focus respectively on malaria, trypanosomiasis and malnutrition. They were chosen for comment because of their intrinsic importance, because the ecology of these diseases has been worked out in more detail than has that of other diseases, and because their role in human affairs in Africa is more clearly perceivable.

II MAJOR FIELDS OF STUDY

1. MALARIA AND THE SICKLE CELL TRAIT

Malaria is the cause of more deaths each year than any other transmissible disease in Africa. In some areas it may be responsible for as much as 10 per cent of infant deaths (Gelfand 1961: 72). The protozoal parasite causing malaria belongs to the genus *Plasmodium*. Of the four species which are pathogenic for man, *Plasmodium falciparum* is by far the most important as it is widespread in tropical Africa and

* Bibliography for this chapter will be found on page 541.

produces the most severe form of the disease known as subtertian or malignant malaria.   It is *falciparum* malaria that will here be discussed.   The malaria parasites are transmitted from person to person through bites from female mosquitoes of the genus *Anopheles*, the species *A. gambiae* being the outstanding vector in Africa, with *A. funestus* also of considerable importance.

In most of West, Central and East Africa, except in drier or elevated parts, and also in southern Asia and the East Indies, *falciparum* malaria is hyperendemic or holoendemic; that is, the parasite is transmitted throughout all or most of the year by anopheline mosquitoes.   The most thorough way of eradicating malaria from a hyperendemic region is to break the cycle of transmission by destroying the mosquito vector, and this has been the ultimate goal of most malaria control programs.   The disease can also be controlled by eliminating the parasite through treating the entire population of an area or by preventing them from being bitten by infected mosquitoes; but as long as the insect vector remains, there is always a potential danger of reinfection through accidental introduction of the parasite into the controlled area.

It has long been known that there are differences between individuals in immunity to malaria.   During the early period of exploration in Africa it was thought that members of the White race were especially susceptible to fatal attacks of malaria; hence the term 'White man's grave' was applied to certain hyperendemic areas.   The discovery by Sir Ronald Ross at the end of the nineteenth century that the mosquito was the vector of transmission had the effect of opening up the continent to White colonisation by indicating the means of preventing or controlling the most serious health danger.   It is now known that immunity to malaria is primarily an acquired condition which results from repeated infections early in life. There is some evidence that Africans are more resistant to malaria than are Europeans for reasons apart from the blood abnormalities which are discussed below. The evidence is not conclusive, however, and Gelfand (1961: 67) states that 'Africans bred in non-malarial regions react in the same way as Europeans when exposed to the disease'.

In endemic areas a newborn infant is relatively resistant to infection and in the first year of life is usually subject only to mild forms of the disease.   In the second year clinical attacks become more severe and there is considerable mortality. Thereafter the child tends to acquire progressive immunity, until by the age of four the host becomes relatively tolerant of the parasite, although parasitæmia may continue (Gelfand 1961: 73).

A new dimension has been added to the understanding of malaria immunity by the discovery that individuals having the sickle-cell trait are more resistant to malaria under certain conditions than normal individuals.   While this has no great practical significance as regards the immediate problems of malaria control, it has implications of great importance for understanding the general biological history of man in Africa.

The red blood cells of certain individuals under conditions of reduced oxygen tension undergo a change from their normal round shape and assume elongated and sickle-shaped forms.   This tendency towards sickling does not seem to cause ill effects in most individuals having the trait, but occasionally the phenomenon is associated with severe hæmolytic anæmia, often fatal in childhood or adolescence. It is generally accepted that the trait is carried by a single gene.   Heterozygous individuals manifest the sickling phenomenon in mild degree but have no anæmia, while homozygous individuals possess the trait in double dose and develop sickle-cell anæmia (Harris 1959: 134–74).

The underlying cause of the sickling phenomenon is now known to be a chemical abnormality in the hæmoglobin of individuals who manifest this trait.   In one of its some 300 amino acid residues, the hæmoglobin of sickle cells (designated as hæmoglobin s) is characterised by a substitution of a valine residue for the glutamic acid residue present in the hæmoglobin of normal individuals (hæmoglobin A). Reduced sickle-cell hæmoglobin is less soluble than reduced normal hæmoglobin, and this evidently provides the explanation for the phenomenon of sickling.   When exposed to atmosphere of low oxygen tension, reduced hæmoglobin s appears to come out of free solution and produce the deformations characteristic of sickle cells (Harris 1959: 137–8).   In homozygotes with sickle-cell anæmia, the concentration of hæmoglobin s is sufficient to cause sickling within the normal range of oxygen tension.   In heterozygotes the red cells contain a mixture of normal hæmoglobin and hæmoglobin s which does not produce sickling under normal physiological atmospheric conditions, though under conditions of abnormally low oxygen tension, such as are encountered in high-altitude flying, sickling may occur.   The proportion of normal hæmoglobin to hæmoglobin s is highly variable in different subjects.   The reason for this is not understood at present, but it suggests that the genetics of this trait may be more complex than was at first supposed (Harris 1959: 141–3).

Hæmoglobin s is only one of a series of abnormal hæmoglobins which have been discovered in recent years.   The identification of these hæmoglobins in large population samples has been facilitated by the relatively simple techniques of paper electrophoresis.   Some of the other abnormal hæmoglobins have been found in combination with sickle-cell hæmoglobin.

The gene responsible for the sickle-cell trait has a remarkable world distribution, being very common in tropical Africa and extremely rare in northern Europe. A high incidence of the gene has been observed in scattered populations in Greece, southern Arabia and India, but its main concentration is in Africa, where perhaps 15 to 20 per cent of all the people living between the Sahara and the Zambesi river show the sickle-cell trait.   In some communities, the incidence reaches as high as 45 per cent (Allison 1961).

This peculiar pattern of distribution raises a difficult problem in population genetics.   Since individuals who are homozygous for the sickle-cell gene suffer from a severe disease which is often fatal in childhood or adolescence, their chances of reproducing are less than those of other individuals, and thus there must be a steady loss of the gene from the population.   Under these circumstances, how does it happen that the gene is carried by between 10 and 40 per cent of some populations? There must be some process counteracting the process of natural selection against it, and this counteraction must vary in intensity from place to place to account for the difference in incidence from population to population.

Since Allison first clearly stated the theory of the relationship, it has been established beyond question that individuals with the sickle-cell trait are less susceptible to malaria than normal individuals (Allison 1961).   The effect of the sickle-cell trait appears to be most marked in the age range of one to four years, which is the period during which children are particularly susceptible to serious attacks of malaria and before acquired immunity has reached protective levels.   The incidence of cerebral malaria, usually fatal, is significantly lower in sickle-cell trait carriers. In older subjects, normally highly immune, the effect of the sickle-cell trait on parasite rates is negligible, being overshadowed by the effects of acquired immunity (Allison 1961: 712–14). The exact mechanism of the resistance to malaria possessed by sickle-cell heterozygotes is not known.

The selective factors which influence the frequencies of the sickle-cell gene in populations are regarded as being in equilibrium. Homozygotes tend to be eliminated from the population before reaching reproductive age through succumbing to sickle-cell anæmia, while heterozygotes have a better than normal chance of reproducing by virtue of their extra resistance to malaria. This situation of equilibrium has been termed *balanced polymorphism*. If this interpretation is correct, the proportion of heterozygotes to either sickle-cell or normal homozygotes should exceed the proportion expected on the basis of random mating alone, since heterozygotes escape the selective effects of both sickle-cell anæmia and malaria. This pattern of gene distribution has actually been found among individuals of reproductive age in several investigations (Allison 1961: 717–18).

Another abnormal blood condition known to confer resistance to malaria is an inherited deficiency in the red blood cell enzyme, Glucose-6-phosphate Dehydrogenase. This defect is inherited as a sex-linked trait with full expression in hemizygous males and homozygous females. Persons with the defect are liable to develop severe hæmolysis upon ingestion of broad beans, *Vicia faba* (hence the name 'favism' sometimes applied to the condition), upon taking primaquine and certain other anti-malarial drugs, and when they have certain virus diseases. The distribution of this trait in Africa tends to correspond to that of subtertian malaria, and field studies have indicated that some resistance to malaria is conferred by the enzyme deficiency. The evidence for this effect, most clearly demonstrated in Sardinia (Siniscalco *et al.* 1961), is less decisive than in the case of the sickle-cell trait (Allison 1961: 716). The enzyme-deficiency gene, therefore, like the sickle-cell gene, is regarded as having a net advantage in areas of hyperendemic *falciparum* malaria. There is a positive correlation between the frequencies of the two genes in population and this suggests that they are not disadvantageous in combination (Allison 1961: 720, Fig. 6).

Another of the abnormal hæmoglobins, hæmoglobin c, produces in homozygous individuals a clinical condition similar to but less severe than a sickle-cell anæmia. This is found in West Africa and reaches its highest incidence in northern Ghana, where 29 per cent of the people are heterozygotes. This high incidence suggests that hæmoglobin c has some selective advantage balancing the disadvantage of the anæmia. Although the distribution of the trait suggested that hæmoglobin c heterozygotes might also be resistant to malaria, investigation has not definitely shown this genotype to have resistance to *P. falciparum*. It is possible that protection against other species of malaria parasites may occur, or some entirely different selective factor may be responsible for the incidence of the trait (Neel 1958, Allison 1961).

A combination of hæmoglobin c and the sickle-cell trait results in an anæmia which is fully as severe as sickle-cell anæmia. Since the genes for the sickle-cell trait and for hæmoglobin c are believed to be either alleles at the same locus or closely linked genes (Harris 1959), individuals with hæmoglobin c sickle-cell disease are in effect double heterozygotes. In West African populations, where both genes occur, there is a negative correlation between their frequencies, as might be expected in view of the disadvantageous effect of the genes in combination.

The finding of these single-gene traits, which reach a high incidence in certain populations and have definite selective advantages and disadvantages, is something essentially new in the study of human genetics and suggests a method of tracing out evolutionary processes in greater detail than was ever before possible. This new method has been used by Neel (1958) in an attempt to determine the sequence of events in the appearance and spread in West Africa of the gene for hæmoglobin c. His primary data are the frequency distributions of this gene and of the sickle-cell gene. In this study he also considered anthropological data which might indicate the length of time the populations involved had occupied their present territories and the patterns of human migrations in the region.

Starting with the reasoned assumption 'that the sickle-cell gene owes its presence in West Africa in whole or in part to an introduction in the not-too-distant past' (Neel 1958: 63), he considers the question of whether the gene for hæmoglobin c had an origin that was pre- or post-migrational with respect to the sickle-cell gene. Without coming to any final decision, he reviews the evidence for both alternatives and indicates the lines of future research which might be able to settle the question.

Livingstone (1958) has carried out an investigation along similar lines but of broader scope. He starts with the observation that in the part of West Africa in which *falciparum* malaria is hyperendemic or holoendemic — roughly the area south of the latitude of the Gambia river — the incidence of the sickle-cell trait varies widely in different populations, often from tribe to tribe. A high incidence is regarded as evidence of stable equilibrium. In some populations the incidence is very low, although malaria is just as severe in these areas as in those with high sickle-cell frequencies. Livingstone deals mainly with two of these areas of very low frequency, coastal Portuguese Guinea and eastern Liberia–western Ivory Coast. To explain the low frequencies he proposes two hypotheses which are suggested by an analysis of the frequency distribution of the trait throughout West Africa (Livingstone 1958: 541).

> (1) The sickle-cell gene has been present in some parts of West Africa for a considerable time, but, due to the comparative isolation of the low frequency populations in Portuguese Guinea and eastern Liberia, is only now being introduced to them.
>
> (2) The environmental conditions responsible for the high frequencies of the sickle-cell gene have been present for a relatively short time among these populations, so that the spread of the sickle-cell gene is only now following the spread of the selective advantage of this gene.

Seeking evidence to support these hypotheses, he reviews relevant linguistic and archæological data. This he interprets as indicating that the populations in question are in line of descent from ancient inhabitants of the region whose economy was originally based upon hunting. These aboriginal populations were among the last peoples to adopt an agricultural mode of life. The first food plants to be culti-vated in West Africa were millet and sorghum, which spread as culture traits through the savannah zone. The hunting peoples were either displaced by agricul-turists or acquired themselves the agricultural complex. Millet and sorghum, however, were ill adapted for cultivation in the forest, especially before iron implements were available for clearing, and it was not until the introduction of the yam that it became possible for cultivators to invade the forest. The increase in the frequency of the sickle-cell trait coincides with the spread of yam cultivation, according to Livingstone's interpretation. From all this he concludes that

> the sickle-cell gene was brought to this part of Africa by the yam cultivators westward from Nigeria, and at present both agriculture and the sickle-cell gene are spreading to the hunting populations, which were in the forests prior to the spread of yam cultivation (Livingstone 1958: 552).

It is not possible here to summarise the detailed evidence that Livingstone considers in arriving at this conclusion. The importance of this research, however, is found in its use of medical data in attacking traditional anthropological problems of racial and cultural history, thus adding a potentially important new dimension to the method of analysis. He goes on to consider the ecology of the mosquito in relation to the epidemiology of malaria. *Anopheles gambiae*, the predominant vector, requires certain conditions for breeding: it does not breed in shaded water or swiftly running water. The unshaded stagnant pools which it requires were uncommon in the uncleared forest occupied by hunting peoples. Under such conditions, he argues, malaria could not be endemic. The introduction of iron tools and yams led to the clearing of the forest and the establishment of agricultural communities where previously the only mode of life had been hunting and gathering. These clearings created conditions favourable to the mosquito vector, and malaria thus became hyperendemic in the forest zone.

Livingstone concludes that the populations upon which his study focuses acquired the yam at a relatively late period, and that they were little affected by gene flow from the migrant peoples, carrying the sickle-cell gene, who originally brought the yam complex from some centre in Nigeria. Even when a strong selective force is acting on an advantageous gene, it requires a number of generations for a high frequency of the gene to be built up in a population. The populations of Portuguese Guinea and eastern Liberia, originally free of the sickle-cell gene, received only a small infusion of the gene through contact with the newcomers from whom they acquired the yam. In making forest clearings for yam cultivation, they also exposed themselves to hyperendemic malaria which gives the sickle-cell heterozygotes a selective advantage over individuals with normal hæmoglobin. Given sufficient time, these conditions should produce an increase in the frequency of the sickle-cell gene until a level of equilibrium is reached. The present low frequencies in these populations are accounted for partly by the small amount of the gene introduced from outside, and partly by the relatively short period of time during which the selective factors favouring an increase in the gene frequency have been operating.

In conventional anthropological thinking, disease as a rule has been viewed as something essentially external to the basic processes of human evolution, both biological and cultural. The tendency has been to regard it as part of the external environment and, therefore, of only contingent interest to anthropology. The recent research dealing with malaria and its relation, the sickle-cell trait, and other inherited conditions of abnormal blood, is of special significance to anthropology in demonstrating that disease may play an important role in the basic evolutionary processes of gene selection within a population. But the research is also of socio-cultural significance. Livingstone has broken through conventional monodisciplinary inhibitions in bringing together data from a wide variety of sources. In doing so, he has demonstrated that man himself, in the course of his cultural evolution, may create the conditions for diseases which then affect his genetic evolution.

The great problem of controlling malaria in Africa is slowly but steadily being solved and in time surely will be solved. Present knowledge also makes it possible to predict with some precision the effects of malaria control on the frequencies of the sickle-cell gene, for these must decrease in a regular manner. In commenting on such a possibility, Neel (1958: 66) states that 'this is probably the clearest example in all human genetics of the effect of an environmental change on the future evolution of man'. He might have added that the agent of environmental change in this case will be man himself.

2. TRYPANOSOMIASIS AND TSETSE FLY

Sleeping sickness was evidently known in Africa at least five centuries ago, a case having been described by a fourteenth-century Arab writer (Nash 1960: 974). The disease was well described in the early nineteenth century, when it was commonly known as 'negro lethargy', although the cause was not determined until the early years of the twentieth century. The prelude was the discovery by David Bruce in 1895 that nagana, a serious cattle disease in Africa, is caused by a protozoal parasite and that it is transmitted from animal to animal by the bite of the tsetse fly. This parasite was later named *Trypanosoma brucei*. Shortly after this an epidemic of sleeping sickness in Uganda reached such alarming proportions, involving hundreds of thousands of people, that a Sleeping Sickness Commission was sent out by the Royal Society to investigate it. By 1903 it was established that the disease was due to a trypanosome transmitted by a tsetse fly, as in the case of nagana of cattle. Since that time a vast amount of research has been devoted to the epidemiology of the disease and the characteristics of the parasite and the insect vector (Wilcocks 1962: 57–91; Burton 1955; Nash 1960).

Trypanosomiasis afflicts both man and his domestic animals in Africa, and both forms have effects on human welfare. At present, animal trypanosomiasis is of far greater economic importance than sleeping sickness; indirectly it is also of greater medical importance, for it results in dietary deficiencies in animal protein which affect far more Africans than does sleeping sickness itself. The study of trypanosomiasis has led to a biological complex in which the principal ecological factors are men, tsetse flies, trypanosomes, cattle and other domestic animals, wild game and vegetation. Still other significant variables in the complex are climate, hydrology, altitude, soils and fire.

Between 15° N. latitude and a line extending approximately from Benguela to Durban, some four and a half million square miles of Africa are infested with tsetse fly, an area one and a half times that of the United States (Nash 1960: 975). Tsetse flies belong to the genus *Glossina*, of which twenty-two species have been distinguished. Most of these species are capable of transmitting trypanosomiasis in cattle. Five species are the principal vectors in human sleeping sickness. The most obvious means of preventing both human and animal trypanosomiasis is to eradicate or control the tsetse fly, and this has been the main goal of research, especially among British workers (Wilcocks 1962: 78). Different species vary considerably in their breeding and feeding habits and their preferred habitats. All tsetse flies, however, require a certain minimum amount of shade, and the principal method of control, therefore, has been to destroy the type of vegetation which provides the shade required by different species of tsetse flies. This has been supplemented by use of insecticides, fly traps, hand catching and various other means. The common tsetse flies feed principally on certain game animals and may infect them with trypanosomes. Most wild animals, however, are immune to the disease in that they appear to suffer no ill-effects from this parasitæmia. As an additional method of tsetse control, therefore, the destruction of game has been carried out in selected areas in Southern Rhodesia, Mozambique and Uganda. This method has aroused opposition from persons concerned with game conservation.

The parasites responsible for human trypanosomiasis are *Trypanosoma gambiense* and *T. rhodesiense*, causing the diseases known respectively as Gambian and Rhodesian sleeping sickness. These two species are morphologically identical and cannot be distinguished microscopically from *T. brucei*, which is pathogenic for livestock but not for man. The two sleeping-sickness parasites have different geographical distributions, a factor which ordinarily facilitates species diagnosis. Where the ranges overlap, or when the place of infection is unknown, differentiation may be difficult; it is then based on the clinical pattern of the disease and on response to therapy, for arsenical drugs are effective against *T. gambiense* but not against *T. rhodesiense*. In the transmission of trypanosomiasis, the trypanosome normally undergoes a cyclical development, requiring about eighteen days in the fly, as it is carried from one infected animal or person to another. It is also believed that mechanical transmissions occasionally may occur, as when a fly, interrupted while feeding on an infected animal, transmits the parasite on its freshly contaminated proboscis to a nearby animal.

Gambian sleeping sickness is more widespread and frequent than the Rhodesian form of the disease. It occurs throughout western and central tropical Africa, extending to Lake Victoria. The disease tends to run a chronic course, involves the central nervous system, and often produces the classical symptoms of progressive lethargy and somnolence in its last stage. The Gambian variety is carried by the riverine flies *G. palpalis* and *G. tachinoides*; these frequent the wooded banks of rivers and lakes, which are also places of concentration for human population. *T. gambiense* is transmitted by the tsetse fly directly from person to person; there is no evidence of a significant non-human reservoir for the parasite.

In the Uganda epidemic of Gambian sleeping sickness in 1901–5, there were over 200,000 deaths in Busoga alone. The epidemic was controlled by removing the entire population of the affected area from the shore of Lake Victoria and from the offshore islands. Methods were later devised for selective clearing of riverine vegetation to eliminate the tsetse flies and prevent their spread, and this procedure has been intensively applied in British West Africa. The preferred method of control in French territories and the Belgian Congo has been drug prophylaxis and early treatment, with the principal aim of eliminating the parasite rather than the carrier (Wilcocks 1962: 75–6). Gambian sleeping sickness continues to be endemic in many areas, but the various control measures have resulted in a steady decrease in the number of new cases reported each year. In 1948 the total was 53,408; in 1957 it had declined to 14,874 (Nash 1960).

A high incidence of Gambian sleeping sickness is maintained only when there is intimate continued contact between individual flies and a human population. Conditions are unfavourable for the disease when a population moves frequently, even though it is repeatedly in intimate contact with flies, because the flies to which it is exposed are constantly changing.   Since permanent human habitations are commonly located near water sources which are also frequented by riverine tsetse flies, the conditions necessary for endemic Gambian sleeping sickness are widespread. As an extreme example of intimate personal contact between people and tsetse flies, Nash (1960) tells of a hamlet of forty-three inhabitants that he investigated among whom the infection rate was 70 per cent.   The total population of *G. palpalis* in the area, which did not exceed a dozen flies, was concentrated near a single water hole that was constantly used by the people.   The same flies repeatedly bit the same people, and when one person contracted sleeping sickness elsewhere, it spread rapidly through the hamlet.

Rhodesian sleeping sickness is a more acute disease.   Symptoms of severe toxicity may develop so rapidly, causing death after only a few months, that there is usually insufficient time for development of the classical cerebrospinal symptoms. The disease occurs in eastern Africa, extending from Kenya and Uganda southwards through Ruanda-Urundi, Tanganyika, Mozambique, the Rhodesias, as far as Bechuanaland.   The incidence of the disease is much lower than in Gambian sleeping sickness.   Excluding occasional large epidemics, Kenya, Uganda and Tanganyika, the territories of greatest prevalence, together notify less than 2,000 cases per year (Nash 1960).   It is nevertheless more dangerous in some respects than the Gambian disease and requires greater vigilance because of its tendency to occur among scattered populations in unexpected outbreaks and explosive epidemics.

The chief vector is *G. morsitans*, which infests thousands of square miles of woodland and whose range is still expanding.   *G. swynnertoni* and *G. pallidipes* are also known to transmit *T. rhodesiense* to man.   These species are all 'game flies' as distinguished from the riverine flies carrying *T. gambiense*.   They live by preference in bush country and woodlands, inhabited by game but with sparse and scattered human populations.   They normally feed on wild game but will attack domestic animals and man on occasion.   It is now definitely established that animals may serve as a reservoir of infection in Rhodesian sleeping sickness.   In experiments on captive animals, *T. rhodesiense* has been maintained for as long as twenty-three years without losing its infectivity for man.   Much epidemiological evidence can only be explained on the assumption of an animal reservoir, and in at least one case *T. rhodesiense* was found in the blood of a wild animal (bushbuck) shot in the bush. Summing up all the evidence, Wilcocks (1962: 75) concludes 'that man may pick up *T. rhodesiense* from game, but that in the great epidemics man is his own reservoir'.

The control of the Rhodesian disease has involved the methods used for Gambian sleeping sickness in addition to some attempts to control game with the purpose of reducing the tsetse flies which feed upon it.   Experience has shown that epidemics are most likely to occur when the human population has the low density of sixteen to eighteen people per square mile.   Where the density is one hundred or more, the farm clearings of most villages are large enough to serve as a protection against contact with the tsetse.   Wilcocks (1962: 72) suggests this historical interpretation of these facts:

> The sequence of events . . . was that before European rule the Africans lived mostly in fairly large and stable communities as a protection against tribal raids, or perhaps Arab slave raids, and they had little contact with tsetse flies. . .   When the Europeans suppressed tribal wars and raids the people spread out into the bush, creating small hamlets there, and infection was

occasionally picked up from some unknown source, possibly from an animal. In their bush villages and hamlets the people were in close contact with flies, and once the infection was introduced it spread quickly among them in the man-fly-man cycle.

The assumption made here is that in pre-European times sleeping sickness was much less prevalent in eastern Africa than in recent years. As yet there is little direct evidence bearing on this assumption, but the supposition regarding earlier settlement patterns is of a kind that can be tested in future ethnological and historical research.

In Tanganyika, where two-thirds of the area is infested with tsetse fly and the population is dispersed, the danger of sleeping sickness epidemics has been particularly acute. The Tanganyika government has taken a leading part in research ever since the creation of its Department of Tsetse Research shortly after the first world war. Under its director, C. F. M. Swynnerton, this organisation has contributed substantially to an understanding of the factors involved in the disease. Faced with an urgent situation, the Tanganyika government decided on a program for concentrating the scattered populations of some of the worst areas. The plan was to resettle these populations in tsetse-free clearings, either created or enlarged natural clearings, large enough to support at least 1,000 taxpayers in close settlement. Clearings of this size expel the tsetse fly and reduce the danger of epidemics to a minimum. In the Western Province alone, 250,000 people have been resettled in sixty-two sleeping-sickness settlements (Wilcocks 1962).

The author had the opportunity of observing a sleeping-sickness settlement at Magugu in Northern Province, which is adjacent to the Wambugwe tribe where he carried out anthropological research for a year in 1950–51 and for a shorter time in 1955. In the early years of the second world war sleeping sickness epidemics in this part of Tanganyika became so severe that a number of European farms in the region had to be abandoned. The Magugu area was at that time uninhabited bush and forest, heavily infested with tsetse fly. This fly belt crossed the great North Road about one hundred miles south of Arusha, and it was feared that the disease might be spread to new areas by people and vehicles travelling up and down the road and transporting infected tsetse flies. It was decided, therefore, to clear the Magugu area of bush and thus to eliminate the vector. Bush clearing is an expensive process, and the shrubs and trees quickly regenerate and again harbour tsetse flies if the cleared area is left uninhabited. The human settlement at Magugu was established primarily to prevent this reinfestation, as well as to bring new land into production.

In 1942 a public announcement was made inviting settlers to take up land, much of which could be irrigated from a local stream. The response was prompt, and soon a prosperous community surrounded by fields of maize, sorghum, rice, sugar cane, manioc and sweet potatoes existed where there had been only wilderness a year or two before. In 1955 the tax register listed 230 taxpayers, and the total population of the settlement exceeded 2,000. The settlers were drawn from all parts of Tanganyika and from neighbouring territories, with seventy-six different tribes being represented.

Although the Magugu settlers are discouraged from entering the surrounding uncleared land, which is still infested with tsetse fly, exposure to infection cannot be entirely avoided, as the people visit the forest to cut timber and firewood, to gather wild honey, and to trap and hunt game.   A ten-bed hospital with an African medical staff was established mainly to treat sleeping sickness.   Scattered cases occur every year, and there are occasional small epidemics: seventy-two cases in 1952, forty-two in 1954.   The mortality rate is relatively low, however, because of the availability of treatment and the alertness of the medical staff.   The aim is to make early diagnosis so that the disease may be cured by treatment.   Specially trained scouts take blood slides of all persons with suspicious symptoms or who have been exposed to tsetse bites.   By these means sleeping sickness is reduced to a disease of manageable proportions with a mortality rate no greater than from other diseases.

Rhodesian sleeping sickness and nagana of cattle are not identical diseases and are caused by different species of the parasite.   They often coexist in the same region, however, and are transmitted by the same vector.   This is the situation, for example, in much of the vast area of Tanganyika infested with *G. morsitans* (Atlas of Tanganyika 1948: 11).   Measures applied for the control of one disease usually also bring the other under control. Thus the clearing program at Magugu, though carried out primarily to control sleeping sickness, made it possible to keep healthy cattle in the settlement.   Another feature common to both types of trypanosomiasis is that wild game may act as a reservoir of infection.

The ecological factors involved in nagana are even more complex than those in sleeping sickness.   Hornby (1952) has described in some detail the inter-relation of the principal factors which, in addition to tsetse flies and trypanosomes, include livestock herding practices, agricultural methods, wild game, natural vegetation and the effect of the widespread custom of burning the grass and bush each year. Whiteside's (1958) paper, presented at an international symposium on animal trypanosomiasis at Luanda, discusses the nagana problem in historical perspective, with special reference to conditions in Kenya.   In this same volume may be found shorter reports on nagana from all the African regions in which it occurs.   Whiteside notes that up to about 1920 the problem of animal trypanosomiasis was one almost incapable of solution with the resources and knowledge available at the time.   Control programs at present are not always aimed at eradication of the vector or total prevention of infection; they may attempt instead to reduce the 'challenge' of the trypanosomes to a level which cattle can withstand.   In the last several decades drugs for curative and prophylactic treatment have been developed which make it feasible to keep cattle in areas of moderate challenge where before this was unprofitable.

Newer methods for controlling tsetse fly and treating trypanosomiasis now offer the promise of opening for ranching vast areas of Africa which in the past have been forbidden to cattle by moderate or heavy infestation.   If such a program were carried through, it might be of immense benefit to many African countries in improved nutrition and general economic advancement.   This optimistic view, however, may overlook some important factors in the complex ecology of the trypanosomiasis problem, and some writers have expressed doubts as to whether any considerable expansion of ranching is possible or desirable.   Darling (1960a), for example, believes that the prospects for the expansion of pastoralism in Africa are limited and uncertain.   As a more promising means of increasing the supply of animal protein, he suggests the rational management and harvesting of wild game, which is now found in much of the tsetse-infested areas and which would be destroyed if the land were cleared for grazing or agriculture.   His argument is that to exchange the wide spectrum of twenty to thirty hoofed animals, living in delicate adjustment to the habitat, for the narrowed spectrum of three ungulates exotic to Africa — cattle, sheep, and goats — is to throw away a bountiful resource and a marvellous ordering of nature (Darling 1960a: 125).

The field observations upon which this interpretation is based are set forth in his book *Wild Life in an African Territory* (Darling 1960b).

The biological history of man in Africa undoubtedly has been profoundly affected by tsetse-borne trypanosomiasis, both of humans and domestic animals, but the limited data makes it difficult to trace this history in detail. It is possible, however, to make some preliminary estimate of the inter-relations between man and trypanosomes in each of the three basic modes of ecological adaptation which have characterised human population in Africa: hunting and gathering, agricultural and pastoral.

Since *T. gambiense* appears to produce sleeping-sickness epidemics only when it is in intimate personal contact with a human population, nomadic hunting bands should not have been seriously affected by the disease. Conditions favouring epidemics would first occur with the appearance of permanent agricultural settlement. It has been noted that sleeping sickness is rare in the West African forest belt — even though *G. palpalis* may be present — except in the drier northern parts. Studies of fly movements in these regions suggest the explanation that in the humid forest areas 'G. palpalis is barely riverine in habit, roving freely throughout the farmland, woodland and forest; consequently the man-fly contact is impersonal, which probably explains the virtual absence of sleeping sickness from this zone' (Nash 1960: 985). This regional epidemiological differentiation in West Africa may have influenced movements of human population at the time that this forest zone was being invaded by agriculturists. Livingstone (1958: 555) has suggested that the forest clearings of the earliest agriculturists created conditions favouring holoendemic malaria. The adverse effects of malaria, however, may have been balanced by a relative freedom from sleeping sickness in the forest zone as compared with the drier regions where early agriculture was also practised. These must remain unproved hypotheses until more is known about the distributions of the insect vectors of both diseases in prehistoric times.

The effects of Rhodesian sleeping sickness on early human populations are more difficult to interpret. The presence of an animal reservoir for *T. rhodesiense*, and the fact that the disease tends to affect scattered rather than concentrated populations would seem to render hunting bands particularly susceptible to the disease. Archaeological evidence, however, indicates that for hundreds of thousands of years hunting populations roamed through central and eastern Africa, the present range of *T. rhodesiense*. Had these populations been continuously exposed to infection, they would presumably have developed the same relative immunity to trypanosomiasis that the game animals of the region have developed. Since the present populations are susceptible to sleeping sickness, it would appear either that they are the descendants of recent immigrants into the region or that the parasite has developed its pathogenicity to man as a fairly recent mutation.

Among the domestic animals kept by man in Africa, the horse is particularly susceptible to trypanosomiasis; this susceptibility has had a significant influence on the course of African history since the introduction of that animal into the Sudan. The mounted forces that played such an important role in the history of the Sudanese kingdoms and empires were barred by tsetse fly from invading deeply into the West African forest zone or from penetrating into central and southern Africa. This factor undoubtedly contributes to a delay of a thousand years or more before the influences of the Mediterranean world reached these parts of Africa with any intensity. The peoples of tropical Africa were also denied the horse as a transport animal mainly because of trypanosomiasis and tsetse flies.

Many herds of cattle are able to survive in tsetse country if the trypanosomiasis challenge is not too great (Hornby 1952; Whiteside 1958). Dwarf breeds of cattle in West Africa, known as Ndama and Muturu, are highly resistant to the local trypanosomes. It is not certain whether this is a congenital immunity or pre-munition, i.e., a chronic state of infection without clinical effects acquired early in life (Baker 1958; Nash 1960). Although under favourable conditions cattle may survive with mild infection, they usually succumb to the disease when subjected to physiological strain, as in periods of drought. Nash (1960: 974) suggests that the absence of the ox-drawn plough and cart in tropical Africa was largely due to the prevalence of nagana, which renders the oxen incapable of exertion. The idea of using draught oxen must have been known along the northern boundary of the tsetse zone as the result of extensive and ancient cultural contacts with the Mediterranean world across the Sahara and up the Nile. After the plough was introduced by Europeans into the Cape Colony, its diffusion northwards as a culture trait was stopped at the tsetse zone. Attempts to introduce the plough in tsetse areas have usually failed; when the oxen are made to pull a plough their resistance breaks, and they succumb to nagana. Nash (1960: 975) has concluded that 'for hundreds of years the tsetse dictated that the economy of the African should be based on the hoe and the head-load, a dictatorship from which only now is he being freed by the petrol engine and railway locomotive'.

A habitual pattern of medical thought is to restrict attention only to the effects of vectors and parasites on man. But the actions of man himself have also influenced the distribution and prevalence of tsetse flies in different parts of Africa. Space limitation permits mention of only one such human action, but it is perhaps the most significant. This is the periodic, often annual, burning of grassland and bush country. Burning of dry vegetation is practised almost everywhere in Africa (Bartlett 1956; Darling 1960b) and appears to be a widespread custom in many other parts of the world among cultivators and pastoralists as well as among hunting peoples. After reviewing the evidence on this question, Stewart (1956: 129) concludes: 'The unrestricted burning of vegetation appears to be a universal culture trait among historic primitive peoples and therefore was probably employed by our remote ancestors.'

It is generally accepted that during late Pleistocene times there was a marked reduction in the forests of central Africa. This retreat of the African forests was part of the ecological trend that Aubréville (1949) terms *désertification*. Burning of vegetation was an important factor in this process. Harroy (1944) lists this first among the human actions contributing to the impoverishment of the vegetation of tropical Africa and the deterioration of the soils. The trend was for high forests to be replaced by savannah woodlands, and this favoured the spread of *G. morsitans*, which later was to be the principal vector in transmitting both Rhodesian sleeping sickness and nagana.

It remains for future research to work out in detail the interaction of man, tsetse fly, vegetation and the other main factors of this ecological complex in historical perspective. Ford (1960) has attempted a tentative historical reconstruction of this kind, based on his own field observations and an imaginative synthesis of existing knowledge. His analysis of prehistorical events in western Uganda, the geographical focus of his study, may be summarised in this necessarily over-simplified manner.

At a time when Central Africa was occupied solely by hunting peoples, a belt of tsetse flies extended across East Africa and the Congo, G. morsitans and the game flies of the savannah meeting with the forest flies at some line in Uganda. How did the first cattle-keeping people bring their cattle southwards through this tsetse belt? The only explanation, according to Ford, is that they were preceded by agriculturists, who settled in the fertile land at the forest margin and cleared a tsetse-free corridor through which cattle could be brought safely. The clearing operation also provided protection against sleeping sickness. 'Tsetse fly does not keep agricultural man out of fertile areas — man keeps out the tsetse fly' (Ford 1960: 12). The agriculturists transformed the forests into grasslands, and the pastoralists brought in their herds of cattle. They then pressed upon the agriculturists to clear more land, thus pushing the forest margin continually to the west. There is historical evidence that this process has been going on for many centuries.

The herdsmen, following their usual practice of firing the dry grass annually, caused their pastures to be invaded by pyrophytic shrubs and trees, and gradually the grasslands were transformed to savannah woodlands, which in time became infected with G. morsitans. Cattle could no longer be grazed safely in these areas, and the pastoralists again pushed westwards in the wake of the agricultural pioneers seeking safe pastures.

A more detailed study of a somewhat different ecological sequence in a small region of northern Uganda (Dodos County) was reported by Deshler (1960). This area was free of tsetse fly until about 1922. As a means of stopping tribal raids the Napore and Nyangeya peoples on the northern border of Dodos County were evacuated by the Uganda government. These people, who hunted a great deal, had kept game from entering the region from the north. Following their departure, buffalo and other game entered the area, and with them came tsetse flies. In three years the tsetse fly advanced eighty miles and infested 1,500 square miles of land. The cattle-keeping people were forced to migrate with their herds to the south and west. This caused overpopulation and overgrazing in the refugee areas, resulting in deterioration of the soil and seriously affecting the health and demography of the population. In 1946 a program of tsetse clearance was started, and in three years two-thirds of the fly belt had been cleared. The newly cleared land was found to be improved for agricultural use as a result of its long period of fallow.

3. THE IMPLICATIONS OF RESEARCH ON NUTRITION

The problem of malnutrition in Africa (CSA 1957) differs in several respects from the problems of malaria and trypanosomiasis which have just been considered. Malnutrition is not a definite condition that one either has or does not have, as in the case of infectious diseases. The definition of malnutrition is largely contingent upon some agreed standard. Conditions of severe malnutrition usually result in some recognised syndrome, such as the classical picture of kwashiorkor. Between this extreme and conditions of entirely adequate nutrition, however, there is a continuum along which it is difficult to evaluate the nutritional status except by reference to an agreed standard.

A relatively simple example is to be found in considerations of caloric intake and energy output. Here the dietary standard is relative to the production of human energy which is needed or expected by certain people in certain situations. In a study of Sotho diet, Ashton (1939) found that the men do not work in the fields for more than five hours, while the women may work for twelve or fourteen hours; he suggests that differences in diet may partly account for this. If these people remain healthy, however, and if their culture operates satisfactorily at this level of energy output, then the caloric 'requirements of the diet would have to be stated with a sex differential'.

In a similar study of Bemba diet — accompanied in this case by a chemical assay of nutritional elements — Richards and Widdowson (1936: 195) came to this conclusion: 'As judged by American standards, the caloric intake was insufficient to provide energy for the work done.' If the accuracy of these data and calculations is assumed, this conclusion implies a difference in energy conversion between Americans and Bemba: an implication which runs counter to the common assumption that physiological processes such as food metabolism, which appear to be free of cultural control, are uniform for human beings everywhere. This paradoxical conclusion will be reconsidered below.

Malnutrition in Africa, more than any other disease, is a problem which tends to be resolved into the general economic problems of the continent. The nutritional status of a population is to a large extent a function of the food supply, which in turn is largely a function of such economic factors as resources, production techniques, and systems of allocation and distribution. The quantity and quality of food actually consumed are influenced, of course, by factors other than the available supply: customary food preferences and avoidances, taboos, ideas about infant feeding, etc. But in the main, the pattern of consumption corresponds to the food supply, which in tribal societies depends on the natural resources of the region and techniques of exploitation. The natural food resources of Africa can in fact be taken as a constant. Not much can be added to them, although unused resources can be exploited through such measures as bush clearing, irrigation and drainage, or elimination of tsetse flies to provide new pastures for livestock.

Techniques of exploitation may vary greatly — as do any culture traits — even between groups inhabiting similar environments, and the variations provide opportunities for deliberate or directed changes. Scientists, such as medical nutritionists and agricultural officers who are involved in practical problems, tend however to assume that diets which do not conform to some scientific standard must be deficient in some respect, and they search for ways of improving and supplementing indigenous diets. Anthropologists, on the other hand, more aware of the unplanned changes which have occurred in most tribal diets, are inclined to find virtue in them and to attribute present nutritional deficiencies to recent changes. Culwick (1943), for example, noted that in East Africa it was customary for women to soak grain for four or five days before grinding it. The ostensible purpose of this treatment was to make the grain easier to manipulate, but, according to the author, it also had the effect of causing the grain partially to sprout, thus enhancing its nutritional value. In many places today the dry grain is ground by mills, and thus the diet has been impoverished.

The crucial question underlying these divergent views seems to be this: had tribal societies in pre-European times evolved patterns of food production and diet — perhaps through trial and error and accumulated experience and under the stimulus of competition with other societies — which provided their members with nutrition adequate for the needs of the society? There is little direct evidence bearing on this question, for by the time researchers have appeared on the scene tribal diets have already undergone some change under the impact of Western economic, political and cultural forces. In one of the most stimulating studies of this kind of problem, Orr and Gilks (1931) made a careful comparative investigation of the physical conditions of the neighbouring Kikuyu and Masai tribes and of the nutritional and other factors affecting them. The pastoral Masai, consuming a diet high in animal protein, were found to be superior in health and physique to the Kikuyu, living on a predominantly vegetable diet. The Masai diet in 1931 may have been little affected by the European occupation of Kenya, but there is no doubt that Kikuyu diet had been considerably altered, and it cannot be assumed that the same difference in nutritional status existed fifty years earlier.

Protein deficiency is the most common defect of African diets and is the principal cause of the widespread syndrome of malnutrition in children known as kwashiorkor. There are various reasons for this protein deficiency. In urban and semi-urban situations it is the result of sheer poverty. In some regions, notably South Africa, maize has largely supplanted millet and sorghum as the staple food because of its higher caloric yield. Because maize is qualitatively inferior to the indigenous cereals in protein content and in certain other nutritional ingredients, this substitution has meant a deterioration in native diet.

Except where fish are abundant, animal protein is generally scarce in those regions in which cattle cannot be kept because of tsetse fly infestation. In these regions, hunting probably provided much more meat in earlier times than at present. Turnbull (1961) describes the cordial hospitality extended to Pygmy bands in the Ituri region by the Negro villagers, who hoped to obtain the meat of game animals in return. The suggestion is that the meat supply was more plentiful at a time before the decline of the Pygmy population and hunting culture put the diet of the agriculturists of the Congo forest into imbalance. The Lele of Kasai, as Douglas (1954) describes them, are intensely interested in hunting and devote much of their time and energy to it, although the production of meat by this means is meagre. The author wonders at this discrepancy between effort and results. In all likelihood game was more abundant in pre-European times but has decreased as a result of the use of firearms and other factors. It may be that Darling's (1960a) plan for the rational harvesting of game in tsetse infested areas proposes not so much an innovation as a restoration of an important food resource of former times.

Although food consumption is the principal correlate of nutritional status, it is not the only inter-related factor. Intestinal infections, prevalent in all parts of Africa, adversely affect the nutritional status of individuals suffering from them, and malnourished individuals are more susceptible to serious intestinal infections (Freeborn et al. 1960: 25, 115 ff.). In the case of malarial infections there is some evidence that subnormal hæmoglobin levels resulting from inadequate nutrition may even inhibit the multiplication of parasites (Allison 1961: 725). This protective effect, however, may be offset by a general lowering of resistance to malaria in malnourished individuals.

Nearly every country in Africa has — or had until recently — one or more research organisations working primarily in the field of nutrition, and an immense amount of research is now being devoted to nutritional problems. These organisations and the work they are doing are described in CSA (1957). Most of this nutrition research is clinically oriented. Different syndromes of malnutrition are conceived of as diseases to be attacked by the usual clinical procedure of discovering causative factors, pathogenesis, clinical manifestations, preventive or protective measures and remedial treatment. There is not space here to discuss this medical research, and in any case it is difficult to generalise about its relevance for social research in Africa. Attention may be directed, however, to one general interpretation of malnutrition which has been proposed by two South African medical workers, J. and T. Gillman (1951).

The Gillmans' theory is based on clinical investigations of human subjects and on animal experiments. Their findings suggested to them that the reaction of an organism to its diet at any given stage of its life history tends to be modified by its previous nutritional experience, including prenatal experience. Innate differences between individuals or populations tend to be neglected in this theory, because they appear to be overshadowed by acquired conditions of nutritional reactivity. The theory is focused on the concept of a 'life-track', which encompasses the biological experience of an organism from fertilisation to senescence and death. The life-track, as the Gillmans conceive of it, is primarily, though not exclusively, concerned with nutritional experience. This conception is best explained in their own words:

> Since a great number of alternative possibilities are open to the organism, and since only a restricted number are actually realized, the organism, at various stages along its life-track, finds itself, so to speak, at crossroads in respect to its future course of development. At each 'crossroad' the future course of development of the organism is determined by the prevailing metabolism and by the previous events in development. As each new direction of it is registered, the life-track gradually converges on a more specific part of the spectrum of phenotypes. The more general direction of the life-track at birth is steadily converted into a more specific one in adulthood and in senescence (1951: 11).

The nutritional experiences of different organisms in prenatal existence and infancy vary considerably even within a single cultural milieu, and the individual life-tracks begin to follow divergent directions at an early age. This 'individuality of metabolism means that no two infants utilise food in the same way' (1951: 13). More significant from an anthropological viewpoint is the fact that different cultural groups may have markedly different nutritional life-tracks. The Gillmans have mainly explored the difference in nutritional patterns between South African Bantu and Whites under conditions of urban life. Upon moving from a Native Reserve to the city to work as labourers, many Bantu adopt a diet quite different from that to which they were habituated. This means a sharp change in their life-track, with repercussions in their nutritional status and health. It renders them particularly susceptible to liver pathology, which is the focus of the Gillmans' clinical research.

This theory of nutrition, if corroborated by a wider range of medical investigations, might usefully be applied to anthropological problems in Africa. The theory of the life-track, for example, might explain the paradoxical findings of Richards and Widdowson which were considered above. If the nutritional life-tracks of Bemba and Americans are quite different — a reasonable supposition — then, according to the Gillmans, individuals of these two groups would utilise food in different ways; it should not be surprising, therefore, if some of the metabolic processes of adult Bemba — in this case energy conversion — failed to conform to American standards.

A basic postulate of anthropological theory is that the possession of *culture* is a fundamental difference between man and other animals, including the non-human primates. Strictly speaking, this term, culture, should be used in the plural, for there is no uniform set of cultural usages characterising all groups of the species. Each society has its own distinctive culture, and — of even greater interest — societies with no great difference in the genetic composition of their populations and occupying similar natural environments, may have cultures which differ sharply in certain respects. This is true, for example, of the Kikuyu and Masai. The culture of every society includes among its elements some of the major determinants of the society's diet: techniques for production and preparation of food, economic system, food preferences and avoidances, and so forth. The cultural features related to nutrition in a sense form a channel or track through which an individual passes during his life. Barring environmental or social catastrophes, this nutritional track must in the long run provide an adequate diet for most of the members, if the society is to maintain enough vigour to succeed and survive.

One effect of the life-track principle would be to retard the process of cultural change with respect to diet. If an individual has already started on a nutritional program which has been successfully tested by his society for generations, there is no assurance that he can change the direction of his life-track or switch to a different nutritional program in mid-career without serious consequences to his health and vigour. As the Gillmans have shown, the metabolism of an organism and its mode of food utilisation are partly determined by its past nutritional history. A society, therefore, could not with impunity change its food habits too rapidly. This insight has implications for the deliberate planning of changes in diets as well as theoretical implications for anthropological concepts of culture. On the basis of his nutritional studies in South Africa, T. Gillman (1958: 19) issues this warning: 'There is scarcely any other way whereby it is possible, wittingly or unwittingly, to inflict such widespread bodily harm on so many people as by tampering, incorrectly, with a nation's diet.' T. S. Eliot has perceived this same principle on the basis of poetic intuition. In his *Notes Towards a Definition of Culture*, he writes: 'If we take culture seriously, we see that a people does not need merely enough to eat . . . but a proper and particular cuisine' (p. 24).

III *SOME POSSIBILITIES FOR FUTURE RESEARCH*

Consideration of a concrete situation — which in the past has been mainly the concern of social research — may demonstrate the way in which some of the ideas discussed in the foregoing pages may be applied. Ruanda-Urundi recently achieved independence as two nations, but it did so under a cloud of strife between Tutsi and Hutu sections of the population. Most analyses of the problems have been sociological in nature, they have dealt with the structure of Ruanda society and particularly with the relationship between the two castes: the agricultural Hutu and the pastoral Tutsi. The penetrating study by Maquet (1961) is the most recent of these.

Ford's (1960) study of trypanosomiasis and the tsetse fly in that part of Africa, however, indicates how analysis of another dimension can increase understanding of the situation in Ruanda.   As noted in a previous section, the agriculturists of this region have been clearing the eastern margin of the Congo forest for centuries, creating grasslands for the herds of pastoral people.   The grasslands in time were invaded by tsetse fly, thus increasing the pressure on the agriculturists to push into the forests and provide new pastures.   Having in mind this ecological process, Ford (1960: 18) writes that

> although it may be that it is the 'wind of change', one suspects that the recent rebellion in Ruanda of the agricultural Bahutu against their Batussi overlords, has as its fundamental cause the pressure of the longhorn Sanga cattle for more grazing and the compulsion on the agricultural peasantry to provide tsetse free pastures.

This interpretation might be further expanded by applying the Gillmans' theory of the life-track.   The nutritional life-tracks of agricultural and pastoral peoples are quite different, and it may be more difficult than is commonly thought to change from one dietary regime to another.   Nutritional factors, therefore, may well be reinforcing the sociological and ecological factors which have maintained and even extended the separation between the Hutu and Tutsi.

III

PSYCHO-CULTURAL STUDIES

14

Psychology *   Leonard W. Doob

I INTRODUCTION†

PSYCHOLOGY IN AFRICA is underdeveloped because the study of the African environment and of the social groups living there has seemed to be more compelling and important to European and African scholars than the study of problems posed by identifiable individuals.   Clearly the continent must be grasped geographically before exploration can occur and political boundaries be fixed; historically before the present can be understood and the past either forgotten or glorified; anthropologically and politically before people can be ruled and changed; and sociologically before intergroup struggles can be mitigated and urban living improved.   It is often more efficient to study groups rather than particular people: the emerging generalisations are believed to have wider applicability.   Hospitals in most areas of Africa are so crowded and understaffed that perforce a higher priority must be given to sick bodies than to disturbed minds; hence psychiatry in Africa lags even further behind the other medical disciplines than it does in Western countries, and psychiatric attention has had to be focused upon socially disturbing psychoses rather than upon the milder neuroses.   Until recently, educational facilities in Africa have been so sparse and the supply of African labour so great that there has been little incentive to develop psychological tests for schools and in-dustry or government.   Finally, many European residents of Africa have convinced

* Dr Simon Biesheuval, while director of the National Institute for Personnel Research, generously supplied copious materials and insights.   At his suggestion Dr D. H. Reader prepared a summary of the Institute's current activities, with special emphasis upon its unpublished research; frequent references are made to this document.   Professor Marshall H. Segall has offered provocative suggestions and has permitted me to read his unpublished materials on perception.   Professor Irvin L. Child has placed his data on socialisation at my disposal and has patiently helped me in organising them.   Mrs Margaret M. Nagle has valiantly and conscientiously hunted for, and discovered relevant reports which she has then dissected with more skill than my frequently hesitating directions deserved to command.   The Concilium on International Studies at Yale University allocated Ford Foundation funds which enabled me to depend upon Mrs Nagle.   Professor Robert A. LeVine has published such an excellent account (1961) of certain psychological problems in Africa that, to avoid discouragement, I have had to refuse to digest his views until finishing what I fear, nevertheless, may be in part only a repetition of the major points he has scored.   To avoid confusion I have deliberately adopted the forms proposed by Murdock (1959) in naming African societies, even when the investigators themselves use different ones.   No claim is advanced that every important investigation has been located and then surveyed up to the time of the completion of the manuscript (May 1962), but the search has been intensive.
† Bibliography for this chapter will be found on page 543.

themselves that, through practical experience over the years, they 'understand Africans' and are not likely to profit from the generalisations of psychological research. Symptomatic of the status of psychology in Africa is the fact that, save for the universities in South Africa, no university south of the Sahara has a department or faculty of psychologists. Whatever psychologists there are usually either lurk within a faculty of education or some other social science, or operate outside academic institutions in industry or government.

Much of the responsibility for the status of psychology in Africa must be traced to psychologists themselves and to the nature of their craft. Psychologists are not normally content to collect and analyse a set of facts; they seek to transcend those facts by extracting a principle or generalisation. Africa has not been a challenge to them as it has been to other social scientists whose interest in the continent can be aroused just because there are new data to be collected there. In contrast, European and American psychologists are generally convinced that they have enough unsolved problems at home, among both animals and human beings, and that hence they do not need to plunge into the exotic phenomena of Africa. On that continent, moreover, they feel that they can have little or no opportunity to employ the experimental method to which with great justification they are addicted (Segall 1961).

This chapter, therefore, is based upon admittedly inadequate information. By and large too little is known about the behaviour of Africans to be able to supply answers to the critical questions about them which psychological research must raise. Under these circumstances, the cry on behalf of future research is herewith, not surprisingly, sounded loudly. In order to spare the reader's sensibilities, that cry will not be frequently repeated, although it should be raised at the conclusion of every topic.

Except in passing or as a basis for comparison, no reference is made to studies of Arabs in North Africa or of Europeans and other ethnic groups living south of the Sahara. Basic or applied research by psychologists, especially in South Africa, is excluded when it is unrelated to Africans; some of the work on electro-encephalography by Mundy-Castle (1953), for example, could very well have been conducted in London or Los Angeles rather than in Johannesburg. But other of his research, such as that which compares the brain waves of Africans and Europeans either incidentally (1951) or deliberately (Mundy-Castle, McKiever and Prinslov 1953), is clearly germane. The hero of this chapter, in short, is the sub-Saharan African; all other characters play minor roles.

The presentation to follow has been facilitated by a simple distinction between *theoretical* and *sequential* research. What happens when A occurs? Let it be assumed that B appears. When the investigator merely indicates that B has been shown to be a consequence of A, his research is sequential: B follows A, it is stated, and the report is finished. But when in advance B is predicted as a consequence of A on the basis of an explicitly stated theory, or when the sequence of A-B is shown to confirm or refute some theory, then the research is theoretical. The distinction of course is relative, not absolute. In some cases the theory related to the research may be quite unimportant or be oriented towards a practical principle restricted to a narrow series of situations; in others the established sequence, though not at the moment related to a theory, may turn out to have very significant theoretical implications.

Much of the psychological research in Africa can be shown to involve a recurrent question: in what ways and for what reasons are Africans different from other ethnic groups? The question can often be answered sequentially: under condition A, Africans do B; Europeans under the same condition do or do not do B. The problem also has important theoretical implications, because the presence or absence of differences can indicate the possible significance of biological or cultural factors in explaining behaviour. It should be noted, however, that existing comparisons between African and other ethnic groups are almost never satisfactory from a sampling standpoint; usually, for example, too few African societies have been sampled or, within a given society, too few Africans have been examined. Such an elementary deficiency is discouraging.

One final introductory note on methodology stems from the sampling problems just mentioned. In describing research procedures or in presenting results, many investigators lump together subjects or informants from different societies and speak of 'Bantu', 'non-white', or 'Africans'. Such a mode of presentation may be used for several reasons. The researcher may be prejudiced and imagine that all Africans are so similar that finer discriminations are not necessary. Sometimes the nature of the research problem requires only the crude category, and preliminary analysis may reveal so little variability among the Africans that statistically they may be considered as a single group. In some instances too few subjects, informants or patients from each society have been obtained — or were obtainable — to justify separate statistical treatment. A single illustration is offered to show that such coalescing can be misleading. In 1934 a Maze Test was administered to various groups of Africans with the following results expressed in terms of mean mental age for the indicated number of subjects: 29 Thonga in the Transvaal, 11·7; 32 Karanga, 11·6; 43 Ndau, 11·4; 25 Xhosa, 10·8; 25 Thonga in Mozambique, 9·3; 28 Chopi, 8·3; and 25 Bushmen, 7·6 (Porteus 1937: 257). To have called all these subjects Africans, as unfortunately the same author did in a few instances (e.g., p. 301), would have obscured the interesting differences.

For another reason, too, the practice of identifying a group as 'African' is to be roundly condemned: without knowing the precise societal affiliation of Africans, the results of a study cannot be related to the cultural background, and they cannot be easily or sensibly joined with data collected in other research. To enlighten the reader of this chapter and to chastise the investigator — sometimes sympathetically, sometimes not—each study guilty of the transgression is made to wear in brackets, as a symbol of disgrace, one or two asterisks whose meaning is herewith declared to be the following:

* The societies to which the Africans belong are mentioned but are then neglected in offering the results and in drawing conclusions which are derived by combining all the data into one statistical group.

** The society or societies to which the Africans belong are not even mentioned.

II MAJOR QUESTIONS FOR AFRICAN PSYCHOLOGICAL STUDIES

1. GENETIC DIFFERENCES?

From a political standpoint, the most impertinent variant of the basic question is: are Africans genetically different from Europeans? Of course they are with respect to certain physical attributes such as skin colour and type of hair. But are they born with bodies that cause them to behave differently from Europeans regardless of, or in conjunction with, cultural factors? The answer here must be, as it has been for a generation or more in scientific circles, *No*. At the same time the possibility cannot be excluded for all eternity, and the precise way in which so-called culture functions to produce the obtained differences is by no means completely clear.

The discussion can begin on what appears to be a very basic physiological level, *viz.*, brain action. A high proportion of Guinean soldiers stationed in Marseilles [**] revealed abnormal brain-wave patterns; this electro-encephalographic finding was attributed by the investigators to 'l'existence d'une immaturité neuronique avec tendance aux paroxysmes spontanés et provoqués' and in turn to 'une intégration psycho-biologique en rapport avec le site physiographique simplifié du cadre de vie de nos sujets' (Gallais *et al.* 1951). Such a potentially important discovery, however, has not been confirmed among urban Africans from various societies [*] in southern Africa, although the records of the adults — but not those of the children — reveal 'minor significant differences' in comparison with groups of Europeans (Mundy-Castle *et al.* 1953; Reader 1961). These latter investigators believe that 'a normal EEG pattern appears to be very much a heredito-constitutional affair', but they do not deny the unproven possibility that the obtained differences may reflect cultural influences upon Africans either over time or, conceivably, in the laboratory at the moment of measurement. The fact that an EEG measure, alpha frequency, has been found to be correlated with performance on one particular intelligence scale both in a normal European population and in an isolated, homogeneous, rather abnormal group of Europeans (Mundy-Castle and Nelson 1960) can, however, be interpreted as a tentative argument supporting the cultural hypothesis, if it is believed that intelligence so measured is environmentally determined. Both the EEG and intelligence may in turn be affected by some sort of genetic proclivity; thus the investigators point to possible inbreeding among the isolated Europeans as a factor.

A psychiatrist has speculated concerning 'the possibility of actual structural differences in the brains of Africans — particularly in the diencephalic-frontal system'. He flatly asserts that East Africans in Tanganyika [**] show 'little variation' in physique in the Kretschmerian sense of somatotype (Smartt 1956: 446, 462–63). Admittedly he has no evidence for the speculation and he offers none for the assertion.

Figures on disease incidence in Africa are unreliable principally because medical services are overtaxed, and only the diseases of patients seeking medical care can be recorded. In one series of extremely careful, well-designed studies, however, the blood pressure of rural Zulu has been shown to be significantly lower than that of urban Zulu and of white and Negro groups in the United States. Such a difference cannot be attributed to genetic factors, because both African groups belong to the same stock. Instead a variation in 'social stress' is offered as an explanation (Scotch 1960; Scotch *et al.* 1961). These investigators also indicate that existing literature on hypertension among Africans is contradictory: the disturbance allegedly is rare in some African societies (especially East Africa) but occurs often in South Africa and, according to another authority (Lambo 1958: 134), in West Africa. The Zulu research, moreover, demonstrates that, unless members of the society at the time of measurement are living under almost identical conditions, the intrasocietal differences may be as great as, or even greater than the intersocietal ones. The authors just cited are tentatively convinced that another culturally determined factor, that of diet, which does not seem to mediate the difference in blood pressure among the Zulu, may account for the relatively late age of the onset of the meno-pause as reported by a small sample of Zulu women (Abramson *et al.* 1960a). They also offer convincing evidence of a connection between diet and the serum protein pattern of urban Zulu adults (Abramson *et al.* 1960b). At the moment the behavioural correlates of these physiological processes are not adequately known, but because the processes are affected by diet and because African diets often differ from those of Europeans, the establishment of any significant and consistent relation could lead to the conclusion that diet accounts for some of the behavioural differ-ences between Africans and Europeans. It is believed, for example, that 'quiet-ness and docility' among children is associated with the protein-deficiency disease of kwashiorkor (Welbourn 1954). The data seem to favour not a genetic but a cultural explanation.

An African psychiatrist has 'the impression' that 'organic psychiatric condi-tions that are usually associated with senescence in European and American countries occur much earlier in the indigenous population of Nigeria'. Such a difference he immediately attributes to 'racial or constitutional predisposition to vasomotor sensitivity'. But he also indicates that the disturbances may be 'pre-cipitated by associated factors, e.g., malnutrition, avitaminosis, and recurrent malaria' (Lambo 1958: 134–5). The latter factors, of course, are clearly environ-mentally determined.

Impatiently and in accordance with an ancient tradition of research, it must be asked whether this question of genetic *versus* cultural factors cannot be settled empirically be examining infants at birth, when cultural factors supposedly have not yet begun to operate. Alas, no clear-cut studies in Africa — or elsewhere — are at hand. Of relevance, however, is the following: 'In a small group of new-born African infants ($N = 8$), responses to photic stimulation suggested the possibility of a higher level of neuropsychological maturity at birth than Euro-peans; but this must be regarded as extremely tentative' (Reader 1961). The most dramatic results so far have been obtained by measuring the psychomotor development and co-ordination of African infants and children from birth to the age of six by means of standardised tests: those of Thomas *et al.* and Gesell. A large sample of 252 children was examined in Uganda, some more than once at different ages; most but not all were Ganda [*]. The research has been repeated, and the findings apparently replicated, on samples of thirty children each in Senegal and South Africa [**]. In her most complete summary to date, the investigator states: 'Quelle que soit la tribu du petit Africain, quel que soit son milieu social, son développement psycho-somatique est remarquablement précoce, et l'avance est d'autant plus marquée que l'enfant est plus jeune, toutefois cette avance est moindre dans les milieux non traditionnels' (Geber 1960: 103). 'From the first days', for example, 'the child when drawn up to a sitting position could keep his head from falling back': a feat attained normally by European infants about six weeks later (Geber 1958b). 'Much of the activity' among the newly born Africans corresponded to an age of four to six weeks, but some was even 'more precocious' and not to be expected until between six and eight weeks; 'the advance was shown chiefly by a lesser degree of flexion, by a remarkable control of the head, and by the frequent absence of primitive reflex activity. . . In many children, even in the first days, moving objects could be followed with the eyes, and rotation of the head accompanied the pursuit' (Geber and Dean 1957b). The Ganda child is reported to walk at ten months and to run by fourteen; 'a 11 mois, il est capable de prendre avec exactitude un très petit objet (pastille) en pince fine entre le pouce et l'index' (Geber 1960: 103).

The preceding paragraph contains copious quotations in order to suggest the positive tone of the investigator. Few actual figures, however, are ever reported in the many, usually repetitive, summaries that have appeared in British, American and French scientific journals. The one set of tables that has been provided (Geber 1960: 108–10) is confined to displaying only the distribution of the Developmental and Intelligence Quotients and hence does not offer details on such specific activities as walking, running and grasping. The data therein are presented in such a form that adequate statistical analysis by interested scholars is impossible. Careful reading of them, however, indicates that they support all the author's conclusions except for one pertaining to acculturation which will be mentioned below.

On the whole, therefore, Geber's findings seem solid. In addition, except for visual perception, which apparently she did not measure, they have been replicated in another laboratory (Biesheuvel 1959b: 9). How, then, can these findings be explained? Altitude and climate can be excluded: when fifteen European and sixty Indian newborn infants were measured at the same site in Uganda, 'exactly the results that have been found in Europe' were obtained (Geber and Dean 1957b). It may well be, therefore, that genetic tendencies are operating here; if not, environmental or cultural factors must again be invoked.

Possibly such factors function pre-natally. Will the developing organism, for example, be affected *in utero* when the mother is suffering from kwashiorkor? A well-controlled experiment on rats has demonstrated that on a specially designed piece of apparatus the exploratory behaviour of the offspring of mothers raised on a protein-deficient diet was not affected, but their 'intelligence' was (Cowley and Griesel 1959). Later work has indicated that such animals not only had 'impaired learning ability and temperamental defects (e.g., in responsiveness to fear-producing stimuli)' but also that the 'impairment' persisted even when they were changed at birth to mothers which had been fed a normal diet (Reader 1961). It is not now known whether similar results occur among human beings. For this and other reasons, the National Institute for Personnel Research has been planning a long-term project in which expectant African mothers and later they and their children will be continuously examined and observed over a long period of years. Conceivably the allegedly relaxed and joyful attitude of African mothers during pregnancy may 'lessen the retarding effects of the birth trauma' (Biesheuvel 1959b: 9).

The view that culture has a post-natal influence is supported by more substantial evidence. Geber herself points out again and again that the loving concern of African mothers for their children after birth — including the attention given them during the administration of the tests — may facilitate development, but in a manner, however, that has not been specified. African children reared 'in the European way' are not precocious after the first month, nor do they show a 'falling-off' in intellectual development by European standards on both the Gesell and Terman-Merill tests after the age of two or after weaning as do children from more traditional African homes (Geber and Dean 1957a and 1958a). The pattern of development, possibly including brain waves, is different in children suffering from kwashiorkor (Nelson and Dean 1959). Geber attributes the disappearance of precocity after the first two years to the weaning process, which she describes in such unequivocal terms that one is forced to wonder, as will be suggested later in this chapter, whether the Ganda really follow such a distinct pattern: 'j'ai relié cette transformation totale du petit Africain au *sevrage*.   Celui-ci est extrêmement brutal dans le milieu traditionnel en Ouganda' (Geber 1960: 105).

Geber's stimulating research, like the other evidence surveyed in this section, provides still another push in the direction of a predominantly cultural explanation but leaves the problem of genetic influence unsettled.   At this tantalising point, the problem must be temporarily abandoned.

2. PERCEPTION

Do Africans and Europeans perceive the external world differently?   A precise answer to such an unprecise question must be: *yes*, a number of them do, but only in certain respects.   Some Africans, it appears, are less susceptible to various visual illusions than are Europeans or, from another standpoint, these Africans make more accurate judgments concerning the stimulus figures.   The quite varied evidence can be quickly summarised by indicating for each study the Africans who served as subjects and the type of stimulus to which they were exposed.   West African adolescents who were studying drawing [**] reacted to the shape or size of a geometric figure (Beveridge 1935).   African soldiers from the Soudan and Guinea [*] reacted to a set of standard illusions (Heuse 1957).   Rural Zulu reacted to an illusion involving the rotating of a trapezoidal window with attached objects, but they were less subject to this illusion only under 'suboptimal conditions' (Allport and Pettigrew 1957).   'Illiterate black mine labourers' in South Africa [*] and Bushmen reacted to the classical Müller-Lyer illusion in which two equal lines appear unequal when short, distracting lines at their ends face inwards and outwards; but non-susceptibility was less in the case of the Bushmen and, for both groups, less or not at all when similar and also dissimilar illusions were offered (Morgan 1958b).   The data from the last investigation are now being combined with those obtained under the same conditions from eleven other African societies (including both children and adults) and from Americans; similar results emerge (Segall and Campbell 1962).   Finally, the responses of large samples of Europeans, Bashi and Mbuti Pygmies to the Müller-Lyer illusion have been systematically tested.   With one technique, not feasible among the Pygmies and only slightly different from that employed in the two studies just cited, the Bashi were less susceptible than the Europeans; with another, both African groups were no different from the Europeans (Bonte 1959).

Since only tendencies to be less susceptible to some but not to all illusions are reported for some but not for all Africans, and since urban Zulu were more susceptible than rural Zulu to the trapezoidal illusion, some complicated cultural factors rather than genetic ones must be offered as the explanation.   The effect of the trapezoidal illusion depends in part upon how the shape of the rotated 'window' is perceived; hence the investigators point to the relative absence of square or rectangular forms in traditional Zulu society as a possible determinant, and they also establish a statistical connection between susceptibility to the illusion and an expressed preference for circular form.   In the comprehensive study of Europeans and samples from thirteen African societies a similar view is offered 'In the carpentered Western world such a great proportion of artifacts are rectangular that the habit of interpreting obtuse and acute angles as rectangular surfaces extended in space is a very useful one.'   This type of cultural explanation,

however, faces a number of difficulties.   Although the results which indicate that
Africans in the thirteen societies are less susceptible to two of the illusions are
certainly in line with the hypothesis, the negative results on the test of an illusion
involving perspective may not be.   Since few Europeans and few Africans in any
society perceived this illusion, however, its physical construction may have
prevented cultural factors from exerting an influence.   In addition, the differences
between the African samples, a few of which reach the required level of statistical
significance, must be accounted for; and so an index of the 'degree of carpentered-
ness' of the societies is being sought on the basis of ethnographic materials from
those societies.   The susceptibility of the Bashi to the Müller-Lyer illusion when
measured with one but not with another method may be very difficult to relate to
cultural background.

Finally, it is necessary to ask how cultural factors in fact operate to affect
perception.   They may determine the frequency with which certain perceptions
are made or certain stimulus-attributes are noted.   If so, on an *a priori* basis it is
strange to note that, except for Bushmen, South African miners were less susceptible
to the Müller-Lyer illusion than any of the other African societies and that they were
least susceptible of all to a similar illusion called the Sander Parallelogram (the
Bushman sample was not tested).   If the milieu of mines and mine 'reservations' in
South Africa provides a frequent opportunity to perceive the Western carpentered
world and its rectangular forms, could it be that the cultural factors which most
influence perception operate during childhood and that the adult experiences of
these men, therefore, are less important?   It may be, too, that cultural factors
affect the manner of perceiving at a given moment.   The responses of the African
miners and the Bushmen (Morgan 1958b), for example, were reported to be
'quicker and more spontaneous' than those of Europeans.   Although it is not at all
clear why deliberation increases and spontaneity decreases susceptibility to the
illusion, such a way of perceiving may well be related to the modal behaviour in a
society.

The validity of such speculation is exposed when the behaviour of subjects in
the Congo study is noted.   For among the typical Bashi, 'en général, on observe
une très grande simplicité, son attention est généralement soutenue', and 'tous
étaient intéressés à l'épreuve et un grand nombre, particulièrement désireux de
la subir'.   In contrast, 'chez les Européens, l'attitude était sensiblement différente.
Un grand nombre de filles presentait une certaine excitation, une agitation motrice
considérable, et une logorrhée accentuée. . .   Chez les garçons au contraire,
l'attitude était en général calme, réfléchie, et l'attention très soutenue'(Bonte
1959: 89–90).   It would appear that groups can behave differently and yet be either
equally susceptible to the illusion (European boys and European girls — the author
reports no sex differences) or not susceptible to it (Bashi *versus* South African
miners and Bushmen).

After this unsuccessful encounter with a cultural explanation, the discussion
moves on to another area.   Africans sometimes have difficulty perceiving visual
figures, but that difficulty tends to disappear with increasing opportunity to perceive
Western stimuli.   A fairly consistent relation has been shown to exist between the
degree of presumed acculturation among Africans in southern Africa [**] and the
ability to report the third dimension in a specially prepared series of drawings and
photographs.   The acculturating experience, however, must be 'ongoing' or
reinforced, for both European and African adults who were out of school for some

time reported the third dimension less frequently than did school children of their own ethnic group.   This ability to note distance in depth on a flat surface, moreover, is attributed to intelligence-as-measured-by-a-test and to experience with similar materials in printed media (Hudson 1960).   In line with an explanation which stresses differential experience is the finding that the ability to recognise representational silhouettes increased with age among South African children [*]. But then why did their projective ability to find 'objects' in non-representational silhouettes show a reverse tendency and decrease with age (Hector et al. 1961)? The experience hypothesis would hold that the latter ability ought also to improve with age: as people mature, there are more opportunities to perceive representations of objects, etc.   The findings may possibly suggest that the reactions to external stimuli become fixed with repetition, and hence the older children were less imaginative.

Once again it seems necessary to try to indicate the precise effect of past experience upon perception in the present.   Here two broad possibilities exist. First, the stimuli may in fact be perceived differently.   One investigator, for example, found that a small group of illiterate Chewa from Nyasaland, in reproducing a series of drawings, rotated them to a significantly greater degree than educated Africans and various English groups (including normal, brain-damaged, and imbecilic adults).   He believes the Chewa had failed to 'integrate' the drawing with their surroundings either through lack of attention or through previous experience (Shapiro 1961).   Second, it is possible that Africans perceive drawings and photographs no differently from anyone else, but that, from lack of experience or embarrassment in the interviewing situation, they are unable to express or report their percepts (Doob 1961: 198–200, 269–75).

Existing differences between Europeans and Africans with respect to perception may disappear with increasing education.   At this point in historical time, however, the differences are practically or sequentially significant when Africans fail to grasp the content of printed materials either correctly or readily.   It has been noted in this connection that 'posters relying on serial or cause-and-effect for their pictorial impact tend to be atomised perceptually' by Africans in South Africa [**], 'so that their coherence and message are lost' (Reader 1961).

Brief attention will now be paid to a special form of perceiving, viz., dreaming. It can be stated that Africans dream and that the ways in which they perceive and interpret their dreams are not unique.   Each society has culturally stereotyped interpretations that are attached to dreams (Chaplin 1958).   In West Africa, for example, 'the Ga connect dreams with their spiritual relatives, the sky-family from which a man comes at birth and to which he returns at death'; etc. (Parrinder 1951: 185–97).

Such variation suggests that there is no characteristically African way of interpreting dreams.   A cross-cultural survey of dreams in a world-wide sample of cultures, however, reveals a marked association between 'the use of dreams to seek and control supernatural powers' and the anxiety which people in a society may be expected to have concerning the possibility of being alone or being self-reliant — as measured by the distance of residence from parents' household after marriage and by the modal way of obtaining food (D'Andrade 1961: 321–7).   The fact that, of the fourteen not necessarily typical African societies included in the sample, nine are reported not to employ dreams for manipulating the supernatural, and the fact that most African societies are not dependent upon hunting and gathering or fishing (Murdock 1959: 18), may possibly indicate that by and large Africans do not consider dreams to be supernatural weapons.   It is not known whether all Africans are like the Akan peoples who think that dreams are 'highly important and when vivid or frightening give the dreamer great anxiety till a satisfying interpretation is found' (Field 1960: 131).

From the standpoint of research, the dreams of Africans may be used as bases for making deductions about the dreamer and his problems.   In this regard the psychiatrist just cited reports that 'most of the dreams' which neurotics among the Akan peoples ask to have interpreted at traditional shrines 'have a manifest content very little removed from the latent content'.   It would be splendid to know whether this finding is valid for other African peoples.   One intensive study among the Zulu indicates that dreams are symptomatic of the dreamer's unresolved problems as intuited by the investigator from his status or role in the society or as independently ascertained by a form of the TAT and by clinical interviews.   The dreams may contain culturally determined details, and their manifest content is interpreted by the dreamer and his contemporaries, often in terms resembling the orthodox Freudian.   One unique finding of this survey indicates that the content of women's dreams is 'derived almost exclusively from areas of social experience permitted by the culture *in the indigenous system of sanctions*, of some fifty to one hundred years ago' (Lee 1958: 270, italics his).   Here perhaps is a method for measuring the strength of the culture, inasmuch as the old strains must still be present, either at the moment or during the early socialisation of the new generation, in sufficient strength to have such a permanent effect upon dreams.

3. INTELLIGENCE AND APTITUDES

A return is now made to an intriguing, oft-repeated, and politically provoking query: are Africans basically less 'intelligent' than Europeans?   Without question, the mean intelligence of samples of Africans, as measured by a conventional European intelligence test, is always below that of the corresponding European norm: in IQ the difference is usually twenty or even thirty points (Biesheuvel 1943: 223) and in mental age from four to five years (Biesheuvel 1952a: 18).   The performance of Africans on tests measuring some capacity presumably related to intelligence, moreover, is more often than not inferior to that of Europeans.   A sample of African soldiers from the Soudan and Guinea [*], for example, was measured with respect to the following: memory for form, colour, rhythm, time and numbers; attention in a standard laboratory situation; the learning of mazes and other mechanical tasks; and the ability to carry out instructions on tasks requiring some kind of abstract thought.   In all instances, the mean performance was either poorer or slower than that obtained from normal and abnormal French adults and, in some instances, children (Heuse 1957).   Certain intelligence tests are too difficult to be used in African societies which, according to one investigator, have had little contact with 'la culture des blancs' (Ombredane 1957: 5).

There is no justification, however, for attributing obtained differences to 'un phénomène differentiel que a certainement un fondement génétique, anatomo-physiologique' (Heuse 1957: 58).   The differences must be ascribed to the tests themselves.   In their present stage of development, another analyst has observed, these tests 'do a useful job in revealing differences in those intellectual capacities which are valued by white middle-class culture' in Europe (Vernon 1959: 100).   Other classes in Europe and America and also non-literate societies are handicapped by emotional, perceptual, motivational, attitudinal, educational, nutritional and other experience-derived factors, and hence their performance is lower. The behaviour of African subjects on a test, when examined carefully, reveals how unfamiliar they are with the materials or the problem at hand. Katanga children [**] may serve as an illustration:

> . . . The old form-board of Séguin comprises a cross, a diamond, a circle, a star, a hexagon, a half-circle, a square and an oval, which they must replace as fast as possible in the corresponding openings. This very simple task presents considerable difficulties to the people of the bush. For example, they do not differentiate clearly between the star with five points and the cross, and they repeatedly attempt to place one in the space intended for the other. In the case of failure, they do not see their error immediately, but they persevere for several seconds with the obviously wrong response. Generally, they have to engage in much trial and error activity to find the openings that correspond to the given forms. This indicates that these simple forms are entirely strange to them. . . (Verhaegen and Laroche 1958: 255).

The conclusion coming closest to the facts, it is felt, has been expressed by an investigator in the Congo who believes that 'il n'existe aucune différence qualitative entre l'intelligence des Noirs et celle des Blancs'. He has shown that 'si la fréquence des fautes commises par les Blancs et les Noirs n'est pas la même, la *nature* des erreurs est cependant *rigoureusement identique*'. 'Le primitiv' may commit the same type of error as 'le malade' by giving concrete rather than abstract responses but, unlike the ill individual, the African changes his mode of responding with an improvement in educational status (Maistriaux 1955: 445; 1956: 134, 135; italics his).

To make a fair comparison between Europeans and Africans, representative samples of each group must either be carefully equated with respect to previous, relevant experience or be given a culture-free test. The equating of experience so far has been impossible; in Africa, for example, the quality of schooling varies enormously and the 'educational standards claimed by Africans are often unreliable' (Reader 1961). Some adults, moreover, are not certain of their chronological age.

Attention has consequently turned to the development of culture-free tests. Most recently a group of investigators has seized upon the fact that people everywhere, regardless of culture, experience symmetry as a result of the construction of their bodies and of many natural phenomena. It should be easy, therefore, to suggest to anyone that he should compose or construct a symmetrical pattern. This Pattern Completion (PATCO) test, as it is called, uses a simple pantomime or a film to instruct the subject to complete in various symmetrical ways sixty incomplete patterns formed by simple oblong figures. The test has been administered successfully to Europeans, to illiterate 'black miners' and 'black labourers' [**], and to Kalahari Bushmen. In each instance the correlations between these results and those from other tests presumably related to intelligence were relatively high (Fridjhon 1961). Thus far, however, no claim has been made that this test, straightforward though it is, really does present the same challenge or difficulty to people from different societies. In fact the existence of a positive correlation between performance on the PATCO by Europeans and their artistic achievement as measured by art grades in school arouses the suspicion that the differences between groups reflect aesthetic rather than institutional factors.

It might similarly be thought that Africans who know how to use a pencil ought to fare as well as Europeans when intelligence is measured by the 'Draw-a-Man Test'. Nevertheless, even when the drawings are scored so that the Africans [**] are not penalised (according to the European scoring method) for failing to draw enough clothes, the Africans' mental age is four years below that of a group of Europeans (Haward and Roland 1945: 87). These investigators note that the 'lack of synthetic ability shown in the drawings [of the Africans] is typical of the general inability to synthesise which forms a marked feature of African education', a tendency which, if substantiated, undoubtedly could be traced to the culture. Other work has shown that the size and kind of human figure drawn under these conditions is related to the educational status of the informants (Ainsworth and Ainsworth 1962: 395–6).

Although obtained differences in intelligence or aptitude apparently have no theoretical implications, they are of real practical significance. Especially in South Africa and, to a lesser degree, in West Africa, standardised tests are being employed to measure 'the occupational suitability of Africans as they are here and now' (Biesheuvel 1952b: 3, italics his). The procedure is sequentially quite straight-forward: tests are either devised or borrowed with modification from Western precedents; they are administered to applicants seeking employment or admission to an institution; the results thus obtained are subsequently correlated with actual performance on the job or in the institution; if the correlation is high, the test may be used for assessing the ability of other applicants in the future. The National Institute for Personnel Research in South Africa has repeatedly demonstrated the reliability, the utility, and — even on a mass basis — the practicality of this procedure for industry and government. Mime and films enable the examiners to circumvent the barrier resulting from the presence of many different languages in South Africa. Then refined research of a limited, technical kind seeks to improve testing details; it has been shown, for example, that the addition of colour to a demonstration film does not affect the performance of a task involving the discrimination of colours (Hudson 1958). In the gold mines outside Johannesburg, a 'practical intelligence test' is administered to a candidate by placing before him a stile without steps and giving him the following instructions in Fanakalo, the lingua franca of the mines: 'Take the bucket of water across. Climb across here. Do not spill the water. Do not walk here. Do not climb here. Devise a plan. Use the material lying here. Work fast.' (National Institute for Personnel Research 1950: 68.) For use in mining and other industries, the Institute has designed what it calls a General Adaptability Battery which consists of eight performance tests, such as sorting screws, washers and nails in accordance with directions (Lake and Böhr 1960: 3). A simplified form is now being sought, because the test itself 'takes about $2\frac{1}{2}$ hours to administer and requires expensive equipment and a specially designed locale' (Reader 1961).

What do these tests reveal about African abilities? Since testing procedures have proven successful, at least in those areas of Africa which can afford them, the abilities of Africans, even of those arriving at a Western-type institution for the first time, are shown to be measurable. Applicants comprehend and execute instructions and, in doing so, reveal that they too possess some central trait which can be sampled by means of the tests. Occasionally, of course, difficulties arise; thus experience in South Africa suggests that 'the "face-value" of a test for African mine-workers, i.e., its similarity to the actual work required, was far more important than for white workers' (Reader 1961). Even when Africans such as the Bushmen (Reuning 1959) appear to be living in a uniform environment, the tests indicate that they possess varying degrees of ability: a fact which demonstrates that a single statistical figure for mean performance can be as unrevealing in Africa as anywhere else.

Another conclusion supported by these results is that cultural elements figure prominently in the abilities being tested. This view is implicitly stressed whenever statements like the following are made: with reference to secondary schools in Ghana and Nigeria, but with probable applicability throughout Africa, it has been judged that 'tests devised outside the local milieu are likely to be of less value than ones developed in West Africa' (Taylor 1962: 171). At the same time, not every cultural difference appears to require a separate test, for the same test has been successfully administered to groups of Africans from varied societies. Such a procedure is, however, purely pragmatic: the men most suited for the job are sought, and the tests serve a useful function if they screen out those who have culturally imposed handicaps. Obtained differences between societies, moreover, may be due to sampling or motivational factors. Both factors, for example, are thought to account for the fact that unskilled labourers from the Cape Province of South Africa and the Sotho persistently receive lower scores on a battery of tests than do Africans from East Africa. As a result of greater competition from other occupations in South Africa, only inferior workers are attracted to the mines; and South African workers in general have 'an adverse attitude towards the tests' (Biesheuvel 1952b).

The cultural factors in the intelligence and aptitude tests undoubtedly explain the fact that the performance of Africans under varying conditions can be appreciably, often dramatically, improved. Past practice and momentary incentive rather than such general factors as 'tribal origin' and 'previous mining experience' affected the learning of three motor-co-ordination tasks by mineworkers in southern Africa (Reader 1961). This result may suggest the very specific nature of some aptitudes, especially those required by Western industry. Improvement on general intelligence tests, furthermore, has been shown to be a function of schooling, age, time allowed to complete the test, and practice. Each of these sub-factors operates somewhat differently and uniquely. For a large sample of Asalampasu, for example, it has been shown that scores on the Raven Colour-Matrix Test did not significantly rise with increased schooling in the younger age ranges, but did increase in the case of adolescents and young adults; for the same group repetition of the test increased the scores only among the older subjects who had had some schooling (Ombredane 1956: 26, 36–7). Among a large sample of Luba, scores on a similar but more difficult test were markedly raised as time for completing the tasks was systematically increased (Ombredane 1957: 16). Such findings are perplexing. Possibly a selective factor is operating whereby the more capable persons receive more education and are thus able to respond to the problems posed by the tests. Since the 'highly significant practice effect' noted in other studies (Jahoda 1956), as well as those just cited, is somewhat at variance with results usually obtained in the West, it may be that the abilities of Africans, previously cultivated in quite different milieux, suddenly can spurt forward after they have been provided with the opportunity to absorb the techniques of Western culture.

The actual performance of the African labour force in Western industries is so diverse that no easy, valid summary is feasible. A careful study of eighteen different South African companies and of data from a sample of 1,200 'black male' Africans [**] suggests that absence and turnover rates did not differ 'very strikingly' from those found in Australia, the United Kingdom or the United States and that turnover — but not absence — rates were clearly related to the degree of urbanisation (Glass 1960). When African [**] and European workers were compared, by some not necessarily unbiased European observers in Nigeria, the Africans were said to be more effective with respect to absorption, less effective with respect to understanding, and about equal in skill (Hudson 1955). Among competent Europeans and Africans there seems to be universal agreement on only one very important point: as a result of deficiencies in the milieu from which they come and the consequent lack of experience, 'Africans should be thoroughly trained for the jobs they are required to carry out' (Northcott 1949: 120). Even this generalisation must be interpreted carefully, for in one study it has been shown that 'effective capacity', as determined by performance in two tasks before training, 'is more important than systematic training in the determination of final output levels' (Hudson, Mokoatle and Mbau 1958: 93). A not unexpected generalisation is that Africans sometimes misunderstood aspects of the industrial system such as fringe benefits, group bonus plans and other incentives. At the same time 'studies in South Africa have shown that the more fully Africans are drawn into an industrial economy, the more their attitudes resemble those of workers anywhere; and this applies at industrial, clerical and professional levels alike' (Reader 1961).

Differences between Africans and Europeans with respect to the specific abilities included in a test of general intelligence are difficult to establish and, when established, about as difficult to explain. Africans are often superior on tests of audition (Biesheuvel 1943: 56), but, although the mean 'mental age' of small samples of Ndau and Karanga was higher when rote memory was tested by auditory rather than by visual means, the reverse result was obtained from a Thonga sample (Porteus 1937: 302–3). Many African people indeed demonstrate 'outstanding musical ability' (Biesheuvel 1952c: 108), yet when compared with Americans of equivalent education on a set of standardised tests ('Seashore Measures of Musical Talent'), a group of East African schoolboys, mostly Kikuyu, was found to be definitely superior with respect to sense of rhythm, time and intensity, and inferior with respect to sense of pitch and of consonance and with respect to memory for tones (Oliver 1932).

A common-sense explanation of an obtained difference in terms of culture may seem reasonable enough on the surface but must be considered unproven or even unprovable. African miners in Kasai [**], for example, drew certain specified patterns more slowly than children in Belgium, regardless of whether the task was relatively easy or difficult. The investigators begin the report of their study with the observation that 'in the Belgian Congo, the slowness of the Bantu population is mentioned by the majority of casual observers'. Later they explain their results by a reference to 'a general lack of interest in speed performance', and yet they do not think that 'a slower operation of mental functions' is involved (Ombredane, Bertelson and Beniest-Noirot 1958). Although the explanation appears reasonable, no actual evidence for the low motivation of the Africans is offered. That cultural factors must play some sort of role is shown by a study in Angola: the speed with which Africans reacted to a series of tests was related to their tribal origins (Athayde 1953).

In other instances, the cultural explanation of differences, though the best available, may be a trifle too facile.   A comparison of scores obtained by very large samples of Europeans and Zulu on the same intelligence test reveals a 'sharp' increase in the size of the differences with increasing education, but within each school grade the differences decrease with increasing age (Dent 1949: 43).   The investigator attributes the finding to 'the earlier maturity of Bantu children', but is it not possible that Africans are less affected by education than Europeans because they must attend inferior schools?   If the opposite result had been obtained, however, and it had been shown that the differences between Europeans and Zulus decrease with increasing education (which often turns out to be the case when Negroes or Indians are compared with other Americans), another cultural argument could have been invoked and made to sound equally plausible: education, even in the Bantu schools of South Africa, gives the children an opportunity to absorb more from the West and hence to perform better on the tests, and so on.   Or when a dozen performance tests were given to fifty Sussu children, the investigators concluded that the subjects did poorly on the items which demanded activities not prevalent in their society, such as those involving 'pictorially representative content', 'symbolic material', and 'the perception of part-whole relationships', whereas they did well on those involving 'imitative functions, immediate memory, perception and retention of visual-kinesthetic cues' (Nissen et al. 1935).   Before such an explanation can be accepted, a detailed analysis of the normal activities of that culture would have to be offered.

The solution to these problems must be an empirical one: after differences have been established, they must be explained through an investigation of some unknown factors in the society.   In a study of ability to engage in abstract thought conducted among Ga, Ewe and Akan male adolescents who had been to school for eight years or more, for example, it was found that performance on one task (Kohs' Blocks), was superior to that on another (Goldstein-Scheerer Cube Test).   Because both tests involve wooden blocks, the explanation must lie not in the materials but in the different manipulations that were required.   On the former test, moreover, the subjects had a tendency not to engage in 'block-by-block matching', which both the instructions and the layout permitted them to do, but instead to rely upon an 'infrequently renewed memory image that was often faulty' (Jahoda 1956: 239). Such an inefficient manner of approach to the problem was sometimes corrected by the subjects themselves as the task became more difficult, and the investigator was somewhat successful in inducing them to use the technique of block-by-block matching.   Still, the same question must be asked again: why did Africans from these societies come to the testing situation with a habit that prevented them from making an empirical check upon their mental image?   Such a 'habit', moreover, is not likely to be universally present in the society itself.   It has been shown, for example, that for a sample of the Asamlampasu the various abilities contributing to the scores obtained on a test of mechanical ability are quite unevenly distributed among very young children and that these abilities improve, though at different rates and in varying degrees, with increasing age (Ombredane 1958: 24–5).

It appears, in short, that, although culture provides an adequate framework for explaining obtained differences between Africans and Europeans or among Africans on intelligence tests, the precise manner in which culture functions has yet to be sequentially delineated.   Conceivably African climate may have both long- and short-term effects upon the performance of Africans and, perhaps even in a different way, upon Europeans.   On this last point, however, adequate studies do not exist.

4. TRADITIONAL PERSONALITY TRAITS

So far attention in this chapter has been directed to rather specific psychological processes, many of which can be measured under laboratory conditions. Now the situation changes radically as larger segments of behaviour are examined, for here measurement is usually even less precise and more unreliable. How can an instrument for measuring personality be devised which can be employed on sufficiently large samples in a large variety of African societies? Tests that ostensibly measure similar behaviour sometimes yield dissimilar results in general or in some societies (Doob 1957–58), so that data transcending both the instruments and the culture are not easy to come by. A penchant towards glib generalisations about Africans is likely to be inhibited by eavesdropping on a not unemotional controversy between two psychologists over the merits and demerits of their respective adaptations of the Thematic Apperception Test for use in the Congo (Leblanc 1958b), or by reading a detailed description of the problems that had to be faced and solved before the same technique could be used among the Swazi in southern Africa (E. T. Sherwood 1957).

Some studies have sought to identify personality traits in various African societies. Differences between very small matched samples of Yoruba and Nupe subjects were established by analysing their immediate reactions to and recollections of pictures and their memory of stories that had been related to them. The Yoruba 'stressed logical and rational elements', the Nupe 'situational facts and connexions of time and place' (Nadel 1937: 211). A comparison between Africans and Europeans or other groups usually appears in such research, because the measuring instruments are standardised upon Europeans. Soldiers from the Soudan and Guinea [*], for example, were found to be more suggestible on standard laboratory tests and to exhibit more extroversion on a paper-and-pencil test than Europeans or Americans (Heuse 1957). A sample of school children in Accra [**], when given direct and semi-projective tests employed in the West and among American Indians, displayed inclinations that seemed to indicate beliefs in animism and immanent justice, but the 'overall incidence' of the former was lower than among American Indians (Jahoda 1958b: 221). In autobiographical essays and on questionnaires, white university students in South Africa revealed an orientation towards private satisfactions, small samples of Africans [**] towards community goals (Danziger 1958a and b). On a projective questionnaire in the same country, white students aspired to improve themselves and their characters, whereas Africans [**] were more interested in changing their social status and in seeking political and social freedom (Bloom 1960).

At the very minimum, piecemeal results such as these prove the presence of individual differences among Africans in every society, in spite of strong tendencies towards conformity. The causes of the differences have not been discovered. Nor is it known whether the differences are associated with particular strata in each society or whether one group — for example, chiefs or shamans — possess traits different from other groups.

Substantively, available studies often seem only to be revealing African traits that could be otherwise observed; at least the reader is left with that impression. Little seems to have been gained, for example, by giving 2,000 Diula a paper-and-pencil task which could be solved only by cheating and to have discovered that '9.85%' of them succumbed to temptation, slightly more in the case of Moslems or heathens, males, and those under thirty years of age, slightly less in the case of

Christians, females, and those over thirty (Thomas 1958–59: 553–4). For the differences are small, and it is impossible to say whether 'la sincérité' so measured reflects some kind of generalised personality trait. A set of concrete data, however, can serve the theoretical objective of confirming or disproving a generalisation. The investigator who studied children in Accra not only ascertained their beliefs but also challenged one of Piaget's assumptions about non-literate peoples by producing data showing that the children's belief in immanent justice declined with increasing age (Jahoda 1958c).

The validity of each personality test must be carefully established. In a study conducted among predominantly Ganda students, the trait of 'rigidity' was less conspicuous in schools clearly oriented towards the West than it was in the more traditional schools; and the African boys as a whole were more 'rigid' than British university students (L. H. Ainsworth 1959). 'Rigidity', however, was measured by means of a single test: a person was classified as rigid if, in solving a simple problem, he continued to use a method which previously had brought him success, but which on the critical trials was either needlessly complicated or inapplicable (the so-called water-jar Einstellung test). That scores from this elementary situation were shown to fluctuate among African subjects under conditions of momentary stress and that in the West such scores are correlated with other measures of personality suggest that some kind of central trait was being tapped. The correlation between the scores and the basic personality trait among Africans, however, may be lower than it is in the West. Another investigator states, moreover, that a sample of Africans from Mozambique [*] was 'more labile and less rigid' than a sample of European pupil pilots in South Africa (Hector and Hudson 1959). This second finding is based upon the differing kinds of figures which the subjects constructed from seven squares and hence reflects another operational definition of rigidity. The relation of the behaviour thus measured to other behaviour in non-test situations is unknown, but presumably some relation exists, because the same test with a different scoring method also discriminated between African clerks and mineworkers [**] (Morgan 1959a). Now surely the reader can appreciate the problem of finding comparable, valid data on African personality traits!

After differences in personality traits between African societies or between an African society and Europeans are established, they must be accounted for. One investigator, who gave 245 Congolese children between the ages of six and thirteen [**] a test seeking to measure reactions to frustration, compared her quantitative results with American data:

> Des différences très significatives existent entre enfants américains et congolais. L'agressivité (E) de ces derniers est plus forte, tandis que l'intra-punivité, l'ego-défense et les catégories relevant du superego pattern sont basses; en contrepoids l'obstacle-dominance et la need-persistence accusent une supériorité. Ce que fait considérer ces sujets comme plus 'task-oriented' que portés aux relations inter-personnelles (Leblanc 1956: 108).

These differences would indeed be challenging and stimulating were it not for one fact: the investigator had to adapt the test to her African subjects. She did so by changing the comic strips in the American version to animal stories presented in the form of silhouettes and by providing situations suggesting different kinds of conflict. It is impossible to say, therefore, whether the differences between the

Congolese and the Americans reflect the alterations in the two forms of the test or are indeed 'real'.

When it is possible to avoid such a methodological difficulty, differences in measured personality traits are usually said to reflect the demands of institutions within the societies being compared. Such common-sense anthropologising, however, is hazardous unless a relation between the traits and the institutions is established by a cross-cultural comparison. Whenever a specific non-cultural factor is invoked as an explanation, other difficulties arise. Consider, for example, the re-lation between climate and the onset of puberty. Although a popular stereotype holds that puberty occurs earlier in the tropics than in the temperate zones, the menarche of adequately large samples of Nigerians girls, largely Yoruba and Ibo from 'a privileged section' of Lagos, was found in fact to occur about a half-year *later* than among British girls in England. An examination of a sample of boys from the same area revealed that pubescence for them began at about the same age as it does for British boys (Ellis 1950). Can the difference in the case of the girls be attributed to climate? The investigator himself indicates that the Nigerian and British girls could not be equated with respect to other environmental conditions, diet or inci-dence of disease. A similar study of girls in Ceylon, which also has a tropical climate, has shown that only the data from girls in rural areas resembled those from the Nigerian girls, whereas girls in urban areas matured earlier, even earlier than the British girls. 'It is evident', these investigators conclude quite correctly, 'that influences other than the climate must be at work' (Wilson and Sutherland 1950).

The next question to raise concerning the personality of Africans is perhaps the most exciting of all: do Africans have in common some central personality trait such as *négritude*? The quick answer must be: although in theory any abstract attribute is discoverable no matter how great the diversity in which it is embedded, characterisations of all sub-Saharan Africans have so far served only the ends of propaganda and are largely undocumented. Attempts to produce generalisations about 'the African' (Carothers 1953; Smartt 1956: 441–6) are vulnerable to anthropological attack (Herskovits 1954). ' "The African Personality" is about as useless a conception as "The African Tree" or "The African Butterfly" ' (Frantz 1960: 461). It may, nevertheless, be argued that successful analyses are not forever precluded, especially if an ascent is made on to a high level of abstraction (Doob 1958), and for this reason attempts to squeeze such general-isations out of existing data should be given a friendly, if sceptical, hearing. An extremely careful investigator has borrowed a concept from a best-seller in the West and intuits that Africans are 'tradition-directed', rather than 'inner-' or 'other-directed' (Biesheuvel 1959b: 30–31). The present writer has the tentative conviction, supported by some data, that traditional Africans tend to seek immedi-ate rather than future rewards to a greater degree than do acculturated Africans or Europeans (Doob 1960: 84–93). On the basis of years of experience in Africa and of the existing literature, another investigator has sought to establish an abstract trait which he thinks characterises the peoples of the Guinea coast and its hinterland:

> Living, then, in a world of forces, all of which may affect men, directly or indirectly, the laws of African tribes englobed not only purely human affairs, but included reference to the working forces which Europeans regard as beyond the control of their powers. Many tabus aimed at preventing the intervention of non-human forces in the life of the individual and of the whole

tribe. Many rites aimed at encouraging such intervention when it was for the good of all. Laws aimed at procuring fertile crops, or at least at preventing the interruption of the working of nature (Parrinder 1951: 15).

If the truth of the abstraction were established, then here would be valuable insight into West Africans: the notion of force is a compelling one in their lives and thus provides, in one kind of psychological terminology, secondary rewards. Although the caveat is less important than validating the generalisation, it is, alas, necessary to note that such a trait must also be embedded differently in each society and in each person.

The suspicion may be uttered that the task of establishing a modal personality for a particular society or for many or most African societies is likely to be facilitated by the development of improved methods for assessing personality. Does this mean simply that the popular projective methods must be perfected? Perhaps, but possibly quite new approaches are called for. Every society, for example, has myths, folklore and some kind of cosmology. Can inferences be made concerning the people who produce and then are affected by such non-material inventions? At the moment the possible validity of the technique has been demonstrated in a study based upon a sample of twelve folk tales that were selected from each of forty-six cultures throughout the world. Agreement between judges who analysed the contents of the tales was not particularly high, and the stories from each society developed different themes. Nevertheless, suggestive, if inconclusive, evidence is offered for possible relationships between the 'achievement themes' of the tales and 'the motives or the general preoccupations of a society' as measured by some of its socialisation practices (Child, Storm and Veroff 1958). An imposing number of unimposing high relations between measures of achievement motivation in folk tales, textbooks and literature, and measures of economic development in a wide variety of countries (almost always non-African) have been offered in a treatise proposing such an achievement-development drive as a theoretical panacea to most of the world's theoretical problems (McClelland 1961: 36–158). Competent studies in a particular society (e.g. Herskovits and Herskovits 1958), on the other hand, concentrate upon the collecting and reporting of the folk materials. Interpretation of these always tends to be artistically subjective, because it involves the methodologically uncharted areas of symbolism and the unconscious.

Other institutionalised aspects of a society may also serve as indices of the modal personalities that exist therein. It is tempting, for example, to use proverbs for this purpose, because they can be so easily collected and, on the surface, seem to suggest the internal rules of behaviour which people follow or try to follow. Unquestionably the structure of a language (e.g., the number of tenses that are distinguished) or its vocabulary (e.g., the areas in which concepts are especially numerous or scarce) must provide some kind of preliminary insight. Or, for that matter, people's own conceptions concerning themselves and their reasons for behaving as they do — the prevailing ethno-psychology — ought to reveal something about the kind of people they are (cf. Thomas 1958–59: 162–97). Leads like these are fascinating and tempting, but they have not yet produced systematic or conclusive knowledge of personality or behaviour.

An additional problem is the gap between well-established anthropological generalisations on the one hand and concrete personality data on the other. Whenever a descent is made from the abstract level of generalisation, the appalling fact of individual differences reappears.   The quotation on the left comes from an anthropologist, that on the right from a Hausa woman describing an incident in her life only slightly over a decade ago:

Polyandry is virtually non-existent in Africa, and monogamy, except for intrusive Europeans and missionized natives, is confined almost exclusively to the Berbers of North Africa, the Monophysitic Christians of Ethiopia, and the remnant hunting peoples. Polygyny preponderates to an over-whelming extent, prevailing in 88 per cent of a representative sample of 154 societies drawn from the continent at large.   Africans have discovered means of making the institution work to the satisfaction of both sexes.   No woman lacks a male provider.   No polygynous wife has trouble finding a helper or a baby sitter in time of need.   Since the first wife normally enjoys for her life-time a position of superior authority and prestige, every woman knows in advance of her marriage what her future status will be and has no fear of being superseded.   Since men almost universally establish each of their wives in a separate dwelling and endow them individually with land and livestock, sources of friction are reduced to a minimum.   Custom normally requires the husband to treat each wife with equal consideration, to eat and sleep with each in regular rotation, so that no married woman suffers public humiliation through any overt manifestations of favoritism.   In consequence of these cultural adjustments, missionaries seeking to institute monogamy in African societies frequently encounter their strongest opposition from the women.   (Murdock 1959: 25–6.)

My younger brother Kadiri had three wives when we came to New Giwa, Gwamma and two others. Gwamma was jealous of the other two and she went to a *malam* [the respected title of a Koranic scholar] at Tatare to get medicine and charms to get rid of them.   She put the medicine into Kadiri's food, but he knew nothing about it.   Within three months he hated her co-wives; one, also called Gwamma, left him, and he turned out the other.

Before this, he had said that he did not like the first Gwamma. Her one co-wife had two children by him, and the latest wife hadn't been there nine months when Gwamma got rid of her, yet earlier he had liked them both so much that he had begun to get tired of Gwamma.   But when she got the medicine and made him very delicious food with the medicine concealed in it, it was she whom he desired.   I used to hear him with each of them; when he went to the hut of one, I heard quarrelling; when he went to the hut of the other, I heard quarrelling; then he went to Gwamma's hut, and I heard laughter. He plagued them with grumbling until the second Gwamma went off to the judge and broke off the marriage. Then the wife with the children was left, she did not feel happy.   He quarrelled with her, then he sent for her mother and said she was to take her away.   He said he did not like her (Smith 1954: 237).

What is needed to study personality traits, one is tempted to say, is a series of detailed life histories.   The sentence sounds true enough as it rolls off a typewriter, but it becomes less convincing when actual documents are examined.   The life history of the Hausa woman just cited or the compelling account of the Manyikan medicine man who migrated to South Africa, who experienced many aspects of

Western culture there, and who eventually was psychoanalysed by a sympathetic, sensitive, melodramatic psychiatrist from the West (Sachs 1947), do indeed dynamically reveal the traits of a particular individual within the context of traditional and changing African society. The revelation, however, is unique, or certainly as unique as each person. Biographies like these may be read with keen interest, but at the end baffling questions must be raised about the typicality of the people and indeed of their societies. Clearly this is not a problem peculiar to African studies, for it arises whenever an attempt is made to evaluate the study of individual people in a broader context. In Africa, though, the query seems particularly poignant because so few life histories are available for systematic study, and hence so little is known intimately or, at any rate, has been communicated concerning the deeper feelings and the personalities of Africans.

5. ABNORMALITY

To date the study of mental abnormality in Africa has produced provocative but inadequately documented hypotheses. Psychiatry in the West, it must be remembered, is a relatively new discipline which has not yet standardised its concepts, theories and procedures. Figures on the incidence of mental illness anywhere in the world are seldom valid or reliable, since they must be gathered from areas where hospitalisation practices vary and from psychiatrists who employ differing modes of diagnosis. These conditions are aggravated in Africa. The low priority accorded psychiatry in the crowded hospitals of Africa has been mentioned in the introductory paragraph to this chapter. Psychiatrists in Africa can rarely afford the luxury of treating a psychoneurotic; instead, rather limited resources must be concentrated upon the severe psychotics who become social nuisances. Linguistic subtleties are especially important in gathering psychiatric data, and in Africa there is usually a language barrier between the patient and the psychiatrist who, until recently, has been a European or who even now is likely to be an African from some other society. Then the psychiatric literature contains assertions that are careless or at least undocumented. One European psychiatrist, for example, after touring mental institutions in the Congo and Ruanda-Urundi for three months, asserts baldly that 'la paranoïa se présente plus particulièrement chez les noirs sous les formes mystiques et mégalomaniaques' (Baudoux 1952: 16). As was observed two decades ago: 'a survey of the literature reveals that the present knowledge of the schizophrenic reaction in non-literate societies is as inadequate as our knowledge of comparative psychopathology in general' (Demerath 1942: 706). Unfortunately the situation remains neither 'claire' nor 'encourageante' (Richelle 1961: 99).

The fact that psychiatrists in Africa all employ the concepts of European psychiatry and European practices in dealing with patients might be interpreted to mean that Africans by and large exhibit the same types of mental abnormality as Europeans. In the psychiatric literature there are indeed flat statements exactly to that effect: 'all varieties of schizophrenia commonly described in Europeans may also be seen in Africans', it has been reported from the Gold Coast (Tooth 1950: 48); and a Canadian psychiatrist after five years of experience in Kenya was convinced that 'by and large the same illnesses are seen throughout the world in all races' (Margetts 1958). Such general conclusions, nevertheless, can be only tentatively accepted and then with reservations. Psychiatrists virtually without exception have been trained in the European psychiatric tradition, and inevitably they must employ the medical paraphernalia they have thus acquired. Published accounts are compelled to quote patients only in translation and to describe their behaviour in Western categories of thought and psychiatry.

Difficulties, moreover, do in fact arise in connection with diagnostic categories from the West. One of the psychiatrists just cited states that 'broadly speaking, it is relatively easy to recognise the standard psychoses when they occur in Africans who have been in contact with Western civilisation, but among the ''bush'' peoples, with few exceptions, diagnosis is less certain' (Tooth 1950: 41). An African psychiatrist feels that he can employ European criteria for diagnosing psychoses among literate but not among non-literate Yoruba, even though some psychotic symptoms are 'common' to both groups in that society (Lambo 1955: 253, 260). Another psychiatrist with experience in East Africa asserts that 'all records of psychiatric material in Africa contain many cases that are not classifiable in standard European categories'; he also believes that 'the lack of integrative elements seen in rural African schizophrenia' may have some kind of cultural explanation (Carothers 1953: 142, 153). And a really sweeping statement once emerged from a psychiatrist in Tanganyika: 'Most writers agree that it is rare to find any great degree of similarity between the various types of mental disorder in Africa and those found in the higher developed Western countries.' In his own work, this man came upon 'no cases, even among literate Africans, that bore any close resemblance to the paranoid form of schizophrenia as it occurs in Europe'. At the same time he noted that cultural differences perhaps account for his own observations: 'The Africans' personality may appear psychopathic through European eyes, but there is no reason to suppose that the European does not appear equally psychopathic through the eyes of a rural African in the bush' (Smartt 1956: 441, 450, 465). Diagnostic difficulties, therefore, may reflect deficiencies in psychiatric techniques or differences in abnormality among Africans; for the moment it is impossible either to accept or reject one of the alternatives.

As anthropologists have been suggesting for decades, it can be extremely hazardous to use a psychiatric category from the West in a non-Western society. A diagnosis like paranoia surely must be made very cautiously in those African societies whose animistic beliefs incline a person anxiously to anticipate an attack by outside forces which he is powerless to resist unless he takes certain institutionalised prophylactic or precautionary measures. Or, from another standpoint, it does not seem fruitful to postulate a modal trait within a society, then to assume a connection between that trait and one with pathological implications in Western society, and finally to draw the conclusion that people in the society that possesses the trait must be pathological *in their context*. Such methodological recklessness can usually be found only in the older literature. A European medical officer, for example, first stated that the Bemba are concerned with witchcraft from 'birth to death' and then concluded that 'the whole of this African tribe is suffering from obsessional neurosis' (Davidson 1949: 76). After studying the Tembu by means of fieldwork, observation in mental hospitals, and reports from officials and the relatives of patients, an investigator suggested, without offering concrete evidence on the particular point, that 'although the scarcity of meat in the diet is no doubt conducive to stock theft, the native's general attitude towards food and his stomach is indicative of powerful oral needs, which reflect the infantile nature of his culture' (Laubscher 1937: 303). The difficulty that arises in transferring psychiatric concepts to another context is well summarised by the previously cited African psychiatrist, who states bluntly that in his work among the Yoruba 'it is not always possible to delineate confidently where normal primitive beliefs cease and paranoid psychosis begins' (Lambo 1955: 247). A prosaic problem complicating the task of diagnosis, finally, is that of the relation between the patient and the psychiatrist and especially the role which the former may believe he is expected to perform. 'Dans les descriptions qu'ils donnent des symptômes de leur maladie, les indigènes sont enclins à employer des termes exagérés, frappants', one psychiatrist has observed of his patients in Ruanda-Urundi (Vyncke 1957: 97). Such behaviour may have sociological rather than psychiatric significance.

'The cultural pattern to which the native belongs', a psychiatrist stated long ago, 'determines the nature of his mental content, but does not affect the particular form of mental disorder, namely its structure, to the extent of making it something different from that which occurs in European culture' (Laubscher 1937: xi). Is the statement true? On the one hand, it appears not the least bit surprising that witches play a prominent role in the delusional systems of patients from societies possessing strong beliefs in witchcraft (Davidson 1949). The general theory often expressed by psychiatrists that each person for largely constitutional reasons has a breaking point which is hastened, delayed, or never reached as a result of conditions in the milieu is in accord with such a view and with a general cultural hypothesis. On the other hand, it has been stated that 'the lack of integrative elements' among schizophrenic Africans from rural areas is 'something more than "content" and may well have connotations for prognosis' (Carothers, 1953: 142). Again evidence — clinical or otherwise — is needed. When cases are at hand, such as the 146 from Ghana that are competently summarised in a single volume (Field 1960: 147–464), the reader is left puzzled: the material is abstracted by means of European concepts, and hence the decision as to whether the raw psychiatric data fit the classical or textbook syndromes of the West cannot be made by anyone who has before him only the summaries and not the data.

Both because psychiatric facilities in Africa are inadequate, and especially because the very theoretical issues here being discussed have not been resolved, one African psychiatrist speaks up against using the common Western technique of hospitalising psychiatric patients. He thinks they should be treated in a clinic during the day but housed at night with their families, either in their own villages or, when this is not practical, in other African villages close to the hospital. 'Where family units are so close and interpersonal relations are so important', he states, 'experience has shown that patients should be treated in as natural an environment as possible'. He reports, without offering control data, that in his experience 'under conditions which we have not yet been able to define satisfactorily, the community group influences in the village are of great therapeutic value' (Lambo 1956: 1389, 1393).

Inconsistent statements appear in the literature which indicate differences in the incidence of certain mental diseases when comparisons are drawn between Europeans and Africans, between various African societies, or between the strata of Africans within a given society. Thus 'obsessive compulsive states' are said to occur rarely in rural Ghana (Field 1958: 1050). Anxiety neuroses are found to be uncommon in a small sample of Bemba (Davidson 1949), but are allegedly more frequent among the Yoruba in Nigeria (Lambo 1955). 'The hysterical reaction is the most common neurotic manifestation in Africa' (Smartt 1956: 547). A psychiatrist who worked for two years among the Zulu indicates that, among the 'Southern Bantu', suicide, depressive psychosis, paranoid schizophrenia, and certain psychosomatic conditions (duodenal ulcer, asthma, coronary thrombosis, hyper-thyroidism, migraine and psoriasis) are relatively rare, but homicides are relatively frequent (Loudon 1959: 364–5).   According to another source, depression is rare and mania frequent 'in the coloured race', at least below the age of forty (Lambo 1958: 141); 'anxiety state is by far the commonest psychological disorder in the primitive'; and involutional psychoses were not observed in Western Nigeria (Lambo 1956: 1391).   The literacy rate among schizophrenics of the Gold Coast was reported to have been four times greater than in the normal population of Africans (Field 1958: 1051).   In various areas of Africa, more males than females obtain psychiatric treatment through Western clinics (Smartt 1956: 448).

Unfortunately, the significance of such findings, even if validated, is not clear. The African psychiatrist so often cited in these pages speaks of 'a "racial" predilec-tion' towards some types of neurosis, but he places the critical words in quotations and clearly notes the importance of cultural factors in the genesis of mental disorders (Lambo 1956: 1393).   It must also be said once again that the psychiatric cate-gories are perhaps not being uniformly interpreted.   The number of cases in most of the studies is too small to command much statistical respect.   A conscien-tious comparison of psychiatric rates in Ruanda-Urundi and elsewhere in Africa (Vyncke 1957) probably reveals almost nothing about the incidence of disorders in these parts of Africa; what it does suggest are the similarities and differences in the patients admitted and committed to hospitals and mental institutions.   The figures themselves, therefore, are quite unimportant, since administrative standards are not uniform.   This approach, however, does make it possible to refute negative statements.   When the same psychiatrist notes, for example, that two British colleagues 'n'ont jamais constaté un cas de mongolisme chez le Noir' but that he himself has tracked down two cases (Ibid.: 89), he at least proves, to anyone interested in a category as broad as 'le Noir', that severe mental deficiency also exists in Africa.   Also of significance are not the precise statistics but the sizeable number of cases in his practice which he has labelled psychoneurotic; 'nos observa-tions permettent de détruire une légende, qui veut que les Noirs, surtout ceux de l'Afrique centrale, ne font pas de psychonévroses' (Ibid.: 91).

Validly and reliably established differences in disease incidence can be ambigu-ous indices of the causal sequences at work.   The higher literacy among schizo-phrenics of the Gold Coast reported above may have been a symptom of their greater acculturation.   But can one conclude that acculturation is accompanied by strains likely to induce the disease?   Or could it be that those Africans either with a proclivity towards schizophrenia or with some kind of predisposition associated with it are drawn to Western culture?   The latter possibility seems far-fetched, but it cannot be completely cast aside.   There is always the possibility, too, that some of the original observations may be faulty: justifiable scepticism, for example, has been expressed concerning instances in which death is said to have resulted as a direct consequence of suggestion, magic or sorcery (Barber 1961).

Occasionally the psychiatric literature contains tantalising surmises concerning the explanation for alleged differences between Africans and Europeans or among Africans.   'Over 95 per cent' of urbanised, hypersensitive Nigerians [**] realised that they were suffering from hypertension, were anxious concerning the possibility of a 'stroke' or other cardiac trouble, and consequently developed psychotic symptoms (Lambo 1958: 135).   Here indeed is an important psychosomatic hypothesis: self-consciousness and the increased knowledge accompanying acculturation may have far-reaching psychiatric consequences. Regretfully, however, no confidence can be placed in the data supporting the idea: only ten patients were involved; the actual numerical division into rural and urban groups is not supplied; in fact, the expression 'over 95 per cent' must be a figure of speech, since 95 per cent of any number below ten must realistically include everybody!

A psychiatric problem of great interest to social science is the complicated relation between abnormality and social institutions. One psychiatrist collected her patients from among people attracted to traditional shrines in Ghana; these shrines, she thinks, have been springing up to satisfy a sense of insecurity induced or accentuated by the growth of the cocoa industry. She believes, consequently, that 'an increase in neurosis, attributable to social and economic changes, has led to an increased preoccupation with witchcraft' and that, in contemporary Ghana and earlier in Britain, people have admitted to witchcraft in order to instigate their own punishment (Field 1955: 833). According to this view, the social institution of witchcraft is thus sustained because it satisfies the needs not of the general population but of a neurotic segment. It has been speculated, too, that the shamans among the Nyima are drawn from that segment and that they are assigned an acceptable role to play (Nadel 1946). The reverse sequence is also historically conceivable: 'many traditional magical procedures were . . . invented by schizophrenics of sufficiently normal aspect to make their statements acceptable to their fellow men' (Field 1960: 38, 317). Such an assumed relation between witchcraft and insecurity is supported by one anthropologist (Ward 1956) but minimised by another (Goody 1957). Unquestionably, therefore, the psychological function performed by institutions, whether to reduce anxiety or to release repressed aggression, is a theme that has been handled frequently but only impressionistically and, though of extreme importance, remains most fuzzy.

Although theoretical issues of this kind cannot exactly be settled, they can at least be more closely considered through empirical research. When it is noted, for example, that football teams among the Zulu in the city of Durban seek to win games by employing magic and sorcery patterned closely after traditional ceremonies (Scotch 1961), not too great an intellectual leap need be made to posit some psychological connection between those practices on the one hand and feelings of insecurity concerning the outcome of the contests on the other. Indeed, the fact that each team employs its own medicine man and that players freely admit that their rivals resort to magic constitutes additional evidence favouring the interpretation.

The needed empirical research must unearth patients or subjects not merely by entering hospitals but through epidemiological surveys of entire communities. In the study mentioned above, most of the seriously disturbed supplicants at the Ghanaian shrines never received formal psychiatric treatment. If more is to be accomplished than merely repeating the anthropological dictum that cultural elements appear in the content of a mental disorder (e.g., Harris 1957), and if generalisations that exceed the actual clinical experience of the psychiatrist (e.g., Carothers 1953) are to be avoided, investigations should be conducted simultaneously by both anthropologists and psychiatrists. These two requirements are admirably satisfied by the Cornell-Aro Mental Health Research Project in Western Nigeria, the data from which were being analysed at the time this chapter was written (Leighton 1960).

Both anthropologists and psychiatrists have noted that in Africa, as elsewhere in the world, people have traditional ways of explaining and of dealing with abnormality. The theories of the Kalabari closely parallel those of Freud with respect to unconscious processes (Horton 1961), and the Bemba have distinctive terms for certain psychiatric conditions which they explain in terms of heredity, congenital syphilis, excessive smoking of hemp, sunstroke, or the failure to keep specified taboos or to perform prescribed rituals, and which they seek to cure with medicines usually having a 'sudorific content' (Brelsford 1950). 'On the whole', one psychiatrist notes, 'Africans are shrewd at diagnosing madness and often know the main differential diagnoses — epilepsy, mental defect ("not clever"), trypanosomiasis, and "spirit-possession" ' (Field 1960: 315).

Traditional therapy, moreover, seems to be administered through heavily sanctioned social institutions. The hysteria which allegedly seizes a Sukuma woman as a medicine man drives away the malevolent spirits of her ancestors is said to have a 'cathartic effect' (Tanner 1955). The 'emotional orgy' following the death of a child or relative in some African societies 'may well protect the individual from the more dangerous effects of solitary grief' (Tooth 1950: 39). The 'Zar' cult in Ethiopia seems to provide a form of 'group therapy', since as an organisation it offers 'security and recognition' to the badly disturbed (Messing 1958: 1125). One psychiatrist, after surveying the problem of abnormality in the Gold Coast, emerges with an unprovable but stimulating conclusion which must be interpreted as either a compliment to African facilities or a rebuke to European psychiatry: 'Africans have evolved a system which cares for quite 80 per cent of their insane under conditions which compare favourably with those provided by the European Authorities, indeed with any that could be provided on purely European lines' (Tooth 1950: 65). An African psychiatrist reports from Western Nigeria [*] that 'in the sphere of psychoneurosis some illiterate patients who have failed to respond to our form of approach have recovered under the influence of "native psychotherapists" at the native treatment centre' (Lambo 1956: 1392). Lest this section end on a concordant note, yet another psychiatrist who has treated patients and conducted research in East Africa is cited: 'There is probably no more reason to fit traditional healing into a mental health programme in this day and age in Africa than in any other country in the world' (Margetts 1960). Notable accomplishments by psychiatry in Africa, it would seem, have yet to be made.

6. SOCIALISATION

Virtually every ethnographer during the last three decades or more has reported certain discrete facts related to socialisation practices in the society he has investigated: the nature of the extended family, the age at which weaning or circumcision modally occurs, the puberty rites through which children pass, and so on. These facts become psychologically relevant only when they are shown to affect the adult personalities that emerge or particular institutions of the society. First of all, however, they must be collected, and relatively few socialisation studies exist for Africa.

Anyone surveying child-rearing practices in Africa (e.g., LeVine 1961: 55–6) eventually asserts that no single generalisation with concrete content is applicable to all or to a majority of the numerous African societies. 'Children are much desired by Africans'; 'Whatever the mother's other duties, the infant, almost from the start, is carried on her back — often in contact with her body — and, at the least whimper, is put to the breast'; 'No attempt is made in early months to control excretory activities' (Carothers 1953: 42-3) — statements such as these that are applied to 'African culture', 'African parents', etc., without reservation, must be branded either premature or in error.   Close observation of the practices in a specific society usually discloses a set of facts that deflate still more one's confidence in the easy generalisation: variability from the norm postulated by tradition and observed by the anthropologist or some outsider is evident.   Among the Ganda, for example, the investigator previously cited who has carefully observed and measured the responses of children in a clinic, has somewhat carelessly described traditional child-rearing practices in that society; she refers to the favourable treatment received during the first year as representing almost a 'symbiose mère-enfant'; the child lives 'dans un monde de satisfaction, de plénitude' (Geber 1958a: 520). Conscientious and contemporaneous investigation of a small sample of Ganda households, however, revealed three different degrees of attachment between mother and child, although almost all the mothers behaved warmly and affectionately toward their children (M. S. Ainsworth 1961).   Western pediatrics has had its effect upon many Ganda women, and yet one must wonder whether the traditional practices were really ever very uniform.

How do socialisation practices in African societies compare with those existing in other societies?   A preliminary answer is provided by a survey of 110 societies which do not represent a cross-section of the world: they have been selected only because perchance sufficiently adequate material concerning their socialisation practices is available (Bacon, Barry and Child 1952).   The present writer has tabulated a small fraction of their data and offers a statistical summary in the Table on page 400.   Of their many categories for describing socialisation practices, he has selected the seven which seem either most critical or interesting; the headings for the rows of the Table had the following meanings:

> Overall infant indulgence: a composite rating based upon 'display of affection toward the infant', 'protection from environmental discomforts', the degree to which the infant's needs are satisfied, 'absence of pain inflicted by the nurturant agent', etc.
>
> Transition anxiety: 'anxiety about dependence developed during the transition period from infantile dependence to status of child'.
>
> Overall childhood indulgence: 'the treatment of the child during the age period following the transition period and prior to puberty'.
>
> Overall nurturance: the extent to which children are given sympathy and are helped in gratifying their needs.
>
> Learning responsibility behaviour: learning to perform 'tasks, duties, or routines which are demanded by the culture'.
>
> Learning of achievement: learning 'to accomplish something difficult', which often means 'to master, manipulate, or organise physical objects, human beings, or ideas'.
>
> Learning obedience: 'learning to do as he [the child] is told by his parents'.

Two judges independently rated the practices on a seven-point scale and assigned the rating of 1 when the practice or condition appeared very weak, 2 when it appeared slightly stronger, and so on to 7, when it appeared strongest of all. The numbers in the body of the Table below are means based upon the sum of these two ratings; thus the theoretical range is from 2 (when each judge rated the practice 1) to 14 (when each judge rated the practice 7).   The number of societies in each category varies, because sometimes adequate data for all of them were lacking. In the Table, the 110 societies have been allocated geographically to Africa, Oceania and North America; the total number from South America, Russia and Asia are so few that they have been combined into the meaningless category of 'remainder'. The twenty-eight societies in Africa are the following: Ashanti, Azande, Bena, Chaga, Chewa, Fon, Ganda, Kikuyu, Kongo, Lamba, Lovedu, Masai, Mbundu, Nuer, Nyakyusa, Pedi, Pondo, Sotho, Swazi, Tallensi, Tanala, Thonga, Tiv, Tswana, Turkana, Venda, Yoruba and Zulu.

MEAN RATINGS OF SOCIALISATION PRACTICES IN A WORLD SAMPLE

	Africa	Oceania	N. America	Remainder
	n = 15–28	n = 17–27	n = 24–30	n = 8–25
Overall infant indulgence	9·7	10·4	10·6	10·3
Transition anxiety	7·6	7·7	7·7	6·5
Overall childhood indulgence	8·0	9·2	8·9	9·7
Overall nurturance	8·8	8·0	8·9	9·1
Learning responsible behaviour	10·1	7·5*	8·3*	8·6
Learning of achievement	10·6	9·3	11·1	9·3
Learning obedience	11·7	9·6*	10·2*	9·7*

* Differs significantly from the mean for Africa, p = <·01, two-tailed test.

Inspection of the Table shows no significant differences between the African sample and the other samples with respect to indulgence during both infancy and childhood, anxiety evoked between infancy and childhood, nurturance, and the learning of achievement. Contrary to its reputation among certain scholars and investigators, *Africa* in the first row is rated not higher but lower in indulgence towards infants than are *Oceania* and *North America*, but the differences are not statistically significant and hence may be a function of sampling fluctuations. This mean of 9·7 for Africa, moreover, is derived from ratings which range from a low of 7 for five societies (Chaga, Fon, Swazi, Thonga and Zulu) to a high of 13 for two of them (Bena, Turkana). The African sample does in fact differ significantly from Oceania and North America only in connection with two practices; more stress is placed upon the learning of responsible behaviour and of obedience. Again the reader is reminded that these data come from not necessarily representative societies and are based upon ratings of not necessarily reliable observations; still, under the circumstances the tentative conclusion must be drawn that African socialisation practices vary considerably and on a world basis may not be particularly unique.

These and other ratings have been employed to determine relationships between socialisation practices on the one hand and personality traits or social institutions on the other hand. In two of the studies the distribution of the African societies that were part of the world sample can be briefly indicated. A positive association was found between the duration of an exclusive relation between mother and infant son and the severity of initiation rites: of the thirteen African societies, nine were classified as providing such exclusive arrangements for at least one year after childbirth; and six of them as having initiation rites at puberty (Whiting, Kluckhohn, and Anthony 1958). Likewise a positive association exists between accumulation as the main attribute of the subsistence economy and an emphasis upon compliance rather than assertion in socialisation: of the nineteen African societies in this survey, all but two tend to emphasise compliance, and all nineteen have an economy stressing animal husbandry or agriculture rather than hunting and fishing (Barry, Child and Bacon 1959). In yet another world survey (based upon from thirty-one to eighty-four societies), those located in Africa — as well as those in North America — tend to train the two sexes differently to a greater degree than those in Oceania (Barry, Bacon, and Child 1957). Although the samples are small, variability in African socialisation practices is evident. The relationships established between these practices and some other social feature, however, are far from clear in either the African or the world-wide samples, and factors other than socialisation are obviously affecting personality and culture.

Other more intensive, less extensive analysis of socialisation has produced sequential results which, though challenging, are of limited applicability and so far merely suggest that the present shape of the tree somehow or other reflects the treatment previously accorded the sapling. It has been pointed out that the Nuer and the Gusii can be considered traditionally stateless, have similar lineage structures, and have been under British administration, though for varying lengths of time. The Nuer seem relatively uninterested in authority, and blood feuds persist among them; in contrast, the Gusii are authoritarian and are attached not to feuds but to litigations in court. An investigator has noted differences in socialisation practices which correspond to the differences in political behaviour and values: the Nuer father tends to be warm and demonstrative, the Gusii remote and punitive; Nuer children are encouraged to settle their disputes by fighting, Gusii to report grievances to their parents (LeVine 1960a). On the basis of observation during a nine-month period, an observer reports that among the Kongo the values and goals to be achieved during socialisation and the techniques employed to achieve them differ markedly from those present in what he calls 'Western culture' (Knapen 1958). When he asserts that these Africans seek 'social values' and Westerners 'individual values' and that the former include as personality traits a 'preponderance of fear of others over sense of guilt' — in contrast to the latter who develop a 'sense of responsibility and regular occurrence of feelings of guilt' — he is speculating excitingly but, in the absence of data from either culture, quite wildly. In contrast, a study of abrupt weaning in a small sample of Zulu inspires confidence that the immediately ensuing pattern of consequences — temporary bewilderment and disturbances were quickly followed by the learning of more mature behaviour — had been established at least for this society, since comparable observations were made upon a control group weaned at an earlier age (Albino and Thompson 1956).

In order to avoid having this section end nowhere, reference can be made to a report which summarises the findings and intuitions of truly qualified experts on socialisation in Africa who agreed upon a set of generalisations at an international conference at Tananarive in 1959 (Biesheuvel 1959b: 8–18) According to them, all or most African societies possess the following traits: human fertility is considered so important that African mothers are happy and eager to be pregnant; during the first year or more or until weaning, African infants are offered 'complete security', and the attitude of African mothers towards their children is best described as loving or indulgent; with few exceptions, African mothers probably are tolerant and gentle with respect to toilet training; after weaning, other relatives in the extended family — especially older siblings — are likely to become important socialising agents; in training children, emphasis is placed upon 'compliance with tradition, backed up by the fear of ancestors or spirits or the fear of breaking taboos' rather than upon an 'internalised set of values represented by the conscience'; and it seems likely that the common factor in the 'ideal personality' sought in African society is 'respect for elders and ancestors, and for accepted forms of behaviour'. Obviously, as the Table in this chapter has suggested, there are exceptions to such generalisations. These experts themselves point out that weaning and puberty rites fluctuate markedly with respect to the age at which they occur and the techniques which are employed, and they also emphasise the great variations in the specific personality qualities encouraged in different African societies. The conferees admit ignorance about the effect of many socialisation practices upon later development and society; for them, too, the problem is vague but inviting. In the meantime, nevertheless, their views must be considered the most promising hypotheses that are available. Though we scowl, let us be grateful and push on.

7. ACCULTURATION

The study of the effects upon Africans of contacts with Europeans is so important that it falls within the province of all the social sciences. For this reason aspects of the problem are considered throughout this book. In the present section, attention is directed to the changes in personality traits, attitudes and behaviour which accompany what sociologists and anthropologists refer to as detribalisation, urbanisation or social change.

At least three critical problems must be faced and resolved before acculturation can be analysed psychologically. First, the people being studied within a society are separated into two or more groups on the basis of a criterion of acculturation which somehow must be justified. In one investigation using the criterion of residence, Congolese [**] in the city of Elisabethville and the smaller community of Kolwezi were given sentence-completion and TAT tests. On the first measure, those from the larger city tended to be somewhat less traditional in outlook, and on the TAT they were more 'productive' and 'optimistic' than those from the smaller town; adult men seemed more traditional than adult women (Leblanc 1958a). That the opportunities for contact with the West in Elisabethville were more numerous than those in Kolwezi is a reasonable but unproven assumption, and the obtained sex difference shows that factors other than residence were influential. In addition, residence as such offers no guarantee of acculturation. In South Africa, for example, miners whose occupation brings them in contact with Europeans and some Western institutions actually remain oriented towards their rural homes, to which they seek to return as regularly and frequently as possible (Reader 1961). Finally, people in a given urban community may respond quite differently to the appeals of the West. One group of Xhosa in East London remains oriented towards their traditional tribal area and another towards the new milieu (Mayer 1961); and among African students in Katanga [**] the reactions to some, though not all, items on two different types of questionnaires pertaining to African and European values significantly fluctuated with age, which in turn was related to amount of education (Richelle 1961: 155-6, 160-4). Since any criterion of acculturation, such as the amount of education at Western schools, presents problems similar to those associated with residence, the solution seems to be to use as criteria either the psychological attitude of the people themselves or various objective features in the same and in different societies. If reasonably consistent trends emerge with the latter approach, it would appear fairly certain that acculturation plays the role thus delineated.

In the second place, obtained differences between more and less acculturated people in a given society cannot immediately be attributed to acculturation, since they may reflect conditions that led originally to acculturation and thus are causes rather than consequences.　One study resolves the problem of alternate interpretations by comparing a rural and urban group of Arabs in Algeria with respect to attributes that both possessed *before* some of those in the rural oasis moved to the city.　Originally the groups differed significantly with respect to only two factors: length of Koranic schooling, and number with polygynous fathers.　Both factors reflected the economic status of the father, and indeed the sons of wealthier fathers had less reason to emigrate.　Neither factor, however, was appreciably related to the many cultural differences between the two groups uncovered during the study. It is reasonable to assume, therefore, that these and other differences between the two groups did not produce but resulted from acculturation (Miner and de Vos 1960: 70–4).　Regrettably, such a clean-cut methodological solution is seldom available; many urban Africans have been born in the cities where they now live, and pre-migration records are rarely obtainable.

The third problem is to select the kinds of behaviour to be measured, and in this respect sheer chaos exists in the literature at hand.　It is fashionable to use some kind of projective test, in large part because the data can thus be relatively effortlessly gathered, but here again scoring categories are not uniform.　And so it is difficult to squeeze generalisations out of the available research.

One generalisation may be regarded as foolproof: every study produces at least one minor surprise.　In the Algerian investigation just cited, for example, more of the urban sample conformed to the French pattern regarding the age at which girls should marry — whether the actual age at which they had married or their stated ideal was considered — but there was no significant difference between the two groups regarding the age at which they believed the seclusion of women should begin and end.　More urban men showed confidence in women and permitted them to have more freedom, but the percentage believing that adultery on the part of women should be punished by death remained approximately the same in both groups.　More of the urban men had learned French, but, by Western standards, they were not observed to be cleaner in physical appearance or to wear cleaner clothes (Miner and de Vos 1960: 66–92).　A comparison of the stories produced by urban and rural children in Ghana [**] substantiates the expectation that the latter were more tradition-minded than the former but also revealed, perhaps unexpectedly, that the changes in the new environment were experienced as not unpleasurable (Lystad 1960b).　In seeming contrast, information collected from a selective source — the letters addressed to an advice-giving columnist in a Ghanaian newspaper [**] — leads to the conclusion that 'the incidence of conflict and anxiety associated with social change is by no means negligible' (Jahoda 1959).

In view of the controversies waged in the West over the effects of modern civilisation upon mental health, it would indeed be sequentially and theoretically important to know what psychiatric changes occur as Africans become acculturated. Existing data, sadly, provide no definitive information.　An obtained difference between the relatively unacculturated and the acculturated may be a statistical artifact.　According to one psychiatrist, 'so long as an African remains at home he is very unlikely to be certified insane, but as soon as he leaves his home his chances of being so certified are much increased' (Carothers 1953: 131).　Psychiatrists working in Africa may hold the intuitively empirical but inadequately supported

opinion that Africans in urban areas undergo strains and tensions leading to maladjustment — one of them categorises the tensions under the headings of economic,
religious and sexual (Tooth 1950: 33–40) — but concrete data are not supplied.
A study of the TAT protocols obtained from 2,500 'urban Africans' [*], largely in
Johannesburg, indicates vividly the 'anxieties and insecurities' under which they
live (de Ridder 1961), but there is no way of knowing whether these psychological
states produce neurotic tendencies or whether they do or do not have analogues in
the traditional milieu from which the people or their ancestors came.   From
anthropological sources and from old informants, a psychiatrist advances the belief
that a Zulu ceremony, in which women abandoned their usual 'modest demeanour'
and temporarily played the roles of men, has virtually disappeared in recent years,
and that simultaneously a disturbance resembling conversion hysteria, often with
anxiety symptoms, has appeared in both sexes but especially among women.   He
then assumes a connection between the two facts and concludes that 'the tensions
created' in the life of Zulu women 'appear to find outlets elsewhere' (Loudon
1959: 366).   When differences in the delusional systems of ten rural and ten
Westernised paranoids among the Yoruba are pointed out — the former centred
on the supernatural and on ancestor cults, the latter on hypochondriacal anxiety
(Lambo 1955) — it is clear that the numbers in each group are far too small to
permit any kind of generalisation.   There seems to be agreement among observers
on only one point (e.g., Biesheuvel 1959b: 27): beliefs in witchcraft, sorcery and
magic survive even among highly acculturated Africans, not only because they
continue to serve important psychological functions, but also because they operate
in areas of human affairs where science is far from being omniscient.   Most diseases
have a scientific explanation, but it is not always possible to isolate the factors that
cause one person and not another to succumb; here sorcery can be a much more
intelligible theory than chance or a multivariable analysis.

'Suicide is rare in the primitive community', an African psychiatrist reported
from Western Nigeria, 'while it is not uncommon in Westernised Africans' (Lambo
1956: 1391); the only evidence supplied is a reference to 'a survey of nine villages'
which showed that the elders therein had never heard of a case of suicide [*].   A
really careful examination of existing court records revealed that suicide rates in
seven different African societies 'vary from moderate to low' (Bohannan 1960:
264).   In fact, a finding among the Soga is contrary to the hunch about Western
Nigeria: 'the breaking down of traditional institutions appears to reduce the frequency of homicide and suicide rather than to increase it' (Fallers and Fallers 1960:
84, italics theirs).   This last statement again highlights the fact that the changes
produced by acculturation must be viewed in the context of people in particular
societies.   Estimates of the percentages of homicides committed by people of
eighteen Uganda societies outside their home districts 'show that Western impact
situations may have a very different effect on the homicide rates and practices of
one tribe than on others' (Bohannan 1960: 265).

In the absence of a baseline provided by a knowledge of traditional personality
traits in African societies, it is impossible to chart the changes in personality that
may or may not occur with increased acculturation.   Many interesting sequential
questions remain unanswered: what kinds of changes are most and least likely to
take place? Is conformity greater or less as the society changes? Do new kinds
of personality traits or personalities begin to appear? Can it possibly be true, as
one writer has imaginatively speculated (Biesheuvel 1959a: 18–19), that Africans

are leaping directly from the so-called tradition-directed stage to the other-directed phase without going through a period of inner-directedness? Anyone who has touched ground in Africa, if only at an airport or two, has an opinion on these matters, but nobody so far has impressive evidence in support of that opinion.

Anthropological and sociological studies of acculturation are available, but they usually either ignore psychological changes or else assume that such changes automatically occur. A long, excellent account of the traditional and modern Fang and Kongo peoples is able to draw the conclusion that 'il est incontestable que ces deux sociétés n'ont pu réagir de même manière et avec la même intensité à la situation coloniale' (Balandier 1955: 487), without prcviding any specific references to the reactions of the people themselves, other than to imply that institutional shifts have altered them and that new religious cults of protest have appeared among the Fang. Sometimes an institution in the society is selected for analysis, and its traditional form is compared with the modified one observable in urban areas of Africa. In one instance an investigator has divided his discussion of preparation for marriage, married life and divorce among the Luba into sections bearing titles such as 'l'ancien temps' and 'les temps actuels'. Without doubt there have been changes in these practices, but the evidence on 'le conflit psychologique actuel', which is said to exist among members of the society in Elisabethville (Forthomme 1957: 43), is not documented. There is only the implication that conflict in customs inevitably gives rise to psychological conflict, and this may or may not be so.

For two unrelated reasons, an aspect of acculturation — the attitude of Africans towards Europeans — will now be considered in some detail. It may be assumed that Africans acquire more or less distinctive feelings towards the carriers of Western culture; and the study of attitudes falls squarely within the traditional jurisdiction of psychology. Systematic investigations, however, are few, undoubtedly because they are difficult to carry out. Non-literate Africans are unaccustomed to paper-and-pencil questionnaires and pollsters; they sometimes have subtler and less direct ways of providing information about themselves; and they may be frightened by European investigators or offer them polite rather than truthful replies in order to demonstrate hospitality or good will (Marwick 1956). Consequently, the validity of a survey among Africans must be questioned even more conscientiously than it should be in Western countries (Biesheuvel 1958: 170-1), and it is not always sensible to assume that an attitude scale is valid merely because African informants, particularly in colonial days, were willing or able to express hostility towards Europeans. As is true in any kind of attitude research, the type of question that is employed can have an effect upon the outcome. Thus slightly or markedly varying results were obtained in three African societies from a blunt question concerning Europeans, from a semi-projective one which enabled informants to choose whether they wished to express their sentiments, and from a projective TAT-type drawing in which they were asked to report the conversation between an African and a European (Doob 1960: 287).

Most of the published work on African attitudes towards Europeans comes from South Africa, perhaps because that country possesses both racial conflicts and psychologists competent to investigate them. Let a quick glance be cast at some of the studies conducted there. More than a decade ago, a sample of nineteen Africans [**] wrote life histories in which they were asked to emphasise the origin and development of their attitudes towards Europeans; they revealed deep antagonism towards Afrikaners but almost favourable attitudes towards English-speaking South Africans (McCrone 1947).   Later, in c. 1958, from 105 to 110 'African intellectuals' [**], who were given a social-distance questionnaire and later interviewed by African personnel, expressed hostility towards all Europeans in South Africa (Crijns 1959: 114–17).   In two recent surveys a clear-cut majority of mine workers [**] preferred African to European supervisors (Reader 1961).

The emphasis in other South African investigations has been on ascertaining, not the direction, but the content of the attitude or the reason for it.   About 1956, a group of seventeen African [**] and nineteen Indian university students, combined statistically to form a 'non-white group', explained differences between themselves and Europeans in terms of social conflict rather than of tradition or inferiority; European students reversed the priority given the explanations (Danziger 1958a).   About a year later a similar 'non-white' group of university students [**] reacted less favourably to the idea of 'white civilisation' than did European students (Danziger 1958b).   Autobiographies and questionnaires of fifty-one 'Bantu' university students [**] collected in 1950 showed the group to be 'pessimistic' about achieving racial equality (Gillespie and Allport 1955: 37).   A detailed study of close to 300 'Bantu' clerical and professional workers [**] in the middle 'fifties suggests that 'an important source of job dissatisfaction' for them was 'the discrimination on racial grounds to which they are subjected' (R. Sherwood 1959).   In essays on 'What I expect from an efficient Bantu clerical worker', 'Bantu' clerks themselves [**] in Johannesburg naturally had expectations different from those of white personnel (e.g., 31 per cent of the former, but 70 per cent of the latter, expected the clerks to be 'respectful, obedient to European authorities').   According to the overall analysis, although the Africans were aware that their behaviour was expected to conform both to African and European standards, they were more concerned with the reactions of their fellow Africans (R. Sherwood 1958).

Each of these studies may be interesting in its own right, but little more is obtained from the collection beyond the quantified impression that Africans are not particularly fond of Europeans or of some European values.   There is, furthermore, no continuity between them, so that even sequentially trends cannot be detected. Different investigators use different techniques on samples of Africans whose tribal origins are seldom specified and, when specified, are not related to the expressed attitude.   Differences between two sets of findings may reflect differences in techniques, in sampling, or in the attitudes themselves.   The statistical data, moreover, cannot be correlated with the personality traits of Africans, the nature of their society, or the type of contact they have had with Europeans, for the simple reason that such information is not provided.   On a more positive side, however, two not world-shaking conclusions can be squeezed out of the research.   First, African attitudes can be measured with the same techniques as those used in the West or anywhere else in the world.   Secondly, when the attitude data are scaled, modal tendencies emerge, but there are always deviations from the central tendency. The moral of this research is clear: continuous studies of African attitudes are desperately needed.

In the meantime some solace can be obtained from attitude studies which do attempt to be analytical.   In 1937 a group of 912 relatively well-educated Africans in South Africa [**], when asked to pass judgment on how and why Africans should behave in a series of situations, revealed their attitudes not only towards Europeans but also towards European moral and legal standards. In fact, their judgments tended to be based on ethico-legal and religious bases rather than on standards involving compliance or non-compliance with European practices and codes (Biesheuvel 1955). Workers in the South African mines at first prefer only members of their own society; then they generally grow to feel more tolerant towards Africans from other societies, but they are likely to remain unchanged in their hostility and suspicion towards Europeans and European supervisors (Reader 1961). The 'images of marriage partners' of young boys and adolescents and the 'self-image' of girls in Ghana [**] were ascertained on a projective test; one item determined that, with increasing age, drawings of women in African dress came to be preferred more/less. (The reader who believes that quantification demonstrates only the obvious is asked to complete the sentence by choosing between the adverbs 'more' and 'less'.) Preference for African dress in fact increased (Jahoda 1958a). The results of this sequential research have been presented in such a melodramatic manner in order to highlight again the fact that neither commonsense nor theory can inevitably predict the outcome — or that either can be used to rationalise whatever happens.

The ability of various ethnic groups to recognise the racial identity of briefly exposed stereoscopic photographs has been investigated in South Africa. The Zulu recognised photographs of Africans more accurately than they did those of Afrikaners, English, Coloureds or Indians, but their accuracy in judging Africans was less than that of the other groups. The Zulu and the Coloureds were also less accurate in judging the identity of the other races: a result attributed not to differences in formal education but to 'exceptionally restricted contact with other races' on the part of the Zulu and the Coloureds (Pettigrew, Allport, and Barnett 1958).

Attitude studies of Africans are in one respect no different from any other approach to specific people: an adequate interpretation usually demands a knowledge of the cultural norm. It is quite conceivable, for example, that a projective or non-projective study of the Ibo would reveal that they have a decided preference for paler colours, including the pigmentation of human skin. The conclusion might well be that European influence accounts for this; for centuries Europeans have enjoyed a superior status; perhaps lighter Ibo have been treated more graciously by colonial rulers, etc. Such a conclusion, however, is likely to be false, for there is clear-cut evidence indicating that 'the presence of Europeans has only accentuated an indigenous preference in which probably smoothness, gloss, and light reflecting colouring were criteria for beauty in any object, where other things are equal' (Ardener 1954: 73).

The best available study of African attitudes towards Europeans, in the opinion of the present writer, was conducted in Ghana just prior to independence in 1952-55 (Jahoda 1961). Three samples of boys [**] were interviewed and asked to write essays: 149 boys were in a primary school, 140 in a middle school, and 74 in a secondary school; 200 adults [**], whose 'tribal distribution . . . roughly corresponded with the general pattern in the country' except for the northern part, were also interviewed. Concerning the latter 'no significant tribal differences in responses' are reported to have been discovered (pp. 137–40). By means of such samples, it is possible to survey changes in stereotype and attitude with age and education. Among the boys, for example, as education increased, progressively fewer mentioned 'physical appearance' and progressively more 'customs' among the 'ways in which Africans and Europeans are different'. There was also an increase in the number referring to 'hospitality and community life' as attributes of African superiority, and to 'punctuality, thoroughness, and orderliness' as better European 'moral qualities' (pp. 137–8). More of the adults with some or considerable schooling than those who were illiterate considered 'education' a benefit brought to Africa by Europeans, but there was little difference in percentage between the best educated and the illiterate groups with respect to calling promiscuity and prostitution the greatest evils introduced by Europeans (pp. 51, 53). 'No less than four-fifths' of the adults 'thought that whites had a poor opinion of Africans'. The stereotypes concerning Africans that were attributed to Europeans by the Ghanaians can be grouped as follows: 'animals, not human'; 'inferior, to be looked down on, not respect'; 'low, stupid, backward'; 'slaves, here to serve them, to be kept down'; 'they dislike us, don't mean well, just pretend to be nice'; and 'they like us, respect us, wish us well, want to help us' (pp. 54–6). In a subjectively sensitive manner, the investigator also examined the reflection of African attitudes in speeches delivered in the legislative assembly and in industrial disputes; he recorded his own personal experiences as illustrative data; and he sought to relate his survey data to historical events and especially to the frequency and types of contacts between Africans and Europeans in the past and at the time of his study. Toward the end of his monograph he emerged with 'a tentative typology' through which with broad strokes he organised his carefully collected materials as well as his historical and sociological observations. Type I has a 'value-system' that is 'tribal', contains people with no 'formal education' whose 'orientation to whites' is thought on the whole to be 'dependent'. The values of Type II are 'divided', education is 'intermediate', and orientation to whites 'inferior'. Finally, Type III has 'integrated' values, 'high' education, and an 'autonomous' orientation (p. 108). The investigator obviously has displayed more intellectual audacity and originality than reliable information; his methodological presentation is spotty; but he has provided a most stimulating framework within which to formulate hypotheses concerning this aspect of acculturation in Africa.

The analysis of African attitudes towards Europeans might well be advanced by yet other approaches which so far have been only foreshadowed by projective techniques. It would be fruitful, for example, to examine the kind of literature being produced by educated Africans in order to catch the spirit of their feelings regarding Europeans and other problems in their lives. For the moment, however no systematic research of this kind seems to have been conducted, and existing anthologies (e.g., Hughes 1960; Rutherford 1960) emphasise, of course, literary merit rather than social-science relevance. African art exists in abundance, but there is no accepted or objective way to make deductions concerning the attitudes or other attributes of the creators or their audience from the products.

The present writer has made an overly ambitious effort to offer a set of twenty-seven hypotheses concerning acculturation which stem in part from his own studies of limited samples of Ganda, Luo and Zulu, as well as from an examination of existing literature on acculturation in various parts of the world (Doob 1960). Some of the hypotheses are considered causal when they indicate factors inducing people to become acculturated; others are called sequential when they suggest the consequences of acculturation; and a third group of hypotheses is thought to be interactional, since they relate to factors that simultaneously incite to and result from acculturation. In content they refer to the following processes or areas: motivation, including aggressiveness; attitudes towards people, particularly the family, traditional leaders and outsiders; beliefs and values; intelligence, aptitude and skill; and personality.   The first, the middle and the last hypotheses are cited as samples:

> In comparison with those who remain unchanged or who have changed, people changing from old to new ways are likely to be more discontented.
> In a society having outside contacts, beliefs and values are likely to change at similar rates unless old ones are particularly satisfying or unsatisfying, or unless new ones are particularly attractive or unattractive.
> Basic changes in personality are likely to occur as people become adequately civilised.

Such hypotheses are pitched at this high level of abstraction in order to include the details of each specific situation and then to transcend them.   Concrete knowledge concerning traditional and Western components in a particular society can be obtained only by consulting anthropological studies, such as the one devoted to the behaviour of African women in Johannesburg (Langmore 1959); but the broad outlines of any study ought to be anticipated from the hypotheses, provided, of course, they are really valid and not simply banal.

III PSYCHOLOGY AND THE SOCIAL SCIENCES

The substantive contributions which psychology and psychiatry have made to knowledge concerning Africans and hence to general social science have been out-lined in the previous sections of this chapter.   As research in Africa continues, what additional contributions can be anticipated?   In the first place, the concepts, the theories and the interests of psychologists can broaden the perspective of other social scientists by suggesting types of data which they might overlook or neglect. Anthropologists, for example, are alerted or made more sensitive to the problems of socialisation; sociologists to the dynamics of small groups and associations; political scientists to modes of communication; economists to the strength of certain habits reflected in consumer demand.

Psychology's second contribution is methodological.   Since they are often but not always self-conscious about their methods, other social scientists can be reminded of points they once acknowledged and now perhaps disregard.   Psychology becomes their gadfly.   Thus the need for a representative sample, when the generalisation pertains to a universe of informants, or for quantitative or qualitative evidence to support an assertion has only to be stated to receive assent.   'Looking back', a reputable anthropologist writes, 'the Zulu regard the first years of White rule as happy and have made this the traditional basis of a preference for English, as against Boer, rule' (Gluckman 1958: 43).   More than a quibble is involved when it is wondered just how many Zulu hold this view and whether the fact from the distant past actually plays the suggested role in the modern attitude. Undoubtedly this particular investigator has simply failed to communicate the adequate information in his possession, or he is convinced that it would be super-fluous or boring to do so.   Material of this sort can certainly be quantified and at the same time reveal meaningful details concerning the patterning of people's thoughts and feelings.   By statistically and sensitively analysing essays written by African children in Northern Rhodesia [**], one investigator has shown quantitatively and qualitatively how the 'self-image' of these Africans has been affected by European standards and how their 'image' of Europeans reflects the inter-relations between the two ethnic groups (Powdermaker 1956).

Techniques for investigating personality or personality traits — especially Rorschach plates and variations of the Thematic Apperception Test — have been borrowed from psychology and psychiatry for more than two decades. The projective methods have had the greatest appeal because they appear less culture-bound, at least with respect to their administration, and because investigators can learn them easily and use them to collect data relatively quickly. Detailed responses for a group of 162 Africans in what was then French West Africa [**] have been tabulated (Peiffer 1959). The TAT technique has been adapted to Africans; sets of drawings, with manuals for administration and scoring, have been devised for use in the Congo and South Africa (Lee 1953; Ombredane 1954; E. T. Sherwood 1957). In his manual, Lee suggests that the Test has proven profitable — in descending order of importance — in the following aspects: the determination of conscious and unconscious reaction-patterns, needs and attitudes; of creative imagination; of relative intelligence; and of general verbal ability. Ombredane has given impressionistic illustrations of how protocols from twelve subjects reveal sociological problems among the Suku and has asserted that the test also has been useful in assessing whether Africans have 'des qualités de caractère' for work in the mines. The validity of still another form of the TAT has been demonstrated in Johannesburg where a 'blind analysis' of the protocols significantly discriminated among 163 African bus drivers [*] with respect to their previously established accident and disciplinary records; and in an unspecified manner the protocols from 2,500 other males [*] provided generalisations about 'the urban African' (De Ridder 1960).

Among Rorschach and TAT devotees, the pragmatic view prevails that, in the absence of other guides, the shaky norms established for projective tests administered to people in the West are useful in Africa or in any non-Western society. These norms are the only criteria available. The blunt fact, however, seems to be that so far there is little justification for the assumption or the procedure, even when the interpretations are most cautious. The successful blind TAT analysis just mentioned must be put alongside an unsuccessful effort to match Rorschach protocols and cultural data from the samples of rural and urban Arabs in Algeria, although in the latter instance there was some significant agreement in matching personality traits independently ascertained by a Rorschach expert and an anthropologist who knew the men personally. The investigator concluded that 'factors external to the basic personality structure contribute so much to the determination of specific cultural forms that prediction of the latter becomes impossible on the basis of knowledge of general behavioral predispositions' (Miner and de Vos 1960: 180).

A standardised test yields at the very least objective and reliable scores which *then* may be interpreted either in accordance with Western experience or in the light of the conditions under which they have been obtained. There can be no doubt that the analyst must be thoroughly acquainted with the culture of a subject — particularly the 'usual pattern story', the 'stereotyped plot from literary tradition', the 'folk tales', and the 'stories taken direct from books or the cinema' (Lee 1953: 12–14) — before he can possibly decide whether he is confronted with a cultural or an idiosyncratic phenomenon in a particular protocol. Although in the Algerian study cited above cultural traits could not be predicted from Rorschach responses, the rural and urban samples did differ objectively with respect to the distribution of various Rorschach coding categories. The investigators then interpreted these differences by considering tentative American norms, the actual testing situation, and their own anthropological knowledge. They emerged with provocative if not rigorously derived insights, such as the following:

> In the oasis, where the social order is more stable and beliefs more firm, the Arabs develop a more secure, though highly restricted, personality. Those who move to the Casbah live in more stressful surroundings. Some Arabs internalize these stresses; others achieve a more adequate adaptation to their new, half-Western world; but the lack of development of more objective controls is still quite apparent (Miner and de Vos 1960: 189).

Projective instruments, moreover, may provide suggestions, however preliminary, concerning psychological procesess. A group of adolescent Ghanaian schoolboys, presumably Ashanti and living at the time in the city of Kumasi, were asked to 'paint pictures of whatever they wished'. These paintings were found to contain no city scenes and essentially no Western elements. Such an objective fact by itself proves nothing but, as the investigator suggests, it does 'raise problems for future research regarding the rate of social change in Ghana and also regarding the stability and satisfactions which still accrue from traditional patterns' (Lystad 1960a).

Projective instruments should be employed, therefore, only when they yield material not obtainable or not so easily obtainable in other ways. When it is stated that the maternal uncle was mentioned in five out of 120 protocols obtained from twelve Suku subjects in the Congo — each one reacted to ten plates, and for some strange and unrevealed reason all the data were combined — and that in those protocols the uncle 'apparaît surtout comme un être protecteur auquel il est normal de faire des cadeaux quant on revient de loin' (Ombredane 1954: 201), the investigator should have indicated the significance of the fact that so few protocols referred to the uncle; he should also have shown whether or not the attitude expressed projectively differed from the cultural phrasing of, or observations concerning, the relationship. Did the TAT thus tell him something he had not already known?

In some situations no subtle projective test is needed: simple, straightforward interviewing of informants suffices. When Temne men were asked why they were willing to undertake 'the expensive, time-consuming, and potentially dangerous training' involved in joining a secret society, their replies could be classified under the headings of money, prestige, power and intellectual curiosity (Dorjahn 1961). Depth interviewing or subtle Rorschach interpretations might have uncovered unconscious motives and perhaps have differentiated psychologically among those willing and unwilling to join the societies, but on the level of the interview it appears that very adequate information was obtained.

The concept of levels suggests definitely the need for psychological instruments if complete understanding is to be attained. An anthropologist, for example, has suggested that a ceremonial can be interpreted either by the people themselves or by someone who feels he understands its role in the society and in their lives. The information obtained from the people may often be different from that which is deduced, because, for example, 'ritual may have a number of practical effects which are not at all intended by the performers and of which they or the majority of them are not aware' (Richards 1956: 112–20).   Techniques that may possibly induce people to reveal information about themselves from which shrewder deductions can be made concerning their motives obviously would be helpful.   At the same time not even the most thorough psychoanalysis of a large sample of informants can reveal all the societal functions performed by an institution.

One final word about measuring instruments in psychology: ingenuity and patience, it appears, can produce a battery of tests for any kind of society and can induce subjects to take the tests with pleasure or at least without too much suspicion.   On a recent expedition, for example, adequate samples of Bushmen in the Kalahari willingly submitted themselves to five standardised psychological tests and to an improvised one, finger-drawing in sand, which was clearly adapted to their talents (Reuning 1959) and which subsequently could be scored in a useful, meaningful manner (Reader 1961).

The third service offered by psychology to the social sciences in Africa is that of pure theory: as has been shown above in connection with the cross-cultural approach, two sets of social data can be conceptually connected by means of some psychological theory and their relationship, preferably stated explicitly in advance, can be tested statistically.   A principle of stimulus generalisation, once used to establish an association between kinship terminology and the residential relationship of a newly married pair to their parents (Murdock 1949), has more recently been invoked to show a connection between the political and the class structure of a society: societies with an hereditary aristocracy or with a system of complex stratification tend to have centralised political organisations or states, and vice versa (LeVine 1960b).   The tendency is especially strong in the African societies about which information is available.   These relationships might be discovered without invoking psychological explanations, but such explanations, being derived from the functioning of people on an individual level, have the additional advantage of suggesting how the connection might have evolved over generations and how it might be continuously sustained.

The connection between sets of social data is often established *ex post facto*, and then the theorist can be accused of 'psychologising' his data.   There is nothing sinful as such about psychologising, provided that the procedure in each instance is fully explained; but abuses do occur.   A physician, for example, tries to explain the 'somewhat arrested' mental development of Africans as a consequence of 'long and excessive indulgence as a nursling ended by a sudden shock at weaning' (Davidson 1949: 77).   Two assumptions are here being made; *viz.*, that child-rearing practices in the indicated respects are uniform in all African societies, and that such practices will have the postulated effect on adult personality.   The first assumption is patently false, the second is based upon an unproven psychological theory.

It sometimes appears that there is no alternative to psychologising if one is to go beyond existing facts, secure greater understanding, and make predictions.   One analyst, for example, has addressed himself to the problem of 'anti-European violence' in Africa by borrowing a psychological hypothesis which states, in effect, that the tendency towards aggression is likely to be strengthened when the impulses of a person are in conflict.   The hypothesis for Africa means that anti-European violence is likely to occur when European-run governments arouse 'conflicting expectations' regarding political autonomy, that is, when African hopes are simultaneously or alternately inflated and punctured.   There follows a discussion which organises the facts around the hypothesis and which makes sense for the period up

to the time of writing (April 1959).   The Mau Mau outbreak is considered to have
been a result of Britain's benevolent attitude towards both the Kikuyu and European
settlers; Africans never knew what to anticipate from the colonial power (LeVine
1959a).   The presumption remains that the postulated psychological tendency
operates within many Africans and so the presence or absence of anti-European
violence, though also dependent upon a quasi-military organisation and other
complicated interactions, can be traced in large part to that process.   Many of the
writer's predictions have been vindicated in the meantime, but in the less successful
cases (e.g., Angola) he prepared his alibi in advance by quite justifiably calling
attention to factors that make prediction difficult: changes in European policies,
inadequate information concerning events, and the diffusion of ideas to Africans
from the newly independent nations.   Psychologising is undoubtedly helpful, but
in a multivariant situation it must be judiciously employed in conjunction with an
analysis of other factors which are operating simultaneously.

Witchcraft, sorcery and magic have previously been identified in this chapter
as tempting topics for which psychological and especially psychoanalytic explanations can be glibly supplied.   A generation of speculation, however, has been quite
sterile, except perhaps for producing the assertion that social institutions have
psychological functions.   Such speculation develops little new knowledge, because
it uses psychological theory to 'interpret' one set of data — those pertaining to the
institution being analysed — rather than to connect two sets of data, such as the
institution and socialisation practices.   Perhaps, therefore, the psychologising of
only a single set unaccompanied by some other set ought to be gently outlawed.

A dash of psychologising, while adding only flavouring, is sometimes completely optional and undamaging.   A clear-cut demonstration that the use of a
chemical fertiliser increased the yield of millet and ground-nuts over 30 per cent did
not prove convincing to a group of Kanuri cultivators.   Why?   According to the
analysis by an anthropologist, the Agricultural Officer, though a Kanuri himself,
phrased and executed the change in a Western manner which the people rejected;
in the past they had had unfavourable experience with the same fertiliser because
they had misused it; they considered the change unimportant since traditionally
important actions demanded not voluntary co-operation as in this instance but
compulsory obedience; and no cultivator was given the opportunity to report on
the success that had been obtained (Cohen 1961).   It seems at first to matter little
whether one notes, as the investigator does, that 'all technology is imbedded in a
welter of cultural accretions', which were here disregarded, or whether stress is
placed upon the motivational and perceptual factors which were absent.   A combination of anthropological and psychological concepts presumably could produce
a set of systematic principles useful in dealing with this and with various other
instances of social change or resistance to it.

In concluding this excursion on psychologising, an impertinent question must
be raised: how much longer is it necessary to use psychological principles to show
connections between sets of social data?   In the present chapter reference has
already been made to studies involving kinship names, dreams, initiation rites and
political organisation; it has even been suggested (LeVine 1959) that such a sweetly
innocent subject as rape has deep, deep sociological, economic, political and interpersonal roots.   If rape, then any aspect of behaviour that is modally present in a
society can be subject to similar analysis.   Why go on?   The question is legitimate
when all that is accomplished is to add additional illustrations supporting the

doctrine of determinism.   In the future, consequently, such studies ought also to provide new insight into more specific principles of social science.

The effect of the social sciences upon psychology demands final attention, not merely because the author of this chapter is a psychologist, but because any improvements in psychology, it is hoped, eventually can be transmitted to other social scientists toiling in the vineyard of Africa.   The greatest service to be rendered psychology by research in Africa is so obvious that psychologists pay lip-service to it and then return to their animals or college sophomores: Africa, like any other place outside the West, provides a different cultural setting and hence different people for testing the universality of psychological theories.   Thus it may eventually be necessary to revise theories concerning the role of genetic and environmental factors in perception as a result of the experimental work now being carried on among Africans.   Any theory concerning basic or innate drives obviously must be based upon an examination of people everywhere, including Africa.   The avoidance of scientific ethnocentrism, moreover, has certain positive gains.   For roughly three decades, social scientists have concerned themselves with the problem of 'culture and personality'.   Apart from producing literally thousands of illustrations which demonstrate that there is a complicated interaction between individual and social factors — and in some guises only a slightly revised statement of the interaction between heredity and environment has been proposed — there can be relatively little gain until concrete relationships, again as illustrated by the cross-cultural approach, have been investigated.   More systematic exploration ought to result in faster progress.

The writer must confess, however, that so far psychological research in Africa has made little or no contribution to psychological theory.   In part this is due to psychological theory itself: so many different principles exist in contemporary psychology that it is always possible for at least one of them to embrace almost any set of new facts.   It appears, moreover, that psychological theory has been seldom if ever rigorously tested in Africa; most psychologists, indeed most social scientists in Africa, have been content to be guided, not by hypotheses, but by the stimulating kind of sequential empiricism that merely says in effect: 'let us see how these Africans react. . .'   Rarely is research experience in Africa utilised in Europe as it was in the following instance: the fact that a verbal explanation by Congolese subjects of their responses on an intelligence test generally resulted in 'une amélioration considérable du score' inspired a study whose purpose was to compare changes in score among Belgian children when they were asked to provide similar explanations or when they took the same test a second time (Ombredane and Robaye 1953).

In studying sequences for the sake of more general theory, it is well to note the social context in which a sequence occurs.   On the one hand, Africa may offer students of socialisation unique opportunities to investigate the effects of abrupt weaning upon subsequent development; in the West the practice may be observed too infrequently to be studied, but in some African societies it may be the modal method of child-training.   On the other hand, the attending conditions may be quite different: abrupt weaning may have one set of consequences when the child is reared in the extended family of an African society and have quite other consequences when he is part of a simple nuclear family in California.

What are the unique opportunities which Africa offers for collecting data to test psychological hypotheses?   One astute investigator has noted certain cultural characteristics which he thinks are 'distinctively African, although they are neither limited to Africa nor universal throughout it', *viz.*: pastoralism; large and dense populations; highly developed prestige economy and acquisitive culture patterns; centralised political institutions and institutionalised leadership; unilineal descent groups; bridewealth; polygyny and the mother-child household; initiation rites and genital operations; ancestor cults; witchcraft and sorcery; and the important role of proverbs in folklore (LeVine 1961: 52–3). Additions to the list can easily be made, such as: climate; tropical diseases; malnutrition; the existence of a number of societies that have been divided by the arbitrary boundaries of the Europeans and hence subjected to different colonial rulers; the rapid emergence of an elite; the British policy of indirect rule; particular structural peculiarities of certain African languages; etc. Clearly from such standpoints Africa is psychologically inviting.

It is not inconceivable that data from African societies can force psychologists to formulate conceptual frameworks which they have up to the present not even adequately noted. Any theory of learning, for example, can function only when its variables are weighted in particular situations. How is learning theory then applicable to social change? The assumption must be made that some people in the society learn the innovation and that the new or the modified form is immediately or eventually transmitted from generation to generation. Charting the course of the change, however, does not necessarily reveal the dynamics of the learning process. For learning on the adult level is likely to result from a complicated interaction between innumerable people who then in turn do, or do not, engage in transmitting the change to their children. It is perfectly obvious that over a period of time the vocabulary or structure of a language changes, and certainly people produce and reflect the changes; but only rarely is it possible to identify the precise innovators and the precise interactions leading to changes. Can an advance along such lines occur in connection with African research?

Psychologists in Africa might conceivably also improve their methods for studying, not only Africans, but also people in the West. It has been repeatedly noted throughout this chapter that research in Africa places a challenging strain upon the conventional interpretations that implicitly or explicitly accompany projective tests. Being more or less unique, each research situation, moreover, usually requires some modification of existing methods; hence African research stimulates such inventions. Experimentation, the method with the highest prestige among psychologists because it enables them to come closest to establishing causal sequences, may possibly be applied to wider areas outside the laboratory in connection with some field investigations in Africa. Within a given society, it is extremely difficult to find two completely equivalent communities, one of which can serve as an experimental and the other as a control group; but the ideal of equivalent groups can be roughly approximated. In an interviewing schedule, it is possible to introduce and manipulate an experimental variable so that alternate informants who are interviewed can be subjected to differential treatment.

Improvements in theory and method may also result from psychological research conducted by investigators other than psychologists. For theories and methods from psychology diffuse to other social scientists, who can then gather psychological data. Whether an anthropological fieldworker is assisted by psychological preparation or whether a psychologist has anthropological guidance, for example, is an issue to be decided by the temperament of each investigator. Only one points seems certain: additional research in Africa inevitably benefits all the disciplines.

15

Linguistics   Joseph H. Greenberg

I INTRODUCTION*

ALL THE SCIENCES and humanities deal in some manner with data which are
linguistic; to cite but a few examples, the documents of the historian, the
informant statements of the ethnologists, the very materials of folklorist and literary
studies are linguistic in form (Hockett 1958; Gleason 1961).[1] Even the physical
sciences share at least one linguistic preoccupation with disciplines concerned with
human and therefore largely verbal behaviour: namely, a concern with the language
of the science itself.   However, all these other areas of study deal with language
as a means to an end.   Only linguistics studies languages as an end in itself.   The
distinction between the linguistic system as such, describable by a set of rules, and
the system in actual use has been variously phrased as *langue* versus *parole*, syntactic
versus pragmatic or, in accordance with the recent vogue of information theory, as
code versus message (Morris 1949; Wilson 1954).[2]   However stated, it serves to
delimit in a general way the province of linguistics as against the linguistic aspects
of all other fields of study.

Linguistics is a social science.   The very notion of language presupposes a
social group which employs it as a means of communication.   Linguistics, therefore,
deals with the speech of an individual as representative of that of a social group,
often called the speech community.   Further, language as a highly complex body
of learned behaviour forms a part of the cultural heritage of the community which
uses it.   Indeed it has a central role as the fundamental vehicle of transmission of
other cultural traits within and across social groups.   From this point of view,
linguistics may be considered a specialised branch of the science of cultural anthropology.

The primary interest of the linguists is in spoken language.   Writing and
similar systems are viewed by virtually all linguists as derivative phenomena.[3]
Speech has priority over reading in the life history both of the individual and the
race.   Writing always implies some spoken form, but the converse does not hold.
A further reason for assigning priority to the study of spoken language has to do
with the study of language change.   Writing systems are highly stable whereas
spoken languages constantly change.   Hence the changes in a writing system can be

* Notes and bibliography for this chapter will be found on page 549.

understood by reference to the spoken language but not vice versa. The effect of writing on speech in the form of spelling pronunciations is a real but relatively insignificant factor. Although his attention is thus centred on spoken language, the linguist cannot but be concerned with the relation between spoken and written forms. All our knowledge of past languages comes from texts which must be subject to linguistic interpretation in terms of a primary written source. In setting forth the results of descriptive analysis, moreover, the linguist himself employs a written transcription. He may also become involved in the practical problem of devising orthographies.

Linguistics is divided into two main branches: descriptive and historical — or, as they are sometimes called, synchronic and diachronic. Linguistic science in its recognisably modern form arose in the first decades of the nineteenth century as a basically historical discipline chiefly concerned with the specific problem of the reconstruction of the ancestral Indo-European language. Interest tended to shift to problems of language description with the rise of various 'structural' schools from approximately 1920 onwards. The relation between these two main fields of study is complementary, not hostile. The degree of success of historical enquiry is in the final analysis dependent on the reliability and completeness of descriptive data. On the other hand, while a language can be described without reference to its own past, like other cultural phenomena it is a product of this past, and fuller understanding is only possible when the time dimension is taken into account. A clear distinction between these two types of investigation is necessary for clarity of exposition. Many traditionally oriented grammars tend to interweave historical or often pseudo-historical interpretations with descriptive statements in such fashion that observed phenomena are not clearly distinguished from inferences, and no clear picture of the language for a specified time locus emerges.

The aim of a scientific language description is to state as accurately, completely and elegantly as possible the structure of a language at a particular time. There are a number of differing theoretic approaches to the problems of language description characteristic of various 'schools' of linguistics. In spite of these differences, the descriptions themselves are largely convertible from one theoretic framework to another. While these differences are no doubt of considerable significance, they will seem, particularly to the outsider, less extensive than the shared common ground. The differences are at least partly terminological. Occasionally the treatment of a particular linguistic topic will be very nearly unintelligible without orientation in the theoretical literature of the school concerned. For the non-specialist interested in utilising the linguistic literature on Africa, such differences need not be a significant handicap. The majority of linguists are eclectic and not likely to introduce a term used by a restricted circle of linguists without preliminary explanations. Some of the most elaborate grammatical theories, moreover, have seldom or never been applied to overall descriptions of African languages. Thus, two of the approaches most widely discussed at the present time — that of the glossematic school of Copenhagen (Hjelmslev 1953), and American transformational theory (Chomsky 1957) — have not, at the time of writing, been applied to the description of an African language. In fact, the vast majority of full-fledged descriptions of individual languages have up to now been carried out by individuals with limited or non-existent technical training. They therefore follow traditional models, and the approach and terminology should be sufficiently familiar from exposure to conventional English grammar and foreign language instruction.

In view of these differences of approach, any attempt to describe the analytic methods of the linguist for the non-specialist must steer through the Scylla of all-inclusiveness, going far beyond the purpose and scope of the present exposition, and the Charybdis of a biased presentation based on a single theory. In what follows, therefore, the attempt will be made to set forth some of the basic methods which are very generally employed by linguists. The orientation will be towards problems rather than specific solutions. The overall purpose will be to sharpen the non-linguist reader's awareness regarding some of the fundamental issues debated by linguists and to acquaint him in a preliminary way with linguistic concepts and terminology most frequently encountered in the linguistic literature of Africa.

II DESCRIPTIVE LINGUISTICS

There are three main aspects of any linguistic description, and it would seem that, on any showing, they have a certain irreducible distinctiveness which cannot be eliminated theoretically and in practice lead to quite different sets of problems. These are *phonology* (the study of sound systems), *grammar* (the study of the rules governing arrangements of meaningful elements), and *semantics* (the study of meaning). There are, of course, interconnections, and indeed one issue which has divided linguists is the problem known as the mixing of levels. One possible formulation of this problem is the extent to which considerations drawn from one area can or should be taken account of in dealing with another. [4]

1. PHONOLOGY

All contemporary structuralist schools distinguish in some manner between a level of description based on sounds (phonetics) and a more abstract level involving analytical procedures operating upon phonetic data and designed to yield a description in terms of functioning units of the language structure (phonological level).

The basis of any description of this aspect of language, then, is an accurate description of the sounds of the language. The indispensable tool for accomplishing this is training in the theory and practice of articulatory phonetics. The theoretical framework of this phonetics developed in its essentials in the course of the nineteenth century. In effect, this system provides a set of co-ordinates, almost all stated in terms of articulatory processes, that is positions and movements of the speech organs, by means of which all possible speech sounds may be defined (Heffner 1949). [5] Thus the English *b* sound in this system would be described (in a highly oversimplified fashion for purposes of illustration) as a bilabial voiced stop, each of these three terms referring to features of articulation, contact of the lips (bilabial), vibration of the vocal cords (voiced) and completeness of the closure (stop). [6] A very few features are, however, *faute de mieux*, described in terms of acoustic impression rather than articulations. Thus pitch or fundamental frequency depends in its articulation upon the frequency of vibration of the vocal cords; this cannot be measured by non-instrumental methods.

The training of the practical phonetician increases the understanding of the theoretical framework of this system and the ability to place any sound accurately within it. The technique is largely one of mimicking and introspective analysis of the matching sound thus produced. Visual observation, e.g., of the lip movements of the informant, plays a definite but minor role. The tape recorder, by providing a virtually permanent, indefinitely repeatable, record of speech sounds, has been of great practical importance in the more accurate application of such methods. Finally, the practical phonetician must learn to apply a standard method of transcription in order to codify his results and make them understandable to others.

A second set of fundamental methods is that of laboratory phonetics. To a certain degree, these methods simply provide more objective data about articulations. By the use, for example, of the palatogram — essentially an artificial palate covered with a removable substance — it is possible to discover what part of the palate has been subject to contact in a specific articulation. In particular, recent developments in X-ray photography promise much in the area of objective observation of speech articulations. The heart of laboratory phonetics, however, is acoustic analysis of the sound wave itself as employed in speech: a source of information obviously not available without instrumental means. Fundamental advances have occurred during the last two decades largely through the invention of the sound spectograph. From a sound input this instrument produces a spectogram in which the relative amplitude within each of a number of frequency bands is indicated by the darkness of the impression on the paper. The subsequent invention of a speech synthesiser, by which the process is reversed so that hand-painted spectograms are utilised as inputs with synthetic sound as output, provides another basic tool in acoustic research. Synthetic sounds can be judged by subjects, while the acoustic cues utilised in perception are subject to manipulation by the experimenter.

Such laboratory methods are obviously of considerable relevance to the linguist-phonetician involved in the description of specific languages. However, if only for practical reasons of time, expense, and the absence of servicing facilities under field conditions, such instrumental methods cannot as yet replace the traditional methods of practical phonetics. No one as yet has been able to analyse the sounds of a language by purely instrumental means, although individual points of doubt in the analysis can often be clarified by such methods. Outside of any such practical help in linguistic analysis, it is clear that research into the acoustic nature of speech is of fundamental importance to linguistics and communication studies.

A method very different from those already described is required in those cases where the only evidence regarding a language is in the form of written texts from a past period. The methods employed consist of highly complex inferences based on comparative linguistic methods, transcriptions of loan words into and borrowings from other langt ages, and the contemporary phonetic facts when study is being made of an earlier stage of a language still spoken. The results are necessarily both more uncertain and less detailed than when direct observation is possible (Sturtevant 1920).[7]

The basic unit derived by the application of analytic methods to the phonetic data has usually been the phoneme, the principle of which is foreshadowed in the pre-scientific invention of alphabetic writing. It might be thought that a single simple analytic principle, implicit in the popular notion of 'phonetic alphabet', would suffice: namely, the consistent assignment to each individual sound of a symbol. In this case the analytic unit would simply correspond to the phonetic notion of a distinct sound as defined by the co-ordinates of articulatory phonetics as described earlier. In fact, however, there is often a multiplicity of sounds, consistently distinguishable by a trained phonetician but intuitively regarded as the same sound unit by the average speaker. For example, the average speaker of

English, untrained in phonetics, is unlikely ever to have noticed that the sound spelled *t* in 'stop' (unaspirated) is distinct from the *t* in 'top' (aspirated). It is not enough to say that the difference is small, for this precise difference of aspiration or lack of aspiration of *t* and other stops is evidently phonetic in Hindi, Chinese and many other languages.

If the approach to a foreign language is naïve, a response will be made only to those sound differences which are structurally relevant in the learner's language. He will thus ignore relevant differences in the foreign language where he is not accustomed to respond to them and will sometimes erroneously assume that the differences are relevant when they coincide with differences familiar to him from his own language. Thus an untrained observer will tend to arrive at essentially the same sound system for any language he describes, and two untrained observers with different first languages will describe the same foreign language in different ways.

Phonetic training is the necessary but not sufficient condition for transcending this built-in linguistic ethnocentrism. In the pre-structural period of descriptive linguistics, the stated aim was to transcribe phonetically in an attempt to reproduce as accurately as possible the sounds of the language to be investigated. The result was an ever-growing mass of structurally irrelevant phonetic detail. The develop-ment of instrumental phonetics hastened the realisation that this procedure leads to a dead end, for it became apparent that the actual sounds were not identical even in two different renderings of the 'same' utterance in the same language.

In order to discover which sound differences are distinctive, various analytic procedures are employed. A basic one is the notion of complementary distribution (Block and Trager 1942; Gleason 1961).[8] By the distribution of any sound is meant the set of environments in which it occurs. For example, in 'Stop the ceremony!' the environment of the unaspirated *t* is 's-op the ceremony!' Two sounds are said to be in complementary distribution if it can be shown by means of a simple rule that they never occur in the same environment. Thus in English a sample of environments of unaspirated and aspirated *t* shows that all of the environ-ments of the former are marked by an *s* preceding the unaspirated *t*, while the latter never occurs in such environments. Because the choice between the two is therefore always determined by the environment, they are incapable of distinct contrasts. Other phonetic variants of the /t/ phoneme in other environments could also be demonstrated. Such variant sounds which are grouped together as members of the same phoneme are frequently called allophones of the phoneme.[9]

Even in the present brief presentation, it is necessary to point out that an analysis which seeks to account for all structurally relevant differences in sound sequences must reckon with additional entities beyond the phoneme unless, of course, the term 'phoneme' is extended by definitional fiat to include quite heterogeneous phenomena. Along with the succession of discrete sound units or phonemes are various elements characteristic of the syllable, word, phrase or sentence which are, as it were, superimposed on this underlying sequence and can only arbitrarily be assigned a position within it. In American linguistics such units have been called prosodic features, in contrast to the segmental units or phonemes proper. An example is the intonation (pitch pattern) of a statement as opposed to a question. In England, the 'prosodic' school of J. R. Firth has emphasised such phenomena and tended to reduce the role of segmental entities (called 'phonematic units') in their terminology. Because sentence, phrase and word are grammatical units, this is another example of the problem of 'mixing of levels' mentioned earlier.

2. GRAMMAR

The basic strategy of phonologic analysis has been described as the attempt to develop a method which isolates the functionally relevant features of the sound system and thus overcome the biases resulting from the individual speech background of each observer. It might be maintained that the most significant advances of grammatical theory have been along the same lines. The aim has been to develop techniques through which the functional categories of each language emerge in place of an *a priori* set derived from traditional models of Latin grammar as applied to Western languages. It was, indeed, the challenge of 'exotic languages', differing drastically in type from European languages, which exposed the inadequacies of traditional methods of grammatical analysis.

The basic problem of grammatical theory may be characterised as the generation of an infinity of grammatically possible sentences from a grammar based on a necessarily finite set of given utterances (the 'corpus') and by means of a necessarily finite set of rules or formulae. If the number of grammatical sentences in a language was finite, they could be ordered in degree of length, and there would be some one or more finite number of sentences of maximum length. But, in fact, from a sentence of any length a still longer sentence can always be formed by the addition of co-ordinate clauses, insertion of additional modifiers, e.g., adjectives, and by still other methods. Although each sentence is itself of finite length, the number of sentences in any language forms what mathematicians call a countable infinity. Grammars, therefore, cannot take the form of a simple finite enumeration of sentences; they are necessarily predictive in that the rules permit the construction of new sentences not contained in the original corpus. This is confirmed by everyday experience in that persons constantly understand and make up sentences which they have never encountered in their previous experience.

The possibility of a grammar which generates an infinity of sentences arises through the existence of constructions in which the same finite class of words can occur repeatedly without limit (e.g., adjectives modifying a single noun). It follows then that, in order to deal with this infinitude of possible sentences, grammatical statements must be in terms of classes. Traditional grammar has made us familiar with the most inclusive of these classes, the so-called parts of speech. The most common variants of traditional grammar, based on a fixed set of parts of speech and even on a fixed order of the chapters dealing with them, has furnished the ground plan of innumerable grammars.

Such a grammar consists of two kinds of statements. The first, or morphological, concerns variations in form, that is the constituent sounds, particularly those connected with the functioning of the same part of speech in different constructions (inflection). Here then belong the tables of conjugation and declension. The second type of statement has to do with the use rather than with the form of the parts of speech. In fact, it becomes a statement regarding the meanings of inflectional categories. The two types of statement indicate a dichotomy between form (morphology) and use (syntax). Thus, in a traditional Latin grammar a morphological section states that, say, the ablative singular of *vir* ('man') is *virō*, while the syntactic sections describe the uses of ablative under such rubrics as 'the ablative of separation', 'the ablative of instrument', etc.

The heart of this doctrine is obviously the notion of part of speech. It presupposes a universally valid set of categories (noun, verb, adjective, etc.) believed to be present in all languages because they are necessary to human thinking. The definition is thus necessarily semantic. Thus the verb is delimited in terms of activity, the adjective designates qualities, etc. It has long been felt that this approach does not do justice to the functional grammatical categories even of very familiar language, e.g., English (Fries 1940, 1952).[10]

The reaction against this scheme has largely developed in terms of a rejection of universal *a priori* semantically based definitions for isolating the classes of elements to be employed in grammatical description. In consequence a formal (i.e., non-semantic) approach to the definition of grammatical categories has arisen. Such classes are defined in terms of morphological behaviour; for example, by their occurrence in certain inflectional categories as marked by afformatives of specified phonemic shapes, or by their occurrence in the same or similar environments, environment being defined here in essentially the same manner as that described earlier in reference to phonologic theory. To say that elements occur in the same environment is tantamount to saying that one can substitute for another. Hence the definition of classes by substitution has become a key operation in modern structural linguistics, particularly in its American version. Despite certain difficulties, the formal (i.e., non-semantic) techniques described have led to the isolation of differing parts of speech in differing languages which often depart widely from the traditional model of the parts of speech.

Still other procedures of structuralism undermine even more decisively the very concept of parts of speech which constitutes the core of the traditional scheme. It is obvious that traditional analysis requires that the basic unit of grammatical description be the 'word'. Morphology is the study of the formal (phonologic) internal structure of the word, and syntax has reference to its use in the sentence. It should be noted that in this usage some term such as paradigm is perhaps more appropriate than word. Thus in the traditional view *man*, *man's*, *men* and *men's* are all variants (accidents or inflectional forms) of the same underlying word. But the search for a minimal unit of phonological analysis led to the postulation of a unit smaller than the word as the basis for grammatical theory. This unit, first introduced by Bloomfield, is the morpheme, defined by him as the minimum meaningful unit (Bloomfield 1933: 161). Thus a word such as 'farmers' would consist of three morphemes: *farm-*, *-er* and *-s*. In this way inflectional elements likewise become morphemes, so that the above-mentioned paradigm of *man* is dissolved into morpheme combinations.

A consistent attempt was made to develop an overall theory of linguistic description based on the phoneme and morpheme as the two basic minimal units and with a good deal of parallelism in the analytic procedures involved in both. This finds its classic expression in a paper by Z. Harris, in which, by repeated substitution procedures on higher and higher levels, there is a *gradus ad Parnassum* from the morpheme to the sentence (Harris 1947). The word level appears here only tacitly, so that for all practical purposes the old morphology-syntax division disappears. Form variations formerly handled in declensional and conjugational tables with words as units are treated as allomorphs (i.e., variants) of the same morphemic unit, e.g., *-en* in the environment . . . *ox-*. . . The statement of all such varying forms of the same morpheme is termed morphophonemics and forms a distinctive compartment of the grammar in the scheme. The connection with phonemics is via what Hockett has named the principle of accountability, according to which every phoneme is assigned to one and only one allomorph in a context.

The general model just sketched has been widely influential, even if it has seldom been carried out with completeness in an overall grammar of a language. It was soon realised, for example, that, for languages with highly complex and irregular morphologies, the analyst would be faced with the necessity of highly arbitrary and difficult choices which are often avoided by the traditional method of the paradigm (Greenberg 1957: 18–27).[11]

The recently proposed transformational type of grammar differs in certain fundamental respects from the phoneme-morpheme model (Gleason 1961: 171–94).[12] Some of its features can be illustrated from its characteristic treatment of the problems of morphophonemics discussed above. In its most common current version such a grammar provides for three fundamental sections, considered as levels: phrase-structure, transformational and morphophonemic. One of the distinctive attributes of such a grammar is that it manipulates abstract symbols which do not directly represent sound sequences. The final section provides formulae for converting the sequences of symbols, in this case called the 'terminal strings', into symbols representing sounds. Although at higher levels the symbols are usually abbreviations of familiar grammatical terms, in principle it would make no difference if, for example, arbitrary numerals or Greek letters were used instead.

The transformational grammar is a subclass of the generative type of grammar. In general, the notion of a generative grammar requires use at the start of a set of primitive symbols, usually a single one generally symbolised s (= sentence). By various rewritings in accordance with given rules, a succession of strings, consisting of symbols, is generated until a terminal string is converted into one symbolising an actual sentence. A grammatical sentence is by definition one which is generated from a given grammar by this procedure. The first or phrase-structure section consists of rewrite rules of the form $(x) + A + (y) \longrightarrow (x) + B + (y)$, where x or y or both may be null and A stands for a single symbol but B is under no such restriction. A string which already is of the form $(x) + A + (y)$ may then, in accordance with this rule be rewritten as $(x) + B + (y)$. From strings generated in this fashion according to phrase-structure rules others may be formed by transformational formulae; these permit changes more drastic than those allowed by the rewrite rules of phrase-structure.

These transformational formulae, which form the second section of the grammar, may produce change of the order of symbols within a string, may join parts of two strings to form a new one, etc. Not all sentences are necessarily generated with the intervention of transformational rules. A set of particularly simple structure, known as the kernel, consists of terminal strings produced solely within the phrase-structure part of the grammar.

Any string, whether phrase-structure only or originating through one or more transformations applied to a phrase-structure string, is a terminal string if it consists of symbols subject to the rules which convert the string into a set of phonologic symbols representing an actual sentence. The rules for converting such terminal strings into phonologic symbols form the third, or morphophonemic, section of the grammar. The terminal strings contain symbols which in principle are abstract and for which any arbitrary set could be substituted. In practice they consist of sequences of phonemic symbols or names for grammatical categories. Thus, in a sentence containing 'took', the terminal string might contain somewhere the sequence . . . {take} + {past}. . . Under the rules in the morphophonemic section of the grammar, it would be stated that this sequence may be replaced by the phoneme sequence /tuk/, i.e., 'took'. It would, of course, not matter in principle if {156} had been used instead of {take} and {372} instead of {past}; the rule would then read that {156} + {372} is replaced by /tuk/. Note that there is no question of phonemic accountability here, because individual phonemes of /tuk/ cannot be traced to either of the constituent elements {take} or {past}.

3. SEMANTICS

The chief descriptive problem in semantics, the third basic aspect of language, is the statement of meanings in terms of definitions, whether the language of description is the same (periphrasis) or different from (translation) the object language. This is primarily the task of the lexicographer or dictionary-maker. The division between the written productions commonly called grammars and dictionaries, however, does not completely coincide with the division of subject matter into grammar and semantics. Certain kinds of meanings, e.g., those of inflections, are treated at least in traditional grammars and are almost never found in dictionaries. On the other hand, the assignment of words to paradigm classes, e.g., the gender of nouns in French and irregularities of morphological formation, particularly the former, is regularly performed by dictionaries. Thus a grammar of French will describe the phenomenon of grammatical gender and give rules relating to agreement in gender, but it will not normally list all masculine and feminine nouns.

Partly because of the stress on formal (i.e., non-semantic) approaches in recent linguistic theory and partly because the field itself is not inherently as highly structured as grammar and phonology, semantics, in spite of certain recent developments (Lounsbury 1956; Conklin 1962), has hardly been touched by the more recent theoretic trends in these other aspects of descriptive linguistics.[13] Lexicography is still very much an art learned by apprenticeship or unguided imitation of existing dictionaries with relatively little in the way of codified principles or theoretic elaborations. It is significant, in the present context, to point out that the lexicographic aspects of hitherto unwritten languages or of those with a minimal written literature are quite different from those of established and standardised literary languages. African languages, for example, are parts of non-Western cultures with which the dictionary-maker or non-indigenous user may well not be familiar. The lexicographer, who uses informants' spoken usage as his ultimate source, finds his task, therefore, extraordinarily close to that of the ethnographic fieldworker. Indeed, a really first-rate dictionary cannot be compiled under these circumstances without coincident investigation of non-linguistic culture and is itself an ethnographic document of first-rate importance.

III   COMPARATIVE LINGUISTICS

Great as is the value of descriptions of the thousands of the world's languages from both the practical and the theoretic point of view, it can be argued that description is but the initial task of linguistic science. Only by comparisons of languages can either law-like generalisations or specific historical conclusions be derived from linguistic study.

I. HISTORICAL METHOD

One basic type of comparison is that of two or more historical stages of the same language. This, the direct historical method, depends on the existence of documentation for the earlier periods of the language. It is therefore of limited use in Africa where, except for the northern part of the continent, such cases are rare. Historical depth can also be attained by the comparative method, which involves the systematic comparison of related languages in order to reconstruct the ancestral language from which they have sprung. A specialised aspect of the comparative historical method is the intensive study of dialect variation within a single language, for such interdialectal relationship can be considered the limiting case of closest relationship. This field, which has a highly developed set of techniques, is called dialect geography. Its characteristic production is the dialect atlas, in which the geographical distribution of linguistic features within the total language area is mapped (Pop 1950).[14] In principle, social stratification of linguistic forms on class and occupational lines is likewise an aspect of linguistic variability within the bounds of a single language, but this area of study is still in its infancy.

The concept of genetic relationship of languages, the bases of comparative historical linguistics, is an extension of the notion of dialectic divergence over a longer time span. The dialects of one period become the separate but related languages of a later time. Language is always changing, and no language spoken over an extensive area can maintain full and equal communication within the entire speech community. A further factor in language change is migration, which may result in a community of speakers who are permanently removed from frequent and easy communication with the home community, i.e., Dutch in South Africa which evolved into a separate language, Afrikaans. Under the conditions just outlined, linguistic innovations, which may occur in all aspects of language, tend not to diffuse over the communication barriers; the results are local differentiation or dialects, as they are called. As the process continues, the dialects shift further apart beyond the point of mutual intelligibility. Each of the new languages which arises in this way may itself once more undergo the same splitting process.

The recovery of this sequence of events leads to the postulation of a family tree or genetic classification of languages. Hypotheses of this kind are based on shared resemblances which are retentions, though often in a modified form, from the original period of linguistic unity. The systematic comparison of such related languages leads to the reconstruction, as far as may be possible, of the traits of the ancestral language and the processes of change in the languages during the intervening period. A fundamental part of this method is the technique of determining sound correspondences. Sound change is regular in that a phoneme in a particular language changes to another phoneme virtually without exception under stated conditions, these conditions themselves being phonetic. Sometimes all instances of a phoneme change under all conditions (so-called unconditional sound change). An example of a conditioned change is the shift from earlier *t* in German to *s* (written *ss*) in non-initial position and to *ts* (written *z*) in initial position. Since in English *t* did not change under these circumstances, there have resulted two sets of correspondences between English and German. Initially, German *ts* = English *t*, as in *zwei*: *two*; *Zunge*: *tongue*, etc.; non-initially, German *s* = English *t*, as in *beissen*: *bite*; *schiessen*: *shoot*, etc. An example of an unconditioned change is the shift of Anglo-Saxon *ā* to modern English *o*, e.g., *hām*: *home*; *stān*: *stone*, etc.

An understanding of regular sound change and a number of other processes of change permits, by a kind of triangulation, the determination of features of the parent language. Such comparative study is most advanced in the case of the Indo-European languages, but it has been applied successfully to closely related groups of languages, including Bantu, in many parts of the world, even in the absence of earlier written records.[15]   An incidental but important by-product is the sorting out of resemblances among both related and non-related languages which result from borrowing rather than descent with modification from a form in the ancestral language.

It is evident that the most important contributions of linguistics to historical research lie in this area (Sapir 1949).[16]   Until recently conclusions of this kind have lacked the all-important aspect of absolute chronology.   Since about 1950, however, Swadesh and others have developed a method called glottochronology which attempts to fill this gap (Hymes 1960).   The fundamental assumption of glottochronology is that the rate of change by replacement within a standard vocabulary list is reasonably constant for all languages.   The absolute value is calculated from a number of documented cases from earlier and later stages of the same languages in Europe and the Near East.   If it is hypothetical that attrition in related languages is occurring independently at this rate, then there will be an expected number of common retentions, the so-called cognate forms.   From the percentage of cognates in such cases it is possible to derive an estimate of the chronological date at which divergence within the original unified speech community began.   Recently both the empirical and mathematical bases of the theory have come under sharp attack.[17]

2. TYPOLOGIC METHOD

Another type of comparison has come into renewed prominence in recent years. This is typologic comparison and classification in which the criteria employed refer to similarities which may arise without any necessary implication of historical connection through either contact or common origin.   Languages can have noun case systems, for example, which considerably resemble each other in the semantic categories but which do not have corresponding similarities in the sound sequences which express these categories.   Thus certain Australian, Caucasian, Indo-European, Amerind, and other languages in all probability have independently developed systems of case inflection in the nouns.   To cite but a few instances of a widespread phenomenon in phonology: Ewe in West Africa, Chinese in Eastern Asia, and Zapotecan in Mexico, make use of pitch distinctions in their phonemic systems although the languages have had no historic connection.

Non-historical comparison using such criteria leads to classification of languages into types.   The complete absence of certain logically possible types and the significantly different frequencies of others evidently lead to generalisations about human language as a whole.   In the past there has been a tendency to confuse typological and genetic criteria for resemblances, but the growing clarification of this problem has tended to elucidate the legitimate role of typological comparison in the development of both synchronic law-like generalisations and diachronic regularities governing the change of type.

IV   OTHER LINGUISTIC DISCIPLINES

In addition to the two core fields of descriptive and comparative linguistics just outlined, a number of more or less peripheral, though definitely related, topics possess the common characteristic of having fairly direct relevance to other disciplines. In certain instances the area of common interest is sufficiently extensive to have given rise to nascent subdisciplines, notably psycholinguistics and ethnolinguistics. In the present context the emphasis is on common ground with other social sciences, and no consideration need be given to such fields as semantic analysis, an important joint interest of linguistics with logic.

Because language is a part of culture, and linguistics, from this point of view, may be considered a branch of cultural anthropology, the relationship between language and other aspects of culture has naturally become a concern of anthropological linguistics. This rather vague area of knowledge is often called *ethnolinguistics*. Among its basic problems is the determination of the role of language in the transmission of culture from one generation to another (enculturation) and from one culture to another (acculturation). Studies have been made, for example, of the changes induced in one language by contact with another in the context of the general culture-contact situation, including its non-linguistic aspects. Another set of problems has to do with possible correlations between language, particularly in its semantic aspect of classification of concepts, and non-linguistic cultural behaviour. The by now classic anthropological topic of the relation between kinship terminology and patterned kinship behaviour is an example of this. But the sharpest issues in this area have been raised through the largely posthumous interest in the writings of Benjamin Whorf (Carroll 1956; Hoijer 1954).[18] The Whorfian thesis or 'linguistic Weltanschauung hypothesis', as it has been called, in its most extreme interpretation would assert that the general 'world view' of its speakers is determined by, or at least mirrored in, the categories of the language which they speak. This thesis has aroused wide interest and has been the stimulus both for analytic discussion and for cross-cultural psychological experimentation.

Like ethnolinguistics, the merging subdiscipline of *psycholinguistics* does not as yet have a clearly delineated set of problems or techniques (Osgood and Sebeok 1954).[19] In order to give a general notion of its contents, a number of topics generally considered relevant may here be mentioned. These include the psychological processes in language-learning, whether of first or subsequent languages, and in language-loss in the pathological condition known as aphasia; the study of sound perceptions in speech; and the psychological aspects of meaning interpreted as the reaction of subjects to words operating as stimulus objects. This last type of interest has given rise to the semantic differential as an instrument to measure meaning as response along a set of dimensions (Osgood, Suci, and Tannenbaum 1957).[20]

Even more recent is the interest in what has come to be called *sociolinguistics*, including such topics as: the relation of language differences to social class; the differential social roles of different languages co-existing in the same society; the development and spread of lingua francas as auxiliary languages in multilingual situations; the factors involved in the differential prestige ratings of languages; the role of language as a sign of ethnic identification; language in relation to nationalism; and problems of language policy, e.g., in education. This area has become a focus of interest largely because of problems arising in developing areas and is therefore of particular interest to social scientists concerned with Africa (Ferguson and Gumperz 1960).[21]

Still another aspect of language, namely, its employment as a *medium of aesthetic expression*, must also be considered. There is a purely linguistic side to the characterisation of individual and folk style in written and unwritten literature. Linguistic considerations also enter into the description and analysis of differences between prose and various poetic types of language. The study of one particular poetic device, metre, cannot be analysed without reference to strictly linguistic factors. The use of language in song, for example, the relation between linguistic and musical pitch patterns in tone languages, raises at least partly linguistic considerations. Departing somewhat from the strictly aesthetic aspect, one may also consider the ritual use of language, secret languages, the linguistic aspect of drum and other communication based on language and the playful modification of language involved in tongue-twisters, dog-Latins and similar devices.

With this outline of some of the main features of linguistic science and its relationship to other disciplines, consideration may now be given to linguistics in its specifically African setting.[22]

V AFRICAN LINGUISTICS

A significant knowledge of the languages spoken in sub-Saharan Africa begins, for all practical purposes, in the seventeenth century. The humanistic interests aroused in the Renaissance, the broadening horizons about the world as a whole, and the voyages of exploration and discovery evidently produced an attitude of curiosity about man which had, as one of its facets, an interest in the languages of 'exotic' peoples. This stands in marked contrast to the attitude of the Greeks and Romans in such matters. In a letter reproduced in Chamberlayne's collection of Lord's Prayers in many languages, Leibnitz, himself a pioneer in the classification of the languages of Europe, states: '. . . and it is to be deplored that the ancients never thought of anything similar by which there might have been transmitted information about ancient languages which now have perished. . .' (Chamberlaynius 1715). Among the people of antiquity, the Babylonians were outstanding in providing bilingual word lists and paradigms of Akkadian and Sumerian and even a word list of Cassite, but of course this was not known until the decipherment of cuneiform writing in the nineteenth century.

The Arabs occasionally cite individual words from African languages, but they never collected vocabularies or wrote grammars or dictionaries, and almost everything remains to be done on the collection and interpretation of African words in Arabic sources. M. Delafosse (1912) has discussed the African terms in Ibn-Batūtah, and C. Meinhof (1919–20) has treated a few expressions in al-Hamadhānī and al-Mas'ūdī.

In Western Europe, the practical demands of evangelisation soon led to more intensive studies of individual languages, but only sheer intellectual curiosity and the nascent stirrings of a concept of man as the object of scientific study can explain why, for example, Pigafetta (1923: 74) records a vocabulary from the aborigines of Tierra del Fuego in his report of Magellan's voyage (1519–22): an activity unparalleled in the whole literature of the ancients.[23]

Until the development of modern phonetics in the course of the nineteenth century, recordings of African languages were highly impressionistic and based on the apprehension of sounds in terms of the sound system of the observer; the orthography was based on that of the language of the investigator. Where an indigenous orthography already existed, as in some instances in Ethiopia, greater accuracy was attainable. In constructing a grammar, the European student of African languages could draw on two traditions: the classical, which already formed the basis for pioneer grammatical analysis of Western vernaculars; and an oriental tradition, known to European scholars from Arab and Jewish sources, which provided an approximate framework for the study of languages of the Semitic type. The range of language available for study during the seventeenth and eighteenth centuries was severely limited, of course, by the nature of the contact of Europe with Africa in this period. Word lists or more extensive works on African languages published in the seventeenth century appear to be confined to the following languages: Fanti (Mueller 1675), Kikongo (Brusciottus 1659), Kimbundu (Pacconio and Do Conto 1642), Hottentot (T. Herbert in Esquier 1643), Nubian (Carradoi 1635), Geez — classical Ethiopic — (Ludolfus 1661), Amharic (Ludolfus 1698), and Malagasy (De Flacourt 1658). A number of vocabularies collected in Senegal in 1650 were published in 1845 by the Société Ethnographique de Paris, and Schebesta (1919–20) has published on seventeenth-century Chisena.

Two of these linguistic works of the seventeenth century are outstanding and, indeed, unequalled until the earlier part of the nineteenth century. They are Job Ludolfus' studies of Geez and Amharic and Father Brusciotto's grammar of Kikongo. The former provides a powerful illustration of the value of the oriental tradition in approaching the study of hitherto unknown Semitic languages. As early as 1590 Gregorius Weigenmayerus (1590) professor of Hebrew at Tuebingen, had provided an essentially correct grammatical analysis of the Geez translation of the Psalms and Song of Songs, which he perforce treated as representing a Semitic language of unknown provenance, because the language was mislabelled Chaldean. Ludolfus states that, had he known this work, he would have saved himself much trouble. The chief defect of Weigenmayerus' work was that he thought every Geez root must have exactly the same meaning as the corresponding Hebrew root. Jacob Wemmers (1638) subsequently produced the first real grammar and lexicon of Geez. Ludolfus' *Lexicon aethiopico-latinum* (1st edition, 1661), however, marks a great advance in scope and accuracy over the work of his predecessors. Ludolfus was an accomplished Semitic scholar with a thorough knowledge of Hebrew and Arabic and was able, therefore, to organise his grammar along familiar lines. For example, he numbers the verbal derivative conjugations in close parallelism with those of Arabic yet modifies them in order to conform more closely to the facts of Geez. In his lexicon the order is that of the root consonants, and he cites the third person masculine perfect of the root conjugation as the quotation form in accordance with standard Semitic practice. Doubled consonants and stress accent, not indicated in the Geez script, are sometimes marked in his transcriptions on the basis of contemporary pronunciation. He was doubtless aware of these two linguistically relevant facts about Geez, because he expected them on the basis of cognate Hebrew and Arabic forms, and because doubled consonants are expressed in Hebrew and Arabic orthography and stress is expressed in Hebrew. On the other hand, the appendix to the work in 1661 by J. M. Wansleben, giving comparisons with other languages, shows the primitive state of comparative linguistics at the time. Although the vast majority of correspondences are with other Semitic languages, words borrowed from Greek — including even proper names like Herodias — are entered on the same basis; nor, of course, is there any notion of regular correspondence of sound: a notion which first appears in the work of Grimm in the early nineteenth century.

The task faced by Brusciotto in his description of Kikongo was, of course, much more difficult. There was neither an indigenous orthography nor a suitable grammatical model on which to build. The most obvious problem was that of the typically Bantu noun-class system. Brusciotto treated the prefixes as articles after the manner of Italian. He had no clear statement of the principle of agreement in class among various parts of speech, but he did accurately enumerate the classes themselves and the correspondences between singular and plural classes. His analogy, however, was with Latin cases rather than genders. Struck by the fact that the class prefixes precede rather than follow, as is the case with the inflections of European languages, he called these markers *principationes*. In spite of its defects, his treatment of Bantu grammar was unequalled until fairly well into the nineteenth century.

Throughout the eighteenth century there was a slow, gradual increase in knowledge of African languages. From this period came the first information about the Berber of North Africa, a number of vocabularies and more extensive works on the Bantu languages of the coastal areas of Central, South and East Africa, and further investigations on Hottentot. A new chapter in the knowledge of African languages begins to unfold at the turn of the nineteenth century. This new impulse was partly due to the opening up of the interior of the continent, which began with the explorations of Park, Bruce, Salt and others and which had as a by-product the collection of vocabulary data from hitherto uncontacted languages. Indeed the collection of comparative vocabularies had become a linguistic fashion of the times. The earliest of the period, the *Glossarium Comparativum Linguarum Totius Orbis* of 1787, was sponsored by Catherine the Great and contained data from thirty African languages in the revised edition of 1790 and 1791. Other collections of this nature followed, e.g., the *Catalogo* of Hervas (1800) and the *Mithridates* of Adelung and Vater (1806).

The publications of the period are not confined to mere collection. The study of languages as forming families based on common origin — the master conception which underlies the systematic development of comparative linguistics as a science — begins in this period. The statement in 1786 of William Jones (1788) regarding the relationship of Sanskrit, Greek, Latin, Gothic, and other languages in an Indo-European family is usually cited as the decisive step inaugurating the modern period of comparative linguistics. That this general idea was already in the air, however, can be shown particularly from the precocious activities of William Marsden, who in 1758 gathered material from a Makua slave of Mozambique and deduced the relation between East African languages and Kikongo. In 1781, on the basis of linguistic material assembled during Captain Cook's voyages, Marsden (1782) came to a clear conception of a Malayo-Polynesian family extending from Madagascar to Polynesia. Indeed Marsden's statement (1783) is quite modern in its conception (and superior in clarity to Jones' celebrated pronouncement): '. . . that general language which is found to prevail and to be indigenous to all the islands of the eastern sea; from Madagascar to the remotest of Captain Cook's discoveries; comprehending a wider extent than the Roman, or any other tongue yet boasted'. A reading of this and of his earlier essay shows how easily the idea of a language with local dialect variation slips into the notion of still less similar languages as former dialects of the same language, i.e., as related languages. Indeed Marsden, as can be seen from the above passage, views the various Malayo-Polynesian languages as variants of a 'general language' aptly compared to what we today call the Romance languages as forms of Latin.

There is thus apparent a new organising principle by means of which the first attempts at grouping languages into larger units are undertaken. The third volume of *Mithridates* (1812) already incorporates these and similar suggestions in its survey of African languages. Such hypotheses were pursued eagerly during this period because of light they might shed on the origin and dispersion of mankind, and, because groupings based on language were uncritically equated with those based on race, they played an important role in the raging controversy concerning the monogenetic and polygenetic theory of human origins.

The data were not yet sufficient for general classifications of African languages but the progress of more limited hypotheses and the inevitable extrapolations by bolder spirits can be most easily traced through the successive editions of Prichard's *Inquiry into the Physical History of Mankind* and his *Natural History of Man* (1855). Although there were considerable differences in details, and no really complete overall classification of African languages was advanced in the first half of the nineteenth century, certain generally accepted conclusions did emerge. The results of the classificational efforts of this period were of fundamental importance in that certain basic results were attained which have stood the test of subsequent research. Even where such solutions were not forthcoming, it was during this period that almost all the questions were posed to which later investigators addressed themselves. The chief results attained up to approximately 1860 were as follows:

1 The term Semitic, introduced by Schloezer in 1781, received a definition approximating present usage (Eichhorn, n.d.). The existence of an Ethiopian branch of the family, including the extinct Geez (Classical Ethiopic) as well as certain modern languages (e.g., Amharic, Tigrinya), was established.

2 It was recognised that certain languages of North and East Africa resembled Semitic and were probably related to it. These languages were sometimes called Sub-Semitic and, later, Hamitic (Renan 1855).[24] Berber, ancient Egyptian, the Cushitic languages of the Horn (e.g., Somali, Galla, Saho) and, less frequently, Hausa were generally assigned to this group.

3 A clear distinction was made between Hottentot and Bushman languages on the one hand and the South African, or Kaffir languages, as they were frequently called, on the other. The existence of a relatively homogeneous group of languages including these latter and covering almost all of Central, South and East Africa was generally accepted. The name Bantu for this family was introduced by Bleek (1862).

4 The large groups of languages mainly in the western and eastern Sudan, not accounted for as Bantu, Semitic, Hamitic, or Bushman, were often called Negro languages and variously treated. Their classification was recognised as a basic unsolved problem. The generally confident Norris stated that some Negro groups 'elude classification' and that 'The Negroes hitherto have been considered as constituting one race rather from physiological than philological evidence' (Prichard 1855: I: 427).

5 The affiliation of Malagasy to Malayo-Polynesian was advanced early and had won general acceptance.

In accordance with the interest in classification, the first half of the nineteenth century saw a succession of large comparative vocabularies such as those of Clarke

(1848), Kilham (Norris 1841), and Norris (1841) prepared for the use of the Niger Expedition.   By far the most important of these and a true landmark in the history of African linguistics is the *Polyglotta Africana* of S. W. Koelle (1854).   Unlike other works based on secondary collections which, therefore, varied in the specific words collected, in the methods of transcription, and in general reliability, Koelle compiled this material at first hand from repatriated slaves in Freetown, using a standard word list and a uniform method of transcription based on the as yet unpublished system of Lepsius (1858), which appeared a few years later in the latter's *Standard Alphabet.*   The *Polyglotta* contains about 250 words and phrases in approximately 200 languages.

The first half of the nineteenth century saw not only the remarkable increase in the number of African languages for which at least minimal vocabulary became available, but also a whole series of grammars and dictionaries of individual languages which both quantitatively and qualitatively far exceeded the sum total of what was produced in the preceding centuries.   These works were all produced in response to the linguistic needs of the rapidly growing missions and were in general carried out by men who were not primarily interested in linguistic study for its own sake. During the first half of the nineteenth century, linguistics had few professionals, and these were almost all occupied with questions of Indo-European comparative linguistics based on works with written documents.   On the other hand, and in considerable independence of this trend, the bases of articulatory phonetics were being worked out chiefly in England and Germany.   In African linguistics certain individuals might be singled out as professionals in the sense that, while fully in sympathy with the movement for the evangelisation of Africa, they were mainly moved by a scientific interest in the languages for their own sakes and were not confined to the study of one or at most two languages which almost inevitably accompanied missionary interest in language.   Barth, the explorer, and Koelle might be mentioned as professionals, while a borderline case like Christaller — a true virtuoso in language description — shows how uncertain was the dividing line between professional and non-professional.

The difference was indeed more one of interest and outlook than of presence or absence of professional training, for, in descriptive linguistics at least, there was little training to impart.   Under these conditions, the untrained specialist working in 'exotic' languages during this period might have more to impart than to learn. This situation can be documented from the important matter of tonal distinctions in African languages.   The vast majority of African languages are now known to be tonal.   Tonal distinctions are particularly important in many of the West African languages which were among the first objects of study.   In spite of the fact that the phenomenon as such was long familiar in the case of Chinese, contemporary phonetic theory provided no framework for the recognition and analysis of tonal systems. Tone is not indicated by Koelle in his *Polyglotta*, nor is it found in the *Standard Alphabet* of Lepsius, intended as an application of the most advanced phonetic knowledge of the time to the orthography of African and other non-European languages.

Tone seems in fact to have been noted first by native speakers of African languages or to have been brought to the attention of European investigators by African informants.   Probably the first example of recognition of tone is in a translation into Gã of the Gospels of Matthew and John, published in 1843 and composed by A. W. Hanson, a mulatto who was a native speaker of Gã.   Bishop Crowther (1852, 1864), himself a Yoruba, was likewise a pioneer in the recognition of tone not only in his native Yoruba but in other African languages. The true founder of African tonal studies is, however, J. G. Christaller (1893) who in his studies of Twi first put tonal analyses on a firm basis. Christaller himself tells us that his attention was first drawn to the subject by an African.

In spite of its disregard of tone (and it seems likely that Lepsius ignored it because he did not consider it necessary to indicate it in an orthography), the two editions of the *Standard Alphabet* represent a considerable achievement. The state of knowledge regarding African languages had now reached a point where individual unco-ordinated orthographic decisions, frequently based on the differing ortho-graphic practice of European languages, could no longer be tolerated. This was particularly the case where differing orthographies and standardised linguistic forms for the same language were propagated by different missions. When the Secretary of the Church Missionary Society wrote to his Parisian counterpart announcing the glad news of the translation of the New Testament and Psalms into the Chwana language, the latter replied: 'But is it not sad that these thousands of copies already published are entirely unavailable and sealed to our French missionaries who labour among the same people, and to all those who have received instruction from them, simply because they make use of another orthography?' (Lepsius 1863: 29).

The CMS was the prime instigator in the movement for standard orthographic practice for African languages and officially adopted the Lepsius system. Greatly helped by these powerful auspices, the *Standard Alphabet* was widely diffused and held the field as the only commonly accepted system of transcription until well into the twentieth century. As with later attempts, however, it often failed to dislodge already well-accepted orthographies. In addition to its gradual obsolescence in the face of advancing phonetic knowledge, it suffered from a further handicap. Lepsius, in his passionate espousals of the principle of one symbol for each sound and his opposition to new invented symbols, necessarily resorted to the use of numerous diacritics. The psychological and social factors involved in writing systems, of course, were not realised by Lepsius and those associated with him. In practice the use of diacritics has often encountered opposition and tended to be disregarded in actual use even when officially part of an orthographic system.

The *Standard Alphabet* was significant in yet another respect. The appendix to the second edition of 1863 contains, along with similar material from other parts of the world, a table of African languages containing a virtually complete classification of the languages of the continent. Earlier classificatory essays had all left considerable areas of vagueness. This first version of Lepsius' classification was followed in only a few years by the first version of its chief rival, that of Friedrich Müller (1867).

Lepsius' classification was set forth in revised form in his elaborate *Einleitung über die Völker und Sprachen Afrikas* to his Nubian grammar (1880). The key principle of Lepsius' classification was the typological criterion of noun classification systems, particularly the presence or absence of sex gender. Sex gender was present in Indo-European (Japhetic), Semitic and Hamitic, and was viewed as an advanced trait. Chiefly for this reason Lepsius posited their ultimate relationship in a 'Noahite' speech family. In this general approach he followed the earlier work of Bleek, and like Bleek he assigned Hottentot to Hamitic because of its possession of sex gender. Among basically Negro languages he considered Bantu with its non-sex gender as fundamental, while the remaining Negro languages were considered to be mixed, having undergone Hamitic influence. Lepsius, then, lists

African languages under four rubrics: 1 Bantu; 2 Mixed Negro; 3 Hamitic; 4 Semitic. These are viewed as forming two fundamental groupings: (a) Bantu and Mixed Negro; and (b) Hamitic and Semitic.

Friedrich Müller's revised classification is found in his *Grundriss der Sprachwissenschaft* (1884) in which all of the world's known languages are classified on the assumption of a thorough-going coincidence between race and language. The various grand divisions of Muller's comprehensive work are called 'the languages of the straight-haired peoples', 'the languages of the woolly-haired peoples', etc. On this assumption Hottentot, in contrast to Lepsius' treatment of it as Hamitic, is considered ultimately to be related to the languages of the frizzly-haired Papuans. The bulk of African languages spoken by Negroes are divided into African Negro and Kaffir (i.e., Bantu) of which, in diametric opposition to Lepsius, he considered the former primary and the latter derivative. A number of languages spoken by Negroes considered to be culturally more advanced were separated from the bulk of Negro languages and assigned to a new Nuba-Fulah group whose speakers were considered racially allied to Dravidians and Mediterraneans as curly-haired. A classification grounded on Müller's work, but without the substructure of racial theory and the accompanying extra-continental connections, was set forth in R. N. Cust's well-known work, *A Sketch of the Modern Languages of Africa* (1883), and in this guise Müller's work was popularised in the English-speaking world. In Cust's version there were six families in Africa: 1 Semitic; 2 Hamitic; 3 Nuba-Fulah; 4 Negro; 5 Bantu; 6 Hottentot-Bushman.

The same decade which saw the first version of the Müller and Lepsius classifications was also noteworthy for the appearance of the first comparative historical grammar of a group of languages, the pioneer work of W. H. I. Bleek (1862–69) on Bantu. The appearance of two general classifications and of the first comparative work within the same decade is a significant indicator of the impressive accretions to the knowledge of African languages during the first half of the nineteenth century. That Bantu should have been the first language group to receive comparative treatment is not surprising. The historical linguistic method is most easily applicable — particularly in the absence of early written documentation — to an extensive group of closely related languages; and Bantu was the only one to fulfil this requirement. Bleek's methodology still recalls the pioneer Indo-European comparative method of the period of Bopp and Grimm. Although superseded by the later work of Meinhof (1932, 1948), it can still be read with profit by the professional linguist.

The remainder of the nineteenth century and the first decade of the twentieth century were marked, both quantitatively and qualitatively, by a steady growth of descriptive knowledge. Classificational problems were temporarily in abeyance as it became apparent that, in spite of the great increase in descriptive knowledge, only the surface had been scratched and a vast world of African linguistic phenomena still remained for investigation. During this period the extent of professionalisation increased, and for the first time systematic efforts were undertaken to provide linguistic training of missionaries and professional linguists with a primary regional interest in Africa. By now scientific phonetics and the methods of training by which this knowledge might be applied had advanced to the point where they could provide important aid to those who had to deal with African languages. In consequence there was now a significant difference in the results obtained by trained as against untrained observers. During this period the first journal devoted chiefly to African language studies made its appearance in Germany: the *Zeitschrift für Afrikanische Sprachen*, founded in 1887. It lasted only until 1890, however, and was followed by the equally abortive *Zeitschrift für Afrikanische und Oceanische Sprachen* (1895–1903). In 1910 the *Zeitschrift für Kolonial-Sprachen* was established. It continues at the present time under the name, *Afrika und Uebersee*.

In comparative linguistics by far the most important contribution was that of Carl Meinhof. His *Grundriss der Lautlehre der Bantusprachen* (1899) is still the basis for historical research in Bantu linguistics. For the first time the concept of sound correspondence was systematically exploited and proto-Bantu forms reconstructed. An important part of this work was an extensive set of such reconstructed forms of substantial and verbal roots. This phonological work was followed by a treatment of comparative Bantu grammar in his *Grundzüge einer vergleichenden Grammatik der Bantusprachen* (1906).

The publication of two important works within a year of each other — Diedrich Westermann's *Die Sudansprachen* (1911) and Meinhof's *Die Sprachen der Hamiten* (1912) — signalled a revived interest in problems of classification. In the former work, whose basic outline was apparently developed in conjunction with Meinhof, Westermann sought to establish a far-flung Sudanic stock, embracing practically all the vast variety of languages that could not be assigned to the relatively well-established Semitic, Hamitic, Bantu or Bushman groups. This work, like Meinhof's comparative Bantu, employed sound correspondence and reconstructed *Urforms*. In his work on the languages of the Hamites, Meinhof (1912) sought to extend the membership of this family beyond more or less traditional bounds with definite overtones of Hamitic racial superiority. He did not find it possible to reconstruct proto-forms because of the very small proportion of vocabulary resemblances found among some of the languages. Although the fivefold scheme which emerged from Meinhof and Westermann's investigations of this period (Semitic, Hamitic, Sudanic, Bantu, Bushman) was for long the standard one, it did not remain unchallenged during the period of its dominance. In particular, Meinhof's assertion regarding the Hamitic affiliations of such languages as Fulani, Masai and Hottentot encountered opposition. Westermann himself in his *Die Westlichten Sudansprachen und Ihre Beziehungen zum Bantu* (1927) limited his earlier notion of a general Sudanic unity to the languages of West Africa, and the relation of this more restricted group to Bantu was, in effect, asserted. Indeed Sir Harry H. Johnston, in his monumental work on Bantu and Semi-Bantu (1919–20), had treated many of the West African languages as affiliated with Bantu (i.e., his 'Semi-Bantu'), though he did so only if they had noun-class prefixes. In spite of these and other dissents, the two works cited earlier — those of Westermann on Sudanic and Meinhof on Hamitic — were of.fundamental importance in that, taken together, they rendered obsolete the earlier efforts of Lepsius and Müller and ushered in the modern period of classification. These combined results of Meinhof's and Westermann's earlier work were largely disseminated in English-speaking countries by the writings of Alice Werner (1915, 1930) and became standard in anthropological and linguistic textbooks and standard reference works.

Brief references may be made at this point to several other classifications of the period following 1910 which did not, with the possible exception of that of Delafosse, attain wide currency. One of these is the classification of A. Drexel (1921–22, 1923–24, 1925), who brought African linguistic stocks into consonance with the ethnologic conclusions of the *Kulturkreislehre* (Culture-Historical School).

Drexel's results in slightly modified form were espoused by W. Schmidt (1926), at the time the acknowledged leader of this school, in his general work *Die Sprach-familien und Sprachkreise der Erde*.   The well-known French Africanist, M. Delafosse, grouped Negro-African languages into sixteen branches in his chapter, 'Les langues du Soudan et de la Guinée' in Meillet and Cohen's *Les Langues du Monde* (1924).   In contrast to the German investigations of the time, Hamitic was reduced to a minimum of Berber, Egyptian and Cushitic, and all other non-Semitic, non-Khoisan languages were treated as forming a single vast Negro-African family.   In addition to the sixteen non-Bantu branches enumerated in his article, Delafosse evidently considered that Bantu also was a part of this Negro-African unity.   Delafosse's nomenclature for specific branches and something of his general point of view are still current among some French linguists.   Starting in her earlier work from this same notion of a single Negro-African family, Mlle Homburger (1941) ultimately espoused a theory of Egyptian and, without being viewed as contradictory, even a Dravidian origin for all African-Negro languages.   Although this point of view has found some echoes in current pan-African theorising, it seems to have acquired no adherents among scholars professionally concerned with the study of African languages.

In descriptive method, the period subsequent to 1910 saw increased application of the methods of phonetic science to the analysis of African languages.   A memorandum of the International African Institute (1927), entitled *Practical Ortho-graphy of African Languages*, resumed the task of the unification of transcriptional practice and the standardisation of orthographies to replace the long obsolescent *Standard Alphabet* of Lepsius.   Both in theoretical approach and in the actual symbols suggested, this work was in close conformity with the principles of the International Phonetic Association.   The state of professional phonetic knowledge of African languages during this period is most clearly reflected in D. Westermann and I. C. Ward's *Practical Phonetics for Students of African Languages* (1933), still an indispensable work.

The tonal studies of I. C. Ward in Efik (1933), Ibo (1936) and Yoruba (1938), the various grammars and dictionaries of R. C. Abraham, starting with his collabora-tive study with J. Bargery, on Hausa in the 1930s, and the remarkable phonetic study by D. M. Beach of Hottentot (1938) introduced a new level of phonetic accuracy and attention to detail.   These and other works of the period between the first and second world wars, however, reflect the normal time gap between theoretic linguistic developments in the centres of research and their application to Africa; they show practically no evidence of the new structuralist tendencies in linguistics or of the key concept of its initial period: the phoneme.   In grammatical analysis, however, C. M. Doke (1935) was a pioneer in seeking to develop grammatical categories which would more accurately reflect Bantu linguistic structure than did those of traditional grammatical analyses.   His work in a manner independently paralleled that of F. Boas' even earlier concern with discovering the functionally relevant categories of Amerindian languages.   Structural methods in phonology began to be applied mainly after the second world war by American structuralists, such as Welmers (1945), by members of the British Firthian school, and by certain Belgian, and more recently by French, linguists (Meeusen 1954; De Rop 1958).

In the period following 1910, the completion of the effective occupation of Africa by the colonial powers brought with it a need for information about local language distributions and, in some situations, a demand for knowledge of these languages for administrative purposes. In particular the policy of Indirect Rule in certain British-administered areas had a linguistic corollary. The use of African languages in an educational system in which government rather than the traditional mission assumed an increasing rcle and in which official status was given to certain languages (e.g., Hausa in northern Nigeria and Swahili in parts of East Africa), created a demand for systematic linguistic research and language instruction. These tendencies were by no means confined to British areas but were perhaps more pronounced here because of their close connection with an explicitly formulated policy. German centres, such as that at Hamburg, had existed, but the School of Oriental and African Studies of London University (founded in 1916), contrasted with such earlier centres by developing a particularly strong emphasis on instruction in African languages along with an emphasis on research into the indispensable background of the languages. The School of Oriental and African Studies, of course, is not exclusively linguistic. In other metropolitan countries and in response to similar needs, research institutes were organised in which linguistics had an important place and which in some cases (e.g., Institut Français d'Afrique Noire in Dakar), were located in Africa itself.

The political events of the period following the second world war, particularly the sweeping decolonisation which reached its climax in 1960 and 1961, have as yet had relatively minor repercussions in the field of African linguistics. The rapidly increasing involvement of the United States in Africa, as in other non-Western areas, produced the need for practical language instruction with its correlates of efficient instructional material based on linguistic research and the training of linguists specialised in African languages. Governmental efforts, particularly those initiated under the National Defense Educational Act and various university programs in African studies, usually with Foundation support, have served to advance African linguistic studies in the United States to the point where American efforts can be considered of major significance. British and European continental centres have even increased their efforts, despite disengagement from direct political responsibilities. Russian and other East European states have significantly expanded their facilities for the study of African languages; they are, however, as yet little developed as compared to those of Western Europe and the United States. As in other areas of scholarship, African activity is beginning to make itself significantly felt, but the advanced level of academic training required for professional linguistic activities and their relative remoteness from the practical needs of developing countries have thus far limited this participation. The efflorescence of African interest in things African, however, as evidenced by the founding of programs of African studies in African universities, and the demand for a place for the study of African languages in the curriculum, are producing a demand for linguistic specialists which cannot but stimulate the scientific study of African languages by African scholars in the immediate future.

The marked increase in scholarly activity connected with African language in the period after the second world war is evidenced by *Afrika und Uebersee*, the post-war continuation of the older *Zeitschrift für Eingeborenen-Sprachen*, and by the founding of two new journals. *African Language Studies* was instituted in 1960 as an organ of the staff of the School of Oriental and African Studies of London University. In 1962 the *Journal of African Languages* was founded as an international venture with an editorial board of broad representation under the editorship of Professor Jack Berry, also of the School of Oriental and African Studies. In South Africa *African*

Studies continues a well-established tradition of linguistic researches concentrated on languages of that area.

Paralleling its well-known *Ethnographic Survey of Africa* series, the International African Institute has sponsored the *Handbook of African Languages*: a set of survey volumes which began in 1947 and has already covered all of Africa south of the Sahara. The purpose of this series is to furnish information regarding the geographical distribution, population statistics, linguistic classification and basic bibliography of African languages.

In descriptive research, the application of structuralist methods, particularly to phonology, in the period following the second world war has already been mentioned. The application to African language research of the phonetic instrumental methods which developed in the post-war period, particularly the sound spectrograph, is still in its infancy. However, several African institutions of learning now have well-equipped laboratories, and significant results may be anticipated.

In comparative reconstruction linguistics, the only well-developed field has been, as in the past, that of Bantu studies. Significant extensions and corrections of the basic work of Meinhof have appeared in the post-war period in the work of Meeusen (1954, 1960), de Rop (1960), Greenberg (1955, 1963) and others. The vast Bantu etymological project of Malcolm Guthrie (1948, 1953) of the School of Oriental and African Studies — which involves the identification for a large number of languages of original Bantu roots as well as those of more recent data in more restricted Bantu areas — promises important results for the subgrouping of Bantu as well as for other comparative Bantu problems.

In the classification of African languages, the post-war period was marked by the appearance of a new overall general classification: that of the present writer (Greenberg 1955, 1963). Some of the features of this classification were already adumbrated in the work of other scholars. It was noted earlier that Westermann himself in his work, *Die Westlichen Sudansprachen und Ihre Beziehungen zum Bantu* (1927), had pointed to the relationship of Western Sudanic to Bantu and had in effect destroyed the by then orthodox system which classified the basic language families of Africa as Hamitic, Semitic, Sudanic, Bantu and Bushman. The present writer has sought to identify linguistic stocks by criteria which reflect actual historical common origin and clearly to distinguish such results from those which employ typological resemblances. The basic assumption is that only resemblances simultaneously involving sound and meaning are relevant for historically valid classifications; the use of sound only (as in such classificational rubrics as tonal versus non-tonal languages) or meaning only (as in the concept of non-class or gender languages) do not of themselves lead to genetic classifications.

A significant recent trend is the interest in the hitherto neglected Creoles, pidgins and lingua francas. With occasional exceptions, linguists had reflected the popular disdain for such forms of speech and therefore had not considered them worthy objects of study. It is now realised that the rise and spread of such languages is an important socio-linguistic phonemenon which has become intensified with urbanisation and industrialisation. The purely linguistic attention to these languages, therefore, is inextricably connected with the recent interest in socio-linguistic problems in general.

At several points of the historical résumé presented here, the time lag between the development and application of theoretic linguistic insights to Western European languages and their appearance in African linguistic studies was noted. This peripheral status, of course, is found to an even greater degree in Oceanic and Amerind linguistic studies. It is shared with other disciplines with the exception of anthropology, whose very raison d'être has been the study of non-Western areas. As in these other disciplines, there has been a particularly marked increase of interest in non-Western areas in recent years, but linguistics as a whole — excluding its anthropological branch — is still largely limited in its interest to a single language family: Indo-European; this is particularly the case with respect to comparative studies.

The study of non-Western areas by all the social sciences involves in part the extension of already well-developed techniques on a scale comparable to their employment in Western areas. Beyond this, however, the characteristic contrasts with phenomena encountered in a more familiar cultural setting constitute a challenge to existing theory, a stimulus to the development of new, cross-culturally oriented methods, and the formulation of generalisations valid for all areas, Western and non-Western alike. This challenge of the unfamiliar, of course, is not totally new in linguistics. At the very outset of modern linguistic science, it was the encounter with Sanskrit which led to the formulation of the Indo-European hypothesis, even though the data from more familiar languages in Europe had in fact long been sufficient for its development.

In the light of the factors just enumerated, some of the major desiderata for further linguistic research in Africa may be indicated. The following may be mentioned as applications of basic techniques. In Africa, as in other non-Western areas, we still lack in many instances the most elementary information of all: the geographical distribution, degree and type of dialect variation and population statistics of individual languages. In descriptive linguistics, the number of first-rate grammars and dictionaries, even of major languages, is still not in any way equal to our knowledge of comparable phenomena in Europe. The more advanced and specialised studies of particular syntactic phenomena are almost totally lacking. Such studies, of course, stand in a special relation to the technical study of African literary style, which has barely begun. The technique of dialect geography, so highly developed in Europe and the United States, has received only marginal applications. The descriptive data asked for here, it should be pointed out, are not only fundamental to linguistic studies as such, particularly to comparative studies, but are also important to the provision of the practical bases on which administrators can formulate intelligent policies towards linguistic-tribal groupings and plan the development and implementation of educational programs.

The large contributions, past and present, of relatively untrained investigators, particularly those connected with missions, has come in for repeated mention. The level of professional competence of such workers has risen greatly in the recent past, and the increase of systematic advanced training for them has great potential value. The archiving of existing, but only locally known, material and the exploitation of local knowledge of linguistic distributions can add greatly to the store of generally available knowledge in the areas just mentioned.

As has been evident from the foregoing survey, in the field of comparative linguistics only the Bantu languages have enjoyed a development at all comparable to that of historical linguistic studies elsewhere. There has also been some comparative study of a preliminary nature directed towards a few more restricted groupings, notably the Mende group of Niger-Congo and Nubian (Welmers 1958;

Zyhlarz 1949–50). Westermann's etymologies (1927), used in conjunction with the large amount of etymological work already accomplished in Bantu, can serve as a preliminary basis for comparative Niger-Congo studies. In the Afro-Asiatic (Hamito-Semitic) languages, the relatively high development of comparative Semitic studies and Semitic-Egyptian comparisons provide a framework for the historical study of the whole family. In particular the expected further extensions in knowledge of the numerous Chad languages promise to widen significantly the basis of comparative Afro-Asiatic studies. Here and elsewhere the greatest need is for large-scale, phonologically accurate dictionaries as the foundation of etymological studies.

In the virtual absence of early written records (ancient Egyptian, Old Libyan, or Berber, Meroitic, Geez and medieval Nubian are almost the only exceptions), early European transcriptions and the records of African languages spoken by New World slaves can contribute importantly to historical studies. Here almost everything remains to be done. It is likely that there exists a fair number of as yet undiscovered sources of this kind which will supplement the known materials which have not yet been edited or otherwise made generally available to scholars.

Even in the present state of historical linguistic knowledge, there exists the possibility of the careful application of reliable techniques to specific culture-historical problems on a scale much wider than that previously used. Linguistics is in a position to make important contributions to our knowledge of African history. Glottochronology up to now has been applied only on a limited scale to Bantu problems and to the question of the date of separation between Malagasy and the other Malayo-Polynesian languages (Meeusen 1956; Coupez 1956; Olmsted 1957; Dyen 1953). Provided it weathers its present theoretical and methodological crisis, it can provide key information for certain problems of culture history. Even without glottochronology much can be done in the methodologically well-developed areas of the study of loan-words and of the cultural content of proto-vocabularies; this would replace the free-wheeling speculation about ethnic and place names which in the past has unfortunately constituted nearly the sum total of linguistic contributions to African history.

All of the areas just mentioned by and large come under the rubric of the application of well-attested techniques to African subject matter. It is particularly in the interdisciplinary areas such as psycholinguistics and sociolinguistics that, in many instances, problems are still not sufficiently clearly formulated and techniques remain for the most part undeveloped. But it is in these areas that the challenge to creative thinking is greatest and that African problems can play an essential role. A few randomly chosen possibilities may be cited. Word association techniques have thus far been applied only to a few languages and not at all to African languages. Important here is not only the question of the specific associations but also the role of grammatical classes in association. The study of African noun-class systems in this respect opens up new possibilities. Study of the semantic differential, which has never been tested on speakers of African languages, offers still another area. The South-West Project of the Social Science Research Council has devised tests — applied to monolingual and bilingual speakers of Amerind languages, Spanish and English — which are designed to probe possible effects of linguistic structure on psychological processes. Similar or newly designed tests could be applied in the African situation. In sociolinguistics, detailed studies of the social role of first languages and auxiliary languages, social psychological measures of attitude towards different languages, and the degree and type of multilingualism found in the rapidly growing multi-ethnic urban centres of Africa are but a few of the topics that might be mentioned.

The work already accomplished in the study of African languages, extensive as it is, is thus hardly more than a preliminary sounding into the depths that remain to be penetrated within the vast world of African languages.

16

The Visual Arts   Roy Sieber

> The mind of the Western research-worker is accustomed, by his work on the classics, to
> a reasonable number of new fragments discovered annually by a select band of archaeolo-
> gists. Sudden shocks are coldly received and the select few flee from an avalanche of
> facts. It is admitted that centuries of erudition have amassed materials about the
> Greeks, from which vast edifices have been built. We are accustomed to see these ancient
> bits of masonry slowly rising against the background of our culture: the least stone found is
> transmitted by respectful hands to the workers on the roof. But let thousands of exotic
> cities suddenly spring up, let unusual, strange and shocking façades arise, and they
> depreciate in value through their very number. This excess repels us and, turning our
> backs resolutely on the deluge, we take refuge in our convenient clichés. (*Griaule* 1950.)

I   INTRODUCTION*

TRADITIONAL AFRICAN ART, like most art in the history of the world, was
predominantly a reflection and a reinforcement of values centring on the
security of the individual and the group. From spiritual authority focused in a
mask to worldly prestige demonstrated in architecture or clothing, the arts echoed
the positive aspects of a world view and served actively in the fulfilment of material
and spiritual needs. The tribal artist presented, usually without question, the
normative values of his culture expressed in styles and modes that to a great extent
were fixed. Because of this cultural integration the arts more closely approached
those of Egypt, Greece and the Middle Ages in Europe than more recent arts of the
Western world. This analogy is not totally apt, however, for the arts of royal
prerogative, characteristic of those cultures, were relatively exceptional save
among the Ashanti, Fon, Yoruba of Ife, and in Benin. For the most part, tribal
arts seem to have emerged from the group and not from an aristocratic unit within
that group and imply comparatively broad usage within the tribe.[1]

In view of the high artistic value placed upon African arts by the Western world
in the last half century, it is necessary to note that there is no more validity in the
a priori application of Western aesthetic standards to African art than there is in
applying Western value criteria to African ethics or economics. The non-revolu-
tionary character of the values expressed in African art and the cultural constraints
on the 'freedom' of the artists contradict current Western aesthetic concepts based
on individuality, freedom, invention and protest. It is thus evident that the term
'fine arts', as used in the Western world, is inapplicable to African art, for it tends
to remove the objects from their cultural context and to predicate a non-utilitarian
role. Few if any African arts are conceptualised as inutile. Their significance
and importance relate so directly to their function that comparative aesthetic (in

* Notes and bibliography for this chapter will be found on page 555.

the strict sense of 'beauty') evaluations are difficult to obtain; importance in a functional sense over-rides excellence in a formal sense.

More extensive knowledge of African aesthetics — taken here to mean the relative value placed on various modes and types as well as the explicit and implicit evaluation of the formal (beauty) aspects — most probably will lead to a reassessment of aesthetic values as they obtain in Africa.   Such analyses may also lead to a revaluation of Western aesthetics, which often propounds 'universals' that are in fact conclusions drawn from the limited body of Western art and thought.

There is no culture in Africa which does not have an aesthetic dimension.   Although the visual arts may appear to a minimal degree in some groups, they do not seem to be totally absent anywhere on the continent.   Broadly speaking, some form of visual art, from simple decoration to extensive complexes of sculpture, costume or architecture, is evident in every tribe.

The arts of North Africa are predominantly non-African in orientation.   The archaeological arts of Egypt are African in a geographic sense and to some degree may be African in origin, in so far as certain of the elements contributing to the pre-dynastic mixture that gave rise to Egyptian art and culture were African in origin.   The arts of Egypt may also be of potential interest because of their relationship to sub-Saharan arts (usually overly romanticised) and influence on them (usually overestimated).   Until these problems are solved archaeologically, however, the arts of ancient Egypt are best seen in the light of other Mediterranean and Near Eastern developments.   Similarly, the Roman arts of North Africa are reflective of the developments that occurred on the north coast of the Mediterranean Sea.

Islamic-influenced arts and crafts are found over much of sub-Saharan Africa, particularly in the Sudan and East Africa, and merit study as a part of the larger Moslem world extending from the Near East to Spain.   (This influence, incidentally, carried from Spain to the New World, produced curious parallels between post-conquest decorative motifs of the Indians of the Americas and those of the Sahara and the Sudan.)

Islamic motifs occur predominantly in the decorative arts, including horse-trappings and costume, and in architecture.   This is not unexpected in view of the iconoclasm and concomitant emphasis on the decorative and architectural arts throughout the Islamic world.   Nor is it surprising that the influences of Islam on the figurative arts of sub-Saharan Africa are almost totally negative and destructive. Moslem missionising equated figurative arts exclusively with heathen activities and encouraged — or insisted upon — destruction of existing works and cessation of the production of masks and figurines in particular.

Western influences, particularly those of missionaries, were similarly inimical to the figurative arts.   As early as the sixteenth century, Pigafetta (1597) reports the wholesale destruction of 'idoles' after the conversion of the king of Kongo. Thus for the most part traditional figurative arts have tended to disappear in the wake of systematic conversion either to Christianity or to Islam.   Decorative arts, especially those that are neither figurative nor overtly ritual in character, more easily survived the conflict of religious ideologies.   They often succumbed, however, to the more material aspects of the alien cultures.   The novelty and prestige associated with foreign decorative motifs, clothing, tools, utensils and architecture, despite an often doubtful practicality, gave rise to the *mélange* of North African,

European and traditional fashions in these arts. Only recently, and to a small extent, have traditional or quasi-traditional modes been reinstated: evidence, perhaps, of a growing awareness of the values of heritage.

It is pertinent to divide the arts into those of permanent or semi-permanent materials (stone, terra-cotta, metal) and those of perishable materials (wood and other vegetable materials, unfired clay or mud).   The former are accessible to archaeological investigation: that aspect of art history that concerns itself with the origins, sequences, dates, distribution and movements of materials, modes and styles. Unfortunately there has been little systematic archaeology of this sort in sub-Saharan Africa.   As a result there is little to report except to note that what is known raises a series of provocative questions that indicate the pressing need for more work.   The terra-cotta figurine complex of the Nok culture of Northern Nigeria (900 BC–AD 200), for example, awaits systematic investigation and analysis, including an assessment of its possible relationship to the early art of Ife.   The history of metals needs sorting out, as in the cases, for example, of tin working at Nok and of copper and brass casting by the lost-wax process.   The earliest examples of the latter, recently discovered in the Congo, appear to be decorative copper pieces dated at about AD 700.   The history of iron in sub-Saharan Africa is of great potential importance for what it will reveal about the craft itself and about the industry as a source of tools for other craftsmen and artists.   The nature and character of wood carving, decorative or sculptural, is greatly dependent upon the iron adze.   Because iron thus becomes an adjunct to the history of wood carving, the significance of further research in the history of iron-working can hardly be overemphasised.

So little is known of stonework — at best a rare commodity — that it is possible to note only that it is found, primarily in the form of sculptures of apparently varying age, thinly and discontinuously scattered over much of the sub-continent.   No known examples seem to relate closely to Egypt or the classical world; their origins and derivations are unclear.

Pottery and terra-cotta are widespread, but again there are few systematic studies of distribution or sequence.   Concomitantly, attempts at relative dating encounter extremely difficult problems, for there are few long-inhabited sites such as the *tells*, those archaeological godsends of the Near East.   Nevertheless, until the problems are approached intensively and imaginatively, an *a priori* pessimism is distinctly out of order.   It is perhaps necessary to recall that the archaeological methods developed for Egypt, the Near East, Europe and the Americas came to differ as the demands of given situations differed, and as it became apparent that the distinctive aspects of the terrain and the cultures themselves required modified or new modes of attack.

The arts in perishable materials are rather better known and more extensively reported.   Much of the material is imbedded in anthropological reports and is usually descriptive of one moment in time and space.   Data extracted and compiled from such published reports combined with museum collection data (of itself often unpublished) form the basis of most published surveys of African art.   The materials are arranged geographically, by area and tribal styles, in the classic works of Kjersmeier (1935–38), Olbrechts (1959), Wingert (1950) and von Sydow (1954), and those of Fagg and Elisofon (1958), Trowell (1954, 1960), Leuzinger (1960) and Himmelheber (1960).   With one exception these surveys deal exclusively with sculpture; the other arts are almost totally neglected.   The exception is Trowells' work (1960), which, although admirable as a beginning, has the disadvantage of attempting too much and accomplishing too little.

Certainly this horizontal approach is valid. Perhaps it is, for the moment, the only valid method for a survey. What is known of historical sequence, influences and cultural functions, furthermore, can be imbedded as small vertical digressions in the presentations.

It is increasingly evident that a tremendous amount of work remains to be done in the study of the arts. Shockingly little has been published on any area except sculpture: a situation which stems, no doubt, from the ethnocentric heritage of Western aesthetic attitudes. Next to nothing exists in print about architecture, weaving, pottery, painting or costume. Even in the realm of sculpture, few field studies delimit styles and sub-styles, describe types, and explore the cultural function and the value context of the objects. It seems imperative that such data be collected where it is still possible to obtain a relatively clear picture of the traditions of style, mode, function and context.

In short, what now exist as minor vertical digressions in horizontal surveys, must become the subjects of major studies. Research and analysis of this nature are not totally absent, but little of it is definitive. At best, hints as to the direction research must take are to be found, for example, in the corpus of material now becoming available for Ife, in the writings of Bernard Fagg, William Fagg (1960), and Frank Willett; in the depth studies of the Dogon by Griaule (1938: Forde 1954); or in Beier's study of the carvings in one Yoruba town (1957). Of itself *African Worlds* (Forde 1954) points a direction of great use to the art historian, as does Fr. Tempels' study of Bantu philosophy (1956). It is significant that these studies are not conducted in the manner of the traditional, Western, specialist-oriented disciplines of art history or anthropology; instead they seem to anticipate a methodology essentially interdisciplinary in character.

In order to discuss methodology it is first necessary to posit a discipline, and, as William Fagg (1960: 463) has pointed out:

> We must first note that we have already begged a very large question by using the word 'discipline', for it is hard indeed to detect any quality of discipline when we look at most of the publications and activities in the field of tribal art in the past few years. Much confusion reigns because of the lack of any generally accepted principles of study and criticism and for the more positive reason that the recent and current popularity of African art has been based in large part not on genuine scholarly interest but on fashion — a fashion which may suitably go under the name of *négrérie*. We may ask ourselves where Oriental studies would be today if they had been as largely based on the ignorant *chinoiserie* and *japonaiserie* of eighteenth century society.

Early studies (better, 'appreciations') of African arts were based on two different levels of approach. On the first level, the sculptures in particular became fuel for expressionist fires early in the twentieth century. Artists, out of their rejection of the classical and naturalistic modes of Western art, embraced the new and exciting world of forms that African (and other co-called 'primitive') arts offered, quite ignoring the cultural and historical *milieux* from which they sprang and from which, most probably, much of their admired vitality derived.

The concept of the 'noble savage', which had caught the fancy of nineteenth-century artists, was pushed outward from the peasants of Millet to Gauguin's Pacific natives.   This segment of the romantic movement was predominantly focused on exotic *subject matter* — the unfamiliar, displaced in time or space — presented in a realistic manner that was totally European in origin.   Although a few non-Western stylistic or compositional devices were borrowed near the end of the century (as in Gauguin's conscious use of Egyptian and Cambodian sources), it was not until early in the twentieth century that the aesthetic merit of the *arts* of the 'savages' became generally accepted.

Significantly this occurred at almost the same moment that Palaeolithic cave art came to be regarded as genuine and meritorious.   Thus, at a single blow, these arts were accepted as art, and the evolutionist use of 'early', 'simple', 'primitive', 'crude', or 'unsophisticated', as nearly synonymous terms applicable to both prehistoric and recent 'primitive' arts (the one ancient, the other frozen anciently), lost validity.   This acceptance, possibly more than any other attitude, contributed an antidote to the missionary-inspired attitude of repugnance and to the accusations of spiritual darkness that was thought to surround the traditional arts of the 'benighted savage'.   Certainly the missionary zeal that placed the origin of these arts in spiritual darkness, and the view that the objects themselves were akin to the most advanced experimental and expressionist modes of contemporary art, effected a curious situation.

The second early approach to the arts of sub-Saharan Africa (and to the arts of Oceania on which, indeed, rather more work was done), was the collection of scientific evidence and the interpretations of data that would serve to correct both of the afore-mentioned attitudes.   Work of this nature, begun by nineteenth-century anthropologists and museologists, unfortunately withered in the face of the undisciplined exuberance of the artists and critics.   Despite certain interpretational shortcomings that now seem obvious (as, for example, the *in situ* evidence of evolution where all steps in the development of a type were discerned in contemporaneous manufacture), the cessation of those studies left a gap that it may already be too late to fill.

Whatever the loss, it is evident that to avoid an ethnocentric bias—aesthetic or ethical — in the attempt to understand the arts of Africa, it is crucial that the methods and tools developed by the anthropologist be adapted for use by the art historian.

Herskovits has stated:

What [ethnology] now offers students of art history and art processes parallels what it has offered to those with other interests traditionally centred in our own culture, who seek to understand materials from other cultures.   Such understanding can obviously be arrived at only if it is recognized that the approach to be applied must cut across specialities no less than across cultures. From this point of view, it becomes apparent that while the student of the arts has a background, a training, even an idiom that the ethnologist does not control, yet by the same token the student of culture has a method of gathering the facts concerning peoples of differing ways of life that are his by virtue of his special training.   The study of African art must today be thought of, then, as the analysis of a cross-cultural phenomenon which cannot be adequately understood unless its aesthetic values are fully related to its cultural background. (Herskovits 1945.)

The traditional modes of both anthropology — especially those aspects that deal with material culture and values (including religion) — and of art history (particularly stylistics) must be modified or enlarged and combined in order to cope effectively with the arts. The traditional methods of art history that use written documentation to explore iconography, historical sequence and dating, and the like, must now be augmented by anthropological techniques of acquiring data and their interpretation: the collection of oral traditions and the use of field techniques. Anthropologists must become aware of the degree of pervasiveness of the arts; a new look must be taken at material culture studies in the light of the value structures expressed (or symbolised) in the arts and crafts in particular. The time has come for review and revaluation of the entire area of material culture.

The visual arts may be approached from a number of points of view. Just as the structure of music may be analysed in terms of pitches organised into temporal patterns and dance in terms of choreography, the visual arts may be analysed in terms of elements of form, principles of design, and stylistics. Stylistics is that study of art which attempts to define those characteristic formal aspects or details that differentiate the works of one period, place or artist from all others. It is evident that such studies emphasise the work of art as an entity, as a thing in itself. Taken by themselves, structural and stylistic analyses take little note of art as the product of human behaviour and even less of its relationships to human actions and reactions.

There can be no argument about the validity of intensely specialised structural studies as constituting one aspect or level of analysis. The work of art is the point of departure and the point of return for all studies legitimately to be included in the discipline. But the more fully all facets of the work are known — from the most intensively specialist dissection of a motif to the broadest exploration of its cultural role — the more fully is it understood. Conversely, the more limited the mode of attack, the less useful is that knowledge for broad comparative studies in the history of world arts, or, for that matter, in the history of aesthetics.

For reasons such as this, it is in the realms of studies of creativity and of the 'ramifications of art in the society at large' (Report of the Committee of Fine Arts and the Humanities 1961: 22) that studies of general value may be expected.

> All forms of cultural anthropology, including the morphological or technological study of objects of material culture, are in the last resort studies of human behavior. The study of artists is, I suppose, the ultimate purpose of research in African art, and if in field studies we could learn all that there is to know about African artists, then there would be little or no need for other methods of study. But what can still be learnt from the carvers themselves has been reduced by time and the advance of civilization to a rather small compass. As with the Sibylline books in early Rome, this shrinking of source material only enhances the need and urgency of collecting it. (Fagg 1960: 464.)[2]

Of particular importance in studies of the artist and of creativity as an aspect of human behaviour

> . . . are the conceptualizations of the product and the process of creation, as well as the multiple problems of who the creators are, why people produce

art objects, the attitudes toward creation and contemplation, the role of the creator in the society, and other like matters. (Report of the Committee of Fine Arts and the Humanities 1961 : 22.)

Surprisingly few reports deal, even in part, with the artist. Himmelheber's *Negerkünstler* (1935) is the only extensive published study of artists and of their modes of training and work. Griaule, in *Masques Dogon* (1938), Herskovits, in *Dahomey* (1938), and William Fagg, in *De l'Art des Yoruba* (1951), include descriptions or notes that add significantly to the small corpus of knowledge. Because the descriptions infer the techniques employed, they are also useful in preparations for field studies.

Three attitudes seem to have combined to limit if not negate research into the cultural functions of the arts: First, missionaries for the most part saw many of the arts, sculpture in particular, as the accoutrements of heathenism. Secondly, current Western aesthetics severely limits the role of the 'fine arts' to a single cultural dimension. These two points have already been touched on. Thirdly, academic specialism to a great extent precluded the examination of the interactions of art, religion, values, law, economics and politics. These attitudes must be re-examined if future research is to avoid covert but nonetheless significant ethnocentric commitments which, because they are unidimensional, have severely limited past studies in depth of African art.

The study of the arts in their cultural context is of particular importance with regard to Africa because of the degree to which the arts traditionally interpenetrated with other aspects of life. 'Context' may be understood as the cultural environment in which an aspect of culture — in this instance, art — exists. This environment is more than a simple time and place setting: it includes both individual and group responses, associations, and behavioural patterns related to the work of art.[3]

In the light of the general observation that three levels of approach exist — the technical, the processual, and the contextual — some reference to the relevance of this approach to disciplinary and interdisciplinary studies seems in order. Perhaps this can best be indicated by an outline that purports to be no more than suggestive in nature.[4]

II DISCIPLINARY STUDIES

I. PURE RESEARCH WITHIN THE SUB-DISCIPLINE

Studies of this kind, conducted within that segment of world art which refers particularly to sub-Saharan Africa, are the backbone of all later interpretative analyses, although both can be designated as primary research.

(i) Field studies for the collection and collation of data about the object, its author, and its cultural context (tribe, sub-tribe, village, artist, age, material, indigenous aesthetics, behaviours, concepts, value patterns, attitudes, roles, functions).[5]

(ii) The correlation of field studies with the data of other disciplines; for example, history, anthropology, archaeology, economics, political science.

(iii) The analyses of the field data: technical, functional, processual, aesthetic, etc.

4. Descriptions, interpretations, and conclusions based on field studies and their correlations and analyses.

It is probable that most studies will be horizontal, that is, fixed to a fairly recent time phase, because the basic data does not exist in historical depth. It has been noted that most studies of African art have been horizontal, presented predominantly in terms of the geographic distribution of tribal styles. This is perhaps inevitable, because the tribal arts of Africa for the most part have been compounded of perishable materials. The climate and the termites have taken an almost total toll of objects older than a few generations at most, and this means that much of the past is lost to the historian. At the same time it is quite possible that the arts have maintained a vitality and an inventiveness because of the absence of fixed prototypes and the loss of spirit through slavish copies of such prototypes. Where the latter has — exceptionally — occurred, as with Benin brasses, imitative degeneration is apparent. In short, 'the termite insures that each generation shall carry on the tradition of skill' (Goodwin 1958: 95).

There is no evidence that African arts were in the past fixed, frozen or unchanging. Indeed, one of the greatest challenges to the student of African art is the reconstruction, where possible, of the unrecorded history of change, development and cross-influences of tribal styles. The art historian, however, must be at least reasonably respectful of his data, and to this point, he can establish a realistic picture of the arts — in perishable materials at any rate — only as it existed within the past century or two. This, then, he must treat as his base line in order to analyse the visible nature of changes in materials and style; he must also treat it as the base line for studies in the meaning and function of art.

Any object or skill or concept which was once 'out of context' — that is, which at a given point in time was not part of an associative complex — can, in time acquire a fixed place. It will reach that stage of acceptance that no longer identifies its external origin or its grafted character. From the evidence available, it seems that this process of adaptation was quite slow in Africa.

There is some evidence, furthermore, that Yoruba style changed little over 250 years. Thus, without desiring to over- or underestimate its pace, it may be suggested that traditional tribal arts in Africa in most cases were fairly resistant to change. Except in instances of a massive exterior force, such as Islam or Western civilisation, or occasionally an empire-building group, such as the Bini or Jukun, the pace seems sufficiently slow to permit taking as reasonably fixed the base line which, with some degree of predictable success, can be established.

2. COMPARATIVE STUDIES WITHIN THE CONTEXT OF WORLD ART STUDIES

Disciplinary studies of this kind constitute an area wherein pure research and interpretation can find a larger significance.

(i) The results of primary studies constitute an element in the construction of theories of the pattern of historical sequence; an inductive approach to theories of history. They can serve, furthermore, as a check upon existing hypotheses based for the most part on the studies of the Western arts.

(ii) Similarly, they will constitute an element in the construction of theories of aesthetics (including considerations of object, artist and audience). They can also serve as a check upon existing aesthetic theories, which for the most part are based on studies of Western aesthetics often assumed to be universal in application.

III INTERDISCIPLINARY STUDIES

'The social sciences deal with man as a social animal and the ways in which he solves his social problems in daily living, while the humanities take man beyond his social living into his own distillations of his life experiences' (Merriam 1962: 14–15).

'We can only understand the social system to which it has intimate connections, we can only make real and final sense out of the social system if we understand the humanistic elements through which man makes his comment upon and his distillation of his social experience' (Merriam 1962: 23).

1. THE SOCIAL SCIENCES

(i) *Anthropology:* the relation of the arts to other aspects of culture; functional studies including the arts as mechanisms of social control; the study of cultural dynamics.

(ii) *Economics:* studies of the role of the object and the artist in terms of the economics of specialism; the arts as part of the total economy; patterns of distribution, stimuli to production (or overproduction); luxury or prestige items, conspicuous consumption.

(iii) *Political Science:* art objects as reflective and/or validation symbols of political status, aspirations, succession or prerogative; the use of arts in war.

(iv) *Psychology:* the investigation of the nature of conceptualisations, mental constructs and images as they relate to style and role analyses; art as symbolic of security.

2. THE OTHER HUMANITIES

(i) *Religion:* art and cults, divination, ancestor worship; the interactions of religion, political structure, economics and the arts.

(ii) *Philosophy:* art as an expression of the basic philosophic system; the philosophy of aesthetics.

(iii) *History:* art as an element of historic construction; as one of the content materials of history.

(iv) *The other arts:* the inter-relationships and interdependence of the arts: music, dance, literature.

Much needs to be explored in the adaptation, sharpening and application of methods and tools. Exactly what use can historical linguistics play in the analyses of the distribution and history of style, type or function? Just how can existing records of religion be used to help describe the role of a mask? How do kinship and inheritance patterns affect the transfer of objects or the choice and training of specialists? How are the 'expectations' of an audience with reference to style, type, function and relative excellence to be discerned in order to record these unvoiced aspects of their aesthetic?

These and literally hundreds of other questions spring to mind. As examples they are significant only in that they emphasise that the answers can be found only through an interdisciplinary approach. They also indicate the degree to which anthropologists, linguists, economists, political scientists, and specialists in law and religion can be of immeasurable aid to the art historian. Conversely, he can be of use to them. It is to be doubted that the political scientist can ignore the traditional symbols of authority — the regalia of office, the mask, for example, that symbolises or focuses the spiritual authority of the ancestors vested in the chief-tainship — any more than the British could, finally, ignore the Golden Stool of Ashanti.   Nor can the economist ignore the obvious economic aspects of specialised crafts or the less obvious role of a mask that adjudicates debt disputes.

At the outset it would perhaps be argued that problems of method stand in the way; that is, that the social sciences are objective and scientific, while the humanities are subjective and non-scientific.   This does not seem to me to be a particular problem, for the social sciences are probably less scientific than they might wish to be, and the humanities can afford to bring more of the scientific method into its studies.   Neither side is in such a position that it cannot afford its concessions.   What seems of basic importance in the matter is that both the humanities and the social sciences are interested inevitably in human behavior, and this is the bridge between the two that must never be forgotten (Merriam 1962: 18–19).

Although this paper has been conceived predominantly in terms of traditional, essentially tribal arts, much of it is pertinent to the study of contemporary arts as well.   The need for studies of the traditional arts is imperative, for they have changed or are changing rapidly under the impact of Western influences.   The nature of the contemporary arts, furthermore, can be understood only in the light of the past; that is, viewed in relation to the base lines which the methodology here indicated could supply.

17

Music and the Dance*   Alan P. Merriam

I INTRODUCTION†

DESCRIPTIONS OF AFRICAN music and dance appear in the general literature concerning Africa almost from the earliest publications. Traders, explorers, missionaries, travellers, colonialists—all seem to have had at least a passing interest in the means that Africans use to express themselves in sound and motion, and as a result references to these forms of expression can be counted in the thousands. Yet any sort of systematic study has been long in coming, and it was not until approximately the 1920s that detailed investigations of specific forms of music and dance, or generalisations that sought to reach the essence of these forms, were undertaken. Even of the more scholarly studies, some kinds have tended to take precedence over others, and thus the systematic study of African music and dance is only now beginning to be realised.

The earliest accounts of African music and dance tended to be simply descriptive, and even contemporary studies have continued largely in this vein. Thus the literature on music instruments is enormous—though in most cases non-technical from the standpoint of instrument organology — and purely emotional descriptions of music performances abound. Although contemporary studies of music instruments are couched in much more direct and technical terms and although generalisations about the content of music style are on a highly technical and sophisticated level, these two areas of study still tend to dominate the literature.

Within the last few years, however, ethnomusicologists and ethnochoreographers interested in African studies have begun to realise the broader potentials of their studies, and some students are now analysing music as a guide to human behaviour. In short, the student of the African humanities is increasingly aware today of a dual responsibility that his field of study impresses upon him. His most pressing problems are still those which relate to his own discipline — that is, to the

* Information concerning the Bashi and Basongye people, cited in this paper, was collected during the course of field research in the Congo and Ruanda Urundi in 1951–52 and 1959–60. Grateful acknowledgment is made to the sponsors of this research: the Belgian-American Educational Foundation, the Wenner Gren Foundation for Anthropological Research, the National Science Foundation, and the Program of African Studies, Northwestern University. In addition, appreciation is expressed for the co-operation in the field of l'Institut pour la Recherche Scientifique en Afrique Centrale, and l'Université Lovanium.

† Bibliography for this chapter will be found on page 556.

technical description of the artistic product and its relationships to analogous products in other parts of the world, and to the human behaviour that produces this sound or motion product and the conceptualisations underlying the behaviour. At the same time, he has a second responsibility — in this case to students of other disciplines — to use his knowledge of the humanities in Africa to shed light on other facets of human behaviour, such as the social, political and economic.

Of these two responsibilities or directions of study, more progress has been made in the first. But even here, the relationship of the product to the behaviour that produces it has been little studied, which means, in turn, that the second responsibility has not begun to be probed on more than a superficial level. Further, the study of African music has proceeded much further than that of dance; indeed, little but the most superficial information is known of African dance, though refined techniques for its description and analysis do exist.

This essay, then, will be devoted primarily to the study of African music, though dance will enter wherever possible, and it will be concerned with the major areas of study noted above. Finally, it will confine itself primarily to Africa south of the Sahara, for the two parts of Africa divided by the desert region are represented by two markedly different sound and motion styles. North of the Sahara, music and dance are Arabic, and this influence seems to have begun at a very early date although it is difficult to establish proof of more than physical contact. Archaeological evidence points to very early trade between Yemen and Somaliland, and Egypt was apparently conquered by the Arabic Hyksos as early as *c.* 1700 BC. With the establishment of Islam by Mohammed the Prophet, the Arabic world was unified and Egypt was taken finally and firmly into the Arabian orbit by the seventh century AD. In 1056, the Berber Almoravides became a political force in North Africa in general, and surely from this period at the latest Arabic music and dance styles were firmly established in Africa north of the Sahara (Farmer 1957: 430). Thus in speaking of Africa as a whole, two distinct styles must be considered: the Arabic and the Negro African. It is the Negro African which is of primary interest here.

II   MUSIC AND DANCE AS ARTISTIC PRODUCT

The study of African music as a product rests upon the assumption that any piece of music is a structured entity. This assumption, in turn, refers to cultural fact — i.e., that music is defined as essentially repetitive behaviour which draws together regulated pitch in time in such a manner that the result is pleasing to the people who produce it. There seems to be no reason to contradict this view of the patterned nature of music, for as in any other kind of human behaviour, musical sound can vary only within the limits imposed upon it by the cultural conventions of those who create and listen to it; without patterning, music would become a chaotic succession of noises. Music, then, always has a patterned structure, and the problem of those whose interest lies in the study of the product is to isolate the various aspects of the structure and the inter-relationships among them. In order to do this successfully, emotionally evaluative and subjective approaches, so common in music studies in general, must be discounted and replaced by the most rigorous and objective analyses possible. To this end, ethnomusicologists have devised a series of objective measurements and observations of music structure which are highly technical, often expressed in arithmetic and even statistical terms.

The description of any African music style usually contains observations concerning tonal range, melodic level, melodic direction, melodic contour, melodic intervals and interval patterns, ornamentation and special melodic devices, melodic metre and durational values, formal structure, scale, mode, duration tone and subjective tonic, tempo, rhythm, metre, accompaniment, and various other structural characteristics. Although it is not our purpose here to describe in detail the problems of music structure, the explicit description of the approach to one or two of these problems may perhaps make clearer the nature of this kind of observation.

In analysing melodic level, for example, the student determines the total tonal range of the piece of music, which he expresses in terms of semitones; let us assume, in this case, a range of ten semitones or, expressed in Western terms, an augmented sixth. The student then determines the position of the beginning tone of the song in this total range and expresses that position by a percentage of the total tonal range; if the song begins seven semitones above the lowest tone in the range, the figure is then expressed as $70°$. The position of the ending tone of the song is similarly obtained; in this case, let us assume that the ending tone lies three semitones above the lowest tone, or at the $30°$ point. Thus, the level formula for this particular piece of music is $70° : 30°$, and the level difference is $-40°$. The levels for all songs in a given body of music under analysis are then averaged and a final result reached for the songs as a group.

This particular measurement yields three different bits of information concerning the structure of a piece of music: the position of the beginning tone in relation to the total range; the position of the ending tone in relation to the total range; and the degree of overall melodic movement from beginning to end. The question involved, of course, is the significance of the measurements; without subjecting it to statistical tests of validity, we can say that comparisons among song bodies indicate significant differences. Thus, Kolinski (1949: 208, 210) indicates the following level formulae:

Group	Level Formula	Level Difference
Dahomey	$59° : 26°$	$-33°$
Ashanti	$58° : 28°$	$-30°$
Menominee	$89° : 4°$	$-85°$
Pawnee	$90° : 6°$	$-84°$
Ute	$88° : 9°$	$-79°$

A comparison of these figures indicates a clear relationship between the two West African groups (Dahomey and Ashanti) on the one hand, and a similar relationship among the three American Indian groups on the other. Further, the level formula for a group of Yovu songs from Ruanda (Merriam, 1957b: 937-8) lies between these two groups at $59° : 9°$, with a level difference of $-50°$, indicating that this particular tool of structural measurement apparently distinguishes not only between broad music styles, but also within such styles. This is but a single example of an arithmetic expression of an element of music structure; such examples could be multiplied considerably (Merriam, Whinery and Fred 1956).

The further question here is whether measurements of this kind are statistically reliable; that is, whether such elements of music structure as can be isolated are truly characteristic of a particular style and differentiating between styles. To the best of my knowledge, only one attempt has been made to answer this basic question. In a paper by Freeman and Merriam (1956), Fisher's discriminant function was applied to a single measure: the relative frequency of occurrence of major seconds and minor thirds in two bodies of African-derived music in the New World — that of the Ketu cult of Bahia in Brazil, and the Rada cult of Trinidad. The conclusions were that this simple measure alone serves to distinguish between the two styles with only a 0.09 error, and that had more variables been considered the error would have been substantially reduced. In effect, then, the study indicates that the frequency of occurrence of two kinds of intervals in any body of song is statistically significant to a remarkably high degree. This being the case, it would appear that elements of music structure are sharply diagnostic of style. When we consider that objective details of at least one hundred elements of style can be distinguished, we can begin to appreciate the nature of the precision possible in the description of a style.

The same degree of precision is possible, at least, in the recording of dance, although to the best of my knowledge it has not as yet been reduced to arithmetic or statistical precision. Of the various systems in use for the notation of dance, the best known in America appears to be that introduced by Rudolph Laban in 1928; this notation records the motion of every part of the body and shows style or quality precisely through diacritical symbols for flexion or extension, accent, dynamics and effort (Kurath 1960; Hutchinson 1954). It is probable that characteristic and diagnostic elements of the dance can be segregated in much the same way as that indicated for music.

The remarkable precision with which music and dance can be treated has been consistently overlooked by students of other facets of African behaviour. If we can treat music, for example, with such a degree of exactitude, we should be able to note acculturative processes, trace migrations, chart distributions, study variations, and undertake other kinds of problems with an extremely high degree of certainty. At the same time, the potential of this kind of study has not as yet been thoroughly realised by students of music and dance, though such studies seem certain to appear with increasing frequency as further information is gathered in the field.

Not all aspects of sound and motion can be delineated with such precision as those described here, for basic principles underlying structural organisation are not necessarily subject to objective attack. One such problem which has puzzled students of African music is that involved in the concept underlying African rhythmic and metric organisation. W. E. Ward (1927: 217), for example, felt that, although a number of rhythms and metres are in operation at any given time in any piece of African music, a structural basis is to be found in the organisation of sound produced by the largest drum of the ensemble: 'The other rhythms may have no possible similarity to it and no connection whatsoever, but on the first beat of the big drum all must coincide'. Hornbostel (1928: 25–6) sought the rhythmic principle in the motor behaviour of the drummer, and Waterman (1952: 212) has postulated the concept of the 'metronome sense', which refers to the learned habit of the African listener in supplying a basic framework of beats regularly spaced in time, whether or not these beats are actually struck in percussion or melodic tones. A. M. Jones (1954: 28, 40, passim) refers to the combination of rhythms produced by handclapping and drumming, the former acting as 'an inexorable and mathematical background to the song' and the latter represented by a process called 'crossing the beats'. By the latter, he means that rhythm patterns have defined starting and ending points but that they are never begun at the same point in time when more than one drum is playing.

These varying points of view illustrate that it is not always possible to pinpoint all facets of the organisation of African music; yet it is significant that all these theorists emphasise, in one way or another, the idea that in African music the basic and common principle is the simultaneous use of two or more metres. It seems reasonable to assume that the same is true of African dance; it has often been noted, for example, that dancers appearing after the music accompaniment has been well established do not seem to dance in the same tempo or metre as the music. It has further been suggested that multiple metre may well be present in the movement of different parts of the body; thus, while the arms may be moving in one time relationship to the underlying music pulse, the legs may be moving in another relationship, the shoulders in still another, and so forth.

These general observations about the precision in some areas of sound and motion analysis, and the lack of agreement pointing to a lack of precision in others, lead us in turn to a number of problems confronting the descriptive analysis of African music.

Probably the most difficult of these concerns transcription itself — that is, the transference of African music sounds to paper in an acceptable system of music notation. This process formerly depended exclusively upon the ear of the transcriber, but the introduction of various types of sound recording, particularly magnetic tape, has made it possible to repeat a music performance indefinitely. The extremely unreliable process of transcribing direct from the performer in the field has, therefore, been by-passed and a much higher degree of accuracy reached. The same is true of dance notation as cinematographic recording becomes more and more possible. But problems of interpretation remain severe, simply because one transcriber hears a pattern in one way and another in another (Merriam, 1960).

This difficulty is closely connected with a further problem: the reliability — and even the possibility — of translating a non-Western idiom into a Western system of notation. Some of the difficulties have been overcome through the addition of special music notational symbols to the standard system; but precision appears to be virtually impossible, for. African scales not only fail to coincide with our own tempered scale but, indeed, often show considerable flexibility in regard to pitch. Even in instruments of fixed pitch, the scale is apparently never precisely identical with our own (Tracey 1958). The answer to this problem may lie in two directions: on the one hand, it may be possible that Western notation is sufficiently accurate for many, most or all of the technical problems that need to be solved; on the other, the development of electronic equipment giving absolutely precise notation may help. Such equipment is being developed (Seeger 1951, 1957, 1958).

Further problems appear when the question of sampling is considered. Theoretically, at least, the music universe of any given tribe in Africa is infinite; the problem, then, is to determine what size of sample is needed to yield reliable results, and whether a larger sample will yield significantly different results from a smaller one. Further, we are not yet sure whether one type of song in a given culture is significantly different from another, i.e., funeral and war songs; and if so, whether they must be treated separately or lumped together into a general set of results for the entire body of music.

And finally, in this general set of problems involved in sampling and transcription, there is the question of what constitutes 'musical truth'. Which of the versions of a particular song is to be taken as the 'correct' one? Can averages of style be confidently reached? John Blacking (1959) has noted that the anthropologist reaches a generalised conclusion or a consensus of opinion from the various statements given to him by informants and from his own observation, and he suggests that the same procedure applies equally well to music transcriptions. In his study of Venda ocarinas, for example, he notes that 'the four musical transcriptions in this paper do not represent the exact sounds that are made every time two Venda boys play ocarina duets, but are a synthesis of several performances of the same duets' (p. 15). This technique, however, has elicited little comment from the field of ethnomusicology as a whole, and its fate cannot as yet be determined.

In much the same vein, ethnomusicologists are faced with the problem of generalising about traits of African music style as a whole. The most successful studies made to date seem to be those which concern the broadest characterisation of stylistic traits of African music; there has been but one detailed attempt to delineate music areas in Africa (Merriam 1959). Thus questions of generalising on the product level are serious; they represent, probably more than anything else, the scarcity of detailed technical descriptions of music styles.

Despite these problems, it is clear that those students who are pursuing the descriptive, stylistic study of music structure on a product level have developed a number of techniques admirably suited to their purposes. The problems that remain are those of sharpening the details of these techniques and of obtaining enough materials to enable further generalisations to be made.

III   MUSIC AND DANCE AS BEHAVIOUR

The phrase: 'the study of African music and dance as human behaviour', refers to the fact that music sounds or choreographic motion are actually produced through the active behaviour of some individual or group of individuals. Thus the separation between the product on the one hand, and the behaviour that produces the product on the other, can be made on a conceptual basis, though in fact the two are not separable as forms of activity. Further, any facet of human behaviour is supported by underlying sanctions and values, which may be referred to as the 'conceptualisations' supporting the behaviour that, in turn, produces the product. In its turn, the product itself feeds back upon the conceptualisation as judgments are expressed about whether or not the song or dance has been produced according to the criteria of the particular culture concerned. The artistic product, therefore, represents the end result of certain behaviour patterns: in physical terms, as in plucking a stringed instrument; in general terms, as the musician models his life in particular ways because he is a musician; and in conceptual ways, which underly the behaviour and which, in a never-ending cycle, reinforce acceptable behavioural patterns or induce change in response to unacceptable patterns.

As a simple example, we may cite the *kisaghshi* playing of the Basongye people of the eastern Kasai Province of the Republic of the Congo (Leopoldville). The *kisaghshi* is a widespread African idiophone; in its simplest form it consists of a flat sounding board to which are affixed a series of narrow strips of iron or bamboo in varying lengths. One end of the strips runs under a bridge which holds them in fixed positions, but the opposite ends are left free to be plucked by the player's thumbs. The instrument is known generally as *sanza* in western Africa, as *likembe* or variations thereof in central Africa, and as *mbira* in most of southern and eastern Africa.

The particular form of the instrument among the Basongye is of no special concern here; what is important is the music produced. In order to simplify the example, let us assume that recordings have been made of *kisaghshi* music in the field and then given to an ethnomusicologist in the laboratory for analysis. The point is that, without understanding the conceptualisation and behaviour which has produced the *kisaghshi* music, our hypothetical laboratory analyst will almost unquestionably be led to a number of erroneous conclusions. Depending upon what songs have been recorded, he might well suppose that he is dealing with an instrument of an incredible number of keys, or at least with an instrument which can be tuned during the course of performance, since his total body of transcriptions would encompass a chromatic scale of as much as two octaves. But the behavioural fact is that the Basongye tune the instrument to three different scales, depending upon which class of song is to be performed. Thus *kusaka* songs are performed with what I have called tuning #1; *lumba* and *lunkufi* songs with tuning #2; and *kasema* songs with tuning #3. Or, again depending upon which songs had been recorded, our hypothetical student might well decide that he was dealing with an instrument of ten keys. In this, too, he would be in error, for the instrument always has twelve keys; in tunings #1 and #3, however, the player never uses the first two keys on the left, which in fact are left untuned and unused. Thus, while twelve keys are present, musical behaviour calls for the use of but ten of them. Or again, the student in the laboratory might well consider that he was dealing with but a single set of keys; in concept, however, the Basongye musician sees tuning #3, for example, as providing him with two sets or groups of keys, one of which duplicates the other at higher or lower pitch. Thus, looking at the keys in tuning #3 from left to right, we see that #s 1 and 2 are not used, that #s 3, 4, 10, 11 and 12 form one group referred to as the 'little voices' (in our terminology: the higher sounds), and that #s 5, 6, 7, 8 and 9 form a second active group referred to as the 'big voices' (in English: the lower sounds). Further, the musician conceives of these two active groups of five notes each as being tuned in identical internal relationships, whereas in fact they are not; and this could cause our student considerable difficulty, for he would almost inevitably misrepresent Basongye *kisaghshi* music.

The example used here is a simple one, and yet the point is clear. Without a knowledge both of musical behaviour and of the conceptualisation by Basongye musicians of that behaviour, a true picture of the music product cannot be obtained. And examples could be multiplied almost indefinitely. In xylophone music, the Basongye conceptualise every known bass pattern as having definite starting and ending points. These points are not those at which the Western-oriented musician would place them, and thus without knowledge of the Basongye point of view the transcriber would certainly transcribe the song incorrectly.

On a somewhat different level, I have elsewhere called attention to the Basongye conceptualisation of music as a uniquely *human* phenomenon (Merriam 1962a: 27–8). In a series of aphorismic statements, the Basongye summarise the distinctions made in their world between music on the one hand and non-music on the other; for them non-music includes certain kinds of sounds, such as those made by animals or birds, the wind soughing through the trees, and so forth, while music includes other kinds of sounds.

The Basongye 'theory' of music, then, seems to involve three essential features in the distinction between music and non-music; first, the fact that music always involves human beings, and that those sounds emanating from non-human sources are not music. Second, the musical sounds that humans produce are organized; thus a single tap on the drum is not music, but the drums playing together in the patterned forms which the drummers use, do make music. And third, there must be continuity in time; even all the drums struck but once simultaneously do not make music; they must continue over time (pp. 27–8).

This conception of music as a non-mechanistic, humanly produced phenomenon colours the entire attitude of the Basongye towards their music; without this understanding, the outside observer finds himself at a loss at many points in the system.

It is problems such as these that fall into the behavioural and conceptual aspects of the study of music, and they are, of course, equally important in dance analysis. Answers to these problems will help enormously in understanding the music product on the one hand, and on the other, the relationship of music and dance behaviour to other aspects of culture. This being the case, it seems fruitful to discuss further some of the areas of attack that at present are far too infrequently investigated.

The musician or dancer as a subject for study contributes not only to the elucidation of music and dance behaviour but also to the roles these individuals perform in the society of which they are a part. We know little, for example, about the inheritance of artistic ability among Africans, but the problem can be seen from two points of view. The first is the outsider's approach in which, according to the understanding of the problem in the West, musical or other talent is inherited individually. Although the results of various tests of music ability demonstrate this without much question, almost nothing has been done towards attempting to assess the problem in African cultures. This is due partly at least, and with good reason, to the fact that tests of music ability are culture-bound, designed for music as it is known in the Western world. On the other hand, Africans themselves have some definite views on the inheritance of aesthetic ability. Thus Messenger found that the Nigerian Anang consider all individuals to be born with equal inherent talent for aesthetic activity, and believe that it is subsequent training which makes one person more skilled than another. In connection with woodcarving, Messenger (1958: 22) writes:

Once an individual commits himself to this occupation by paying the fee and participating in a religious ritual, he almost never fails to develop the skills which will enable him to enjoy success as a professional. It is simply taken for granted by all concerned that he will become an accomplished and creative artisan. The Anang do recognize that a very few carvers exhibit talents that are somewhat superior to their fellow craftsmen, but at the same time they will not admit, as we tried so hard to get them to, that there are those who lack the requisite abilities. This same attitude applies to other esthetic areas. Some dancers, singers, and weavers are considered more skilled than most, but everyone can dance and sing well, and those who choose weaving as an occupation learn to excel in this activity.

This Anang point of view, which emphasises equal potential at birth, contrasts strongly with the Basongye view, which holds that music ability is definitely inherited. It can come from either the male or female side, and if a child has a musician for a parent the chances of his becoming a musician are greatly increased. For the Basongye, then, there is a concept of the 'gifted' individual.

The two parts of this problem, however, are subjects for study which have been little explored for Africa, or indeed, for any other world area. Yet their importance, both as determining who shall and who shall not become musicians and how this correlates with individual ability, as well as the implications for choice of individuals to do other jobs in the society, cannot be overlooked.

Similarly, the training of the musician or dancer in African societies is relatively unknown, though it would seem to be of the utmost importance in assessing the means acceptable to the society in shaping the musician as well as throwing light upon educational practices in general in any given society. Among the Basongye, again, the neophyte can learn certain instruments by himself, and frequently does, but the key instruments must be learned from a practising expert, who gives several months of instruction. Since the new musician must contribute the entire proceedings of his first few jobs and a proportion of succeeding benefits to his teacher in a pattern that may continue throughout life, a good deal of information about the economics of musicianship can also be obtained from this kind of study.

The professionalism of the musician is another area of study which reveals not only cultural but economic and social information as well. Among the Basongye, there are thoroughly professional musicians who travel widely and who give almost their entire time to performances. They are indispensable at funerals, where they announce the death by sending out gong messages over the area, praise the deceased and his family, play the role of the foil for certain aggressive pantomimes that have to be carried out, and act the clown to raise the low spirits of the villagers. The Basongye, too, recognise various classes of musicians, both male and female. On the male side, the ngomba is the professional of highest standing; the ntundu is a professional of slightly lower grade whose primary accomplishment is the slit gong; the mwiimbi is the player of recognised ability who performs on the rattle and the double metal gong; the nyimba is the song leader; and the abapula compose the singing group. On the female side, a similar ranking obtains, although it varies in a number of details from the male situation.

Finally, in speaking of musicians or dancers, there is the very important question of their attitudes towards themselves and towards others, and of the attitude of the non-musicians of the society towards them. Among the Basongye this is a complex question, but there is much evidence to show that the Basongye musician is the object of considerable stereotyping by non-musicians and that he is aware of this stereotyping and uses it, consciously or unconsciously, to his own advantage. Although non-musicians tend to look on musicians as socially undesirable persons and to place them low in the social order, a village without musicians is unthinkable, and the opportunities for manipulating this situation do not go unnoticed by the musicians.

The musician—as a gifted or non-gifted individual, as the object of specific techniques of education, as a professional or social figure — is important in most African cultures, and these points of attack by no means exhaust or begin to exhaust the possibilities for study. Anthropologists and other social scientists who are not also trained musicians or dancers often consider that it is impossible for them to

study the musical or choreographic aspects of African cultures; yet I hope that it
can be agreed that the problems posed here concerning the musician vary but little
from those one might encounter in studying a chief, a palm-nut cutter, a religious
cult leader, or any other specialist.   Indeed, attention should again be called to the
unfortunate emphasis which has been placed upon strict product analysis in the study
of the African arts; it is clear that behavioural analysis must follow the procedures
and methodology of the social sciences.   Because product analysis has come to be
the means by which those who do not specialise in the arts view them, many
problems of extreme interest and importance in African life have been foregone.

Problems in the behavioural and conceptual spheres of African music and dance
could be cited almost indefinitely.   Innumerable problems centre upon the
question of whether music and dance in African cultures are conceived aesthetically.
What little evidence we have at hand seems to suggest that functionality is the
primary aim of the music or dance performance, but that some approach to
aesthetic attitude is evident in the fact that people make choices, express preferences and include or excise certain songs or dances from the general repertoire.
If we decide, however, that music for Africans is not aesthetic as we understand the
word in Western society — and this conclusion seems probable — then a number of
broader problems are posed.   If we cannot find evidence either of an aesthetic
attitude parallel to our own in African cultures or of clear inter-relationships among
the various fine arts in Africa, the whole problem of an aesthetic attitude may, in
the face of African studies, have to be re-evaluated and recognised as an attitude
that is culturally rather than universally present and defined.

This general question of the aesthetic leads to another series of problems
having to do with the conception of music as a structured system.   Is there, in
African music and dance, any conscious system relating certain sounds or movements to beauty or ugliness?   Is there any concept of formal structure of music
or dance expressed by Africans, and do they play with form for its own sake? We
do not have, so far as is known, any understanding of such problems as intersense
modalities in which concepts from one sense area are transferred to the description
of another.   In our own culture we speak of music as 'hot' or 'cool', 'blue',
'sharp', 'rough', 'shallow', 'high', 'sweet', and use a variety of other terms which
in actuality refer to the senses of sight, touch and taste.   In Africa we find that the
Ashanti refer to music as 'hard' (J. H. K. Nketia, personal communication) and
that the Bashi refer to what we call a high tone as a small or weak tone, and to what
we call a low tone as a big or strong tone (Merriam 1957a: 144).   But these are
mere glimpses into the perception of music by African peoples, and much remains
to be known.

Similarly, such problems as the sources of music — which can throw considerable light upon our understanding of creativity, individuality and the basic concepts
of music — have gone virtually untouched.   The question of what constitutes the
difference between music and non-music, which we have touched upon earlier,
remains unanswered.   We need much more information about people's verbalisa-
tions, inner thoughts and motivations, about the emotions and feelings of the
musician or dancer towards the work he produces, and about the corresponding
emotions which the work produces in him.

In sum, the elucidation of problems which lie on the behavioural and conceptual levels of analysis can and will lead to a far better understanding of two kinds
of phenomena.   On the one hand, the music or dance product itself is not truly

susceptible of accurate description unless the broader underlying factors combining to produce it are known.   On the other hand, the analysis of music and dance on the behavioural and conceptual levels leads to a greatly expanded understanding of other aspects of human behaviour.

IV   RELATIONSHIPS WITH OTHER DISCIPLINES

These, then, are some of the problems that face the student of African music and dance, as well as some of the promising areas of attack through which music and dance analysis can make contributions to the study of other behavioural problems of interest to the Africanist social scientist.   Let us turn now to this latter area to indicate still more clearly where the student of the African humanities meets with the social scientist.

I have elsewhere discussed at some length the relationships between the social sciences and the humanities in African studies (Merriam 1962a), but the crux of the problem can be usefully restated here.   In examining the essential nature of the social sciences on the one hand, and the humanities on the other, we realise that the former deal with problems which stem directly from the biosocial nature of man, and that the latter are devoted to problems of man's extra-biosocial activities. Given the acceptability of this distinction, we then can argue that, although in the nature of their content the two areas of study differ markedly one from the other in emphasis and approach, the central concern of both the social sciences and the humanities is with the understanding of human behaviour.   In these pages I have tried to indicate the sharp conceptual distinction between artistic behaviour and the product of that behaviour, for I wish to stress the point that it is through behavioural studies that we learn why man does what he does.   Product studies, useful in certain kinds of problems, can never go beyond the basically descriptive; from them, we can learn what has happened, but it is difficult to see how they can show us why things happen.

If we look, then, at the relationship of music and dance to other aspects of culture, and assess the uses to which such studies can be put in the broader context, numerous areas of attack appear, of which I should like to discuss four that seem to me to be of particular concern and which I have not previously discussed here.

1.   MUSIC AND DANCE AS SYMBOLIC BEHAVIOUR

The problem here is the level of abstraction upon which the investigator works. At one level we have song — which is supplied with texts — and dance — which is mimetic of specific human actions.   The symbolic nature of music moves to the verbal plane, while that of dance is comprehensible because of the direct nature of the imitative movements.   On another level, however, the problems become more difficult, for the symbolic nature of music as pure sound removed from any considerations of text, and of dance movements which are not mimetic, is much more obscure.   In one sense, music and dance are symbolic of, and even induce, certain attitudes, emotions and aesthetic qualities; thus, in Western art music the introduction of the minor scale immediately suggests sadness, while in dance the rhythmic snapping of the fingers on the second and fourth beats in a relatively fast tempo suggests gaiety.   Indeed, tempo itself carries certain connotations to Westerners, but symbolism of this sort is culturally learned.   The second aspect of 'pure' sound and motion in respect to symbolic content involves the question of whether there are connections between dance patterns, gestures and paraphernalia, for example, and broad cultural ideas. Curt Sachs (1933: 116–17) has suggested an inherent connection and further sees a widespread symbolism in certain ground plans of the dance (pp. 99–119). In connection with music, he has postulated a rather elaborate symbolic scheme involving the correlation of three major types of music material with femininity or masculinity, physical type, size of dance steps, and even such general cultural traits as 'warlike' or 'peace-loving' peoples (Sachs 1933: 127–38). The correlations here are very much open to doubt, not because such correlations necessarily do not exist but because the categories chosen are imprecise.

At a still different level, not precisely symbolic as such but related to it, is the reflection of other aspects of culture found in music and the dance. Kurath (1960: 236–8), for example, considers dance to reflect social organisation, male-female roles, and other organisational principles. Alan Lomax (1959: 950) feels that 'the basic color of a music symbolizes fundamental social-psychological pattern, common to a given culture', and suggests that music (sound) reflects the sexual code, the position of women and the treatment of children in a culture. Finally, Charles Seeger (1961: 40–1) has indicated an approach in which he speaks of 'paradynamism' by which he means

. . . the incorporation, in sound, of dynamic tensions, tonicities and detensions that parallel, reflect or reconstitute those experiences in the individual biological-social life and in the collective social continuum characteristic of a culture.

All these approaches have thus far done little more than express some of the areas of study concerning music and dance and their symbolic role; to date, such problems have hardly been touched in the field of African studies. In one area, however — that of the symbolism of music instruments as forms — Curt Sachs (1940: 52), again, has made some generalised speculations on instruments and the primarily Freudian conception of what they represent.

Tubular wind instruments, straight and elongated like a man's organ, belong to man, and a mixture of symbols arises when a flute is globular instead of tubular, or when a trumpet is made out of a conch shell which is connected with water. . . Sound, also, is a factor as well as form in these connotations. Most of the instruments reserved for men have a harsh, aggressive, indeed ugly tone; most instruments preferred by women have a muffled timbre.

In another passage Sachs speaks of the East African drum as being symbolically feminine, basing his analysis upon information from the Banyankole and the Wahinda, among whom, he feels, drums are equated with 'round, domed enclosure, earth, night, moon and milk, which, in the primitive mind, are connotations of woman and female sex' (p. 36). He further feels that the drumstick in general is a phallic symbol, and makes a particular reference to East African drums 'struck with sticks made of human tibias, which likewise have a phallic significance' (loc. cit.). The extravagant nature of the suggestions gives rise to considerable doubt, although it does not destroy the feasibility of the argument that musical instruments may be symbolic. Indeed, among the Bambara, as reported by Paques (1954: 106–7), the anthropomorphic form of the harp (ngoni) and its symbolic relationship to religious considerations is obvious, striking, and apparently envisaged by the Bambara themselves.

The probable symbolic nature of African music, music instruments, dance, costume, dance structure and so forth, represents an area of investigation that has hardly been touched.   Yet it is likely that further investigation will reveal this kind of symbolism to be extremely significant, for the importance of such correlations to students of other aspects of culture is clear.

2. MUSIC AND DANCE AS FUNCTIONAL BEHAVIOUR

A second area of relationship between studies of African music and dance and other kinds of studies is found in the functional usages to which these forms of behaviour are put.   The functionality of African music, and by extension of dance, has often been emphasised, and on several different levels.   African music is functional in the sense that its practice encompasses large numbers of the population; it is functional in its integration into almost every aspect of culture; and it is also functional in the sense that it appears to be so tightly integrated with other aspects of culture that it is not abstractable from that context (Merriam, 1961: 159–60).

But the extent of this functional integration of music into African life has rarely been commented upon.   It will be recalled that, among the Basongye, musicians are considered to fall low on the social scale; both musicians and non-musicians emphatically state, for example, that they do not wish their children to become musicians.   At the same time, as we noted earlier, people say, 'If there were no musicians in this village, I would move someplace else where there are musicians', and this is a remarkable statement to make in a culture in which heavy reliance is placed upon kinship ties, traditional land ownership, and similar considerations.   In one sense, then, it can be said that for the Basongye, life without music is not to be considered life at all.

More specifically: a major funeral cannot take place among the Basongye without the presence of a professional musician.   Such a funeral extends over a period of seven days, the interment of the body usually taking place on the second day.   The professional musician makes his appearance after the body has been interred and performs the functions described previously (p. 460).   But most important is that he is counted upon by the mourners to fulfil these several functions. Thus there is no other person than him to serve as the foil for the aggressive pantomime carried on by the female relatives of the deceased; the pantomime serves to help establish the magical or non-magical nature of the death, allows the women outwardly to express their inner tensions, and publicises their emotional and innocent involvement in the death of their kinsman.   Without the professional musician, these various expressions would have to be shifted to some other person, but as the funeral is structured at present, it is the musician who performs the function.   Again, it is the musician's role to help the mourners to forget the tragedy of death.   Upon his appearance, the entire course of the funeral is changed: people begin to smile and joke for the first time since the death; social dances whose function is specifically that of helping people to forget are introduced and encouraged by the musician; by acting the clown, the musician contributes heavily to the release of tensions that to this point in the funeral have been very intense. Although other individuals could conceivably perform this role as well as the musician, the point is that in Basongye society other people do not perform it.   The musician is a key figure in the funeral, and in many other aspects of Basongye life as well. Indeed, without the musician, whose numerous roles and functions have been barely touched upon here, the structure of much of Basongye behaviour would doubtless be markedly changed.

The integration, then, of the musician and his music, and of the dancer as well, into the fabric of the society at large is extremely important. It is inconceivable that the study of much of the behaviour of any group of people could be allowed to ignore the musical side.

3. PSYCHOLOGICAL USE OF SONGS

A third important area of study relating aesthetic to non-aesthetic behaviour lies in the psychological uses of music — primarily through verbal expression, i.e., the use of song texts. Of interest here is the fact that in song one can apparently express deep-seated feelings not permissibly verbalised in other contexts. Tracey, for example, in speaking of the Chopi says: 'You can say publicly in songs what you cannot say privately to a man's face, and so this is one of the ways African society takes to maintain a spiritually healthy community' (Tracey 1954: 237). Margaret Green (1947: 199–206) reports for the Ibo that the women of the village occasionally assemble in order to judge a woman suspected of stealing from another member of the group, gathering together at the home of the accused. Green reports that, in order to summon all the women to the judging, the group sang a song: 'Women who will not come out in this place, let millipede go into her sex organs, let earthworm go into her sex organs'. Green comments that 'such things would be said on no ordinary occasion to a woman, but were used here to induce the women strongly to turn out in force' (Green 1947: 201). Among the Bashi people of the eastern Congo (Leopoldville), the present writer witnessed an occasion in which the owner of a coffee plantation was interpreting the texts of songs sung by a group of girl workers on his plantation. Using traditional melodic and rhythmic songs, the girls took the occasion to inform the plantation owner, through song texts improvised on the spot, of a series of grievances that had been troubling them for a considerable length of time. 'The discontent was unknown to the planter; while the girls were unwilling to express their doubts directly to him, they seized the opportunity which presented itself to inform him indirectly of the situation (Merriam, 1954: 41). Thus song texts, because of the special kinds of licence that singing apparently gives in widespread parts of Africa, afford an extremely useful means for obtaining kinds of information not otherwise easily accessible.

This, in turn, suggests that through the study of song texts it may be possible to strike quickly through protective mechanisms to arrive at a basic understanding of the ethos of a given culture or at least to gain some perspective upon psychological problems and processes. In the afore-mentioned study of Bashi song texts, for example, it was found that the texts expressed a general sense of social disorganisation not readily apparent through other kinds of analysis. And the contrast between the expressions voiced in the Bashi texts and those voiced by the Bahutu of Ruanda, neighbours of the Bashi across Lake Kivu to the east, were striking in that they manifested what seemed to be general psychological attitudes towards life.

This leads to the investigation of song texts as they reveal psychological processes in the life of any given culture. Melville J. Herskovits (1934: 76), in a particularly useful paper, proposes 'to indicate certain aspects of the psychology of primitive Negro cultural behaviour which may be better understood when some of the broader simpler concepts of psychoanalysis are applied to their interpretation'.

31—TAW

Taking the concepts of repression and compensation, he points out a number of mechanisms in Negro cultures, both African and New World, and emphasises that 'there exists both a recognition of the neuroses as induced by repression, and of the therapeutic value of bringing a repressed thought into the open' (p. 77). His vehicle for the discussion rests partly upon an analysis of song and dance. Thus, he notes:

> In Dahomey, the institution of the avogan, the dance in the marketplace, is . . . recognized by the natives as affording release for suppressed emotions. At stated periods the people of each of the quarters of the city of Abomey have in turn their opportunity to stage such a dance. Crowds come to see the display and to watch the dancing, but most of all, to listen to the songs and to laugh at the ridicule to which are held those who have offended members of the quarter giving the dance. Names are ordinarily not mentioned, for then fighting may result. In any event, the African relishes innuendo and circumlocution too well to be satisfied with bald, direct statement. However, everyone who is present already knows to whom reference is being made. Thus the song might be:

> > Woman, thy soul is misshapen.
> > In haste was it made, in haste.
> > So fleshless a face speaks, telling
> > Thy soul was formed without care.
> > The Ancestral clay for thy making
> > Was moulded in haste, in haste.
> > A thing of no beauty art thou,
> > Thy face unsuited to be a face,
> > Thy feet unsuited for feet (pp. 77–8).

Such release is also given to co-wives who sing songs against each other, and Herskovits summarises by saying: 'What has been shown is that among the . . . Negroes, both in Africa and the New World, patterned types of psychic purges are recognized as valid; what is important for a psychoanalytic approach to the understanding of these social data is the fact that, in every case, the native explanation of the particular type of behaviour, though ordinarily couched in terms of the supernatural, can be restated in terms of the unconscious' (pp. 82–3).

Such songs of derision, or social control, are rather widely reported from Africa, although no special study has been made of them as a group. Thus, in discussing the 'Nail' (a type of facial marking introduced fairly recently among the Tiv), Akiga reports that 'the younger Tiv are split into two factions, and there is bitter feeling between them. Those with the lumps make up mocking songs about the Nail Men, and the Nail Men about the Lumpy-faced' (East 1939: 46). A similar use of song for social control or as a mechanism of derision is reported for the Chopi (Tracey 1948: 3), Dahomeans (Herskovits 1938: II, 312, 320, 323), Ibo (Madumere 1953: 64–5), Jukun (Meek 1931: 463), and various other groups. The importance of this type of song in Africa is unquestioned; both as a mechanism of social control and as a means of carrying out and resolving social conflict, it is a form of behaviour deserving thorough study.

Song texts serve further functions, of course, in African society functions which may or may not be psychological. John Blacking, for example, discusses the use of music as an enculturative device at initiation ceremonies among the Venda in the northern Transvaal (Blacking 1957: 13, 26, *passim*).   Willard Rhodes indicates the use of songs in furthering political movements in the Federation (Rhodes 1962).   Drums as the symbol of political power among the Tutsi of Ruanda have been noted by a number of authors (Maquet 1954: 147; Pages 1933: 371–2).   The point is clear: the expression of aspirations, values, and social, political, economic, religious and educational relationships, is marked in African song.   The study of song texts deserves far more attention than it has been given by most students.

4. MUSIC AND DANCE AS HISTORICAL PHENOMENA

Waterman and Bascom (1949: 21) have noted that 'songs referring to battles of the 18th century are still current in Nigeria', but perhaps the most direct statement of the case has been made by Herskovits (1938: II, 321) referring to Dahomey.

> Songs were and are the prime carriers of history among this non-literate folk.   In recounting the ritual associated with the giving of offerings to the souls of those who were transported into slavery, this function of song came out with great clarity.   The informant at one point could not recall the sequence of important names in the series he was giving.   Under his breath, to the accompaniment of clicking finger-nails, he began to sing, continuing his song for some moments.   When he stopped he had the names clearly in mind once more, and in explanation of his song stated that this was the Dahomean method of remembering historic facts.   The role of the singer as the 'keeper of records' has been remarked by those who visited the kingdom in the days of its autonomy.

Music can be useful in historic reconstruction in other ways as well.   For example, the distribution of music instruments in the Congo (Leopoldville) correlates almost precisely with the information we have concerning the formation of culture clusters and leads as well to some speculations about the migration of various groups into their present areas (Merriam 1962b).   We have previously remarked upon the statistical precision available to us in the analysis of music structure; although few such studies have been carried out, it is evident that music must offer a remarkably precise set of criteria for judging diffusion paths as well as elements of change and exchange in processes of acculturation as, for example, in the study of Arabic influences on Negro African music.   A. M. Jones (1959) has used such measurements in postulating certain relationships between Africa and Indonesia, and although we may disagree with some of his interpretations, his study is an example of what perhaps can be done with music on a local scale within Africa. There is great promise, then, for the use of music in the reconstruction of African history, particularly in studies of diffusion and acculturation, as well as direct reconstruction in those societies which use music as a device for remembering history.

V   CONCLUSION

This chapter has dealt with three major aspects of the study of African music and dance: as artistic products; as human behaviour; and as aspects of human behaviour in relation to other behavioural aspects.   The study of African dance has barely

Smith, Mary
  1954 *Baba of Karo: a woman of the Moslem Hausa* (London, Faber and Faber; New York, Praeger).
Tanner, R. E. S.
  1955 'Incidence of hysteria in Sukumaland', *Africa*, XXV, 274–8.
Taylor, A., ed.
  1962 *Educational and occupational selection in West Africa* (London, Oxford University Press).
Thomas, Louis-Vincent
  1958–59 'Les Diola: essai d'analyse fonctionnelle sur une population de Basse-Casamance', Memoire de l'Institut Français d'Afrique Noire, Nos. 55 and 56.
Tooth, Geoffrey
  1950 *Studies in mental illness in the Gold Coast* (London, HM Stationery Office).
Verhaegen, P. and J. L. Laroche
  1958 'Some methodological considerations concerning the study of aptitudes and the elaboration of psychological tests for African natives', *Journal of Social Psychology*, XLVII, 249–56.
Vernon, P. E.
  1959 'Race and intelligence', *Eugenics Review*, LI, 99–101.
Vyncke, J.
  1957 'Psychoses et névroses en Afrique Centrale', Académie Royale des Sciences Coloniales, V, No. 5.
Ward, Barbara
  1956 'Some observations on religious cults in Ashanti', *Africa*, XXVI, 47–60.
Welbourn, H. F.
  1954 'Infections among Baganda children attending child welfare clinics', *East African Medical Journal*, XXXI, 321–36.
Whiting, John W. M., Richard Kluckhohn and Albert Anthony
  1958 'The function of male initiation ceremonies at puberty', in *Readings in social psychology*, Eleanor E. Maccoby *et al.*, eds. (New York, Holt).
Wilson, Dagmar C. and Ian Sutherland
  1950 'Age at the menarche', *British Medical Journal*, I, 1267.

Chapter 15: LINGUISTICS (Greenberg)

NOTES

1. The purpose of the first section of this paper is to give a brief introduction to linguistics. For fuller treatments, the reader is referred to standard textbooks of linguistics, particularly Hockett (1958) and Gleason (1961).

2. The distinction of syntactic versus pragmatic is part of Morris's theory of signs; see particularly his *Signs, Language and Behavior* (1949). For an elementary exposition of information theory, the reader may consult Wilson (1954).

3. The approach of the Danish school of glossematics, however, tends to view both speech and writing as equal manifestations of a more abstract underlying structure.

4. For a discussion of these issues from the point of view of the permissibility of such 'mixing', see Pike (1947, 1952).

5. A standard exposition of phonetics to which the reader may be referred is Heffner (1949).

6. This example is highly oversimplified in that a large number of other features would have to be specified.

7. A classic study illustrating the methodology involved in such deductions is Sturtevant (1920).

8. For more detailed expositions of the principles of phonemic analysis, see Bloch and Trager (1942) and Gleason (1961).

9. The present example is oversimplified since other phonetic variants of the /t/ phoneme in other environments are not considered.

10. The revolution in English grammar resulting from the application of structural methods in place of those based on traditional categories is largely associated with the name of Fries (1940, 1952).

11. For a detailed account of morphemic theory, see Greenberg (1957).

12. For an elementary description of transformational theory, see Gleason (1961).

13. Two developments worth noting are componential analysis as applied in kinship terminology and the concept of folk taxonomies. See in particular Lounsbury (1956) and Conklin (1962).

14. For an account of the methods and results of dialect geography, see Pop (1950).

15. Among the language families to which such application has been made in varying degrees are: Semitic, Finno-Ugric, Altaic, Dravidian, Sino-Tibetan, Malayo-Polynesian, Bantu, Algonkian and Oto-Mangue (Mexico and Central America).

16. A still useful account of such methods is contained in Sapir's classic essay, 'Time Perspective in Aboriginal American Culture', reprinted in Mandelbaum (1949).

17. See Bergsland and Vogt (1962) and Chrétien (1962). For a review of glottochronological theory with full bibliography, see Hymes (1960).

18. A convenient collection of Benjamin Whorf's writings is contained in Carroll (1956). The results of a conference in Chicago devoted to a discussion of the Whorfian thesis may be found in Hoijer (1954).

19. The fullest exposition of the methods and problems of this field is Osgood and Sebeok (1954).

20. For a general account of the semantic differential, see Osgood, Suci and Tannenbaum (1957).

21. Some notion of the scope and methods of sociolinguistics may be derived from Ferguson and Gumperz (1960).

22. No general history of African linguistic studies exists. A useful summary treatment in modern Greek is that of Papadoupoulos (1958); Cust (1883) and Delafosse (1922) are useful for the earlier period. Regional surveys include Köhler (1955) and Cole and Doke (1961).

23. Pigafetta's list may be found in convenient form in the French translation of his work (1923).

24. The name Hamitic was proposed by Renan (1855: 189).

BIBLIOGRAPHY AND LITERATURE CITED

Adelung, J. C. and J. S. Vater
    1806–17   Mithridates, 4 vols. (Berlin, Vossische Buchhandlung). The third volume contains material on African languages.
Basset, A.
    1952   La Langue Berbère (London, Oxford University Press).
Bergsland, K. and H. Vogt
    1962   'On the validity of glottochronology', Current Anthropology, III, 115–58.
Bleek, W. H. I.
    1862–69   A comparative grammar of South African languages, 2 vols. (London, Trubner).
Bloomfield, L.
    1933   Language (New York, H. Holt), 161.
Boeck, L. B. de
    1942   'Premières applications de la géographie linguistique aux langues Bantoues', Institut Royal Colonial Belge, Section des Sciences Morales et Politiques, Mémoires, Tome X, fasc. 5 (Brussels).
Bourquin, W.
    1923   'Neue Ur-Bantu-Wortstämme', Zeitschrift für Eingeborenen-Sprachen, Beiheft 5 (Berlin).
Brusciottus, Hyacinthus
    1659   Regulae quaedam pro difficillimi Congensium idiomatis faciliori captu ad grammaticae Normae redactae; Rome; tr. by H. G. Guinnes (London 1882; Hodder and Stoughton).
Bryan, M. A.
    1947   The distribution of the Semitic and Cushitic languages of Africa: an outline of available information (New York and London, Oxford University Press, for the International African Institute).
    1948   Distribution of the Semitic and Cushitic languages of Africa (London, Oxford University Press, for the International African Institute).
Bulck, G. van
    1949   Manuel de linguistique Bantoue, Institut Royal Colonial Belge, Section des Sciences Morales et Politiques, Mémoires, Tomes XVII, fasc. 3 (Brussels).
Burssens, A. F.
    1954   'Introduction à l'étude des langues Bantoues du Congo Belge', Kongo-Overzees Bibliotheek, No. VIII (Antwerp).
Carradoi, Arcangelo
    1635   Ditionario della lingua Italiana e Nubiana; edited up to the letter O by K. J. Zetterseteen, Monde Oriental, V, 42–79, 137–67 (1911); VII, 203–36 (1913).
Carrington, J. F.
    1949   The talking drums of Africa (London, Carey Kingsgate Press).
Chamberlaynius, Johannes
    1715   Oratio Dominica (Amsterdam, G. and D. Goerei), 22.

Chomsky, N.
    1957   *Syntactic structures* (The Hague).
Chrétien, C. D.
    1962   'The mathematical models of glottochronology', *Language*, XXXVIII, 11–37.
Christaller, J. G.
    1893   *Die Töne der Neger-Sprachen und Ihre Bezeichnung* (Basel, Die Basler Mission), 5.
Clarke, J.
    1848   *Specimens of dialects: short vocabulary of languages; and notes of countries and customs in Africa* (Berwick-on-Tweed, D. Cameron).
Cohen, M. S. R.
    1947   *Essai comparatif sur le vocabulaire et la phonétique du Chamito-Sémitique* (Paris, H. Champion).
Cole, D. T.
    1957   *Bantu linguistic studies in South Africa* (Johannesburg, Witwatersrand University Press).
Cole, D. T. and C. M. Doke
    1961   *Contributions to the history of Bantu linguistics* (Johannesburg, Witwatersrand University Press).
Conklin, H. C.
    1962   'Lexicographical treatment of folk taxonomies', in *Problems in lexicography*, ed. by F. W. Householder and S. Saporta (Bloomington, Indiana University), 119–42.
Crowther, S. A.
    1852   *Grammar and vocabulary of the Yoruba language* (London, Seeley).
    1864   *A grammar and vocabulary of the Nupe language* (London, Church Missionary House).
Coupez, A.
    1956   'Application de la lexicostatistique au Mongo et au Ruanda', *Aequatoria*, XIX, 85–7.
Cust, R. N.
    1883   *A sketch of the modern languages of Africa*, 2 vols. (London, Trubner).
Dahl, O. C.
    1951   *Malgache et Maanjan: une comparaison linguistique* (Oslo, Egede-Instituttet).
De Flacourt, E.
    1658   *Dictionnaire de la langue de Madagascar* (Paris).
Delafosse, M.
    1912   *Haut-Sénégal-Niger II* (Paris, Larose), 194–203.
    1922   'L'étude des langues Négro-Africaines de 1822 à 1922', *Journal Asiatique*, Serie 11, Tome XIX, pp. 234–49.
    1952   'Les langues du Soudan et de la Guinée', in A. Meillet and M. Cohen (eds.), *Les langues du monde*, 2nd ed. (Paris, H. Champion), 737–845.
De Rop, A.
    1960   *Les langues du Congo* (Coquilhatville, Editions Aequatoria).
    1958   *Grammaire du Lomongo* (Leopoldville).
De Tressan, Marquis de Lavergne
    1953   'Inventaire linguistique de l'Afrique Occidentale Française et du Togo', IFAN, *Mémoires*, No. XXX (Dakar).
Doke, C. M.
    1935   *Bantu linguistic terminology* (London, Longmans, Green).
    1945   *Bantu: a modern grammatical, phonetical, and lexicographical studies since 1860* (London, P. Lund Humphries, for the International African Institute).
    1954   *The southern Bantu languages* (London, Longmans, Green).
Doke, C. M. and D. T. Cole
    1961   *Contributions to the history of Bantu linguistics* (Johannesburg, Witwatersrand University Press).
Drexel, A.
    1921–22 ⎫ 'Gliederung der Afrikanischen Sprachen', *Anthropos*. Bd. XVI–XVII, 73–108; Bd. XVIII–
    1923–24 ⎬ XIX, 12–39; Bd. XX, 210–43, 444–60.
    1925   ⎭
Dyen, I.
    1953   Review of O. C. Dahl, 'Malgache et Manyaan', *Language*, XXIX, 577–90.
Eichhorn, J. G.
    1777–86   *Repertorium für Biblische und Morgenländische Litteratur* (Leipzig, Weidmanns erben und Reich), viii, 161.
Esquier, T. H.
    1643   *A relation of some yeares travele begunne anno 1626 into Afrique and the greater Asia* (London).
Ferguson, C. A. and J. J. Gumperz (eds.)
    1960   *Linguistic diversity in South Asia* (Bloomington, Indiana University).

Fortune, G.
  1959   *The Bantu languages of the Federation: a preliminary survey* (Lusaka, Rhodes-Livingstone Institute, Communication No. 14).
Fries, C. C.
  1940   *American English Grammar* (New York and London, D. Appleton-Century).
  1952   *The Structure of English* (New York, Harcourt, Brace).
Gleason, H. A.
  1961   *An introduction to descriptive linguistics*, rev. ed. (New York, Holt, Reinhardt and Winston), 171–94; 257–341.
Greenberg, J. H.
  1955   *Studies in African linguistic classifications* (New Haven, Compass Publishing Co.).
  1957   *Essays in linguistics* (Chicago, University of Chicago Press), 18–27.
  1961   'A survey of prosodic systems,' in S. Diamond (ed.) *Culture in history* (New York, Columbia University Press), 925–50.
  1963   *The languages of Africa* (Bloomington, Indiana University).
Guthrie, M.
  1948   *The classification of the Bantu languages* (London and New York, Oxford University Press, for the International African Institute).
  1953   *The Bantu languages of Western Equatorial Africa* (London and New York, Oxford University Press, for the International African Institute).
Harris, Z. S.
  1947   "From morpheme to utterance", *Language*, xxii; 321–43.
Heffner, R.M.S.
  1949   *General phonetics* (Madison, University of Wisconsin Press).
Hervás, Don Lorenzo
  1800–05   *Catalogo de las languas de las naciones Conocidas*, 6 vols. (Madrid, Ranz).
Hintze, U.
  1959   *Bibliographie der Kwa-Sprachen und der Sprachen der Togo-Restvölker* (Berlin, Deutsche Akademie der Wissenschaften; Institut für Orientforschung; Veröffentlichen Nr. 42).
Hjelmslev, L.
  1953   *Prolegomena to a theory of language*, tr. by Francis J. Whitfield (Bloomington, Indiana University).
Hockett, C. F.
  1958   *A course in modern linguistics* (New York, Macmillan).
Hoijer, H., ed.
  1954   *Language in culture* (Menasha, American Anthropological Association).
Homburger, L.
  1941   *Les langues Négro-Africaines et les peuples qui les parlent* (Paris, Payot).
Hulstaert, G.
  1950   'Carte Linguistique du Congo Belge', *Mémoires de l'Institut Royal Colonial Belge*, Tome XIX, No. 5 (Brussels).
Hymes, D. H.
  1960   'Lexicostatistics so far', *Current Anthropology*, I, 3–44.
Johnston, H. H.
  1919–22   *A comparative study of the Bantu and semi-Bantu languages*, 2 vols. (Oxford, Clarendon Press).
Jones W.
  1783   *The History of Sumatra* (London), 164.
  1788   *Asiatic researches*, I (Calcutta), 422.
Koelle, S. W.
  1854   *Polyglotta Africana*, folio (London).
Köhler, O.
  1955   *Geschichte der Erforschung der Nilotischen Sprachen* (Berlin).
Lepsius, K. R.
  1855   *Standard alphabet*, 1st ed. (London, Seeley).
  1863   *Standard alphabet*, 2nd ed. (London, Williams and Norgate).
  1880   *Nubische Grammatik* (Berlin, W. Hertz).
Leslau, W.
  1946   *Bibliography of the semitic languages of Ethiopia* (New York, New York Public Library).
Lounsbury, F.
  1956   'A semantic analysis of the Pawnee kinship usage', *Language*, XXXII, 158–94.
Ludolfus, Job
  1661   *Lexicon Aethiopico-Latinum* (London, Thomas Roycroft).
  1698   *Grammatica linguae Amharicae quae vernacula est habessinorum* (Frankfurt).

Lukas, J.
1936 'The linguistic situation in the Lake Chad area', *Africa*, Vol. VIII, 322–49.
MacDougald, D.
1944 *The languages and press of Africa* (Philadelphia, University of Pennsylvania Press).
Marsden, William
1782 A paper read on February 22, 1781, published in *Archaeologia*, VI, 154–8 (1782).
Meeusen, A. E.
1954 *Linguistische Schets van het Bangubangu* (Tervuren).
1956 'Lexicostatik van het Bantoe: Bobangi en Zulu', *Kongo Overzee*, XXII, 86–9.
1960 Bibliographia del Protobantu, Mimeo (Tervuren).
Meillet, A. and M. Cohen
1924 *Les Langues du Monde*, 1st ed. (Paris), 463–50; reprinted in 2nd ed., 1952 (Paris, H. Champion), 737–845; with addition by A. Caquot.
Meinhof, C.
1912 *Die Sprachen der Hamiten* (Hamburg, L. Friederichsen).
1919–20 'Afrikanische Worte in Orientalischer Literatur', *Zeitschrift für Eingeborenen-Sprachen*, X, 147–52.
1932 *Introduction to the phonology of the Bantu languages* (Berlin, D. Reimer, E. Vohsen).
1948 *Grundzüge einer Vergleichenden Grammatik der Bantu-Sprachen*, 2nd rev. ed. (Hamburg, Eckardt und Messtorf).
Morris, C. W.
1946 *Signs, language and behaviour* (New York, Prentice-Hall).
Müller, F. M.
1867 *Reise der Österreichischen Fregatte 'Novara' um die Erde in den Jahren 1857, 1858, 1859* (Vienna, Linguistischer Teil).
1876–88 *Grundriss der Sprachwissenschaft*, 4 vols. (Vienna). For African languages, see I, 2 (1877) and III, 1 (1884).
Mueller, Wilhelm Johann
1675 *Die Afrikanische auf der Guineischen Gold-Cust Gelegene Landschafft Fetu . . . mit einem Fetuischen Worter-buche Gezieret* (Nürnberg).
Nienaber, G. S.
1956 'Die Vroegste Verslae Aangaande Hottentots', *African Studies*, XV, 29–35.
1962 ' 'N Lysie Hottentotse Woorde uit 1626', *African Studies*, XXI, 28–39.
Norris, E.
1841 *Outline of a vocabulary of a few of the principal languages of Western and Central Africa: compiled for the use of the Niger Expedition* (London, J. W. Parker).
1855 In J. C. Prichard, *The natural history of man*, 4th ed., 2 vols. (London, H. Balliere).
Olmsted, D. L.
1957 'Three tests of Glottochronological theory', *American Anthropologist*, LIX, 839–42.
Osgood, C. E. and T. A. Sebeok, eds.
1954 *Psycholinguistics* (Baltimore, Waverley Press).
Osgood, C. E., G. J. Suci and P. H. Tannenbaum
1957 *The measurement of meaning* (Urbana, University of Illinois).
Pacconio, F. and A. Do Couto
1642 *Gentio de Angola* (Lisbon).
Papadoupoulos, Theodorus
1958 *Zitímata tís Afrikanikís Glossologías* (Wetteren, Belgium).
Pigafetta, A.
1923 *Recueil de voyages et de documents pour servir à l'histoire de la Géographie* (Paris and Antwerp), 74.
Pike, K. L.
1947, 1952 'Grammatical prerequisites to phonemic analysis', *Word*, III, 155–72; VIII, 106–21.
Pop, S.
1950 *La Dialectologie* (Louvain, Bibliothèque de l'Université).
Prichard, J. C.
1855 *The natural history of man*, 4th ed., 2 vols. (London, H. Balliere), I, 427.
Renan, Ernest
1855 *Histoire Générale et Système Comparée des Langues Semitiques* (Paris, Imprimérie impériale), 189.
Sapir, Edward
1949 'Time perspective in aboriginal American culture', reprinted in *Selected writings of Edward Sapir in Language, culture and personality*, ed. by D. G. Mandelbaum (Berkeley and Los Angeles, University of California Press), 389–462.

Schebesta, P., publisher
  1919–20 'Arte da Linguia de Cafre: Eine Bantu-Grammatik aus dem XVII Jahrhundert', *Anthropos*,
  XIV–XV, 764–87.

Schmidt, W.
  1926 *Die Sprachfamilien und Sprachenkreise der Erde* (Heidelberg, C. Winter).

Sturtevant, E. H.
  1920 *The pronunciation of Greek and Latin* (Chicago, University of Chicago Press).

Tucker, A. N.
  1924 *The comparative phonetics of the Suto-Chwana group of Bantu languages* (London).
  1930 *Practical orthography of African languages* (London, International African Institute, Memorandum I).
  1940 *The Eastern Sudanic languages* (London, New York and Toronto, Oxford University Press).

Tucker, A. N. and M. A. Bryan
  1956 *The non-Bantu languages of North-Eastern Africa* (London, Oxford University Press, *for* International African Institute).

Ullendorff, E.
  1955 *The Semitic languages of Ethiopia: A comparative phonology* (London, Taylor's [Foreign] Press).

Van Warmelo, N. J.
  1921 *Die Gliederung der Südafrikanischen Bantusprachen* (Berlin).

Ward, I. C.
  1941 *Ibo dialects and the development of a common language* (Cambridge, W. Heffer).
  1945 *Report of an investigation of some Gold Coast language problems* (London, Crown Agents for the Colonies, *for* the Government of the Gold Coast).

Weigenmayerus, Gregorius
  1590 *Lexicon velpotius Concordantia Psalmorum et Cantici Canticorum* (Tübingen).

Welmers, W. E.
  1945 *A descriptive grammar of Fanti* (Philadelphia, University of Pennsylvania Press).
  1958 'The Mende languages' (Washington, DC, *Georgetown University Monograph Series on Languages and Linguistics*), XI, 9–24.
  1959 'Note on the classification of African languages', Supplement No. 1, *The Linguistic Reporter*, Vol. I, No. 2.

Wemmers, Jacobus
  1638 *Lexicon Aethiopicum . . . cum eiusdem Linguae Institutionibus Grammaticis* (Rome).

Werner, A.
  1915 *The language families of Africa* (London, Society for Promoting Christian Knowledge).
  1930 *Structure and relationship of African languages* (London, Longmans, Green).

Westermann, D. H.
  1927 *Die Westlichen Sudansprachen und ihre Beziehungen zum Bantu*: Seminar für Orientalische Spracher: Mitteilungen. Beiheft, Jahrg. 29 (Berlin, W. de Gruyter).

Westermann, D. H. and I. C. Ward
  1933 *Practical phonetics for students of African languages* (London and New York, Oxford University Press, *for* the International African Institute).

Westermann, D. H. and M. A. Bryan
  1952 *The languages of West Africa* (London and New York, Oxford University Press, *for* the International African Institute).

Whiteley, W. H. and W. H. Gutkind
  1958 *A linguistic bibliography of East Africa*, rev. ed. (Kampala, East African Institute of Social Research).

Whorf, Benjamin
  1956 *Language, thought and reality*, ed. by J. B. Carroll (Cambridge, Mass., Massachusetts Institute of Technology).

Wils, J.
  1935 *De Nominale Klassifikatie in de Negertalen* (Nijmegen, Uitg.-Mij., 'De Gelderlander').

Wilson, K.
  1954 'The information theory approach', in C. E. Osgood and T. A. Sebeok (eds.), *Psycholinguistics* (Baltimore, Waverley Press), 35–49.

Zyhlarz, E.
  1949–50 'Die Lautverschiebungen in Nubischen', *Zeitschrift für Eingeborenen-Sprachen*, XXXV, 1–20, 280–313.

Chapter 16: THE VISUAL ARTS (Sieber)

NOTES

1. I use the past tense throughout, not because the traditional arts of Africa are necessarily dead or moribund, but because the general comments offered in this essay are less generally true at the moment than they were at some point in the recent past. That point is not necessarily constant for different geographical areas or even within the same tribe. In Nigeria, to take but one instance, Nupe arts seem to have undergone a massive change after the Fulani invasion about a century and a half ago; the arts of the Eastern Igala were seriously disrupted by Christian missionaries about 1920; near Shendam certain sculptural modes seem to have successfully survived the encroachments of the Jukun, the Fulani and the British only to begin to crumble in the face of Western technology. At the same time there remain active artistic traditions among the Yoruba, who have been exposed to the Western world for centuries. Although the nature and rate of change differ widely, it is essentially accurate to state that traditional arts in the service of traditional values are quantitatively less than they were in the observed and recorded past.

2. This assessment by William Fagg also includes the caution that

. . . the collection of such material, if it is to give a true account of the spiritual aspects of the art as well as the material ones, cannot be accomplished in short periods of acquaintance such as are adequate for material-culture studies. Training calculated to draw the full benefit from such field studies hardly yet exists, and there is very little time left to develop it. Africans makes less effort than we do to put their aesthetic ideas into words — and in this they are not artistically less advanced but simply more realistic than ourselves; the inquirer who tries to persuade them to do so must have a critical judgment of a high order and considerable experience or understanding of the tribal habits of mind.

3. This point constitutes one of the basic premises of this chapter and has been set forth in the first few paragraphs. Proof lies in the perusal of any good general survey, as, for example, Fagg and Elisofon (1958), wherein nearly every caption contains a description of the use of the object. It is not the premise but the need for and means of documentation, analysis and interpretation in depth that are here under consideration.

4. This outline is a modified version of a portion of the 'Report of the Committee of Fine Arts and the Humanities' (1961: 22–3).

5. A surprising amount of extremely useful data has been collected by other than specialists in the arts. Anyone — no matter his specialisation — who makes photographs and certain basic data available to art specialists is performing a great service.

Good photographs are often hardly less useful to the comparative student than the objects themselves, and since the acquisition of carvings, unless they be freshly made, is generally a lengthy business the field student is probably better employed in expanding and documenting his photographic collection, especially as most of the African territories now rightly restrict the export of their works of art. The photographs must of course be properly documented with the name of the village and of the carver and any other available information about the uses, function, age, etc., of the carvings. Patient inquiry will usually elicit such information, for the carvings themselves do not very often outlast the memories of their makers among the present inhabitants. If it were possible to make such documented photographic records of all the millions of traditional carvings still extant in West Africa, I think that it would be possible by reference to them to identify nearly all the thousands of undocumented works in European and American museums and collections, and to assign them not only to their districts but to their carvers (Fagg 1960: 465).

It is to be lamented that the editors of *Notes and Queries* saw fit not to include in the last edition certain excellent suggestions offered for data collection for the arts.

As a rule of thumb, it is wise to discover as much as possible about any object photographed or collected: *Place* (was it made where it was seen or collected?); *age* (approximations are more useful than no data at all); *artist* (name, tribe, village — the piece might have been imported — age, and training); *owner, change of ownership,* and *role of owner* (important pieces are owned by important men) or *keeper* (a tribal or society piece is often collectively owned); *role of object* (associations with agriculture, chieftainship, a men's society, etc.; its function in more than one context — a men's society mask may also serve a tribal police function); *symbolism*; and, if possible, *aesthetic status* (surprisingly, this quite easily can be discovered in broad terms by asking if the object is a good one — well carved, well shaped, of fine weave, etc. — or if it is as good as or better than any others that are about, especially with reference to examples that are older or newer or by a different artisan). In short, nothing succeeds like curiosity.

BIBLIOGRAPHY AND LITERATURE CITED

Beier, H. U.
   1957 'The story of sacred wood carvings from one small Yoruba town', special publication of *Nigeria Magazine* (Lagos).

Fagg, William
   1951 'De l'art des Yoruba', in *L'Art Nègre* (Paris, Présence Africaine), 103–35.

1960   'The study of African art', in *Allen Memorial Art Museum Bulletin*, Vol. XIII, No. 2 (Oberlin, Ohio, 1956), reprinted in S. and P. Ottenberg, *Culture and societies of Africa* (New York, Random House), 458–73.

Fagg, William and E. Elisofon
1958   *The sculpture of Africa* (New York, Frederick A. Praeger).

Forde, Daryll, ed.
1954   *African worlds* (London, Oxford University Press, *for* International African Institute).

Goodwin, A. J. H.
1958   'The art of Africa: an introduction', in *Africa South*, Vol. II, No. 4, July–September, 94–101.

Griaule, Marcel
1938   'Masques Dogon', *Travaux et Mémoires de l'Institut d'Ethnologie*, XXXIII (Paris).
1950   *Folk art of black Africa* (New York, Tudor Publishing Co.).

Herskovits, Melville J.
1938   *Dahomey*, 2 vols. (New York, J. J. Augustin).
1945   *The backgrounds of African art* (Denver Art Museum); catalogue.

Himmelheber, Hans
1935   *Negerkünstler* (Stuttgart, Strecker und Schroder).
1960   *Negerkunst und Negerkünstler* (Braunschweig, Klinkhardt und Biermann).

Kjersmeier, Carl
1935–38   *Centres de style de la sculpture Nègre Africaine*, 4 vols. (Paris, Editions Albert Morance).

Leuzinger, Elsy
1960   *Africa: the art of the Negro peoples* (New York, McGraw-Hill).

Merriam, Alan P.
1962   *A prologue to the study of the African arts* (Yellow Springs, Ohio, The Antioch Press).

Olbrechts, Frans M.
1959   *Les arts plastiques du Congo Belge* (Brussels, Éditions Erasme); first published as *Plastiek van Kongo* (Antwerp, 1946).

Pigafetta, Philippo
1597   *A reporte of the Kingdom of Congo, a region of Africa*, trans. by Abraham Hartwell (London, John Wolfe).

Report of the Committee of Fine Arts and the Humanities
1961   In *African Studies Bulletin*, Vol. IV, No. 11, May.

Sieber, Roy
1960   'The aesthetic of traditional African art', in *7 metals in Africa* (Philadelphia, University Museum).

Tempels, Placide
1956   *Bantu Philosophie* (Heidelberg).

Trowell, Margaret
1954   *Classical African sculpture* (New York, Frederick A. Praeger).
1960   *African design* (London, Faber and Faber).

Sydow, Eckart von
1954   *Afrikanische Plastik*, ed. by Gerdt Kutscher (New York, George Wittenborn).

Wingert, Paul S.
1950   *The sculpture of Negro Africa* (New York, Columbia University Press).

Chapter 17: MUSIC AND THE DANCE (Merriam)

BIBLIOGRAPHY AND LITERATURE CITED

Blacking, J. A. R.
1957   *The role of music amongst the Venda of the Northern Transvaal* (Roodepoort, International Library of African Music).
1959   'Problems of pitch, pattern and harmony in the ocarina music of the Venda', in *African Music*, II, 15–23.

East, Rupert (translator)
1939   *Akiga's story* (London, Oxford University Press, *for* the International Institute of African Languages and Cultures).

Farmer, H. G.
1957   'The music of Islam', in Egon Wellesz (ed.), *Ancient and Oriental music* (London, Oxford University Press), 421–77.

Freeman, L. C. and A. P. Merriam
  1956 'Statistical classification in anthropology: an application to ethnomusicology', *American Anthropologist*, LVIII, 103–7.

Green, M. W.
  1947 *Ibo village affairs* (London, Sidgwick and Jackson).

Herskovits, M. J.
  1934 'Freudian mechanisms in primitive Negro psychology', in E. E. Evans-Pritchard, R. Firth, B. Malinowski, and I. Schapera (eds.), *Essays presented to C. G. Seligman* (London, Kegan Paul, Trench, Trubner), 75–84.
  1938 *Dahomey: an ancient West African kingdom*, 2 vols. (New York, J. J. Augustin).

Hornbostel, E. M. von
  1928 'African Negro music', *Africa*, I, 1–35 (in reprint).

Hutchinson, Ann
  1954 *Labanotation* (New York, New Directions for the Dance Notation Bureau).

Jones, A. M.
  1954 'African rhythm', *Africa*, XXIV, 26–47.
  1959 'Indonesia and Africa: the xylophone as a culture-indicator', *Journal of the Royal Anthropological Institute*, LXXXIX, 155–68.

Kolinski, M.
  1949 'La musica del oeste Africano', *Revista de Estudios Musicales*, I, 191–215.

Kurath, G. P.
  1960 'Panorama of dance ethnology', *Current Anthropology*, I, 233–54.

Lomas, Alan
  1959 'Folk song style', *American Anthropologist*, LXI, 927–54.

Madumere, Adele
  1953 'Ibo village music', *African Affairs*, LII, 63–7.

Maquet, J. J.
  1954 'La système des relations sociales dans le Ruanda ancien', *Annales* du Musée Royal du Congo Belge, Sciences de l'Homme, Ethnologie, Vol. I (Tervuren).

Meek, C. K.
  1931 *A Sudanese kingdom* (London, Kegan Paul, Trench, Trubner).

Merriam, A. P.
  1954 'Song texts of the Bashi', *Zaïre*, VIII, 27–43.
  1957a 'The Bashi *mulizi* and its music: an end-blown flute from the Belgian Congo', *Journal of American Folklore*, LXX, 143–56.
  1957b 'Yovu songs from Ruanda', *Zaïre*, XI, 933–66.
  1959 'African music', in W. R. Bascom and M. J. Herskovits (eds.), *Continuity and change in African cultures* (Chicago, University of Chicago Press), 49–86.
  1960 Review: A. M. Jones, Studies in African music, *Journal of American Folklore*, LXXIII, 74–6.
  1961 'The music of Africa', in *Africa and the United States: images and realities* (Boston, us National Commission for UNESCO), 155–64.
  1962a *A prologue to the study of the African arts* (Yellow Springs, Antioch Press, Founders Day Lectures No. 7).
  1962b Review: J. S. Laurenty, Les cordophones du Congo Belge et du Ruanda-Urundi, *Ethnomusicology*, VI, 47–9.

Merriam, A. P., Sara Whinery and B. G. Fred
  1956 'Songs of a Rada community in Trinidad', *Anthropos*, LI, 157–74.

Messenger, John
  1958 'Reflections on esthetic talent', *Basic College Quarterly* (Michigan State University), IV, 18–24.

Pages, Reverend Père
  1933 *Un royaume Hamite au centre de l'Afrique*, Institut Royal Colonial Belge, Section des Sciences Morales et Politiques, *Mémoires*, Vol. I (Brussels).

Paques, Viviana
  1954 *Les Bambara* (Paris, Presses Universitaires de France: Monographies Ethnologiques Africaines, Institut International Africain).

Rhodes, Willard
  1962 'Music as an agent of political expression', *African Studies Bulletin*, IV, (May), 14–22.

Sachs, Curt
  1933 *Eine Weltgeschichte des Tanzes* (Berlin, Reimer).
  1940 *The History of musical instruments* (New York, W. W. Norton).

Seeger, Charles
  1951 'An instantaneous music notator', *Journal of the International Folk Music Council*, III, 103–6.

1957 'Toward a universal music sound-writing for musicology', *Journal of the International Folk Music Council*, IX, 63–6.
1958 'Prescriptive and descriptive music writing', *Musical Quarterly*, XLIV, 184–95.
1961 'Music as communication' (abstract), in *Abstracts of American Anthropological Association*, 60th Annual Meeting, Philadelphia, November 16–19, 1961, 40–1.

Tracey, Hugh
1948 *Chopi musicians: their music, poetry and instruments* (London, Oxford University Press for the International African Institute).
1954 'The social role of African music', *African Affairs*, LIII, 234–41.
1958 'Towards an assessment of African scales', *African Music*, II, 15–20.

Ward, W. E.
1927 'Music in the Gold Coast', *Gold Coast Review*, III, 199–223.

Waterman, R. A.
1952 'African influence on the music of the Americas', in Sol Tax (ed.), *Acculturation in the Americas* (Chicago, University of Chicago Press: Proceedings of the 29th International Congress of Americanists), Vol. II, 207–18.

Waterman, R. A. and W. R. Bascom
1949 'African and New World Negro folklore', in Maria Leach (ed.), *Dictionary of folklore, mythology and legend* (New York, Funk and Wagnalls), 18–24.

Chapter 18: FOLKLORE AND LITERATURE (Bascom)

BIBLIOGRAPHY AND LITERATURE CITED

Abraham, D. P.
1959 'The Monomotapa dynasty', *Nada*, Vol. XXXVI, 59–84.
1962 'Maramuca: An exercise in the combined use of Portuguese records and oral tradition', *Journal of African History*, Vol. II, 211–25.

Allen, Samuel
N.d. 'Tendencies in African poetry', in *Africa seen by American Negroes* (Paris, Présence Africaine), 176–98.

Bascom, William
1941 'The sanctions of Ifa divination', *Journal of the Royal Anthropological Institute*, Vol. LXXI, 43–54.
1949 'Literary style in Yoruba riddles', *Journal of American Folklore*, Vol. LXII, 1–16.
1953 'Folklore and anthropology', *Journal of American Folklore*, Vol. LXVI, 283–90.
1954 'Four functions of folklore', *Journal of American Folklore*, Vol. LXVII, 333–49.
1955 'Verbal art', *Journal of American Folklore*, Vol. LXVIII, 245–52.
1957a 'The myth-ritual theory', *Journal of American Folklore*, Vol. LXX, 103–15.
1957b 'Replies and rejoinders', *Journal of American Folklore*, Vol. LXX, 359–61.
1958 'Replies and rejoinders', *Journal of American Folklore*, Vol. LXXI, 155–6.
1962a 'African arts and social control', *African Studies Bulletin*, Vol. V, No. 2, 22–5.
1962b 'Tribalism, nationalism, and Pan-Africanism', *The Annals of the American Academy of Political and Social Science*, Vol. CCCXLII, 21–9.
1964 'Folklore research in Africa', *Journal of American Folklore*, Vol. LXXVII, No. 303, 12–31.

Beattie, John
1960 *Bunyoro* (New York, Henry Holt), 11.

de Bouveignes, O.
1958 'Poètes et Conteurs Noirs' (Antwerp, *Zaïre*), 176.

Cardinall, A. W.
1931 *Tales told in Togoland* (London, Oxford University Press).

Chatelain, Heli
1894 'Folk-tales of Angola', *Memoirs of the American Folk-Lore Society*, Vol. I, 21.

Crowley, Daniel J.
1962 'Symbolism in African oral literature' (unpublished paper read at the annual meeting of the African Studies Association, Washington, DC, October 13).

Derolez, C.
1956 *Quelques Proverbes Judiciaires des Batelela* (Congo Belge, Province du Kasai, District du Sankuru).

Dorson, Richard M.
1962 'Folklore and the national defense education act', *Journal of American Folklore*, Vol. LXXV, 160–4.

Dupire, M. and Marquis de Tressan
  1955 'Devinettes Peules et Bororo', *Africa*, Vol. XXV, 378–9.
Fernandez, James
  1962 'Folklore as an agent of nationalism', *African Studies Bulletin*, Vol. V, No. 2, 3–8.
Gutmann, Bruno
  1932, 1935, 1938 'Die Stammeslehren der Dschagga', *Arbeiten zur Entwicklungs-psychologie*, Vols. 12,
    16, 19, xvi+671; xxi+642; xvii+662.
Helser, Albert D.
  1934 *Education of primitive people* (New York, Fleming H. Revell), 316.
Herskovits, Melville J.
  1938 *Dahomey* (New York, J. J. Augustin), Vol. II, 323.
Herskovits, Melville J. and Frances S. Herskovits
  1958 *Dahomean narrative* (Evanston, Northwestern University Press, Northwestern University
    African Studies, No. 1), 10, 20–1, 56, 62.
Herskovits, Melville J. and Sie Tagbwe
  1930 'Kru proverbs', *Journal of American Folklore*, Vol. XLIII, 228.
Herzog, George and Charles G. Blooah
  1936 *Jabo proverbs from Liberia* (London, Oxford University Press), 2.
Houdas, O. V. (translator)
  1900 'Tarikh es Soudan', *par Abderrahman ben Abdallah ben 'Imran ben 'Amer es-Sa'di, traduit de
    l'Arabe* (Paris, Leroux).
Jadot, J. M.
  1959 'Les Écrivains Africains du Congo Belge et du Ruanda-Urundi', Académie Royale des Sciences
    Coloniales, Classe des Sciences Morales et Politiques, *Mémoire*, Vol. XVII: 2.
Jahn, Janheinz and John Ramsaran
  1959 *Approaches to African literature* (Ibadan, Ibadan University Press).
Jensen, E. and J. D. Krige
  1943 *The realm of the rain queen* (London, Oxford University Press), 5, 304.
Journals of the Reverend James Frederick Schön and Mr. Samuel Crowther
  1842 *Up the Niger, in 1841* (London, Hatchard & Son, Nisbet & Co., Seeleys), 257–344, 371–85.
Lystad, Mary H.
  1960 'Traditional values of Ghanaian children', *American Anthropologist*, Vol. LXII, 454–64.
Malinowski, Bronislaw
  1954 *Magic, science and religion and other essays* (New York, Doubleday, Anchor Book A23), 101.
Meek, C. K.
  1928 'The Katab and their neighbours', *Journal of the African Society*, Vol. XXVIII, 46.
Messenger, John C.
  1959 'The role of proverbs in a Nigerian judicial system', *Southwestern Journal of Anthropology*,
    Vol. XV, 64–73.
Palmer, H. R.
  1920 *Sudanese memoirs* (Lagos, Government Printer), Vol. III.
Porter, Dorothy B.
  1961 'Notes on some African writers', in *Africa and the United States: Images and Realities* (Boston,
    us National Commission for UNESCO; Background Book, 8th National Conference), 165–73.
  1962 'Fiction by African authors: A preliminary checklist', *African Studies Bulletin*, Vol. V, No. 2,
    54–66.
Rattray, R. S.
  1928 'Some aspects of West African folk-lore', *Journal of the African Society*, Vol. XXVIII, 6–7, 7–9.
  1930 *Akan-Ashanti folk-tales* (Oxford, Clarendon Press), ix–x, x–xii.
Raum, O. F.
  1940 *Chaga childhood: A description of indigenous education in an East African tribe* (London, Oxford
    University Press), 214–17.
Rhodes, Willard
  1962 'Music as an agent of political expression', *African Studies Bulletin*, Vol. V, No. 2, 14–22.
Schapera, Isaac
  1941 *Select bibliography of South African native life and problems* (London, Oxford University Press),
    Items E469, L116, L207, L217, L219, L247, L248, L285.
Senghor, Léopold Sédar
  1953 *La Belle Histoire de Leuk-le-lièvre: Cours Élementaire des Écoles d'Afrique Noire* (Paris, Classiques
    Hachette), 175.
Shaw, Flora L.
  1905 *A tropical dependency* (London, James Nisbet).

Smith, H. F. C.
    1959 'The archives of Segu', Supplement to *Bulletin of News*, The Historical Society of Nigeria, Vol. IV, No. 2, 20.
    1962 'Nineteenth-century Arabic archives of West Africa', *Journal of African History*, Vol. III, 333–6.

Snoxall, R. A.
    1942 'Ganda literature', *African Studies*, Vol. I, 55–63.

van Goethem, E.
    1947 'Proverbes judiciaires des Mongo', *Aequatoria*, No. I, 1–8.

Vansina, Jan
    1961a Unpublished discussion on the Congo at the annual meeting of the African Studies Association, New York, October 20.
    1961b 'De la Tradition Orale: Essai de Méthode Historique', *Annales du Musée Royal de l'Afrique Centrale, Sciences Humaines*, No. XXXVI, x+179.

Vilikazi, Benedict W.
    1942 'Some aspects of Zulu literature', *African Studies*, Vol. I, 270–4.

Waterman, Richard A. and William Bascom
    1949 'African and new world Negro folklore', in Maria Leach, ed., *Standard Dictionary of Folklore: Mythology and Legend* (New York, Funk and Wagnalls), Vol. I, 19.

Index of Contents

I HISTORICAL AND SOCIO-CULTURAL STUDIES

1. PREHISTORY   J. Desmond Clark   11
    I. Introduction
        1. The historical background   11
        2. Summary of results obtained during the formative period   14
    II. The establishment of the chronological and climatic framework   15
        1. The use of stratigraphy and fauna in establishing chronology   16
        2. Other relative methods of establishing age   18
        3. Absolute chronologies   26
    III. Determination of environment and climatic change   27
        1. Sedimentation studies   28
        2. Fossil faunas and discontinuous distributions   29
        3. Palaeo-botany, rainfall and vegetation   30
    IV. The archaeological methods — recovery, interpretation and reconstruction
        1. Excavation and field studies   31
        2. Midden analysis   33
        3. Assemblage analysis   33
        4. Distributions   34
    V. Ethno-historical methods   35
    VI. Future needs and problems   35

2. HISTORY   J. D. Fage   40
    I. Introduction   40
    II. Africa's place in historical studies c. 1900–c. 1948   41
    III. The revolution in African historical studies   46
    IV. Written sources   48
    V. Unwritten sources: their nature and problems   50
    VI. Conclusion   55

3. ANTHROPOLOGY   P. H. Gulliver   57
    I. Introduction   57
    II. The development of anthropology in Africa   63
    III. The tribe as the unit of anthropological study   65
    IV. Methods of anthropological study   70
    V. Comparative and cross-cultural studies   73
    VI. Synchronic and diachronic studies and social change   79

VII. *Brief survey of anthropological coverage in Africa*   90
VIII. *The anthropological study of complex urban societies*   96
IX. *Conclusion: trends and problems in anthropology*   100

4. SOCIOLOGY: SOME ASPECTS OF URBAN PLURAL SOCIETIES
                                                    Leo Kuper   107
    I. *Introduction*   107
    II. *The plural society*   113
    III. *The urban context of pluralism*   116
    IV. *Cleavage and integration*
        1. Tribal or ethnic cleavage and integration   119
        2. Race   122
        3. Class   125
        4. Voluntary associations   127

5. POLITICAL SCIENCE   Harvey Glickman   131
    I. *Introduction: the scope of political science*
        1. General concerns   131
        2. Research problems in political science   133
        3. Research problems in African politics   134
    II. *Theoretical considerations*
        1. General concerns   138
        2. Political theory and African research: trends and accomplish-
           ments   140
    III. *Methodological considerations*
        1. General concerns   146
        2. Research methods in African political studies: trends and
           accomplishments   148
    IV. *The results of research in African politics*
        1. A chronology of concerns   151
        2. Subject areas of political studies: achievements and gaps   153
            i. Adaptation and effects of traditional systems   153
            ii. Construction and reconstruction of governmental institutions   154
            iii. Mobilisation of political movements   156
            iv. International and trans-territorial relations   159
    V. *The future of research in African politics*
        1. Some caveats   162
        2. Some suggestions   163

6. LAW   A. Arthur Schiller   166
    I. *Legal pluralism*
        1. Introduction   166
        2. Indigenous law   167
        3. Non-indigenous law   172
        4. Islamic law   174
    II. *Legal policy and its implementation*
        1. Legal policy   176
        2. Implementation of the policy   179
        3. Measures for the directed evolution of the law   180
        4. Cultural and geographical considerations   185
        5. Legal education and the legal profession   189
    III. *Organisation of the courts and the administration of justice*   192
    IV. *The substance of African law*   194
    V. *African law studies in the United States*   197

7. EDUCATION   David Scanlon   199
   I. Introduction   199
  II. The foundation of African education
      1. British Africa   202
      2. French Africa   205
      3. Congo   209
  III. Areas of needed research   212
      1. Africanisation of the curriculum   213
      2. Human growth and development   214
      3. Citizenship training   215
      4. Aptitude testing   216
      5. Teaching of English as a second language   217
      6. Acceleration of teacher training programs   218
  IV. Conclusion   219

8. ECONOMICS AND ECONOMIC DEVELOPMENT
                                        Andrew Martin Kamarck   221
   I. Introduction   221
  II. Policy issues
      1. Defining and measuring the structure of African economies   223
      2. Economic rationality   225
      3. Labour supply and wages   226
      4. Land and agriculture   229
  III. Other key policy issues in economic development   232
      1. Economic dependence   233
      2. Industrialisation   235
      3. Market forces v. government action   236
      4. Trade   238
      5. Federations and common markets   239

II   PHYSICO-BIOLOGICAL STUDIES

9. GEOGRAPHY   Benjamin E. Thomas   245
   I. Introduction: the nature and scope of geography   245
  II. African geography   246
      1. The exploration of Africa   247
      2. General mapping   250
      3. Physical geography   251
      4. Population and settlement geography   251
      5. Medical geography and physiological climatology   254
      6. Land utilisation and land-use surveys   255
      7. Economic geography: agriculture and minerals   257
      8. The geography of transportation and trade   259
      9. Urban and industrial geography   261
     10. Boundaries and political geography   262
     11. Historical geography and geographical history   265
     12. Cultural geography   267
     13. Regional geography of Africa   268
  III. Major trends in research   269

10. DEMOGRAPHY   Frank Lorimer, William Brass and Etienne van de
                                                         Walle   271
    I. Introduction: the population   271
    II. The development of demographic statistics   273
    III. Methods of collecting demographic statistics
        1. Types of demographic data   275
        2. Special problems in Africa   276
           i. Sampling   277
           ii. Retrospective recording   278
           iii. Cross-checks   280
           iv. Field experiment   282
        3. Designs of inquiries and fieldwork   282
    IV. Analysis of demographic trends   283
        1. Population models   284
        2. Sex and age distributions   285
        3. Fertility   288
        4. Mortality   290
        5. Population trends   292
        6. Special demographic studies   293
    V. Nuptiality   293
    VI. Demographic aspects of migration   297
    VII. Conclusion   301

11. BIOLOGICAL STUDIES   Neil C. Tappen   304
    I. Introduction   304
    II. Fossil and living records
        1. Fossil primates   304
           i. Oligocene   305
           ii. Miocene   306
           iii. Pliocene and Pleistocene   306
        2. Living primates   308
        3. Fossil man in the Pleistocene   309
    III. Race classification and relationships
        1. Race classification   311
        2. Relationship of African peoples to other men   313
        3. Relationships of African peoples to each other   314
        4. Studies of populations of African origin in other geographic areas   315

12. AGRICULTURAL RESEARCH   John J. McKelvey, Jr.   317
    I. Introduction   317
    II. Early research   318
    III. Crops in Africa
        1. Cash crops
           i. Palm oil   321
           ii. Cotton   322
        2. Diversification of research   323
        3. Nutrition   325
        4. Food crops
           i. Teff   327
           ii. Neug   327
           iii. Wheat   328
           iv. Sorghum   329
           v. Rice   330
           vi. Corn   331
           vii. Cassava   332
        5. Land tenure and land use   332

IV. *Livestock*
   1. Cattle 337
   2. Small animals and poultry 340
   3. Wild animals 340
V. *Current and future developments*
   1. The new nations and agricultural research 342
   2. The need for review of physical and biological resources 345
   3. Co-operative research 346
   4. Education and research 348
   5. Research problems and trends 350

13. MEDICAL RESEARCH: SOME ANTHROPOLOGICAL ASPECTS
                              Robert F. Gray 352
   I. *Introduction* 352
   II. *Major fields of study* 352
      1. Malaria and the sickle cell trait 352
      2. Trypanosomiasis and tsetse fly 358
      3. The implications of research on nutrition 365
   IV. *Some possibilities for future research* 369

III   PSYCHO-CULTURAL STUDIES

14. PSYCHOLOGY   Leonard W. Doob 373
   I. *Introduction* 373
   II. *Major questions for African psychological studies*
      1. Genetic differences 375
      2. Perception 379
      3. Intelligence and aptitudes 382
      4. Traditional personality traits 388
      5. Abnormality 393
      6. Socialisation 398
      7. Acculturation 402
   III. *Psychology and the social sciences* 409

15. LINGUISTICS   Joseph H. Greenberg 416
   I. *Introduction* 416
   II. *Descriptive linguistics*
      1. Phonology 418
      2. Grammar 421
      3. Semantics 424
   III. *Comparative linguistics* 424
      1. Historical method 425
      2. Typologic method 426
   IV. *Other linguistic disciplines* 426
   V. *African linguistics* 428

16. THE VISUAL ARTS   Roy Sieber 442

   I. *Introduction* 442

II. *Disciplinary studies*
    1. Pure research within the sub-discipline   448
    2. Comparative studies within the context of world art studies   449
III. *Interdisciplinary studies*
    1. Social sciences   450
    2. The other humanities   450

17. **MUSIC AND THE DANCE**   Alan P. Merriam   452
    I. Introduction   452
    II. Music and dance as artistic product   453
    III. Music and dance as behaviour   457
    IV. Relationships with other disciplines
        1. Music and dance as symbolic behaviour   462
        2. Music and dance as functional behaviour   464
        3. Psychological use of songs   465
        4. Music and dance as historical phenomena   467
    V. Conclusion   467

18. **FOLKLORE AND LITERATURE**   William Bascom   469
    I. Introduction   469
    II. Social roles of folklore
        1. Education   469
        2. Conformity to social norms   471
        3. Validation of social institutions and religious rituals   472
        4. Psychological release   473
        5. Cultural continuity   475
        6. Political change   475
        7. Political attitudes   477
        8. Values   478
        9. Law   478
        10. Anthropology   478
        11. Linguistics   479
        12. Psychology   479
        13. Schooling   479
        14. History   479
        15. Independence   480
    III. Studies of African verbal art
        1. Prose narratives   480
            i. Myths   481
            ii. Legends   481
            iii. Folktales   482
        2. Briefer forms of African verbal art
            i. Aphorisms   483
            ii. Riddles   484
            iii. Song texts   484
            iv. Poetry   485
            v. Praise names and praise poems   485
            vi. Tongue-twisters   485
            vii. Verbal formulas   485
    IV. African literature   486

General Index

ABEOKUTA, 487
Abidjan, 342
Abomey, 466
Abri Sefar, 22, 24
Abuja, 87, 88
Accra, 270, 337, 343, 388, 389, 476
Acheulian, 21
Achimota, 477
Addis Ababa, 201, 203, 213, 219, 270, 318, 347, 349
Adiopodoume (Ivory Coast), 342
Ado-Ekiti, 487
Adrar Bous, 20, 22, 24
African Negro (languages), 434
Afrikaans, 425
Afrikaners, 108, 126, 406, 407
Afro-Asiatic (languages), 440
Ain Boucherit, 20, 24
Ain Brimba, 20, 24
Ain Fritissa, 20
Ain Hanech, 20, 24
Akan, 42, 76, 382, 387, 483, 485, 487
Albert National Park, 341
Albertine Rift, 16, 18, 34
Alemaya (Ethiopia), 327
Algeria, 13, 18, 115, 167, 175, 254, 257, 266, 268, 269, 270, 271, 274, 309, 403, 410
Almoravid, 453
Alur, 482
Amadzimba, 23, 24
Amani (Tanganyika), 319, 332
Amharic, 50, 429, 431, 482
Anang, 459, 460
Angola, 30, 34, 35, 91, 178, 250, 272, 274, 276, 292, 343, 348, 386, 413
Arab(s), 22, 91, 126, 248, 249, 319, 339, 358, 360, 374, 403, 410, 411, 428, 429, 453

Arab states, 174
Arabic, 43, 50, 53, 429, 483, 484, 486, 487
Arusha, 324
Asaba (Nigeria), 319
Asalampasa, 385, 387
Ashanti, 41, 46, 49, 83, 91, 142, 178, 252, 293, 294, 340, 400, 411, 442, 451, 454, 461, 473, 474, 482, 487, 489
Aswan, 345
Aterian, 21
Atlantic Coast, 13
Awash River, 345
Axum, 24, 33
Azande, 68, 89, 400. See also Zande

BABUA (Congo), 336
Bachwezi, 55
Bahutu, 314, 369, 465
Bakongo, 477. See also Kongo
Bakuba, 35
Bakweri, 297
Bamako, 337
Bambandyanalo, 23, 24
Bambara, 62, 91, 464, 482, 484
Bambata Cave, 21, 24
Bambesa (Congo), 324
Bamum, 487
Bandama River, 330
Bangweulu, Lake, 30
Bantu, 15, 26, 33, 36, 38, 44, 51, 76, 79, 104, 113, 115, 164, 168, 177, 311, 312, 314, 336, 368, 375, 386, 387, 395, 406, 425, 430, 433, 434, 435, 436, 437, 438, 439, 440, 445, 487
Banyankole, 463
Bara (Malagasy), 482
Barbary states, 266

Bari, 76
Bas-Congo, 324
Basal, 21
Bashi, 379, 380, 452, 461, 465
Basoga, 185. *See also* Soga
Basongye, 452, 457, 458, 459, 460, 464, 465. *See also* Songye
Basutoland, 181, 274
Bathurst, 277
Batutsi, 314. *See also* Tutsi
Baule, 483, 488
Bechuana, 68, 83. *See also* Chwana; Tswana
Bechuanaland, 29, 89, 274, 360
Belgian Congo, 156, 173, 191, 209, 210, 211, 272, 277, 278, 279, 289, 319, 321, 324, 341, 345, 348, 359, 386. *See also* Congo; Congo (Leopoldville); Kongo
Bemba, 89, 91, 102, 187, 366, 368, 394, 395, 398
Bena, 400
Benguela, 358
Benin, 15, 22, 24, 32, 55, 83, 442, 480, 487
Berard, 20, 24
Berber(s), 91, 118, 167, 392, 431, 436, 440, 453, 483
Betsileo, 483
Betsimisaraka, 483
Bigo, 24, 36
Bilin, 483
Bini, 449
Blue Nile, 327. *See also* Nile
Boer, 409
Border Cave, 24
Bornu Province, 329, 346
Boskop, 19, 21, 24
Brazzaville, 38, 98, 99, 207. *See also* Congo (Brazzaville)
Brazzaville group, 161
British Somaliland, 175
Broken Hill, 19, 21, 24, 26
Buganda, 127, 142, 150, 169, 231, 287, 300, 302. *See also* Ganda, Uganda
Bukalasa (Uganda), 322
Bulawayo, 338, 341, 344
Bulu, 483
Bura, 483
Burundi, 183, 225, 272, 273. *See also* Ruanda-Urundi
Bushman, 11, 44, 312, 375, 379, 380, 383, 385, 412, 431, 435, 438, 483
Bushman-Hottentot, 19, 35, 313, 314, 434

C-GROUP, 22

Cairo, 47
Calabar, 319
Cameroon(s) (Cameroun), 188, 209, 272, 273, 274, 289, 292, 297, 299, 302, 342, 343, 477, 480, 489
Cameroon Mountain, 24, 30, 272
Cape Colony, 364
Cape Flats, 18
Cape Province, 11, 385
Cape Verde Islands, 274
Capsian, 21, 22
Cataractes (Congo), 295
Cave of Hearths, 19, 21, 24, 34
Central Africa, 15, 18, 23, 29, 30, 34, 40, 49, 51, 76, 155, 158, 161, 184, 200, 210, 224, 231, 272, 297, 300, 338, 343, 354, 359, 364, 430, 431, 452, 476
Central African Republic, 91, 274, 292, 342
Central Namib Desert, 251
Chad, 19, 272, 329, 342, 440
Chad, Lake, 51, 317, 345
Chaga (Chagga), 90, 400, 470, 483, 484
Chellian, 21
Cherangani, 24, 30
Chewa, 381, 400
Chisena, 429
Chokwe, 477
Chopi, 375, 465, 466
Chwana, 433. *See also* Bechuana; Tswana
Clacto-Abbevillian, 21
Coloured, 407, 489
Conakry, 186
Congo, 14, 16, 38, 40, 76, 91, 159, 161, 195, 196, 200, 201, 209, 211, 212, 213, 272, 294, 295, 296, 319, 330, 336, 337, 340, 346, 364, 367, 369, 380, 383, 388, 389, 390, 393, 402, 410, 411, 414, 444, 452, 477, 484, 488, 489. *See also* Belgian Congo; Congo (Brazzaville); Congo (Leopoldville); Kongo
Congo Basin, 16, 30
Congo (Brazzaville), 274, 342, 485. *See also* Brazzaville
Congo (Leopoldville), 225, 234, 274, 277, 281, 289, 293, 457, 465, 467, 485. *See also* Belgian Congo; Congo; Kongo; Leopoldville
Copper Belt, 98, 99, 120, 121, 122, 187, 240, 300
Cornelia, 21, 24
Creole, 120, 122, 126, 438
Cush, 480
Cushitic, 431, 436

DABBA, 22
Dagomba, 474, 483
Dahomey, 41, 67, 70, 82, 89, 91, 200, 271, 274, 279, 448, 454, 466, 467, 471, 474, 488
Dakar, 36, 39, 48, 206, 208, 209, 270, 300, 348, 437
Dar-es-Salaam, 200, 349
Dar-es-Soltan, 20, 24
Dire Dawa, 19, 20, 347
Diula, 388
Dodos County (Uganda), 365
Dogon, 62, 68, 91, 445, 448, 483, 485
Duala, 483, 484
Durban, 107, 319, 358, 397

EALA (Congo), 319
East Africa, 11, 12, 13, 14, 15, 16, 17, 18, 20, 22, 23, 27, 29, 30, 34, 35, 36, 38, 50, 51, 53, 75, 76, 90, 152, 158, 166, 184, 190, 199, 200, 201, 213, 218, 219, 222, 231, 237, 239, 240, 248, 272, 273, 275, 278, 288, 289, 293, 306, 309, 311, 315, 319, 320, 321, 324, 325, 326, 329, 331, 332, 339, 341, 344, 346, 347, 349, 354, 364, 366, 376, 385, 394, 398, 430, 431, 437, 443, 463
East Central Africa, 272, 273
East Horn (Horn), 34, 35, 431
East London, 120, 121, 402
Eastern Africa, 227, 273, 297, 347, 458
Eastern Highlands, 268
Eastern Rift, 16
Edo, 483
Efik, 436, 481, 483, 484
Egypt, 22, 33, 36, 50, 112, 162, 175, 248, 266, 269, 270, 274, 276, 277, 281, 284, 287, 289, 292, 293, 305, 306, 320, 338, 345, 443, 444, 453, 480
Egyptian, 22, 484
Egyptian, ancient (language), 431, 436, 440
Ekoi, 483
El Guettar, 20, 24
El Mekta, 20, 24
Elandsfontein, 19, 24
Elgeyo, 334
Elisabethville, 196, 324, 402, 405
Elmenteitan, 21
Enderit Drift, 20
Entebbe, 338
Equateur Province, 319
Equator Ranch, 320
Equatorial Africa, French, 156, 209, 272

Equatorial Africa, Spanish, 272
Erg Tihodaine, 20, 24
Eritrea, 175, 183, 271
Erythraean Sea, 50, 248
Et Tera, 21, 22
Ethiopia, 17, 40, 91, 174, 175, 177, 178, 182, 183, 250, 266, 267, 271, 302, 318, 327, 328, 338, 345, 347, 348, 392, 398
Ethiopian (language), 431
Ethiopian (race), 311
Ethiopic (classical), 429, 431. See also Geez
Ewe, 387, 426, 483, 484
Eyasi, Lake, 19, 20, 24, 310

FANAKALO, 384
Fang, 405, 477, 480, 483, 484
Fanti, 429
Fauresmith, 21
Fayum, 22, 24, 31, 305
Federation of Rhodesia and Nyasaland, 223, 233, 240, 272, 324, 349, 467, 477
Fernando Poo, 178
Feti, 23, 24
Fez, 117
Fezzan, 253
Fingo, 487
Fish Hoek, 18
Fish River, 11, 24
Florisbad, 19, 21, 24, 30
Fon, 400, 442, 481, 483, 487
Forest Negro (race), 311
Fort Lamy, 38
Fourah Bay, 199
Freetown, 98, 112, 120, 121, 122, 270, 277, 432
Fula, 122
Fulani, 55, 82, 88, 299, 317, 337, 339, 346, 435, 475, 481, 483, 484, 485, 486
Fulse, 485
Furi, 23, 24

GA, 294, 381, 387, 432
Gabon, 177, 234, 274, 342, 477, 480
Gagu, 483
Galla, 44, 431
Gambia, 46, 343, 489
Gambia River, 356
Gamble's Cave, 19, 20, 24
Gamblian, 16, 17, 20, 26, 28
Ganda, 44, 83, 85, 90, 91, 200, 377, 379, 389, 399, 400, 408, 483, 484, 487. See also Buganda; Uganda

Gandjika (Congo), 324
Gbaya, 483
Geez, 50, 429, 431, 440
Gezira, 231, 322, 323, 324
Ghana, 32, 34, 38, 45, 48, 54, 64, 89, 91,
    115, 127, 151, 157, 168, 180, 181, 186,
    193, 195, 196, 200, 215, 216, 225, 231,
    237, 252, 260, 271, 274, 275, 276, 279,
    281, 282, 292, 293, 294, 295, 300, 302,
    303, 319, 331, 337, 338, 340, 342, 343,
    345, 346, 349, 355, 385, 395, 397, 403,
    407, 408, 411, 474, 477, 478, 480, 489.
    See also Gold Coast
Gimbi (Congo), 324
Gogo, 187, 483
Gold Coast, 42, 46, 49, 149, 150, 183,
    188, 193, 205, 279, 319, 393, 396, 480,
    487. See also Ghana
Gonja, 474
Gouanches, 22
Gregory Rift, 16
Guinea, 40, 51, 175, 178, 179, 186, 196,
    205, 209, 213, 235, 274, 277, 279, 294,
    295, 297, 376, 379, 381, 388, 488, 489
Guinea, Gulf of, 331
Guinea (West Africa), 436
Guinea Coast, 76, 104, 390
Guro, 483
Gusii, 401
Gwari, 473

Ha, 187
Hajj Creiem, 20, 24
Hamitic, 38, 44, 431, 433, 434, 435, 436,
    438
Hamito-Semitic, 440
Hangklip, 24
Harrar, 175
Harrisdale, 24
Hatsa, 483
Haua Fteah, 19, 20, 22, 24
Hausa, 50, 55, 67, 68, 87, 88, 317, 326,
    392, 431, 436, 475, 483, 485
Haya, 170, 183, 187, 194, 483, 484
High Commission Territories, 75, 91, 174,
    272, 274
Hopefield, 21, 24
Hottentot(s), 44, 429, 430, 431, 433, 434,
    435, 436, 483
Hottentot-Bushman, 434. See also Bushman-
    Hottentot
Hova, 483
Howiesons' Poort, 21, 24

Hutu, 314, 369. See also Bahutu

Ibadan, 48, 50, 270, 319, 326, 331, 334,
    337, 338, 339, 340, 349, 487
Ibo, 67, 69, 89, 91, 126, 390, 407, 436,
    465, 466, 481, 483, 484, 488, 489
Ife, 22, 24, 32, 442
Ifni, 178
Ijebu-Ode, 487
Ila, 64, 483
Ilesha, 487
Ilorin, 487
Indian, 120, 406, 407
Inyanga, 24, 32, 34
Isamu Pate, 23, 24
Ishango, 20, 23, 24
Isimila, 20, 24, 31
Ituri, 367
Ivory Coast, 207, 225, 274, 279, 300, 302,
    330, 331, 342, 356, 488, 489

Jaatcha, 22
Jabo, 472, 485
Jebel Irhoud, 19, 20
Jebel Moya, 24, 34
Jimma (Ethiopia), 327
Jinja, 111
Johannesburg, 38, 47, 97, 374, 384, 404,
    406, 409, 410
Jukun, 449, 466

Kabete (Kenya) 338, 340, 341, 349
Kabyle, 483
Kaduna, 347
Kaffir, 431, 434
Kafue River, 345
Kageran, 16, 20
Kaiso, 20, 24
Kalabari, 398
Kalahari, 231, 383, 411
Kalahari Sands, 18, 29
Kalambo Falls, 18, 21, 23, 24, 30, 31, 32
Kalkbank, 24
Kalomo/Choma, 24, 33
Kamasian, 16, 20
Kamba, 483
Kamoa, 24
Kampala, 90, 97, 107, 253, 256, 270
Kanam, 17, 19, 20, 24, 310
Kanjera(n), 16, 17, 19, 20
Kano, 486

Kanuri, 413, 483
Kanyoka, 483
Karanga, 375, 386
Kariandusi, 16, 20, 24
Kasai, 15, 367, 386, 457
Katab, 473
Katanga, 33, 211, 324, 383, 402, 477
Kavirondo Gulf, 17
Kenya, 16, 27, 89, 90, 92, 127, 181, 184, 186, 192, 193, 196, 197, 217, 233, 240, 250, 266, 272, 274, 276, 299, 306, 310, 319, 320, 326, 328, 331, 332, 333, 334, 338, 339, 340, 341, 345, 347, 349, 360, 362, 393, 487
Kenya Capsian, 21
Kenya Rift Lakes, 27
Keyberg, 324
Khami, 24, 28, 32, 34, 36
Kharga Oasis, 20, 24, 31
Khartoum, 24, 270, 322
Khoisan, 436
Kigezi, 299
Kikongo, 429, 430. See also Kongo
Kikuyu, 89, 90, 182, 196, 200, 250, 325, 334, 338, 366, 369, 386, 400, 413, 483, 484, 487
Kimbundu, 429, 483
Kinangop, 24
Kipsigi, 90, 334
Kisale, Lake, 24
Kisalian, 23
Kisantu (Congo), 319
Kisra, 55
Kivu, 324
Kivu, Lake, 465
Klipplaatdrif, 21, 24
Kolo (Niger), 330
Kolwezi, 402
Kongo, 400, 401, 405, 429, 430, 443, 483, 485. See also Bakongo; Congo
Konkomba, 168
Kono, 483
Kosi, 484
Kpe, 483
Kpelle, 483
Kromdraai, 19, 21, 24
Kru, 471, 472
Kulughili, 118
Kumasi, 337, 343, 411
Kundu, 484
Kwadaso (Ghana), 343

La Mouillah, 20, 24

Lac Karar, 20
Laetolil, 16, 20, 24
Lagos, 190, 319, 337, 390, 487
Lake Province (Tanganyika), 325
Lamba, 400, 483, 484, 485
Lanet, 22, 24
Legon, 343
Lele, 367
Leopoldville, 14, 24, 36, 211, 270, 293, 295, 348. See also Congo (Leopoldville)
Levallois-Mousterian, 21
Levalloisian, 21
Liberia, 173, 177, 182, 217, 234, 274, 324, 348, 356, 357, 489
Libya, 175, 233, 274, 345
Libyco-Berber, 22
Limeworks, 24
Limpopo, 29
Lingua franca, 438
Lochard, 24, 29
Lochinvar, 23, 24
Lovedu, 400, 480
Lozi, 68, 169, 171, 187, 483
Luanda, 362
Luangwa Valley, 30
Luanshya, 120
Luba, 385, 405, 483, 484
Luena, 477
Lugbara, 69
Luhya, 90
Luki (Congo), 324
Lulua, 483
Lunda, 477
Luo, 334, 408
Lupembo(an), 21, 23
Lusaka, 335
Lusitu, 23, 24
Lusu, 23, 24

Machili, 23
Madagascar, 271, 305, 430. See also Malagasy; Malgache
Magabengberg, 23, 24
Maghreb, 11, 13
Magosi(an), 18, 20, 21, 23, 24
Magugu (Tanganyika), 361, 362
Maiduguri, 345
Makalian, 16, 20
Makapan, 19, 21, 24
Makerere, 199, 200, 253, 256, 326, 337, 345, 349
Makua, 430

Malagasy, 342, 429, 431, 440, 482, 483, 490. *See also* Madagascar; Malgache
Malayo-Polynesian, 430, 431, 440
Malewa Gorge, 20, 24
Malgache, 183
Mali, 196, 272, 274, 279, 337, 339, 480, 488
Malinke, 483, 484, 488
Mandated territories, 160
Mande, 44, 55, 439
Mandingo, 485, 488
Mandinka, 122
Maniema (Congo), 295
Manyika, 392
Mapungubwe, 23, 24, 34, 51
Marandellos (Southern Rhodesia), 344
Masai, 76, 314, 320, 325, 338, 366, 367, 369, 400, 435, 483
Matjes River, 19, 21, 23, 24
Matopos (Southern Rhodesia), 338, 344
Mauretania, 175, 234
Mauritius, 271, 274
Mazelspoort, 21
Mbundu, 400, 470
Mbuti, 379, 483
Mediterranean, 12, 13, 30, 50, 266, 311, 363, 364, 443
Mehlet, 20
Mende, 439
Meniet, 22, 24
Merimde, 22
Meroe, 15, 22
Meroitic, 440
Mixed Negro (language), 434
Mombasa, 200
Monomotapa, 42, 479, 480
Montagu, 21, 24
Moor Plantation, 319, 343
Morocco, 13, 18, 50, 175, 249, 271, 274, 483
Mossi, 55, 474, 483, 485, 487
Mt. Amba, 23, 24
Mt. Gafula, 23, 24
Mozambique, 91, 178, 272, 274, 276, 292, 322, 343, 348, 359, 360, 375, 389, 430
Mpondo, 82, 487. *See also* Pondo
Mufo, 21, 23, 24
Mugharet el Aliyia, 19, 20, 24
Muguga (Kenya), 319, 340
Mulungu (Congo), 324
Mumbwa Caves, 19, 21, 24
Mvuazi, 324
Mzab, 268

Nachikufu(an), 23, 24
Nairobi, 200, 240, 270, 277, 293, 320, 340, 349
Naivasha, 20
Nakuran, 16, 20
Nambulonge (Uganda), 322, 324
Namib Desert, 251
Nandi, 76, 334
Napore, 365
Natal, 33, 172, 182, 319, 485
Ndau, 375, 386
Ndembu, 69, 169
Ndendenli, 299
Nderit Drift, 24
Negro (language), 434
Negro-African (language), 436
New Kingdom, 22
Ngbandi, 483, 484
Ngoni, 82, 85, 87, 88, 90, 295, 299
Nguni, 485, 487
Niger, 200, 272, 274, 330, 485
Niger Agricultural Project, 333
Niger-Congo, 439, 440
Niger River, 49, 248, 321, 346, 487
Niger River Valley, 329
Nigeria, 32, 38, 45, 48, 52, 55, 69, 82, 87, 89, 91, 126, 169, 176, 179, 180, 182, 184, 185, 188, 193, 195, 196, 200, 205, 216, 217, 231, 233, 237, 238, 246, 260, 273, 274, 278, 281, 317, 319, 321, 322, 324, 326, 329, 330, 331, 333, 334, 335, 337, 338, 339, 340, 343, 345, 346, 347, 349, 357, 377, 385, 386, 390, 395, 396, 397, 398, 404, 437, 444, 459, 467, 471, 473, 479, 480, 484, 485, 487, 488, 489
Nigeria, Eastern Region, 273, 336
Nigeria, Northern Region, 324, 329, 333, 334, 337, 345, 346
Nigeria, Western Region, 231, 273, 335, 340, 477
Nile, 11, 13, 14, 15, 40, 51, 246, 248, 268, 271, 338, 345, 364
Nilo-Hamitic, 76, 314
Nilotes, 76
Nilyamba, 483
Nioka, 324
Njoro, 22, 24, 320, 328, 338, 472
Nkundo, 483, 484, 485
Nok, 22, 24, 444
North Africa, 12, 13, 16, 20, 21, 29, 40, 41, 50, 91, 117, 125, 128, 152, 167, 174, 175, 176, 178, 195, 248, 249, 266, 271, 276, 284, 292, 303, 374, 392, 430, 431, 443, 453, 486

Northeast Africa, 20, 49, 50, 248
Northern Africa, 247, 248, 252, 254, 262, 271
Northern Rhodesia, 29, 31, 32, 33, 34, 35,
    38, 64, 69, 89, 91, 98, 102, 186, 187,
    196, 223, 234, 240, 241, 272, 274, 277,
    300, 331, 335, 336, 344, 345, 409, 477,
    484. *See also* Federation of Rhodesia and
    Nyasaland; Rhodesia(s)
Northwest Africa, 13, 22, 62, 248
Nsongezi, 22, 24
Ntumu, 484
Nubah-Fulah (language), 434
Nubian, 36, 429, 433, 439, 440
Nuer, 72, 89, 91, 94, 168, 400, 401
Nupe, 89, 388, 483
Nyabusoro, 24
Nyakyusa, 68, 72, 88, 90, 91, 400
Nyamwezi, 187
Nyang, 483, 484
Nyanja, 483
Nyanyega, 365
Nyanza, 184
Nyasa, 241
Nyasaland, 29, 92, 195, 240, 241, 272, 293,
    321, 343, 344, 381, 485
Nyiha, 483
Nyima, 397
Nyoro, 472. *See also* Njoro

Oakhurst, 19, 21
Ogbomosho, 487
Oil Rivers, 319
Oil Rivers Protectorate, 321
Old Libyan (language), 440
Oldowan, 21
Olduvai, 14, 15, 16, 17, 18, 20, 24, 27,
    31, 32, 308
Olorgesailie, 16, 20, 24
Omo, 17, 20, 24
Onderstepoort, 338
Ondo, 487
Oranian, 19, 21, 22
Ovimbundu, 91, 483, 484
Owo, 487
Oyo, 24, 32, 487

Pedi, 400, 484, 485
Pemba, 274
Pidgin, 438
Pietersburg, 21
Pneil, 24
Pondo, 107, 400. *See also* Mpondo
Porto Novo, 487

Portuguese Guinea, 274, 276, 356, 357
Pretoria, 12
Pre-Zinga, 19
Principe, 178, 274
Proto-Bantu, 435
Punic, 22
Pygmy, 367, 379, 483

Rabat, 19, 20, 22, 24, 270
Rawi, 17
Red Sea, 480
Reunion, 319, 320
Rhodesia(s), 11, 12, 14, 18, 31, 32, 34, 35,
    82, 87, 88, 99, 122, 272, 279, 288, 290,
    297, 310, 321, 328, 331, 337, 339, 340,
    343, 360, 469. *See also* Federation of
    Rhodesia and Nyasaland; Northern Rho-
    desia; Southern Rhodesia
Richard-Toll Station (Senegal), 331
Rift Valley, 12, 13
Rio Muni, 178
Rokupr (Sierra Leone), 331
Roman, 22
Rose Cottage Cave, 21, 24
Roseires, 345
Ruanda, 225, 314, 369, 454, 465, 467. *See
    also* Ruanda-Urundi; Rwanda
Ruanda-Urundi, 191, 195, 211, 274, 277,
    281, 292, 360, 369, 393, 395, 396, 452.
    See also Burundi; Ruanda; Rundi;
    Rwanda
Rudolph, Lake, 17
Rufiji River, 345
Rufisque, 207
Rukwa Rift, 30
Rundi, 483, 485
Ruwenzori Mountains, 249
Rwanda, 183, 272, 273, 299, 336, 483, 484,
    487. *See also* Ruanda; Ruanda-Urundi

Sahara, 15, 22, 30, 35, 50, 167, 178, 250,
    259, 268, 364, 443
Saho, 431, 483
Sakalava, 483
Saldanha, 18, 310
Salisbury, 36, 39, 331, 344
Samaru (Nigeria), 322, 324, 329, 330, 343
Sambaa, 484
Sangoan, 21
Sao Tome, 178, 274, 319
Saria (Upper Volta), 330
Segu, 487
Sekondi-Takoradi, 98

Semi-Bantu, 435
Semitic, 429, 431, 433, 434, 435, 436, 438, 440
Semitic-Egyptian, 440
Senegal, 38, 45, 177, 206, 233, 272, 274, 319, 327, 331, 342, 377, 479, 485, 488, 489
Senegal River, 248, 329
Senufo, 485
Serakule, 122
Serere (Uganda), 322
Shaheinab, 22
Shambat (Sudan), 322
Shika (Nigeria), 337, 343
Shilluk, 483
Shona, 483
Sidi Abderrahman, 19, 20, 24
Sidi Mansour, 20, 24
Sidi Zin, 20, 24
Sierra Leone, 92, 98, 120, 126, 195, 199, 200, 213, 216, 222, 274, 318, 319, 331, 336, 343, 489
Singa, 19, 20
Smithfield, 21, 23
Soga, 68, 90, 404. See also Basoga
Sokoto, 340, 486, 487
Solwezi, 23, 24
Somali, 67, 91, 311, 431, 483
Somalia, 166, 175, 188, 271, 345, 347
Somaliland, 320, 453
Somaliland, French, 347
Songea (Tanganyika), 299
Songhai, 55, 483, 486
Songye, 483. See also Basongye
Soninke, 483
Sotho, 365, 385, 400, 483, 484, 485, 488, 489
Soudan, 64, 207, 208, 379, 381, 388, 436, 480, 486. See also Sudan
Souf, 268
South Africa, 11, 12, 13, 14, 16, 17, 18, 21, 23, 29, 30, 31, 33, 35, 42, 64, 75, 82, 91, 108, 113, 115, 120, 123, 124, 126, 152, 155, 158, 159, 166, 174, 177, 191, 195, 196, 222, 223, 231, 233, 234, 241, 254, 256, 258, 266, 269, 270, 271, 272, 274, 276, 292, 297, 306, 307, 310, 320, 327, 338, 343, 367, 368, 369, 374, 376, 377, 379, 380, 381, 384, 385, 386, 387, 388, 389, 392, 402, 405, 406, 407, 410, 425, 431, 437, 476, 488, 489
South Central Africa, 76
South West Africa, 30, 34, 75, 91, 272
Southeast Africa, 35, 42

Southern Africa, 15, 18, 29, 31, 75, 104, 152, 184, 227, 246, 252, 262, 272, 273, 297, 376, 380, 388, 458
Southern Rhodesia, 28, 29, 31, 32, 33, 39, 91, 174, 196, 223, 240, 241, 268, 272, 274, 277, 331, 340, 341, 344, 359. See also Federation of Rhodesia and Nyasaland; Rhodesia(s)
Stanleyville, 345
Sterkfontein, 14, 19, 21, 24
Stillbay, 21
Subija, 483
Sub-Semitic, 431
Sudan, 15, 40, 43, 45, 51, 64, 70, 72, 89, 91, 92, 166, 173, 174, 175, 176, 177, 233, 271, 274, 277, 279, 281, 285, 298, 322, 327, 333, 336, 345, 347, 349, 363, 443
Sudanese, 311
Sudanic, 435, 438
Suk, 334
Suku, 410, 411
Sukuma, 90, 183, 187, 195, 398
Susu (Sussu), 387, 485, 488
Suto, 483, 484
Swahili, 50, 217, 437, 483, 484, 485
Swartkrans, 19, 21, 24
Swazi, 388, 400
Swaziland, 234, 274
Syrians, 126

TABORA, 200
Tafo (Ghana), 342
Taforalt, 20, 22, 24
Takoradi, 22, 24, 98
Tallensi, 89, 400
Tana, Lake, 345
Tanala, 400
Tananarive, 401
Tanganyika, 16, 31, 35, 48, 68, 88, 90, 92, 105, 183, 187, 191, 192, 193, 194, 195, 200, 217, 231, 233, 240, 274, 276, 289, 293, 299, 307, 309, 310, 319, 324, 325, 329, 331, 332, 333, 338, 340, 345, 347, 349, 360, 361, 362, 376, 394, 470
Tangier, 249
Tassili, 24, 35
Tatare, 392
Taung(s), 14, 17, 19, 21, 24
Temara, 19, 20, 24
Tembu, 394, 487
Temne, 122, 483
Tenerife, 22

Ternifine, 19, 20, 24
Teso, 76, 90
Tetela, 483
Thembu, 487. See also Tembu
Thonga, 64, 81, 375, 386, 400. See also
    Tonga; Tsonga
Tigre, 484
Tigrinya, 431, 484
Tihodaine, 20
Timbuctu, 50, 486
Tin-Hinan, 22
Tiv, 68, 94, 169, 185, 400, 466, 483
Togo, 273, 274, 342, 345, 488
Tonga, 69, 72, 186, 296, 483. See also
    Thonga; Tsonga
Toucouleur, 55, 300
Transvaal, 14, 17, 28, 29, 34, 375, 467, 483
Trust territories, 160
Tshitolian, 21, 23
Tsonga, 483, 484, 485. See also Thonga; Tonga
Tswana, 89, 91, 169, 171, 181, 400, 484,
    487, 489. See also Bechuana; Chwana
Tuareg, 44, 55, 485
Tunis, 117, 249, 270
Tunisia, 13, 18, 118, 174, 175, 233, 271,
    274, 287
Turkana, 400
Turumba (Congo), 336
Tutsi, 369, 467. See also Batutsi
Twi, 43, 433, 483
Twin Rivers Kopje, 24

Uan Muluggiag, 22, 24
Ubangi, 289
Uganda, 16, 18, 48, 52, 55, 64, 69, 76, 90,
    91, 92, 97, 99, 104, 111, 149, 157, 185,
    196, 199, 200, 205, 213, 217, 230, 232,
    233, 235, 237, 238, 240, 253, 274, 276,
    277, 279, 287, 288, 289, 292, 299, 319,
    322, 325, 327, 331, 332, 338, 340, 345,
    347, 349, 358, 359, 360, 364, 365, 377,
    378, 404, 472
Ukambani (Kenya), 338
Ukiriguru (Tanganyika), 324
Ulanga (Tanganyika), 293
United Arab Republic, 166
Upper Volta, 271, 272, 273, 274, 279, 300,
    329, 330, 485
Usambara Mountains, 319
Usumbura, 211, 300

Vaal Basin, 18, 21
Vai, 483

Venda, 177, 194, 400, 467, 483
Victoria Basin, 16
Victoria, Lake, 17, 90, 324, 359
Volta River, 345, 346
Vom, 347
Voortrekker Republic, 319

Wadi Gan, 20, 24
Wahinda, 463
Wambugwe, 361
Waterberg, 23
West Africa, 15, 22, 31, 34, 49, 50, 52, 53,
    62, 67, 127, 128, 152, 156, 166, 175,
    183, 184, 188, 189, 190, 199, 200, 201,
    205, 206, 207, 208, 237, 249, 268, 272,
    273, 297, 298, 321, 325, 326, 330, 331,
    335, 337, 339, 343, 346, 347, 348, 354,
    355, 356, 359, 363, 364, 376, 379, 381,
    384, 385, 426, 432, 435, 479, 480, 481,
    487, 488, 489, 490
Western Africa, 457
Western Rift, 16
Western Sudan, 486, 487
Western Sudanic, 438
Wilton, 21, 23
Wolof, 483, 485
Wonderboompoort, 24
Wute, 483

Xhosa (Xosa), 120, 121, 126, 177, 375,
    402, 483, 484, 485, 487, 488, 489

Yangambi (Congo), 322, 324
Yao, 293, 483
Yayo, 19, 20
Yoruba, 117, 184, 195, 196, 339, 388, 390,
    394, 395, 400, 404, 432, 433, 436, 442,
    445, 448, 449, 471, 472, 477, 480, 481,
    483, 484, 485, 487, 488, 489
Yovu, 454

Zambesi, 29, 34, 354
Zande, 333. See also Azande
Zanzibar, 200, 272, 279, 289, 292, 331
Zanzibar and Pemba, 274
Zaria, 88, 343
Zazzau, 87, 88
Zimbabwe, 15, 23, 24, 31, 32, 34, 36
Zulu, 43, 83, 85, 91, 107, 126, 177, 182,
    340, 376, 377, 379, 381, 387, 395, 397,
    400, 401, 404, 407, 408, 409, 483, 484,
    488, 489